Advances in Sport Psychology

Thelma S. Horn, PhD
Miami University

Editor

Human Kinetics Publishers

Library of Congress Cataloging-in-Publication Data

Advances in sport psychology / Thelma S. Horn, editor.
   p.   cm.
   Includes bibliographical references and index.
   ISBN 0-87322-364-0
   1. Sports--Psychological aspects. I. Horn, Thelma S., 1949-
GV706.4.A38   1992
796'.01--dc20   91-42061
                                        CIP

ISBN: 0-87322-364-0

The quote on p. 13 is from *The Science Question in Feminism* by S. Harding, 1986, Ithaca, NY: Cornell University Press. Reprinted by permission.

The quote on p. 17 is from "Science, Knowledge, and Sport Psychologist" by R. Martens, 1987, *Sport Psychologist*, **1**, p. 52. Copyright 1987 by Human Kinetics Publishers, Inc. Reprinted by permission.

The quote on p. 18 is from "Lab coat: Robe of Innocence or Klansman's Sheet?" by R. Bleier. In *Feminist Studies, Critical Studies* (pp. 55-66) by T. de Lauretis (Ed.), 1986, Bloomington, IN: Indiana University Press. Reprinted by permission.

Developmental Editor: Christine Drews
Assistant Editors: Laura Bofinger and Elizabeth Bridgett
Photo Editor: Valerie Rose Hall
Copyeditor: Michael Lane
Proofreader: Karin Leszczynski
Indexer: Shroeder Indexing Services
Production Director: Ernie Noa
Typesetting and Text Layout: Angela K. Snyder
Text Design: Keith Blomberg
Paste-Up: Denise Lowry and Tara Welsch
Cover Design: Jack Davis
Cover Photo: Dave Black
Illustrations: Gretchen Walters
Printer: Braun-Brumfield

Printed in the United States of America   10 9 8 7 6 5 4

Human Kinetics
Web site: http://www.humankinetics.com/

United States: Human Kinetics, P.O. Box 5076, Champaign, IL 61825-5076
1-800-747-4457
e-mail: humank@hkusa.com

Canada: Human Kinetics, Box 24040, Windsor, ON N8Y 4Y9
1-800-465-7301 (in Canada only)
e-mail: humank@hkcanada.com

Europe: Human Kinetics, P.O. Box IW14, Leeds LS16 6TR, United Kingdom
(44) 1132 781708
e-mail: humank@hkeurope.com

Australia: Human Kinetics, 57A Price Avenue, Lower Mitcham, South Australia 5062
(088) 277 1555
e-mail: humank@hkaustralia.com

New Zealand: Human Kinetics, P.O. Box 105-231, Auckland 1
(09) 523 3462
e-mail: humank@hknewz.com

Contents

Contributors

Stephen H. Boutcher, PhD
University of Wollongong

Lawrence R. Brawley, PhD
University of Waterloo

Damon Burton, PhD
University of Idaho

Albert V. Carron, EdD
University of Western Ontario

Nigel Chaumeton, MS
University of Oregon

Alison Dewar, EdD
Miami University

Deborah L. Feltz, PhD
Michigan State University

Diane L. Gill, PhD
University of North Carolina at Greensboro

Daniel Gould, PhD
University of North Carolina at Greensboro

Susan L. Greendorfer, PhD
University of Illinois at Urbana-Champaign

Thelma S. Horn, PhD, Editor
Miami University

Douglas P. Jowdy, MS
Virginia Commonwealth University

Vikki Krane, PhD
Bowling Green State University

Edward McAuley, PhD
University of Illinois at Urbana-Champaign

Shane M. Murphy, PhD
United States Olympic Committee

Robin S. Vealey, PhD
Miami University

Maureen R. Weiss, PhD
University of Oregon

W. Neil Widmeyer, PhD
University of Waterloo

Photo Credits

Preface

In its most generic sense, sport psychology can be defined as the psychological study of human behavior in sport and physical activity settings. A close examination of the available literature in the field suggests that sport psychologists are particularly interested in the variation that occurs in the behavior of individuals in such contexts. This includes the variation among different individuals who are placed in the same situation as well as the variation in the behavior of the same individual across different situations. To illustrate variation between individuals, consider the case of two athletes from the same team who are both performing in a rather crucial athletic contest (e.g., a league, state, or regional championship). Despite the fact that both athletes are placed in the same or similar performance context, there may well be differences between them in their behavior in this situation; that is, they may vary considerably in anxiety, confidence, motivation, and actual performance. Equally as interesting to sport psychologists is the variation in behavior that occurs when an individual athlete moves from one situation to another. For example, sport psychologists have consistently noted that the amount of anxiety an individual athlete experiences is highly dependent on the situation (e.g., practice vs. game; home vs. away contest). Similarly, an individual athlete may exhibit a high level of motivation in a soccer practice but then be considerably less motivated to achieve in a softball practice.

To explain such behavioral variation, sport psychologists have identified and examined a number of factors that can be categorized as either individual difference factors or social-environment factors. Individual difference factors refer to rather stable traits, dispositions, or characteristics of the individual, such as age, trait anxiety, motivational orientation, and skill or ability level. These individual difference variables have been used by sport psychologists in an effort to explain and predict the behavior of individual participants in sport and physical activity contexts. From a related perspective, sport psychologists have also found that certain factors within the sport or social environment can affect the participants' behavior. Specifically, characteristics of the group (e.g., size, cohesion, composition) and the behaviors of the group leader (e.g., coach or exercise leader) have been found to affect the behavior of the group members. In addition, the individual participant's sociocultural background (e.g., racial/ethnic background, social class) as well as the nature of the sport structure itself (e.g., program philosophy, organizational goals, program award structure, sport type) will also exert an influence on the individual participant's behavior.

Although much of the research in sport psychology has examined the influence of individual difference and social-environmental factors separately, recent consensus in the field clearly suggests that these two entities exert an interactional effect. In other words, considerable evidence has been accumulated to show that the characteristics of the individual performer interact with factors in the social environment to determine the individual's behavior in specific sport or physical activity contexts.

Within the last two decades, we have accumulated much information concerning the individual and social-environmental factors that affect human behavior in the sport and physical activity settings. However, we still have a considerable way to go before we will truly be able to understand, predict, and modify the behavior of individuals in sport and physical activity contexts.

This book presents a summary of the information we have to date along with clear suggestions for future research. The primary purpose of this edited text is to provide a comprehensive and up-to-date review of the major issues that are of current research interest in sport psychology. It emphasizes a discussion and critical analysis of the current state of knowledge in each topical area combined with recommendations concerning future research directions. It is primarily directed toward graduate students enrolled in research-oriented sport and exercise psychology classes and toward individuals currently conducting research in some area of sport or exercise psychology. Although the book is not intended to serve as a how-to text for practicing sport psychologists or to provide information oriented only toward the enhancement of sport performance, the individual chapters should be useful to current or future practitioners who need to understand the factors that affect the behavior of sport performers before they can hope to effect behavioral change.

The book contains 13 individual chapters organized around the major theme of sport psychology as the study of human behavior in sport and physical activity contexts. The 13 chapters have been divided into four parts. The two chapters that comprise Part I provide a comprehensive introduction to the field of sport psychology (e.g., definitions, history, research methodologies). The five chapters comprising Part II examine the characteristics (i.e., individual difference factors) that affect an individual's behavior in sport and physical activity contexts. These characteristics include personality, arousal/anxiety, self-perceptions, motivational orientation, and gender. The three chapters presented in Part III provide a discussion concerning various factors in the social environment that impinge on the participants' behavior. They discuss the impact of group dynamics, leadership behaviors, and socialization processes. Finally, the three chapters in Part IV examine the extent to which selected intervention techniques can be used to enhance the performance or modify the behavior of athletes and other physical activity participants. Individual chapters discuss the research pertaining to imagery and mental practice, attentional processes, and goal setting.

Despite the fact that the 13 chapters in this edited text were written by different authors, an attempt was made to use a consistent format. Specifically, each chapter begins with a fairly brief introduction to the topic area, defining terms, explaining the scope of the chapter, and outlining the sections comprising the chapter. In the main body of each chapter, the author provides a review of the available research and theory on the chapter topic. This review does not just summarize the research to date but, rather, provides an analysis and, in most cases, a synthesis of the state of knowledge in the area. Finally, a fairly large section of each chapter is devoted to a discussion of future directions.

The production of a textbook of this depth and breadth certainly requires the coordinated efforts of a number of individuals. It seems appropriate at this time to recognize the major contributors. First, it is important to acknowledge the contributions of Rainer Martens, who in his role as president of Human Kinetics Publishers initiated this project and who has obviously provided the resources necessary to get this text into publication. However, at this point in the history of sport psychology, it is also appropriate to recognize Martens's contributions to the field as a whole. As one of its early leaders, he has not only contributed significantly to its growth and development, but also kindled the enthusiasm and commitment of a number of subsequent researchers and scholars. It is perhaps not surprising that four of the 13 chapters in this text were written by individuals who completed their doctoral programs under his supervision. Thus, his contribution to both this project and the field of sport psychology has been most significant.

It is, of course, essential to acknowledge also the contributions of the authors who wrote the individual chapters for this text. Despite extremely busy schedules, the 18 authors and coauthors invested considerable time and effort in writing and rewriting their chapters. As several of them noted, it was not easy to condense the research and theory in each particular topic area into 40 or 50 typewritten pages. In addition, each author was specifically requested to go beyond the current state of knowledge in her or his topic area in an attempt to "push at the boundaries" that have defined, and in many cases limited, our field since its inception. This was certainly a formidable task, but each author accomplished it with distinction.

In soliciting authors for the individual chapters in this book, I found that of the many arguments that I had marshaled to encourage their participation, the one that was consistently the most successful was the one that appealed to their commitment to the field of sport psychology. I am quite convinced that each author's primary motivation in writing was to advance the field and, perhaps more importantly, to stimulate the interest and enthusiasm of current and future researchers. It is our combined hope, then, that this text will be of value to our readers not only in furthering their understanding of the field but also in motivating all of us toward continued and qualitatively better research work. May our passion for sport psychology continue to burn brightly!

Part I

Introduction to Sport Psychology

Despite the early and relatively isolated work of such individuals as Coleman Griffith and Norman Triplett, sport psychology as an area of academic research within the sport sciences did not really begin in earnest until the mid-1960s. As will become evident throughout this book, much has been accomplished over the last 25 years. However, as with any area of academic study, many changes have also occurred with respect to the field itself, so it seems appropriate for this text to begin with two chapters that provide an introduction to, or overview of, the area of study known as *sport psychology*.

In chapter 1, Deborah Feltz compares and contrasts the various perspectives of sport psychology and links these perspectives to divergent research methodologies and objectives. She then offers a historical account of the research paradigms used in sport psychology over the last several decades and concludes by identifying and discussing current issues and future trends in the field.

In chapter 2, Alison Dewar and I critically examine how knowledge is defined and constructed in sport psychology. We begin with a philosophical discussion of science and the dominant ways in which scientific knowledge is obtained and validated. We then present the critiques that have been written concerning these dominant ways of knowing and use this perspective to identify current limitations in our understanding of individuals' behavior in sport contexts.

In combination, these two chapters provide an introduction to, and overview of, sport psychology as an area of academic study. As such, they establish a foundation on which the following more topically oriented chapters will rest.

Chapter 1

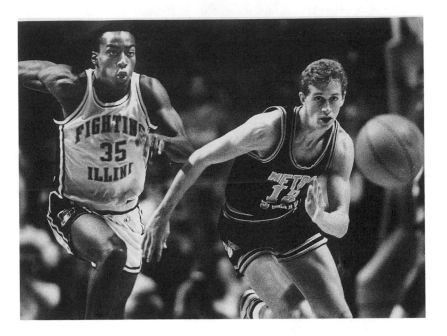

The Nature of Sport Psychology

Deborah L. Feltz
Michigan State University

Describing the nature of *sport psychology* is a difficult task because so many different perspectives on the field exist. Not only are there differences in definitions of the term itself, but there are also differences in the roles that sport psychologists are presumed to play. A content review of the definitions of sport psychology that have been provided in a number of recent books and articles shows that some writers view sport psychology as a subdiscipline of psychology, while others view it as a subdiscipline of sport and exercise science. A brief survey of these definitions is provided in Table 1.1. In addition, other sport psychology writers have differentiated between sport psychology focusing on athletics and *psychology of physical activity* encompassing all movement-related contexts (e.g., Cratty, 1989; Martens, 1974). Finally, some writers have created even more specialized terms, such as *developmental sport psychology* (Duda, 1987; Weiss & Bredemeier, 1983), *psychophysiological sport psychology*

Table 1.1 Definitions of Sport Psychology

Sport psychology is

"the effect of sport itself on human behavior" (Alderman, 1980, p. 4)

"a field of study in which the principles of psychology are applied in a sports setting" (Cox, 1985, p. xiii)

"a subcategory of psychology focusing on athletes and athletics" (Cratty, 1989, p. 1)

"the branch of sport and exercise science that seeks to provide answers to questions about human behavior in sport" (Gill, 1986, p. 3)

"an applied psychology; the science of psychology applied to athletics and athletic situations" (Singer, 1978, p. 4)

(Hatfield & Landers, 1983), and *cognitive sport psychology* (Straub & Williams, 1983). Given such diversity of opinion, it is no wonder that

Dishman (1983) suggested that the field of sport psychology is suffering from an identity crisis.

I shall describe the nature of sport psychology, including different perspectives on the field of study and roles of sport psychologists, and present a historical overview of the research literature from 1950 to the present. Current issues of the field and a presentation of current challenges are also delineated.

Perspectives on Sport Psychology

Sport psychology, when viewed as a subdiscipline within the larger field of psychology, would be defined as an applied psychology or as a field of study in which the principles of psychology are applied. Although sport psychology has not been recognized traditionally as a subdisciplinary area of study within the field of academic psychology, Smith (1989) has recently suggested that sport psychology is ready to be embraced by mainstream psychology. As evidence of this, sport psychology was recently approved as Division 47 within the American Psychological Association in 1986 and has long been recognized as a specialty within psychology throughout Europe.

The view of sport psychology as a subdiscipline within the field of sport and exercise science comes mostly from scientists in physical education (or sport and exercise). Henry (1981), for example, argued that the academic discipline of physical education consists of the study of certain aspects of such fields as psychology, physiology, anatomy, and sociology rather than the *application* of those disciplines to physical activity settings. Dishman (1983), Gill (1986), Morgan (1989), Roberts (1989), and others support this view of sport psychology as a part of the broad area of sport science. Gill (1986) noted that although sport and exercise science is a multidisciplinary field that draws upon knowledge from the broader parent disciplines, the subareas comprising sport and exercise science also draw upon theories, constructs, and measures from each other. In fact, some sport psychology researchers (e.g., Dishman, 1983; Feltz, 1989; Morgan, 1989) have suggested that sport psychology will need to include knowledge from other subdisciplines within sport and exercise science to understand phenomena specific to sport.

These different perspectives concerning sport psychology parallel the situation in social psychology where sociologists and psychologists differ in their definition of social psychology (House, 1977; McCall & Simmons, 1982; Perlman & Cozby, 1983; Stryker, 1977). Social psychology as seen from the psychological tradition emphasizes the individual, while social psychology viewed from the sociological tradition emphasizes the group and social variables. Although there has recently been some convergence between the two traditions, deep divisions are believed to remain regarding fundamentally different assumptions about the nature of human beings in society (McCall & Simmons, 1982). These divergent views pose fundamentally different questions, which define the content of study in terms of topics, methods, and theoretical orientations.

Similarly, whether one views sport psychology as a subdiscipline of psychology or as a subdiscipline of sport and exercise science is an important issue because this perspective determines one's focus of study. For instance, if sport psychology is viewed as a subdiscipline of psychology, the focus of study would generally involve using sport and physical activity as a *setting* to understand psychological theory and to apply psychological principles (see Goldstein, 1979; Martin & Hrycaiko, 1983). If, however, sport psychology is viewed as a subdiscipline of sport and exercise science, the focus of study would more likely involve trying to describe, explain, and predict behavior in sport contexts.

The perspective of this chapter is that Martens's (1974) concept of *psychological kinesiology* offers the most comprehensive view in which to study behavior in sport. Martens defined kinesiology as "the study of human movement, especially physical activity, in all forms and in all contexts" (1989, p. 101). Using this overall definition, psychological kinesiology (sport psychology and motor learning and control) becomes the study of the psychological aspects of human movement. The other areas of kinesiology would then consist of physiological kinesiology (exercise physiology), biomechanical kinesiology (sport biomechanics), social–cultural kinesiology (sport sociology), and developmental kinesiology (motor development). As some sport psychologists (or psychological kinesiologists) have noted (e.g., Dishman, 1983; Feltz, 1989; Gill, 1986; Morgan, 1989), a thorough understanding of behavior in human movement settings requires the integration of knowledge from all the subdisciplines of kinesiology. A schematic representation of kinesiology and some research problems with a psychological focus that can be studied from this cross-disciplinary perspective is shown in Figure 1.1

For instance, in the first example, perceived exertion, exercise addiction, and staleness are examples of research topics that involve physiological and psychological factors. In the second example, a study that actually examined the

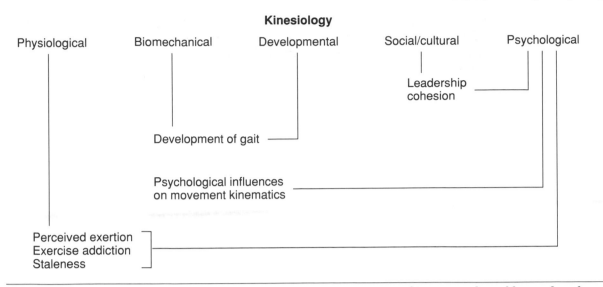

Figure 1.1 A schematic representation of kinesiology and examples of its research problems of study.

psychological influences on movement kinematics was conducted by Beuter and Duda (1985), in which a biomechanical approach (movement kinematics) was used to examine the effect of arousal on stepping movements of children. In the third example, the study of the development of gait patterns could include biomechanical, developmental, and psychological factors. In the last example, a study of the areas of leadership and cohesion necessitate a knowledge of social, cultural, and psychological variables.

Roles of Sport Psychologists

The second major complication in describing the nature of sport psychology is that there exist at least two differing perspectives concerning the role of sport psychologists. One role of the sport psychologist is as a researcher and academician. The other is as a practitioner and service provider. The role of the academic seems to fit most comfortably within the field of kinesiology or sport science, whereas the role of the practitioner seems best categorized within the field of sports medicine. Some of the functions that Nideffer, DuFresne, Nesvig, and Selder (1980) identified as those in which sport psychology practitioners are involved include

- developing performance improvement programs,
- using psychological assessment techniques,
- providing crisis intervention services, and
- providing consultative and program development services for coaches, trainers, and others who work directly with athletes.

Although the two major roles described in the previous paragraph appear to differ considerably, some sport psychologists do play both roles. However, Roberts (1989) has recently expressed concern that a rapidly developing gulf is emerging between the academic and practitioner-oriented sport psychologists. Some sport psychologists have argued that professional services should not be sanctioned until we possess an applied body of knowledge and a reliable technology (Dishman, 1983; Morgan, 1989). Others have contended that the need for professional services in sport psychology is there now and that those providing such service should not "sit idle until scientific evidence has validated their particular application or technique" (Landers, 1989, p. 477). To further widen the gulf between academic and practitioner-oriented sport psychologists, the field is witnessing a growing number of professional journals and organizations that have developed either along scientific research or applied sport psychology lines. In 1989 there were seven prominent professional organizations in sport psychology and five professional journals (LeUnes & Nation, 1989).

Obviously, there is considerable controversy in the field today regarding the basic nature of sport psychology and the roles that sport psychologists can or should play. Roberts (1989) has contended that the controversy in sport psychology is due primarily to the lack of a generally accepted conceptual paradigm to drive the research and applied efforts of sport psychologists. To understand the controversial issues in this field and why sport psychology lacks a generally accepted paradigm, it is necessary to examine where sport psychology has been in the past. Because several individuals have already written excellent historical overviews (e.g., Cox, 1985; Landers, 1983; Ryan, 1981; Wiggins, 1984), I shall present only a brief overview of how the current paradigms in sport psychology evolved, taken from my earlier overview (Feltz, 1989).

Evolution to the Current Paradigms in Sport Psychology

In any area of science, the researchers' choice of topics to investigate, the methods they employ, and the perspective they take are not freely and logically determined. Rather, they are heavily influenced by the sociological forces both within and outside the discipline (Keller, 1985; Shadish, 1985). Sport psychology is no exception, because trends in sport psychology have tended to parallel those in general psychology (Morgan, 1980). As Landers (1983) noted, the research that was conducted in sport psychology during the 1950-1965 time period was characterized by empiricism, and most of the studies investigated personality. This perspective was consistent with the trait approach that was in vogue in the general area of psychology. In contrast, the time period 1966-1976 was characterized by a social analysis approach. Research during this decade consisted of selecting one theory at a time from mainstream psychology and testing that theory in the area of sport and motor performance (Landers, 1983). Such topics as social facilitation, achievement motivation, social reinforcement, and arousal and motor performance were investigated. Much of this research was influenced by Martens's (1970) recommendation of the social analysis approach. Research conducted from the late 1970s to the present has also been influenced by leaders in psychology and sport psychology. Wankel (1975) advocated the application of cognitive approaches to sport psychology issues. These approaches included causal attributions, intrinsic motivation, and self-efficacy/self-confidence.

I shall examine the research perspectives that characterized each of the three time periods in greater detail in an effort to describe the evolution of sport psychology. Specifically, I describe a research topic from within each time period to illustrate the primary focus from that period.

Personality Research From 1950 to 1965

The relationship of personality to participation in sport and physical activity has been one of the most popular research areas in sport psychology. Much of the early research took a trait approach to studying personality profiles in athletes or athletic groups and has been described as being of the "shotgun" variety (Ryan, 1968). Researchers would gain access to a sample of athletes (from high school to Olympic caliber) and test them on the most convenient personality test. This research approach has been labeled the shotgun variety because the researchers typically would have no theoretical rationale for the selection of the personality test used. Few conclusive answers resulted from the hundreds of studies conducted using this approach. This lack of consistency subsequently led to strong criticism of the area by a number of leaders in sport psychology (e.g., Kroll, 1970; Martens, 1975). Most of the criticisms were based on theoretical and methodological shortcomings of the research. The use of univariate instead of multivariate statistics, questionable sampling techniques, and lack of specificity in the operationalization of variables have been some of the major criticisms lodged against the sport personality research. In addition, the applicability of general personality assessment techniques for sport and physical activity that may not have a logical link to participation or performance has been questioned (Kroll, 1970).

This criticism of the personality research led to a general (if temporary) disenchantment with personality as an area of study in sport psychology. Martens (1970, 1975), one of the most vocal critics of this research approach, began advocating the use of a social analysis approach that combined empirical methods with theory. When Martens started testing psychological theories within a motor performance context, many other researchers followed. Most of this research was conducted in controlled laboratory settings and represents the second major stage in the history of sport psychology research.

Social Facilitation and the Arousal-Performance Relationship From 1966 to 1976

A considerable amount of research was conducted during this decade in the area of sport psychology. The typical research paradigm, which was laboratory-oriented, involved taking a social–psychological theory and testing its applicability to motor skill performance. The most popular topics of research during this social analysis period were social facilitation and the arousal–performance relationship. Much of the research in social facilitation and arousal in sport psychology was based on Zajonc's (1965) theory of social facilitation. Zajonc's hypothesis, based on drive theory, was that the presence of an audience creates arousal, which in turn enhances the emission of dominant responses. The dominant response of a complex task is the incorrect response in initial learning but the correct response when the skill is mastered. Martens (1969) initiated a series of laboratory studies on social facilitation using motor skill tasks and found support for Zajonc's theory. A number of other investigators also attempted to extend this research to motor tasks by varying the task, audience, and subject characteristics (e.g., Carron & Bennett, 1976; Haas & Roberts, 1975). Their findings varied, depending on the variables studied. Reviewers of this research have generally concluded that the evidence for a drive theory explanation of social facilitation effects in motor performance has been mixed (Carron, 1980; Landers, 1980; Wankel, 1984). In addition, the size of social facilitation effects has been shown to be very small (Bond & Titus, 1983).

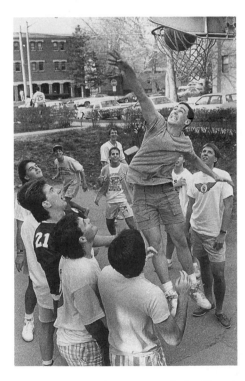

Another aspect of the social facilitation research that investigators found troublesome was the assessment of arousal. Regardless of the particular autonomic arousal measure employed, no clear pattern of results were obtained. Some studies demonstrated increased arousal with the presence of others, and some reported no effect. Some reviewers believed the problem lay in the nature and assessment of arousal, because of its multidimensionality and individual specificity (Carron, 1980; Landers, 1980; Wankel, 1984). Landers (1989) has also noted that one should not

expect much change in physiological measures when the social facilitation effect is so small. Due to these measurement problems, inconsistent results, and the small percent variance accounted for by audience effects, many researchers abandoned the area of social facilitation in search of other psychological theories that might apply to sport.

The most frequently cited alternative to drive theory for social facilitation and arousal–performance research was the inverted-U hypothesis (Carron, 1980). This hypothesis predicted that there was a progressive enhancement in performance as a subject's arousal level increased up to some optimal point, beyond which further increases in arousal progressively decreased performance efficiency. Much of the arousal–motor performance literature of the 1970s also tested the inverted-U hypothesis (e.g., Klavora, 1978; Martens & Landers, 1970). However, just as in social facilitation research, the measurement of arousal was problematic because it was not assessed in terms of its multidimensional nature.

The research conducted during this time period was characterized by use of psychological theories tested in the motor domain and in laboratory settings. However, Landers (1983) noted that the effects achieved with this type of research were small and of questionable generalizability to athletes and the sport setting. This state of affairs led researchers to become dissatisfied with the laboratory-oriented social psychological paradigm and to start looking to cognitive approaches and field methods to answer their research questions.

Cognitive Approaches and Field Methods From 1977 to the Present

In the late 1970s and early 1980s a variety of cognitive models in the sport personality, social facilitation, arousal–performance, and other motivation areas were proposed as a response to the general dissatisfaction with the simplistic and mechanistic drive theory perspective for explaining complex human behavior (Landers, 1980; Wankel, 1975, 1984). For example, Landers (1980) advocated a cognitive arousal–attention model based on Easterbrook's (1959) cue utilization theory. This model suggests that increased arousal leads to a narrowing of attentional focus and cue utilization, thus limiting performance. The concept of objective self-awareness (Duval & Wicklund, 1972) has also been used to interpret audience effects. This theory suggests that the presence of others leads to objective self-awareness (attention directed inward upon the self), which affects task motivation. Baumeister (1984) has suggested that audience-induced pressure increases conscious attention to the performer's own process of performance, which is disruptive to smooth execution.

Wankel (1975) outlined how attribution theory may be used to explain motivation in the presence of an audience. Wankel (1984) also advocated a closer look at Borden's (1980) model, which acknowledges the performer as a proactive, rather than a reactive, individual, who interprets information from the situation, makes predictions about the audience's reactions, and alters behavior accordingly.

Rejeski and Brawley (1983) called for innovative approaches and broader conceptual views to help us understand motivation in sport. The cognitive concepts of perceived ability, self-efficacy, and achievement orientation (Bandura, 1977; Harter, 1978; Maehr & Nicholls, 1980) may play a key role in mediating motivation. These concepts have now been incorporated into the sport psychology research in this area (Ewing, 1981; Feltz, 1982; Roberts, Kleiber & Duda, 1981; Weiss, Bredemeier & Shewchuk, 1986).

At the same time that researchers were dissatisfied with mechanistic drive theory explanations for sport behavior, there was a dissatisfaction with the laboratory-oriented social–psychological paradigm for sport psychology research that had characterized the research during the previous decade. This led some investigators to advocate the use of field research methodology. Martens (1980), in particular, pointed out the limitations of laboratory studies and suggested switching from laboratory settings to field settings in order to observe behavior more accurately and to understand the real world of sport. The publication of this article stimulated many researchers to switch to field research, resulting in a proliferation of field studies conducted during the last decade. However, as Landers (1983) noted, some investigators misinterpreted Martens's position and left theory testing behind, along with the laboratory, when they became field researchers. Some researchers conducted descriptive studies in field settings, but not much theory testing or theory construction (as Martens advocated) had been initiated. Other researchers emphasized intervention studies on applied topics such as mental practice, imagery, psych-up strategies, stress management techniques, and biofeedback. The methodology used in these applied, nontheoretical studies was still based on a technology taken from mainstream (clinical) psychology (Dishman, 1983). In areas where theory testing was being conducted, the cognitive approach that had been developed in mainstream psychology was the focus.

In each of the research time periods described, researchers started with theories (e.g., person-

ality traits, social facilitation, attribution) that were borrowed from psychology. They often obtained mixed results due to theoretical and/or methodological shortcomings. Their discouragement and dissatisfaction led them to abandon either the research area or the methodology and search for a new approach. This historical pattern has contributed to the problems of few programs of sustained research, a lack of a generally accepted conceptual paradigm, and slow growth in advancing knowledge in sport psychology. These problems have become the current issues in the field, for which researchers have begun to offer different explanations and solutions.

Current Issues

Some researchers have offered explanations for the complications and slow growth in sport psychology. Roberts (1989) maintained that the slow growth is due to a lack of a generally accepted conceptual paradigm to drive the research and service effects. He has advocated that we should be using cognitive models to understand behavior in sport and exercise and should become better acquainted with the epistemological concerns of mainstream psychology, where the cognitive paradigm has dominated research since the late 1970s. However, Roberts also conceded that sport psychology researchers should be open to the work of those using other paradigms (e.g., psychobiological). Other writers (Landers, 1989; Morgan, 1989) have suggested that it would be a mistake to shift to one conceptual paradigm. They advocate that broadening the prevailing zeitgeist may provide a better understanding of problems in sport behavior.

Landers (1983) suggested that the reason knowledge in sport psychology has not advanced more rapidly is our approach to testing theory. He contended that we can no longer be content simply to test the relationships outlined by the creator of a theory. Rather, we must develop our own logically formulated alternative explanations and test them against the predictions of the theory. Dishman (1983) argued that sport psychology has been applying general psychology theories and trying to validate general psychology models in sport, rather than developing "applied theories" to answer sport-specific questions. Alderman (1980) noted that although psychology has brought us a long way in increasing our body of knowledge, this knowledge outside or apart from sport can carry us only so far in understanding behavior in sport. As more researchers began to view sport psychology as a subdiscipline within sport science rather than as a field of study in which psychological principles were tested and applied, they also began to advocate the development of theories or conceptual frameworks within sport psychology to further understand sport behavior (Alderman, 1980; Dishman, 1983; Martens, 1980; Morgan, 1989).

For the most part, however, we are not developing the new conceptual frameworks or models within sport that Alderman (1980) and Martens (1980) suggested. The few exceptions are the "iceberg" profile to characterize elite athletes (Morgan & Pollock, 1977) and attempts at concepts such as movement confidence (Griffin, Keogh & Maybee, 1984), sport confidence (Vealey, 1986), and sport enjoyment (Scanlan & Lewthwaite, 1986).

Developing theoretical formulations within the context of sport and exercise does not mean abandoning psychological theory. As Landers (1989) suggests, theory cannot be developed in a vacuum. He contends that we need to continue to borrow theories, methods, and approaches from academic psychology as a starting point from which to examine its applicability and modify it accordingly. However, as was stated in the beginning of this chapter, these models may also be inadequate to understand some of the psychological phenomena specific to sport unless we begin to integrate knowledge from other subdisciplines within sport and exercise science. Dishman (1983) has advocated combining our talents across subdisciplines within sport and exercise science to answer sport and exercise questions of practical impact. Dishman termed this a recycled suggestion, which has more frequently been ignored than followed. I shall provide some examples of such an integrated approach to practical research questions.

In trying to explain why children drop out of youth sports, sport psychology researchers have previously looked entirely for psychological reasons (Ewing, 1981; Feltz & Petlichkoff, 1983; Gould, Feltz, Horn & Weiss, 1982). As a result of such a narrow focus, training and conditioning or maturational explanations for dropping out have often been overlooked. To examine these possibilities adequately, longitudinal, systematic, and interdisciplinary research programs are needed that focus on a number of interrelated questions rather than a single, isolated one. An example of this type of research program was the young runners study conducted by the Institute for the Study of Youth Sports (Seefeldt & Steig, 1986). This study of young, long-distance runners included a battery of tests and assessments: anthropometry, blood sampling (e.g., high- and low-density lipoprotein, triglycerides, and lactic dehydrogenase), cinematographic recording of gaits, densitometry, hand-wrist X ray (biological maturity), history of illness and injuries, motor performance, muscular endurance, nutritional profile, psychological profile, review of activity and competitive history, and treadmill test of work capacity. Assessments of these runners were conducted on an annual basis. Thus, they were followed as some dropped out and others continued in competitive long-distance running. Future analyses of such longitudinal data should provide an interdisciplinary perspective on reasons for continuing or discontinuing sport participation. At this point, it can be hypothesized that explanations for these runners' decisions may be only partially psychological (Feltz & Albrecht, 1986).

Another example of an interdisciplinary approach to examining sport-specific questions is Beuter's and Duda's (1985) analysis of the arousal–motor performance relationship. These researchers used movement kinematics (an assessment of the quality of performance) to examine the effect of arousal on motor performance. This approach allowed them to focus on the process by which arousal influences performance rather than simply on the outcome or *end products* of performance. These types of studies may uncover explanations that a study based solely on psychological models could not provide.

Current Challenges

It seems apparent, therefore, that the development of theoretical models specifically built to answer sport and exercise questions (Alderman, 1980; Dishman, 1983; Martens, 1980) must come from an interdisciplinary sport and exercise knowledge base as well as from psychological theories. In order to achieve this integrated body of knowledge in sport and exercise science, departments may have to change their reward structure so that researchers are rewarded to a greater degree for publishing within sport and exercise science than in their parent discipline (Hoffman, 1985) and are not penalized for doing collaborative research (Mahoney, 1985). In addition, graduate curricular programs would need to be modified to prepare students better for interdisciplinary research (Hoffman, 1985). Rather than taking the majority of their coursework in psychology, students may need to take the majority of their coursework in their degree program. An integrated knowledge of sport and exercise science does not eliminate intensive study in psychology. Both will be necessary if students are to be successful in conducting state-of-the-art research.

References

Alderman, R.B. (1980). Sport psychology: Past, present, and future dilemmas. In P. Klavora & K.A.W. Wipper (Eds.), *Psychological and sociological factors in sport* (pp. 3-19). Toronto, ON: University of Toronto.

Bandura, A. (1977). Self-efficacy: Toward a unifying theory of behavioral change. *Psychological Review, 84*, 191-215.

Baumeister, R.F. (1984). Choking under pressure: Self-consciousness and paradoxical effects of incentives on skillful performance. *Journal of Personality and Social Psychology, 46*, 610-620.

Beuter, A., & Duda, J.L. (1985). Analysis of the arousal/motor performance relationship in children using movement kinematics. *Journal of Sport Psychology, 7*, 229-243.

Bond, C.F., & Titus, L.J. (1983). Social facilitation: A meta-analysis of 241 studies. *Psychological Bulletin, 94*, 265-292.

Borden, R.J. (1980). Audience influence. In P.B. Paulus (Ed.), *Psychology of group influence* (pp. 99-131). Hillsdale, NJ: Erlbaum.

Carron, A.V. (1980). *Social psychology of sport*. Ithaca, NY: Mouvement.

Carron, A.V., & Bennett, B. (1976). The effects of initial habit strength differences upon performance in a coaction situation. *Journal of Motor Behavior, 8*, 297-304.

Cox, R.H. (1985). *Sport psychology: Concepts and applications*. Dubuque, IA: William C. Brown.

Cratty, B.J. (1989). *Psychology in contemporary sport* (3rd ed.). Englewood Cliffs, NJ: Prentice Hall.

Dishman, R.K. (1983). Identity crises in North American sport psychology: Academics in professional issues. *Journal of Sport Psychology, 5*, 123-134.

Duda, J.L. (1987). Toward a developmental theory of children's motivation in sport. *Journal of Sport Psychology, 9*, 130-145.

Duval, S., & Wicklund, R.A. (1972). *A theory of objective self-awareness*. New York: Academic.

Easterbrook, J.A. (1959). The effect of emotion on cue utilization and the organization of behavior. *Psychological Review, 66*, 183-201.

Ewing, M.E. (1981). *Achievement orientations and sport behavior of males and females*. Unpublished doctoral dissertation, University of Illinois at Urbana-Champaign.

Feltz, D.L. (1982). Path analysis of the causal elements in Bandura's theory of self-efficacy and an anxiety-based model of avoidance behavior. *Journal of Personality and Social Psychology, 42*, 764-781.

Feltz, D.L. (1989). Theoretical research in sport psychology: From applied psychology toward sport science. In J.S.

Skinner, C.B. Corbin, D.M. Landers, P.E. Martin, & C.L. Wells (Eds.), *Future directions in exercise and sport science research* (pp. 435-452). Champaign, IL: Human Kinetics.

Feltz, D.L., & Albrecht, R.R. (1986). Psychological implications of competitive running. In M. Weiss & D. Gould (Eds.), *Sport for children and youths* (pp. 225-230). Champaign, IL: Human Kinetics.

Feltz, D.L., & Petlichkoff, L. (1983). Perceived competence among interscholastic sport participants and dropouts. *Canadian Journal of Applied Sport Sciences, 8*, 231-235.

Gill, D.L. (1986). *Psychological dynamics of sport*. Champaign, IL: Human Kinetics.

Goldstein, J.H. (1979). *Sports, games, and play: Social and psychological viewpoints*. Hillsdale, NJ: Erlbaum.

Gould, D., Feltz, D., Horn, T., & Weiss, M. (1982). Reasons for attrition in competitive swimming. *Journal of Sport Behavior, 5*, 155-165.

Griffin, N.S., Keogh, J.F., & Maybee, R. (1984). Performer perceptions of movement confidence. *Journal of Sport Psychology, 6*, 395-407.

Haas, J., & Roberts, G.C. (1975). Effect of evaluative others upon learning and performance of a complex motor task. *Journal of Motor Behavior, 7*, 81-90.

Harter, S. (1978). Effectance motivation reconsidered: Toward a developmental model. *Human Development, 21*, 34-64.

Hatfield, B.D., & Landers, D.M. (1983). Psychophysiology—A new direction for sport psychology. *Journal of Sport Psychology, 5*, 243-259.

Henry, F.M. (1981). Physical education: An academic discipline. In G.A. Brooks (Ed.), *Perspectives on the academic discipline of physical education* (pp. 10-15). Champaign, IL: Human Kinetics.

Hoffman, S.J. (1985). Specialization + fragmentation = extermination: A formula for the demise of graduate education. *Journal of Physical Education, Recreation and Dance, 56*(6), 19-22.

House, J.S. (1977). The three faces of social psychology. *Sociometry, 40*, 161-177.

Keller, E.F. (1985). *Reflections on gender and science*. New Haven, CT: Yale University Press.

Klavora, P. (1978). An attempt to derive inverted-U curves based on the relationship between anxiety and athletic performance. In D.M. Landers & R.W. Christina (Eds.), *Psychology of motor behavior and sport—1977* (pp. 369-377). Champaign, IL: Human Kinetics.

Kroll, W. (1970). Current strategies and problems in personality assessment of athletes. In L.E. Smith (Ed.), *Psychology of motor learning* (pp. 349-367). Chicago: Athletic Institute.

Landers, D.M. (1980). The arousal–performance relationship revisited. *Research Quarterly for Exercise and Sport, 51*, 77-90.

Landers, D.M. (1983). Whatever happened to theory testing in sport psychology? *Journal of Sport Psychology, 5*, 135-151.

Landers, D.M. (1989). Sport psychology: A commentary. In J.S. Skinner, C.B. Corbin, D.M. Landers, P.E. Martin, & C.L. Wells (Eds.), *Future directions in exercise and sport science research* (pp. 475-486). Champaign, IL: Human Kinetics.

LeUnes, A.D., & Nation, J.R. (1989). *Sport psychology: An introduction*. Chicago: Nelson-Hall.

Maehr, M.L., & Nicholls, J.G. (1980). Culture and achievement motivation: A second look. In N. Warren (Ed.), *Studies in cross-cultural psychology* (pp. 221-267). New York: Academic.

Mahoney, M. (1985). Open exchange and epistemic progress. *American Psychologist, 40*, 29-39.

Martens, R. (1969). Effect of an audience on learning and performance of a complex motor skill. *Journal of Personality and Social Psychology, 12*, 252-260.

Martens, R. (1970). A social psychology of physical activity. *Quest, 14*, 8-17.

Martens, R. (1974, March). *Psychological kinesiology: An undisciplined subdiscipline.* Paper presented at the meeting of the North American Society for the Psychology of Sport and Physical Activity, Anaheim, CA.

Martens, R. (1975). The paradigmatic crisis in American sport personology. *Sportwissenschaft, 5*, 9-24.

Martens, R. (1980). From smocks to jocks: A new adventure for sport psychologists. In P. Klavora & K.A.W. Wipper (Eds.), *Psychological and sociological factors in sport* (pp. 20-26). Toronto: Schools of Physical and Health Education, University of Toronto.

Martens, R. (1989). Studying physical activity in context: Sport. In *Big Ten Leadership Conference Report, Chicago* (pp. 101-103). Champaign, IL: Human Kinetics.

Martens, R., & Landers, D.M. (1970). Motor performance under stress: A test of the inverted-U hypothesis. *Journal of Personality and Social Psychology, 16*, 29-37.

Martin, G.L., & Hrycaiko, D. (1983). *Behavior modification and coaching: Principles, procedures, and research.* Springfield, IL: Thomas.

McCall, G.J., & Simmons, J.L. (1982). *Social psychology: A sociological approach.* New York: MacMillan.

Morgan, W.P. (1980). The trait psychology controversy. *Research Quarterly for Exercise and Sport, 51*, 50-76.

Morgan, W.P. (1989). Sport psychology in its own context: A recommendation for the future. In J.S. Skinner, C.B. Corbin, D.M. Landers, P.E. Martin, & C.L. Wells (Eds.), *Future directions in exercise and sport science research* (pp. 97-110). Champaign, IL: Human Kinetics.

Morgan, W.P., & Pollock, M. (1977). Psychologic characterization of the elite distance runner. *Annals of New York Academy of Science, 301*, 382-403.

Nideffer, R.M., DuFresne, P., Nesvig, D., & Selder, D. (1980). The future of applied sport psychology. *Journal of Sport Psychology, 2*, 170-174.

Perlman, D., & Cozby, P.C. (1983). *Social psychology.* New York: CBS College.

Rejeski, W.J., & Brawley, L.R. (1983). Attribution theory in sports: Current status and new perspectives. *Journal of Sport Psychology, 5*, 77-99.

Roberts, G.C. (1989). When motivation matters: The need to expand the conceptual model. In J.S. Skinner, C.B. Corbin, D.M. Landers, P.E. Martin, & C.L. Wells (Eds.), *Future directions in exercise and sport science research* (pp. 71-84). Champaign, IL: Human Kinetics.

Roberts, G.C., Kleiber, D.A., & Duda, J.L. (1981). An analysis of motivation in children's sport: The role of a perceived competence in participation. *Journal of Sport Psychology, 3*, 206-216.

Ryan, e.d. (1968). reaction to "sport and personality dynamics." In *Proceedings of the National College Physical Education Association for Men* (pp. 70-75).

Ryan, E.D. (1981). The emergence of psychological research as related to performance in physical activity. In G.A. Brooks (Ed.), *Perspectives on the academic discipline of physical education* (pp. 327-341). Champaign, IL: Human Kinetics.

Scanlan, T., & Lewthwaite, R. (1986). Social psychological aspects of competition for male youth sport participants: Part 4. Predictors of enjoyment. *Journal of Sport Psychology, 8*, 25-35.

Seefeldt, V., & Steig, P. (1986). Introduction to an interdisciplinary assessment of competition on elite young distance runners. In M. Weiss & D. Gould (Eds.), *Sport for children and youth* (pp. 213-217). Champaign, IL: Human Kinetics.

Shadish, W.R., Jr. (1985). Planned critical multiplism: Some elaborations. *Behavioral Assessment, 8*, 75-103.

Smith, R.E. (1989). Scientific issues and research trends in sport psychology. In J.S. Skinner, C.B. Corbin, D.M. Landers, P.E. Martin, & C.L. Wells (Eds.), *Future directions in exercise and sport science research* (pp. 23-38). Champaign, IL: Human Kinetics.

Straub, W.F., & Williams, J.M. (Eds.) (1983). *Cognitive sport psychology.* Lansing, NY: Sport Science Associates.

Stryker, S. (1977). Developments in "two social psychologies": Toward an appreciation of mutual relevance. *Sociometry, 40*, 145-160.

Vealey, R. (1986). Conceptualization of sport-confidence and competitive orientation: Preliminary investigation and instrument development. *Journal of Sport Psychology, 8*, 221-246.

Wankel, L.M. (1975). A new energy source for sport psychology research: Toward a conversion from D.C. (drive conceptualizations) to A.C. (attributional cognitions). In D.M. Landers (Ed.), *Psychology of sport and motor behavior* (Vol. 2, pp. 221-245). University Park, PA: Pennsylvania State University.

Wankel, L.M. (1984). Audience effects in sport. In J.M. Silva & R.S. Weinberg (Eds.), *Psychological foundations of sport* (pp. 293-314). Champaign, IL: Human Kinetics.

Weiss, M.R., & Bredemeier, B.J. (1983). Developmental sport psychology: A theoretical perspective for studying children in sport. *Journal of Sport Psychology, 5*, 216-230.

Weiss, M.R., Bredemeier, B.J., & Shewchuk, R.M. (1986). The dynamics of perceived competence, perceived control, and motivational orientation in youth sports. In M. Weiss & D. Gould (Eds.), *Sport for children and youth* (pp. 89-102). Champaign, IL: Human Kinetics.

Wiggins, D.K. (1984). The history of sport psychology in North America. In J.M. Silva & R.S. Weinberg (Eds.), *Psychological foundations of sport* (pp. 9-22). Champaign, IL: Human Kinetics.

Zajonc, R.B. (1965). Social facilitation. *Science, 149*, 269-274.

Chapter 2

A Critical Analysis of Knowledge Construction in Sport Psychology

Alison Dewar and Thelma S. Horn
Miami University

Science functions primarily as a "black box": whatever the moral and political values and interests responsible for selecting problems, theories, methods, and interpretations of research, they reappear at the other end of the inquiry as the moral and political universe that science projects as natural and thereby helps to legitimate. In this respect, science is no different from the proverbial descriptions of computers: "junk in; junk out." It is within moral and political discourses that we should expect to find paradigms of rational discourse, not in scientific discourses claiming to have disavowed morals and politics.

—SANDRA HARDING

What does it mean to "know" in sport psychology? When we "know," what version of reality are we accepting as "truth"? In the process of describing, analyzing, and interpreting behavior in sport, whose interests and needs are being served? Whose interests and needs are being ignored? Questions such as these are not often asked by sport psychologists, for they may be deemed unrelated to the subject matter of sport psychology and therefore have little relevance to research and scholarship in the field. We believe otherwise. Much like Sandra Harding, we believe that we must address these questions. In so doing, we will become aware of, and sensitive to, the challenges to modernist conceptions of science and the scientific method that have recently been explicated in the feminist and postmodernist literature.

These challenges question the assumptions that form the basis of mainstream or modernist scientific reasoning and practice. The grand narratives or metatheories of modernist conceptions of science are based on assumptions derived from the Enlightenment, in which individuals are seen as reasoned, stable subjects capable of rational thought processes, which form the basis for objective, reliable, universal representations of the world. It is presumed that "the knowledge acquired from the right use of reason will be 'true'—for example, such knowledge will represent something real and unchanging (universal) about our minds and the structure of the natural world" (Flax, 1990, p. 41).

This chapter will address these questions and present an analysis and critique of how knowledge is defined and constructed in sport psychology. The primary intent of this chapter is to stimulate discussion and debate concerning how we, as researchers, study sport behavior. We do not intend to promote one particular way of knowing at the expense of others. Rather, we will argue that it is important for all sport psychologists to question and critically examine how definitions of what constitutes legitimate knowledge and ways of knowing have been developed in the field. We suggest that these definitions are themselves socially constructed and reflect particular assumptions and beliefs about human beings, behavior, sport, society and their relationships. It is only by examining the nature of knowledge in sport psychology that we can develop an understanding of both the limits and possibilities of the research presented in the literature. Ultimately, discussion and debate about these issues will allow us to develop as self-reflexive scholars who not only know how to generate new knowledge but are aware of the moral, social, and political consequences involved when behavior in sport is explained and analyzed in different ways. Thus, it is our belief that this kind of critical reflection is an integral part of the intellectual process required for the advancement of sport psychology.

This chapter begins with a brief discussion of the dominant ways of knowing and developing knowledge (the orthodoxy) in sport psychology. The assumptions underlying the orthodoxy are examined, and the implications of this for research and knowledge production are identified. In the second section, critiques of the orthodoxy in sport psychology are examined. This discussion focuses on criticisms that have been posed from within the field and examines the assumptions underlying the alternatives suggested. In addition, the subsequent impact of these criticisms on research and scholarship in sport psychology are examined. Specifically, the methodological controversies that currently exist in the field will be outlined in order to identify how researchers have responded to criticisms of dominant, accepted ways of knowing.

Because the criticisms of the orthodoxy that have emerged in the sport psychology literature have, with only a couple of exceptions, been limited primarily to methodological rather than epistemological concerns, the third section of this chapter explores ideas and issues raised outside of the field. This discussion, based on feminist and postmodernist critiques of science, focuses particularly on how primary adherence to, and reliance on, the orthodoxy has seriously limited, and will continue to seriously limit, our understanding of the similarities and differences that occur among and between individuals within the context of sport.

Finally, the chapter concludes with suggestions for future research in sport psychology. We suggest it is important that sport psychologists develop a critical awareness about how knowledge is generated and produced, and then develop ways of knowing that reflect and represent the very real diversity that exists in individuals, sport, and social life.

The Orthodoxy in Sport Psychology: The Social Construction of "Scientific" Knowledge and Ways of Knowing

Although it is typically acknowledged by researchers and scholars that there are many ways to acquire knowledge about human behavior, within the academic discipline of sport psychology there is clearly only one accepted mode. This dominant mode, identified by Martens (1987) as the orthodoxy, not only defines how knowledge is constructed but also sets limits on what counts as legitimate ways of knowing within the field. The orthodoxy in sport psychology is based on ways of knowing that are found in the natural and biological sciences as well as within the behavioral sciences. This way of knowing can be referred to in different ways. For example, it is sometimes called the scientific method, process–product research, research in the empirical analytic paradigm, experimental or quantitative research, or modernist science. Although there are different labels for this orthodoxy in sport psychology, it is important to recognize that there is a set of dominant beliefs that constitute this view of the discipline and that these beliefs have their basis in the philosophical tradition developed during the historical period of the Enlightenment. This philosophical tradition is best known as *logical positivism*.

Logical Positivism as a Modernist Way of Knowing

Logical positivism, or positivism, is a theory of knowledge that is characterized by a distinctive and elaborate definition of what constitutes modernist science and the appropriate methods for generating and discovering scientific knowledge (Jaggar, 1983). This theory of knowledge is more than a method for doing science. It is a set of beliefs about the world and, as such, a prescription for defining and constructing reality through the production of knowledge. In the following paragraphs, a brief description of some of the major assumptions underlying positivism is outlined. This description serves as a way of identifying the basic tenets that underlie the orthodoxy in sport psychology. There is no definitive definition of positivism. The discussion here will center on the characteristics frequently associated with it. (For more detailed analyses of its characteristics, see Cohen, 1980; Giddens, 1979; Jaggar, 1983; and Keat & Urry, 1975.)

Positivism begins with the assumption that reality, whether physical or social, can be reduced to individual, constituent parts. The challenge for positivist science is to identify the parts and to explain their relationships to each other. It is assumed that reality is both orderly and logical and therefore can be described and documented by scientists using the appropriate methods. The scientific method that derives from logical positivism is a method of developing knowledge that has as its aim the development of universal laws about the world. At the root of this method is the belief that in order to study phenomena one has to observe them. The assumption underlying this is that there is an objective reality that can be observed, quantified, explained, and predicted through the careful and systematic use of established procedures and techniques. Logical positivism as a way of knowing is exclusive in that it asserts that knowledge *not* based on directly observable data is meaningless.

One way to think about the scientific method is to see it as a series of steps. Martens (using the work of Lachman, 1960) identified six steps that characterize the scientific method. They are

1. formulation of specific hypotheses or specific questions for investigation,
2. design of the investigation,
3. accumulation of the data,
4. classification of the data,
5. development of generalizations, and
6. verification of the results, both the data and generalizations. (1987, p. 32)

These steps have been developed to provide scientists with a way of collecting reliable and valid data that can then be used to develop generalizable theories and laws of human behavior. This process of theory building and testing is presumed to lead to the development of "truth" because it relies heavily upon the assumed "objectivity" of both the scientists doing research and the process itself. Objectivity is the foundation upon which the scientific method and positivist theory rests.

Objectivity most simply refers to a lack of bias. However, this notion has a number of different aspects to it when it is conceived within positivist definitions of science. First, objectivity implies that the findings of research are verifiable by any scientist. The assumption is that different people following the same accepted rules for analyzing and interpreting data will reach the same scientific conclusions from a set of data. Objectivity is also taken to mean that scientists do not allow their personal values and beliefs to affect their judgments. Rather, they use only the data gathered from their controlled empirical studies to develop their theories and explanations. When used in this sense, objectivity is taken as evidence of value-neutrality (Jaggar, 1983).

Positivism, then, is a way of defining reality and constructing knowledge about the world. The assumptions embedded within this theory provide scientists working within this framework with rules for generating and evaluating knowledge. Jaggar (1983) provides a useful description of the positivist view of scientists and science:

> On the positivist view, therefore, good scientists are detached observers and manipulators of nature who follow strict methodological rules, which enable them to separate themselves from the special values, interests and emotions generated by their class, race, sex or unique situation. (p. 356)

The orthodoxy in sport psychology (i.e., the dominant mode of knowledge production) is based on the premises established by logical positivism, where knowledge from objective, controlled experiments is seen as the basis for developing sound theories about behavior in sport. Although this view of the discipline is clearly the dominant one in the field, it is not universally accepted by sport psychologists and has recently been questioned and criticized.

Something's Wrong That Needs Fixing: Taking on the Orthodoxy in Sport Psychology

Criticisms of the orthodoxy in sport psychology have arisen as a result of concerns that modernist or positivist paradigms for developing knowledge about behavior in sport may have little utility outside of the controlled setting of the research laboratory. In this section, these criticisms are outlined, and the implications for research in sport psychology are discussed.

Developing a Different Form of Research: Moving From the Laboratory to the Field

One of the first criticisms of the orthodoxy in sport psychology was written by Rainer Martens (1979). Martens voiced his concerns about the utility of orthodox research practices for understanding sport behavior. He suggested that sport psychologists needed a different paradigm to guide research and theory building, one capable of building sport-specific theories derived from research conducted in the field, where the behavior of athletes and coaches could be studied in authentic settings.

Although Martens called for a different paradigm for sport-psychological research, his critique was in fact largely *methodological* rather

than *epistemological*. Despite his claims to be disenchanted with logical positivism, Martens's suggestions did not lay the foundation for the development of a new paradigm, or alternative ways of knowing, but simply reconstituted the orthodoxy to allow research to move from the laboratory to the field. This early critique may have had the effect of rocking the boat of logical positivism in sport psychology, but it came nowhere close to sinking it. In effect, this critique called for a redesign of the existing orthodoxy rather than posing a fundamental challenge to the epistemological assumptions underlying it.

Martens's criticisms, however, did have an impact on the field of sport psychology. In the decade following the publication of his article, the number of studies conducted in field settings increased measurably. In addition, Martens's criticisms of the field were followed by considerable debate and discussion about how research ought to be conducted in sport psychology (see, e.g., Feltz, 1987; Landers, 1983; Siedentop, 1980; Thomas, 1980). In retrospect, the discussion in these articles centered primarily around methodological concerns and did not address the more basic issue of how knowledge in sport psychology is constructed. Thus, it is clear that the orthodoxy in sport psychology did not abandon logical positivism as a model for constructing knowledge but simply modified and reconstructed notions of research within the orthodoxy.

Moving Beyond a Methodological Critique: Arguments for a New Paradigm in Sport Psychology

Although Martens's 1979 critique had an impact on how research was conducted in sport psychology, it was not until 1987 that he published an epistemological critique of the field. In this second article he refined his earlier ideas and called for the development of what he termed a heuristic paradigm in sport psychology. In this essay, Martens presented a comprehensive critique of positivism and the scientific method that derives from it. He suggested that the assumptions embedded in this theory do not allow us to study the richness and complexities that characterize human behavior. Thus, he argued, scientists ought to abandon narrow notions of objectivity and value-neutrality and begin to embrace the possibilities that exist when what it means to know is defined experientially and located within the context of the social structures in which behavior occurs. Within this research perspective, scientists are no longer disinterested, neutral outsiders but become an integral and central part of the process of developing knowledge. More specifically, in this way of knowing researchers need to locate themselves within the research process. This means identifying the perspectives and experiences that they bring with them to their work and using these as ways of developing knowledge that are partial, rather than universal, and interested, rather than disinterested. In other words, both researchers and participants are situated and located within the contexts in which the study is occurring and their individual and collective experiences and perspectives are used in understanding the behavior of individuals in particular sport contexts. The purpose of this form of research is to understand the complex ways in which individuals are located within the structures that define their lives—and consequently their experiences and behaviors in sport.

In this 1987 article Martens clearly addressed issues related to how knowledge is constructed in sport psychology. Based on his belief that the orthodox approach presents a limited understanding of human behavior in sport, he argued not only for increased use of alternative methodological procedures but, even *more importantly*, for the development and validation of alternative ways of knowing in sport psychology.

Research in Sport Psychology: The Impact of Critiques of the Orthodoxy

One way to understand the impact of Martens's (1979, 1987) critiques of the field is to examine current research and the controversies as to what constitutes legitimate knowledge in sport psychology and what it means to know and understand human behavior in sport. On the possibilities offered by the heuristic paradigm for sport psychology, Martens (1987) suggested that

> if the heuristic paradigm is embraced by sport psychologists, a shift from the almost exclusive reliance on nomothetic, abstract research to the use of idiographic methods would most assuredly occur. We would find greater emphasis on case studies, clinical reports, and other introspective methods of acquiring knowledge. Also, we would expect to see many more field studies in which the investigator integrated his or her tacit knowledge with the behaviors of those observed. (p. 52)

This statement illustrates the tensions that exist in the field over what constitutes legitimate knowledge. The issues that have arisen in the

context of these debates are presented in a number of different ways. They are often defined as problems of theoretical versus descriptive research, quantitative versus qualitative research, laboratory versus field research, or nomothetic versus idiographic research.

The fact that there are controversies in the field of sport psychology over legitimate ways to construct knowledge about behavior might be seen as a signal that the field is maturing and growing in sophistication. However, it is important to recognize that Martens's critiques of the field have largely been interpreted as *methodological* rather than *epistemological*. This means that attention has been focused somewhat narrowly on questions concerning the "best" methods of collecting data and has largely ignored Martens's more broadly based concern about what it means to know in sport psychology. The fact that much of the controversy that exists in the field remains focused on method suggests either that there is a reluctance to examine how research questions are developed and constructed or that alternatives to modernist orthodox ways of knowing are not seen as important or useful for sport psychologists and their work. Martens's 1987 critique called for much more than an examination of method and suggested that sport psychologists must begin to understand and investigate the possibilities that exist for understanding behavior using paradigms other than logical positivism.

Critiques of modernist science and logical positivism cannot be ignored. They are responsible for generating debate and discussion about the assumptions that underlie how we develop and generate knowledge about the world. Sport psychologists can benefit from these debates and use them to understand much more fully the relationships that exist between *what* we know and *how* we come to know it. Put simply, we need to abandon the belief that there is only one legitimate way of knowing in sport psychology and begin to understand that it is both possible and desirable to examine behavior in different ways.

It is obvious that the critiques of the orthodoxy that have emerged recently in the sport psychology literature have, with only a couple of exceptions, been limited to methodological, rather than epistomological, concerns. In an effort to carry these critical analyses of traditional research perspectives a step further and provide an alternative vision to that outlined by Martens (1987), we next consider a different critique, one that has been developed and presented outside of the sport psychology literature. This discussion, which is based on postmodernist and feminist critiques of science, is presented in an attempt to illustrate how primary adherence to, and reliance on, logical positivism has seriously limited, and will continue to seriously limit, our understanding of the diversity in human behavior that occurs in sport contexts. The *benefits* of using logical positivism are well known and established in the field and therefore do not need to be identified.

Developing a Different Perspective for Sport Psychology: Working Toward Inclusive Ways of Knowing

It is the labcoat, literally and symbolically, that wraps the scientist in the robe of innocence—of a pristine and asceptic neutrality—and gives him, like the klansman, a faceless authority that his audience can't challenge. From that sheeted figure comes a powerful, mysterious, impenetrable, coercive, anonymous male voice. How do we counter that voice?

—RUTH BLEIER

It is clear that logical positivism continues to be the dominant paradigm for constructing knowledge and meaning in sport psychology. Given this situation, questions about the social construction of knowledge may appear to many readers to be unimportant and a distraction from the "important" work that needs to be done to promote a better understanding of human behavior in sport and exercise settings. However, as the discussion in this section will show, traditional research paradigms have not adequately represented the behavioral diversity that exists among individuals who are involved in exercise and sport. Thus, if the knowledge that is constructed in sport psychology is to truly reflect the different perspectives or standpoints of the persons it purports to be studying, then we must reconceptualize what it means to know in sport psychology. One way to do this is to begin to *contextualize* the knowledge that is produced. Rather than searching for universal statements of fact about behavior, we must make explicit the positions that we are adopting in our work by locating ourselves and our own values in the research process.

We need to recognize that sport behaviors cannot be meaningfully isolated and studied independently of the contexts in which they are played. Sports have different meanings for different athletes, and their behaviors are developed within the contexts of these meanings. Sport practices are not neutral and value-free. Rather, as a number of writers have recently explained, sport practices in our culture are clearly based upon, or oriented to, the power, interests and needs of European, middle-class, able-bodied, heterosexual men (Dunning & Sheard, 1979; Fine, 1987; Mangan & Park, 1987). For example, there is evidence to show that sport is used to celebrate particular forms of masculinity (those that stress strength, speed, and power) as natural rather than socially developed (see Messner & Sabo, 1990). When this notion is combined with the idea that sport is fair and just and upholds the liberal democratic ideals of meritocracy (where reward is allocated on the basis of hard work and talent), it is easy for us to think of sport as neutral activity easily accessible to all who are talented and who are prepared to work hard to achieve success. This view of sport is powerful because it suggests that any problems that exist in sport (e.g., the virtual absence of African Americans and working-class individuals in sports like golf and tennis; the existence of rules to prevent girls and women from competing with men in contact sports like wrestling and football; and the underrepresentation of African American coaches, owners, and managers in sports like basketball, football, and baseball despite large numbers of African American players) are the result of problems residing within the individual (e.g., no talent, too lazy, burn out, too anxious) rather than within the structure of sport itself. Thus, in order to fully

understand behavior in sport, it is important to recognize that it does not occur within a neutral context but in a sport world that is designed to celebrate middle-class values of achievement and hard work and dominant notions of ability and skill that are tied to stereotypes about males and females and whites and persons of color.

To illustrate these ideas within the sport psychology literature, we can look at the existing research on children's participation motivation. Specifically, in order to understand why children drop out of youth sport programs, researchers in this area have typically looked for factors either within individual children (e.g., anxiety, motivation, self-esteem) or within the social environment (e.g., socialization). Although this appears to be a reasonable way to conceptualize the problem, it cannot account for the fact that girls, working-class youth, adolescents of color, fat youth, disabled youth, and gay and lesbian youth may leave sport programs because of personal experiences of oppression such as racism, sexism, and homophobia that they encounter while playing sport. These experiences may result in a variety of behavioral responses. The primary issue here is that the behaviors that are evident in certain children (e.g., high anxiety, low motivation) can only be understood if they are seen as *responses* to particular contexts and/or practices within those contexts. It is one thing to say that a child has dropped out of sport because of such personal characteristics as high anxiety, extrinsic motivation, or low self-esteem. But it is quite another thing to realize that if sport is constructed in ways that create racist or sexist practices, certain children may develop responses that manifest themselves in low self-esteem and lack of motivation, which, in turn may cause such children to drop out of sport. If this social context is ignored, then the explanation for discontinuation from sport will only be seen as residing within children rather than as a problem within the structures that constitute youth sport.

Research in sport psychology has tended to treat sport as neutral and unproblematic. This is understandable, given that most of the work in the field is derived from modernist conceptions of science and scientific practice. The problem is that much of the research has used the behavior of white middle-class males (the majority of participants in organized sport) as the standard or norm against which all other behavior is measured. This works well when studying the behavior of white middle-class males but is a problem for any other groups. Any woman or girl who has played sport understands, and can explain only too well, what these problems are. To be told, for example, that you are playing "like a girl" is to be told that you are playing poorly. Yet for girls to be seen playing like the boys means more than simply playing well: It means being answerable to questions about sexuality and feminity. (One need only think of Natasha Dennis, a very skilled 10-year-old soccer player in Texas, who was suspected by some parents of an opposing team of being a boy because her level of skill was viewed as too good for a girl.) The point is not to stop studying behavior in sport but to study it in ways that recognize what happens when we use a single standard to judge all behavior. Because we live in a culture in which white middle-class male values are seen as universal, anything that deviates from these values is not simply defined as different but as a "problem." Not surprisingly, then, problems are often seen as residing within children who are not white, middle-class, and male.

This critique is not a new one. It has been expressed by various feminists in their different attempts to illustrate how knowledge in the biological and behavioral sciences has represented white middle-class male perceptions of the world as universal and therefore representative of all reality. (For examples of feminist critiques supporting our arguments, see Bleier, 1986, 1987; Collins, 1989; Harding, 1986; Jaggar, 1983; and a special issue of *Women's Studies International Forum* on feminism and science—12[1989].) The purpose of this critique is to challenge the assumption embedded in logical positivism that there is an objective reality that can be discovered and represented in a way that is neutral and value-free. This is Bleier's point as quoted on page 18. Our work is neither neutral nor innocent. It reflects particular beliefs about the world and the best ways to understand and represent that world. Unfortunately, in both science generally and psychology in particular, there is evidence that supposedly "objective" research on individuals and groups other than white men is neither innocent nor neutral (see Harding, 1986, 1987). Under the guise of scientific neutrality, negative stereotypes about women, people of color, and gays and lesbians have been presented as "the facts" and thus representative of the truth about the characteristics of individuals belonging to these groups.

Examples of how objectivity and neutrality can be, and have been, abused in the name of science are being exposed by the works of, among others, feminists, African Americans, and gays and lesbians who are challenging and critiquing knowledge that misrepresents and distorts the realities of their lives. An example of such a critique is provided by Stephen Gould's *The Mismeasure of*

Man (1981), in which he illustrates how knowledge developed in the behavioral sciences has been used to reproduce oppression of women and people of color. For example, Gould shows how the theories developed by individuals such as Yerkes, and Gustave Le Bon were based on scholarship that is at best highly suspect and questionable. For example, Gustave Le Bon wrote in 1879:

> In the most intelligent races, as among the Parisians, there are a large number of women whose brains are closer in size to those of gorilla than to the most developed male brains. This inferiority is so obvious that no one can contest it for a moment; only its degree is worth discussion. All psychologists who have studied the intelligence of women, as well as poets and novelists, recognize today that they represent the most inferior forms of human evolution and that they are closer to children and savages than to an adult civilized man. (Gould, 1981, p. 104)

And Yerkes, writing in 1921, suggested from his measures of "innate" intelligence obtained from results of Binet tests that

> the negro lacks initiative, displays little or no leadership, and cannot accept responsibility. Some point out that these defects are greater in the southern negro. All officers seem to further agree that the negro is a cheerful, willing soldier, naturally subservient. (Gould, 1981, p. 197)

It is tempting to look at these examples as problems of an earlier period in history and continue to believe that sport psychology today is in fact objective and does not reflect blatantly sexist and racist meanings. This is a mistake. We must examine our own work for sexism, racism, classicism, heterosexism and other forms of thinking that are oppressive. We need to understand and question the consequences of our work and critically analyze the questions we ask and the measures and standards we use in our attempts to answer them. We need to ask why we continue to focus on sex-differences research or on research that compares the achievements and motivations of white athletes to black athletes. We need to understand that in doing such work, irrespective of the methods we choose to study the differences, we risk reproducing sexism and racism if we use white males as the standard against which the behavior and responses of women and African Americans are judged. The danger in this is that we will explain any differences that exist in terms of "problems" within those who are different and fail to ask what it is

about the sport experience that may elicit such differential behaviors.

The critiques that have been outlined in this section are ones that can be made about all forms of research. In addressing questions such as the ones raised in this section, the possibilities have been expanded for developing alternative ways of knowing that can adequately represent the diversity of behavior in sport. By avoiding the problems that occur when we use false universals about behavior, it will be possible to create ways of knowing and understanding sport that help us to better understand the behavior of all individuals in sport and exercise settings.

Future Directions for Research and Scholarship in Sport Psychology

This chapter began with a discussion and explanation of the dominant way of knowing or constructing knowledge in sport psychology. This description of what it means to know within the orthodoxy in sport psychology was then used to outline and develop criticisms of this dominant construction of knowledge. Unfortunately, these arguments are not typically discussed or debated within sport psychology. Most of the arguments and debates in the field have focused on methodological questions rather than epistemological ones. Although methodological questions are extremely important, they, too, need to be located within the context of larger epistemological debates about what it means to know. We do not believe that our critique means abandoning all or even many of the research methods that are being used in sport psychology but only rethinking how we use these methods and what we can say about the knowledge and understanding that is obtained from the data that we collect.

Suggestions for future research and scholarship in sport psychology are offered in the final section. These recommendations are provided as a response to the concerns raised in the previous discussion about the pursuit of knowledge in sport psychology. Thus, they illustrate how a critical analysis of how knowledge is constructed and validated can and should be used to inform our research practices.

Recommendation Number 1

We must be willing, individually and collectively, to question how knowledge about sport behavior is developed and created in sport psychology. We must explore alternative ways of understanding and explaining behavior in sport and treat these as credible and useful contributions to the field. Thus, it is important to view questions of epistemology and methodology together rather than separately. If this occurs, it will be possible to judge research based not only on the particular methodology employed but also (and perhaps more importantly) on how such research interprets and contextualizes the data gathered in the study.

Inherent in the recommendation that we need to critically analyze both what we know and how and why we know it is the notion that our field must move away from a strict adherence to modernist conceptions of research. This recommendation is based in part on the philosophical issues raised earlier but is also made in response to the methodological (rather than epistemological) controversies that have surfaced in our literature within the last several years. These controversies include such issues as

- the relative value of field or laboratory research contexts,
- the relative reliability and/or validity of self-report versus observational or physiological measurement systems, and
- the relative value of quantitative versus qualitative research methodologies.

We suggest that these controversies are misguided because they begin with the modernist conception that it is both possible and desirable to produce metanarratives (grand theories) about behavior in sport and because they frame the debates in terms of how much each of these methodological strategies enable the production of such a narrative. The question is not which particular methodology can contribute most to theory or narrative building but rather whether or not it is possible to produce a grand narrative for sport behavior. What are the consequences if we continue to try to do so in the light of all the evidence suggesting that such research will only succeed in misrepresenting and oversimplifying the very complex and multiple forms of reality that constitute sporting experiences and behavior (see Nicholson, 1990)? We suggest that most topics in sport psychology cannot be adequately addressed without using a variety of methods and interpretive strategies that will allow researchers to compare and contrast the results obtained through different ways of knowing.

Recommendation Number 2

Sport psychologists must recognize that human behavior in sport (as in any other context) is complex and multifaceted. As Roberts (1989) noted,

> The conceptual models we erect to describe psychological functioning fail to capture the true complexities of bidirectional causality, the use of feedback mechanisms, and the constellation of cognitions that characterize individuals in exercise and sport. The problem with both theory-driven and practice-driven hypotheses currently tested in exercise and sport is that both fail to attend to the complexities with which the variables are organized in the individual and social systems. (p. 80)

In response to this criticism, Roberts recommended increased use of multivariate, time-series designs as well as nonparametric procedures that are more apt to capture the complexity

of human behavior. While we agree with the need to use more inclusive research methodologies in order to assess the whole of human behavior adequately, we note again that when these methods are all assumed to help produce a better metanarrative or grand theory, all we shall have achieved is a different *method* for knowing in the same (orthodox) way. What is needed is a recognition of the alternative ways of knowing and a production of alternative narratives—some perhaps complementary, others seemingly oppositional. If we can begin to understand how these come together so as to reflect that behavior is dynamic and develops within the structures and contexts that themselves give meaning to behavior, we can then celebrate both the similarity and the diversity that characterizes behavior in sport.

Recommendation Number 3

As sport psychologists, we need to interpret the results of our behavioral research in ways that are sensitive to the social and political contexts of sport in U.S. culture. We need to strive to develop research and knowledge that is inclusive. This means that we must be sensitive to how our work may construct oppressive images, practices, and policies. We must be clear about contextualizing our findings to ensuring that our work does not invoke white middle-class male standards as universal and normative. In an attempt to develop inclusive ways of knowing, we need to recognize and celebrate the complexity and diversity that characterizes behavior in sport in order to develop ways of knowing that reflect this complexity and richness.

Conclusion

We have illustrated the importance of understanding what it means to know in sport psychology and the consequences of developing particular conceptions of, and methods for, knowing. We believe that the future of sport psychology will be an exciting one if we can critically analyze not only what we are doing but how and why we are electing to do it in particular ways. Developing critical, reflective ways of knowing will allow us to develop knowledge that is inclusive and that reflects the complexity of the problems we are attempting to solve. This is not an easy challenge, but we believe it can and will shape the future of sport psychology as a field.

References

Bleier, R. (1986). Lab coat: Robe of innocence or Klansman's sheet? In T. de Lauretis (Ed.), *Feminist studies, critical studies* (pp. 55-56). Bloomington, IN: Indiana University Press.

Bleier, R. (Ed.). (1987). Feminist approaches to science. Elmsford, NY: The Athene Series, Pergamon Press.

Cohen, P. (1980). Is positivism dead? *Sociological Review,* **28**(1), 141-76.

Collins, P.H. (1989). The social construction of black feminist thought. *Signs,* **14**(4), 743-745.

Dunning, E., & Sheard, K. (1979). *Barbarians, gentlemen, and players.* New York: New York University Press.

Feltz, D. (1987). Advancing knowledge in sport psychology: Strategies for expanding our conceptual frameworks. *Quest,* **39**, 243-254.

Feminism and science [Special issue]. (1989). Women's Studies International Forum, **12**.

Fine, G.A. (1987). *With the boys: Little League baseball and preadolescent culture.* Chicago: University of Chicago Press.

Flax, J. (1990). Postmodernism and gender relations in feminist theory. In L.J. Nicholson (Ed.), *Feminism/postmodernism* (pp. 39-62). New York: Routledge & Kegan Paul.

Giddens, A. (1979). Positivism and its critics. In T. Bottomore & R. Nisbet (Eds.), *A history of sociological analysis* (pp. 361-474). London: Heinemann.

Gould, S. (1981). *The mismeasure of man.* New York: W.W. Norton.

Harding, S. (1986). *The science question in feminism.* Ithaca, NY: Cornell University Press.

Harding, S. (Ed.) (1987). *Feminism and methodology.* Bloomington, IN: Indiana University Press.

Jaggar, A.M. (1983). *Feminist politics and human nature.* Totowa, NJ: Rowman & Allanheld.

Keat, J., & Urry, J. (1975). *Social theory as science.* London: Routlege & Kegan Paul.

Lachman, S.J. (1960). *The foundations of science.* New York: Vantage.

Landers, D. (1983). Whatever happened to theory testing in sport psychology? *Journal of Sport Psychology, 5,* 135-151.

Mangan, J.A., & Park, R. (Eds.) (1987). *From 'fair sex' to feminism: Sport and the socialization of women in the industrial and postindustrial eras.* London: Frank Cass.

Martens, R. (1979). About smocks and jocks. *Journal of Sport Psychology, 1,* 94-99.

Martens, R. (1987). Science, knowledge, and sport psychology. *Sport Psychologist, 1,* 29-55.

Messner, M., & Sabo, D. (Eds.) (1990). *Sport, men, and the gender order.* Champaign, IL: Human Kinetics.

Nicholson, L.J. (Ed.) (1990). *Feminism/postmodernism.* New York: Routledge, Champman and Hall.

Roberts, G. (1989). When motivation matters: The need to expand the conceptual model. In J. Skinner, C. Corbin, D. Landers, P. Martin, & C. Wells (Eds.), *Future directions in exercise and sport science research* (pp. 71-84). Champaign, IL: Human Kinetics.

Siedentop, D. (1980). Two cheers for Rainer. *Journal of Sport Psychology,* **2**(1), 2-4.

Thomas, J. (1980). Half a cheer for Rainer & Daryl. *Journal of Sport Psychology,* **2**(4), 266-267.

Part II

Individual Differences and Sport Behavior

A major focus in the sport psychology research literature over the past 25 years has been on the identification of particular characteristics or traits of individuals that can be used to explain and predict their behavior in sport and physical activity contexts. As noted in the preface, such individual difference factors usually consist of relatively stable traits, dispositions, or characteristics of individuals that can be measured in participants with varying degrees of ease and accuracy. It is, of course, assumed that individuals' scores on these individual difference measures will vary on a continuum and that this variability can explain at least a portion of the differences observed among individuals in sport and physical activity contexts.

Part II will examine the research and theory that have been conducted to test the hypothesized relationship between selected individual difference factors and subsequent sport behavior. It will begin with a chapter by Robin Vealey providing an overall perspective on the reciprocal relationship between personality and sport behavior. Vealey begins her chapter by defining personality and outlining the corresponding theories that have been developed to explain the relationship between personality and behavior. She then critically reviews the research procedures that have been used both to measure personality and to examine the personality and sport behavior relationship. She concludes this chapter by summarizing the current status of knowledge in this area and outlining potential directions for future research. Due to this comprehensive overview, Vealey's chapter provides an excellent foundation for chapters 4-7, which focus on more specific aspects of personality.

In chapter 4, Maureen Weiss and Nigel Chaumeton review the research and theory that have been developed to explain how individuals can differ in motivational orientation or style and how such orientations or styles may affect their sport behavior. Individual differences in motivational orientation are examined from three different perspectives: participation and discontinuation motivation, intrinsic/extrinsic motivational orientation, and competitive goal orientation. Weiss and Chaumeton conclude their chapter by outlining an integrated model of sport motivation that they suggest can be used to guide future research on motivated behavior in sport and physical activity contexts.

In chapter 5, Edward McAuley reviews the literature on self-referent thought in sport and exercise participants, with particular attention directed toward self-efficacy cognitions and performance attributions. His chapter begins with an explanation and critical review of the theory and research in both of these areas. He then synthesizes the two approaches to illustrate how causal attributions and self-efficacy cognitions reciprocally affect each other and how both are integrally related to behavior in sport and exercise contexts.

In chapter 6, Daniel Gould and Vikki Krane examine individual differences in anxiety and arousal and again use this variability to explain and predict subsequent differences in performance and behavior. Gould and Krane focus particularly on the research and theory pertaining to the arousal–performance relationship and critically review a number of theories that have been developed to explain this relationship. Noting that there has been considerable inconsistency in the sport psychology literature in the use of arousal-related terminology, Gould and Krane offer a conceptual model for integrating arousal construct terminology and then use this model to suggest future directions for research on anxiety, arousal, and sport performance.

Finally, in chapter 7, Diane Gill examines the impact of gender and gender roles on sport and exercise behavior. Gill writes her review of the available research and theory from a chronological perspective. She begins with an examination of the early work on sex differences in sport and exercise behavior and progresses through a review of the literature on gender role orientation and achievement cognitions. Gill concludes her review by arguing for the need to consider gender within the context of sociocultural history and the current social environment rather than merely as a characteristic of individuals that affects their sport and exercise behavior. This approach is then used to suggest future research directions.

Although all of the chapters in Part II are written from the perspective that individual difference factors can serve as predictors of sport behavior, each of these authors clearly recognizes that these individual difference factors must be used in combination with situational factors if an adequate understanding of sport behavior is to be obtained. As Vealey, for example, notes in chapter 3, research has consistently shown that sport behavior is codetermined by intrapersonal and situational or environmental factors. Thus, although Part II focuses on individual difference characteristics while Part III will focus on factors in the sport and social environment, the overriding theme of each chapter is the interactional approach to the study of behavior in sport and physical activity contexts.

Chapter 3

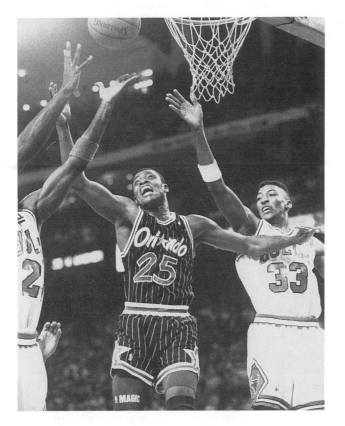

Personality and Sport: A Comprehensive View

Robin S. Vealey
Miami University

The human body is a machine; it is a great chemical laboratory; it is an achievement of engineering; but it is also a self. The ancients believed that the body was merely the dwelling place of a spiritual being, and that this being looked out through the eyes as one would look through a window to get knowledge of the external world. They believed that this soul was responsible for all that the body did, and that no matter how fatigued the body or how great the obstacle, the soul could by sheer "mental resolve" or "will power" drive the body to further work or to overcome any obstacle. We now know that the ancients were rather crude and unscientific in many of their beliefs. While we cannot accept their explanations of self or personality, the facts which they sought to explain are still before us and we must now come to terms with them.

—COLEMAN GRIFFITH

Historically, one of the most popular issues in sport psychology concerns the relationship between personality and sport participation.

From an intuitive perspective, it seems logical that certain personality attributes (e.g., competitiveness, self-confidence) are important to achieving success in sport. Another popular belief is that certain personality attributes (e.g., self-esteem, emotional control) may be developed or modified through sport participation. Both of these issues have been extensively investigated over the last three decades. Ruffer (1975, 1976a, 1976b) identified 572 research studies that have examined the relationship between personality and sport. Fisher (1984) found that well over one thousand studies have been conducted on personality and sport behavior. However, does this plethora of research support the popular perceptions of the relationship between personality and sport behavior? Are there born winners or personality profiles that relate to success in sport? Does sport build character or serve to develop desirable personality characteristics in individuals?

The purpose of this chapter is to review theory and research on personality and sport, beginning with a discussion of definitional, theoretical, paradigmatic, and methodological issues regarding the study of personality. Following this introductory discussion, the empirical research examining the reciprocal relationship between personality factors and participation in sport is reviewed. This chapter takes a more comprehensive view of sport personality than has been advanced in previous reviews of this literature (e.g., Kane, 1978; Martens, 1975; Morgan, 1980b; Silva, 1984). This comprehensive view is based on the perspective that the very nature of personality psychology causes it to underlie much of social psychology (Carlson, 1984; Malloy & Kenny, 1986; Snyder, 1983). Thus, the perspective taken in this chapter is that personality involves considerably more than just personality traits and descriptive personality profiles. Although many people have stated that sport personality research is dead, an alternative view suggests that much of what is studied in sport psychology could be called the study of personality in sport (Vealey, 1989).

The chapter is divided into seven sections. The first four provide an introduction to the area by defining *personality*, examining theories and paradigms of personality, and outlining approaches and methods in personality assessment. The next two review the existing research on sport personality. The final section examines problems in the sport personality area and offers future directions for research.

Defining Personality

Even a cursory examination of the personality literature indicates that there is little consensus as to the definition of *personality*. Allport defines it as "the dynamic organization within the individual of those psychophysical systems that determine his [sic] characteristic behavior and thought" (1961, p. 28). Guilford simply defines it as "a person's unique pattern of traits" (1959, p. 5). Maddi more extensively defines it as "a stable set of characteristics and tendencies that determine those commonalities and differences in the psychological behavior (thoughts, feelings, and actions) of people that have continuity in time and that may or may not be easily understood in terms of the social and biological pressures of the immediate situation alone" (1976, p. 9). Lazarus and Monat define it as "the underlying, relatively stable, psychological structure and processes that organize human experience and shape a person's activities and reactions to the environment" (1979, p. 1).

These definitions illustrate the diversity that exists among theorists in their definitions of personality. Obviously, this diversity makes it difficult to clearly understand what personality is and may in part explain the controversy, contradictory findings, and debates that have raged in the personality literature. Pervin (1970) asserts that how individual investigators define personality reflects the kind of behavior they measure and the type of techniques they use to study behavior. For example, Allport's definition states that the focus of personality should be on behaviors that are characteristic of an individual and that these behaviors are explained by "psychophysical systems." Guilford speaks of traits but not of any behavioral consequences of these traits. Maddi, with Lazarus and Monat, speak of personality as involving stable characteristics and impinging on behavior, experiences, or reactions. Maddi also accounts for commonalities as well as differences in behavior; defines behavior as encompassing thoughts, feelings, and actions; and explains that personality is often overshadowed by situational factors. Clearly, researchers who study personality in sport might use very different approaches, depending upon which definition of personality they choose to follow. Although the various definitions of personality do serve the purpose of operationalizing variables for study, they do not, unfortunately, provide a consensual definition of personality.

Given the diversity among theorists in their definitions of personality, it seems useful to identify common features that pervade most definitions. Two theorists have conceptualized approaches or models that identify components common to most all specific definitions of personality. The first approach to understanding personality is offered by Levy (1970), who states that three conditions are necessary when speaking of personality:

1. Personality by nature always involves behavior based on characteristics defining an important aspect of a person's identity, which may be labeled by psychologists as traits, styles, needs, motives, or cognitions; but all of these terms represent a means by which the identity of an individual may be established.
2. Personality is concerned with behavior influenced by an internal locus of causation or behavior that cannot be entirely explained in terms of the external situation; for example, the startle reflex or the "fight or flight" response to danger would not be considered as areas of study in personality.
3. This behavior must possess some degree of organization or structure; that is, various human behaviors should appear to fit into a meaningful pattern, and although behavior may not be perfectly consistent, it is not random.

The second approach or model for understanding personality is conceptualized by Hollander (1967). Many definitions of personality refer to the existence of a core that contains personality components that are for the most part stable and unchanging (e.g., Allport, 1937; Eysenck, 1960; Maddi, 1976). Theorists have also conceptualized peripheral characteristics of personality that emanate from the core (Allport, 1937; Maddi, 1976). Hollander (1967) incorporates the notion of core and peripheral personality structure in a model that includes a psychological core, typical responses, role-related behaviors, and the social environment (see Figure 3.1).

The psychological core is based on early interactions with the social environment and includes perceptions of the external world as well as perceptions about self. According to Hollander, an individual's self-concept is the centerpiece of the psychological core. At the next level are typical responses that are fairly predictable behaviors that emanate from our core characteristics. The outermost ring in the model represents role-related behaviors that are behaviors we engage in daily, based upon the influence of the social environment. Role-related behaviors exemplify the dynamic aspect of personality, since they include behaviors that are situationally variable. Role-related behaviors for athletes are predicted to result from the complex relationship between core characteristics, typical responses, and the unique social characteristics of sport (e.g., public evaluation, salient rewards). Like Levy (1970),

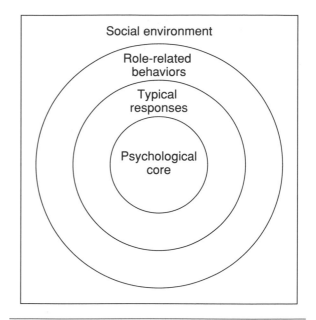

Figure 3.1 Hollander's model of personality.
Note. From *Principles and Methods of Social Psychology* by Edwin P. Hollander. Copyright © 1967 by Oxford University Press, Inc. Reprinted by permission.

Hollander (1967) does not specifically define personality but, rather, provides a model in which personality can be understood as consistent yet dynamic, internal yet manifested externally, and intrapersonal yet influenced by the social environment.

Thus, although personality is too broad to be defined in one particular way, theorists such as Levy (1970) and Hollander (1967) have provided useful models of personality that may serve as frameworks for the systematic study of personality in sport.

Theories and Paradigms of Personality

The goal of sport personality research is to explain the role of personality in sport in a way that is systematic, replicable, and predictive. To achieve this goal, a theoretical perspective is needed. Theories are simple systematic explanations of phenomena that are derived from the accumulation of empirical evidence. Due to the broad nature of personality psychology, numerous theories have been proposed (similar to the numerous definitions of personality). In this section, these theories will be broadly categorized into four major theoretical approaches (psychodynamic, dispositional, phenomenological, and learning) and will briefly outline example theories that characterize each of these approaches. Later in this chapter, research which has been conducted to test the applicability of these theories to sport are reviewed. The discussion of personality theory presented in this section of the chapter is by no means exhaustive but, rather, represents a general and necessarily brief overview of the available literature. This section ends with a discussion of the paradigmatic person–situation debate in the personality literature and the resultant endorsement of the interactional paradigm as that which is most appropriate for understanding personality and sport behavior.

Psychodynamic Approaches

Although psychodynamic approaches are very complex, only a cursory description of them is provided here. There is no need to go into detail, since these theories have had little direct impact on sport personality research, due to their clinical and psychopathological focus. However, psychodynamic theory has had an enormous influence on the field of psychology and is often used by clinical consultants in psychological intervention with athletes.

Originating with the work of Sigmund Freud (1900/1953, 1901/1960), the psychodynamic approach is based on the premise that personality is a dynamic set of processes always in motion and often in conflict. This approach is also deterministic in that behavior is seen to be determined for individuals instead of by individuals. To psychodynamic theorists, personality is greatly influenced by early experiences and behavior is viewed as being determined by unconscious processes. Freud's psychoanalytic theory is based on the continuous interaction and conflict between his proposed three parts of the psychic structure: id, ego, and superego. The adult personality is shaped by the resolution of these conflicts in early life as the ego mediates between the unconscious impulses of the id and the values and conscience of the superego. Several neo-Freudians, such as Alfred Adler (1929), Erik Erikson (1950), Erich Fromm (1947), Karen Horney (1924), and Carl Jung (1926), continued the psychodynamic approach by proposing various modifications in Freud's original theory. Generally, these neo-Freudians incorporated social and cultural forces into their psychodynamic theories, as opposed to Freud's emphasis on instinctual drives.

Dispositional Approaches

Dispositional theories emphasize consistency in behavior over time and across situations. These theories contend that an individual's personality is essentially a collection of dispositional characteristics. Included in this category of theories are trait theories, biological theories, and motive/need theories.

Trait Theories

Trait theories of personality most clearly exemplify the dispositional approach and have generated a tremendous amount of research in psychology as well as sport psychology. Traits are relatively enduring and highly consistent internal attributes (Allport, 1937); that is, traits are intrapersonal characteristics that account for unique yet stable reactions to the environment. These theories emphasize the person as opposed to the situation; thus, personality is seen as a function of a set of enduring traits that make one person different from another. Trait theories emphasize consistent differences among individuals in their responses to the same situation.

Gordon Allport (1937) was an early influential trait theorist who emphasized individuality and uniqueness in each personality. According to Allport, traits never occur in different people in exactly the same way; rather, he suggested, traits operate in unique ways in each person. It is this unique pattern of traits, or overall "personality structure," that Allport felt determined behavior; that is, each person's behavior is determined by his or her particular trait structure. However, Allport did admit that through social interaction, individuals tend to develop some types of common traits.

Another proponent of trait theory was Raymond B. Cattell (1965), who also theorized that traits underlie human behavior. Like Allport, Cattell distinguished between "common traits," possessed by all people, and "unique traits," which occur only in a particular person and cannot be found in another in exactly the same form. Through extensive factor analysis procedures, Cattell proposed that personality is composed of 16 dimensions or primary factors (see Table 3.1). Cattell parsimoniously reduced these 16 primary factors into four second-order factors that efficiently represented the primary factor components (see Table 3.2).

Like Cattell, J.P. Guilford (1959) subdivided traits into categories, but his categories represent different interests, aptitudes, needs, and attitudes. Guilford also distinguished between traits represented by behavior (behavior traits) and those represented by physical makeup (somatic traits). He defined personality as a unique pattern of traits and emphasized individual differences by stating that the best way to know personalities is to compare them with one another. Guilford's individual difference approach is in contrast to Allport's position that personality

Table 3.1 Primary Factors of the 16PF Questionnaire

A	Warm, sociable vs. aloof, stiff
B	Mentally bright vs. mentally dull
C	Mature, calm vs. immature, emotional
E	Aggressive, competitive vs. mild, submissive
F	Enthusiastic vs. prudent, serious
G	Conscientious vs. casual, undependable
H	Adventurous vs. shy, timid
I	Sensitive, effeminate vs. tough, realistic
L	Suspecting, jealous vs. accepting, adaptable
M	Imaginative vs. practical
N	Sophisticated vs. simple, unpretentious
O	Timid, insecure vs. confident, self-secure
Q1	Radicalism vs. conservatism
Q2	Self-sufficiency vs. group adherence
Q3	Controlled vs. uncontrolled, lax
Q4	Tense, excitable vs. phlegmatic, relaxed

Table 3.2 Second-Order Factors of the 16PF Questionnaire

Second-order factor	Primary factor components
Anxiety (high vs. low)	C, H, L, O, Q3, Q4
Introversion vs. extroversion	A, E, F, H, Q2
Tough-minded vs. tender-minded	A, C, E, F, I, M, N
Independence vs. subduedness	A, E, G, M, I, Q2

is so unique that it cannot be studied by making comparisons among people.

Hans Eysenck (1967, 1970) extended the search for personality dimensions to the area of abnormal behavior and, like Cattell, utilized factor-analytic techniques. Eysenck theorized that there are two superordinate type or trait dimensions in personality: introversion–extroversion and emotionality–stability. These superordinate types are further subdivided into component traits that lead to habitual responses (e.g., extroversion is broken down into sociability, impulsiveness, activity, liveliness, and excitability). Although Eysenck and Cattell derived their structures of personality quite differently, their theories have distinct similarities. Both theories include introversion versus extroversion, and Eysenck's *emotional stability* is similar to Cattell's *anxiety dimension*. Eysenck also includes a third personality dimension called *psychoticism*, which relates to the development of psychopathologies; but this dimension is referred to far less in the literature than the other two.

Biological Theories

A second group of theories that represent the dispositional approach to personality are biological theories. Like trait theories, biological theories involve human dispositions predicted to influence behavior across situations. However, these theories postulate that human dispositions are related to biological processes. Based on the writings of Hippocrates and Galen, ancient Greeks believed that there were four basic body fluids, or "humors," that all individuals possessed in varying proportions. Different temperaments, or personalities, of individuals were seen as reflective of the different proportions of these humors. For example, yellow bile was related to irritable behavior, while black bile was associated with sadness or melancholy.

Personality has also been related to body configuration. Sheldon (1942) built upon the earlier work of Kretschmer (1925) to define three somatotypes that are theorized to predispose individuals genetically toward certain types of behaviors. Ectomorphy refers to a linear and lean body type and is associated with cerobrotonia (tenseness, inhibition, and introversion). Endomorphy describes a round or plump body type and is associated with viscerotonia (sociability, warmth, and complacency). Mesomorphy is defined as a muscular body type and is associated with somatotonia (assertiveness, risk-taking, and high levels of energy). Although Sheldon found initial support for his theory, additional research proved equivocal; and the theory has never gained wide acceptance. Also, social expectancy effects based on stereotypes of body configurations have been offered as an alternative explanation to the genetic predisposition to behave a certain way based on somatotype (Carver & Scheier, 1988).

As discussed in the previous section, Eysenck's (1967, 1970) trait theory was based on two trait dimensions: extroversion–introversion and emotionality–stability. Eysenck also provided a biological analysis of these personality dimensions. First, he suggested that introverts and extroverts differ from each other in the brain functioning of the ascending reticular activating system (ARAS). The ARAS is responsible for activating or deactivating higher portions of the brain. When the ARAS is functioning at a high level, individuals feel alert, when at a low level, they feel drowsy. Eysenck (1981) proposed that the base levels of ARAS activation of introverts are higher than those of extroverts. Thus, because introverts have higher base levels of arousal, they avoid further stimulation, while the lower base level of extroverts may induce them to seek additional stimulation. Eysenck also proposed a neural basis for the emotionality–stability dimension. It is beyond the scope of this chapter to discuss nervous system functioning in any more detail, but it is important to note that Eysenck anchored his trait theory in brain functions.

Like Eysenck, Zuckerman (1971, 1979, 1987) attempted to link the personality characteristic of sensation seeking with nervous system functioning. Individuals high in sensation seeking search for experiences that are exciting, risky, and novel. Zuckerman originally hypothesized that people differed from each other in levels of cortical arousal but refined the theory to suggest that sensation seekers possess stronger orienting responses than other individuals. The orienting response is an individual's first reaction to a new or unexpected stimulus. It is a tendency toward sensory intake and is contrasted to defense responses, which attempt to screen out stimuli. Research has substantiated stronger orienting responses among sensation seekers (Neary & Zuckerman, 1976), as well as a link between sensation seeking, brain-wave response (Zuckerman, Murtaugh & Siegel, 1974) and the production of endorphins (Johansson, Almay, von Knorring, Terenius & Astrom, 1979).

Motive or Need Theories

A third class of dispositional theories consists of motive or need theories, which essentially propose that behavior is influenced by underlying needs. To these theorists, personality differences are a function of individual differences in need patterns.

The earliest and most influential need theorist was Murray (1938), who proposed that individuals possessed two types of needs: viscerogenic, or primary, needs and psychogenic, or secondary, needs. Viscerogenic needs are primary because they are somatic in nature (e.g., food, sex, avoidance of pain). Murray proposed 28 psychogenic needs (e.g., achievement, autonomy, dominance, deference, affiliation), each with characteristic desires and feelings that drive behavior. Although closely allied with psychoanalytic theory, Murray's need theory does not incorporate psychoanalytic assumptions about the instinctual origins of human behavior. Murray emphasized that the environment plays an important role in behavior, coining the term *environmental press*. Just as an internal need increases motivation, thus creating behavioral action, an environmental press can do the same thing. For example, being in an environment in which achievement is rewarded and modeled appropriately may increase an individual's desire to achieve. Sport psychologists have linked the importance of understanding and meeting individuals' needs to participation motivation and attrition in sport (Ewing, 1981; Gould & Petlichkoff, 1988).

Of Murray's original 28 needs, the need for achievement has received the most attention in the psychological literature. McClelland (1961) and Atkinson (1957) are well known for their theory and research using the need for achievement as the basis for understanding motivation. The need for control has also sparked interest in the psychological literature, due to its proposed link to the Type A behavior pattern. Friedman and Rosenman (1974) defined the Type A personality as characterized by competitiveness, hostility, and time urgency. Glass (1977) proposes that the underlying basis for the Type A behavioral characteristics is the need for control over the environment; that is, competing is seen

as controlling a situation, time urgency is related to the fear of losing control, and hostility may result when control of a situation is blocked.

Phenomenological Approaches

Phenomenological approaches to personality focus on individuals' subjective experience and personal views of the world and self; that is, behavior is seen to be determined by the individual's understanding of self and environment rather than by predetermined or dispositional responses to external events. Phenomenology developed from the writings of the philosopher Edmund Husserl (1911/1965), who believed that too much emphasis had been placed on interpreting and classifying human experience instead of studying what human experience actually is. Other sources for the emergence of this approach were the early writings of Jung and Allport, Gestalt psychology, Kurt Lewin's (1935) field theory, and existential philosophy.

According to Carver and Scheier (1988), phenomenological approaches can be divided into two categories. The first set of theories focuses on the striving of individuals to actualize, or to fulfill, human potential and be self-determining. The second group of theories represent the cognitive approach to personality, whereby individuals actively process external events and their own behavior in order to make sense of things that take place around them. This approach emphasizes the uniqueness of each person's world view and assumes that individuals actively construct reality for themselves.

Actualization/Self-Determination Theories

Carl Rogers's (1961) self theory and Abraham Maslow's (1968) hierarchy of needs are examples of phenomenological approaches that emphasize self-determinism and the human tendency toward growth and self-actualization. The central idea behind these theories is that all persons have the potential for positive growth and change and that behavior is the result of an individual's tendency toward growth or actualization. Although Maslow's hierarchy-of-needs theory would seem to fit under the motive/need theories of the dispositional approach, Maslow was not interested in categorizing individuals according to their dominant motives or needs. Maslow theorized that all people have the same kind of motives or needs, but differ in how completely their various motives or needs are satisfied at a given time.

Though not a basic personality theory, Deci's (1975, 1980) theory of intrinsic motivation is an example of self-determination theory in that people are viewed as having an intrinsic interest in actively engaging with their environment. To Deci, motivational behavior is not a function of internal motives, instinctual needs, or desired external reinforcement but rather of the need for competence and self-determination. Deci's intrinsic motivation theory has received a great deal of attention in the sport psychology literature (Ryan, 1980; Ryan, Vallerand & Deci, 1984; Vallerand, 1983; Weinberg, 1984).

Another theory that has emerged from this approach is the concept of hardiness. Hardiness is related to Rogers's (1961) view that congruence between perceived self and actual experience leads to active engagement in life and thus to actualization, or an integrated personality. Incongruence between self and experience (termed alienation) is believed to lead to psychological problems. Hardiness (the opposite of alienation) is used to describe this level of engagement with, and commitment to, life experiences resulting from the congruence between self and experience. Research has indicated a negative relationship between hardiness and stress and illness susceptibility (Kobasa, 1979; Kobasa, Maddi & Kahn, 1982).

Cognitive Theories

Cognitive theories view individuals as novice behavioral scientists attempting to understand, or construct, behavior and events in meaningful ways. George Kelly's (1955) personal construct theory most clearly reflects cognitive theory. While trait approaches attempt to explain personality by the individual's place on a personality dimension derived by the theorist, personal construct theory attempts to understand human behavior by studying what dimensions of personality individuals subjectively construct for themselves. Kelly believes that people do not experience the world directly or in the same way. Rather, personal constructs that each of us develops serve as a lens, or filter, through which we view external events and our own behavior. People continuously evaluate the predictive efficiency of their personal constructs, and these constructs remain stable as long as they allow the person to interact successfully with the environment.

Emanating from personal construct theory, cognitive consistency theories are based on the premise that individuals attempt to achieve consistency and reduce dissonance in their perception of important concepts or cognitions

(Festinger, 1957; Heider, 1958). Thus, behavior is based on people's striving to reduce cognitive dissonance and regain cognitive consistency among personal beliefs. These theories have generated an enormous amount of experimental research in psychology.

Schema theory has also emerged from the personal construct approach of Kelly. Schema theory is concerned with the influence of cognitive structures on the selection and organization of information in individuals (Markus, 1977, 1983). Self-schemas are used to organize new and incoming information; thus, they are guides to the processing of self-related information obtained through social interactions with the environment. These cognitive structures, or schema, are theorized to be predictive of future behavior.

Like schema theory, attribution theory is another example of behavioral explanation based on the processing of self-related information. Attribution theory posits that the ways in which individuals judge the causes of particular events or outcomes impinge significantly on future motivation and behavior (Kelley, 1973; Weiner, 1974, 1985). Attribution theory has sparked considerable research in sport psychology (for a detailed discussion, see chapter 5).

Learning Approaches

Theories of personality based on the learning approach emphasize that learning accomplished through interactions with the environment explains human behavior. Seen from this perspective, personality is an accumulation of learned behavior. Learning approaches to the study of personality may be subdivided into conditioning and social learning theories.

Conditioning Theories

In conditioning approaches to personality, behaviors are "conditioned" by consequences that either strengthen or extinguish the behavior. Miller and Dollard (1941) were the first to describe personality in terms of conditioned behavior. They are often called "psychodynamic behavior theorists" (Mischel, 1971) because they included a motive or drive component in their theory. However, they represent the learning theory perspective because they attempted to account for psychoanalytic phenomena in learning theory terms (Carver & Scheier, 1988).

In his "radical behaviorism" approach, B.F. Skinner (1938, 1953) postulated that drives and motives are unnecessary to understanding behavior. Radical behaviorists such as Skinner describe behavior as one of two stimulus conditions:

deprivation or satiation. Both of these phenomena are viewed as observable, measurable, and completely unrelated to internal personality components.

Social Learning Theories

In contrast to conditioning theories, which focus on personality and behavior as the act of working for reinforcement, the learning approach to personality and behavior was expanded as theorists realized that unlike animals, humans may engage in social learning without any apparent direct reinforcement (Bandura, 1977b; Mischel, 1968). These social learning theories extend the concepts and principles of learning to interpersonal, social contexts.

J.B. Rotter's (1954) social learning formulation includes a cognitive element to personality-oriented learning theories. Rotter contends that the probability that a particular pattern of behavior will occur depends on the individual's expectancies concerning the outcomes to which his or her behavior will lead and the perceived values of those outcomes. These generalized expectancies are assumed to be consistent and stable across situations; thus, they are similar to traits, although they are construed as learned expectations. Rotter (1966) also conceptualized the term *locus of control* to describe the cause-effect connection between individuals' perceptions of their behavior and reinforcement that occurs afterward. Rotter contends that people who expect their outcomes to be determined by their actions (internal locus of control) learn from reinforcers and that people who expect their outcomes to be unrelated to their actions (external locus of control) do not learn from reinforcers.

Bandura's (1977a) self-efficacy theory is based on Rotter's theme of the importance of expectancy in influencing behavior. Derived from his clinical experiences, Bandura asserts that a sense of personal efficacy is necessary for persistent behavioral striving. Self-efficacy is the self-perceived ability to carry out desired behaviors, and Bandura argues that this construct is central to human behavior. Other theories emphasize social learning through observation (Bandura, 1969; Mischel, 1968). Observational learning refers to learning without any direct rewards or reinforcement. People learn and behave by observing other persons and events and not merely from the direct consequences of what they themselves do. A considerable amount of research in sport psychology has utilized the social learning approach (e.g., the effects of modeling or observational learning on skill acquisition and competitive behavior, locus of control related to sport behavior, and self-efficacy in sport).

The Person–Situation Debate

The theories reviewed in the previous section were grouped into psychodynamic, dispositional, phenomenological, and learning approaches because these groupings effectively categorize the theories based on similar structural and dynamic properties. An alternative way to view the study of personality is based on the distinction between dispositional, situational, and interactive approaches. As discussed previously, dispositional approaches focus on relatively stable, consistent attributes that exert generalized causal effects on behavior. In contrast, situationism is best characterized by the radical behaviorism of Skinner (1938, 1953), in which behavior is explained by examining environmental stimuli and individuals' responses to these stimuli. Finally, interactionism posits that behavior is codetermined by intrapersonal and situational factors (Bowers, 1973; Magnusson & Endler, 1977). The cognitive and social learning theories previously discussed are examples of interactional approaches to personality.

The dispositional, situational, and interactional categories may be thought of as paradigmatic thrusts or trends in personality research (Malloy & Kenny, 1986; Smith & Vetter, 1982; West, 1986). A paradigm is an accepted scientific practice that becomes a model for subsequent scientific inquiry in a particular area (Kuhn, 1970). Clearly, the adoption of a particular paradigm is the most critical feature of research, as the paradigm defines how the research question is addressed and pursued. The so-called person–situation debate arose from these paradigmatic trends in personality psychology.

The person–situation debate received its impetus from Walter Mischel's *Personality and Assessment* (1968), in which he reviewed 50 years of personality research and challenged the assumption that stable dispositions or traits could effectively predict behavior. Mischel coined the term *personality coefficient* to describe the weak relationship ($r=.30$) he found between self-report and behavioral measures. Mischel asserted that this weak personality coefficient indicates that behavior is situationally determined. Thus, he advocated a social learning approach rather than a traditional trait approach. Mischel's book stimulated two decades of diverse reactions regarding what became known as the person–situation debate (e.g., Bem, 1972; Bem & Allen, 1974; Buss, 1989; Craik, 1969; Epstein, 1979; Houts, Cook & Shadish, 1986; Kenrick & Funder, 1988; Magnusson & Endler, 1977; Pervin, 1985; Zuroff, 1986). The person–situation debate has raged in the sport psychology literature as well (Carron,

1980; Fisher, 1976, 1984; Martens, 1975; Morgan, 1980a, 1980b; Rushall, 1972; Silva, 1984); that is, sport psychologists have debated over which personality paradigm is the most efficacious approach to understand and predict behavior in sport.

Careful examination of the literature suggests that the person–situation debate is a pseudo-issue (Carlson, 1984; Endler, 1973; Houts et al., 1986). As Endler (1973) noted, this question is like asking whether air or blood is more essential to life. Pervin (1985) and Zuroff (1986) state that it is erroneous to think that trait theorists believe that people will behave the same way in all situations. In fact, they note that Allport was in fact an interactionist, since he asserted that different traits are aroused to different degrees in different situations. From a critical multiplistic perspective, Houts and colleagues (1986) suggest that the camps traditionally viewed as opposing in the person–situation debate actually agree and have simply discussed different versions of the same paradigmatic question. Mischel (1973) agreed that personality psychology should adhere to an interactional perspective, although he argued that the person component should be cast in terms of cognitive constructs instead of enduring traits. A provocative analogy is provided by Baron and Boudreau (1987) whereby intrapersonal characteristics are seen as "keys" in search of the right environmental or situational "locks." Baron and Boudreau emphasize that personality and social psychology are inextricably bound, with personality theorists specifying the nature of keys and social psychologists focusing on the nature of locks. Clearly, the door behind which the understanding of human behavior is found requires the study of both locks and keys. Thus, most personality psychologists agree that behavior is best explained by accounting for both situational and intrapersonal characteristics (i.e., by assuming an interactional perspective).

The Interactional Perspective

The person–situation debate in the personality literature has culminated with general acceptance of the interactional perspectives as the paradigm of choice in sport personality research. Reviewing the sport personality literature from 1950 to 1973, Martens (1975) concluded that the interactional paradigm was the direction that sport personality research should take. He based this conclusion on the premise that situationism was an overreaction to the trait paradigm and that sport behavior could best be understood by concurrently studying the effects of environmental and intrapersonal variables. However, the adoption of the interactional paradigm for sport personality research involves understanding various issues involved in studying personality within this paradigm. This section briefly addresses some of these issues, such as the cognitive approach within the interactional paradigm, the dispositional approach within the interactional paradigm, and the distinction between personality traits and states. The section ends with an examination of Vealey's (1989) updated review of the sport personality literature to see whether Martens's (1975) urging for the adoption of the interactional paradigm in sport personality has been heeded.

Cognitive Approach

As discussed previously in this chapter, cognitive approaches are based on the premise that humans are information-processing organisms who appraise and interpret environmental stimuli before responding. Fisher (1976) states that the cognitive theoretical approach may be categorized within the interactional paradigm, since it is based on the sport performer's (with his or her unique individual differences) first interpreting, and then reacting to, the situation. Several contemporary psychologists support the cognitive approach as the most fruitful way to advance personality research (Bem, 1983; Hogan, DeSoto & Solano, 1977; Mischel, 1977a, 1977b; Snyder, 1983), although others question the zeitgeist of cognitive psychology (Neisser, 1980; Skinner, 1987). However, the important point to be made is that the "person" component in the person–situation interaction of this paradigm is not necessarily represented by personality *traits*. Fisher's (1976) argument is that consistency in behavior across situations can be explained within the cognitive theoretical perspective. This perspective is represented in the sport psychology literature by work in attribution theory, perceived competence, and self-efficacy, all of which fall within the interactional paradigm.

Dispositions

Besides the cognitive approach to personality, another way of explaining consistency in behavior across situations within the interactional perspective is to use the term *disposition* as opposed to *trait*. The terms *trait* and *disposition* are never clearly differentiated in the literature, but the difference appears to be one of degree versus kind; that is, dispositions are less rigid and enduring than traits and may be thought of as tendencies to respond in certain ways in certain

situations (Hollander, 1967), summary statements about past behavior (Buss & Craik, 1983), or regular or expected responses to certain situations (Hempel, 1960). However, even the view of traits as rigid, underlying forces that dictate behavior is not held by contemporary personality psychologists, who tend to define traits as "recognizable typical responses" (Hollander, 1967, p. 281) or "cross-situational tendencies" (Kendrick & Funder, 1988, p. 23). Sport psychologists have utilized this dispositional approach in the conceptualization of sport-specific personality dispositions. For example, Martens (in Martens, Vealey & Burton, 1990) conceptualizes competitive trait anxiety as a competitive anxiety disposition, or a tendency to perceive competitive situations as threatening (see chapter 6). Although Martens speaks of competitive *trait* anxiety, he clearly views this construct as a disposition. Similarly, Vealey (1986) conceptualizes a sport-specific dispositional construct of self-confidence called *trait* "sport-confidence."

Traits (Dispositions) Versus States

An important issue to understand within the dispositional interactional perspective is the difference between personality dispositions (popularly referred to as *traits* in this distinction) and personality states. Coleman Griffith (1926) made an early distinction between traits and states by describing personality in terms of persistency as well as insistency. Griffith stated that habits (his term for personality characteristics) are persistent in lasting over a period of time but can also be insistent as they are actively manifested in specific situations. Fridhandler (1986) outlines four dimensions that define the distinguishing aspects of trait and state concepts. Most sport psychologists cite temporal duration (traits as enduring over time and states as brief) as the distinction between traits and states, but Fridhandler also separates traits and states based on continuous versus reactive manifestation, concreteness versus abstractness, and situational causality versus personal causality. Dispositional (trait) personality constructs such as competitive trait anxiety are viewed as enduring over time, reactive only to relevant circumstances (the keys only fit into certain locks), abstract in that they must be inferred from behavior, and representative of behaviors that emanate from within the person. State personality constructs are viewed as short-lived, manifested continuously in reaction to relevant situations (the key is *in* the lock), directly detectable, and resulting from immediate situational factors. The theoretical conceptualizations of sport-specific anxiety (Martens et al., 1990) and self-confidence (Vealey,

1986) utilized interactional perspectives in which person and situational factors combine to create a personality state that is predicted to influence behavior most directly.

Adoption of the Interactional Approach in Sport Research

Although specific research in sport personality is reviewed later, it seems important to address at this point whether the interactional paradigm that Martens recommended in 1975 has been adopted or not. To answer this question, Vealey (1989) extended Martens's (1975) review of the literature to examine paradigmatic trends in sport personality research from 1974 to 1988. She found that 55% of the personality literature utilized an interactional approach, compared to 45% that utilized a trait approach. However, within the interactional category there was a greater trend toward cognitive approaches (35%) as opposed to trait–state approaches (20%). In terms of trends across time, the trait approach in sport personality decreased markedly from 1974 to 1981, whereas the cognitive interactional approach showed a marked increase during this time. The trait–state interactional approach has increased from the early 1970s, yet it has not demonstrated the popularity of the trait and cognitive interactional approaches. Mischel (1968) states that the cognitive approach has overshadowed the trait–state approach to interactionism because, although the trait–state approach is conceptually logical, it is difficult to validate empirically. Others have attacked the trait–state approach as an "arbitrary" distinction with no conceptual or empirical viability (Allen & Potkay, 1981). Problems in predicting sport behavior (particularly performance) using the trait–state approach have been discussed frequently in the literature (e.g., Burton, 1988; Gould, Petlichkoff, Simons & Vevera, 1987; Sonstroem & Bernardo, 1982) and have usually been attributed to inappropriate measurement and operationalization of variables.

A Final Word on Theories and Paradigms in Personality

The definitional, theoretical, and paradigmatic issues, which were discussed in this section represent an enormous part of the personality literature. How should personality be defined? What theoretical perspective best articulates the structure and dynamics of personality? Which paradigmatic approach provides the most appropriate framework for the study of personality in sport? Although these questions were not definitively answered, it is important that they were addressed. As with any area of theoretical inquiry, the acquisition of definitive answers in personality psychology is probably an unrealistic goal. The advancement of knowledge in science is not based on "proving" that a particular theoretical approach is "right" but instead involves devising, testing, and refining multiple hypotheses to test alternative theoretical approaches to a particular phenomenon (Platt, 1964; Popper, 1959). Landers (1983) provides an excellent overview of this approach to theory testing in sport psychology. Also, Landers (1983), like other sport psychologists, urges sport personality researchers to develop their own logically formulated alternative hypotheses rather than simply test the relationships proposed by the original theorists (Alderman, 1980; Dishman, 1983; Feltz, 1987; Martens, 1979, 1987). It is imperative that we follow this model of science in our attempt to advance knowledge and understand personality and behavior in sport.

Approaches to Personality Assessment

Definitional, theoretical, and paradigmatic issues in personality have sparked continuous debate in the literature. Similar debate has occurred over methodological approaches to the *assessment* of personality. *Assessment* simply refers to the process of measuring personality. In this section, methodological approaches that influence assessment are examined and discussed relative to the study of personality in sport. First, the purposes of personality research are outlined, and second, the context of personality research is discussed.

Purposes of Personality Research

What methodological approach to the study of personality should be used? What are the reasons we engage in personality research? These questions seem important to address as Mischel (1977b) states that a source of confusion in personality psychology is the failure of researchers to specify the goals or objectives of their research endeavors clearly. Methodological approaches to the study of personality are categorized in different ways, three of these will be discussed:

- Idiographic versus nomothetic approaches to the study of personality
- Differences in experimental, correlational, and clinical methods of personality research

- The different purposes of personality research in terms of description, prediction, and intervention

Idiographic Versus Nomothetic Approaches to Personality

The idiographic versus nomothetic issue raised by Allport (1937) asks the question: What should be the focus of personality research? In the idiographic approach to personality assessment, the individual is studied intensively and extensively in order to arrive at laws of behavior unique to that individual. The nomothetic approach studies individuals by comparing them to each other in order to arrive at laws of behavior that hold for all individuals. The nomothetic approach assumes that a common set of descriptors, dispositions, or trait dimensions can be used to characterize all persons and that individual differences are to be identified with different locations on those dimensions. In contrast, the pure idiographic approach assumes that a different set of descriptors is needed for each person. Thus, idiographic assessment focuses on the uniqueness of personality and nomothetic assessment focuses on similarities in personality. Based on the idiographic study of personality, Murray (1938) popularized the term *personology* as the study of personality that focuses on persons as whole units and emphasizes intrapersonal characteristics as opposed to externally observable behavior.

Bem (1983) advocates moving beyond the idiographic–nomothetic debate and distinguishing between variable-centered and person-centered research. The variable-centered approach is concerned with the relative standing of persons across variables, while the person-centered approach is concerned with the salience and configuration of variables within the individual. Allport moved toward this new distinction in 1962, when he replaced his earlier term *idiographic* with the term *morphogenic*, which means dealing with the intra-individual patterning of variables. Bem argues that researchers can be morphogenic or person-centered while still assuming nomothetically that there is a common set of descriptors for all persons.

Allport (1937, 1962) maintains that both idiographic and nomothetic approaches are necessary to the study of personality but argues that personality theorists and researchers have relied almost exclusively on the nomothetic approach. It is safe to say that the nomothetic approach has dominated personality psychology in general and sport personality research in particular over the past three decades. One explanation for this domination by nomothetic work is that it is seen as the goal of science, whereas the idiographic approach has been called nonscientific (Martens, 1987). However, particularly because personality research focuses on the functioning of the individual, both methodological approaches are warranted in personality research.

In general, personality psychologists agree that for answering questions about within-subject variation, an idiographic perspective is warranted (Bem & Allen, 1974; Bem & Funder,1978; Mischel, 1977b), while a nomothetic perspective is probably more useful for answering questions about central tendencies in the behavior of people in general (Epstein, 1979; Mischel, 1979). Bem (1983) asserts that a successful interactional paradigm in personality includes the morphogenic or person-centered approach to the study of personality; that is, it does not search for a unique set of variables for characterizing each person (the traditional idiographic approach) but is concerned with the unique salience and configuration of a common set of variables within the person rather than with the relative standing of persons across those variables. Bem (1983) notes that this will result in more of a type theory of personality (as opposed to traditional trait theory), in which the focus of inquiry is on understanding "how certain *kinds* of persons behave in certain *kinds* of ways in certain *kinds* of situations" (p. 566). In this way, the structure or description of personality is studied idiographically, while the process or dynamics of personality is studied nomothetically.

An example of this idiographic–nomothetic combination in sport personality is the work of Scanlan and colleagues (Scanlan, Ravizza & Stein, 1989; Scanlan, Stein & Ravizza, 1989). In these studies, elite figure skaters were first interviewed using a idiographic approach to understand enduring sources of enjoyment that these athletes derived from their competitive experiences. Through content analysis, the skaters' responses were organized into thematic categories that represented various sources of enjoyment. This content analysis, then, provided a nomothetic picture of the data. Another example of combining idiographic and nomothetic approaches in sport personality is a study conducted by Sadalla, Linder, and Jenkins (1988) to investigate the factors underlying preferences for participation in particular sports. Sadalla and colleagues used an idiographic phase in which subjects generated personality descriptors related to sport preferences about hypothetical individuals. In a following nomothetic phase, another sample of subjects rated a hypothetical individual said to be a participant in a particular sport on the dimensions of personality generated in the idiographic phase. Sadalla and colleagues' (1988) results indicated that specific personality characteristics are consistently attributed to individuals described as preferring certain sports.

Experimental, Correlational, and Clinical Methods

Another distinction between methodological approaches in the study of personality was developed by Carlson (1971). Based on the writing of Kluckhohn and Murray (1949), Carlson described the three major methods used in the study of personality as

- experimental (an individual is like all other individuals),
- correlational (an individual is like some other individuals), and
- clinical (an individual is like no other individuals).

Experimental methods seek to discover general laws of human behavior by manipulating social–environmental factors and deemphasizing intrapersonal factors. Correlational methods seek to discover existing differences in personality characteristics among different kinds of individuals without any experimental manipulation. Clinical methods seek to understand the uniqueness of personality characteristics or the organization of personality within individuals. In his review of the sport personality literature between 1950 and 1974, Martens (1975) found that 89% of the studies used correlational methods, 10% used experimental methods, and 1% used clinical methods. Vealey's (1989) follow-up review of the sport personality literature between 1974 and 1988 indicated that 68% of the studies used correlational methods, 28% used experimental methods, and 4% used clinical methods. Thus, although correlational methods are still the most widely practiced, the literature appears to be moving toward more methodological balance. Vealey also noted there that methodological and paradigmatic approaches were related because the trait and trait–state (interactional) paradigms used primarily correlational methods, while studies within the cognitive interactional approach utilized all three methods.

Description, Prediction, and Intervention

Personality researchers may adopt either idiographic or nomothetic approaches and utilize either experimental, correlational, or clinical methodology in their study of personality. What, then, are the reasons that they engage in personality research? Psychologists (Eysenck & Eysenck,

1985; Fiske, 1988; Mischel, 1977b), as well as sport psychologists (Silva, 1984; Singer, 1988), have identified several objectives of personality research that can be divided into three categories, each of which represents a particular purpose of personality research.

The first purpose is *description*—the static, noncausal description of personality. Descriptive studies focus on "what people are like" and examine elements of personality (e.g., traits, states, dispositions, cognitions, needs) and how they are related within the individual or between groups. An example of a descriptive research objective in sport personality would be to determine whether individual sport athletes differ from team sport athletes in competitive anxiety. The second purpose is *prediction*, or "what people do." These types of studies are causal, since they examine the dynamic relationship between personality and behavior. Predictive studies in sport psychology examine the influence of personality characteristics on sport behavior, as well as the influence of sport participation on personality. An example of a predictive research objective in sport personality would be to determine whether high-competitive-trait-anxious athletes differ in state anxiety and performance level from low-competitive-trait-anxious athletes in competitive situations. The third purpose is *intervention* to examine "how people change." Intervention studies examine how personality characteristics and behavior may be modified through various intervention strategies. This category differs from the prediction category in that some type of manipulation or treatment is induced, and the effect measured, as opposed to predicting the natural effects of sport participation on personality. An example of an intervention research objective in sport personality would be to determine the effects of a seasonal psychological skills training program on the self-esteem and self-confidence of athletes.

Based on an analysis of the sport personality literature between 1974 and 1988, Vealey (1989) found that 48% of the studies focused on prediction, 44% on description, and 8% on intervention. However, in examining yearly trends, Vealey found that predictive research has declined since 1982, that intervention research has increased over the same time period, and that descriptive research has remained fairly constant. The increase in intervention studies is the result of the upsurge of interest in applied sport psychology, while the decline in predictive studies suggests a lack of theory development and testing (Landers, 1983). Vealey also noted difficulty in categorizing studies by objective, since the purpose of the research was often unclear and/or unstated.

Thus, there is a need for clear definitions of, and congruence between, paradigm, theoretical framework, and purpose in sport personality research.

The Context of Personality Research

Nearly all of the early research in personality that was reviewed and criticized by Mischel (1968) utilized correlational methods. This methodological approach, however, came under increasing criticism in the 1960s, particularly following the publication of Campbell and Stanley's (1966) classic book on experimental design. As a result of these occurrences, the number of experimental personality research studies conducted in the laboratory increased (West, 1986). This historical pattern was also reflected in sport personality research (Landers, 1983; Martens, 1979) as researchers in the 1970s strived for the privileged status afforded to true experimental research. However, probably as a reaction to Martens's (1979) plea for more external validity, field research in sport personality has increased since the 1970s (Vealey, 1989).

Clearly, the strength of laboratory research is in the maximization of control and internal validity. However, the primary weakness of this approach is the lack of external validity, or generalizability of results to situations outside of the experimental setting. Researchers indicate that this is particularly a problem in personality research. West (1986) and Buss (1989) assert that the prediction of behavior from person variables is maximized in environments in which situational constraint is low. This is clearly antithetical to experimental control and laboratory research.

Potential design alternatives to the traditional lab–field dichotomy are needed. First, laboratory settings that minimize situational constraint are needed to facilitate the emergence of personality factors. For example, individuals' choices and modifications of situations can be investigated as *dependent* variables in contrast to traditional designs, in which situations are static variables that only have effects on individuals (Buss, 1989; Snyder, 1983). Examples might be to have subjects choose levels of competition, types of competitors, or methods of evaluation. Mischel (1977b) states that the most striking differences between persons may be found not by studying their responses to the same situation but by analyzing their selection and construction of situational conditions. Malloy and Kenny (1986) have advocated the social relations model as a personality framework that focuses on the study of social interactions within a laboratory format. A second design alternative is the adoption of a quasi-experimental approach in field research to identify and control threats to internal validity within the real-world setting. Third, researchers need to engage in "full cycle social psychology" (Cialdini, 1980), in which personality research can move systematically back and forth between the real world and the laboratory by interweaving controlled laboratory methods, naturalistic field observation, personality inventories, and biographical/archival data. This has been similarly argued by Landers (1983) in the sport psychology literature. Fourth, personality researchers should take great care in examining various contextual factors that mediate the relationship between personality and sport behavior. Sundberg (1977) provides an excellent overview of assessment of persons in context and suggests that assessment take into account the physical, social, interpersonal, organizational, and symbolic environments of an individual in the study of personality. Clearly, the relationship between personality factors and sport behavior is influenced by such factors as gender, ethnicity, socioeconomic status, and age.

Methods and Techniques of Personality Assessment

As stated previously, assessment involves the measurement of personality. In the previous section, various methodological approaches that influence personality assessment were examined. In this section, specific methods and techniques of personality assessment (particularly those used in sport) are examined. Because the bulk of personality research has utilized psychological inventories as the method of choice, this section focuses mainly on the use of these inventories. However, it is important to realize that there are methods of personality assessment other than psychological inventories, and various alternative assessment techniques are also identified.

Properties of Psychological Inventories

A psychological inventory, or test, is "an objective and standardized measure of a sample of behavior" (Anastasi, 1988, p. 23). Anastasi's definition emphasizes objective measurement and the fact that a test measures only a sample of an individual's behavior. Anastasi also emphasizes that standardization implies uniformity of procedures in developing, administering, and scoring inventories. Three characteristics are important when evaluating a psychological inventory or any other assessment technique: validity, reliability, and normative data.

Validity

The most important property of a psychological inventory is validity, or the degree to which a test actually measures what it purports to measure (Anastasi, 1988). A test is never valid in general, it is valid *for* something, such as heart rate, intelligence, or trait anxiety (Sundberg, 1977); that is, a test's validity must be established with reference to the particular use for which the test is being considered. Three types of validity can be differentiated: content, criterion, and construct. *Content validity* involves the extent to which the contents of the test are representative of the behavior domain to be measured. In attempting to provide evidence for content validity, personality researchers must systematically analyze the behavioral domain to be tested to make certain that all major aspects are represented by test items and in the correct proportion (Anastasi, 1988). It is common practice in the development of tests to submit the inventory to knowledgeable experts in the area so they may judge the content validity of the test. Anastasi (1988) cautions that content validity should not be confused with *face validity*, which is really not validity in the technical sense. Face validity is concerned with whether the test "looks valid" and refers to what the test superficially appears to measure. *Criterion validity* indicates the effectiveness of a test in predicting individuals' performance on a specified activity, or criterion. Two types of criterion validity may be identified. If the test is administered and the criterion measurement is obtained at the same time, the term *concurrent validity* is used. If the criterion measurement is obtained at a later time, the term *predictive validity* is used to indicate the extent to which test scores predict the criterion measure (Sundberg, 1977). From a theoretical standpoint, the most important kind of validity is *construct validity*, or the relation of test results to the theoretical concept that the test is trying to measure (Cronbach & Meehl, 1955). Construct validity is demonstrated by an accumulation of evidence that the construct the test purports to measure is related to other constructs consistent with theoretical predictions.

Reliability

Another important psychometric property of a test is reliability, which refers to the consistency, reproducibility, or accuracy of the results (Sundberg, 1977). *Test–retest reliability* is determined by administering the test to the same individual at two different points in time (Anastasi, 1988). An inventory that has a high degree of test–retest reliability will yield scores on the retest (e.g., one day or one week later) that are similar to the scores obtained on the original test. Test–retest reliability implies stability over time. Another form of reliability is termed *internal consistency*, which pertains to reliability at a single point in time. Internal consistency indicates to what degree individuals' responses are similar across the items of the scale (Anastasi, 1988). Internal consistency is computed using various statistical procedures such as the Kuder–Richardson method or Cronbach's (1970) alpha coefficient (see Anastasi, 1988). Using behavioral observation methods of personality assessment, it is important to demonstrate *interobserver reliability*, or the relationship (expressed as a correlation) between two independent observations of the same behavior. The larger the reliability coefficient and the smaller the standard error of measurement, the more reliable the test is. Anastasi (1988) as well as Sundberg (1977) indicate that a reliability coefficient in the .80s or .90s is necessary to have confidence in the reliability of the test.

Norms

In addition to validity and reliability, a third characteristic of a psychological inventory is its normative data, or norm; that is, in order to understand what an individual's test score means, it should be compared with the test scores of other people. For that comparison to be meaningful, information must be provided about the kinds of people included in the norm groupings. Normative data must be representative of the population for which the test is designed (Sundberg, 1977). Usually, the test developers provide norms in the form of percentile and standard scores.

The process of developing a reliable, valid measurement tool to assess personality requires rigorous and extensive psychometric procedures. Examples of this process in sport psychology research include the validation of the Sport Competition Anxiety Test and Competitive State Anxiety Inventory–2 (Martens et al., 1990). Researchers are urged to carefully select and/or develop reliable and valid instrumentation with which to study personality in sport.

Examples of Personality Assessment Techniques

In this section, various assessment techniques that have been used in the study of personality are identified. Because theory and method are often inextricably related, the discussion of various inventories and techniques is organized around the theories of personality already discussed. The techniques and inventories identified here are only *representative* of typical personality assessment approaches and should not be seen as a complete listing. A more comprehensive listing of psychological inventories used in sport psychology research has been compiled by Anshel (1987).

Psychodynamic Theories

Many of the methods assessing unconscious processes within the psychodynamic approach are termed *projective techniques*. These techniques are based on the assumption that significant aspects of personality are not open to conscious thought and thus cannot be reliably measured through self-report. These techniques are thought to let the subjects "project" their personality characteristics into interpretations of various kinds (Frank, 1939). Examples of projective techniques used in personality assessment are the Rorschach Inkblot Test, the Thematic Apperception Test, and various sentence completion or drawing tasks (Sundberg, 1977). Projective techniques were popular in the 1940s and 1950s, when psychoanalysis was a predominant force in *personality*. These techniques are used very little in the study of sport personality. Other techniques used in the psychodynamic approach are life history or biographical data and various types of interviewing methods.

Dispositional Theories

Trait or dispositional theorists have traditionally used objective personality inventories in which subjects respond to paper-and-pencil scales by assigning numerical weights to represent their responses on various items. Objective personality inventories involve direct quantification without any intervening interpretation of the subjects' responses (as in projective techniques). Objective trait or dispositional personality inventories have clearly been the most popular technique of personality assessment in psychology and sport psychology since the 1960s.

Three popular trait inventories in psychology are the Minnesota Multiphasic Personality Inventory (MMPI; Hathaway & McKinley, 1943), the 16 Personality Factor Questionnaire (16PF; Cattell, 1946), and the Eysenck Personality Inventory (EPI; Eysenck & Eysenck, 1975). The MMPI was developed to differentiate among various psychiatric categories and contains 10 clinical scales (e.g., depression, hypochondria,

paranoia) and four validity scales. The 16PF measures 16 factors (traits) thought by Cattell (1946) to be descriptive of personality. The EPI measures the personality dimensions of neuroticism and introversion–extroversion. These trait inventories and similar others (e.g., California Psychological Inventory, Edwards Personal Preference Schedule) were used extensively in sport personality research in the 1960s. The 16PF was a particularly popular inventory used in the early sport personality research.

Inventories such as the 16PF, the MMPI, and the EPI provide an overall assessment of an individual's personality. Other trait inventories have been developed to measure only selected personality characteristics. Examples of these types of inventories that have been used extensively in sport personality research are the State–Trait Anxiety Inventory (STAI; Spielberger, Gorsuch & Lushene, 1970), the Measure of Achieving Tendency (Mehrabian, 1968), and the Manifest Anxiety Scale (Taylor, 1953). Based on the interactional approach to the study of personality, state personality scales also were developed. For example, the STAI contains a trait and state scale of anxiety (Spielberger et al., 1970). The Profile of Mood States (POMS; McNair, Lorr & Droppleman, 1981) was developed to measure six dimensions of subjective mood states: tension–anxiety, depression–dejection, anger–hostility, vigor–activity, fatigue–inertia, and confusion–bewilderment. Although the initial intent of the POMS was to assess moods in psychiatric patients, it has been used extensively in sport personality research (LeUnes, Hayward & Daiss, 1988).

Sport-specific personality inventories based on the trait or dispositional approach were developed as researchers began to question the applicability of global personality tests in predicting behavior in sport. The first sport-specific trait personality inventory, the Athletic Motivation Inventory (AMI), was developed by Tutko, Lyon, and Ogilvie (1969) to provide an overall assessment of an athlete's personality. The AMI assesses 11 personality traits predicted to be related to athletic success: drive, aggressiveness, determination, guilt proneness, leadership, self-confidence, emotional control, mental toughness, coachability, conscientiousness, and trust. Sport-specific measures of single personality dispositions include the Sport Competition Anxiety Test (SCAT; Martens et al., 1990), the Sport Orientation Questionnaire (Gill & Deeter, 1988), and the Trait Sport-Confidence Inventory and Competitive Orientation Inventory (Vealey, 1986, 1988). Sport-specific state personality measures include the Competitive State Anxiety Inventory–2

(Martens et al., 1990) and the State Sport-Confidence Inventory (Vealey, 1986).

Phenomenological Theories

Phenomenological measurement involves the person as his or her own assessor. In this area of personality, subjects are asked directly how they feel or will behave. Structured questionnaires have been the most widely adopted strategy for assessing cognitions (see Clarke, 1988). Prominent cognitive measures used in sport personality research include the Test of Attentional and Interpersonal Style (TAIS; Nideffer, 1976), the Intrinsic Motivation Inventory (Ryan, 1982), the Causal Dimension Scale (Russell, 1982), and the Self-Perception Profile for Children (Harter, 1985). Sport-specific cognitive measures that have been developed include the Psychological Skills Inventory for Sports (PSIS; Mahoney, Gabriel & Perkins, 1987), the Intrinsic/Extrinsic Motivation Scale (Weiss, Bredemeier & Shewchuk, 1985), and the Physical Self-Perception Profile (Fox & Corbin, 1989).

Besides questionnaires, alternative assessment techniques in phenomenology include interviewing, self-monitoring, thought sampling, and Q-sort techniques (Block, 1961) which provide a measure of how individuals organize their thoughts. The Role Construct Repertory Test was developed by Kelly (1955) to assess the cognitive construct systems of individuals.

Learning Theories

Obviously, early conditioning theories based on radical behaviorism focused exclusively on observable behavior. However, with the expansion of the learning approach to incorporate social learning, self-report measures became useful. Examples of self-report measures of personality characteristics based on social learning theory include the Internal–External Locus of Control Scale (Rotter, 1966), the Bem Sex-Role Inventory (Bem, 1974), and the Physical Self-Efficacy Scale (Ryckman, Robbins, Thornton & Cantrell, 1982).

Issues Regarding Personality Assessment Techniques

Similar to the theoretical, paradigmatic, and broad methodological issues previously discussed, the use of specific personality assessment techniques also raises various issues. Included in these issues are the limitations of self-report inventories, ethical concerns over the use of personality tests and the use of inventories in the sport context that were originally validated for psychopathological purposes.

Limitations of Self-Report Techniques

The use of self-report psychological inventories in sport personality research has been widely criticized. Self-report assessment techniques have been criticized by researchers who feel that individuals do not know themselves well enough to give accurate assessments, that test items are open to misrepresentation (Vane & Guarnaccia, 1989), and that dispositional scales focus not on properties of individuals' personalities but on value judgments placed on them by the researchers (Hogan et al., 1977). Another criticism of self-report measures is that they are susceptible to social desirability response bias (i.e., individuals falsify their responses to make themselves appear more socially desirable; Vane & Guarnaccia, 1989). Finally, Hogan and colleagues (1977) assert that personality tests encourage mindless research by marginally competent investigators who "discover" significant relationships without establishing any substantive a priori hypotheses.

Certainly, these criticisms are warranted to some degree; however, there is a place in sport personality research for self-report inventories. First of all, as McGrath (1982) argues, all research techniques have limitations, and research needs to utilize multiple assessment techniques to overcome individual methodological weaknesses. The meaning of personality or behavior may not be the same in different measurement contexts, so multiple measures are needed. For example, sport anxiety research has lacked consistent agreement between self-report and physiological measures (Karteroliotis & Gill, 1987; Yan Lan & Gill, 1984). However, this does not mean that the physiological measures are more valid than self-report or that self-report has no place in sport psychology research. Second, self-report inventories that meet the psychometric criteria of reliability and validity and are based on relevant theory have met rigorous scientific standards and are no less precise than any other assessment method. Third, the use of "anti–social desirability instructions" has been shown to lessen social desirability response bias in sport personality research (Martens et al., 1990); and the inclusion of scales to detect social desirability tendencies in subjects (Crowne & Marlowe, 1960) is also advocated in personality studies. Fourth, using an idiographic approach to personality inventory development, researchers are encouraged to use interview and open-ended techniques to identify relevant and salient personality descriptions of individuals in sport (e.g., Sadalla et al., 1988; Scanlan, Ravizza & Stein, 1989; Scanlan, Stein & Ravizza, 1989). For example, the development of the PSIS (Mahoney et al.,

1987) was based on the extensive experiential knowledge of athletic personality characteristics gained by Mahoney in his consulting work with athletes. This type of experiential knowledge is important in developing relevant, appropriate techniques of personality assessment in sport psychology (Martens, 1987). Finally, although the existence of personality inventories may provide easy weapons for "mindless" research, perusal of the literature in any scientific area of study indicates that mindless research is not limited to those who use self-report personality inventories.

A provocative and seemingly valuable approach to self-report is the use of *ipsative* or *idiothetic* forms of self-report as compared to normative self-report. Using Allport's (1937, 1962) argument that personality characteristics are best studied in an intra-individual rather than an interindividual context, Block (1957) proposed the ipsative approach to personality assessment, in which an individual's responses on a rating scale are interpreted relative to his or her responses on other scales, under other conditions, or at other times. Thus, if individuals rate themselves on a given characteristic above their average rating on other characteristics, they are viewed as possessing a high level of that characteristic, regardless of the value of the rating relative to those provided by others. From a slightly different perspective, Lamiell (1981) has proposed an idiothetic measurement model, in which responses are interpreted with reference to the maximum and minimum possible responses that an individual could make in a given measurement situation.

In support of the value of an ipsative approach, Chaplin and Buckner (1988) asked subjects to describe themselves on a set of attributes that span the domain of personality (implicit rating). They then rated themselves on the same attributes according to instructions that specified a normative, ipsative, or idiothetic standard. The results indicated that ipsative ratings were most similar to implicit ratings, and that normative ratings were significantly more midscale with fewer extreme responses than the ipsative and idiothetic ratings. These results suggest that self-report ratings in personality assessment may be better represented by a model other than the traditional normative one. This ipsative self-rating method has been utilized by a few researchers in the sport anxiety research area (e.g., Gould et al., 1987; Sonstroem & Bernardo, 1982), and the results indicate that this assessment method may be of value for sport personality researchers.

Ethical and Appropriate Uses of Personality Inventories

The second issue related to personality assessment techniques in sport concerns the use and misuse of personality inventories. Personality tests are often misused in two ways. First, personality inventories may be used to screen or select individuals for inclusion on sport teams. The use (or misuse) of personality inventories for sport selection is based on the general belief that desirable personality attributes should be related to success in sport. The validity or accuracy of this proposed relationship is examined further later, but from an assessment perspective the use of personality inventories for this reason is ethically questionable. As Singer (1988) states, the ethical use of personality tests for team member selection assumes that we know

- which personality characteristics are relevant,
- what the ideal level of that characteristic is,
- how much athletes can compensate in some characteristics for the lack of others, and
- that the particular test being used provides a valid and reliable measure of these attributes.

A second ethical problem involves the use of personality inventories as a means to diagnose "problems" or to provide information about special needs of athletes. The ethical concerns with diagnosis are similar to those regarding selection. Is the test a valid measure of relevant characteristics? Who decides what constitutes "normal" versus "problem" behaviors or characteristics in sport?

The early use of the AMI (Tutko et al., 1969) has been challenged based on the ethical considerations just presented (Gill, 1986). First of all, the AMI was marketed in a way that indicated that test scores were predictive of success in athletes, although no evidence of reliability and validity was published in the scientific literature. Second, the AMI is a trait scale and in no way considers the influence of situational factors on athletes' behavior. However, a book was published based on work with the AMI that identified "problem athletes" and provided guidelines as to how to deal with these types of athletes without considering any environmental, social, or cultural characteristics (Ogilvie & Tutko, 1966). Third, even if the traits measured by the AMI are related to sport success, this still does not demonstrate causality; that is, these traits were not shown to *cause* success in sport. Overall, these points indicate that the AMI has limitations in its ability to predict sport behavior, as does any measurement technique. What was problematic, however, was that these limitations were not clearly identified. In fact, the scale has been described as "totally perfected" (Tutko, 1986, p. 55).

This discussion is not presented to discourage the use of personality inventories in sport psychology but rather to encourage that they be used ethically and appropriately. Guidelines for the development and appropriate use of psychological tests have been established by the American Psychological Association (1974) and should be followed. Appropriate use of personality tests means that tests should be used only in situations in which they are valid. Many psychological assessment techniques are used by clinical psychologists to diagnose psychopathology; these instruments have been validated for that purpose and the psychologists are trained—even licensed—to use these tests in clinical settings. However, most of the personality tests developed in sport psychology have been validated for research purposes only. For example, the SCAT (Martens et al., 1990) has been validated to predict competitive A-state but not clinical anxiety and certainly not success in sport. Batteries of sport-specific psychological tests may be given to athletes to provide vague sport-psychological profiles, but it would be inappropriate as well as unethical to use these test results for the purpose of team selection or diagnosis of "problems." As with research, the multimethod approach would be more useful in profiling athletes by combining personality inventories, interview techniques, behavioral observation, self-monitoring, and so on to provide a more comprehensive perspective of athletes' personalities.

Related to the appropriate use of personality inventories, Kroll (1976) questions the use of inventories developed and validated for clinical populations in sport psychology research. He contends that these types of tests emphasize a psychopathological view of personality that appraises normal personality in terms of susceptibility to maladjustment. Holtzman (1965) argues that the MMPI, developed for identification of psychiatric populations, is poorly suited to the examination of personality structure in normal populations. A similar criticism could be leveled against the use of the POMS in sport research, because this inventory was developed to assess mood in psychiatric patients (although it has been validated for use with normal college-age subjects).

Even if the validity of using tests such as the MMPI with athletes is not questioned, the information provided by these tests only examines the relationship between psychopathology (or lack of it) and sport behavior. Kroll (1976) states, "Just as we recognize that health is more than the absence of disease, we must recognize that athletic personality is more than the absence of psychiatric deficiencies" (p. 379). Thus, we need to move beyond the use of clinically derived instrumentation and even beyond general psychological inventories (e.g., TAIS, STAI) to develop and utilize sport-specific personality assessment inventories based on the unique characteristics of the sport environment. Sport psychologists have demonstrated increased behavioral prediction when using valid, sport-specific personality measures as opposed to general psychological measures of the same attribute (e.g., Gill & Deeter, 1988; Martens et al., 1990; Vealey, 1986).

Sport Personality Research

The previous sections have attempted to provide understanding about the definitional, theoretical, paradigmatic, and methodological foundations and issues in personality research. In this section, specific research in sport personality is examined. This review of completed research is organized according to the various theoretical approaches to the study of personality.

A main point of this chapter is that personality involves much more than just the trait approach. That is, research that is based on trait or dispositional theories represents only one part of the study of personality. As discussed at the beginning of the chapter, a comprehensive view of sport personality should include research conducted in all of the theoretical areas of personality. Much of the research discussed in chapters 4–7 of this book concerns specific aspects of personality (e.g., attributions, motivational orientations, self-perceptions). Thus, the results of this research will not be extensively reviewed here. However, the specific areas of sport personality research related to each theoretical approach will be briefly identified.

Psychodynamic Approaches

As discussed previously, specific and relevant hypotheses based on the psychodynamic perspective have not been generated and tested in the sport context. Although limited in its application to sport, the psychodynamic or deterministic approach has been applied in one way in that sport personality researchers have suggested that individuals with certain personality types may "gravitate" toward participation in certain sports (Bird, 1979; Kane, 1978; Kroll, 1970; Morgan,

1972, 1980b; Williams, 1978). No research has provided definitive evidence to support this suggestion.

Dispositional Approaches

The dispositional approaches represent most of the early research conducted in sport personality, and these approaches remain popular today. The sport research that has been conducted from a dispositional perspective can be categorized into trait–state, biological, and motive/need approaches to the study of personality.

Trait Theory

Research using this approach can be categorized into (a) trait-descriptive personality profiles of different groups of athletes or nonathletes, and (b) studies that have examined the relationship between personality traits and various sport behaviors. People usually associate sport personality research with the work done in this area.

Most of the studies in the trait area have focused on the *description* of personality based on hypothesized differences between three comparison groups: athletes versus nonathletes, athletes of one sport type versus athletes of another sport type, and the comparison of athletes based on different ability or success levels. The basic premise underlying these studies is the conception that these different groups of individuals possess unique and measurable personality traits. The prototypical study of this type used the 16PF or MMPI and compared the personality profiles of different groups to each other or against population norms for that particular inventory (see Fisher, 1976 or Morgan, 1980b for examples of these studies). Although several types of personality differences (e.g., athletes more extroverted and emotionally stable than nonathletes) have been found between various groups, no clear pattern can be discerned from this research.

This tendency to find "insignificant significant differences" in trait-descriptive sport personality research is illustrated in a study in which athletes from a variety of sports and schools were compared using a standard personality inventory (Lakie, 1962). As expected, personality differences were found between different groups of athletes (e.g., between baseball and track and field athletes); but the differences between groups of athletes were not consistent across schools! Morgan (1980a, 1980b) has argued that this failure to find consistent descriptive differences in personality traits is due to methodological problems such as inadequate operationalism,

small samples and poor sampling procedures, misuse of theory, inappropriate statistical procedures, and disregard of response distortion. These methodological limitations are clearly evident in the literature and have muddied the findings in this area (e.g., in one study multiple regression analysis was conducted using six predictor variables with a sample size of 33).

A study by Schurr, Ashley, and Joy (1977) illustrates a sound methodological approach to trait-descriptive sport personality research. Schurr and colleagues classified almost two thousand athletes according to sport type (team/individual, direct/parallel, long/short duration) and participation status (letter winner, non–letter winner, nonathlete) and then compared the various athletic groups using the second-order factors from Cattell's 16PF. Multivariate statistical analysis indicated that no personality profile differentiated athletes from nonathletes. However, significant interactions between participation status and sport classification were found. Specifically, direct sport athletes were found to be more extroverted and independent than nonathletes; and parallel sport athletes appeared to be less anxious and less independent than nonathletes. The methodological sophistication of this study provided some evidence for trait personality differences between various groups of athletes and nonathletes. However, the differences were not simple but were based on complex interactions between certain types of athletes in sports characterized by different task demands.

Overall, the findings using the trait approach in an attempt to describe differences in personality among various groups in sport has indicated some differences (e.g., Schurr et al., 1977). However, a great deal of the research in this area has been plagued by methodological, statistical, and theoretical problems; and the findings indicate no consistent results. Furthermore, no consistent pattern of personality traits have been identified as representative of an "athletic personality." Vanek and Cratty (1970) summarized this area of personality research as follows:

> The findings of recent studies. . . indicate that the identification of a typical personality trait pattern expected to appear in an 'athlete' is a tenuous undertaking. The trait patterns isolated in these investigations indicate that within certain sport groups, traits may often be identified. But the delineating of some ubiquitous 'animal' called an athlete cannot be done with any degree of certainty. (p. 82)

The research described in the previous paragraphs was conducted to *describe* personality differences in existing groups of athletes and nonathletes. Other researchers have focused more on the *prediction* of sport behavior (particularly successful sport performance) using personality traits as predictors. Debate over the ability of personality traits to predict sport behavior has been referred to as the "credulous–skeptical argument" (Morgan, 1980a). Proponents of the credulous argument believe that personality traits may predict success in sport, while proponents of the skeptical argument believe that traits are not predictive of sport success. Similar to the person–situation debate, this argument has been called a pseudo-issue (Morgan, 1980a). Morgan (originally in the credulous camp) admits that traits alone are not predictive of sport behavior and success. However, Morgan argues that traits should not be abandoned but should be used for prediction purposes in conjunction with other types of data such as personality state, cognition, and physiological measures.

Trait–State Theory

Trait–state approaches employ an interactional perspective in which dispositions (commonly called traits) are combined with situational factors to create a personality state that is predicted to influence behavior most directly. Apart from Griffith's (1926) distinction between personality "persistency and insistency," the earliest study examining the influence of personality states on sport behavior was Jackson's (1933) analysis of the effects of "fear" on muscular coordination (conducted under Griffith's direction at the University of Illinois Laboratory for Research in Athletics in partial fulfillment for the degree of master of arts in education). Jackson noted, "There seems to be some correlation between the mental and physical state of the performer, his performance, and his susceptibility to fear. A subject who is depressed, or who is tired or ill, can seldom perform as well as he will under more ideal conditions" (p. 79). Another early study by Johnson examined "pre-contest emotion" and concluded that this tension has "a decided deleterious effect in terms of performance and well-being during and after competition" (1949, p. 77).

Morgan (1985b) has proposed a "mental health model" in which the presence of positive mood states in athletes is associated with higher performance levels as compared to the performance levels of athletes possessing less positive mood states; that is, the mental health model asserts that positive mental health and athletic success are directly related, while psychopathology and success are inversely related. In separate studies with college rowers (Morgan & Johnson, 1978),

college swimmers (Morgan, Brown, Raglin, O'Connor & Ellickson, 1987), and elite wrestlers (Morgan & Johnson, 1977), Morgan demonstrated that successful athletes possessed more positive mood states than less successful athletes. The pattern of mood states associated with positive mental health has been termed the *iceberg profile* by Morgan, and is operationalized by scores on the six mood dimensions of the POMS (McNair et al., 1981). The iceberg profile is characterized by scores above the population norm on vigor and below the population norm on tension, depression, anger, fatigue, and confusion (see Figure 3.2). This profile has been supported with various athletic samples (e.g., Frazier, 1988; Fuchs & Zaichkowsky, 1983; Furst & Hardman, 1988; Hagberg, Mullin, Bahrke & Limberg, 1979; Morgan, O'Connor, Ellickson & Bradley, 1988; Morgan & Pollock, 1977).

Morgan's (1985b) mental health model is an important contribution to the study of personality and sport. However, like any research approach, it has limitations. First, the iceberg profiles of athletes do not necessarily indicate that positive mood states (personality) cause success in sport; rather it may be that success in

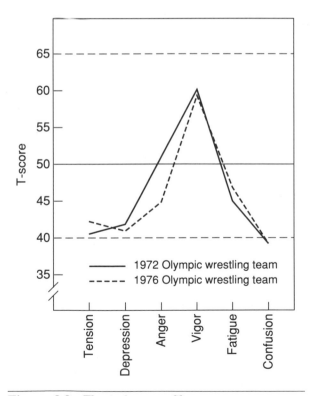

Figure 3.2 The iceberg profile.
Note. This figure is reprinted with permission from the *Research Quarterly for Exercise and Sport* vol. 51, no. 1, 1980, p. 64. *The Research Quarterly for Exercise and Sport* is a publication of the American Alliance for Health, Physical Education, Recreation and Dance, 1900 Association Drive, Reston, VA 22091.

sport elicits positive moods. At this point, the evidence indicates only an association between success in sport and positive mood states; but interpretation of this as a causal relationship is premature. Second, although the iceberg profile is characteristic of successful athletes on the average, there are substantial individual differences; and many world-class athletes have exhibited less positive profiles on the POMS (Gill, 1986; Mahoney, 1989). Third, there is some confusion regarding the use of the POMS as a trait or state measure. McNair and colleagues (1981) indicate that the POMS is designed to measure "typical and persistent mood reactions to current life situations" (p. 5) and state that the standard instructions of having subjects rate their moods during the past week may be modified to time sets such as "right now" or "today." However, even though McNair and colleagues are interested in tapping "typical and persistent" moods, the POMS is clearly not designed as a trait scale and should not be confused as such. Morgan (1980b) himself added to this confusion by alluding to the POMS mood states as "traits" and suggesting that the evidence supporting the mental health model provides support for the "credulous" argument that traits are predictive of sport behavior. Finally, Gill (1986) states that it is not surprising that psychopathology (less-than-desirable mood patterns on the POMS) is negatively related to success in sport, since psychopathology is negatively related to success in most achievement situations. The relationship between mental health and sport performance was supported by Jackson as early as 1933. Thus, prediction in sport personality research should now move beyond the mental health model and toward a focus on attributes of personality other than the absence of psychopathology.

Within the trait–state approach to personality and sport, sport-specific conceptualizations and measurement instruments have been developed in the areas of anxiety (Martens et al., 1990) and self-confidence (Vealey, 1986, 1988; Vealey & Campbell, 1988). Furthermore, these constructs have been shown to predict various sport behaviors. In particular, the work of Martens and colleagues in modifying Spielberger's (1966) trait–state anxiety distinction for sport generated an enormous amount of research in sport personality with regard to the anxiety–behavior relationship (see Martens et al., 1990 for review). Gill and colleagues have developed a sport-specific measure of the disposition of competitiveness that has been shown to predict achievement choices and behavior in sport (Gill & Deeter, 1988; Gill, Dzewaltowski & Deeter, 1988). Vealey

and Gill also included sport-specific goal orientation constructs in their respective conceptualizations of self-competitiveness and self-confidence to account for tendencies to strive for certain goals in sport.

Biological Theory

Two psychobiological approaches to understanding sport behavior have been introduced in the sport literature. In the psychophysiological approach, inferences of psychological processes and emotional states are derived from the examination of psychophysiological measures such as heart rate and brain (electroencephalograph) or muscle (electromyograph) activity (see Hatfield & Landers, 1983 for review). An example of this type of research approach is that which has examined the relationship between the Type A behavior pattern and psychophysiological responses to stress (e.g., Hardy, McMurray & Roberts, 1989; Rejeski, Morley & Miller, 1983). Hatfield and Landers (1983) assert that the psychophysiological approach can uniquely contribute to the understanding of sport behavior by focusing on the process, or underlying mechanisms, of behavior, as opposed to outcome research, which only assesses resultant behavior. The second biological approach to sport personality uses biological measures in conjunction with different types of personality measures to improve behavioral prediction in exercise settings (e.g., Dishman, 1982, 1984) and sport settings (e.g., Silva, Shultz, Haslam & Murray, 1981). This multivariate approach to understanding behavior is particularly pertinent for understanding how behavior in sport and exercise is simultaneously influenced by biological, psychological, and social factors.

Motive/Need Theory

The motive/need theory that has sparked the greatest amount of research in sport personality is Atkinson's (1957) achievement motivation theory, which is interactional but contains a motive construct known as the need for achievement (nACH). Differences in risk-taking and performance behaviors have been examined based on differences in nACH (e.g., Healey & Landers, 1973; Ostrow, 1976; Roberts, 1972, 1974; Ryan & Lakie, 1965).

Sensation seeking, or the need for adventure or risk, has also been examined in relationship to sport based on the work of Zuckerman (1971, 1979). Sensation seeking has been shown to describe participants in high-risk sports (Fowler, Knorring & Oreland, 1980; Hymbaugh & Garrett, 1974; Straub, 1982). Rowland, Franken, and

Harrison (1986) extended the earlier descriptive studies of sensation seeking to demonstrate that sensation-seeking predicts not only choice of, but also degree of involvement in, various sports.

Phenomenological Approaches

Phenomenological approaches to the study of personality in sport have become extremely popular as sport psychology has followed psychology in moving away from the dispositional approach toward cognitive theory and measurement. Phenomenological approaches to the study of personality and sport may be categorized into the areas of actualization/self-determination and cognitive theory.

Actualization/Self-Determination Theory

Deci's (1975, 1980) theory of intrinsic motivation has received a great deal of attention in the sport psychology literature (e.g., McAuley & Tammen, 1989; Ryan, 1980; Ryan et al., 1984; Vallerand, 1983; Weinberg, 1984). This research is discussed in greater detail in chapter 4. Also relevant to actualization theory, athletes have been found to be higher than nonathletes in psychological well-being and life satisfaction (Snyder & Kivlin, 1975). Similarly, athletes have been characterized as conformist, group-oriented, and concerned with belonging and popularity in terms of ego development (Malmisur, 1976).

Cognitive Theory

Currently, the cognitive approach to the study of personality in sport is flourishing. Studies examining cognitive–descriptive personality differences in athletes (Gould, Weiss & Weinberg, 1981; Highlen & Bennett, 1979, 1983; Mahoney & Avener, 1977; Meyers, Cooke, Cullen & Liles, 1979; Rotella, Gansneder, Ojala & Billing, 1980) have taken the place of the trait-descriptive personality difference studies of the 1960s to determine whether successful athletes differ from less successful athletes on various cognitive characteristics. Overall, successful athletes appear to have more positive cognitive self-perceptions (e.g., self-confident) and to utilize more productive cognitive strategies (e.g., attentional focusing). Research also indicates that cognitive intervention strategies enhance performance behaviors and coping skills in sport (see Greenspan & Feltz, 1989 for review). The cognitive strategies of association and dissociation have also been examined in an attempt to understand their influence on sport performance (e.g., Masters & Lambert, 1989).

Two studies have utilized personal construct theory in the study of sport personality. Lerch (1976) utilized an idiographic approach to study four athletes' unique perspectives within their specific environmental context across the course of the competitive season. The results emphasize unique differences in personality functioning within an athletic context. Sadalla and colleagues (1988) utilized construct theory to examine factors that underlie preferences for participation in particular sports. Their results indicated that specific personality characteristics are associated with preferences for certain sports.

Cognitive attribution theory has generated a tremendous amount of sport research (see chapter 5). The important construct of *perceived ability* (Nicholls, 1984) has emerged from the attribution literature and has been hailed by many as the personality construct that is the central mediator of behavior in sport (Roberts, 1984a, 1984b). Research has indicated that perceived ability is a significant predictor of persistence and attrition in sport (see chapter 4). The increased focus on the achievement goal orientation of individuals has advanced our understanding of sport behavior from a nomothetic perspective of motivated behavior to an idiographic perspective in which sport behavior is examined relative to personal goals or intent (see chapter 4). Cognitive consistency theory has been used to demonstrate that sport performance is positively associated with less conflict and the use of cognitive conflict reduction mechanisms, whereas sport dropouts are characterized by cognitive conflict (Volp & Keil, 1987). Utilizing a personal investment theory approach (Maehr & Braskamp, 1986), Duda, Smart, and Tappe (1989) found that personal incentives, sense of self, and perceived behavioral options predicted adherence to injury rehabilitation programs. Clearly, the cognitive approach has been adopted by numerous researchers who are interested in the relationship between personality and sport behavior.

Learning Approaches

Research based on conditioning theories has focused mainly on behavior modification. Although this area has important implications for influencing behavior in sport (Rushall & Siedentop, 1972), it is not discussed here, since it is not directly related to intra-individual characteristics of personality. A considerable amount of research in sport personality has utilized the social learning theoretical approach. Bandura's

(1977a) self-efficacy theory has been tested repeatedly in sport (see chapter 5) and Rotter's (1966) locus-of-control construct has also been included in sport personality research (see Cox, 1990). Some evidence exists that performance is facilitated by an internal locus of control (Chalip, 1980). Based on the premise that one of the most powerful roles we learn in life is our gender role, the relationship between perceived gender role and behavior in sport is also a critical area of study within the social learning approach to personality (see chapter 7 and Gill, 1986).

A Comprehensive View of Personality and Sport

The comprehensive view of personality assumed in this chapter reviews personality from several theoretical approaches. Table 3.3 encapsulates the various ways personality is studied in sport into a coherent "big picture." This table outlines the theoretical approaches to the study of personality by identifying brief characteristics of each theory, the paradigm with which each is associated, examples of sport research areas within each, and examples of assessment techniques used in these research areas. The trait–state theoretical perspective is added under the dispositional approach to emphasize that the interactional paradigm can operate within this approach to the study of personality. Motive/need theories can be categorized as within either the trait or the interactional paradigm, depending on the specific theory (e.g., Atkinson's, 1957, theory of achievement motivation is interactional). The placement of theories in particular categories may be arguable, but the intent of the categorization is to provide a comprehensive overview of the study of personality, particularly as it has been investigated in the sport context.

Table 3.3   Theoretical Approaches to Personality

Approach/theory	Characteristics	Paradigm	Sport research	Assessment
Psychodynamic	Deterministic, instinctual, unconscious processes	Trait	"Gravitational theory"	—
Dispositional				
Trait	Consistent internal attributes stable across time	Trait	Personality profiles	16PF, MMPI
Trait–state	Trait, state, and situation influence on behavior	Interactional	Mental health model, competitive anxiety	POMS, SCAT/CSAI–2
Biological	Relatedness of physiology and personality	Trait	Psychophysiology	Heart rate
Motive/need	Underlying motives, need patterns	Trait/interactional	nACH, sensation seeking	Mehrabian scale, Zuckerman scale
Phenomenological				
Actualization/self-determination	Self-fulfillment, self-determinism	Interactional	Intrinsic motivation	Observation, Ryan scale
Cognitive	Personal meaning, subjective construction	Interactional	Attribution theory, cognitive strategies, attentional style	Russell scale, PSIS, TAIS
Learning				
Conditioning	Working for reinforcment, observable behavior, no intrapersonal construct	Situational	Behavior modification	Observation
Social learning	Socialization influence on self-perception	Interactional	Locus of control, self-efficacy, gender role	Rotter scale, efficacy estimates, Bem scale

Influence of Sport and Exercise on Personality

Although most sport personality research has focused on the description of personality characteristics in athletes and the influence of personality on sport behavior, the study of the effects of sport and exercise participation on personality development and change has also been an important area of research. This perspective was seemingly derived from the traditional physical education philosophy that participation in physical activities and sports enhances psychological as well as physical development. In this section, two areas of research are reviewed. First, the literature concerned with developing positive personality attributes, or "building character," through sport participation is examined. Second, research that examines the influence of exercise or fitness training on personality characteristics is reviewed.

"Character" Development Through Sport

The construct "character" was originally referred to as personality structure (Freud, 1901/1960), but the term was subsequently modified to reflect culturally valued attributes that reflect morality as defined by society (Allport, 1961; Peck & Havighurst, 1960). The notion that "sports builds character," or that valued personality attributes may be developed through sport participation, has been traditionally espoused in U.S. society. However, this claim has not been well substantiated in the research literature. In fact, laboratory research has shown that competition serves to reduce prosocial behavioral tendencies such as helping and sharing (Barnett & Bryan, 1974; McGuire & Thomas, 1975) and serves to increase antisocial tendencies (Estrada, Gelfand & Hartmann, 1988; Rausch, 1965). Furthermore, both of these effects are magnified by losing. Socialization in U.S. sport is clearly a factor, since U.S. children have been shown to become more irrationally rivalrous and competitive with age than non-U.S. children (Kagen & Madsen, 1972).

Kleiber and Roberts (1981) examined the effects of sport competition on the prosocial behaviors of cooperation and altruism in a field experiment with children. They found that sport competition has a negative effect on the occurrence of prosocial behavior and that children more experienced in competitive sports are significantly less altruistic than the less experienced. This is consistent with Webb's (1969) research indicating that fairness as a sport value becomes subordinate to competence and winning

as age and experience in sport increases. Ogilvie and Tutko (1971) dispute the claim that sport builds character and contend that the personality characteristics associated with character in athletes are probably established before they begin involvement in sport (although their claim is unsubstantiated by research evidence). Two sets of researchers using the 16PF found no significant changes in personality characteristics of college athletes over four years (Werner & Gottheil, 1966) or over the course of a season (Rushall, 1976). Thus, the literature indicates that sport participation increases rivalrous, antisocial behavior and does not build "character" or socially valued personality attributes.

Influence of Exercise or Fitness Training on Personality Characteristics

Echoing the idea that "sport builds character," exercise or fitness training has also been popularly associated with positive personality change. However, with regard to changes on global trait measures of personality (e.g., 16PF), the research indicates rather modest changes or no changes following fitness training (Buccola & Stone, 1975; Ismail & Young, 1973, 1977; Tillman, 1965; Young & Ismail, 1976). Folkins and Sime (1981) state that global personality traits as measured by the 16PF are probably not permeable enough to be modified through fitness training. They suggest that specific personality characteristics identified as target variables should be the focus of modification through physical training or exercise. For example, Duke, Johnson, and Nowicki (1977) found a significant increase in internal locus of control in children during an eight-week sport fitness camp.

The personality characteristic that has been most frequently examined in this type of research is self-concept or self-esteem (see reviews by Folkins & Sime, 1981 and Sonstroem, 1982). Research has generally confirmed that fitness training improves self-concept in children (Koocher, 1971; Martinek, Cheffers & Zaichkowsky, 1978), adolescents (Collingwood & Willett, 1971; McGowan, Jarman & Pederson, 1974), and adults (Collingwood, 1972; Hanson & Nedde, 1974; Kowal, Patton & Vogel, 1978). Interestingly, several researchers assert that these changes in self-concept may result from perceived, as opposed to actual, changes in physical fitness (Heaps, 1978; Leonardson, 1977; Sonstroem, 1982). This assertion has important implications for fitness training programs in that mere involvement may not lead directly to enhanced self-esteem. Sonstroem (1982) emphasizes that it is critical that the participant

interpret fitness gains in terms of controllable success experiences and personal growth in competency. Although some studies have found no effect of fitness training on self-concept (Bruya, 1977; Mauser & Reynolds, 1977), these studies have been criticized for methodological limitations (Folkins & Sime, 1981; Sonstroem, 1982).

Exercise has also been associated with changes in affect and state anxiety. Most individuals admit that under normal circumstances, they "feel better" or "feel good" after vigorous exercise. Research substantiates that state anxiety and tension is reportedly reduced up to five hours following acute physical activity (Bahrke & Morgan, 1978; Morgan, 1985a). Berger, Friedmann, and Eaton (1988) have demonstrated reductions in self-reports of tension, depression, and anger after intense physical activity. Chronic physical activity is also associated with significant decreases in depression and alleviation of depressive symptoms in individuals who are clinically depressed at the outset of the exercise treatment (Mihevic, 1982). Several hypotheses have been advanced to explain these changes. The "distraction hypothesis" maintains that it is the attentional distraction from stressful stimuli, as opposed to the actual effect of exercise, that reduces anxiety and tension (Bahrke & Morgan, 1978). Other explanations (e.g., monamine hypothesis, endorphin hypothesis) have focused on physiological parameters to explain the effects of exercise on affective states (see Morgan, 1985a).

Current Status and Future Directions in Sport Personality Research

Clearly, personality in relation to sport and exercise has been studied using a variety of approaches and methods to ask a variety of questions. Research has been conducted to describe differences in personality based on groupings of individuals in sport, to predict various behaviors in sport and exercise (e.g., performance, adherence, choice), and to examine how personality characteristics may be mediated through participation in sport and exercise or through specific intervention programs. In this section, broad conclusions regarding what we know about personality and sport are drawn, and possible directions for future research are offered.

Current Status of Knowledge

Based on a review of the available research on personality in sport and exercise, several general conclusions may be offered.

• *No distinguishable "athletic personality" has been shown to exist.* There are no consistent research findings showing that athletes possess a general personality type distinct from the personality of nonathletes.

• *No consistent dispositional personality differences between athletic subgroups (e.g., team versus individual sport athletes, contact versus noncontact sport athletes) have been shown to exist.* Although personality differences between various athletic subgroups have been identified in some studies, the findings are inconsistent overall. Much of this research has failed to employ large subject samples, appropriate personality measures, and precise consideration and operationalization of unique situational variables. Such research sophistication is necessary in order to understand complex personality–behavior interactions.

• *Success in sport seems to be facilitated by positive mental health, positive self-perceptions, and productive cognitive strategies.* Successful athletes have been shown to possess the iceberg profile (Morgan, 1985b) of positive mental health, more positive cognitive self-perceptions (e.g., self-confidence), and more productive cognitive strategies (e.g., attentional focusing, anxiety management), as compared to less successful athletes. It is noteworthy that personality differences between successful athletes and less successful athletes have been found in mood states, cognitions, and coping abilities, as opposed to more enduring personality traits and dispositions.

• *Cognitive intervention strategies enhance performance behaviors and cognitive coping skills in sport but are less effective in inducing change in personality traits or dispositions.*

Again, it is significant that cognitions, as opposed to traits or dispositions, have been shown to mediate sport behaviors and performance.

• *Participation in sport does not build "character," or socially valued personality attributes.* In fact, research indicates that sport participation increases rivalrous, antisocial behavior.

• *Exercise and fitness training enhances self-concept and reduces negative affective states but has little influence on global personality traits.* Thus, although fitness training seems to influence personality with regard to self-perceptions and mood, the global and stable personality traits as measured by the 16PF seem to be less adaptable to change via physical training.

• *We know a great deal about specific personality characteristics or content areas with sound theoretical underpinnings and valid measurement instrumentation* (see chapter 4 on motivation, chapter 5 on attribution theory, and chapter 6 on anxiety). Thus, we should continue to test theory as it applies to sport and exercise contexts but also develop and test theory and assessment techniques that are specific to sport and exercise.

Future Directions

Although many researchers in sport psychology feel that the area of sport personality research has yielded no useful findings, it may be argued that this is not true. The conclusions stated in the previous section illustrate that the sport personality research of the last three decades has progressed across paradigms, theories, and assessment methods to provide sport psychologists with some definitive findings; that is, if we look into its depths, the water is not as muddy as we might have thought. It seems important to avoid criticizing early personality research for its lack of sophistication and realize that early attempts in all scientific areas involve less than precise theories and methods. The early work in sport personality, while lacking in scientific rigor, did in fact generate tremendous interest in sport psychology and was a major impetus for the emergence of the field as an academic subdiscipline of physical education. However, it is imperative that sport psychologists now move forward to extend paradigmatic, theoretical, and methodological approaches to the study of personality in sport.

Several points were discussed that hopefully will serve to stimulate future research in sport personality. In this section, some additional directions for future research are discussed. These include the adoption of a comprehensive approach to the study of personality in sport, accounting for moderator variables in the study of personality and the utilization of a life-span approach in studying personality development and change.

Comprehensive Approach

A comprehensive view of personality takes the perspective that personality is structured in multiple layers or levels and that it can be studied using many different approaches. Hollander's (1967) model (see Figure 3.1) provides a framework for this perspective by structuring personality into a psychological core, typical responses, and role-related behaviors and also accounts for the influence of social environment on these components. Those who believe that personality research only encompasses the study of traits are focusing on only one narrow dimension or approach within the study of personality. To understand personality in sport contexts, a cross-theoretical, multimethod perspective is needed in which the various levels of personality are examined to understand their interrelationships, their influence on different behaviors, and their structure and function in relation to the social environment. Maddi (1984) supports this comprehensive approach by emphasizing that personality researchers must generate and test hypotheses regarding peripheral, developmental, and core characteristics of personality.

A hypothetical example illustrates how various personality characteristics could be structured and examined within Hollander's (1967) model. The psychological core might include an individual's self-concept, perceived ability in relation to sport, and achievement goal orientations. These basic, underlying personality foundations would then influence various typical responses (or traits/dispositions) of the individual, such as self-confidence, competitive trait anxiety, and locus of control. The individual's role-related behaviors would be influenced by the trickle-down of core and dispositional characteristics as well as the specific situational influences on behavior at that moment. Role-related behaviors might be competitive state anxiety, cognitive strategies, physiological manifestations of stress, and performance. Sophisticated statistical techniques such as structural equation modeling (Dwyer, 1983) could be used to test proposed causal models of relationships between networks of personality and social variables as seen in this example. Another assessment strategy would be to employ an idiographic approach to attempt to understand how personality is constructed within these various layers or levels of functioning.

Within this comprehensive approach, the cognitive aspects of personality functioning in sport has taken center stage in the sport psychology literature. This is due to the fact that the cognitive approach has improved behavioral prediction in sport when compared to the traditional trait approaches. For example, Mahoney and Avener (1977) found that successful athletes are better able to use anxiety as a means to stimulate performance than are less successful athletes, even though traditional trait research could not establish any significant differences between successful and less successful athletes in trait anxiety. The point is that although successful and less successful athletes may not differ at the trait level of anxiety, successful athletes seem to be more cognitively skilled in controlling anxiety that is manifested in stressful situations. Researchers should continue to study the cognitive processes involved as athletes prepare for competition, actually compete, and postcompetitively appraise their performances. However, this research should be extended to study how personality is constructed and related at all levels of Hollander's (1967) model.

An example of sport personality research using a comprehensive approach is the work of Morgan, O'Connor, Ellickson, and Bradley (1988), who studied the psychological characteristics of a sample of elite runners. The runners were assessed on global personality traits (EPI), specific personality traits (STAI), and mood states (POMS). Structured interviews were also conducted to assess motivation, cognitive strategies, precompetition arousal levels, and training staleness. All of these parameters were examined in relation to their effects on a performance measure. This study used trait, trait–state, and cognitive approaches and various assessment techniques to provide a multiplistic view of the relationship between personality and performance.

Moderator Variables

An important consideration in personality research is the influence of moderator variables, which may be defined as personal or situational characteristics that influence or moderate the valid measurement of personality. For example, a psychological inventory may be a better predictor of criterion performance for men than for women, meaning that in this case gender is a moderator variable, since it moderates the validity of this particular inventory.

Several moderator variables that influence the study of personality have been identified in the literature and seem to be important considerations in the study of personality in sport. *Trait relevance* can be identified as a moderator variable based on Allport's (1937) original contention that not all trait dimensions apply equally well to all people; that is, individuals differ not only according to their levels of a given trait but also according to which trait dimensions they possess (Paunonen, 1988). Baumeister and Tice (1988) coined the term *metatrait* to describe the trait of having versus not having a particular trait or the presence versus absence of the associated trait dimension in a person's personality. Baumeister and Tice advanced the "metatrait hypothesis," which states that many past empirical studies of trait–behavior relationships have underestimated the true strength of the relationship because these studies have included persons to whom the trait dimensions did not apply. They compare these studies to a hypothetical study in which the relationship between diet and menstrual cramps is studied in males. Ideally, researchers should eliminate untraited individuals from their samples to conduct more precise tests of their hypotheses. Although the term *trait* is used here, the metatrait approach can be applied to various other personality characteristics, such as attitudes, orientations, values, and styles. In principle, all personality characteristics have metatraits associated with them.

Several methods of assessing metatraits have been advocated (Baumeister & Tice, 1988). The first method involves asking subjects to rate their behavioral consistency with regard to the particular trait under analysis. Second, the extremity of self-ratings on the trait dimension can be examined. People with extremely high or low ratings are classified as being traited on this dimension, while people with intermediate scores are classified as untraited on this dimension. Third, new scales could be constructed to measure behavioral consistency on various dimensions. The fourth approach involves an "ipsatized variance index" developed by Bem and Allen (1974). In this method, several traits are simultaneously assessed, then a ratio is computed of the inter-item variance on the target dimension to the inter-item variance on all dimensions for each subject. The fifth approach simply computes inter-item variance of scale responses on the scale of interest. Low variance signifies that the person responded consistently on the dimension and so is traited on that dimension. High variance indicates that the person responded erratically or inconsistently to the different items, suggesting that he or she is untraited on that particular dimension. Empirically, metatraits may be used to construct a sample or to compare the responses of traited versus untraited subjects. Baumeister and Tice (1988) suggest two possibilities when comparing responses: either the metatrait moderates the effects of the trait or the metatrait predicts behavior directly, independent of trait. Future research in sport personality could examine metatraits in individuals to ascertain if there are metatraits unique to athletes or metatraits that are important behavioral predictors in sport.

A second moderator variable that may be important to personality research is *self-schema*. Related to metatraits, self-schema are knowledge structures about the self that are acquired from past experience that organize and guide the processing of the self-relevant information contained in the individual's social behavior (Markus, 1977, 1983). Self-schema develop around aspects of an individual's life that are personally significant, so they represent areas that are very salient for that particular individual. This approach is based on the premise that individuals are not equally invested in, nor do they feel equally responsible for, all of their actions. Specifying self-schema, or the self-relevant domains of personality, is critical in understanding and predicting behavior in individuals. A particularly fruitful area of research utilizing this approach involves the study of how individuals' goals influence how information is processed and thus how behavior is driven (Cohen & Ebbesen, 1979; Jeffery & Mischel, 1979). Dweck and Elliot (1983) propose that the goals individuals pursue create a personal framework within which they interpret, and react to, events. Research has indicated that personal goal orientation is more important in predicting behavior than perceptions of ability (Dweck & Leggett, 1988). These findings seem to have important implications for the examination of goal orientations in sport research.

Another moderator variable that may influence the study of personality in sport is *self-monitoring*, or the processes by which individuals plan and enact their behavioral choices in social contexts (Snyder, 1983). High-self-monitoring individuals are described as those who monitor and regulate their behavioral choices on the basis of situational information. Snyder states that for high-self-monitors, the influence of situational and interpersonal cues of social appropriateness is strong. Thus, the relationship between behavior and underlying personality characteristics should be minimized in high-self-monitors. Conversely, low-self-monitoring individuals are described as those who monitor or guide their behavioral choices on the basis of information from relevant internal states, so they are predicted to be less responsive to situational and interpersonal specifications of behavioral appropriateness (Snyder, 1983). Thus, the behavior of low-self-monitors should show substantial cross-situational consistency and the relationship between behavior and underlying personality characteristics should be maximized in low-self-monitors. Empirical evidence has supported the influence of self-monitoring on behavior, and the Self-Monitoring Scale has been validated as a measure of this tendency (Snyder, 1974). The phenomenon of self-monitoring has not been studied in sport and would seem to be an important moderating variable to study in relation to the prediction of sport behavior by personality.

Life-Span Approach

Another fruitful area for future research that falls nicely within the comprehensive framework of personality study advocated in this chapter is a life-span approach. Neugarten (1977) advocates the study of personality within the broader context of life span, which emphasizes that there is a continually changing basis within the individual for perceiving, and responding to, events. Individuals learn behavior regarded as appropriate for a particular life period, so a comprehensive understanding of personality and behavior must account for social and historical events that may influence personality. For example, personality can be studied across the life span to understand successful aging or individuals' different capacities for coping with changing life situations. This would seem to have implications in sport to understand personality factors that influence retirement from sport or the movement from one level of sport to another (e.g., college to professional sport). Along these lines, Ryff (1984) suggests using retrospective research strategies to attempt to understand what the person perceives as important in different periods of his or her past.

Conclusion

Overall, a comprehensive view of personality is advocated in which sport psychology moves beyond the measurement of traits to a multitheory, multimethod approach to understanding the structure and process of personality as it relates to sport and exercise. In this regard, Maddi (1984) suggests a shift from actuality to possibility. He states that personality research has followed a trivial, narrow model of science and that the quest for scientific credibility through narrow construct validation has precluded the study of more important and relevant questions. Research in sport personality should now move forward past our early scientific inferiority complex into an era of inquiry that examines significant and meaningful relationships between personality characteristics and behavior in sport.

References

Adler, A. (1929). *The science of living*. New York: Greenberg.

Alderman, R.B. (1980). Sport psychology: Past, present, and future dilemmas. In P. Klavora & K.A.W. Wipper (Eds.), *Psychological and sociological factors in sport* (pp. 3-19). Toronto: University of Toronto.

Allen, B.P., & Potkay, C.R. (1981). On the arbitrary distinction between states and traits. *Journal of Personality and Social Psychology, 41*, 916-928.

Allport, G.W. (1937). *Personality: A psychological interpretation*. New York: Holt.

Allport, G.W. (1961). *Pattern and growth in personality*. New York: Holt.

Allport, G.W. (1962). The general and the unique in psychological science. *Journal of Personality, 30*, 405-422.

American Psychological Association. (1974). *Standards for educational and psychological tests*. Washington, DC: American Psychological Association.

Anastasi, A. (1988). *Psychological testing*. New York: Macmillan.

Anshel, M.H. (1987). Psychological inventories used in sport psychology research. *Sport Psychologist, 1*, 331-349.

Atkinson, J.W. (1957). Motivational determinants of risk-taking behaviors. *Psychological Review, 64*, 359-372.

Bahrke, M.S., & Morgan, W.P. (1978). Anxiety reduction following exercise and meditation. *Cognitive Therapy and Research, 2*, 323-333.

Bandura, A. (1969). *Principles of behavior modification*. New York: Holt.

Bandura, A. (1977a). Self-efficacy: Toward a unifying theory of behavioral change. *Psychological Review, 84*, 191-215.

Bandura, A. (1977b). *Social learning theory*. New York: Prentice-Hall.

Barnett, M.A., & Bryan, J.H. (1974). Effects of competition with outcome feedback on children's helping behavior. *Developmental Psychology, 10*, 838-842.

Baron, R.M., & Boudreau, L.A. (1987). An ecological perspective on integrating personality and social psychology. *Journal of Personality and Social Psychology, 53*, 1222-1228.

Baumeister, R.F., & Tice, D.M. (1988). Metatraits. *Journal of Personality, 56*, 571-598.

Bem, D.J. (1972). Constructing cross-situational consistencies in behavior: Some thoughts on Alker's critique of Mischel. *Journal of Personality, 40*, 17-26.

Bem, D.J. (1983). Constructing a theory of the triple typology: Some (second) thoughts on nomothetic and idiographic approaches to personality. *Journal of Personality, 51*, 566-577.

Bem, D.J., & Allen, A. (1974). On predicting some of the people some of the time: The search for cross-situational consistencies in behavior. *Psychological Review, 81*, 506-520.

Bem, D.J., & Funder, D.C. (1978). Predicting more of the people more of the time: Assessing personality of situations. *Psychological Review, 85*, 485-501.

Bem, S.L. (1974). The measurement of psychological androgyny. *Journal of Consulting and Clinical Psychology, 42*, 155-162.

Berger, B.G., Friedmann, E., & Eaton, M. (1988). Comparison of jogging, the relaxation response, and group interaction for stress reduction. *Journal of Sport and Exercise Psychology, 10*, 431-447.

Bird, E.I. (1979). Multivariate personality analysis of two children's hockey teams. *Perceptual and Motor Skills, 48*, 967-973.

Block, J. (1957). A comparison between ipsative and normative ratings of personality. *Journal of Abnormal and Social Psychology, 54*, 50-54.

Block, J. (1961). *The Q-sort method in personality assessment and psychiatric research*. Springfield, IL: Thomas.

Bowers, K.S. (1973). Situationism in psychology: An analysis and a critique. *Psychological Review, 80*, 307-336.

Bruya, L.D. (1977). Effect of selected movement skills on positive self-concept. *Perceptual and Motor Skills, 45*, 252-254.

Buccola, V.A., & Stone, W.J. (1975). Effects of jogging and cycling programs on physiological and personality variables in aged men. *Research Quarterly, 46*, 134-139.

Burton, D. (1988). Do anxious swimmers swim slower? Reexamining the elusive anxiety–performance relationship. *Journal of Sport and Exercise Psychology, 10*, 45-61.

Buss, A.H. (1989). Personality as traits. *American Psychologist, 44*, 1378-1388.

Buss, D.M., & Craik, K.H. (1983). The dispositional analysis of everyday conduct. *Journal of Personality, 51*, 393-412.

Campbell, D.J., & Stanley, J.C. (1966). *Experimental and quasi-experimental designs for research*. Chicago: Rand McNally.

Carlson, R. (1971). Where is the person in personality research? *Psychological Review, 75*, 203-219.

Carlson, R. (1984). What's social about social psychology? *Journal of Personality and Social Psychology, 47*, 1304-1309.

Carron, A.V. (1980). *Social psychology of sport*. Ithaca, NY: Mouvement.

Carver, C.S., & Scheier, M.F. (1988). *Perspectives on personality*. Boston: Allyn & Bacon.

Cattell, R.B. (1946). *Description and measurement of personality*. Yonkers-on-Hudson, NY: World.

Cattell, R.B. (1965). *The scientific analysis of personality*. Baltimore: Penguin Books.

Chalip, L. (1980). Social learning theory and sport success: Evidence and implications. *Journal of Sport Behavior, 3*, 76-85.

Chalip, W.F., & Buckner, K.E. (1988). Self-ratings of personality: A naturalistic comparison of normative, ipsative, and idiothetic standards. *Journal of Personality, 56*, 509-530.

Cialdini, R.B. (1980). Full-cycle social psychology. In L. Bickman (Ed.), *Applied social psychology annual* (pp. 69-102). Beverly Hills, CA: Sage.

Clarke, D.A. (1988). The validity of measures of cognition: A review of the literature. *Cognitive Therapy and Research, 12*, 1-20.

Cohen, C.E., & Ebbesen, E.B. (1979). Observational goals and schema activation: A theoretical framework for behavior perception. *Journal of Experimental Social Psychology, 15*, 305-329.

Collingwood, T.R. (1972). The effects of physical training upon behavior and self attitudes. *Journal of Clinical Psychology, 28*, 583-585.

Collingwood, T.R., & Willett, L. (1971). The effects of physical training upon self-concept and body attitudes. *Journal of Clinical Psychology, 27*, 411-412.

Cox, R.H. (1990). *Sport psychology* (2nd ed.). Dubuque, IA: Brown.

Craik, K.H. (1969). Personality unvanquished. *Contemporary Psychology, 14*, 147-149.

Cronbach, L.J. (1970). *Essentials of psychological testing* (3rd ed.). New York: Harper.

Cronbach, L.J., & Meehl, P.E. (1955). Construct validation in psychological tests. *Psychological Bulletin, 52*, 281-302.

Crowne, D.P., & Marlowe, D. (1960). A new scale of social desirability independent of psychopathology. *Journal of Consulting Psychology, 24*, 349-354.

Deci, E.L. (1975). *Intrinsic motivation*. New York: Plenum.

Deci, E.L. (1980). *The psychology of self-determination*. Lexington, MA: D.C. Heath.

Dishman, R.K. (1982). Contemporary sport psychology. In R.L. Terjung (Ed.), *Exercise and sport science reviews* (Vol. 10, pp. 120-159). Philadelphia: Franklin Institute Press.

Dishman, R.K. (1983). The identity crisis in North American sport psychology: Academic and professional issues. *Journal of Sport Psychology, 5,* 123-134.

Dishman, R.K. (1984). Motivation and exercise adherence. In J.M. Silva & R.S. Weinberg (Eds.), *Psychological foundations of sport* (pp. 420-434). Champaign, IL: Human Kinetics.

Duke, M., Johnson, T.C., & Nowicki, S., Jr. (1977). Effects of sports fitness camp experience on locus of control orientation in children. *Research Quarterly, 48,* 280-283.

Duda, J.L., Smart, A.E., & Tappe, M.K. (1989). Predictors of adherence in the rehabilitation of athletic injuries: An application of personal investment theory. *Journal of Sport and Exercise Psychology, 11,* 367-381.

Dweck, C.S., & Elliot, E.S. (1983). Achievement motivation. In E.M. Hetherington (Ed.), *Handbook of child psychology: Vol. 4. Social and personality development* (pp. 643-691). New York: Wiley.

Dweck, C.S., & Leggett, E.L. (1988). A social-cognitive approach to motivation and personality. *Psychological Review, 95,* 256-273.

Dwyer, J.H. (1983). *Statistical models for the social and behavioral sciences.* New York: Oxford University Press.

Endler, N.S. (1973). The person versus the situation—A pseudo issue? A response to Alker. *Journal of Personality, 41,* 287-303.

Epstein, S. (1979). The stability of behavior: On predicting most of the people most of the time. *Journal of Personality and Social Psychology, 37,* 1097-1126.

Erickson, E.H. (1950). *Childhood and society.* New York: Norton.

Estrada, A.M., Gelfand, D.M., & Hartmann, D.P. (1988). Children's sport and the development of social behaviors. In F. Smoll, R.A. Magill, & M.J. Ash (Eds.), *Children in sport* (3rd ed., pp. 251-262). Champaign, IL: Human Kinetics.

Ewing, M.E. (1981). Achievement orientations and sport behavior of males and females. (Doctoral dissertation, University of Illinois). *Dissertation Abstracts International, 42,* 2559A.

Eysenck, H.J. (1960). The effects of psychotherapy. In H.J. Eysenck (Ed.), *Handbook of abnormal psychology: An experimental approach.* New York: Basic Books.

Eysenck, H.J. (1967). *The biological basis of personality.* Springfield, IL: Thomas.

Eysenck, H.J. (1970). *The structure of human personality* (3rd ed.). London: Methuen.

Eysenck, H.J. (1981). *A model for personality.* Berlin: Springer-Verlag.

Eysenck, H.J., & Eysenck, M.W. (1985). *Personality and individual differences.* New York: Plenum.

Eysenck, H.J., & Eysenck, S.B.G. (1975). *Manual of the Eysenck Personality Inventory.* London: Hodder & Stoughton.

Feltz, D.L. (1987). Advancing knowledge in sport psychology: Strategies for expanding our conceptual frameworks. *Quest, 39,* 243-254.

Festinger, L.A. (1957). *A theory of cognitive dissonance.* New York: Harper & Row.

Fisher, A.C. (1976). *Psychology of sport: Issues and insights.* Palo Alto, CA: Mayfield.

Fisher, A.C. (1984). New directions in sport personality research. In J.M. Silva & R.S. Weinberg (Eds.), *Psychological foundations of sport* (pp. 70-80). Champaign, IL: Human Kinetics.

Fiske, D.W. (1988). From inferred personalities toward personality in action. *Journal of Personality, 56,* 815-833.

Folkins, C.H., & Sime, W.E. (1981). Physical fitness training and mental health. *American Psychologist, 36,* 373-389.

Fowler, C.J., Knorring, L. von, & Oreland, L. (1980). Platelet monoamine oxidase activity in sensation seekers. *Psychiatric Research, 3,* 273-279.

Fox, K.R., & Corbin, C.B. (1989). The Physical Self-Perception Profile: Development and preliminary validation. *Journal of Sport and Exercise Psychology, 11,* 408-430.

Frank, L.K. (1939). Projective methods for the study of personality. *Journal of Psychology, 8,* 389-413.

Frazier, S.E. (1988). Mood state profiles of chronic exercisers with differing abilities. *International Journal of Sport Psychology, 19,* 65-71.

Freud, S. (1953). *The standard edition of the complete psychological works of Sigmund Freud: Vols. 4 and 5. The interpretation of dreams.* J. Stachey, (Ed.). London: Hogarth. (Original work published, 1900).

Freud, S. (1960). *The standard edition of the complete psychological works of Sigmund Freud: Vol. 6. The psychopathology of everyday life.* J. Stachey, (Ed.). London: Hogarth. (Original work published, 1901).

Fridhandler, B.M. (1986). Conceptual note on state, trait, and the state–trait distinction. *Journal of Personality and Social Psychology, 50,* 169-174.

Friedman, M., & Rosenman, R.H. (1974). *Type A behavior and your heart.* New York: Knopf.

Fromm, E. (1947). *Man for himself.* New York: Holt.

Fuchs, C.Z., & Zaichkowsky, L.D. (1983). Psychological characteristics of male and female bodybuilders: The iceberg profile. *Journal of Sport Behavior, 6,* 136-145.

Furst, D.M., & Hardman, J.S. (1988). The iceberg profile and young competitive swimmers. *Perceptual and Motor Skills, 67,* 478.

Gill, D.L. (1986). *Psychological dynamics of sport.* Champaign, IL: Human Kinetics.

Gill, D.L., & Deeter, T.E. (1988). Development of the Sport Orientation Questionnaire. *Research Quarterly for Exercise and Sport, 59,* 191-202.

Gill, D.L., Dzewaltowski, D.A., & Deeter, T.E. (1988). The relationship of competitiveness and achievement orientation to participation in sport and nonsport activities. *Journal of Sport and Exercise Psychology, 10,* 139-150.

Glass, D.C. (1977). *Behavior patterns, stress, and coronary disease.* Hillsdale, NJ: Erlbaum.

Gould, D., & Petlichkoff, L. (1988). Participation motivation and attrition in young athletes. In F. Smoll, R.A. Magill, & M.J. Ash (Eds.), *Children in sport* (3rd ed., pp. 251-262). Champaign, IL: Human Kinetics.

Gould, D., Petlichkoff, L., Simons, J., & Vevera, M. (1987). Relationship between Competitive State Anxiety Inventory–2 subscale scores and pistol shooting performance. *Journal of Sport Psychology, 9,* 33-42.

Gould, D., Weiss, M.R., & Weinberg, R.S. (1981). Psychological characteristics of successful and nonsuccessful Big Ten wrestlers. *Journal of Sport Psychology, 3,* 69-81.

Greenspan, M.J., & Feltz, D.L. (1989). Psychological interventions with athletes in competitive situations: A review. *The Sport Psychologist, 3,* 219-236.

Griffith, C.R. (1926). *Psychology of coaching.* New York: Scribner.

Guilford, J.P. (1959). *Personality.* New York: McGraw-Hill.

Hagberg, J., Mullin, J., Bahrke, M., & Limburg, J. (1979). Physiological profiles and selected physiological characteristics of national class American cyclists. *Journal of Sports Medicine, 19,* 341-346.

Hanson, J.S., & Nedde, W.H. (1974). Long term physical training effect in sedentary females. *Journal of Applied Physiology, 37,* 112-116.

Hardy, C.J., McMurray, R.G., & Roberts, S. (1989). A/B types and psychophysiological responses to exercise stress. *Journal of Sport and Exercise Psychology, 11*, 141-151.

Harter, S. (1985). *Manual for the Self-Perception Profile for Children*. Denver: University of Denver.

Hatfield, B.D., & Landers, D.M. (1983). Psychophysiology—A new direction for sport psychology. *Journal of Sport Psychology, 5*, 243-259.

Hathaway, S.R., & McKinley, J.C. (1943). *MMPI manual*. New York: Psychological Corporation.

Healey, R.R., & Landers, D.M. (1973). Effect of need achievement and task difficulty on competitive and noncompetitive motor performance. *Journal of Motor Behavior, 5*, 121-128.

Heaps, R.A. (1978). Relating physical and psychological fitness: A psychological point of view. *Journal of Sports Medicine, 18*, 399-408.

Heider, F. (1958). *The psychology of interpersonal relations*. New York: Wiley.

Hempel, C.G. (1960). Operationism, observation, and scientific terms. In A. Danto & S. Morgenbesser (Eds.), *Philosophy of science* (pp. 101-120). Cleveland: World.

Highlen, P.S., & Bennett, B.B. (1979). Psychological characteristics of successful and nonsuccessful elite wrestlers: An exploratory study. *Journal of Sport Psychology, 1*, 123-137.

Highlen, P.S., & Bennett, B.B. (1983). Elite divers and wrestlers: A comparison between open- and closed-skill athletes. *Journal of Sport Psychology, 5*, 390-409.

Hogan, R., DeSoto, C.B., & Solano, C. (1977). Traits, tests, and personality research. *American Psychologist, 32*, 255-264.

Hollander, E.P. (1967). *Principles and methods of social psychology*. New York: Holt.

Holtzman, W.H. (1965). Personality structure. *Annual Review of Psychology, 16*, 119-156.

Horney, K. (1924). On the genesis of the castration complex in women. *International Journal of Psychoanalysis, 5*, 50-65.

Houts, A.C., Cook, T.D., & Shadish, W.R. (1986). The person-situation debate: A critical multiplist perspective. *Journal of Personality 54*, 52-105.

Husserl, E. (1965). *Phenomenology and the crisis of philosophy*, Q. Lauer (Ed. and trans.). New York: Harper Torchbooks. (Original work published 1911).

Hymbaugh, K., & Garrett, J. (1974). Sensation seeking among skydivers. *Perceptual and Motor Skills, 38*, 118.

Ismail, A.H., & Young, R.J. (1973). The effect of chronic exercise on the personality of middle-age men by univariate and multivariate approaches. *Journal of Human Ergology, 2*, 47-57.

Ismail, A.H., & Young, R.J. (1977). Effect of chronic exercise on the personality of adults. *Annals of the New York Academy of Sciences, 301*, 958-969.

Jackson, C.O. (1933). An experimental study of the effect of fear on muscular coordination. *Research Quarterly, 4*, 71-80.

Jeffery, K.M., & Mischel, W. (1979). Effects of purpose on the organization and recall of information in person perception. *Journal of Personality, 47*, 397-419.

Johansson, F., Almay, B.G.L., von Knorring, L., Terenius, L., & Astrom, M. (1979). Personality traits in chronic pain patients related to endorphin levels in cerebrospinal fluid. *Psychiatry Research, 1*, 231-239.

Johnson, W.R. (1949). A study of emotion revealed in two types of athletic sports contests. *Research Quarterly, 20*, 72-79.

Jung, C.G. (1926). The structure and dynamics of the psyche. In H. Read, M. Fordham, & G. Adler (Eds.), *Collected works of C.G. Jung* (Vol. 8). Princeton, NJ: Princeton University Press.

Kagen, S., & Madsen, M.C. (1972). Experimental analyses of cooperation and competition of Anglo–American and Mexican–American children. *Developmental Psychology, 6*, 49-59.

Kane, J.E. (1978). Personality research: The current controversy and implications for sports studies. In W.F. Straub (Ed.), *Sport psychology: An analysis of athlete behavior* (pp. 228-240). Ithaca, NY: Mouvement.

Karteroliotis, C., & Gill, D.L. (1987). Temporal changes in psychological and physiological components of state anxiety. *Journal of Sport Psychology, 9*, 261-274.

Kelley, H. (1973). The process of causal attribution. *American Psychologist, 28*, 107-128.

Kelly, G. (1955). *The psychology of personal constructs*. New York: Norton.

Kenrick, D.T., & Funder, D.C. (1988). Profiting from controversy: Lessons from the person–situation debate. *American Psychologist, 43*, 23-34.

Kleiber, D.A., & Roberts, G.C. (1981). The effects of sport experience in the development of social character: An exploratory study. *Journal of Sport Psychology, 3*, 114-122.

Kluckhohn, C., & Murray, H.A. (1949). *Personality in nature, society, and culture*. New York: Holt.

Kobasa, S.C. (1979). Stressful life events, personality, and health: An inquiry into hardiness. *Journal of Personality and Social Psychology, 37*, 1-11.

Kobasa, S.C., Maddi, S.R., & Kahn, S. (1982). Hardiness and health: A prospective study. *Journal of Personality and Social Psychology, 42*, 168-177.

Koocher, G.P. (1971). Swimming, competence, and personality change. *Journal of Personality and Social Psychology, 18*, 275-278.

Kowal, D.M., Patton, J.F., & Vogel, J.A. (1978). Psychological states and aerobic fitness of male and female recruits before and after basic training. *Aviation, Space, and Environmental Medicine, 49*, 603-606.

Kretschmer, E. (1925). *Physique and character*. New York: Harcourt.

Kroll, W. (1970). Personality assessment of athletes. In L.E. Smith (Ed.), *Psychology of motor learning* (pp. 349-367). Chicago: Athletic Institute.

Kroll, W. (1976). Current strategies and problems in personality assessment of athletes. In A.C. Fisher (Ed.), *Psychology of sport* (pp. 371-390). Palo Alto, CA: Mayfield.

Kuhn, T.S. (1970). *The structure of scientific revolutions* (2nd ed.). Chicago: University of Chicago Press.

Lakie, W.L. (1962). Personality characteristics of certain groups of intercollegiate athletics. *Research Quarterly, 33*, 566-573.

Lamiell, J.T. (1981). Toward an idiothetic psychology of personality. *American Psychologist, 36*, 276-289.

Landers, D.M. (1983). Whatever happened to theory testing in sport psychology? *Journal of Sport Psychology, 5*, 135-151.

Lazarus, R.S., & Monat, A. (1979). *Personality* (3rd ed.). Englewood Cliffs, NJ: Prentice-Hall.

Leonardson, G.R. (1977). Relationship between self-concept and perceived physical fitness. *Perceptual and Motor Skills, 44*, 62.

Lerch, H.A. (1976). Four female collegiate track athletes: An analysis of personal constructs. *Research Quarterly, 47*, 687-691.

LeUnes, A., Hayward, S.A., & Daiss, S. (1988). Annotated bibliography on the Profile of Mood States in sport. *Journal of Sport Behavior, 11*, 213-240.

Levy, L.H. (1970). *Conceptions of personality: Theory and research*. New York: Random House.

Lewin, K. (1935). *A dynamic theory of personality*. New York: McGraw-Hill.

Maddi, S.R. (1976). *Personality theories: A comparative analysis*. Homewood, IL: Dorsey.

Maddi, S.R. (1984). Personology in the 1980s. In R.A. Zucker, J. Aronoff, & A.I. Rabin (Eds.), *Personality and the prediction of behavior* (pp. 7-41). New York: Academic.

Maehr, M., & Braskamp, L. (1986). *The motivation factor: A theory of personal investment*. Lexington, MA: Lexington Books.

Magnusson, D., & Endler, N.S. (1977). Interactional psychology: Present status and future prospects. In D. Magnusson & N.S. Endler (Eds.), *Personality at the crossroads: Current issues in interactional psychology* (pp. 3-31). Hillsdale, NJ: Erlbaum.

Mahoney, M.J. (1989). Psychological predictors of elite and non-elite performance in Olympic weightlifting. *International Journal of Sport Psychology*, **20**, 1-12.

Mahoney, M.J., & Avener, M. (1977). Psychology of the elite athlete: An exploratory study. *Cognitive Therapy and Research*, **2**, 135-141.

Mahoney, M.J., Gabriel, T.J., & Perkins, T.S. (1987). Psychological skills and exceptional athletic performance. *Sport Psychologist*, **1**, 181-199.

Malloy, T.E., & Kenny, D.A. (1986). The social relations model: An integrative method for personality research. *Journal of Personality*, **54**, 199-225.

Malmisur, M.C. (1976). Ego development stages of a sample of college football players. *Research Quarterly*, **47**, 148-153.

Markus, H. (1977). Self-schemata and processing information about the self. *Journal of Personality and Social Psychology*, **35**, 63-78.

Markus, H. (1983). Self-knowledge: An expanded view. *Journal of Personality*, **51**, 543-565.

Martens, R. (1975). The paradigmatic crisis in American sport personology. *Sportwissenschaft*, **1**, 9-24.

Martens, R. (1979). About smocks and jocks. *Journal of Sport Psychology*, **1**, 94-99.

Martens, R. (1987). Science, knowledge, and sport psychology. *Sport Psychologist*, **1**, 29-55.

Martens, R., Vealey, R.S., & Burton, D. (1990). *Competitive anxiety in sport*. Champaign, IL: Human Kinetics.

Martinek, T.J., Cheffers, J.T., & Zaichkowsky, L.D. (1978). Physical activity, motor development, and self-concept: Race and age differences. *Perceptual and Motor Skills*, **46**, 147-154.

Maslow, A.H. (1968). *Toward a psychology of being* (2nd ed.). Princeton, NJ: Van Nostrand.

Masters, K.S., & Lambert, M.J. (1989). The relations between cognitive coping strategies, reasons for running, injury, and performance of marathon runners. *Journal of Sport and Exercise Psychology*, **11**, 161-170.

Mauser, H., & Reynolds, R.P. (1977). Effects of a developmental physical activity program on children's body coordination and self-concept. *Perceptual and Motor Skills*, **44**, 1057-1058.

McAuley, E., & Tammen, V.V. (1989). The effects of subjective and objective competitive outcomes on intrinsic motivation. *Journal of Sport and Exercise Psychology*, **11**, 84-93.

McClelland, D.C. (1961). *The achieving society*. Princeton, NJ: Van Nostrand.

McGowan, R.W., Jarman, B.O., & Pederson, D.M. (1974). Effects of a competitive endurance training program on self-concept and peer approval. *Journal of Psychology*, **86**, 37-52.

McGrath, J.E. (1982). Dilemmatics: The study of research choices and dilemmas. In J.E. McGrath, J. Martin, & R.A. Kulka (Eds.), *Judgment calls in research* (pp. 69-102). Beverly Hills, CA: Sage.

McGuire, J., & Thomas, M.H. (1975). Effects of sex, competence, and competition on sharing behavior in children. *Journal of Personality and Social Psychology*, **32**, 490-494.

McNair, D.M., Lorr, M., & Droppleman, L.F. (1981). *Profile of mood states*. San Diego: Educational and Industrial Testing Service.

Mehrabian, A. (1968). Male and female scales of the tendency to achieve. *Educational and Psychological Measurement*, **28**, 493-502.

Meyers, A.W., Cooke, C.J., Cullen, J., & Liles, L. (1979). Psychological aspects of athletic competitors: A replication across sports. *Cognitive Therapy and Research*, **3**, 361-366.

Mihevic, P.M. (1982). Anxiety, depression, and exercise. *Quest*, **33**, 140-153.

Miller, N.E., & Dollard, J. (1941). *Social learning and imitation*. New Haven, CT: Yale University Press.

Mischel, W. (1968). *Personality and assessment*. New York: Wiley.

Mischel, W. (1971). *Introduction to personality*. New York: Holt.

Mischel, W. (1973). Toward a cognitive social learning reconceptualization of personality. *Psychological Review*, **80**, 252-283.

Mischel, W. (1977a). The interaction of person and situation. In D. Magnusson & N.S. Endler (Eds.), *Personality at the crossroads: Current issues in interactional psychology* (pp. 333-352). Hillsdale, NJ: Erlbaum.

Mischel, W. (1977b). On the future of personality measurement. *American Psychologist*, **32**, 246-254.

Mischel, W. (1979). On the interface of cognition and personality: Beyond the person–situation debate. *American Psychologist*, **34**, 740-754.

Morgan, W.P. (1972). Sport psychology. In R.N. Singer (Ed.), *The psychomotor domain: Movement behaviors* (pp. 193-228). Philadelphia: Lea & Febiger.

Morgan, W.P. (1980a). Sport personology: The credulous–skeptical argument in perspective. In W. Straub (Ed.), *Sport psychology: An analysis of athlete behavior* (pp. 330-339). Ithaca, NY: Mouvement.

Morgan, W.P. (1980b). The trait psychology controversy. *Research Quarterly for Exercise and Sport*, **51**, 50-76.

Morgan, W.P. (1985a). Affective beneficence of vigorous physical activity. *Medicine and Science in Sports and Exercise*, **17**, 94-100.

Morgan, W.P. (1985b). Selected psychological factors limiting performance: A mental health model. In D.H. Clarke & H.M. Eckert (Eds.), *Limits of human performance* (pp. 70-80). Academy Papers, no. 18. Champaign, IL: Human Kinetics.

Morgan, W.P., Brown, D.R., Raglin, J.S., O'Connor, P.J., & Ellickson, K.A. (1987). Psychological monitoring of overtraining and staleness. *British Journal of Sports Medicine*, **21**, 107-114.

Morgan, W.P., & Johnson, R.W. (1977). Psychologic characterization of the elite wrestler: A mental health model. *Medicine and Science in Sports*, **9**, 55-56.

Morgan, W.P., & Johnson, R.W. (1978). Psychological characteristics of successful and unsuccessful oarsmen. *International Journal of Sport Psychology*, **11**, 38-49.

Morgan, W.P., O'Connor, P.J., Ellickson, K.A., & Bradley, P.W. (1988). Personality structure, mood states, and performance in elite male distance runners. *International Journal of Sport Psychology*, **19**, 247-263.

Morgan, W.P., & Pollock, M.L. (1977). Psychologic characterization of the elite distance runner. *Annals of the New York Academy of Science*, **301**, 382-403.

Murray, H.A. (1938). *Explorations in personality: A clinical and experimental study of fifty men of college age*. New York: Oxford University Press.

Neary, R.S., & Zuckerman, M. (1976). Sensation seeking, trait and state anxiety, and the electrodermal orienting reflex. *Psychophysiology*, **13**, 205-211.

Neisser, U. (1980). On "social knowing." *Personality and Social Psychology Bulletin*, **6**, 601-605.

Neugarten, B.L. (1977). Personality and aging. In J.E. Birren & K.W. Schaie (Eds.), *Handbook of the psychology of aging* (pp. 626-649). New York: Van Nostrand.

Nicholls, J.G. (1984). Achievement motivation: Conceptions of ability, subjective experience, task choice, and performance. *Psychological Review, 91*, 328-346.

Nideffer, R.M. (1976). Test of Attentional and Interpersonal Style. *Journal of Personality and Social Psychology, 34*, 394-404.

Ogilvie, B.C., & Tutko, T.A. (1966). *Problem athletes and how to handle them*. London: Palham Books.

Ogilvie, B.C., & Tutko, T.A. (1971). Sport: If you want to build character, try something else. *Psychology Today, 5*, 60-63.

Ostrow, A.C. (1976). Goal-setting behavior and need achievement in relation to competitive motor activity. *Research Quarterly, 47*, 174-183.

Paunonen, S.V. (1988). Trait relevance and the differential predictability of behavior. *Journal of Personality, 56*, 599-619.

Peck, R.F., & Havighurst, R.J. (1960). *The psychology of character development*. New York: Wiley.

Pervin, L.A. (1970). *Personality: Theory, assessment, and research*. New York: Wiley.

Pervin, L.A. (1985). Personality: Current controversies, issues, and directions. *Annual Review of Psychology, 36*, 83-114.

Platt, J.R. (1964). Strong inference. *Science, 146*, 347-352.

Popper, K.R. (1959). *The logic of scientific discovery*. New York: Basic.

Rausch, H.L. (1965). Interaction sequences. *Journal of Personality and Social Psychology, 2*, 487-499.

Rejeski, W.J., Morley, D., & Miller, H. (1983). Cardiac rehabilitation: Coronary-prone behavior as a moderator of graded exercise test performance. *Journal of Cardiac Rehabilitation, 3*, 339-343.

Roberts, G.C. (1972). Effect of achievement motivation and social environment on performance of a motor task. *Journal of Motor Behavior, 4*, 37-46.

Roberts, G.C. (1974). Effect of achievement motivation and social environment on risk taking. *Research Quarterly, 45*, 42-55.

Roberts, G.C. (1984a). Children's achievement motivation in sport. In J.G. Nicholls (Ed.), *The development of achievement motivation* (pp. 251-281). Greenwich, CT: JAI.

Roberts, G.C. (1984b). Toward a new theory of motivation in sport: The role of perceived ability. In J.M. Silva & R.S. Weinberg (Eds.), *Psychological foundations of sport* (pp. 214-228). Champaign, IL: Human Kinetics.

Rogers, C.R. (1961). *On becoming a person*. Boston: Houghton Mifflin.

Rotella, R.J., Gansneder, B., Ojala, D., & Billing, J. (1980). Cognitions and coping strategies of elite skiers: An exploratory study of young developing athletes. *Journal of Sport Psychology, 2*, 350-354.

Rotter, J.B. (1954). *Social learning and clinical psychology*. Englewood Cliffs, NJ: Prentice-Hall.

Rotter, J.B. (1966). Generalized expectancies for internal versus external control of reinforcement. *Psychological Monographs, 80* (1, Whole No. 609).

Rowland, G.L., Franken, R.E., & Harrison, K. (1986). Sensation seeking and participation in sporting activities. *Journal of Sport Psychology, 8*, 212-220.

Ruffer, W.A. (1975). Personality traits in athletes. *Physical Educator, 32*, 105-109.

Ruffer, W.A. (1976a). Personality traits in athletes. *Physical Educator, 33*, 50-55.

Ruffer, W.A. (1976b). Personality traits in athletes. *Physical Educator, 33*, 211-214.

Rushall, B.S. (1972, January). *The status of personality research and application in sports and physical education*. Paper presented at the Physical Education Forum, Dalhousie University, Halifax, NS.

Rushall, B.S. (1976). Three studies relating personality variables to football performance. In A.C. Fisher (Ed.), *Psychology of sport* (pp. 391-399). Palo Alto, CA: Mayfield.

Rushall, B.S., & Siedentop, D. (1972). *The development and control of behavior in sport and physical education*. Philadelphia: Lea & Febiger.

Russell, D. (1982). The causal dimension scale: A measure of how individuals perceive causes. *Journal of Personality and Social Psychology, 42*, 1137-1145.

Ryan, E.D. (1980). Attribution, intrinsic motivation, and athletics. In C.H. Nadeau, W.R. Halliwell, K.M. Newell, & G.C. Roberts (Eds.), *Psychology of motor behavior and sport—1979* (pp. 19-26). Champaign, IL: Human Kinetics.

Ryan, E.D., & Lakie, W.L. (1965). Competitive and noncompetitive performance in relation to achievement motive and manifest anxiety. *Journal of Personality and Social Psychology, 1*, 342-345.

Ryan, R.M. (1982). Control and information in the intrapersonal sphere: An extension of cognitive evaluation theory. *Journal of Personality and Social Psychology, 45*, 736-750.

Ryan, R.M., Vallerand, R.J., & Deci, E.L. (1984). Intrinsic motivation in sport: A cognitive evaluation theory interpretation. In W.F. Straub & J.M. Williams (Eds.), *Cognitive sport psychology* (pp. 231-242). Lansing, NY: Sport Science Associates.

Ryckman, R.M., Robbins, M.A., Thornton, B., & Cantrell, P. (1982). Development and validation of a physical self-efficacy scale. *Journal of Personality and Social Psychology, 42*, 891-900.

Ryff, C.D. (1984). Personality development from the inside: The subjective experience of change in adulthood and aging. In P.B. Baltes & O.G. Brim, Jr. (Eds.), *Life-span development and behavior* (Vol. 6, pp. 243-279). New York: Academic.

Sadalla, E.K., Linder, D.E., & Jenkins, B.A. (1988). Sport preference: A self-presentational analysis. *Journal of Sport and Exercise Psychology, 10*, 214-222.

Scanlan, T.K., Ravizza, K., & Stein, G.L. (1989). An in-depth study of former elite figure skaters: Part 1. Introduction to the project. *Journal of Sport and Exercise Psychology, 11*, 54-64.

Scanlan, T.K., Stein, G.L., & Ravizza, K. (1989). An in-depth study of former elite figure skaters: Part 2. Sources of enjoyment. *Journal of Sport and Exercise Psychology, 11*, 65-83.

Schurr, K.T., Ashley, M.A., & Joy, K.L. (1977). A multivariate analysis of male athletic characteristics: Sport type and success. *Multivariate Experimental Clinical Research, 3*, 53-68.

Sheldon, W.H. (1942). *The varieties of temperament: A psychology of constitutional differences*. New York: Harper.

Silva, J.M. (1984). Personality and sport performance: Controversy and challenge. In J.M. Silva & R.S. Weinberg (Eds.), *Psychological foundations of sport* (pp. 59-69). Champaign, IL: Human Kinetics.

Silva, J.M., Shultz, B.B., Haslam, R.W., & Murray, D. (1981). A psychophysiological assessment of elite wrestlers. *Research Quarterly for Exercise and Sport, 52*, 348-358.

Singer, R.N. (1988). Psychological testing: What value to coaches and athletes? *International Journal of Sport Psychology, 19*, 87-106.

Skinner, B.F. (1938). *The behavior of organisms*. New York: Appleton.

Skinner, B.F. (1953). *Science and human behavior*. New York: Macmillan.

Skinner, B.F. (1987). Whatever happened to psychology as the science of behavior? *American Psychologist, 42*, 780-786.

Smith, B.D., & Vetter, H.J. (1982). *Theoretical approaches to personality*. Englewood Cliffs, NJ: Prentice-Hall.

Snyder, E.E., & Kivlin, J.E. (1975). Women athletes and aspects of psychological well-being and body image. *Research Quarterly, 46*, 191-198.

Snyder, M. (1974). The self-monitoring of expressive behavior. *Journal of Personality and Social Psychology, 30*, 526-537.

Snyder, M. (1983). The influence of individuals on situations: Implications for understanding the links between personality and social behavior. *Journal of Personality, 51*, 497-516.

Sonstroem, R.J. (1982). Exercise and self-esteem: Recommendations for expository research. *Quest, 33*, 124-139.

Sonstroem, R.J., & Bernardo, P. (1982). Intraindividual pregame state anxiety and basketball performance: A reexamination of the inverted-U curve. *Journal of Sport Psychology, 4*, 235-245.

Spielberger, C.D. (1966). *Anxiety and behavior*. New York: Academic.

Spielberger, C.D., Gorsuch, R.L., & Lushene, R.L. (1970). *Manual for the State-Trait Anxiety Inventory*. Palo Alto, CA: Consulting Psychologists.

Straub, W.F. (1982). Sensation seeking among high- and low-risk male athletes. *Journal of Sport Psychology, 4*, 246-253.

Sundberg, N.D. (1977). *Assessment of persons*. Englewood Cliffs, NJ: Prentice-Hall.

Taylor, J. (1953). A personality scale of manifest anxiety. *Journal of Abnormal and Social Psychology, 48*, 285-290.

Tillman, K. (1965). Relationship between physical fitness and selected personality traits. *Research Quarterly, 36*, 483-489.

Tutko, T.A. (1986, February). Dr. Tutko on the marriage of psychology and sport. *Scholastic Coach*, pp. 55-57.

Tutko, T.A., Lyon, L.P., & Ogilvie, B.C. (1969). *Athletic Motivation Inventory*. San Jose, CA: Institute for the Study of Athletic Motivation.

Vallerand, R.J. (1983). Effect of differential amounts of positive verbal feedback on the intrinsic motivation of male hockey players. *Journal of Sport Psychology, 6*, 94-102.

Vane, J.R., & Guarnaccia, V.J. (1989). Personality theory and personality assessment measures: How helpful to the client? *Journal of Clinical Psychology, 45*, 5-19.

Vanek, M., & Cratty, B.J. (1970). *Psychology and the superior athlete*. Toronto: Macmillan.

Vealey, R.S. (1986). Sport-confidence and competitive orientations: Preliminary investigation and instrument development. *Journal of Sport Psychology, 8*, 221-246.

Vealey, R.S. (1988). Sport-confidence and competitive orientation: An addendum on scoring procedures and gender differences. *Journal of Sport and Exercise Psychology, 10*, 471-478.

Vealey, R.S. (1989). Sport personology: A paradigmatic and methodological analysis. *Journal of Sport and Exercise Psychology, 11*, 216-235.

Vealey, R.S., & Campbell, J.L. (1988). Achievement goals of adolescent figure skaters: Impact on self-confidence, anxiety, and performance. *Journal of Adolescent Research, 3*, 227-243.

Volp, A., & Keil, U. (1987). The relationship between performance, intention to drop out, and intrapersonal conflict in swimmers. *Journal of Sport Psychology, 9*, 358-375.

Webb, H. (1969). Professionalization of attitudes toward play among adolescents. In G.S. Kenyon (Ed.), *Aspects of contemporary sport sociology* (pp. 141-167). Chicago: Athletic Institute.

Weinberg, R.S. (1984). The relationship between extrinsic rewards and intrinsic motivation. In J.M. Silva & R.S. Weinberg (Eds.), *Psychological foundations of sport* (pp. 177-187). Champaign, IL: Human Kinetics.

Weiner, B. (1974). *Achievement motivation and attribution theory*. Morristown, NJ: General Learning.

Weiner, B. (1985). An attributional theory of achievement motivation and emotion. *Psychological Review, 92*, 548-573.

Weiss, M.R., Bredemeier, B.J., & Shewchuk, R.M. (1985). An intrinsic/extrinsic motivation scale for the youth sport setting: A confirmatory factor analysis. *Journal of Sport Psychology, 7*, 75-91.

Werner, A.C., & Gottheil, E. (1966). Personality development and participation in college athletics. *Research Quarterly, 37*, 126-131.

West, S.G. (1986). Methodological developments in personality research: An introduction. *Journal of Personality, 54*, 1-17.

Yan Lan, L., & Gill, D.L. (1984). The relationships among self-efficacy, stress responses, and a cognitive feedback manipulation. *Journal of Sport Psychology, 6*, 227-238.

Young, R.J., & Ismail, A.H. (1976). Personality differences of adult men before and after a physical fitness program. *Research Quarterly, 47*, 513-519.

Zuckerman, M. (1971). Dimensions of sensation seeking. *Journal of Consulting and Clinical Psychology, 36*, 45-52.

Zuckerman, M. (1979). *Sensation seeking: Beyond the optimal level of arousal*. Hillsdale, NJ: Erlbaum.

Zuckerman, M. (1987). A critical look at three arousal constructs in personality theories: Optimal levels of arousal, strength of the nervous system, and sensitivities to signals of reward and punishment. In J. Strelau & H.J. Eysenck (Eds.), *Personality dimensions and arousal* (pp. 217-231). New York: Plenum.

Zuckerman, M., Murtaugh, T.M., & Siegel, J. (1974). Sensation seeking and cortical augmenting-reducing. *Psychophysiology, 11*, 535-542.

Zuroff, D.C. (1986). Was Gordon Allport a trait theorist? *Journal of Personality and Social Psychology, 51*, 993-1000.

Chapter 4

Motivational Orientations in Sport

Maureen R. Weiss and Nigel Chaumeton
University of Oregon

Within the sport psychology literature, motivation has been seen as a topic so pervasive, so complex, and even so curious that its general definition as "the direction and intensity of effort" (Gill, 1986a) appears too simplistic and nondescript in nature. Questions such as, Why do people participate? Why do people discontinue participation? What intrinsic and extrinsic factors influence effort and persistence behaviors? and What achievement goals influence participation and performance? abound in the research literature. Similar questions have also been asked by practitioners, who desire to structure sport and exercise settings in ways that will maximize motivation in populations ranging from children through older adults. Obviously, understanding motivated behavior is one of the key issues pursued by sport psychologists and educators for reasons related to both theoretical development and effective and successful programming applications.

Within the social-psychological viewpoint of sport behavior, motivation has been studied from two major perspectives. First, motivation has been examined as an outcome variable, which is usually measured or operationalized in the form of choice, effort, and persistence behaviors. From this vantage, motivation is also considered to be the product of the interaction between characteristic individual differences and physical and social environmental factors (Alderman, 1978; Carron, 1984; Gill, 1986a). For example, Smith, Smoll, and Curtis (1979) found that children who played for coaches exhibiting a "positive approach" in the form of frequent encouragement, mistake-contingent reinforcement, and technical instruction reported a greater desire to continue their participation the following season and higher levels of enjoyment than children who played for coaches who exhibited these behaviors less frequently. Moreover, these coaching behaviors had the most dramatic positive impact on children who started the season with the lowest levels of self-esteem.

An alternative approach to studying motivation in sport psychology has been to view it as an individual difference factor. From this stance, interest is focused on how individuals who vary in levels of motivational characteristics differ on self-perception and participation behaviors. For example, Klint and Weiss (1987) found that young gymnasts who assigned higher importance ratings to skill-related participation motives were also higher in perceived physical competence than those who rated skill-related reasons as less important. This relationship between participation motives and perceived competence, in turn, is predicted to result in continued effort and persistence in physical activity.

The central focus of this chapter will be on the study of motivation as an individual difference factor that can be used to explain the behavior of participants in sport and physical activity settings. However, it is important to note that there is a very strong connection between motivation as an individual difference factor and motivation as an outcome variable. For example, individuals who differ in particular motives (e.g., levels of intrinsic motivation or achievement goals) can be distinguished on a variety of self-perception variables such as perceived competence, locus of control, causal attributions, and affect. Ultimately, however, these motivational orientation and self-perception distinctions manifest themselves in motivated behavior, which differs in terms of approach and avoidance tendencies, activity choices, effort, and persistence. And so the cycle continues. Thus, while the central focus of this chapter will be on the examination of motivation as an individual difference factor, resultant variations in motivation as an outcome variable will also be of interest.

Individual motivational orientations will be explored from three different theoretical perspectives. These include participation and discontinuation motives, intrinsic and extrinsic motivation, and achievement goal orientations. Participation motivation refers to reasons individuals adopt for initiating, continuing, and sustaining involvement in physical activity, as well as reasons individuals choose to discontinue involvement. Intrinsic and extrinsic motives reflect incentives primarily determined by the inherent desire and curiosity of embracing optimal skill challenges in the sport setting versus incentives primarily determined by external sources, such as adult and peer approval, material rewards, and a competitive emphasis on winning. Finally, the area of achievement goal orientations emphasizes a contrast between individuals who are task- or personal mastery-oriented with regard to participation and performance goals versus individuals who are ego- or outcome-oriented with these goals and how these orientations manifest themselves in future motivated behavior.

The ultimate goal of sport and physical activity programs is to nurture an emphasis on intrinsic motives that meet the developmental needs of participants and are, in turn, the primary determinant of future participation behavior and performance. To accomplish this objective, it is imperative to understand, from both theoretical and applied perspectives, such individual differences in motivational orientations as participation incentives, perceived competence, and self-determination as indicators of levels of intrinsic motivation, and mastery-oriented versus outcome-oriented goals. Understanding the nature of these constructs will move us toward a clearer conceptual model of motivation in physical achievement settings, as well as sound recommendations for teaching and coaching behaviors. The contemporary theory and research contained in this chapter should be used to stimulate ideas concerning how to optimally challenge all participants as they strive to attain achievement goals. These ideas should ultimately result in the development of various individual and group-instructional techniques aimed at fostering adherence to physical activity and sport.

This chapter has been divided into four sections. In the first section, the research and theory pertaining to participation and discontinuation motives will be reviewed, with a focus on both descriptive and theoretically based research studies. Intrinsic and extrinsic motivational orientations are covered in the second section, with particular emphasis on cognitive evaluation and competence motivation theories. The third section targets the literature concerning achievement goal orientations which, to date, has predominantly been examined within academic achievement settings. Finally, in an attempt to bring parsimony to motivation as an individual difference factor, the fourth section attempts to consolidate the common themes from the several theories and weave them together into an integrated model of sport motivation. Future research possibilities within any given motivational orientation theory are provided in each of the separate sections.

Participation and Discontinuation Motives

The area of participation motivation addresses the general questions of how and why people become actively involved in sport. More importantly, beyond initial reasons for becoming socialized into sport, sport psychologists seek to understand why individuals continue and sustain their involvement and, conversely, what factors cause permanent attrition from sport or temporary withdrawal from a particular sport or intensity level. The topics of *participation* and *discontinuation motivation* go hand in hand, so they will be discussed together. Research interest in participation and discontinuation motives first emerged in the 1970s with an exploratory study on participation motivation conducted by Alderman and Wood (1976) and an attrition study conducted by Orlick (1973, 1974). Sapp and Haubenstricker (1978) were the first researchers to study participation and discontinuation motives concurrently using the same homogeneous population of over a thousand athletes, nonathletes, and sport leavers from Michigan.

A position paper written by Gould (1982), which summarized the current status of research in the youth sport area and outlined future research directions, provided a strong impetus for the sudden interest and productivity in the area of participation in, and attrition from, youth sport involvement. In this paper, Gould noted that the key psychological studies conducted on youth sport phenomena (a) contributed to the development or extension of psychological theory and (b) asked questions of practical significance. In an effort to identify important questions of both a theoretical and practical nature, Gould surveyed both youth sport practitioners and researchers. Surprisingly, consensus was found between the two groups in that the top-ranked psychological issue of importance was "why young athletes stop participating in youth sports." The question of "why young athletes participate in youth sports" was also ranked highly by both groups. The steady publication of studies on participation behavior that followed from this influential article conformed to Gould's two criteria for conducting youth sport research that counts; that is, these studies asked questions of practical significance and made significant contributions to theory development.

Descriptive Studies of Participation Motivation and Attrition

The majority of studies on participation and discontinuation motives have been descriptive in nature and constitute an excellent example of a topical area that has proceeded from a social empiricism to a social analysis stage of research (Iso-Ahola, 1980; Landers, 1983). That is, as a topic that initially had little or no knowledge base, it was necessary to gather data to describe and understand the phenomenon before hypotheses could be formulated and theories developed and tested. Thus, the wealth of information gleaned from these early studies have laid the groundwork for more contemporary research

that is more theoretically based (e.g., Klint & Weiss, 1987; Petlichkoff, 1988), couched within conceptual models (Brown, 1985; Gould & Petlichkoff, 1988), and life span–oriented (Brodkin & Weiss, 1990; Heitmann, 1985; Maehr & Braskamp, 1986).

Descriptive research on participation motivation can be classified as either sport-general (Gill, Gross & Huddleston, 1983; Longhurst & Spink, 1987; Wankel & Kreisel, 1985) or sport-specific (Brodkin & Weiss, 1990; Gould, Feltz & Weiss, 1985; Klint & Weiss, 1986) in nature. A review of these descriptive studies on participation motivation in young athletes reveals several common themes. First, data reduction techniques conducted on multi-item questionnaires have identified a fairly consistent set of motivational factors. These include competence (learn and improve skills, achieve goals), fitness (get in shape or get stronger), affiliation (be with friends or make new ones), team aspects (be part of a group or team), competition (win, be successful), and fun (excitement, challenge, action). A second common finding is that children and adolescents typically indicate that several, rather than only a few, of these motives are salient as reasons for participation. Third, minimal age, gender, experience level, and sport type differences have been found. However, because these studies have not been conceptualized within a theoretical framework, age groups have not typically been selected based on underlying cognitive criteria but, rather, on issues such as sample size and subject availability. This practice may affect how findings are interpreted with regard not only to age but to gender, skill level, and competitive experience as well.

The majority of participation motivation studies have been conducted on youth populations in the United States. However, descriptive studies have also been conducted in various cultures such as England (White & Coakley, 1986), Canada (Fry, McClements & Sefton, 1981; Wankel & Kreisel, 1985), Australia (Longhurst & Spink, 1987; Robertson, 1981), and Israel (Weingarten, Furst, Tenenbaum & Schaefer, 1984). The social context surrounding these different cultures is likely to have an impact on participation motives. For example, in an investigation of Israeli youngsters Weingarten and colleagues (1984) found that motives such as achievement/competitiveness, affiliation, competence, future success orientation, and family/social expectations were rated as significantly more important by city children than by kibbutz children. The authors concluded that Israeli youth are motivated to compete in sport based on the opportunities it provides for actualizing independence, taking on responsibility, and making decisions. These results suggest that motives for participation may vary as a function of sociocultural factors. In addition, it might be hypothesized that motives may vary as a function of race, social class, and ethnicity. Thus, although consistent findings pertaining to participation motives have been identified in the descriptive research, generalizations to diverse youth populations would be premature at this time.

The descriptive research on discontinuation motives has paralleled that for participation motives. The early attrition research by Orlick (1973, 1974) sent some shock waves through the sport psychology and youth sport communities. In his interviews with 60 former Canadian sport participants, ranging in age from 7 to 18 years, Orlick (1974) found that the majority of children who indicated that they would not continue their participation the following year cited negative experiences such as lack of playing time, the competitive emphasis of the program, and dislike for the coach. Orlick also found age differences in discontinuation motives, with children under 10 years of age reporting lack of playing time and lack of successful experiences and children older than 10 reporting conflicts of interest such as other extracurricular activities or responsibilities with work.

These discouraging findings were not replicated in a large-scale study initiated by the Michigan Youth Sports Institute (Sapp & Haubenstricker, 1978). Youths between the ages of 11 and 18 years (N = 1,183) and parents of children 6 to 10 years (N = 418) were asked about their future participation patterns. The percentage of children who reported they would not continue with their sport the following year was high, with 37% of older children and 24% of younger children being identified as potential dropouts. However, the types of negative sport experiences identified by Orlick accounted for less than 15% of the reasons cited for sport withdrawal in the Michigan study. The most frequent reason given was "other interests" by the younger children and "work" by the older children.

Subsequent studies have called into question the meaning of the term *dropout* as an accurate or even appropriate descriptor of individuals who discontinue sport involvement. For example, Klint and Weiss (1986) found that 95% of the former competitive gymnasts they interviewed were either participating in another sport or were still participating in gymnastics but at a lower level of intensity. Similarly, Gould, Feltz, Horn, and Weiss (1982) found that 68% of the youth who withdrew from competitive swimming programs were active in other sports and 80%

planned to reenter swimming the following year. Finally, in a qualitative study of 13-to-23-year-old English participants and "nonparticipants" in youth sport programs, White and Coakley (1986) concluded that "dropout" and "nonparticipant" were inappropriate descriptions of young people who decide not to participate in organized sports activities. Through extensive interviews, they discovered that for most youths, changes in participation patterns and leisure activity priorities were normal and that discontinuation from sport was often a developmentally constructive decision even when it meant doing nothing for a period of time. Such decisions were often made based on a consideration of their future in various adult roles, concerns about personal competence, and constraints related to money, parents, and friends. Based on these few studies, it is apparent that the phenomenon of discontinuation may range on a continuum from being a sport transfer (e.g., discontinue one sport to try another or the same sport at a different level of intensity) to totally withdrawing from sport in general (based on a variety of practical, developmental, or negative reasons).

The notion of whether a dropout is really a dropout would appear to be an important question and a major consideration for future research on participation behaviors. Dishman's (1986) treatment of the same issue in regard to research in the exercise compliance area allows some interesting parallels to be drawn to the youth sport literature. First, Dishman suggests that researchers interested in motives for discontinuation need to look beyond supervised, organized exercise programs and toward unstructured exercise programs in which people are involved. The same criticism could be made of the participation behavior literature, which has focused only on children's participation in structured, competitive programs. Based on studies by Klint and Weiss (1986) and White and Coakley (1986), it is clear that children and adolescents participate in a number of different sporting pursuits, ranging from recreational to competitive, from unstructured to highly structured, and from developmental to elite levels.

Dishman's second point about the definition of dropouts is that a dropout in one program may actually be a complier in another program. This is similar to the finding of "sport transfers" in studies by Klint and Weiss (1986) and Gould and colleagues (1982). To this end, it becomes a critical issue for future researchers to monitor the participation patterns of individuals involved in specific programs, in order to document the transitory or permanent nature of the discontinuation process. Dishman's third point is that

100% compliance to exercise prescriptions is an unrealistic goal; rather, our focus should be on the percentage of individuals who are sedentary in their life-styles. Perhaps a parallel understanding would be identifying children and youth who are truly "nonparticipants," kids who do not participate in physical activity or some form of sport involvement whatsoever. Because sport is thought to contribute to the physical, social, and cognitive development of individuals (Holland & Andre, 1987; Horn, 1987; Weiss, 1987), future research that targets such individuals may provide important insight into the development of children and youth who are not involved and how they can become involved to a greater extent. Finally, Dishman suggests that a physician's influence may be quite salient in participation decision making. A parallel issue in the area of youth sport would be the influence of significant others such as parents and peers on the participation and discontinuation motives of young athletes. Surprisingly little research has examined the role of significant others in the participation motivation and attrition processes even though it has been frequently encouraged as a prime area of study by sociologists (Brown, 1985; Lewko & Greendorfer, 1988).

In sum, the descriptive research on sport attrition has identified multiple reasons given by children and adolescents for discontinuing involvement. The most frequent reasons given center around conflicts of interest or the desire to pursue other activities. However, reasons such as injuries, lack of fun, lack of skill improvement, dislike for the coach, competitive pressure, and too time consuming also emerge as important reasons for individuals. It appears that reasons for discontinuation differ for younger (under 10 years), as compared to older, children (e.g., Orlick, 1974; Sapp & Haubenstricker, 1978); but these results need to be replicated in future research, preferably within a cognitive-developmental framework (Duda, 1987; Weiss & Bredemeier, 1983).

Theory-Based Studies of Participation Motivation and Attrition

The numerous descriptive studies cited in the previous section have provided a solid knowledge base from which to gain an initial understanding about sport participation and attrition. However, in order for scientific knowledge to advance, researchers need to focus on testing and modifying existing theories (Gould, 1982; Landers, 1983). Recent research in the participation motivation

and attrition areas have assumed this approach. To date, three general theoretical models have been tested and modified in relation to describing and explaining the participation behavior process. These theories include competence motivation (Harter, 1978, 1981a), achievement goals (Maehr & Nicholls, 1980; Nicholls, 1984), and social exchange/cost–benefit analysis (Smith, 1986; Thibaut & Kelley, 1959). Theoretical studies of both participation and attrition motives will be consolidated here for a more coherent look at these related phenomena.

To date, perhaps the most productive theory for studying youth sport participation motives has been competence motivation theory (Harter, 1978, 1981a). According to Harter, individuals are motivated to demonstrate competence in an achievement area and do so by engaging in mastery attempts (i.e., learn and demonstrate sport skills). If successful, these mastery experiences result in feelings of efficacy and positive affect, which, in turn, result in continued motivation to participate. Central to theory predictions are the constructs of perceived competence and perceived performance control as contributors to positive affect and motivation. Based on competence motivation theory, individuals high in perceptions of competence and internal control will exert more effort, persist at achievement tasks longer, and experience more positive affect than individuals lower on these characteristics. The underlying conceptual framework of Harter's theory is particularly attractive for application to sport, and several empirical studies have provided support for its suitability to the physical domain (see review paper by Weiss, 1987).

Six studies have tested Harter's theory of competence motivation in relation to participation motivation (Feltz, Gould, Horn & Weiss, 1982; Feltz & Petlichkoff, 1983; Frazer & Weiss, 1991; Klint, 1985; Klint & Weiss, 1987; Roberts, Kleiber & Duda, 1981). In an early study, Roberts and colleagues (1981) compared sport participants and nonparticipants (defined as children who did not participate in that particular program) on perceptions of competence, general self-worth, and success expectations. Participants were found to score significantly higher on perceived cognitive and physical competence, general self-worth, and expectations for future success than did nonparticipants. Feltz and Petlichkoff (1983) reported similar findings for participants versus dropouts in interscholastic sport. However, Klint (1985) found exactly the opposite pattern; that is, former gymnasts reported higher perceptions of physical and social competence than did current gymnasts. This led Klint and Weiss (1987) to conduct a follow-up study that investigated the relationship between perceptions of competence and particular motives for participating in competitive gymnastics. Results revealed that children high in perceived physical competence were more motivated by skill development reasons, while gymnasts high in perceived social competence were more motivated by affiliation aspects of sport. Thus, in accordance with Harter's theory, children were motivated to demonstrate competence in those areas for which they perceived themselves to have high abilities. These findings may explain, at least in part, the discrepant results previously reported pertaining to perceived competence and participation motivation status.

Although most of the theory-based research in the participation and discontinuation motivation area has been based on Harter's competence motivation theory, achievement goal orientation theories (Maehr & Nicholls, 1980; Nicholls, 1984) have also provided a backdrop for participation motivation and attrition studies (Burton & Martens, 1986; Ewing, 1981; Petlichkoff, 1988; Vealey & Campbell, 1988). According to the achievement goal orientation theory posited by Maehr and Nicholls (1980), individuals are primarily motivated by one of three goal orientations: Ability, task, and social approval orientations. Ability-oriented individuals strive to demonstrate skills in relation to others, so social comparison is a primary source of information for these individuals. Task-oriented individuals adopt mastery-oriented goals and evaluate their sport ability in relation to their own past performance, rather than the performance of others. Finally, the individual primarily oriented by social approval goals is directed toward obtaining positive feedback from significant others for the effort put forth during participation, regardless of performance outcome.

Sports File/Tony Henshaw

Only two studies to date have tested the notion that achievement goal orientations are related to sport persistence in children and youth. Ewing (1981) developed the Achievement Orientation Questionnaire (AOQ) and administered it to 452 14-to-15-year-old adolescents who had been identified as participants, nonparticipants, and dropouts. Subjects were asked to list three experiences in which they felt they had been successful. For each experience, they rated 15 items on a 5-point scale to indicate how strongly each item completed the statement, "I felt successful because. . . ." The 15 items from each of the three experiences were factor analyzed separately, and in each case different factor structures and number of factors emerged. Ewing also found that current participants were more highly oriented toward social approval goals, while the dropouts were more highly oriented toward ability-related goals. Speculations about these results have been given; but because no replications or extensions of the study have been conducted, it is difficult to make conclusive remarks about the results.

A second study based on achievement goal orientations was conducted by Petlichkoff (1988), as part of an extensive study of 557 interscholastic athletes. Achievement goal orientations were assessed from starters, nonstarters, survivors (who had minimal playing time), cuttees (who voluntarily withdrew), and "dropouts" at three times during the season: preseason, precompetition, and postseason. Differences among the participant groups occurred only during the precompetition and postseason measures. Specifically, starters were more ability- and task-oriented than the other four groups at precompetition, and more ability-oriented at postseason. Starters and nonstarters were significantly higher than both survivors and cuttees on task orientation at the postseason assessment. More importantly, while achievement goal orientations were related to athletes' level of satisfaction with their sport experience, they were not found to be related to sport persistence.

The absence of a relationship between achievement orientations and sport persistence in Petlichkoff's study may not necessarily mean that ability-, task-, or social approval–oriented goals do not distinguish participant status groups. Rather, the nonsignificant results may likely be due to issues regarding measurement of the achievement orientation construct. Little psychometric information about the AOQ was reported by Ewing; and subsequent studies using the AOQ (Petlichkoff, 1988; Vealey & Campbell, 1988) have resulted in different factor structures and number of factors than those found by

Ewing. In addition, a study designed specifically to assess the validity and reliability of the AOQ found little evidence of construct, factorial, and predictive validity or test–retest reliability (Pemberton, Petlichkoff & Ewing, 1986). The authors concluded that more work was needed in developing the scale before it could be considered a valid and reliable instrument to test achievement goal orientations. Thus, the issue of accuracy and consistency of measurement of motivational orientations is a central one for the continued theoretical testing of participation behaviors in sport.

Nicholls (1984) takes achievement goal orientation theory as conceptualized by Maehr and Nicholls (1980) one step further by considering the interaction among goal orientations, perceived ability, and task difficulty. Specifically, Nicholls theorized that individuals with primarily an ability (or ego-involved) orientation and high perceptions of physical competence will demonstrate high levels of effort and persistence in sport, while ability-involved individuals with low perceptions of ability may be susceptible to withdrawing from sport (Duda, 1987, 1992). This reasoning is based on the fact that the ability-oriented youngster is motivated to demonstrate high ability and avoid demonstrating low ability, with comparison to others being the salient feature of this individual's definition of success and failure. Thus, individuals who value winning as the most important goal in sport but who have self-doubts concerning their capabilities for being successful will avoid or discontinue involvement rather than risk the demonstration of low ability. Similar to ego-involved individuals with high-ability perceptions, the task-oriented child would be expected to persist in sport as long as realistic goals are set and progressive improvements in skill are made. These predictions hold true whether the task-involved individual is high or low in perceived ability. Despite the intuitive theorizing about the relation between goal orientations and participation behaviors based on Nicholls's conceptualizations, little empirical evidence exists to support these contentions.

Nicholls's theory is also developmentally oriented. Conceptions of ability, task difficulty, and effort are posited to have different meanings to individuals based on their cognitive maturity, personal disposition, and situational factors (Duda, 1987). For young children of ages 7 to 9 years, for example, performance outcomes on tasks of varying difficulty are based on one's effort or how hard they tried on the task. By ages 9 to 10, conceptions of ability, effort, and task difficulty are partially differentiated in that less effort on a task is sometimes seen by the child as equated with higher ability. Not until ages 11 to 12 are ability and effort completely differentiated, with children conceiving of ability as more of a capacity and reasoning that an individual who performs better with equal effort or as well without trying as hard is judged as more competent. Although considerable theorizing has been advanced in relation to Nicholls's developmental formulations (Duda, 1987), research examining the relation between achievement goals and participation is sparse. Thus, numerous research questions remain unanswered. For example, even though children 8 and 9 years of age are capable of engaging in social comparison, recent research suggests that these children prefer to use adult evaluation and performance outcome as informational sources in which to judge personal competence (Horn & Hasbrook, 1986, 1987; Horn & Weiss, 1991). And although children of ages 11 and 12 can differentiate ability and effort as causal influences of performance, it is not known what types of attributions they prefer and on what dimensions (e.g., locus of causality, controllability, stability) these attributions lie.

A final theoretical approach to participation motivation and discontinuation motives that has been advocated is social exchange theory (Thibaut & Kelley, 1959) which was reconceptualized within a cognitive–affective model of athletic burnout by Smith (1986). The basic premise of social exchange theory is that social behavior is motivated by the desire to maximize positive experiences and minimize negative experiences. Individuals will remain in relationships or activities as long as the outcome is favorable. Furthermore, this favorability is considered to be a function of benefits and costs. The decision to remain involved in a current situation is not merely a function of benefits and costs but rather includes two levels of satisfaction: satisfaction with the current activity and satisfaction with alternative activities. Thus, an individual weighs the costs, benefits, and satisfaction of a current situation with those of alternative situations and makes a decision accordingly.

To date, only Petlichkoff (1988) included a cost–benefit analysis in an examination of predictors of sport persistence. She found that starters and nonstarters had higher levels of satisfaction than did survivors, dropouts, or cuttees and that survivors had lower levels of satisfaction than did dropouts. Perhaps those who were motivated to "hang on" despite the minimal likelihood of being able to play in games were willing to put up with higher levels of dissatisfaction than those who dropped out. Being on a team may have been a major benefit, which was not outweighed by the cost of low perceptions of ability based on lack of playing time.

The notion of a cost–benefit analysis mediating the relationship between participation motives and the decision to persist is intuitively appealing. However, it appears that this construct needs considerably more conceptualizing on an operational level before it can be considered a viable contributor to understanding sport persistence. Merely measuring satisfaction levels may be too simplistic and may not get at the entire picture of a cost–benefit analysis of participation. In addition, children and adolescents may not have the cognitive sophistication for engaging in an evaluation process such as weighing costs and benefits, minimal comparison levels, and comparison levels of alternatives.

Future Research Directions in Participation Motivation

The research conducted to date in the area of participation and discontinuation motives has provided a great deal of insight into why children and youth remain involved or drop out from sport. There are many recommendations for future research, however, that would provide direction and substance to the information gleaned from such studies. In a recent paper, Weiss and Petlichkoff (1989) note that an often underlying assumption about sport withdrawal is that it is a negative or abnormal phenomenon. This assumption, however, is unfounded, because studies have demonstrated that discontinuation of a sport program is usually not permanent (Gould et al., 1982; Klint & Weiss, 1986; White & Coakley, 1986), that it is typical of youth pursuing developmental activities to prepare them for adulthood (Holland & Andre, 1987; White & Coakley, 1986), and that reasons for attrition are not necessarily related to an individual's initial reasons for becoming involved (Gould et al., 1982, 1985; Klint & Weiss, 1986). To this end, Weiss and Petlichkoff identified "missing links" in the sport participation/attrition research literature. Only some of these missing links will be discussed here (see Weiss and Petlichkoff, 1989, for further explanation and clarification of these research directions).

The literature on participation behavior has been plagued with inconsistent operational definitions of *participation, dropout*, and *nonparticipant*. Care must be taken to determine whether a "dropout" is one who has withdrawn from sport altogether or only from a particular program. Also, is the nonparticipant really not participating in any activities? In the study by Klint and Weiss (1986), only two children in an entire community could be labeled as actual nonparticipants (i.e., not active in any kind of sporting pursuit), even though their peers who were involved in sport identified them as such. White and Coakley (1986) also found that the terms *dropout* and *nonparticipant* were labels characterized by negative connotations and were usually unreflective of the active lifestyle, albeit in unstructured programs, of these individuals. In some studies, participant status has been defined along a continuum, such as starters, nonstarters, survivors, cuttees, and dropouts (Frazer & Weiss, 1991; Petlichkoff, 1988; Robinson & Carron, 1982). Further research is needed to distinguish achievement characteristics and motivational orientations of participants based on more refined categories such as these. In addition, the youngster who is forced to withdraw from a sport team (the cuttee) is in need of intensive study. Do these individuals become permanent or temporary dropouts? What effect does being cut from a team have on self-perceptions of ability, attitude toward physical activity, and subsequent motivated behavior in sport?

Another very important missing link in the current sport psychology literature is how the social context interacts with individual motives to produce persistence or withdrawal behavior. For example, the impact of significant others such as parents, peers, and coaches on young athletes' participant motives and their persistence has been neglected (Brustad, 1992). For example, Brown (1985) found that social support for the sport role from parents, teammates, and friends was positively related to participant status, with current female swimmers receiving significantly more positive reinforcement and encouragement for their swimming involvement than former swimmers. In a follow-up study, Brown, Frankel, and Fennell (1989) found that the degree to which physical activity involvement is maintained in adolescent females is positively related to the amount and type of influence received from mothers, fathers, and male and female peers. Similarly, White and Coakley (1986) found in their interview of English adolescents that decisions about sport participation reflect support and encouragement from significant others, most notably parents and friends. These studies were more sociological in nature and serve as a reminder that motivation as a psychological construct can be better understood by considering the variety of social, cultural, and physical parameters that may influence participation orientations.

Another recommendation for future research is to adopt a more life-span developmental perspective to the study of participation motivation and discontinuation (Brodkin & Weiss, 1990; Heitmann, 1985). Brodkin and Weiss (1990), for example, found that older adults scored significantly lower on competitive motives than all other age groups, while older children and high school/college-aged swimmers scored higher on social status motives. Fun was rated most important by younger children and older adults, while health and fitness motives were deemed most important by young and middle-aged adults. Results from further studies would lend substantive evidence leading toward a life-span approach to participation motivation, as well as specific information for practical application to particular sport settings.

Intrinsic and Extrinsic Motivational Orientations

Most individuals participate in sport and physical activity for the sheer joy, pleasure, fun, curiosity, and personal mastery involved with the experiences. These can be classified as intrinsic or internal motives for participation. There may also be external reasons for participation behavior, such as social approval from adults and peers, material rewards, and social status. Indeed, the participation motivation literature reviewed in the last section shows that the overriding reasons cited by children and adolescents for their sport participation are intrinsic in nature. These motives included skill improvement, the inherent challenges of the sport, the excitement and thrills, and the achievement of personal performance goals. Reasons more extrinsic in nature, such as winning, receiving trophies and awards, and pleasing others were rated by children as less important motives for participation.

In both the psychology and sport psychology literatures, two theoretical approaches have been adopted to study intrinsic and extrinsic motivational orientations. Cognitive evaluation theory (Deci, 1975; Deci & Ryan, 1985) has been studied extensively in the sport domain (Ryan, Vallerand & Deci, 1984; Vallerand, Deci & Ryan, 1987) by researchers who employed primarily an experimental paradigm to examine the effects of external rewards, positive and negative feedback, or competition on intrinsic motivation. Within this approach, novel laboratory tasks have been dominant, and intrinsic motivation has been operationalized most frequently as time on task in a postexperimental free choice activity period. Although intrinsic motivation within the cognitive evaluation stance has been employed as a dependent or outcome variable, the theory and research will be reviewed here because the subsequent intrinsic and extrinsic motivational changes that individuals experience

have a substantial effect on their perceived competence, perceived control, and tendencies to approach or avoid similar achievement situations.

The second common approach to studying intrinsic/extrinsic motivational orientations have been theories that focus on mastery and competence in relation to specific achievement domains (Harter, 1978, 1981a; White, 1959). Extensive research has also been conducted in sport psychology using this theoretical approach, primarily with the study of children and adolescents in sport. Typically, nonexperimental research designs conducted within field settings have been employed, in contrast to the experimentally oriented tests of cognitive evaluation theory. Intrinsic and extrinsic motivational orientations are examined as they relate to the interaction of social support, affect, and self-perceptions of success, competence, and performance control. Individuals' preferences for easy versus optimal challenges, curiosity, and independent versus dependent mastery are tapped in particular achievement domains in relation to these other constructs, predominantly using paper-and-pencil measures designed to determine the underlying cognitions involved in evaluating personal and situational characteristics. Studies examining the relationships among the various constructs in Harter's model have most frequently included the relationships of perceived competence and perceived performance control with constructs such as intrinsic/extrinsic motivational orientation, positive and negative affect, participation motivation, coaches' reinforcement behaviors, and the informational sources used to judge competence in the physical domain (Weiss, 1987).

Both the cognitive evaluation and competence motivation theoretical approaches have provided a great deal of empirical information and practical implications for sport psychologists and educators. Each approach has its unique theoretical components, research design preferences, operational definitions, measurement instruments, and practical applications. However, just as important are their commonalities, which include an emphasis on perceived competence, self-determination (perceived control), mastery at optimal challenges, and the role of the social environment (significant others, competitive structure, external rewards) in developing intrinsic and extrinsic motivation. Thus, each of these theoretical approaches and the sport-related research will be systematically presented here, with summaries to consolidate common themes, results, and applications.

Cognitive Evaluation Theory

The major tenet of cognitive evaluation theory (Deci, 1975; Deci & Ryan, 1985) is that intrinsic motivation is maximized when individuals feel competent and self-determining in dealing with their environment. Deci and Ryan (1985) believe that sport and physical activity settings provide many opportunities for persons to compare their skills and competencies against a standard, thus enhancing the likelihood of meaningful feedback and positive changes in intrinsic motivation. Similarly, physical achievement settings often allow for the creative expression of a variety of physical and social behaviors over which individuals feel internal control. This sense of control also increases the probability of enhanced intrinsic motivation. However, just as sport offers these opportunities for positive changes in perceived competence, self-determination, and intrinsic motivation, it can also frequently be structured so as to provide negative feedback about one's competencies or so as to exert pressure on individuals to conform to standardized rules and behaviors, resulting in decrements to intrinsic motivation and the internalization of a more extrinsic orientation.

According to cognitive evaluation theory, any event that affects individuals' perceptions of competence and feelings of self-determination will ultimately have an impact on their level of intrinsic motivation. Additionally, these events, which may include the distribution of rewards, the quantity and quality of feedback and reinforcement, and how situations are structured, consist of two functional components: a controlling aspect and an informational aspect. The controlling aspect of an event relates to an individual's perceived locus of causality within the situation. If an event or situation is seen as controlling one's behavior, then an external locus of causality and a low level of self-determination are developed. These negative self-perceptions, in turn, cause a decrease in intrinsic motivation. For example, many stories pertaining to college football and basketball players seem to suggest that the pressure to win, compete for scholarships, conform to coaching demands and expectations, and be chosen for the professional ranks have resulted in feelings of being controlled by powerful others, such as coaches, institutions, and team owners, and subsequently in decreased levels of interest, enjoyment, and pleasure in the activity. Conversely, if an event is seen as one that contributes to an internal locus of causality, intrinsic motivation will increase. In this case, people feel a high level of self-determination and perceive that their behavior is determined by their own personal goals. For example, sport and exercise programs that provide individuals with opportunities for input about choice of activities, personal performance goals, and team or class objectives and rules should result in higher intrinsic

motivation on the part of its participants (Gould, 1986; Thompson & Wankel, 1980).

In contrast to the controlling aspect of events, the informational aspect of an event relates to the perceived competence of the individual. If an event provides positive information about an individual's competence, then intrinsic motivation for an optimally challenging activity will be enhanced. For example, successful achievement of a goal that was determined based on individual competencies signifies positive information about personal competence and should result in the likelihood of continued goal setting, effort, and persistence at the task. Events that provide negative information about competence, however, should result in lowered perceived competence and intrinsic motivation. For example, a coaching style that is predominated by criticism and put-downs may be internalized by some athletes as information about their value and worth as team members, and they may not look forward to practices and competitions, learning and improving skills, and the enjoyment of the sport as much as they did previously. The practice of choosing up sides for games that still occurs in youth sport programs or physical education classes is a very visible and powerful means for conveying information about peers' evaluations of ability and affects perceptions of competence and intrinsic motivation.

In addition to the controlling and informational aspects of events, a third major element to cognitive evaluation theory is what is termed the *functional significance* of the event (Deci & Ryan, 1985). More specifically, most events contain both controlling and informational elements and thus have the potential for affecting perceived locus of causality, perceived competence, and intrinsic motivation. However, the aspect of the situation perceived as more *salient* by the individual will determine whether locus of causality will be perceived as internal or external, whether competence will be perceived as high or low, and (subsequently) whether intrinsic or extrinsic motivation is nurtured. It is the relative salience of these aspects that determines the functional significance of an event to a person. Deci and Ryan conclude that choice and positive feedback result in the salience of the informational aspect; and rewards, time deadlines, and surveillance result in the controlling aspect being most salient. As an example, a local high school wrestling coach came to one of us (Weiss) for advice regarding the participation behavior of one of his athletes. He claimed that the boy had a great deal of potential and was one of the most talented members of the team. Furthermore, the athlete had performed well and won most of his matches and had received a lot of positive feedback from his teammates, coach, and the community. As a team captain he had participated in some of the decision making with regard to team rules, travel protocols, and practice regimens. Despite the vast amount of positive information conveyed about his wrestling competence and the occurrence of events that should have promoted an internal locus of causality, this coach was baffled by the lack of positive affect, effort, persistence, and overall desirable athletic behavior on the part of the boy. It was only later that we learned that the boy's father had exerted considerable pressure on him to join the wrestling team and was now living vicariously through his son's successes, and constantly criticized him at home for performance errors. It appears from this scenario that the wrestler perceived the controlling aspect as most salient, which resulted in an external perceived locus of causality, the undermining of intrinsic motivation, and the promotion of extrinsic compliance and defiance.

A substantial amount of psychology and sport psychology research has been conducted to test hypotheses based on cognitive evaluation theory. The two major questions addressed by this research have been, What factors are likely to enhance versus undermine intrinsic motivation for sport activities? and, How do extrinsic motivators typically used in the sport setting affect sport experiences? Studies related to the controlling and informational aspects of events on intrinsic motivation have typically fallen into three categories: (a) the effects of external rewards, (b) the quantity and quality of feedback, and (c) competitive structure. The findings gleaned from these studies have generally provided support for cognitive evaluation hypotheses and have resulted in practical applications for sport settings. However, the nature of the physical domain is unique and much more complex in comparison to the typical experimental manipulations employed in most of these studies. Thus, in addition to reviewing the extant literature in this area, criticisms and future research considerations will be provided.

External Rewards and Intrinsic Motivation

The early research in this area by Lepper and Greene (Greene & Lepper, 1974; Lepper & Greene, 1975; Lepper, Greene & Nisbett, 1973) attempted to test what they termed the *overjustification hypothesis*, namely, that an expectation of a reward for an inherently interesting activity would produce less interest in that activity when the reward was subsequently unavailable. That is, the reward comes to overjustify intrinsic interest in the activity. The experimental design for such studies consisted of a pretest period, during which an initial score on the activity (e.g., drawing, puzzles) was obtained. Then, children were randomly assigned to expected, unexpected, or no-reward conditions. In the expected reward condition, children were told they would get a good-player award for completing the activity. Children in the unexpected reward condition received the same good-player certificate (which they did not anticipate) after completing the task, while children in the no-reward condition neither anticipated nor received a reward. During a subsequent time period, children were observed during a free-choice activity session to determine the degree of interest on the same drawing activity. Results revealed that children in the expected reward condition showed significantly less interest, or time on task, than children in the other two conditions, thus supporting the overjustification hypothesis. The authors concluded that external rewards can undermine intrinsic motivation for activities that were initially seen as interesting and enjoyable.

Orlick and Mosher (1978) extended this experimental design to the physical domain. Specifically, they examined the influence of reward and no-reward conditions on children's (ages 9 to 11) motivation to perform on a stabilometer balance task. After establishing a baseline level of interest in the activity using amount of time spent during a free-choice period, children were either given a trophy or no trophy for participating in the activity. During a post-test assessment period, children in the reward condition showed a decrease, while children in the no-reward condition showed an increase, in time on task from pre- to post-test activity. Orlick and Mosher reached the same conclusion as Lepper and Greene, namely, that external rewards for an interesting motor activity may undermine children's desire to sustain interest and participation in the future.

The results of these early experimental studies were used by a number of researchers and practitioners to discourage the use of material or other external rewards in classrooms (e.g., grades, gold stars) and sport teams (e.g., trophies, ribbons) as a means of motivating children and adolescents. These concerns, however, may have been premature, since the research to substantiate such claims is limited and also involves problems that pertain to the unique nature of competitive sport. We believe that many of these research limitations persist today, leaving the question about the function of external rewards in sport motivation still an enigma.

At least three criticisms can be raised to the conclusions reached in the studies by Lepper and Greene, Orlick and Mosher, and others of similar approach (see Deci & Ryan, 1985). First, activities used in these experiments were established as ones in which children were already inherently interested and, with minimal exposure, could perform at some level of competency. However, in the world of motor skill and sport activities, individuals may not have such initial interest and may, in fact, find certain physical activity experiences unattractive (e.g., jogging, swimming laps). This level of interest may also likely be related to the level of competence the individual possesses for the activity.

The issue of interesting versus uninteresting activities is a salient one for sport and exercise settings. Children who have not experienced certain activities or adults who have been sedentary most of their lives may not choose to engage in sport, leisure, or fitness pursuits on their own. However, external rewards in the form of tangible commodities (e.g., money, T-shirts), social support, or status may be seen as necessary motivators to initiate participation behaviors, with the intent that once involved, the activity itself becomes the source of motivation that is intrinsic in nature. For example, when 10-K road runs first became popular in the 1970s, many individuals were attracted to this novel activity to obtain the T-shirt that was given to all participants, which may have symbolized some social status amid the "fitness boom" era. However, for many individuals, the activity of running to stay fit or get in shape became more salient than the tangible reward. To test whether external rewards affect motivation differently based on the inherent interest in the activity, Calder and Staw (1975) randomly assigned subjects to reward (money) and no-reward conditions and to interesting-puzzle and uninteresting-puzzle groups. Results revealed that the reward resulted in decreased enjoyment for subjects in the interesting-puzzle group, replicating results of earlier studies. However, individuals solving the uninteresting puzzle expressed greater enjoyment as a result of receiving the reward. Thus, it was concluded that external rewards can increase intrinsic motivation for activities initially perceived as uninteresting by individuals.

The issue pertaining to attractiveness of physical activity is a salient consideration facing researchers and practitioners. If sport is to be embraced for its potential to contribute to motor skill development, physical fitness, health, and psychosocial development, some individuals may need to be motivated through external means to initiate participation. These external means may be in the form of material awards such as certificates or being able to select favorite activities. Because physical educators and coaches understand the need to maximize the intrinsic desire on the part of individuals to participate, however, activities should be structured in order to develop competence, enjoyment, and the opportunities to offer input and make choices such as team and individual goals. Eventually, the activity itself is now seen as interesting, enjoyable, and self-satisfying in and of itself; and the external rewards can be gradually removed.

A second criticism about the early studies is that rewards were generally not given contingent to performance on the activity. Rather, children were given good-player awards or trophies for merely engaging in the activity. In sport and physical activity, external rewards are usually given contingent to a minimal participation level or quality of performance. Rewards given in this manner usually convey positive information about the individual's competence and should increase intrinsic motivation. Studies examining the use of contingent and appropriate feedback and reinforcement from teachers and coaches, for example, have shown a positive influence on perceptions of competence and control, enjoyment, and motivation in the form of task persistence (see Horn, 1987). Thus, it is insufficient to investigate the effects of rewards on intrinsic motivation without also determining how contingent the rewards were to participation and performance. A few studies have attempted to examine this issue in the physical domain.

Thomas and Tennant (1978) specifically investigated the effect of giving contingent and noncontingent rewards for performance on an athletic task. Boys (N = 424), who were either 5, 7, or 9 years of age, were randomly assigned to one of four reward conditions. Children in the contingent group were told that a monetary reward would be given to them that was directly related to how well they performed on a throwing task. The more points they scored on the task, the greater the amount of money they would receive. Children in the noncontingent reward group were told to perform as well as they could and that for performing the task for 5 minutes, they would receive a reward of some money. An unexpected reward group was told to perform as best as they could, but they were not told about the reward, which they did receive after participating for 5 minutes. Boys in the noncontingent and unexpected reward groups were actually yoked to boys in the contingent reward group to determine how much money they would receive. Finally, a control group was merely told they could play with a chosen task for 5 minutes. A post-test assessment of the percentage of time on target activity clearly revealed that the contingent reward group scored significantly higher than noncontingent, unexpected, and control groups. Thus, intrinsically motivated behavior differed depending upon whether the reward was contingent or noncontingent to performance.

The final criticism about the early overjustification studies is that the effect of rewards on motivation may vary as a function of cognitive-developmental differences in the way individuals attach meaching to the function or value of rewards in relation to participation in interesting activities (Halliwell, 1978; Thomas & Tennant, 1978). However, conclusions in these studies were made based on a single behavior measure: amount of time spent on the activity in a free-choice period. Given that perceived locus of causality and perceptions of competence are hypothesized to play a role in the effects of rewards on motivation, it is imperative to determine how developmental level mediates these effects.

Of special interest in the Thomas and Tennant (1978) study were the results pertaining to developmental differences in perceptions of the reward and subsequent scores on the intrinsic motivation measure. Among the 5-year-old children, the contingent and noncontingent reward groups recorded similar scores; and these were higher than the unexpected and control group scores. Thus, children were said to employ an additive principle in attaching meaning to the function of external rewards: The reward was viewed as

a bonus for activities which were already fun, regardless of whether or not it was given according to some criterion performance level. At age 7, the contingent reward group was significantly higher in time on task than all other groups, which did not differ. The noncontingent reward, therefore, was being discounted as a means for increasing motivation on the task. By age 9, children in the noncontingent reward group engaged in a higher level of discounting in that they viewed the money as a bribe to participate in the task: Children in the noncontingent reward group spent significantly less time on task than both the unexpected reward and control groups. Thus, the effects of contingent or noncontingent rewards on children's intrinsic motivation appear to vary as a function of the child's age or level of cognitive maturity.

The studies conducted to test cognitive evaluation theory discussed so far have primarily focused on children and/or have involved laboratory procedures. E.D. Ryan was especially interested in testing hypotheses based on Deci's (1975) theory in the natural sport setting and using intercollegiate athletes. A pair of intriguing field studies examining the effect of rewards on intrinsic motivation were conducted by Ryan (1977, 1980). He was interested in examining the possible effects of college scholarships on athletes' intrinsic motivation as measured through athletes' inherent interest, enjoyment, and desire to continue sport participation. In the first study, Ryan surveyed male scholarship and nonscholarship athletes at two institutions. He hypothesized that athletes on scholarship would report less intrinsic motivation than nonscholarship athletes, because they were being paid to participate in an activity that was already intrinsically pleasing. Results supported his contention, with scholarship athletes citing more extrinsic reasons for participation and lower enjoyment levels than nonscholarship athletes.

In a replication and extension of this study, Ryan (1980) sampled athletes from 12 institutions, including male football and wrestling athletes, as well as female athletes across a variety of sports. Results revealed that the football players on scholarship scored lower on intrinsic motivation items than nonscholarship football athletes but that both male wrestlers and female athletes on scholarship were higher on intrinsic motivation measures than their nonscholarship teammates. These results were explained within a control-versus-informational distinction of cognitive evaluation theory. Ryan suggested that both wrestlers and female athletes viewed their scholarship as an affirmation of how competent they were since all wrestlers and female athletes did not receive scholarships (at least at the time of this study). Football players, on the other hand, may have viewed their scholarship from more of an external control saliency; for all football players on the team had scholarships, and scholarships are often seen as a means of controlling athlete behavior (i.e., retract the scholarship based on performance or behavior). Due to the field study design, however, causality cannot be inferred regarding the relationship between scholarship/nonscholarship status and intrinsic motivation. Given the changing trends in both men's and women's collegiate sport during the 1980s, more studies investigating the differential nature of reward distributions on intrinsic motivation, academic orientations, enjoyment, and sport persistence are needed.

Feedback and Intrinsic Motivation

Research on rewards and intrinsic motivation has focused primarily on the controlling aspect of intrinsic motivation, or how events affect changes in individuals' perceived locus of causality. Conversely, research related to feedback and intrinsic motivation has focused mainly on the informational aspect of intrinsic motivation, or how positive and negative information from significant others affects the perceived competence of the individual. To date, only a handful of studies in sport psychology have examined the nature of feedback, changes in perceived competence, and subsequent intrinsic motivation to participate.

Vallerand (Vallerand, 1983; Vallerand & Reid, 1984) conducted two studies to investigate the effects of feedback on perceived competence and intrinsic motivation. In the first study, Vallerand (1983) assigned adolescent hockey players (N = 50) to feedback conditions varying in amount of positive comments (0, 6, 12, 18, 24) in response to decision making in simulated hockey situations. Results revealed that feedback groups were significantly higher in perceived competence and intrinsic motivation; but there were no differences based on amount of feedback. The authors concluded that positive feedback, regardless of the absolute quantity involved, enhanced athletes' perceptions of competence and intrinsic motivation when compared to no informational feedback.

In the second study (Vallerand & Reid, 1984), male adults (N = 115) were randomly assigned to positive feedback, negative feedback, and no-feedback conditions on a stabilometer balance task. Results revealed that subjects in the positive feedback condition scored higher on the intrinsic motivation measure (Mayo Task Reaction Questionnaire) than subjects in the no-feedback condition, who scored higher than those in the negative feedback condition. In addition, path analyses revealed that the effects of feedback on intrinsic motivation were mediated by changes in perceived competence. These results offered strong support for cognitive evaluation theory.

Whitehead and Corbin (1991) recently applied cognitive evaluation predictions for feedback and intrinsic motivation to a youth fitness setting. Children (N = 105) in grades 7 and 8 were assigned to experimental conditions of positive, negative, or no-feedback in an agility run. Subjects in the positive feedback condition were told that their scores were above the top 80th percentile for students their age, while those in the negative feedback condition were told that their scores were in the bottom 20th percentile. In this study, intrinsic motivation was measured using the Intrinsic Motivation Inventory (IMI; Ryan, 1982) with subscale scores on perceived competence, interest–enjoyment, effort–importance, and pressure–tension. Results revealed a significant main effect for feedback condition. Specifically, subjects in the positive feedback group recorded significantly higher scores on perceived competence, effort–importance, and interest–enjoyment and lower scores on pressure–tension than the negative feedback group. However, these scores were significantly higher than the no-feedback group only on perceived competence.

On the basis of the results of these studies, many writers have concluded that positive feedback will always be facilitative of perceived competence and intrinsic motivation. For example, Deci and Ryan state, "It seems clear that positive feedback increases and negative feedback decreases perceived competence and intrinsic motivation" (1985, p. 320). However, based on research from educational and other sport psychology studies, this may be an overgeneralized statement. Moreover, the results reported by Vallerand (1983) on amount of positive feedback must be viewed with some caution. Inappropriately high amounts of positive feedback can be as detrimental to motivation, self-perceptions, and participation behavior as high amounts of negative feedback. Thus, more important than the *quantity* of feedback given, serious consideration must be given to the *quality* of feedback given for performance. Horn (1984a, 1984b, 1985, 1986, 1987) has provided strong evidence that it is the quality of feedback in terms of contingency and appropriateness to a criterion performance level that is crucial to subsequent psychological development. The mere distribution of feedback that is positive or negative and the quantity of verbal statements made in response to performance are less important than feedback quality.

Such feedback quality can appear in the form of contingency to a criterion (e.g., praise for attaining a personal goal), appropriateness to the level of performance (e.g., not giving excessive praise for success at an easy task that the majority of individuals can do), and attributions that imply an internal locus of causality and personal controllability (Horn, 1987).

For example, Horn (1985) found that coaches' use of more frequent positive reinforcement resulted in lower perceived competence in youth softball players, while higher amounts of mistake-contingent criticism were related to higher levels of perceived competence. Horn explained these results by suggesting that the use of liberal praise in this case was not contingent to prescribed levels of performance and thus may have been perceived by the players as an upper limit on their ability to perform. Conversely, players receiving contingent performance-related criticism, including information on how to perform better in the future, may have been given the message that higher levels of performance are possible. Thus, the quantity and quality of informational feedback is an area in need of more research, especially as it relates to intrinsic motivation.

To date, studies on feedback and intrinsic motivation have only examined information conveyed by adults in the form of positive or negative verbal comments. However, many sources of information are contained in the sport setting (Horn & Hasbrook, 1986, 1987; Horn & Weiss, 1991), including internal criteria (e.g., self-improvement), social comparison (e.g., comparison to peers), event outcome (e.g., win/loss), and affect (e.g., attraction to the activity). Future research studies are needed to examine the relationship between these other feedback sources and intrinsic motivation. For example, it could be hypothesized that individuals high in intrinsic motivation utilize internal criteria and affect more often as sources of information than do individuals who are more extrinsically oriented. Those higher in extrinsic motivation, in contrast, may be more likely to use event outcome, others' feedback, and social comparison as sources of information. In the sport domain, social comparison is necessarily an inherent part of competition. It is not surprising, therefore, that the topic of the effects of competition on intrinsic motivation has been a popular focus of study.

Competition and Intrinsic Motivation

The effects of competitive outcomes on intrinsic motivation is especially salient in the sport domain. Competitive events contain both controlling and informational aspects and thus have the potential to influence either or both perceived locus of causality and perceived competence in athletes. If winning is the primary competitive orientation, the controlling aspect may be the functionally salient feature of the situation that is affected. If, however, a task or mastery orientation to achieving competitive goals is adopted, in which individuals focus on the process and not the outcome of performance, then the informational element may be perceived as the most salient feature of the situation. Either way, it is clear that the controlling and informational aspects inherent within competition will need to be separated out in order to determine how competition accounts for differences in intrinsic motivation level. Again, only a handful of studies have explored this relationship.

In an early study, Deci, Betley, et al. (1981) compared the effects of face-to-face competition with self-competition in the presence of another subject on solving puzzles. Results on a post-test free-choice measure revealed that subjects in the direct competition group showed decreased intrinsic motivation for the activity relative to those who competed against a standard. Furthermore, these findings were particularly strong for females. In what at first appeared to be contradictory results, Weinberg and Ragan (1979) found that males who competed against either another person or a standard showed increases in intrinsic motivation. Similar to the Deci, Betley, et al. study, Weinberg and Ragan found gender differences, in that competition had the effect of decreasing intrinsic motivation in females. Deci and Ryan (1985) explain the discrepant findings for males in the Weinberg and Ragan study as due to conceptual differences in the dependent measure of intrinsic motivation used. While Deci and colleagues (1981) assessed the motivation of subjects to do the activity in the absence of competition, Weinberg and Ragan (1979) in essence measured subjects' willingness to pursue the task in the future in the presence of competition.

The objective competitive outcomes of winning and losing on intrinsic motivation have been examined in two studies (Vallerand, Gauvin & Halliwell, 1986a; Weinberg & Jackson, 1979). In both of these studies, subjects competing on laboratory tasks who were in the losing (failure) condition evidenced lower levels of intrinsic motivation (and perceived competence in the case of the Vallerand et al. study) than subjects in the winning (success) condition. However, a recent study by McAuley and Tammen (1989) suggests that it is the subjective evaluation of success that more dramatically affects intrinsic motivation than objective success (i.e., winning and losing).

In this study, subjects were matched on ability and paired in a basketball-shooting competition, after which they completed items on the IMI assessing perceived competence, effort–importance, interest–enjoyment, and pressure–tension. Individuals who perceived that they were more successful recorded significantly higher scores on effort–importance, perceived competence, and interest–enjoyment than those who perceived themselves as less successful. However, the analysis comparing objective winners and losers on the intrinsic motivation dimensions only *approached* significance. These results are important in that they relate to individuals' own definitions of success and failure and raise the issue of whether competitors adopt a more task (mastery)- or ability (outcome)-oriented view of their competitive experiences.

The effects of competitive structure on perceived competence and intrinsic motivation were examined in a study of 10-to-12-year-old children by Vallerand, Gauvin, and Halliwell (1986b). Children (N = 26) were randomly assigned to either an interpersonal competition or intrinsic mastery group, and asked to perform on a stabilometer balance task. Children in the competition group were told that they should try to perform as best as they could because they were competing against other children their age and their performance would be compared relative to others at a later date. Conversely, children in the intrinsic mastery condition were encouraged to perform as well as they could by exploring several strategies for balancing on the stabilometer. Intrinsic motivation was assessed by time spent on the stabilometer during a free-choice period. Subjects in the competition condition spent significantly less time on the task than subjects in the intrinsic mastery condition, but the two groups did not differ on levels of perceived competence. Thus, these results provided an initial comparison of competitive orientation differences.

Sport psychology research based on cognitive evaluation theory has focused on both the controlling and informational aspects of situations and has examined the effects of external rewards, adult feedback, and competitive outcomes on intrinsic motivation. The results of these studies suggest that several events can influence both perceptions of locus of causality and perceptions of competence and that these self-perceptions are likely to be mediators of the relationship between these external events and motivational orientations. Areas that must be addressed by future researchers include the measurement of intrinsic motivation, the salience of tasks or activities used, gender and developmental differences, and the salience of the reward, feedback, or competitive orientation experimentally manipulated.

Competence Motivation Theory

An alternative approach to an understanding of intrinsic and extrinsic motivational orientations has been effectance or competence motivation theory, which was originally conceptualized by White (1959), and later refined, extended, and operationalized by Harter (1978, 1981a). White's thesis was that individuals are intrinsically motivated to deal effectively or competently within their social and physical environment and do so by engaging in mastery attempts. If these mastery attempts result in successful or competent performance outcomes, feelings of efficacy and inherent pleasure are experienced; and these feelings, in turn, maintain or enhance one's intrinsic or competence motivation. White viewed the urge toward mastery, challenge, curiosity, and exploratory play as examples of behaviors that result in feelings of efficacy and intrinsic motivation.

A notable shortcoming of White's theoretical model was the lack of operational definitions for constructs such as competence motivation, feelings of efficacy, and intrinsic pleasure. Thus, despite the attractive and intuitive appeal of White's theory for explaining intrinsic motivation, it lay dormant to empirical testing for nearly 20 years. At that time, Susan Harter (1978) provided a refinement and extension of White's original formulations to include several components that should influence an individual's motivational orientation. In addition, Harter and her colleagues (Connell, 1985; Harter, 1981c, 1982, 1985, 1986; Harter & Pike, 1983; Neemann & Harter, 1986) put on psychometric laboratory coats and developed valid and reliable measures for pertinent model constructs that opened the floodgates for subsequent empirical testing.

Harter (1978, 1981a) views competence motivation as a multidimensional construct that influences both the initiation of mastery attempts in particular achievement domains and the development of characteristic achievement behaviors such as perceived competence, perceptions of performance control, and affect. These constructs, in turn, serve to maintain, increase, or decrease competence motivation or, alternatively stated, influence the development of a primarily intrinsically or extrinsically oriented person.

Six components are integral to the multidimensional model of competence motivation. These are:

- Domain-specific mastery attempts (i.e., cognitive, social, physical)
- Influence by significant others in the form of modeling and reinforcement

- Performance outcome in relation to task difficulty (i.e., the notion of optimal challenges)
- Sources of information used for judging and reinforcing personal competence (internal vs. external criteria) and the adoption of certain performance goals (mastery vs. externally defined goal)
- Perceived competence and perceptions of performance control
- Affective outcomes

In general, Harter contends that the intrinsically oriented individual is one who embraces opportunities to demonstrate ability by engaging in mastery attempts; uses internal criteria and mastery goals to evaluate success and guide judgments about level of competence; has high levels of perceived competence and an internal sense of personal control; and experiences positive affect as a result of successful mastery attempts under optimal challenges. The extrinsically oriented person, in contrast, is one who may avoid mastery attempts in order to minimize the probability of demonstrating low ability; depends upon external criteria to evaluate performance outcomes and adopts external standards or performance goals (e.g., winning, parental reinforcement); possesses low perceived competence and an external perceived locus of control; and experiences anxiety in mastery situations. Each of these components is salient to the physical achievement domain (see Weiss, 1987 for an extensive discussion). Thus, Harter's theory has been an attractive model for examining the antecedents and consequences of intrinsic and extrinsic motivational orientations, as defined in the pursuit of competence or mastery.

During the 1980s, empirical testing of Harter's competence motivation theory in the physical achievement domain flourished. Strong support has been found for the hypothesized relationships among several of the components of the model, with particular importance found for the influence of perceived competence upon various achievement-related characteristics and motivational orientation. Sport-specific studies of competence motivation can be divided into several categories:

- The relation between perceived competence and participation motives
- Influence by significant others on perceptions of competence and performance control
- The relation between perceived competence and other achievement-related characteristics
- Antecedents and consequences of positive and negative affect in sport
- Sources of information that are used to evaluate physical ability

- Psychometric studies to develop measures of physical achievement constructs

These studies will be reviewed to demonstrate the knowledge base in this area. In addition, suggestions concerning future research to test competence motivation theory in the physical domain will be provided.

Perceived Competence and Participation Motives

Six studies reviewed earlier (see p. 65) have tested the relationship between perceived competence and participation motives in the physical domain (Feltz et al., 1982; Feltz & Petlichkoff, 1983; Frazer & Weiss, 1991; Klint, 1985; Klint & Weiss, 1987; Roberts et al., 1981). However, a few key points will be repeated here to highlight the focus on domain-specific mastery attempts and their relation to the central construct of perceived competence.

According to Harter, intrinsically motivated individuals will strive to demonstrate ability in the specific achievement areas in which they feel most competent. The study by Klint and Weiss (1987) was specifically designed to test this hypothesis and found support, in that individuals high in perceived physical competence identified skill development or competence-related participation motives as more important, while those high in perceived social competence indicated that affiliation-related participation motives were most salient. Studies that compared participants and nonparticipants (Roberts et al., 1981) or participants and "dropouts" (Feltz & Petlichkoff, 1983; Klint, 1985) may have erroneously assumed that children who are no longer involved in sport have discontinued because their perceptions of *physical* competence are lower than those who have remained involved. However, there are many and varied reasons given for participating in sport besides skill development and for discontinuing sport besides low perceptions of success and competence (see p. 69).

Future studies of participation motivation and attrition might attempt to look at particular participation motives and perceived competence (similar to Klint and Weiss, 1987), or the relation among other constructs in the model in combination with participation motives. This might include the influence of parental expectations and beliefs about their children's abilities on perceived competence and participation behaviors (see Parsons, Adler & Kaczala, 1982 for an example of research in the academic domain), or the relation between coaching behaviors such as reinforcement patterns and decision-making styles on perceptions of control, perceived competence, and changes in participation motives over the course of a season. Another line of research could explore the sources of information used to judge personal competence and its relation to sport persistence. For example, are children and adolescents who primarily depend upon social comparison information and who have low perceived ability more susceptible to dropping out? These relationships and others are likely to shed additional light on why youth participate and discontinue their sport involvement.

Influence by Significant Others

Harter (1981a) states that the most critical addition to White's (1959) formulation involved the effects of the child's socialization history. More specifically, the influence of significant others in reinforcing an intrinsic versus extrinsic motivational orientation via judgments of personal competence and performance control is especially critical during the childhood and adolescent years. Parents, peers, coaches, and teachers all appear to be salient individuals who are used as sources of information by children and adolescents in the competitive sport environment for judging ability and making decisions about future participatory behavior. However, despite the central role afforded by Harter in her model, sport psychologists have neglected the socialization history of the child in understanding motivational orientations (Brustad, 1992).

To date, only two studies have examined the influence of significant others' behavior on self-perceptions of ability within Harter's theoretical framework. Horn (1985) investigated how coaches' reinforcement patterns influenced female adolescent softball players' perceptions of competence and performance control in both practice and competitive settings. She found that certain coaching behaviors over the course of a season contributed, above and beyond skill improvement, to changes in perceived softball competence but not to perceptions of performance control. Specifically, players who received more frequent positive reinforcement and nonreinforcement in response to desirable performances scored lower in perceived physical and cognitive competence; and players who received higher frequencies of criticism in response to performance errors had higher perceptions of competence in relation to their counterparts. Although the results for positive reinforcement and criticism may at first appear contradictory to expected relationships, Horn (1985) explained the results by arguing that contingent and appropriate feedback conveyed to those who received

more criticism, that their performances could improve in the future, while those who were merely positively reinforced for desirable performances may have inferred that their demonstrated level of performance was the best the coach expected. More recently, Black and Weiss (1991) recorded perceptions of coaches' behaviors and examined them in relation to perceptions of ability and motivation in competitive age-group swimmers (ages 10 to 18). The results supported those of Horn (1985), by finding that contingent praise and information following successful performances and contingent encouragement and corrective information following performance errors were associated with athletes who were higher in perceived success and competence, as well as higher in their enjoyment of the sport and preference for optimal challenges.

Empirical testing of the pathway from significant others to other dimensions of Harter's model is wide open. It is surprising that the role of the coach in the psychological development of youth is given so much importance in the literature (Gould, 1988; Martens, 1987) although so little research has established just how important coaching behaviors are. Future research should focus on the influence of coaches, parents, and peers on self-perceptions, affect, and motivational orientations of participants of various ages, gender, and skill levels in order to determine what communication styles and behaviors are most conducive to positive psychological development and intrinsic motivation (Brustad, 1992). For example, Deci, Schwartz, Sheinman, and Ryan (1981) found that classroom teachers who were more autonomy-oriented in their teaching style produced students who were more intrinsically motivated and had higher self-esteem at the end of the school year than did students of teachers with a more controlling orientation. We have a long way to go in understanding the relationship between social support, psychological development, and motivational orientations in the sport domain; but competence motivation theory provides an attractive resource for initiating such investigations.

Perceived Competence and Achievement-Related Characteristics

The pathways in Harter's model suggest that intimate relationships should exist among actual success, perceptions of performance success, competence, and control, affect, and motivational orientation. Four studies to date have supported hypothesized relationships among some or all of these constructs (Klint, 1988; Weiss, Bredemeier & Shewchuk, 1986; Weiss & Horn, 1990;

Weiss, McAuley, Ebbeck & Wiese, 1990). Weiss and colleagues (1990), for example, examined the relationship between children's perceptions of competence and their attributions for performance success in both physical and social domains within a 7-week summer sports program. Results revealed that children high in perceived competence made attributions for physical competence (and interpersonal success) that were more internal and stable and higher in personal control than their low-perceived-competence peers. Thus, children with positive self-perceptions of ability adopted a more intrinsic orientation to explaining their performance ratings; and these attributional patterns are likely to lead to positive affect and future success expectations.

Weiss and Horn (1990) were interested in how the accuracy of children's perceived competence related to achievement characteristics such as perceived control, motivational orientation, and anxiety. Children were divided into accuracy groups based on difference scores between teachers' ratings of their actual physical competence and perceptions of their competence. Children whose perceived competence fell into the lower quartile of difference scores were considered to be underestimators; children whose perceived competence fell into the upper quartile of difference scores were overestimators; and children whose perceived competence fell into the middle 50% of the frequency distribution of discrepancy scores were accurate estimators. A significant gender-by-accuracy interaction effect revealed that underestimating girls were lower in intrinsic motivation, higher in anxiety, and more external in their control perceptions than accurately estimating or overestimating girls. Underestimating boys were higher in perceived unknown control than accurately estimating and overestimating boys. It was concluded that children who seriously underestimate their perceived physical competence follow an extrinsic motivational pattern, making them likely candidates for sport withdrawal and/or low levels of physical achievement.

The results of these two studies suggest that children with high levels of perceived competence follow a pattern of functional achievement behaviors, reflected in their success perceptions, causal attributions for performance, motivational orientation, and affective outcomes. Moreover, Weiss et al. (1986) used causal modeling procedures to examine the relationships among perceived competence, perceived control, physical achievement, and motivational orientation. Results revealed significant causal influences from perceived competence and perceived control to motivational orientation and actual motor performance scores. Specifically, children high in

perceived competence and low in perceived unknown control evidenced higher achievement scores and a more intrinsic motivational orientation than children low on these self-perception characteristics.

Taken together, these studies demonstrate strong support for the links among several central constructs in Harter's competence motivation model. Future research might examine the perceived competence–causal attributions–affect–motivation link through observational measures of children's effort and persistence under optimal but challenging physical achievement situations. Also, intervention studies are needed to determine whether attribution-retraining or self-esteem-enhancing instructional strategies can make a difference with extrinsically motivated children on achievement and persistence behaviors in the physical domain.

Antecedents and Consequences of Affect

Most studies of affect in children's sport have centered on trait and state anxiety in competitive settings (Passer, 1988). Not until recently have empirical investigations of positive affect been initiated (Brustad, 1988; Klint, 1988; Scanlan & Lewthwaite, 1986; Scanlan, Stein & Ravizza, 1988; Wankel & Sefton, 1989). However, only a few studies of affective outcomes in competitive sport have been couched within a motivational theoretical framework. Four studies have specifically been grounded in Harter's theory (Brustad, 1988; Brustad & Weiss, 1987; Klint, 1988; Weiss, Bredemeier & Brustad, 1987).

The studies by Brustad and Weiss (1987) and Weiss and colleagues (1987) were designed to examine the relationship between negative affect in the form of competitive trait anxiety (CTA) and perceptions of competence, perceptions of control, motivational orientation, and characteristic worry perceptions in youth sports. Brustad and Weiss reported gender differences, in that low-, medium-, and high-CTA girls did not differ on any of the self-perception characteristics but high-CTA boys could be distinguished from low-CTA boys on general self-worth and frequency of performance-related worries. Gender differences were also found by Weiss and colleagues; but this time a stronger relationship was found for Harter's theory, in that anxiety was found to be related to several achievement-related characteristics. Specifically, high-CTA girls reported lower levels of perceived physical competence, a more external perception of control, and lower levels of intrinsic motivation in the form of challenge seeking than did low-CTA girls. For the boys, those high in trait anxiety reported lower perceptions of competence and a more external perception of control than low-CTA boys.

Brustad (1988) extended his previous study by investigating predictors of negative and positive affect in competitive youth sport. Predictor variables included perceived competence, perceived parental pressure, general self-worth, motivational orientation, performance-related worries, and negative-evaluation-related worries. Unlike the two previously reported studies, identical findings emerged for boys and girls. High levels of intrinsic motivational orientation and low perceptions of parental pressure to perform were related to season-long enjoyment ratings, although only general self-worth was significantly related to trait anxiety levels. However, high perceived parental pressure for boys and low perceived physical competence for girls approached significance in the regression analyses. Finally, high-CTA boys and girls were significantly higher on performance-related worries and worries about negative evaluation from coaches, parents, and peers than were low-CTA youngsters.

Finally, Klint (1988) was interested in examining which antecedent variables in Harter's model were most predictive of affect, using measures of enjoyment, anxiety, pride, excitement, and happiness to reflect positive and negative aspects of affect. Competitive female gymnasts (N = 156) completed measures of self-perceptions, motivational orientation, and affect in relation to how they usually felt about participating in gymnastics. A significant relationship was found between psychological characteristics and affect, with an intrinsic motivational orientation emerging as the strongest contributor to levels of enjoyment, excitement, pride, and anxiety. A subsequent analysis was conducted to determine the effects of self-perception and affect variables on choice, effort, and persistence as measures of motivation. High levels of enjoyment, excitement, and perceived competence were the strongest contributors to all three motivation measures. The results of this study supported Harter's theoretical predictions; however, only 9% and 14% of the variance in the criterion variable set was explained in these two analyses, respectively. This suggests that other variables must be considered in order to explain and predict affect and motivation.

These studies provide initial support, albeit small, for the pathways linking various self-perceptions, affective outcomes, and motivational orientation in Harter's model. Harter (1981a, 1981b) has argued that *affect* be given center stage in the study of intrinsic motivation; but for this to happen, more empirical research is essential in order to understand affective outcomes in competitive sport. In addition to enjoyment and anxiety, Weiner (1985) detailed a host of other emotions that should be related to perceptions of success, causal attributions, and causal dimensions for performance outcome. These included pride, happiness, excitement, surprise, and confidence. Thus, future studies should not only explore multidimensional affects in relation to sport participation but also to specific contexts. For example, all the studies on affect reported here asked children to report how they characteristically feel about participating in youth sport. A more context-specific understanding of the role of emotions in sport can be gained by testing the relationship among self-perceptions, affect, and motivational orientation immediately following specific experiences, such as practice and competitive events that vary in importance, time of season, or other characteristics. In this way, objective and subjective measures of success can be obtained; and causal attribution and emotion measures related specifically to these perceptions.

Sources of Information Used to Judge Physical Ability

An important component in Harter's model is the preference for sources of information to reinforce one's mastery attempts and successes, as well as to establish a set of goals or standards. The individual who is intrinsically motivated comes to internalize a self-reward system and a set of mastery goals as a result of positive socialization experiences. In this orientation, the need for, and dependency on, external social reinforcement decreases with age. Conversely, the individual who is extrinsically motivated comes to depend upon external approval and reinforcement to judge one's ability and also comes to depend upon externally defined goals for behavior. This is based on a socialization history predominated by lack of reinforcement or disapproval for independent mastery attempts in combination with reinforcement for dependency on adults. In this orientation, the need for external social approval and reinforcement persists or increases developmentally.

Horn and her colleagues (Horn & Hasbrook, 1986, 1987; Horn & Weiss, 1991) have investigated the relationship between preferred sources of competence information and various constructs identified in Harter's intrinsic motivation model. Three studies (Horn & Hasbrook, 1986, 1987; Horn & Weiss, 1991) have consistently found a relationship between age and the sources of information used to judge physical competence. Specifically, children 8 and 9 years of age more frequently indicated that they used game outcome and adult feedback and evaluation as sources of information than did children 10 to 14 years of age. In contrast, these older children identified peer comparison and evaluation as a more salient source of information than did younger children.

Horn and Hasbrook (1987) also examined the relationship between self-perceptions, as measured by perceived physical competence and perceived performance control, and sources of information used to judge personal abilities. They found a non-significant relationship between perceptions of competence and control with sources of competence information in 8-to-9-year-old children but a significant relationship for 10-to-11- and 12-to-14-year-old children. This implies that a certain level of cognitive-developmental sophistication is necessary for hypothesized relationships in the motivational model to be accurate. The significant relationships found for children in the two older age groups were generally in accordance with theoretical predictions. Specifically, children who were high in perceived competence and an internal sense of control identified internal criteria (e.g., self-improvement in skills) and peer comparison as preferred sources of information. Children low in perceived competence and high in perceived external control preferred information that was more external in nature, such as feedback and evaluation from parents and teachers. A logical extension of this study would be to examine both cognitive and behavioral motivational orientations of these two types of youngsters. Do children who are low in perceived competence and external in their control perceptions actually report that they prefer easy, rather than optimal, challenges and that they depend upon parents and teachers for help, rather than engage in independent mastery? Do their behaviors in physical achievement settings actually validate these self-perceptions and motivational orientations?

Additional age-related findings pertaining to accuracy of perceived competence and preference for informational sources of competence were reported by Horn and Weiss (1991). Correlations between perceptions of competence and actual competence, as measured by teachers' ratings of sport performance, revealed that children become more accurate in their perceived competence with age, with children of 8 to 9 years less accurate than children of 10 to 13 years. Moreover, these differences in accuracy could be linked, at least in part, to the informational sources children used to judge their performance capabilities. Younger children indicated a dependence upon feedback and evaluation from parents and teachers more than older children,

although the older children primarily relied upon peer comparison and evaluation for information about their competence. Thus, studies by Horn and her colleagues suggest a developmental pattern regarding sources of information used to judge physical ability.

Psychometric Developments

Although Harter and her colleagues have developed valid and reliable measures of perceived competence, perceived control, and motivational orientation, some of these instruments needed modification before they could be considered appropriate for the physical activity setting. In other cases, measures had to be developed for specific constructs of interest. For example, Ulrich (1987) built upon the Pictorial Scale of Perceived Competence and Social Acceptance for Young Children (Harter & Pike, 1983) by including depictions of fundamental motor skills (e.g., throwing, catching) and motor abilities (e.g., strength) to complement some of the more general skills (e.g., climbing) included in the original scale. Horn and Hasbrook (1986) modified Minton's (1979) Competence Information Scale to produce a Sport Competence Information Scale and further modifications have been made since (Horn, personal communication).

A preliminary measure of Motivational Orientation in Sport has been developed through the use of confirmatory factor-analytic techniques (Weiss, Bredemeier & Shewchuk, 1985; Weiss & Shewchuk, 1985). Subsequent studies have provided construct and/or factorial validity, as well as internal consistency reliability (Weiss et al., 1987; Weiss et al., 1986; Weiss & Horn, 1990). However, as with any measure, further studies are essential to provide additional evidence of accurate and reliable assessments of constructs.

A discouraging note has been the inconsistency of the Multidimensional Children's Perceptions of Control Scale (Connell, 1985). Some studies in which the physical subscale has been modified to be sport-specific have reported inadequate internal consistency values, resulting in the scores being deleted from further analyses (Brustad & Weiss, 1987; Glenn & Horn, 1991). It may be possible that when general physical abilities are translated to sport-specific ones, item intercorrelations and reliabilities of the individual items are affected negatively. Moreover, Connell's (1985) research resulted in internal, powerful others, and unknown subscales consisting of four items each. However, two of the items depict successful outcomes, and two depict failure outcomes. Based on knowledge from attribution theory and research, individuals are likely to assign aspects related to locus of causality and personal controllability differently for success and failure outcomes (see chapter 5). Thus, future psychometric testing must be conducted to solidify valid and reliable measures for assessing self-perceptions and motivational orientation across the life span.

In sum, the issue of valid and reliable measurement of motivational constructs is one that pervades the field of sport psychology. It seems to have been explicitly addressed by Harter and colleagues and offers a good model for sport psychologists to emulate. It is clear that efforts to develop instrumentation that accurately and reliably taps self-perception and motivational constructs are critical to the maturity of the area of motivational orientations.

Weiss's (1987) book chapter summarized Harter's theory and the sport-related research to that date. The number of research studies that can be added here are numerous, and the direction for continued growth in this area most encouraging. The use of a competence or mastery orientation to study intrinsic motivation is a viable alternative to a cognitive evaluation theory orientation. However, it should be noted that the two theories are much more similar than different. For example, perceptions of competence and the informational sources available to judge ability are central constructs related to intrinsic motivation for both approaches. The notions of self-determination and perceptions of performance control are quite similar, with the salient feature residing in the individual's perceived locus of causality for participation behavior: internal or external. Both theories highlight the importance of success at optimal challenges as essential to maximizing perceived competence, internal locus of control, and intrinsic motivation. Finally, both approaches highlight the importance played by reinforcement from significant others or from rewards inherent in competitive experiences in ensuing motivation orientation levels.

Achievement Goal Orientations

One of the prominent features of sport is the variation in individuals' achievement behaviors. Some participants choose challenging tasks, exert appropriate effort while striving for success, and persist through the adversity of learning new sport skills. Others, in contrast, select less optimally challenging goals, exhibit minimal effort, and lack the persistence behaviors that would result in reaching maximal performance potential. A number of social cognitive theories have been proposed and refined in an attempt to explain and predict such behavioral variations in terms of the goals or motivational orientations of individuals. These theories have been primarily tested in the academic achievement domain, but recent research and theoretical discussion indicate that these theories may also be applicable to the physical domain.

Theoretical models of achievement motivation have been formulated by a number of theorists (e.g., Ames, 1984; Dweck, 1986; Dweck & Elliott, 1983; Elliott & Dweck, 1988; Maehr & Nicholls, 1980; Nicholls, 1984, 1989; Spence & Helmreich, 1983). Each of these theoretical viewpoints share a number of common themes. First, the concept of ability is central to each theory. In fact, achievement situations are often defined as those in which the primary concern of the participant is his or her personal competence to meet the situational demands. Second, in contrast to early theorizing about achievement motivation as a unitary construct (Atkinson, 1977; McClelland, 1961), each of these contemporary theories considers achievement motivation as multidimensional in nature. From this stance, each theory consists of a number of salient personal disposition, social environmental, and developmentally related parameters. Finally, in each of these conceptualizations, "goals" are central determinants of achievement behavior, with individuals defining success and failure in terms of how well these goals were attained. Each of these unique, yet related, theories and sport-related research are now presented.

Maehr and Nicholls

Maehr and Nicholls (1980) contend that achievement motivation may take a variety of forms, which are derived from individuals' primary goals for participatory behavior, as well as the meanings they attach to success and failure. From this perspective, attainment of a goal is thought to imply something desirable about the person, for example, that he or she is competent. Maehr and Nicholls's theory, therefore, emphasizes the qualitative variations in goals instead of quantitative differences in motivation. The aim of this research was to define a comprehensive and universal classification of achievement behaviors, with the categorization of behaviors based upon certain particular goals. Three categories of achievement goal orientations were derived from Maehr and Nicholls's analysis: *ability-oriented*, *task-oriented*, and *social approval–oriented* behaviors.

Ability-oriented behavior is characterized as the desire to maintain favorable perceptions of ability. The goal of the behavior is to maximize the probability of demonstrating high ability or to minimize the probability of demonstrating low ability. Performance outcomes attributed to high ability will be subjectively experienced as success and will result in positive affect and expectations of future success in similar situations. Conversely, outcomes attributed to low ability will be perceived as failures, resulting in negative affect and expectancies that future mastery attempts will result in the demonstration of low ability. Social comparison is the overriding source of information used in this goal orientation to judge performance successes and failures, defined in terms of demonstrated ability.

Task-oriented behavior focuses on the process, rather than the outcome, of involvement in achievement situations. This may include developing a more adequate understanding of a task or to engage in problem solving, rather than an emphasis on demonstrating ability. Examples of task-involved goals in sport include attempts to improve personal performance standards or to perform a skill in a technically correct manner. The criteria against which such performances are evaluated are inherent in the task itself or based on previous individual performances, rather than the performance of others. Success defined in these terms is experienced as intrinsic motivation derived from the mastery of the task itself.

In social approval–oriented behavior, the goal of the individual is to maximize the probability of demonstrating virtuous intent and thereby gain social approval for these intentions. Maehr and Nicholls, as well as researchers in the sport domain (Ewing, 1981; Petlichkoff, 1988; Roberts, 1984), have emphasized the role of effort in such behaviors. Effort is seen as being under the voluntary control of individuals and an indicant of social conformity. Hence, it is proposed that persons who are motivated to obtain social approval for their actions will demonstrate high levels of effort.

Limited research has been conducted to investigate the relationship between achievement goal orientations and sport achievement behaviors in accordance with Maehr and Nicholls's theory. Duda (1981, 1985) found evidence for cultural variations in achievement goals, with both ethnic and gender differences emerging on sport achievement orientations. In general, males are more ability-oriented than females (Duda, 1986a; Ewing, 1981) and Anglo males are more ability-oriented than either Anglo females, or native Americans or Mexican–Americans of either sex (Duda, 1985).

Ewing (1981) and Petlichkoff (1988) have both examined the relationship between sport persistence and achievement orientations using a sport-specific measure of achievement orientations. They have identified factors that correspond to the ability, task, and social approval orientations identified by Maehr and Nicholls. However, Vealey and Campbell (1988) found only two orientations with their sample: a task orientation and a combined social approval and ability orientation. Additional psychometric testing revealed low validity and reliability indexes (Pemberton, Petlichkoff & Ewing, 1986). Thus, despite the intuitive appeal of Maehr and Nicholls's theory for the physical domain, limited research has been conducted, and measurement of the goal orientations has been called into question.

Nicholls

Nicholls built upon the notions of ability-oriented and task-oriented motivational orientations introduced earlier with Maehr (Maehr & Nicholls, 1980). Nicholls proposed that both goal orientations relate similarly to the concept of ability. However, the concept of ability was viewed as holding different meanings for ability-oriented and task-oriented individuals. Specifically, Nicholls suggested that how individuals construe ability varies developmentally but that individual differences within developmental level exist depending upon personal dispositions and situational factors.

According to Nicholls, young children do not differentiate between the concepts of ability and effort, or between the concepts of ability and task difficulty (Nicholls, 1978; Nicholls & Miller, 1983). Up until about the age of seven years, children tend to use their expectations of successful task completion as the basis for evaluating task difficulty, and do not use information from social comparison sources. Tasks which these children are unsure of being able to perform adequately are evaluated as being difficult. Because difficult tasks are viewed as requiring greater effort for successful completion, young children tend to view greater ability as being demonstrated when higher effort expenditure results in successful performance. Nicholls terms this view an undifferentiated conception of ability, because the child perceives that a positive relationship exists between the concepts of ability and effort. Inferences of high ability are thus expected within situations in which the child tries hard and successfully completes tasks perceived to be personally difficult.

Not until about the age of 11 years, Nicholls posits, are difficult tasks evaluated as being those

that few people are able to perform. At this level, ability is conceived as a capacity, wherein the concepts of ability and effort are differentiated from each other. In this view, one's ability limits the impact that additional effort can have on increased performance. Thus, if two individuals achieve equal performance outcomes but one exerts greater effort in the process, he or she is seen as possessing less ability than the individual who exerted less effort. Finally, once ability is viewed as a capacity in this differentiated perspective, it is recognized that trying harder than others to complete a task successfully may be risking the demonstration of low ability.

Nicholls (1984) proposes that once the conception of ability as capacity has been attained by a person, he or she will be able to utilize either the differentiated or undifferentiated conception of ability. The probability of invoking either conception is dependent upon the personal disposition of the individual and situational cues. Specifically, situations that emphasize evaluation (Butler, 1987, 1988), self-awareness (Carver & Scheier, 1982), and interpersonal competition (Ames, Ames & Felker, 1977; Butler, 1989) are likely to invoke social comparison processes and the differentiated conception of ability. Under conditions of low social evaluation, indirect competition, or noncompetitive pursuits, the undifferentiated conception of ability is likely to be adopted (Nicholls, 1984). More recently, Nicholls (1989) emphasized that in any given situation, individuals may fluctuate between using each of the conceptions of ability.

According to Nicholls, these different conceptions of ability are also linked to variations in achievement goals. When the undifferentiated conception of ability is utilized, the individual is said to be task-involved, and personal competence relative to others is not a primary concern. The central focus is to master the task. Task involvement is analogous to the task orientation in Maehr and Nicholls's (1980) theory. When an individual is task-involved, greater learning is predicted to result in enhanced perceptions of competence, as task difficulty and ability judgments are self-referenced. Because greater effort is seen as resulting in greater learning, tasks seen as requiring the greatest effort provide the greatest opportunity for learning and feelings of competence. Alternatively, when a person's goal is to demonstrate high ability relative to a comparison group, he or she invokes the differentiated conception of ability and is said to be ego-involved in goal orientation. Under this condition, success on tasks that few are able to achieve is required for inferences of high ability to be made. When a person is ego-involved, expectations of failure on normatively easy tasks will lead to feelings of incompetence.

Dweck

Like Nicholls, Dweck has investigated variations in achievement behavior in the academic domain. She proposes that children's conceptions of intelligence direct them toward adopting specific academic achievement goals (Dweck, 1986; Dweck & Bempechat, 1988; Dweck & Elliott, 1983; Elliott & Dweck, 1988). Children who view intelligence as being a global and stable "entity" are predicted to set goals emphasizing the demonstration of personal adequacy and the avoidance of the display of low ability. Because intelligence may be inferred only through performance,

Dweck terms the goal of demonstrating competence a *performance goal*. A second conception of intelligence is the "incremental" view, whereby intelligence is conceived as a broad variety of skills that may be developed with practice and effort. Individuals operating under this conception of intelligence are predicted to set goals emphasizing the enhancement of present abilities, which Dweck terms *learning goals*.

Central to Dweck's propositions are two distinct behavioral patterns with which students respond to failure (Diener & Dweck, 1978, 1980). Mastery-oriented individuals respond as if the failure to attain a goal is a temporary setback. Instead of internalizing failure as a permanent personal characteristic, they focus on personally controllable factors that may change the course of action in the future, such as increasing effort, adopting an alternate strategy, and selectively attending to salient task features. In this view, positive affect and expectancies are maintained, and performance is subsequently improved. Conversely, helpless-oriented individuals attribute their failures to lack of ability, exhibit negative affect, and show deterioration in effort and persistence, resulting in performance decrements. Dweck argues that the incremental and entity conceptions of intelligence are associated with mastery- and helpless-oriented behavioral responses, respectively.

Nicholls and Dweck: A Reconciliation

Formulations based on Nicholls's and Dweck's understanding of conceptions of ability and subsequent achievement behaviors contain similar components. Dweck's predictions for the achievement behavior of individuals who set learning goals align with the predictions Nicholls makes for task-involved individuals. Those who view ability or intelligence as being controllable and who are concerned with the development of competence are primarily focused on the processes of an activity. The basic question of concern to such a person is, How can I solve this task? Criteria used in performance evaluation are self-referenced, rather than normative, and emphasize progression toward a long-term goal. Because task difficulty and ability assessments are self-referenced, it is predicted that individuals will select personally challenging tasks. Such tasks are most attractive because they require effort for successful completion, and therefore provide the greatest opportunities for developing feelings of competence. A task in which one is uncertain of one's ability to succeed is viewed as a challenge, instead of a threat; and errors incurred during performance of the task are viewed as an integral part of the learning process. Most importantly, regardless of the person's confidence in his or her ability compared with others, learning- or task-involved goals are proposed to be related to mastery-oriented behavior characterized by the selection of, and striving to succeed in, personally challenging tasks, persistence, and high performance attainment.

Similarly, the predictions Dweck makes for the achievement behaviors of individuals operating under performance goals are similar to Nicholls's formulations for ego-involved individuals. These predictions are somewhat more complex than those made for task involvement and learning goals. The goal in the ego-oriented and performance-oriented conditions described by Nicholls and Dweck, respectively, is to maximize the probability of demonstrating high ability and minimize the probability of displaying low ability. In ego and performance orientations, competence evaluations are made relative to the performance of others.

Ego-involved and performance-oriented individuals who possess high perceptions of ability or intelligence will expect to succeed in moderately difficult tasks. Therefore, it is predicted that these individuals will display the same mastery behaviors seen in task- and learning-oriented individuals. Because success on tasks that are normatively difficult implies high ability, individuals who are confident of their ability are predicted to select challenging tasks, exert maximal effort, and persist under the struggle of achieving task goals. However, this behavioral pattern is not predicted for ego- or performance-oriented individuals who are not confident of their ability. Instead, the helpless pattern of behavior may be induced. Ego-involved individuals who have low perceived ability will expect to fail at tasks of moderate difficulty. Failure at such tasks will be perceived as a demonstration of incompetence. Therefore, it is predicted that these individuals will perceive challenging tasks as threatening and will attempt to avoid a possible display of incompetence by selecting very difficult or very easy tasks. More specifically, Nicholls (1984, 1989) predicts that when an ego-involved person is certain that he or she possesses very low ability, he or she will choose to engage in an extremely easy activity in an attempt to avoid the demonstration of low ability. If, however, a person whose ability is low wishes to establish him- or herself as competent in this domain, then selection of an extremely difficult task is predicted. Successful completion of such a task, although highly unlikely, will imply that the person is highly competent.

Individuals who are ego- or performance-oriented and low in perceived ability are predicted to exert the greatest effort in tasks of extremely low or high difficulty. In tasks of intermediate difficulty, performance and effort are predicted to be the poorest because perceived threat to feelings of competence are expected to be highest. Failure in such tasks, from an ego-involved perspective, will be construed as a demonstration of incompetence. Although trying hard may increase the probability of successful performance, exertion of maximal effort under conditions where failure is anticipated will only ensure the display of low ability. Because it is more difficult to assess an individual's ability accurately when he or she withholds effort, this person may choose not to try hard. Ironically, although this ploy may prevent the person from displaying incompetence, it also maximizes the probability that the individual will not increase his or her actual skill competence. However, Nicholls (1989) argues that if the person continues to strive to establish competence, he or she will maintain effort but may evidence negative affect, impaired performance, and divided attention. Additionally, this person may come to devalue the activity and direct less effort to performance or avoid involvement in activities in which he or she perceives low ability.

Achievement Motivation Research in Sport

Roberts (1984) and Duda (1987, 1989a) have advocated the utility of Nicholls's (1984, 1989) theory in explaining variations in children's sport behaviors. To date, researchers investigating achievement constructs in the physical domain have provided limited evidence for the hypothesized links between goal orientations and the achievement behaviors of participation (Duda, 1986a, 1988b), performance (Burton, 1989), and intensity (Duda, 1988a). Duda's (1986a, 1988a) research has demonstrated a consistent pattern of results. Individuals who participate in sport most extensively—and who persist longest—appear to be both highly ego-involved and highly task-involved. Persons who are highly ego-involved but low on task involvement tend not to persist in sport for as long as those who are high in both goal orientations.

More recently, Duda (1989b) presented evidence suggesting that a relationship exists between an individual's goal orientations and his or her perceptions of the purpose of sport. Specifically, ego-involved high school athletes tended to perceive the purpose of sport as being instrumental (to develop social status and self-esteem),

whereas those who were task-oriented believed that sport should enhance self-esteem but also teach individuals socially desirable behaviors such as trying to the best of one's ability, cooperation, and being a good citizen.

Most of the basic tenets of Nicholls and Dweck's theories remain untested. Specifically, the development of children's understanding of the concepts of effort and ability has scarcely been addressed in the physical domain, despite considerable theorizing about developmental capabilities and subsequent motivated behavior (Duda, 1987). Moreover, the influence of motivational goal orientations on achievement behaviors must be considered together with perceptions of ability in order to adequately test Nicholls and Dweck's theories, as it is a central construct mediating the relationship between goal orientation and sport persistence. To date, only Petlichkoff (1988) has done so. Future research possibilities abound with regard to the hypotheses that emanate from these two similar theories.

Ames

Ames (1984) has emphasized the influence of reward structures within educational environments upon children's use of different achievement goals. She proposes that competitive, cooperative, and individualistic reward systems pose situations in which success and failure take on different meanings for individuals. A competitive reward structure is a situation in which a negative interdependence of rewards exists: When an individual attains a reward, he or she precludes others from receiving this reward. In a cooperative reward system, a positive interdependence of rewards is said to exist: A person's attainment of a reward is dependent upon the performance and attainment of rewards of other members of the group. Thirdly, Ames (1984) describes an individualistic reward structure as being a situation where each individual's attainment of rewards is independent of the attainment of rewards by others, in that performance is evaluated in terms of personal mastery, not in relation to the performance of others.

Ames argues that competitive, cooperative, and individualistic reward systems involve the use of different motivational processes, because success and failure outcomes are defined differently under each of these structures. Specifically, she proposes that competitive and individualistic reward systems engender, respectively, the ego-involved and task-involved motivational orientations as described by Nicholls (1984) and that the cooperative reward system relates to a moral motivational orientation. Ames's own research in the academic domain (Ames, 1978, 1981; Ames & Ames, 1981; Ames, Ames & Felker, 1977; Ames & Archer, 1988; Ames & Felker, 1979) suggests that reward structures influence the salience of various informational sources in self-evaluations of ability, the affective value of success and failure, and perceptions of individual differences in ability. For example, Ames (1984) contends that success in competitive situations increases the salience of social comparison as a source of information in self-evaluations. Ames and Ames (1981) found that previous performance success was a salient source of information used for self-evaluation in individualized settings, where the purpose of the goal is self-improvement. However, this was not the case in competitive situations.

Along with variations in self-evaluations that occur as a function of social context, affective responses to success and failure and perceptions of individual differences in ability also vary (Ames, 1981; Ames, Ames & Felker, 1977). Satisfaction in cooperative—but not competitive—settings appears to be influenced by group outcomes. Thus, an individual's personal dissatisfaction with poor performance may be compromised by successful group performance; and satisfaction accompanying high performance levels may be attenuated by an unsuccessful group performance. Finally, because competitive contexts encourage individuals to compare personal performance attainments to others, perceptions of individual differences in ability are more likely in competitive than in individualistic or cooperatively structured settings, where the performance of others is not relevant to performance evaluation.

To date, no research studies have purposely tested Ames's contentions in the domain of sport. Some studies have, however, examined differences among competitive, cooperative, and individualistic contexts on physical and psychological outcomes (Giannini, Weinberg & Jackson, 1988; March & Peart, 1988). Giannini and colleagues (1988) experimentally manipulated competitive, cooperative, and mastery goal instructions to recreational basketball players and found nonsignificant group differences on basketball performance. It could be argued that despite being assigned to particular goal groups, players may have utilized their own characteristic goal orientation on the task; but this possibility was not ascertained. Marsh and Peart (1988) examined the effects of competitive and cooperative exercise programs on adolescent girls' physical fitness and multidimensional self-concepts. Results revealed that both programs enhanced physical fitness levels but that only the cooperative-oriented program produced positive changes in self-concept dimensions

of ability and physical appearance, while the competitive program lowered them.

Research in sport psychology has not pursued the utility of competitive, cooperative, and individualistic goal structures as conceptualized by Ames (1984) on physical achievement, self-perception, and motivated behaviors. One possible research direction is to extend the work of Horn (Horn & Hasbrook, 1986, 1987; Horn & Weiss, 1991) on sources of information used to judge personal competence to contexts varying in competitive, cooperative, and individualistic goal structures. It is possible that contextual cues may interact with developmental level to influence the sources of information that children, adolescents, and adults use to evaluate physical ability.

Spence and Helmreich

An alternative approach toward achievement orientations has been provided by Spence and Helmreich (1983). They view achievement motivation as a multidimensional construct as well as a stable personality characteristic that varies in strength among individuals. Like Dweck, Maehr and Nicholls, and Nicholls, Spence and Helmreich (1983) define achievement behaviors as those in which performance may be evaluated relative to either normatively referenced (social comparison) or self-referenced (personal standards) criteria. In an attempt to explain differences in achievement behavior of males and females, they (Helmreich & Spence, 1978) constructed a multidimensional measure of achievement motivation, the Work and Family Orientation Questionnaire (WOFO). Factor analyses revealed four factors, which were labeled *Work* (the desire to work hard and to perform well), *Mastery* (the desire for challenge and the attainment of personal goals), *Competitiveness* (the enjoyment of interpersonal competition and the desire to succeed in competitive situations), and *Personal Unconcern* (a lack of concern for negative performance evaluation).

Spence and Helmreich (1983) have found that females tend to score higher than males on the Work subscale, and that males score higher than females on the Mastery and Competitiveness subscales of the WOFO. In academic and work situations, performance quality measured in terms of academic grades (elementary school students), citations (research psychologists), and salary (employees) has been positively related to the Work and Mastery motives but negatively related to subjects' scores on the Competitiveness subscale. These results for Competitiveness are especially true when high scores on this subscale are combined with high scores on the Mastery and Work subscales (Helmreich, Beane, Lucker & Spence, 1978; Spence & Helmreich, 1983).

Spence and Helmreich (1983) suggested that the influence of competitiveness on athletic performance is a potentially fruitful research topic. Gill and her colleagues (Gill, 1986b, 1988; Gill & Deeter, 1988; Gill & Dzewaltowski, 1988; Gill, Dzewaltowski & Deeter, 1988) validated a sport-specific measure of achievement orientations modeled after the WOFO. The Sport Orientation Questionnaire (SOQ) contains three subscales:

- Competitiveness (the desire to strive for success in competitive sport situations)
- Win orientation (the desire to win in interpersonal competition)
- Goal orientation (the desire to attain personal goals)

Gill and her colleagues have found that males score significantly higher than females on the Win and Competitive achievement orientations, while females score higher than males on the Goal subscale. Additionally, athletes score significantly higher than nonathletes on both sport-specific and general achievement orientations, but these differences are primarily explained by scores on the Competitiveness orientation.

Future Research Directions in Achievement Motivation

Only a limited range of behaviors has been investigated with regard to the relationship between goal orientations and achievement motivation. Nicholls (1984, 1989) specifies hypothesized relationships between goal orientations, perceived ability, and the achievement behaviors of task choice, effort, performance, and persistence. Few investigations have included task choice and effort as variables in their analyses, yet these are central components in Nicholls's theory. In addition, the whole area of participation motivation and attrition is conducive to investigations based on Nicholls's theory. For example, are children who are primarily ego-involved and low in perceived ability more susceptible to discontinuing their participation?

If certain goal orientations are associated with long-term performance variations, then the mechanisms by which these occur need to be investigated. Both Dweck (1986) and Nicholls (1989) suggest that attention, affect, and intrinsic motivation are related to performance in the academic domain. If these contentions also generalize to the physical domain, it may become

necessary to seek ways to help athletes adopt a more mastery-oriented or task-involved approach to sport achievement. This raises the question, Can achievement goal orientations be changed? Moreover, if motivational orientations can be changed, how might this be achieved? Burton (1989) provided preliminary evidence that a goal-setting program designed to highlight a task, rather than an ego, orientation to performance can positively affect self-perceptions, motivation, and performance in collegiate swimming teams.

In a review of Nicholls's developmentally based theory of achievement motivation, Duda (1987) offered a number of research suggestions in the domain of sport. Two suggestions deserve special recognition. First, very little research has focused on how conceptions of ability vary among individuals, and especially how such ability conceptions might vary with developmental level. Duda (1987) notes that in the realm of sport, the nature of ability, effort, and task difficulty are more readily apparent than in the academic domain; that is, both performance processes and outcomes are observable to the participant him- or herself, as well as to a host of significant others such as parents, peers, and coaches. It may be possible, therefore, that the processes underlying conceptions of ability in the physical domain are quite different from those in the academic domain. For example, in a recent study by Watkins and Montgomery (1989), children and adolescents in grades 3, 6, 9, and 12 were interviewed about their beliefs concerning contributors to athletic ability. Findings provided support for Nicholls's hypotheses about children's capabilities for viewing ability as differentiated or undifferentiated from effort, as well as Dweck's hypotheses about ability conceived as an entity or as incremental in nature.

A second major research question highlighted by Duda (1987) is the need to investigate the influence of the situation or the social context on an individual's goal orientations and perceived ability. Ames's work provides a model for such research. Situations that vary in their emphasis on competitive, cooperative, and individualistic goals may be defined differently by individuals who are characterized by task- or ego-involved achievement orientations. A competitive goal structure may invoke an ego orientation, whereas a situation that stresses personally referenced goals and performance processes may be more conducive to eliciting a task orientation. For example, in the classic Robber's Cave Experiment (Sherif & Sherif, 1953), an emphasis on direct competition between the two groups resulted in ego-involved performance goals and a "win at all costs" attitude. When more of a cooperative structure was invoked through the use of superordinate goals, a mastery goal orientation that considered the good of all was achieved.

Finally, a general area in need of investigation is to establish how the differently labeled, yet strikingly similar, constructs within the several achievement motivation theories relate to one another. For example, there are clear similarities between the terms *task orientation* (Maehr & Nicholls, 1980; Nicholls, 1989), *learning goals* (Dweck, 1986), *work/mastery goal orientations* (Spence & Helmreich, 1983), *goal orientation* (Gill & Deeter, 1988), and *performance orientation* (Vealey, 1986). Are these constructs getting at the same underlying cognitive processes? If so, a common language should be adopted. If they are distinct, similarities and differences should be highlighted. Similarly, there are clear similarities between the terms *ability orientation* (Maehr & Nicholls, 1980), *ego-involved goals* (Nicholls, 1989), *performance goals* (Dweck, 1986), *competitiveness* (Spence & Helmreich, 1983), *win orientation* (Gill & Deeter, 1988), and *outcome orientation* (Vealey, 1986). Moreover, Duda (1989a) has suggested that the Competitiveness and Win subscales and the Goal subscale of the SOQ (Gill & Deeter, 1988) are similar to the Ego and Task subscales, respectively, on the newly developed Task and Ego Orientation Scale Questionnaire (Duda, 1992). It is certainly a worthwhile venture to ascertain the relationships between the various subscales of sport motivational orientation inventories, in an attempt to reveal more clearly how individuals conceive of achievement motivation in sport and to arrive at a common language for both theory development and practical applications.

Toward an Integrated Model of Motivational Orientations in Sport

In previous sections of this chapter, three major research approaches to the study of motivational orientations were reviewed. These approaches included participation and discontinuation motives, intrinsic and extrinsic motivational orientations, and achievement goal orientations. Within each of these approaches, nine theories were discussed relative to their unique and cojoint contributions to understanding sport motivation. Moreover, various terms have been used for similar or even synonomous constructs (e.g., *task-involved* and *learning goals; ego-involved* and *performance goals*). This variety of terms used to describe similar constructs may be a

source of unnecessary confusion to researchers interested in studying motivation in sport and physical activity contexts. Thus, it is time to try to introduce parsimony to our understanding of motivational orientations in sport by conceptualizing a model that integrates the various theoretical perspectives and provides a common or unifying language for similar constructs.

A proposed integrated model of sport motivation is depicted in Figure 4.1. It is initiated at the bottom with a consideration of the motivational orientation of the individual, then proceeds to mastery attempts and performance outcomes, responses by significant others, and the internalization of a reward system and a standard of goals. The predominant use of internal criteria for reinforcement (i.e., self-reward) and mastery goals versus dependence on external approval and goals defined by others influences the individual's perceptions of competence and control, positive and negative affective outcomes, and (ultimately) motivated behavior in the form of levels of persistence in the physical achievement domain. This "core" of the model accounts for the greatest amount of shared variance among the cognitive, affective, and behavioral constructs of the various theories discussed. Lurking in the shadows of this model are a variety of individual difference and contextual factors that are explicitly or implicitly contained within individual theories that help to explain motivational processes. A brief discussion of each of the model components will clarify its origin and provide a rationale for its inclusion.

The Core of the Integrated Model

In the introduction of this chapter, it was stated that motivation in sport has been studied in two ways: as an individual difference factor and as an outcome variable. Although the focus of this chapter has been on how individuals who differ in motivational orientation vary in self-perceptions and participation behaviors, the point was made that ultimately we are interested in changes in motivation in the form of activity choices, effort, and persistence. The model presented here reflects the interconnectedness of the two views of motivation. Motivational orientation as an individual difference factor signifies the starting block of the model, and motivated behavior as an outcome variable represents the finish line. In-between lie the hurdles that individuals traverse in their pursuit of intrinsically motivated behavior and high levels of sport persistence.

Motivational Orientation

In our integrated model, we have adopted the terminology of intrinsic or mastery orientations

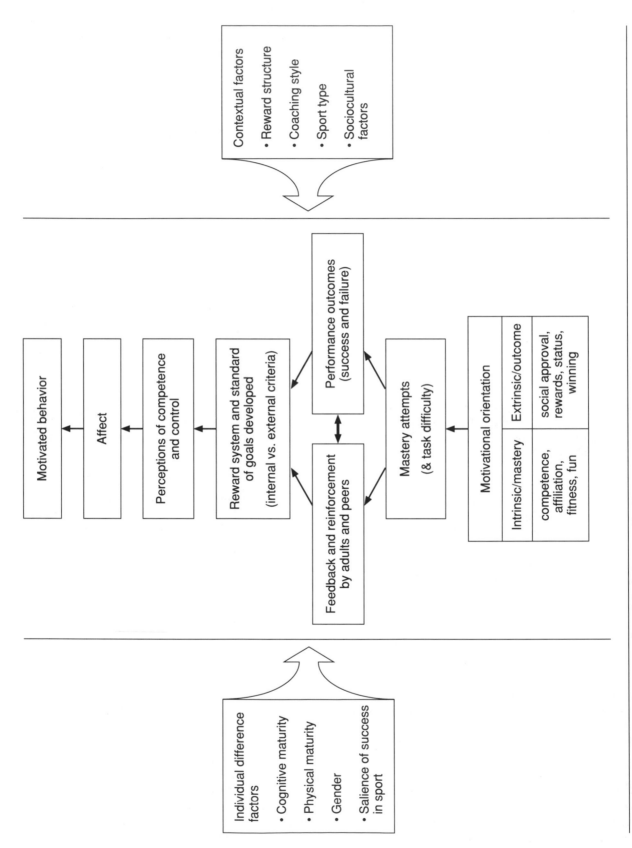

Figure 4.1   A proposed integrated model of sport motivation.

versus extrinsic or outcome orientations to describe individuals' characteristic outlook in relation to their involvement in physical activity. We propose that the terms *intrinsic* and *mastery* imply an emphasis on the *process* of participation, such as reasons related to developing competence (e.g., improve skills), affiliation (e.g., social aspects), fitness (e.g., get stronger, stay in shape), and the sheer fun of participating in sport. Conversely, the terms *extrinsic* and *outcome* imply an emphasis on the *product* of participation, such as reasons related to winning, gaining social status or recognition, receiving rewards, and seeking social approval. Thus, we have classified the major categories identified in the participation motivation literature under the umbrella terms of *intrinsic/mastery* and *extrinsic/outcome* and consolidated the numerous terms used for these constructs in the achievement motivation literature.

Mastery Attempts (Plus Task Difficulty)

According to all the theories reviewed in this chapter, an individual's mastery- or outcome-oriented motivational stance should dictate his or her desire to demonstrate ability through engagement in mastery attempts. Individuals who reflect a mastery orientation tend to choose optimally challenging activities, ones that are at the "cutting edge" of their capabilities. These challenges are difficult but realistic, and these individuals will exert maximal effort and persistence to attain success at these activities. Individuals identified as more outcome-oriented in their motivation may choose very easy or very difficult tasks in order to maximize the demonstration of high ability or avoid demonstrating low ability. To choose an optimally challenging activity might increase the risk of demonstrating low ability.

Performance Outcomes

In sport, objective performance outcomes have traditionally been defined in terms of winning and losing. However, the motivational orientation theories have all highlighted the importance of subjective performance outcomes, which are reflected by the individual's perceptions of success and failure. The individual who is mastery-oriented, for example, is likely to focus on whether he or she showed performance improvements in relation to previous standards of athletic performance. Thus, the objective outcome of winning or losing may not be as meaningful to personal definitions of success and failure as the individual level of performance demonstrated in particular achievement situations. The outcome-motivated individual, in contrast, is likely to define success and failure based on objective competitive outcomes, especially as they relate to the performance of others. In this case, winning comes to signify high ability, and losing low ability; and this conceptualization has implications for subsequent components in the model.

Feedback and Reinforcement by Adults and Peers

The role played by significant others in the psychological development of children and adolescents is given special prominence in most of the motivational orientation theories. The quantity and, more importantly, the quality of the feedback and reinforcement given by significant others will have salient consequences for cognitions, affective outcomes, and behavioral variations with regard to sport persistence. The quality of communication behaviors may refer to modeling behaviors (approval or disapproval of mastery attempts and/or outcomes) on the part of parents, coaches, and peers; praise in response to desirable behaviors and mistake-contingent criticism; and the type of attributions made for successful performance (correct skill performance or winning) and unsuccessful performance (failure to achieve a personal goal or losing). The salience with which certain socializing agents are regarded at various developmental levels is an important consideration as well. While parents seem to play a central role in early and middle childhood, peers become increasingly more important in the later childhood and adolescent years.

Development of a Reward System and a Standard of Goals

As a product of intrinsic/extrinsic motivational orientation and the sources of information provided by performance outcomes and significant others, individuals internalize either a self-reward system and a set of mastery goals or an external reward system and dependence upon externally defined goals. The mastery-oriented person who seeks optimal challenges, uses self-improvement to define success, and is reinforced by significant others for independent mastery attempts is hypothesized to develop a reward system and standard of goals based on internal criteria. The outcome-oriented person, in contrast, who seeks less than optimal challenges, defines success in terms of performance relative to others, and is reinforced by significant others primarily for performance outcome and develops a reward system and goals based on external criteria. The development at this stage, then, is linked to the sources of information available in the sport environment and the preferences individuals show with regard to judging their physical ability.

Perceptions of Competence and Control

Perceived competence or ability is a central construct in all the motivational theories discussed in this chapter. The degree to which an individual feels that he or she is capable of succeeding at a task is a powerful predictor of performance and participation behavior. Perceived competence, of all the constructs in the model, has received the most support through empirical research testing cognitive evaluation, competence motivation, and achievement motivation theories. The construct *perceptions of control* refers to the degree to which individuals feel that they (internal) or others (external) are responsible for success or failure in certain achievement contexts. Within a cognitive evaluation theory framework, this construct is called *perceived locus of causality* or *self-determination*. In achievement motivation theories, causal attributions for success and failure are reflective of this construct, and competence motivation theory uses the term *perceptions of performance control* (or *locus of control*).

Perceptions of both competence and control are shaped as a result of one's history of successes and failures, as well as by the characteristic feedback and reinforcement from significant others. Individuals who primarily employ internal criteria as informational sources about competence and who adopt mastery goals will have high perceptions of competence and internal control, while those who utilize external criteria to judge their physical ability and who develop externally defined goals will have low perceptions of competence and an external perceived locus of control.

Affect

Most contemporary theories of motivation include affect or emotion as a salient influence of motivated behavior and performance. Positive affect in the form of enjoyment, happiness, pride, excitement, and pleasure are posited to maintain and enhance motivation and future mastery attempts, whereas negative affect in the form of anxiety, embarrassment, shame, sadness, and disappointment would appear to attenuate future participation motivation. Intrinsic- or mastery-oriented individuals are more likely to experience positive affect in their participation based on their emphasis on the process or learning of sport skills, whereas extrinsic- or outcome-oriented individuals are likely to experience positive affect only under conditions of winning. These individuals are also prone to higher anxiety in achievement situations, which may result in performance decrements and lowered motivation. This construct has perhaps received the least attention in the sport psychology literature but holds unlimited potential as a possible mediator of the self-perceptions–motivation link.

Motivated Behavior

Ultimately, the goal of positive psychological development is the demonstration of persistence or adherence behavior in sport. The topic of motivation in sport necessarily focuses on how to maximize participation rates through an emphasis on intrinsic motives, mastery goals, and enjoyment through active involvement. The last component in the model signifies the individual who chooses to exert maximal effort and persistence in sport versus the one who chooses to discontinue his or her participation. The mastery-oriented individual who finds joy and feels successful in achieving personal goals is likely to persist in sport. The outcome-oriented individual who defines success only in terms of others will persist as long as he or she is "successful" (i.e., wins) and maintains a high perception of ability. The outcome-oriented individual who falls short in comparison to others and experiences decreased perceived ability is hypothesized to eventually drop out from sport activities.

Individual Difference Factors

In addition to the central constructs that comprise the integrated motivation model, several of the motivational orientation theories identify or imply certain individual difference factors which mediate the relationships in the model. First, many of the theories discussed in this chapter are developmentally oriented, with cognitive maturity a major consideration in the ability to analyze behavioral outcomes. How individuals assign attributions of ability and effort to success and failure experiences, the salience with which adults and peers are regarded as information sources to judge ability, and the preference for internal and external criteria to evaluate physical competence are all examples of cognitive-developmental influences on the motivational orientation process.

An individual difference factor particularly relevant to the physical achievement area is physical maturity. Although the motivational theories do not explicitly address physical maturity, this is not surprising because all the theories evolved primarily as a means of explaining academic achievement behavior. Thus, while cognitive maturity is a natural and necessary concern for school achievement, physical maturity plays a prime role in athletic achievement endeavors. For example, Malina (1988) reported that early-maturing boys and late-maturing girls are more likely to experience sport success. Early success is then likely to be strongly related to sport persistence. Other considerations, such as parental beliefs about, and expectations of, performance, and degree of peer acceptance and support for the athletic role are likely to influence this relationship. The factor of physical maturity and how it affects the sport motivation process is a topic desperately in need of attention in future research.

Gender has been found to mediate the relationships among the constructs in the model to various degrees. For example, research has consistently shown that males are more outcome-oriented than females, whereas females are more mastery-oriented in their motivation. Competition appears to affect females' intrinsic motivation negatively while increasing that of males. Minimal or no gender differences have been found to date with regard to the sources of information used to judge physical ability, predictors of affective outcomes such as enjoyment and anxiety, and the relationship between accuracy of perceived competence and other achievement-related characteristics. Nevertheless, continued research is necessary to identify when and how gender may affect these processes.

The salience of being successful in the physical domain is a construct that has been rarely considered. Harter (1985) strongly suggests that perceived competence should be examined in combination with how much importance individuals attach to being successful in a particular achievement domain. She hypothesizes that individuals who have low perceived competence in the physical domain but who do not consider athletic excellence salient to a definition of their overall self-worth will not show dysfunctional achievement behaviors. However, achievement domains for which an individual assigns central importance will result in that person's showing significant changes in self-perceptions and persistence behaviors as a consequence of successful or unsuccessful performances.

In sum, a number of intrapersonal factors such as cognitive maturity, physical maturity, gender, and salience of achievement areas may affect the pathways in the motivational model. Future research is needed to delineate how the links among behavioral tendencies, self-perceptions, and motivated behavior are affected by variations in these factors.

Contextual Factors

Similar to the influence of individual differences, social contextual factors also have the potential for mediating relationships in the motivational model. Variables such as reward structures, coaching styles, type of sport, and sociocultural influences are just some of these factors identified by the theories discussed in this chapter. Both cognitive evaluation theory and Ames's approach to achievement motivation identify reward structures as potential mediators of the motivational orientation–self-perceptions–motivated behavior link. For example, Ames hypothesized that competitive, cooperative, and individualistic structures were all likely to invoke particular goal orientations. Moreover, direct (performance against an opponent) and indirect (performance against a standard) competitive structures are expected to invoke different motivational orientations and, consequently, offer implications for sport persistence or withdrawal.

A second contextual factor that likely influences the motivational orientation model is coaching orientation or style; that is, the degree to which coaches primarily implement a controlling style (e.g., autocratic) or an informational style (e.g., frequent instructions, positive feedback) can influence self-perceptions and motivated behavior. Additionally, the motivational orientation of the individual should interact with preferred coaching style; that is, an intrinsically oriented person would be more compatible with a coach who provides information on how to improve, reinforces mastery attempts, and incorporates opportunities for shared decision making. In contrast, the extrinsically oriented individual should prefer a coaching style that is more autocratic in nature, where compliance with the coach's orders is expected and reinforced and competitive outcome is the salient definition of successful performance. Preliminary evidence for a relationship between motivational orientation and coaching preference was found in a study by Horn and Glenn (1988). They found that athletes with an external perception of control exhibited a greater preference for autocratic coaches, whereas athletes with an internal locus of control preferred coaching styles characterized by high frequencies of training and instruction behavior, as well as positive feedback contingent to performance successes and errors.

Some sport type differences in participation motivation and attrition have been found. To date, these have not been tied to a particular motivational theory per se, but one might expect that inherent characteristics about particular sports would influence the process described in the model. For example, elite versus competitive versus recreational sport, team versus individual sports, contact versus noncontact sports, and co-acting versus interdependent sports, to name a few, would appear to emphasize different motivational orientations and the adoption of certain reinforcement systems and goals. Research of this type is nonexistent but would be an interesting addition to the literature in this area.

Finally, sociocultural factors such as race, ethnicity, and social class impinge on the motivation model. This is an area desperately in need of further research. A handful of studies examining participation and discontinuation motives have been conducted in other cultures. Additionally, Duda's (1981, 1985, 1986a, 1986b) research comparing achievement goals of Anglo, black, and Hispanic adolescents represents the only work to cross ethnicity boundaries. Given that all the motivational orientation theories advocate that individual difference *and* situational factors influence the various constructs related to motivational orientation (e.g., perceived competence), we must broaden our selective sampling of white, middle-to-upper-class, well-educated participants and explore how achievement behavior distinguishes individuals of varying ethnicity, race, and social class categories.

The model of motivational orientation in sport proposed in this section is intended to pull together the common themes of the various theories, incorporate findings from the empirical research, and initiate a process of thoughtful considerations about the factors affecting sport motivation. It is our hope that future researchers will use the opportunity to test the various facets of the model in order to better understand theoretical notions as well as practical applications of the model.

Conclusion

Motivational orientation in sport is a multidimensional construct that can be approached from a variety of theoretical approaches. It was the intent of this chapter to provide an extensive review of each of these theoretical approaches and empirical research to date, to identify some concerns with this research or possible gaps that exist in the knowledge base, and to provide suggestions for future research in the physical achievement domain. Moreover, we concluded that the motivation theories that abound share commonalities with regard to the underlying processes describing and explaining the effect of motivational orientation on self-perceptions and sport persistence. Thus, an integrated model of motivation in sport was proposed in an attempt to consolidate these shared ideas and bring parsimony to an understanding of key relationships.

One of the major goals of sport psychology is to determine what factors maximize participation and performance in the physical domain. Thus, our research pursuits should focus on identifying factors that maximize the probability that individuals will sustain their active involvement across the life span. In doing so, individuals will be more likely to obtain the physical, psychological, and social benefits that sport participation can offer. It appears that a critical element affecting whether individuals persist or discontinue is their motivational orientation. An intrinsic- or mastery-oriented individual embraces optimal challenges in which he or she can learn and improve skills and adopt a self-reward system and a standard of mastery goals. This results in enhanced perceptions of competence and internal control, positive affect, and the probability that the individual will continue to choose sport activities and will approach them with appropriate effort and maximal persistence. The extrinsic- or outcome-oriented individual, in contrast, selects less-than-optimal challenges and focuses on the outcome (winning) as a means of judging personal capabilities. This individual may come to depend primarily upon external forms of information, such as adult evaluation, to judge physical ability; and this results in the development of a reward system that depends on external criteria and the adoption of outcome goals. Perceptions of competence may be attenuated, and perceptions of external control and feelings of anxiety in mastery situations nurtured. The result may be decrements in persistence behavior and perhaps dropping out altogether from physical activity.

Scholars of sport psychology and practitioners who face challenges related to program adherence and sport persistence must understand the underlying processes that explain motivation in physical achievement settings. A better conceptualization of these processes will lead to continued research that both contributes to theory development and asks questions of practical significance. It is our hope that the theoretical and empirical issues that were presented in this chapter will stimulate researchers and educators to pursue these objectives with a mastery orientation and positive affect.

References

Alderman, R.B. (1978). Strategies for motivating young athletes. In W.F. Straub (Ed.), *Sport psychology: An analysis of athlete behavior* (pp. 136-148). Ithaca, NY: Mouvement.

Alderman, R.B., & Wood, N.L. (1976). An analysis of incentive motivation in young Canadian athletes. *Canadian Journal of Applied Sport Sciences, 1,* 169-176.

Ames, C. (1978). Children's achievement attributions and self-reinforcement: Effects of self-concept and competitive reward structure. *Journal of Educational Psychology, 70,* 345-355.

Ames, C. (1981). Competitive versus cooperative reward structures: The influence of individual and group performance factors on achievement attributions and affect. *American Educational Research Journal, 18,* 273-287.

Ames, C. (1984). Competitive, cooperative, and individualistic goal structures: A motivational analysis. In R. Ames & C. Ames (Eds.), *Research on motivation in education: Student motivation* (pp. 177-207). New York: Academic.

Ames, C., & Ames, R. (1981). Competitive versus individualistic goal structures: The salience of past performance information for causal attributions and affect. *Journal of Educational Psychology, 73,* 411-418.

Ames, C., Ames, R., & Felker, D. (1977). Effects of competitive reward structure and valence of outcome on children's achievement attributions. *Journal of Educational Psychology, 69,* 1-8.

Ames, C., & Archer, J. (1988). Achievement goals in the classroom: Students' learning strategies and motivation processes. *Journal of Educational Psychology, 80,* 260-267.

Ames, C., & Felker, D. (1979). An examination of children's attributions and achievement-related evaluations in competitive, cooperative, and individualistic reward structures. *Journal of Educational Psychology, 71,* 413-420.

Atkinson, J.W. (1977). Motivation for achievement. In T. Blass (Ed.), *Personality variables in social behavior.* Hillsdale, NJ: Erlbaum.

Black, S.J., & Weiss, M.R. (1991). *The relationship among perceived coaching behaviors, perceptions of ability, and motivation in competitive age-group swimmers.* Manuscript submitted for publication.

Brodkin, P., & Weiss, M.R. (1990). Developmental differences in motivation for participation in competitive swimming. *Journal of Sport and Exercise Psychology, 12,* 248-263.

Brown, B.A. (1985). Factors influencing the process of withdrawal by female adolescents from the role of competitive age group swimmer. *Sociology of Sport Journal, 2,* 111-129.

Brown, B.A., Frankel, B.G., & Fennell, M.P. (1989). Hugs or shrugs: Parental and peer influence on continuity of involvement in sport by female adolescents. *Sex Roles, 20,* 397-412.

Brustad, R.J. (1988). Affective outcomes in competitive youth sport: The influence of intrapersonal and socialization factors. *Journal of Sport and Exercise Psychology, 10,* 307-321.

Brustad, R.J. (1992). Integrating socialization influences into the study of children's motivation in sport. *Journal of Sport and Exercise Psychology, 14,* 59-77.

Brustad, R.J., & Weiss, M.R. (1987). Competence perceptions and sources of worry in high, medium, and low competitive trait anxious young athletes. *Journal of Sport Psychology, 9,* 97-105.

Burton, D. (1989). Winning isn't everything: Examining the impact of performance goals on collegiate swimmers' cognitions and performance. *The Sport Psychologist, 3,* 105-132.

Burton, D., & Martens, R. (1986). Pinned by their own goals: An exploratory investigation into why kids drop out of wrestling. *Journal of Sport Psychology, 8,* 183-197.

Butler, R. (1987). Task-involving and ego-involving properties of evaluation: Effects of different feedback conditions on motivational perceptions, interest, and performance. *Journal of Educational Psychology, 79,* 474-482.

Butler, R. (1988). Enhancing and undermining intrinsic motivation: The effects of task-involving and ego-involving evaluation on interest and performance. *British Journal of Educational Psychology, 58,* 1-14.

Butler, R. (1989). Interest in the task and interest in peers' work in competitive and noncompetitive conditions: A developmental study. *Child Development, 60,* 562-570.

Calder, B.J., & Staw, B.M. (1975). Self-perception of intrinsic and extrinsic motivation. *Journal of Personality and Social Psychology, 31,* 599-605.

Carron, A.V. (1984). *Motivation: Implications for coaching and teaching.* London, ON: Sports Dynamics.

Carver, C., & Scheier, M. (1982). Outcome expectancy, locus of attribution for expectancy, and self-directed attention as determinants of evaluations and performance. *Journal of Experimental and Social Psychology, 18,* 184-200.

Connell, J.P. (1985). A new multidimensional measure of children's perceptions of control. *Child Development, 56,* 1018-1041.

Deci, E.L. (1975). *Intrinsic motivation.* New York: Plenum.

Deci, E.L., Betley, G., Kahle, J., Abrams, L., & Porac, J. (1981). When trying to win: Competition and intrinsic motivation. *Personality and Social Psychology Bulletin, 7,* 79-83.

Deci, E.L., & Ryan, R.M. (1985). *Intrinsic motivation and self-determination in human behavior.* New York: Plenum.

Deci, E.L., Schwartz, A.J., Sheinman, L., & Ryan, R.M. (1981). An instrument to assess adults' orientations toward control versus autonomy with children: Reflections on intrinsic motivation and perceived competence. *Journal of Educational Psychology, 73,* 642-650.

Diener, C.I., & Dweck, C.S. (1978). An analysis of learned helplessness: Continuous changes in performance, strategy, and achievement cognitions following failure. *Journal of Personality and Social Psychology, 36,* 451-462.

Diener, C.I., & Dweck, C.S. (1980). An analysis of learned helplessness: II. The processing of success. *Journal of Personality and Social Psychology, 39,* 940-952.

Dishman, R.K. (1986). Exercise compliance: A new view for public health. *Physician and Sportsmedicine, 14,* 127-145.

Duda, J.L. (1981). *A cross-cultural analysis of achievement motivation in sport and the classroom.* Unpublished doctoral dissertation, University of Illinois at Urbana-Champaign.

Duda, J.L. (1985). Goals and achievement orientations of Anglo– and Mexican–American adolescents in sport and the classroom. *International Journal of Intercultural Relations, 9,* 131-155.

Duda, J.L. (1986a). A cross-cultural analysis of achievement motivation in sport and the classroom. In L. VanderVelden & J. Humphrey (Eds.), *Current selected research in the psychology and sociology of sport* (pp. 117-131). New York: AMS.

Duda, J.L. (1986b). Perceptions of sport success and failure among white, black, and Hispanic adolescents. In J. Watkins, T. Reilly, & L. Burwitz (Eds.), *Sport Science* (pp. 214-222). London: E. & F.N. Spon.

Duda, J.L. (1987). Toward a developmental theory of motivation in sport. *Journal of Sport Psychology, 9,* 130-145.

Duda, J.L. (1988a). The relationship between goal perspectives and persistence and intensity among recreational sport participants. *Leisure Sciences, 10*, 95-106.

Duda, J.L. (1988b). Goal perspectives, participation and persistence in sport. *International Journal of Sport Psychology, 19*, 117-130.

Duda, J.L. (1989a). Goal perspectives and behavior in sport and exercise settings. In C. Ames & M. Maehr (Eds.), *Advances in motivation and achievement* (Vol. 4, pp. 81-115). Greenwich, CT: JAI.

Duda, J.L. (1989b). Relationship between task and ego orientation and the perceived purpose of sport among high school athletes. *Journal of Sport and Exercise Psychology, 11*, 318-335.

Duda, J.L. (1992). Motivation in sport settings: A goal perspective approach. In G.C. Roberts (Ed.), *Motivation in sport and exercise*, (pp. 57-91). Champaign, IL: Human Kinetics.

Dweck, C.S. (1986). Motivational processes affecting learning. *American Psychologist, 41*, 1040-1048.

Dweck, C.S., & Bempechat, J. (1988). Children's theories of intelligence: Consequences for learning. In E.M. Hetherington & R.D. Parke (Eds.), *Contemporary readings in child psychology* (3rd ed., pp. 608-621). New York: McGraw-Hill.

Dweck, C.S., & Elliott, E.S. (1983). Achievement motivation. In E.M. Hetherington (Ed.), *Socialization, personality, and social development* (pp. 643-691). New York: Wiley.

Elliott, E., & Dweck, C.S. (1988). Goals: An approach to motivation and achievement. *Journal of Personality and Social Psychology, 54*, 5-12.

Ewing, M.E. (1981). *Achievement orientations and sport behavior of males and females*. Unpublished doctoral dissertation, University of Illinois at Urbana-Champaign.

Feltz, D.L., Gould, D., Horn, T., & Weiss, M. (1982, May). *Perceived competence among youth swimmers and dropouts*. Paper presented at the meeting of the North American Society for the Psychology of Sport and Physical Activity, College Park, MD.

Feltz, D.L., & Petlichkoff, L.M. (1983). Perceived competence among interscholastic sport participants and dropouts. *Canadian Journal of Applied Sport Sciences, 8*, 231-235.

Frazer, K.M., & Weiss, M.R. (1991). *Initial, continued, and sustained motivation in adolescent female athletes: A season-long investigation*. Unpublished manuscript, University of Oregon, Eugene.

Fry, D.A.P., McClements, J.D., & Sefton, J.M. (1981). *A report on participation in the Saskatoon Hockey Association*. Saskatoon, SK: SASK Sport.

Giannini, J.M., Weinberg, R.S., & Jackson, A.J. (1988). The effects of mastery, competitive, and cooperative goals on the performance of simple and complex basketball skills. *Journal of Sport and Exercise Psychology, 10*, 408-417.

Gill, D.L. (1986a). *Psychological dynamics of sport*. Champaign, IL: Human Kinetics.

Gill, D.L. (1986b). Competitiveness among females and males in physical activity classes. *Sex Roles, 15*, 233-247.

Gill, D.L. (1988). Gender differences in competitive orientation and sport participation. *International Journal of Sport Psychology, 19*, 145-159.

Gill, D.L., & Deeter, T.E. (1988). Development of the Sport Orientation Questionnaire. *Research Quarterly for Exercise and Sport, 59*, 191-202.

Gill, D.L., & Dzewaltowski, D.A. (1988). Competitive orientations among intercollegiate athletes: Is winning the only thing? *Sport Psychologist, 2*, 212-221.

Gill, D.L., Dzewaltowski, D.A., & Deeter, T.E. (1988). The relationship of competitiveness and achievement orientation to participation in sport and nonsport activities. *Journal of Sport and Exercise Psychology, 10*, 139-150.

Gill, D.L., Gross, J.B., & Huddleston, S. (1983). Participation motivation in youth sports. *International Journal of Sport Psychology, 14*, 1-14.

Glenn, S.D., & Horn, T.S. (1991). *Psychological predictors of leadership behavior in female soccer athletes*. Manuscript submitted for publication.

Gould, D. (1982). Sport psychology in the 1980's: Status, direction and challenge in youth sports research. *Journal of Sport Psychology, 4*, 203-218.

Gould, D. (1986). Goal setting for peak performance. In J.M. Williams (Ed.), *Applied sport psychology: Personal growth to peak performance* (pp. 133-148). Palo Alto, CA: Mayfield.

Gould, D. (1988). Your role as a coach. In V. Seefeldt (Ed.), *Handbook for youth sports coaches* (pp. 17-32). Reston, VA: American Alliance for Health, Physical Education, Recreation and Dance.

Gould, D., Feltz, D., Horn, T., & Weiss, M. (1982). Reasons for attrition in competitive youth swimming. *Journal of Sport Behavior, 5*, 155-165.

Gould, D., Feltz, D., & Weiss, M. (1985). Motives for participating in competitive youth swimming. *International Journal of Sport Psychology, 6*, 126-140.

Gould, D., & Petlichkoff, L. (1988). Participation motivation and attrition in young athletes. In F. Smoll, R. Magill, & M. Ash (Eds.), *Children in sport* (3rd ed., pp. 161-178). Champaign, IL: Human Kinetics.

Greene, D., & Lepper, M.R. (1974). Effects of extrinsic rewards on children's subsequent intrinsic interest. *Child Development, 45*, 1141-1145.

Halliwell, W.R. (1978). The effect of cognitive development on children's perceptions of intrinsically and extrinsically motivated behavior. In D.M. Landers & R.W. Christina (Eds.), *Psychology of motor behavior and sport—1977* (pp. 403-419). Champaign, IL: Human Kinetics.

Harter, S. (1978). Effectance motivation reconsidered. *Human Development, 21*, 34-64.

Harter, S. (1981a). A model of intrinsic mastery motivation in children: Individual differences and developmental change. In W.A. Collins (Ed.), *Minnesota Symposium on Child Psychology* (Vol. 14, pp. 215-255). Hillsdale, NJ: Erlbaum.

Harter, S. (1981b). The development of competence motivation in the mastery of cognitive and physical skills: Is there still a place for joy? In G.C. Roberts & D.M. Landers (Eds.), *Psychology of motor behavior and sport—1980* (pp. 3-29). Champaign, IL: Human Kinetics.

Harter, S. (1981c). A new self-report scale of intrinsic versus extrinsic orientation in the classroom: Motivational and informational components. *Developmental Psychology 17*, 300-312.

Harter, S. (1982). The perceived competence scale for children. *Child Development, 53*, 87-97.

Harter, S. (1985). *Manual for the self-perception profile for children*. Denver: University of Denver.

Harter, S. (1986). *Manual for the self-perception profile for adolescents*. Denver: University of Denver.

Harter, S., & Pike, R. (1983). *The pictorial scale of perceived competence and social acceptance for young children*. Denver: University of Denver.

Heitmann, H.M. (1985). Motives of older adults for participating in physical activity programs. In B.D. McPherson (Ed.), *Sports and aging* (pp. 199-204). Champaign, IL: Human Kinetics.

Helmreich, R.L., Beane, W.E., Lucker, G.W., & Spence, J.T. (1978). Achievement motivation and scientific attainment. *Personality and Social Psychology Bulletin, 4*, 222-226.

Helmreich, R.L., & Spence, J.T. (1978). The Work and Family Orientation Questionnaire: An objective instrument to assess components of achievement motivation and attitudes toward family and career. *Journal Supplement Abstract Service Catalog of Selected Documents in Psychology, 8*, 35.

Holland, A., & Andre, T. (1987). Participation in extracurricular activities in secondary school: What is known, what needs to be known? *Review of Educational Research, 57*, 437-466.

Horn, T.S. (1984a). Expectancy effects in the interscholastic setting: Methodological considerations. *Journal of Sport Psychology, 6*, 60-76.

Horn, T.S. (1984b). The expectancy process: Causes and consequences. In W.F. Straub & J.M. Williams (Eds.), *Cognitive sport psychology* (pp. 199-211). Lansing, NY: Sport Science Associates.

Horn, T.S. (1985). Coaches' feedback and changes in children's perceptions of their physical competence. *Journal of Educational Psychology, 77*, 174-186.

Horn, T.S. (1986). The self-fulfilling prophecy theory: When coaches' expectations become reality. In J.M. Williams (Ed.), *Applied sport psychology: Personal growth to peak performance* (pp. 59-73). Palo Alto, CA: Mayfield.

Horn, T.S. (1987). The influence of teacher–coach behavior on the psychological development of children. In D. Gould & M.E. Weiss (Eds.), *Advances in pediatric sport sciences: Vol. 2. Behavioral issues* (pp. 121-142). Champaign, IL: Human Kinetics.

Horn, T.S., & Glenn, S. (1988, June). *The relationship between athletes' psychological characteristics and their preference for particular coaching behaviors.* Paper presented at the meeting of the North American Society for the Psychology of Sport and Physical Activity, Knoxville, TN.

Horn, T.S., & Hasbrook, C.A. (1986). Information components influencing children's perceptions of their physical competence. In M.R. Weiss & D. Gould (Eds.), *Sport for children and youths* (pp. 81-88). Champaign, IL: Human Kinetics.

Horn, T.S., & Hasbrook, C.A. (1987). Psychological characteristics and the criteria children use for self-evaluation. *Journal of Sport Psychology, 9*, 208-221.

Horn, T.S., & Weiss, M.R. (1991). A developmental analysis of children's self-ability judgements in the physical domain. *Pediatric Exercise Science, 3*, 310-326.

Iso-Ahola, S.E. (1980). *The social psychology of leisure and recreation.* Dubuque, IA: William C. Brown.

Klint, K.A. (1985). *Participation motives and self-perceptions of current and former athletes in youth gymnastics.* Unpublished master's thesis, University of Oregon, Eugene.

Klint, K.A. (1988). *An analysis of the positivistic and naturalistic paradigms for inquiry: Implications for the field of sport psychology.* Unpublished doctoral dissertation, University of Oregon, Eugene.

Klint, K.A., & Weiss, M.R. (1986). Dropping in and dropping out: Participation motives of current and former youth gymnasts. *Canadian Journal of Applied Sport Sciences, 11*, 106-114.

Klint, K.A., & Weiss, M.R. (1987). Perceived competence and motives for participating in youth sports: A test of Harter's competence motivation theory. *Journal of Sport Psychology, 9*, 55-65.

Landers, D.M. (1983). Whatever happened to theory testing in sport psychology? *Journal of Sport Psychology, 5*, 135-151.

Lepper, M.R., & Greene, D. (1975). Turning play into work: Effects of adult surveillance and extrinsic rewards on children's intrinsic motivation. *Journal of Personality and Social Psychology, 31*, 479-486.

Lepper, M.R., Greene, D., & Nisbett, R.E. (1973). Undermining children's intrinsic interest with extrinsic rewards: A test of the "overjustification" hypothesis. *Journal of Personality and Social Psychology, 28*, 129-137.

Lewko, J.H., & Greendorfer, S.L. (1988). Family influences in sport socialization of children and adolescents. In F. Smoll, R. Magill, & M. Ash (Eds.), *Children in sport* (3rd ed., pp. 287-300). Champaign, IL: Human Kinetics.

Longhurst, K., & Spink, K.S. (1987). Participation motivation of Australian children involved in organized sport. *Canadian Journal of Sport Sciences, 12*, 24-30.

Maehr, M.L., & Braskamp, L.A. (1986). *The motivation factor: A theory of personal investment.* Lexington, MA: D.C. Heath.

Maehr, M.L., & Nicholls, J.G. (1980). Culture and achievement motivation: A second look. In N. Warren (Ed.), *Studies in cross-cultural psychology* (Vol. 3, pp. 221-267). New York: Academic.

Malina, R.M. (1988). Growth and maturation of young athletes: Biological and social considerations. In F. Smoll, R. Magill, & M. Ash (Eds.), *Children in sport* (3rd ed., pp. 83-102). Champaign, IL: Human Kinetics.

Marsh, H.W., & Peart, N.D. (1988). Competitive and cooperative physical fitness training programs for girls: Effects on physical fitness and multidimensional self-concepts. *Journal of Sport and Exercise Psychology, 10*, 390-407.

Martens, R. (1987). *Coaches guide to sport psychology.* Champaign, IL: Human Kinetics.

McAuley, E., & Tammen, V.V. (1989). The effects of subjective and objective competitive outcomes on intrinsic motivation. *Journal of Sport and Exercise Psychology, 11*, 84-93.

McClelland, D.C. (1961). *The achieving society.* New York: Free Press.

Minton, B. (1979, April). *Dimensions of information underlying children's judgments of their competence.* Paper presented at the meeting of Society for Research in Child Development, San Francisco.

Neeman, J., & Harter, S. (1986). *Manual for the self-perception profile for college students.* Denver: University of Denver Press.

Nicholls, J.G. (1978). The development of the concepts of effort and ability, perceptions of own attainment, and the understanding that difficult tasks require more ability. *Child Development, 49*, 800-814.

Nicholls, J.G. (1984). Achievement motivation: conceptions of ability, subjective experience, task choice, and performance. *Psychological Review, 91*, 328-346.

Nicholls, J.G. (1989). *The competitive ethos and democratic education.* Cambridge, MA: Harvard University Press.

Nicholls, J.G., & Miller, A. (1983). The differentiation of the concepts of difficulty and ability. *Child Development, 54*, 951-959.

Orlick, T.D. (1973, January/February). Children's sport—A revolution is coming. *Canadian Association for Health, Physical Education, and Recreation Journal*, pp. 12-14.

Orlick, T.D. (1974, November/December). The athletic dropout: A high price for inefficiency. *Canadian Association for Health, Physical Education, and Recreation Journal*, pp. 21-27.

Orlick, T.D., & Mosher, R. (1978). Extrinsic rewards and participant motivation in a sport related task. *International Journal of Sport Psychology, 9*, 27-39.

Parsons, J.E., Adler, T.F., & Kaczala, C.M. (1982). Socialization of achievement attitudes and beliefs: Parental influences. *Child Development, 53*, 310-321.

Passer, M.W. (1988). Determinants and consequences of children's competitive stress. In F. Smoll, R. Magill, & M. Ash (Eds.), *Children in sport* (3rd ed., pp. 203-228). Champaign, IL: Human Kinetics.

Pemberton, C.L., Petlichkoff, L.M., & Ewing, M.E. (1986). *Psychometric properties of the Achievement Orientation Questionnaire.* Paper presented at the meeting of the

North American Society for the Psychology of Sport and Physical Activity, Scottsdale, AZ.

Petlichkoff, L.M. (1988). *Motivation for sport persistence: An empirical examination of underlying theoretical constructs*. Unpublished doctoral dissertation, University of Illinois at Urbana-Champaign.

Roberts, G.C. (1984). Achievement motivation in children's sport. In J. Nicholls (Ed.), *The development of achievement motivation* (pp. 251-282). Greenwich, CT: JAI.

Roberts, G.C., Kleiber, D.A., & Duda, J.L. (1981). An analysis of motivation in children's sport: The role of perceived competence in participation. *Journal of Sport Psychology, 3*, 206-216.

Robertson, I. (1981). *Children's perceived satisfactions and stresses in sport*. Paper presented at the Australian Conference on Health, Physical Education, and Recreation; Adelaide, Australia.

Robinson, T., & Carron, A.V. (1982). Personal and situational factors associated with dropping out versus maintaining participation in competitive sport. *Journal of Sport Psychology, 4*, 364-378.

Ryan, E.D. (1977). Attribution, intrinsic motivation, and athletics. In L.I. Gedvilas & M.E. Kneer (Eds.), *Proceedings of the National Association for Physical Education of College Men National Conference Association for Physical Education of College Women National Conference*. Chicago: University of Illinois at Chicago Circle.

Ryan, E.D. (1980). Attribution, intrinsic motivation, and athletics: A replication and extension. In C.H. Nadeau, W.R. Halliwell, K.M. Newell, & G.C. Roberts (Eds.), *Psychology of motor behavior and sport—1979* (pp. 19-26). Champaign, IL: Human Kinetics.

Ryan, R.M. (1982). Control and information in the intrapersonal sphere: An extension of cognitive evaluation theory. *Journal of Personality and Social Psychology 45*, 736-750.

Ryan, R.M., Vallerand, R.J., & Deci, E.L. (1984). Intrinsic motivation in sport: A cognitive evaluation theory interpretation. In W.F. Straub & J.M. Williams (Eds.), *Cognitive sport psychology* (pp. 231-242). Lansing, NY: Sport Science Associates.

Sapp, M., & Haubenstricker, J. (1978). *Motivation for joining and reasons for not continuing in youth sport programs in Michigan*. Paper presented at the meeting of the American Alliance for Health, Physical Education, Recreation, and Dance, Kansas City, MO.

Scanlan, T.K., & Lewthwaite, R. (1986). Social psychological aspects of competition for male youth sport participants: Part 4. Predictors of enjoyment. *Journal of Sport Psychology, 8*, 25-35.

Scanlan, T.K., Stein, G.L., & Ravizza, K. (1988). An in-depth study of former elite figure skaters: Part 2. Sources of enjoyment. *Journal of Sport and Exercise Psychology, 11*, 65-83.

Sherif, M., & Sherif, C.W. (1953). *Groups in harmony and tension*. New York: Harper & Row.

Smith, R.E. (1986). Toward a cognitive–affective model of athletic burnout. *Journal of Sport Psychology, 8*, 36-50.

Smith, R.E., Smoll, F.L., & Curtis, B. (1979). Coach effectiveness training: A cognitive–behavioral approach to enhancing relationship skills in youth sport coaches. *Journal of Sport Psychology, 1*, 59-75.

Spence, J.T., & Helmreich, R.L. (1983). Achievement-related motives and behaviors. In J.T. Spence (Ed.), *Achievement and achievement motives* (pp. 7-74). San Francisco: W.H. Freeman.

Thibaut, J.W., & Kelley, H.H. (1959). *The social psychology of groups*. New York: Wiley.

Thomas, J.R., & Tennant, L.K. (1978). Effects of rewards on children's motivation for an athletic task. In F.L. Smoll & R.E. Smith (Eds.), *Psychological perspectives in youth sports* (pp. 123-144). Washington, DC: Hemisphere.

Thompson, C.E., & Wankel, L.M. (1980). The effect of perceived activity choice upon frequency of exercise behavior. *Journal of Applied Social Psychology, 10*, 436-443.

Ulrich, B.D. (1987). Perceptions of physical competence, motor competence, and participation in organized sport: Their interrelationships in young children. *Research Quarterly for Exercise and Sport, 58*, 57-67.

Vallerand, R.J. (1983). The effect of differential amounts of positive verbal feedback on the intrinsic motivation of male hockey players. *Journal of Sport Psychology, 5*, 100-107.

Vallerand, R.J., Deci, E.L., & Ryan, R.M. (1987). Intrinsic motivation in sport. In K.B. Pandolf (Ed.), *Exercise and sport sciences reviews* (Vol. 15). New York: Macmillan.

Vallerand, R.J., Gauvin, L.I., & Halliwell, W.R. (1986a). Effects of zero-sum competition on children's intrinsic motivation and perceived competence. *Journal of Social Psychology, 126*, 465-472.

Vallerand, R.J., Gauvin, L.I., & Halliwell, W.R. (1986b). Negative effects of competition on children's intrinsic motivation. *Journal of Social Psychology, 126*, 649-657.

Vallerand, R.J., & Reid, G. (1984). On the causal effects of perceived competence on intrinsic motivation: A test of cognitive evaluation theory. *Journal of Sport Psychology, 6*, 94-102.

Vealey, R.S. (1986). Conceptualization of sport-confidence and competitive orientation: Preliminary investigation and instrument development. *Journal of Sport Psychology, 8*, 221-246.

Vealey, R.S., & Campbell, J.L. (1988). Achievement goals of adolescent figure skaters: Impact on self-confidence, anxiety, and performance. *Journal of Adolescent Research, 3*, 227-243.

Wankel, L.M., & Kreisel, S.J. (1985). Factors underlying enjoyment of youth sports: Sport and age group comparisons. *Journal of Sport Psychology, 7*, 52-64.

Wankel, L.M., & Sefton, J.M. (1989). A season-long investigation of fun in youth sports. *Journal of Sport and Exercise Psychology, 11*, 355-366.

Watkins, B., & Montgomery, A.B. (1989). Conceptions of athletic excellence among children and adolescents. *Child Development, 60*, 1362-1372.

Weinberg, R.S., & Jackson, A. (1979). Competition and extrinsic rewards: Effect on intrinsic motivation and attribution. *Research Quarterly, 50*, 494-502.

Weinberg, R.S., & Ragan, J. (1979). Effects of competition, success/failure, and sex on intrinsic motivation. *Research Quarterly, 50*, 503-510.

Weiner, B. (1985). An attributional theory of achievement motivation and emotion. *Psychological Review, 92*, 548-573.

Weingarten, G., Furst, D., Tenenbaum, G., & Schaefer, U. (1984). Motives of Israeli youth for participation in sport. In J.L. Callaghan (Ed.), *Proceedings of the International Symposium "Children to Champions,"* (pp. 145-153). Los Angeles: University of Southern California.

Weiss, M.R. (1987). Self-esteem and achievement in children's sport and physical activity. In D. Gould & M.R. Weiss (Eds.), *Advances in pediatric sport sciences: Vol. 2. Behavioral issues* (pp. 87-119). Champaign, IL: Human Kinetics.

Weiss, M.R., & Bredemeier, B.J. (1983). Developmental sport psychology: A theoretical perspective for studying children in sport. *Journal of Sport Psychology, 5*, 216-230.

Weiss, M.R., Bredemeier, B.J., & Brustad, R.J. (1987, June). *Competitive trait anxiety in children's sport: The relationship to perceived competence, perceived control, and motivational orientation*. Paper presented at the meeting of the North American Society for the Psychology of Sport and Physical Activity, Vancouver, BC.

Weiss, M.R., Bredemeier, B.J., & Shewchuk, R.M. (1985). An intrinsic/extrinsic motivation scale for the youth sport setting: A confirmatory factor analysis. *Journal of Sport Psychology, 7*, 75-91.

Weiss, M.R., Bredemeier, B.J., & Shewchuk, R.M. (1986). The dynamics of perceived competence, perceived control, and motivational orientation in youth sports. In M.R. Weiss & D. Gould (Eds.), *Sport for children and youths* (pp. 89-101). Champaign, IL: Human Kinetics.

Weiss, M.R., & Horn, T.S. (1990). The relation between children's accuracy estimates of their physical competence and achievement-related characteristics. *Research Quarterly for Exercise and Sport, 61*, 250-258.

Weiss, M.R., McAuley, E., Ebbeck, V., & Wiese, D.M. (1990). Self-esteem and causal attributions for children's physical and social competence in sport. *Journal of Sport and Exercise Psychology, 12*, 21-36.

Weiss, M.R., & Petlichkoff, L.M. (1989). Children's motivation for participation in and withdrawal from sport: Identifying the missing links. *Pediatric Exercise Science, 1*, 195-211.

Weiss, M.R., & Shewchuk, R.M. (1985, June). *The motivational orientation in sport scale: A replication and validation*. Paper presented at the meeting of the North American Society for the Psychology of Sport and Physical Activity, Gulfport, MS.

White, A., & Coakley, J. (1986). *Making decisions: The response of young people in the Medway towns to the "Ever thought about sport?" campaign*. London: Sports Council.

White, R. (1959). Motivation reconsidered: The concept of competence. *Psychological Review, 66*, 297-333.

Whitehead, J.R., & Corbin, C.B. (1991). Youth fitness testing: The effect of percentile-based evaluation feedback on intrinsic motivation. *Research Quarterly for Exercise and Sport, 62*, 225-231.

Chapter 5

Self-Referent Thought in Sport and Physical Activity

Edward McAuley
University of Illinois at Urbana-Champaign

In the course of the past 15 years, psychological research focusing on sport, exercise, and physical activity has adopted a largely cognitive orientation. Within this cognitive framework, a number of theoretical approaches have been embraced, but few have been as systematically applied as attribution theory and self-efficacy theory (Landers, 1983). Attribution theory is predominantly concerned with how individuals cognitively appraise the outcomes of achievement situations in terms of causality. Self-efficacy theory (Bandura, 1977, 1986) focuses on the mediational

role played by perceptions of personal agency in affecting diverse aspects of human functioning and behavior. Common to both theories, however, is their foundation in self-referent thought; that is, both theories assume the individual to be capable of exercising control over thought processes, motivation, and behavior (Bandura, 1986).

With few exceptions, these two cognitive theories of behavior have been examined orthogonally with researchers interested in understanding human behavior as it relates to sport, exercise, and physical activity focused *either* on

Note. The preparation of this chapter was facilitated by a grant from the National Institute on Aging (AG07907).

the impact of outcomes on the process of causal search (attribution theory) *or* on the influence of perceptions of personal capabilities on performance (self-efficacy theory). Very seldom has the approach been taken that a relationship exists between one's efficacy expectations and the causal ascriptions one makes for achievement outcomes or how, in turn, these latter cognitions shape future efficacy expectations. Bandura (1986), theorizing from a social cognitive perspective on human behavior, observes that in spite of the large body of attribution research, scant attention has been directed toward the effects of causal ascription on self-evaluation. Furthermore, Bandura suggests that percepts of personal efficacy help shape causal ascriptions for future behavior. For example, attributing a successful tennis performance to personal, stable, and controllable qualities leads to enhanced self-efficacy cognitions for future tennis matches. These positive perceptions, in turn, tend to facilitate the continued use of stable self-related attributions in future success situations. Thus, self-referent thought plays a very important role in human behavior and functioning.

The first objective of this chapter is to present a general overview of attribution theory with respect to the sport and physical activity literatures. In so doing, a conceptual framework will be presented first. This framework will be employed to discuss some sport and physical activity applications, methodological considerations, and future research directions. The second objective of this chapter is to consider causal attributions and self-efficacy cognitions as *process* variables. In so doing, the notion that these cognitions reciprocally determine each other will be pursued. A chapter summary will conclude the discussion of self-referent thought in sport and physical activity.

Attribution Theory in Sport and Physical Activity

Although other models such as Kelly's (1973) analysis of variance model and Jones and Davis's (1965) correspondent inference theory exist, empirical investigation of attribution theory with respect to achievement in sport has been predominantly driven by Bernard Weiner's (1972, 1979, 1985) attributional model of achievement motivation and emotion. Weiner's model—in particular his recent reformulation (Weiner, 1985, 1986)—represents an elegant and sophisticated attempt to explain the individual's interpretation of achievement outcomes and to understand how that interpretation may influence his or her future behavior.

Conceptual Framework

The foundation of Weiner's model is built upon the premise that following an achievement outcome, individuals will engage in causal search to determine why a particular outcome occurred. For example, missing a crucial free-throw in the waning moments of an important basketball game might be attributed to "freshman nerves" or to being distracted by unruly, placard-waving, abuse-chanting fans of the opposing team. The reasons employed to explain and understand achievement outcomes are commonly referred to as causal attributions. In his original attributional model, Weiner and his colleagues (Weiner et al., 1972) identified *ability, effort, task difficulty*, and *luck* as the four causal attributions most commonly ascribed to achievement outcomes. However, subsequent research and theory development has clearly demonstrated that in addition to the four "classic elements" (which Weiner, 1983, takes care to point out need not be the only ones) there are numerous other ascriptions in which causality might be inferred. This is particularly true in the case of such domains as sport and physical activity (see Bukowski & Moore, 1982; Roberts & Pascuzzi, 1979).

Central to Weiner's (1985) reformulated theoretical model is the supposition that causal attributions by and of themselves are largely unimportant. Weiner (1985, 1986) maintains that although causal attributions may directly influence future behaviors, it makes more sense to try and identify common properties or dimensions that underlie all causal ascriptions. Empirical research has consistently reported the existence of at least three causal dimensions. The three most frequently identified include the *locus of causality, stability*, and *controllability* dimensions (e.g., Meyer & Koelbl, 1982; Passer, 1977). The locus of causality refers to whether the cause of the performance or achievement outcome is perceived to reside within, or is external to, the attributer; the stability dimension concerns the relative variability of the cause over time; and the control dimension determines whether the cause is deemed to be under the control of the attributer or other people. Let us consider how a causal attribution for a performance might be translated into dimensional space. Consider, for example, the novice golfer who, on his opening drive, unceremoniously hooks the ball far beyond the fairway and into the rough. Causality for such an event might well be ascribed to a biomechanically flawed swing, a typical problem with beginning (and some seasoned) golfers. From a dimensional perspective, the aberrant drive might be ascribed to internal causes, (something about the golfer), unstable causes (it can, with practice, be improved), or controllable causes. (Although this $2 \times 2 \times 2$ taxonomy of dimensional structure is well supported, Weiner, 1985, concedes that other dimensions, e.g., intention and responsibility, may well exist.)

The core of Weiner's (1979, 1985) reformulated model (see Figure 5.1) lies in the mediational role played by emotions and expectancy between causal dimensions and future behavior. Weiner proposes the attribution process to proceed in the following manner. Following an achievement outcome, the individual experiences some immediate affective reactions that are almost "automatic" reactions to outcome and are termed *outcome-dependent* affects (Weiner, Russell & Lerman, 1979). Such affects take the form of feeling good when one is successful and feeling bad when one fails. The individual then engages in causal search, in an effort to determine "why" the outcome occurred (Heider,1958). Once an attribution has been formulated, it is processed in terms of its relative dimensional placement with respect to locus of causality, stability, and control. These dimensions, Weiner proposes, impinge upon future behavior through the mediation of affective reactions and future expectancies. More specifically, Weiner identifies the stability dimension as being instrumental in the formation of future expectancies and the locus of causality and control dimensions to be the predominant antecedents of affective reactions. These latter reactions have been termed *attribution-dependent* affects (Weiner et al., 1979). It should be noted, however, that a number of researchers have shown all three causal dimensions to be related to emotions (e.g., Forsyth & McMillan, 1981; McAuley & Duncan, 1990a; McAuley, Russell & Gross, 1983; Vallerand, 1987; see Figure 5.1).

The last 15 years have spawned a number of empirical investigations of the attribution process in sport (see Rejeski & Brawley, 1983, and McAuley & Duncan, 1990b, for more thorough reviews of this area). The following sections will focus on four areas of contemporary attribution research:

- Methodological issues
- Causes of personal outcome in sport
- Objective versus subjective outcomes
- The attribution–emotion link in sport

Methodological Issues

In any research endeavor accurate measurement is of paramount importance. However, much of the research on attributional theory has relied upon measurement systems that were based on a rather limited perspective of the attributional process. Specifically, virtually all of the sport attribution research conducted prior to 1983 relied upon Weiner's (1972) early two-dimensional taxonomy (locus and stability dimensions) and the basic four causal elements initially proposed. Despite the advent of Weiner's reformulated attributional model (1979, 1985) and criticism in the sport psychology literature concerning the limitations of restricting causal ascriptions to four elements (Bukowski & Moore, 1982; Roberts & Pascuzzi, 1979), many of the empirical investigations that have been conducted in the last several years have suffered from these shortcomings. The problems implicit in such approaches will be detailed, as will recent solutions to measurement issues.

A crucial methodological and theoretical flaw inherent in many sport attribution studies has been the failure to consider the respondent's perception of the link between specific causal attributions and their corresponding causal dimensions, a perception that may be radically different from that of the investigator. Consider our beginning golfer. Suppose that he was asked why he had placed very low among the field in

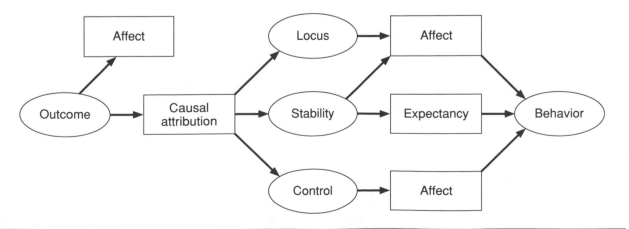

Figure 5.1 Schematic diagram of the causal attribution process (Weiner, 1986).

his first tournament. Such a poor showing might be attributed to lack of golfing ability. Typically, such an attribution would be classified by attribution researchers as a stable ascription. However, it is clear that such is not the case in sport and that low ability or skill can be *changed* with practice. In many contemporary sport attributional studies, investigators, endeavoring to associate different attributional elements with their respective causal dimensions, have often, through the use of raters and judges (e.g., Auvergne, 1983; Martin & Huang, 1984; Riordan, Thomas & James, 1985) arbitrarily assigned elements to dimensional space. In effect, these researchers are committing what Russell (1982) has referred to as the "fundamental attribution researcher error" by assuming that the investigator can accurately predict how the subject perceives an attribution in terms of causal structure. Such an approach ignores the individual phenomenology by excluding a factor fundamental to the attribution process, that is, the subject as an active agent (McAuley & Gross, 1983; Rejeski & Brawley, 1983; Russell, 1982).

In an effort to rectify this problem Russell (1982) developed the Causal Dimension Scale (CDS), a measure of how individuals perceive causes. The CDS represents an important advance in the measurement of causal attributions in that it allows the respondent to make an open-ended attribution and then classify that cause along the causal dimensions *locus of causality, stability*, and *control*. McAuley and Gross (1983) designed the first study utilizing the CDS in the sport domain to assess attributional patterns following a competitive table tennis match. Since this initial investigation, a large number of studies utilizing the CDS have appeared in the literature (e.g., Mark, Mutrie, Brooks & Harris, 1984; McAuley, Duncan & McElroy, 1989; McAuley et al., 1983; Schoeneman & Curry, 1990; Vallerand, 1987).

Although these studies, and a considerable number from other achievement domains, provide evidence for the utility of the CDS in involving the subject as an active agent, the measure has not been without criticism. McAuley and Gross (1983) found the locus of causality and stability dimensions to be quite reliable but the control dimension to be suspect. They suggested that control may be less clear-cut and more difficult to assess in sporting situations than in academic situations. Vallerand and Richer (1988) also called into question the properties of the control dimension, suggesting that the items did not accurately reflect control but in actuality represented other possible constructs, such as intention and responsibility. Russell, McAuley,

and Tarico (1987), in a multitrait–multimethod approach to the measurement of attributions, have acknowledged the weakness of the control dimension of the CDS but have nonetheless demonstrated it to be superior to other commonly employed methods for assessing attributions.

McAuley, Duncan, and Russell (in press) have recently revised the Causal Dimension Scale (CDSII) addressing both the problem of aberrant nonrepresentative items and the inability of the original control items to differentiate between control by the attributer versus control by other individuals. In essence, McAuley et al. (in press) argued that control may be better assessed if considered from the perspectives of personal control and external control. McAuley and his colleagues reported data from five studies ranging from academic to exercise-related achievement situations to support their contention. Employing structural equation modeling, they demonstrated, via multigroup confirmatory factor analyses, construct validity and reliability for the four dimension CDSII. Moreover, they clearly showed the four-factor model to be superior to other models composed of other combinations of dimensions. At this point, then, the CDSII appears to be a reliable instrument, and some evidence is available to support its construct validity as a measure of how individuals perceive outcomes in terms of causal dimensions. However, continued psychometric testing is warranted.

Another issue of concern relative to attribution research in sport and physical activity is that of incomplete model testing (McAuley & Duncan, 1989). In order to test Weiner's model fully, the researcher has to go beyond simply looking at differential attributional patterns; that is, it is important to try to determine whether the relationships between causal dimensions and affective reactions, expectancies, and future behaviors in sport do follow the theoretical directions suggested by Weiner (1985). As we shall subsequently observe, only a handful of researchers have attempted to examine these relationships in sport.

Causes of Personal Outcomes

One of the most common approaches to investigating attributional processes in sport has been to try to determine whether there exist differential patterns among the attributions made for achievement outcomes in sport; in other words, do winners and losers ascribe outcome differently? This body of research, particularly the laboratory research, has generally shown that winners tend to make dispositional attributions for outcomes, whereas losers identify situational causes for outcomes. This pattern of responses, identified as a hedonic or self-serving bias (Bradley, 1978; Zuckerman, 1979) is commonly interpreted from a motivational perspective (Brawley & Roberts, 1984), whereby one's need for the preservation of self-esteem governs one's attributional thinking; with success leading to internal attributions (e.g., ability) that serve to enhance one's self-esteem, and failure producing attributions that attempt to protect self-esteem (e.g., did not try hard, opponent was too difficult). However, a recent meta-analytic review of 22 sport-related studies suggests that the motivational, self-presentational bias is weakest at the level of questions focusing on individual performance, which is contrary to what one would expect (Mullin & Riordan, 1988).

Miller and Ross (1975) have suggested previously that although a hedonic bias may be present in the case of successful outcomes, self-protective attributions are not prevalent in the case of failure. It is wholly possible that such attributional patterns are inferred by the *researcher* as a function of classifying raw attributions along dimensional taxonomy (McAuley & Duncan, 1990b; Russell, 1982). As we have pointed out elsewhere (Russell et al., 1987), external attributions are a very rare phenomenon when the subject is allowed to classify the attribution along causal dimensions. This underscores the previous point that causal attributions per se are relatively unimportant. How the attributer perceives the cause in terms of causal dimensions is much more meaningful.

Objective and Subjective Outcomes

Many studies in the sport attribution literature have made the erroneous assumption that *absolute* outcomes, (e.g., winning and losing) are analogous to the *perceived* outcomes of success and failure. In some ways this error parallels the problem of researchers assuming that their interpretation of the subject's phenomenology, with respect to causal attributions and dimensions, is accurate and similar to the respondents' own (Rejeski & Brawley, 1983). Employing Maehr and Nicholls's (1980) conceptual framework of success and failure as psychological states, Spink and Roberts (1980) have demonstrated that perceived and absolute outcomes are not isomorphic. This, of course, suggests that the relationship between causal ascriptions and perceived success is as important as the relationship between causal ascriptions and the absolute outcome.

McAuley (1985a) examined these relationships in a sample of female intercollegiate gymnasts competing in an invitational tournament. Subjects made causal attributions for their performance in each of four Olympic events including vault, floor exercise, balance beam, and uneven parallel bars. A commonality analysis was conducted to determine the relative influence of perceptions of success and absolute success (actual score) on each causal dimension for each event. With the exception of floor exercise, causal dimensions for all events were significantly influenced by perceptions of success rather than actual score. The findings from this study are consistent with those of Maehr and Nicholls (1980) and Spink and Roberts (1980) suggesting that *perceptions* of success are important antecedents of causal ascriptions. Although representing only a small percentage of the sport attribution literature, these studies emphasize how little we know about causal attributions and sport outcomes if we restrict our definition of outcome to simply winning or losing (Brawley & Roberts, 1984).

The Attribution–Emotion Link

One of the primary components of Weiner's (1985, 1986) model is emotion. Affective reactions are proposed to mediate the link between causal dimensions and future behavior. Despite the fact that the whole spectrum of affective reactions is displayed in the context of sport, little research attention has been paid to the role of emotion in sport (Silva & Hardy, 1984; Vallerand, 1983). Recently, a few studies have been conducted that examine the attribution–emotion relationship proposed by Weiner (1985). The first study to be conducted in the sport domain examined the relationships between causal dimensions and affect following table tennis performance (McAuley et al., 1983). Weiner's (1979) early theoretical formulations had suggested that *locus of causality* was the dimension chiefly responsible for affect generation, whereas McAuley and his colleagues (1983) reported the *control* and *stability* dimensions to be instrumental in predicting affect, a finding that was consistent with Forsyth and McMillan's (1981) examination of these same issues in an academic situation. The McAuley et al. (1983) study revealed a number of interesting results relative to the attribution–affect relationship. First, subjects apparently cared about their performance, demonstrating affective reactions to outcome. Second, successful outcomes elicited more intense affective reactions, a finding consistent with that of Weiner and his colleagues (1979). Finally, the fact that the control dimension was responsible for evoking affects suggests that settings such as sport contests, which involve interpersonal competition and ego involvement, may increase the salience of the control dimension.

Vallerand (1987) conducted two studies, one in a laboratory and one in a field setting, to examine the relationship between causal dimensions and self-related affects following performance. In general, Vallerand (1987) demonstrated support for the notion that these two constructs are related. Furthermore, his results suggest that the subjective perception of outcome, not the objective outcome, is related to affect generation. Vallerand (1987) also reported the stability and control dimensions to be more predictive of affect than the locus of causality.

McAuley and Duncan (1990a), Robinson and Howe (1989), and Vallerand (1987) have also examined the attribution–affect relationship from a slightly different perspective, examining the effects of intuitive appraisal (perceptions of success) and causal dimensions on affective reactions in a variety of physical activity settings. The combined findings of these researchers suggest that both reflective (attributional) and intuitive appraisal are implicated in the generation of affect.

It appears therefore that causal dimensions do indeed mediate affective reactions to achievement outcomes (Weiner, 1985). However, this does not mean that we must blindly accept the proposition that affect occurs only as a function of postoutcome causal search. As the findings of Vallerand (1987), McAuley and Duncan (1990a), and Robinson and Howe (1989) suggest, other cognitive processes appear to influence postoutcome affect. Moreover, Rejeski and his associates (Hardy & Rejeski, 1989; Rejeski & Brawley, 1983; Rejeski & Sanford, 1984) have suggested that affect is also generated as a ramification of task difficulty. How such affect impinges upon subsequent causal ascription would be worth exploring.

In summary, emotion is clearly an important part of the sport experience, and causal ascriptions appear to mediate affect generation. However, it is also clear that emotion is a complex phenomenon (Vallerand, 1987) and that sport psychologists have merely scratched the surface with respect to the underlying cognitive processes that augment emotional reactions in sport.

Other Attributional Approaches

This section introduces two neglected areas of research that hold promise for attributional analysis but have been virtually ignored: exercise and the developmental process. Although little attributional research exists in either of these areas, the utility of studying the attributional

process in understanding behavior in these contexts will be detailed.

There has been a considerable growth of research activity in the general area of exercise psychology in the past few years. One of the most commonly studied—and perhaps least understood—aspects of exercise is the problem of sustaining adherence to prescribed programs once they have been initiated. Indeed, well-documented statistics indicate that the attrition rate from exercise programs approximates 50% within the first six months (Dishman, 1982; Oldridge, 1982). This attrition rate parallels the compliance dilemma in other areas of modern medicine (e.g., smoking cessation, weight control) and is considered to be one of the most serious problems encountered in disease control and health promotion (Epstein & Cluss, 1982). Interestingly, much of this exercise adherence/attrition research is concerned with the basic attributional question *why*; that is, it is concerned with why people adhere to, or drop out of, exercise programs. However, in spite of some promising attributional approaches to other health behaviors in the literature (Michela & Wood, 1986), such as smoking cessation (Eiser, Van der Plight, Raw & Sutton, 1985), few empirical reports exist that document the role of attributional processes in exercise behavior.

McAuley, Poag, Gleason, and Wraith (1990) have recently examined the relationships among causal attributions and affective reactions to attrition from exercise programs in middle-aged adults. McAuley et al. (1990) were able to demonstrate that all three causal dimensions were predictive of negative affective reactions experienced as a function of dropping out of exercise programs. Furthermore, Schoeneman and Curry (1990) have recently reported that causal attributions are implicated in successful and unsuccessful exercise behavior change. These results, in combination with results linking attributions and health behavior (Michela & Wood, 1986), are promising insomuch as they suggest attribution processes to be at the very core of these complex behaviors. Future exploration of this important research area is to be encouraged.

Although Brawley (1984) cogently argued that it is impossible to have a developmental psychology of attributions until the attributions that occur in play, sport, and physical activity are more thoroughly studied, very little sport attribution research exists that is developmental in nature. An early study by Bird and Williams (1980) examined the relationship between attributions and sex roles as a function of increasing age. Although young subjects (7 to 12 years) of both sexes offered similar attributional explanations for the outcomes of sport scenarios, older males (13 to 18 years) attributed performance to effort, whereas females were more likely to use luck as a causal ascription. Such findings suggest, then, that gender differences in attributions were a developmental phenomena. Weiss, McAuley, Ebbeck, and Wiese (1990) recently attempted to examine the relationship between self-esteem and causal attributions for physical and social competence in sport with 8-to-13-year-old children. Although somewhat restrictive in the range of developmental stages, Weiss et al. were able to demonstrate that children high in self-esteem used more internal, stable, and personally controllable patterns of attributions for physical and social competence. Fielstein and colleagues (1985) have also reported some modest findings suggesting a link between self-esteem and attributions in young children. However, their results were restricted to *hypothetical* social, athletic, and academic scenarios. Although several other studies have assessed causal attributions given by children in sport and athletic situations (e.g., Bukowski & Moore, 1982; Roberts, 1978; Scanlan & Passer, 1981), the three previously discussed studies remain the sole developmental attempts to explore this seemingly fertile area of inquiry.

The Future of Attribution Theory in Sport

In a review of the sport attribution literature Brawley and Roberts criticize sport researchers' "single-minded devotion" (1984, p. 211) to the Weinerian model, suggesting it to be a limited viewpoint, allowing too few questions to be examined. It should be noted that Brawley and Roberts were criticizing research that had relied almost exclusively on the early Weiner (1972) model. However, given the advances in both theory development and measurement over the past decade, it might be appropriate to state that we still actually know very *little* about the attribution process. A large part of the sport attribution literature is post hoc, researcher-biased, poorly conceptualized, and methodologically suspect. Aspects of Weiner's attributional model of achievement motivation and emotion, such as the role of causal dimensions, the dimension–affect link, and (of most importance but least studied) the attribution–behavior link in sport have gone largely unexplored. The developmental sport attribution literature is virtually an empirical wilderness. The role of the attributer as an active agent in the attribution process has only just begun to be examined from both a measurement and phenomenological perspective. Moreover, attribution processes lie at the very heart of many

theories of behavior change (e.g., learned helplessness, cognitive behavior modification) but for the most part are studied independent of such theories.

Weiner's (1985, 1986) model offers many intriguing possibilities for future study in the sport domain both from the perspective of testing theoretical links in the model and—on a grander scale perhaps—fully testing the causal process from raw attribution through to future behavior (Duncan & McAuley, 1989) and on to attributions for that behavior. This is not to say that we *should* blindly accept Weiner's model. Rather, it is recommended that it be *fully tested* to determine how much utility it has for understanding sport behavior. Indeed, as we shall subsequently see, causal attributions may be better understood from the perspective of how they are related to *other* cognitive variables with respect to behavior.

Self-Efficacy, Sport, and Physical Activity

This section offers a general overview of self-efficacy theory in the context of the sport and physical activity literatures, first outlining a conceptual framework, which is then used to discuss applications, methodology, and possibilities for future research.

Conceptual Framework

A theoretical approach to understanding behavior that holds considerable promise for the sport and exercise domain is self-efficacy theory (Bandura, 1977, 1986). Self-efficacy cognitions represent the convictions or beliefs that one can successfully execute a course of action to produce a certain behavior. In very simple terms self-efficacy represents a form of situation-specific self-confidence. For example, an individual may feel very confident of his or her ability to perform on the basketball court but be completely intimidated at the thought of public speaking. These judgments of personal capabilities have been shown to be important determinants of individuals' choice of activity, how much effort they expend in those activities, and how long they persist in the face of aversive stimuli (Bandura, 1977, 1986). When faced with stressful stimuli, low-efficacious individuals tend to give up, attribute failure internally, and experience greater anxiety or depression (Bandura, 1982).

Expectations of personal efficacy are culled from four major sources of information: past performance accomplishments, vicarious experiences, social or verbal persuasion, and physiological arousal (Bandura, 1977). Past performance or mastery accomplishments are the most dependable and influential sources of efficacy information. For example, a history of previous successes in sport will facilitate efficacy expectations, whereas previous failures result in lowered perceptions of personal capabilities in that domain. Vicarious experiences are sources of efficacy information derived through observing or imagining others engaging in the task to be performed. These modeling effects, although generally weaker than mastery experiences, have been shown to be a dependable source of efficacy information across a variety of situations (e.g., Bandura & Adams, 1977; Feltz, Landers & Raeder, 1979; McAuley, 1985b). Social persuasion is a technique commonly employed by teachers, coaches, and peers to bolster individuals' personal efficacy but is less powerful than information based on personal accomplishments. Finally, physiological arousal is postulated to affect behavior through the cognitive evaluation (efficacy expectations) of the information conveyed by the arousal; that is, increased arousal can be interpreted as inability to carry out a course of action successfully (Bandura, 1986). For example, perceiving increased respiration rate as physiological stress rather than psychological readiness can lead to decreases in personal efficacy.

Self-efficacy theory is a social-cognitive approach to behavioral causation that postulates behavior, physiological and cognitive factors, and environmental influences to operate as interacting determinants of each other (Bandura, 1986). This theory of reciprocal determinism posits that behavior and human functioning are determined by the interrelated influences of individuals' physiological states, behavior, cognition, and the environment. Self-efficacy theory focuses on the role of self-referent thought on psychosocial functioning and provides a common mechanism through which people demonstrate control over their own motivation and behavior. Self-efficacy cognitions have been consistently shown to be important determinants of physical activity and sport behavior (see Feltz, 1988a), exercise behavior (see McAuley, 1992a), as well as social, clinical, and health-related behaviors (see O'Leary, 1985). It is important to realize that self-efficacy is not concerned with the skills an individual has but rather with the judgments of what an individual can do with the skills he or she possesses (Bandura, 1986).

Bandura (1977, 1986) has argued that the measurement of self-efficacy cognitions should be conducted in a microanalytic fashion by assessing efficacy along three dimensions: level,

strength, and generality. *Level* of self-efficacy concerns the individual's expected performance attainment or the number of tasks he or she can perform. For example, the performance of a complex twisting dive from a high platform requires the mastery of a number of skill components before the whole movement can be successfully completed. Such components represent the various levels of self-efficacy for that skill. *Strength* of self-efficacy determines the certainty with which the individual expects successfully to attain each level. In the diving task, one might feel completely certain about being able to dive from the side of the pool, less certain about diving from several meters, and completely uncertain about one's ability to execute any type of dive necessitating a twisting motion. *Generality* refers to the number of domains in which individuals consider themselves efficacious. For example, divers may also consider themselves quite efficacious in other types of activities requiring acrobatic skills (e.g., tumbling, trampolining, gymnastics). Some evidence exists in the sport and exercise literature to support this notion of self-efficacy cognitions generalizing across events (e.g., Brody, Hatfield & Spalding, 1988; Holloway, Beuter & Duda, 1988; McAuley, Courneya & Lettunich, 1991). However, this particular aspect of self-efficacy theory is not as well substantiated as other tenets of the theory.

Assessments of self-efficacy are generally developed with a view to tapping what Bandura terms the "generative capabilities" (1986, p. 397) with respect to a task rather than singular acts that collectively comprise the task. In other words, to assess skiing self-efficacy it is necessary to determine individuals' confidence with respect to making crisp turns; negotiating icy moguls at speed; maneuvering through deep, soft, powder snow; and avoiding or approaching other possible challenges. Simply asking, "How confident are you in your skiing ability?" is insufficient because it fails to address the many components that are relevant to judging skiing self-efficacy.

Somewhat in contrast to such recommendations, Ryckman, Robbins, Thornton, and Cantrell (1982) have developed the Physical Self-Efficacy Scale, which purports to measure the individual's perceived physical self-confidence. This scale consists of items assessing (a) the individual's perceived physical ability and (b) physical self-presentation confidence. Together, the two subscales represent a measure of the individual's efficacy expectations across a variety of physical abilities (e.g., speed, strength, reaction time). Although the scale has been applied in a variety of physical tasks in a laboratory (Ryckman et al., 1982) and in such field contexts as marathon running (Gayton, Matthews & Burchstead, 1986) and competitive gymnastics (McAuley & Gill, 1983), this global measure of physical self-efficacy has been shown to be less predictive of skilled performance than have more task-specific measures (McAuley & Gill, 1983). Bandura (1986) has asserted that particularized, or task-specific, measures of self-efficacy are more predictive of behavior and offer more explanatory power than do more generalized measures.

Having presented a basic theoretical framework from which to understand the construct of self-efficacy and its measurement, the remainder of this section reviews efficacy-related research in the areas of sport, exercise, and physical activity. Also briefly discussed is what Bandura (1986) refers to as *collective self-efficacy* and consideration of what the future may hold for self-efficacy research in sport and physical activity.

Sport and Physical Activity Research

As Feltz (1988a) has established in her review of self-confidence and sport performance, the majority of the extant literature linking sport and self-efficacy has primarily focused on (a) the influence of self-efficacy on performance and (b) the effects of differential sources of information on efficacy expectations and performance. The relevant results from these two areas of research will be summarized.

The research that has investigated the effects of the various sources of information on efficacy expectations and performance has rather consistently shown that performance-based treatment modalities or techniques appear to be the most robust source of information for enhancing efficacy cognitions (Brody et al., 1988; Feltz et al., 1979; Hogan & Santomeier, 1984; McAuley, 1985b). Similar but weaker relationships have been evidenced when vicarious techniques are employed (Corbin, Laurie, Gruger & Smiley, 1984; Gould & Weiss, 1981; Weinberg, Gould & Jackson, 1979). In contrast, the empirical trials that have tested the effectiveness of emotional arousal and verbal persuasion as facilitators of self-efficacy have been less convincing. Kavanagh and Hausfeld (1986) attempted to determine whether negative or positive mood states influenced self-efficacy for performance of a physical task. Although mood changes and self-efficacy were related, no clear picture emerged as to the mediational role that efficacy cognitions are theorized to play between arousal and performance. Wilkes and Summers (1984) employed a variety of cognitive preparation techniques,

including positive efficacy self-talk, and were also unable to demonstrate a mediational effect of efficacy cognitions between this form of verbal persuasion and performance. Finally, Feltz (1982) and Feltz and Mugno (1983) reported perceived autonomic arousal to be a significant predictor of self-efficacy but less so than previous performance.

In an attempt to explain these findings, Feltz (1988a) hypothesized that failure to show a mediational effect among informational sources, self-efficacy, and performance may be due, in part, to past performance effects. Subjects' previous performance experience may override or interfere with the treatment effects in multiple trial studies, especially where trials are temporarily close together. Solving this dilemma would require studies that span longer periods of time, to give treatments time to take effect. Such a perspective calls into question many efficacy studies where one-time measurements of the construct are expected to predict variance over time (McAuley, 1992b). By theoretical definition, efficacy cognitions are dynamic. Various sources of information are theorized to reduce or increase self-percepts of personal agency. In sport and physical activity contexts, where experience, learning, physiological adaptations, and diverse degrees of task difficulty can all vary, self-efficacy has the potential to change dramatically over time. Thus, we need more studies that assess self-efficacy at multiple time points and in more complex tasks and behaviors before we can fully understand the role such cognitions play in physical activity.

It has been established that various sources of information can influence self-efficacy perceptions. But what of the subsequent effect of self-efficacy on performance? For the most part, studies of the efficacy–performance relationship have not been designed to determine the causal links between these two variables. However, Feltz and McAuley (Feltz, 1982, 1988b; Feltz & Mugno, 1983; McAuley, 1985b) have employed path analysis to determine the strength of some of the causal relationships suggested by Bandura (1977, 1986). Although the mechanisms are not completely clear in terms of the effects on performance of variables other than self-efficacy, it appears from this handful of studies that self-efficacy is an important causal agent in physical performance. Feltz's studies have employed complex multitrial path models comparing the theorized pathways to alternative models, including an anxiety-based model and a respecified model (Feltz, 1982) that incorporates self-efficacy and previous performance as direct influences on back-diving performance. Feltz

(1982, 1988; Feltz & Mugno, 1983) has presented evidence to suggest that the principal predictions of her respecified model warrant further attention.

McAuley (1985b) contrasted self-efficacy-based and anxiety-based models of gymnastic performance and reached conclusions similar to those of Feltz (1982), namely, that the self-efficacy model was superior to the anxiety-based model and efficacy cognitions were demonstrated to be significant predictors of performance. However, direct effects between performance-based treatments and gymnastic performance suggested that other mechanisms, in addition to self-efficacy were in effect, as previously suggested by Bandura and Cervone (1983).

Deeter (1989) has also verified a causal link, albeit modest, between both general and task-specific self-efficacy and performance in physical activity classes. Deeter, employing structural equation modeling, attempted to test Eccles and colleagues' (1983) cognitive expectancy value model of achievement behavior in a physical activity setting. Deeter's results showed that self-efficacy was influenced by trait sport confidence (Vealey, 1986) and perceived competence for the task. Self-efficacy, in turn, mediated performance and instructor influence.

A considerable number of studies exist in the sport and physical activity domain that show some support for the relationships (a) between various sources of information and self-efficacy, and (b) between self-efficacy cognitions and performance. Further research is now called for to address the independent and co-joint causal roles that self-efficacy and other mechanisms play in sport and physical activity.

Exercise-Related Research

The areas of behavioral medicine and health psychology have provided some impressive testimony to the tenability of self-efficacy theory (O'Leary, 1985). Of particular interest are the studies in this area that have included exercise as either an independent variable or an outcome variable. Secondary prevention studies, in the area of cardiac rehabilitation with an exercise focus, offer some compelling evidence for the predictive value of self-efficacy in the adoption and maintenance of health-promoting activity. Ewart, Taylor, Reese, and DeBusk (1983) reported that the more efficacious postmyocardial infarction (PMI) patients were in their perceived physical capabilities (i.e., mastering increasing treadmill workloads), the more effort they exerted, which in turn fostered recovery and a more aggressive pursuit of normal activities. Ewart

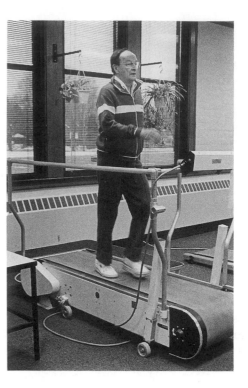

and colleagues (1986) demonstrate that PMI patients' efficacy cognitions predicted compliance with prescribed exercise programs, whereas their physical capabilities did not. Furthermore, Taylor, Bandura, Ewart, Miller, and DeBusk (1985) reported that the cardiac expectations of patients in a rehabilitation program and those of their spouses have been shown to be significant predictors of cardiac function. The combined findings of these studies suggest that perceptions of past accomplishments may be better predictors of future health behaviors than actual physical skills or activity levels. This is consistent with Bandura's (1986) theoretical contention that it is not the skills or capabilities themselves that are important but the individual's beliefs in what he or she can accomplish with those skills.

A number of recent studies have also suggested links between self-efficacy and physical activity/exercise (see McAuley, 1992a, for a review). Sallis and colleagues (1986) reported that efficacy cognitions predicted change in intensity levels of activity within a community sample of elderly adults. Similarly, McAuley and Jacobson (1991) were able to demonstrate, in a sample of sedentary adult women, a modest relationship between self-efficacy (with respect to overcoming barriers to activity) and program attendance, as well as regularity and duration of exercise at follow-up. Auley and Rowney (1990) found similar results in a sample of self-described "unfit" young females enrolled in aerobic dance classes. McAuley (1989) employed structural equation modeling to examine the effects of efficacy expectations on continued exercise participation over the course of a 10-week program and for 3 months after program termination. The model revealed that self-efficacy and intention to participate in other physical activities influenced attendance during the program and perceptions of success at the end of the program. Self-efficacy also influenced self-reported exercise behavior at follow-up. McAuley (1992b) has also demonstrated that self-efficacy predicted exercise adherence over a 5-month period for middle-aged, sedentary adults. Adopting a perspective that viewed exercise as a dynamic process, McAuley showed efficacy cognitions to predict exercise behavior at 3 months but not at 5 months. In the latter instance, previous exercise behavior was the major predictor at the end of the program. Finally, Dzewaltowski (1989) and his colleagues (Dzewaltowski, Noble & Shaw, 1990) have found that self-efficacy explained a significant amount of variation in self-reported exercise behavior of college undergraduate students.

Exercise psychology is a rapidly developing area of sport psychology that holds great promise for contributing to our knowledge of effective and healthy human functioning. The group of studies previously discussed suggests that the application of self-efficacy theory may contribute substantially to our understanding of such complex phenomenon as adoption, adherence, and attrition in exercise behavior in both asymptomatic and diseased populations (Klug, McAuley & Clarke, 1990). Future studies must, however, address the role of efficacy cognitions and exercise behavior at multiple time points. Social cognitive theory (Bandura, 1986) proposes that our perceptions of personal capabilities are continually influenced by environmental, cognitive, and behavioral variables. Thus, longitudinal studies are necessary to verify the role that efficacy perceptions may play in this behavior. Moreover, normal (asymptomatic) sedentary populations need to be studied, because they comprise the bulk of the population, as do children, who, as a study population, have been all but ignored in the exercise literature. What role efficacy cognitions play in the development of attitudes toward physical activity and the adoption of a healthy lifestyle at an early stage needs to be documented. Finally, we need experimental studies that attempt to manipulate or facilitate efficacy cognitions in an effort to influence exercise and physical activity participation and compliance.

Collective Self-Efficacy

Like most discussions of self-efficacy, the previous sections have been directed at personal or individual efficaciousness and its effect on subsequent behavior. However, as Bandura (1986) pointed out, the surmounting of challenges and barriers or difficulties is often accomplished through the collective efforts of groups of individuals. Just as self-efficacy influences the choice, effort, and persistence exhibited by the individual, collective efficacy, it is proposed, markedly affects how the group behaves. Little research exists at the present time to confirm the existence of such a construct in sport; nonetheless, it is a wholly tenable idea.

Feltz and her associates (Feltz, Bandura, Albrecht & Corcoran, 1988; Feltz, Corcoran & Lirgg, 1989) have conducted some exploratory studies suggesting that beliefs in group capabilities do indeed influence performance. These researchers examined the relationship between individual and team (collective) efficacy and team performance over the course of one 32-game hockey season. Correlational analysis of the data indicated that individual efficacy was more closely related to team performance in the first game than was team efficacy. However, over the span of eight games, team efficacy was more strongly correlated to team performance than was individual efficacy. Although exploratory in nature, these data suggest an interesting pattern of collective efficacy taking time to develop but eventually proving to be a stronger predictor of group behavior than individualized confidence in personal capabilities. This development and the obvious link that could be made with such group processes as team cohesion warrants further exploration and presents numerous possibilities for future research endeavors. Indeed, Spink (1990) has recently examined the relationship between collective efficacy and group cohesion, finding differential results for elite and recreational performers. Clearly, this area is in need of further investigation.

The Future of Self-Efficacy in Sport and Physical Activity

If one can draw any conclusion from the sport literature that deals with situation-specific self-confidence and sport, it may be that the relationship is quite robust. This is particularly cogent when one considers the variety of measures, definitions, environments, and designs that have been used to investigate self-efficacy. However, we must now move beyond the simple bivariate relationship and scrutinize in more depth the complexities of self-efficacy and its relationship, both as antecedent and consequence, with sport, exercise, and physical activity.

One direction that future researchers might take is to begin examining self-efficacy in relation to other psychological variables associated with performance. A considerable number of techniques and cognitive variables have been empirically linked to skilled performance; but little effort has been made to explore how—or whether—these variables are related to self-efficacy. For example, a number of studies exist that have examined the effectiveness of goal setting as a technique for positively enhancing sport performance (e.g., Burton, 1989; Hall & Byrne, 1988; Hall, Weinberg & Jackson, 1987; Miller & McAuley, 1987; Weinberg, Bruya & Jackson, 1985). Bandura (1986) has proposed that goals play an important part in the development of self-efficacy. Proximal goals, once achieved, provide mastery information that serves to enhance efficacy cognition (Bandura & Schunk, 1981). Thus, the effects of goal setting on behavior are mediated, in part, by self-efficacy cognitions formed as a function of cognitive comparison (Bandura & Cervone, 1983). Such relationships have yet to be reliably demonstrated in the sport domain.

Equally important to determine is the extent to which self-perceptions of efficacy are related to other cognitive variables. For example, Sonstroem and Morgan (1989) have recently proposed a model in which physical self-efficacy is considered an essential step in the formation of self-esteem through exercise and physical activity. Although at the time of writing no evidence exists to support such a model, it is only a matter of time before tests of such a process are conducted. Similarly, cognitive evaluation theory (Deci & Ryan, 1980, 1985) posits that evidence of competence and self-determination leads to intrinsically motivated behavior. Social cognitive theory (Bandura, 1986) would postulate that such competence is the direct result of beliefs in one's ability to exercise personal agency, or being self-efficacious. Indeed, in a recent study McAuley, Wraith, and Duncan (1991) report self-efficacy to be significantly related to dimensions of intrinsic motivation in aerobic dance participants. More efficacious exercisers perceived themselves to enjoy exercise more, put forth more effort, experience less pressure-tension, and feel more competent than their less efficacious counterparts. Again, the relationships between these variables need to be further investigated in the sport, exercise, and physical activity domain.

In summary, it appears that much work is still to be done in clarifying the role self-efficacy plays in the explanation and prediction of individual and group behavior in sport and exercise contexts. Based upon research across diverse domains of functioning, it is evident that self-efficacy is related not only to performance but also to many other psychological and behavioral variables of interest. Examination of such relationships in physical activity contexts is necessary if we are to better understand the role of self-efficacy as a mediator of behavior change.

The final section of this chapter takes such an approach. The attributional process, it is argued, is at the foundation of many cognitive theories of behavior change and, as such, weaves into social cognitive theory with little difficulty.

Causal Attributions and Efficacy Cognitions as Process Variables: A Social Cognitive Perspective

The chapter thus far parallels the general approach that has been taken toward both attribution theory and self-efficacy theory research with respect to sport and physical activity; in essence, they have been treated in the main as separate theoretical entities. However, incorporating the broader framework of Bandura's (1986) social cognitive theory of human behavior suggests that causal attributions and efficacy cognitions are reciprocal determinants of each other and are, therefore, intimately related as process variables.

To recap, social cognitive theory characterizes human functioning as the product of reciprocal determinism, in which behavior, cognitive and other personal factors, and environmental events interact to determine each other. Central to this conceptualization is the notion that behavior is purposeful and is regulated by forethought. This forethought is, in essence, the derivative of self-reflection. Attributional search is a self-reflective process.

Self-reflective processes are, of course, at the heart of self-efficacy theory. It is at this point that we must consider how attribution and self-efficacy processes might reciprocally determine each other. Although Weiner (1979, 1985) has theorized that causal attributions influence future performance through the mediation of affective reactions and expectancies, Bandura has suggested that the relationship may be more complex. Specifically, Bandura (1986) argues that in addition to influencing behavior or performance, percepts of efficacy also provide information from which causal attributions are formed. Highly efficacious children have been shown to attribute failure to lack of effort, whereas less efficacious children ascribe failure to a lack of ability (Collins, 1982). Thus, there are two distinct steps in the process to be examined. The first is the effect of efficacy expectations on subsequent causal attributions for achievement outcomes; the second concerns the role that those causal attributions play in the formation of future efficacy expectations. Bandura's social-cognitive framework, therefore, takes into consideration the bidirectional relationship between efficacy cognitions and causal attributions. Figure 5.2 details in its most simplistic form the proposed relationships.

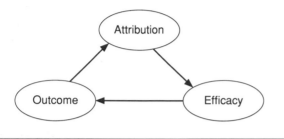

Figure 5.2 Proposed relationship between causal attributions and self-efficacy expectations.

In an effort to determine the veridicality of these relationships, a number of studies in the social, educational, and sport psychology literature will now be examined. To be consistent with the temporal flow outlined, the effects of causal attributions on efficacy expectations will be examined first, the role played by efficacy cognitions in the formation of subsequent causal attributions, second.

The Attribution–Efficacy Link

Schunk and his colleagues (Schunk, 1984; Schunk & Cox, 1986; Schunk & Gunn, 1986) have conducted a series of studies examining the relationships among efficacy cognitions, causal attributions, and young children's arithmetic performance. By manipulating attributional feedback concerning performance, Schunk and his associates were able to influence ensuing self-efficacy expectations. Specifically, effort feedback concerning performance led to increases in self-efficacy (Schunk & Cox, 1986) as did attributions of success to ability (Schunk, 1984; Schunk & Gunn, 1986). Both types of attribution signify causal mechanisms that are internal and subject to personal control—key aspects of perceptions of self-efficacy.

McAuley (1990) examined the effects of causal ascriptions for previous exercise attrition on exercise behavior through the mediation of affective reactions and self-efficacy. Of primary concern here is, of course, the role that attributions play in the formulation of efficacy cognitions for subsequent exercise behavior. Subjects making unstable and controllable attributions

for attrition from previous exercise programs had stronger efficacy expectations with respect to overcoming possible barriers to future exercise participation. It is apparent that reflective appraisal processes such as causal attributions, although linked to more general expectancies (as Weiner's model would suggest), are also implicated in the formation of the more specific efficacy cognitions implicated in Bandura's (1986) social-cognitive framework.

The Efficacy–Attribution Link

A few studies exist that document the effects of efficacy cognitions on causal attributions. Alden (1986) has reported that subjects classified as high and low in interpersonal efficacy with respect to social relations differed in the types of attributions that they made for feedback for social interactions. High-efficacy subjects receiving negative feedback made significantly more external attributions than either high-efficacy subjects receiving positive feedback or low-efficacy subjects receiving negative feedback. Further, low-efficacy subjects receiving positive feedback attributed the outcome to external factors more than did low-efficacy subjects receiving negative feedback. Alden interprets her results from a consistency bias perspective, in that subjects appraised the feedback in terms of their perceived efficacy and attributed the outcomes accordingly.

In a physical activity setting, McAuley and his colleagues (Duncan & McAuley, 1987; McAuley, Duncan & McElroy, 1989) employed an exercise bicycle ergometer task to determine the relationship between self-efficacy and subsequent causal attributions. Self-efficacy information and performance outcomes of children (McAuley, Duncan & McElroy, 1989) and young adults (Duncan & McAuley, 1987) were electronically manipulated to examine the proposed relationships. Highly self-efficacious children tended to make significantly more controllable and stable attributions for their performance on the ergometer than low-efficacious children (McAuley et al., 1984). However, no relationship emerged between efficacy cognitions and causal attributions under similar circumstances with young adults (Duncan & McAuley, 1987). This latter failure to support the proposed relationship might be explained by subject involvement in situations that are not naturally occurring (e.g., manipulated laboratory experiments); that is, subjects may feel less personally involved and less responsible for the eventual outcome (see Harvey, Arkin, Gleason & Johnson, 1974). As a consequence, this lack of personal involvement and responsibility might well alleviate the individual's predisposition to causal search.

Finally, in a recent path analysis study, McAuley (1991a) investigated the relationships among causal attributions, self-efficacy cognitions, and affective reactions relating to exercise progress in a sample of previously sedentary adults. As Bandura (1986) had suggested, efficacy expectations were related to causal dimensions and these causal dimensions, in turn, were predictive of affective responses. Moreover, self-efficacy has a direct effect and an indirect effect on affect reactions through the dimension of personal control.

The results of the previous studies, although by no means conclusive, suggest some preliminary support for Bandura's (1982, 1986) contentions that efficacy cognitions influence the types of causal attribution made following achievement outcomes. Clearly, further investigation of the relationship between these important constructs and their influence on sport, exercise, and physical activity is warranted.

Although attribution theory and self-efficacy theory are considered to be two of the more systematically examined theoretical models in contemporary sport psychology (Landers, 1983) and although both can be considered theories of social cognition (Brawley, 1984), the challenge for future researchers must lie in examining these constructs and others together from an interactive process perspective (McAuley, 1991b). Such an approach will require solid methodology, rigorous measurement, and appropriate statistical treatment if the reciprocal determinism suggested by Bandura (1986) is to be thoroughly tested. Moreover, it will allow sport scientists to pursue two prominent sources of self-referent thought that may, it has been theorized, be intimately linked, rather than pursuing either theory in a singular manner. After all, human functioning is influenced by numerous mechanisms, such as goal mechanisms, self-efficacy mechanisms, and attributional or self-evaluative mechanisms (Bandura & Cervone, 1983). Therefore, it behooves us, as researchers interested in understanding and predicting sport and exercise behavior, to employ such approaches as Bandura's (1986) social-cognitive theory in an attempt to link antecedents and consequences of such behavior in a reciprocal, rather than unidirectional, manner.

Conclusion

This chapter reviewed some of the more current work in attribution and self-efficacy theories with respect to sport and physical activity and attempted to draw together the two approaches from a social-cognitive perspective. Reviews of self-efficacy (Feltz, 1988b; McAuley, 1992a) and attribution theory (McAuley & Duncan, 1990b; Rejeski & Brawley, 1983) currently exist in the literature, and the reader is directed to these works for a more detailed review of each area.

The section on attribution theory focused on four broad categories of interest: methodology, causes of personal outcomes, objective versus subjective outcomes, and the attribution–emotion relationship. More specifically, the failure to employ the subject as an active agent in the attribution process and the development of new attributional measures were discussed. The self-serving bias (see Bradley, 1978) has long been a staple interpretation for personal outcomes, with subjects purportedly making self-protective ascriptions for failure and self-enhancing attributions for success. However, it is suggested that if attributions are accurately assessed, the identification of external causes in achievement situations is a very rare phenomenon. It is further suggested that if we are to understand the role of self-reflective processes in sport behavior more fully it will be necessary to differentiate between causal explanations proffered for objective outcomes and those that reflect subjective interpretations of outcome (Maehr & Nicholls, 1980; Spink & Roberts, 1980). Finally, it was argued that Weiner's (1985) model of achievement motivation and emotion has yet to be adequately tested in the sport domain; the relationship between causal explanations for sport-related outcomes and affective reactions has been given, at best, cursory attention by sport psychologists and the link between attributions and behavior has largely gone unexamined.

In this chapter the basic tenets of Bandura's (1977, 1986) self-efficacy theory were outlined, and the general conclusion suggested that performance-based treatment modalities are the most powerful source of efficacy cognitions. The causal role played by efficacy cognitions has received limited attention and must be more thoroughly documented. The role of efficacy expectations in exercise behavior was discussed with the suggestion that future research must address how exercise self-efficacy changes over time, how it affects the behavior of diverse populations, and how efficacy-based interventions might be devised to facilitate exercise behavior. A new area that holds promise for research in sport and physical activity concerns collective or group self-efficacy. Little research has been conducted to date in this area, although the literature with respect to group dynamics in sport is considerable (see chapter 8).

The final objective was to draw together self-efficacy and attribution theory, arguing from a social-cognitive perspective that these two theoretical approaches are not orthogonal but intimately related in a reciprocally determining manner. Attributions made for achievement outcomes influence perceptions of personal capabilities in the future, which in turn, impact upon causal ascriptions for that future outcome. Attributing a positive sport outcome to factors that are perceived as personally controllable, internal, and relatively stable (although this can be variable; e.g., ability can improve with practice) leads to enhanced efficacy congitions. Highly efficacious individuals are likely to attribute the outcomes of future performances to causes within their control. The sequence of these social cognitions has been only partially examined by a handful of researchers. It is recommended that the association between these two important theories be more fully examined as they apply to sport, exercise, and physical activity. Moreover, perceptions of personal control are hypothesized to play an important role in other mechanisms purported to influence behavior, such as intrinsic motivation, goal mechanisms, and social support (Duncan, 1989; Duncan & McAuley, in press).

Self-efficacy and causal attributions should be studied as interdependent rather than separate entities. Self-efficacy beliefs are widely held to exert an important influence on human behavior across myriad domains. However, at the most fundamental level, causal attributions are intimately involved in cognitive processing of information and thereby cognitive theories of motivated behavior. Detailed examination of causal attributions and self-efficacy perceptions as bidirectional influences is likely to enhance and deepen our understanding of sport and exercise behavior.

References

Alden, L. (1986). Self-efficacy and causal attributions for social feedback. *Journal of Research in Personality*, **20**, 473.

Auvergne, S. (1983). Motivation and causal attribution for high and low achieving athletes. *International Journal of Sport Psychology*, **14**, 85-91.

Bandura, A. (1977). Self-efficacy: Toward a unifying theory of behavioral change. *Psychological Review*, **84**, 191-215.

Bandura, A. (1982). Self-efficacy in human agency. *American Psychologist*, **37**, 122-147.

Bandura, A. (1986). *Social foundations of thought and action*. Englewood Cliffs, NJ: Prentice Hall.

Bandura, A., & Adams, N.E. (1977). Analysis of self-efficacy theory of behavioral change. *Cognitive Therapy and Research*, **1**, 287-310.

Bandura, A., & Cervone, D. (1983). Self-evaluative and self-efficacy mechanisms governing the motivational effects of goal systems. *Journal of Personality and Social Psychology*, **45**, 1017-1028.

Bandura, A., & Schunk, D.H. (1981). Cultivating competence, self-efficacy, and intrinsic interest through proximal self-motivation. *Journal of Personality and Social Psychology*, **41**, 586-598.

Bird, A.M., & Williams, J.M. (1980). A developmental–attributional analysis of sex-role stereotypes for sport performance. *Developmental Psychology*, **16**, 319-322.

Bradley, G.W. (1978). Self-serving biases in the attribution process: A reexamination of the fact or fiction question. *Journal of Personality and Social Psychology*, **36**, 56-71.

Brawley, L.R. (1984). Attributions as social cognitions: Contemporary perspectives in sport. In W.F. Straub & J.M. Williams (Eds.), *Cognitive sport psychology* (pp. 212-230). Lansing, NY: Sport Science Associates.

Brawley, L.R., & Roberts, G.C. (1984). Attributions in sport: Research foundations, characteristics, and limitations. In J.M. Silva & R.S. Weinberg (Eds.), *Psychological foundations of sport* (pp. 197-213). Champaign, IL: Human Kinetics.

Brody, E.B., Hatfield, B.D., & Spalding, T.W. (1988). Generalization of self-efficacy to a continuum of stressors upon mastery of a high-risk sport skill. *Journal of Sport and Exercise Psychology*, **10**, 32-44.

Bukowsi, W.M., & Moore, D. (1982). Winners' and losers' attributions for success and failure in a series of athletic events. *Journal of Sport Psychology*, **2**, 195-210.

Burton, D. (1989). The impact of goal specificity and task difficulty on basketball skill development. *Sport Psychologist*, **3**, 34-47.

Collins, J. (1982, March). *Self-efficacy and ability in achievement behavior*. Paper presented at the meeting of the American Educational Research Association, New York.

Corbin, C.B., Laurie, D.R., Gruger, C., & Smiley, B. (1984). Vicarious success experience as a factor influencing self-confidence, attitudes, and physical activity of adult women. *Journal of Teaching in Physical Education*, **4**, 17-23.

Deci, E.L., & Ryan, R.M. (1980). The empirical exploration of intrinsic motivational processes. In L. Berkowitz (Ed.), *Advances in experimental social psychology* (Vol. 13, pp. 39-80). New York: Pergamon.

Deci, E.L., & Ryan, R.M. (1985). *Intrinsic motivation and self-determination in human behavior*. New York: Plenum.

Deeter, T.E. (1989). Development of a model of achievement behavior for physical activity. *Journal of Sport and Exercise Psychology*, **11**, 13-25.

Dishman, R.K. (1982). Compliance/adherence in health-related exercise. *Health Psychology*, **1**, 237-267.

Duncan, T.E. (1989). *The influence of social support and efficacy cognitions in the exercise behavior of sedentary adults: An interaction model*. Unpublished doctoral dissertation, University of Oregon.

Duncan, T.E., & McAuley, E. (1987). Efficacy expectations and perceptions of causality in motor performance. *Journal of Sport Psychology*, **9**, 385-393.

Duncan, T.E., & McAuley, E. (1989, April). *Cognition and emotion following sport performance: A causal model*. Paper presented at the meeting of the American Alliance for Health, Physical Education, Recreation and Dance; Boston.

Duncan, T.E., & McAuley, E. (in press). Social support and efficacy cognitions in exercise adherence: A latent growth curve analysis. *Journal of Behavioral Medicine*.

Dzewaltowski, D.A. (1989). Toward a model of exercise motivation. *Journal of Sport and Exercise Psychology*, **11**, 251-269.

Dzewaltowski, D.A., Noble, J.M., & Shaw, J.M. (1990). Physical activity participation: Social cognitive theory versus the theories of reasoned action and planned behavior. *Journal of Sport and Exercise Psychology*, **12**, 388-405.

Eccles, J.S., Adler, T.F., Futterman, R., Goff, S.B., Kaczala, C.M., Meece, E.L., & Midgley, C. (1983). Expectancies, values, and academic behaviors. In J.T. Spence (Ed.), *Achievement and achievement motions: Psychological and sociological approaches* (pp. 75-146). San Francisco: Freeman.

Eiser, J.R., Van der Plight, J., Raw, M., & Sutton, S.R. (1985). Trying to stop smoking: Effects of perceived addiction, attributions for failure and expectancy of success. *Journal of Behavioral Medicine*, **8**, 321-341.

Epstein, L., & Cluss, P.A. (1982). A behavioral medicine perspective on adherence to long-term medical regimens. *Journal of Consulting and Clinical Psychology*, **50**, 950-971.

Ewart, C.K., Stewart, K.J., Gillian, R.E., Keleman, M.H., Valenti, S.A., Manley, J.D., & Kaleman, M.D. (1986). Usefulness of self-efficacy in predicting overexertion during programmed exercise in coronary artery disease. *American Journal of Cardiology*, **57**, 557-561.

Ewart, C.K., Taylor, C.B., Reese, L.B., & DeBusk, R.F. (1983). Effects of early post myocardial infarction exercise testing on self-perception and subsequent physical activity. *American Journal of Cardiology*, **51**, 1076-1080.

Feltz, D.L. (1982). Path analysis of the causal elements of Bandura's theory of self-efficacy and an anxiety-based model of avoidance behavior. *Journal of Personality and Social Psychology*, **42**, 764-781.

Feltz, D.L. (1988a). Gender differences in the causal elements of self-efficacy on a high avoidance motor task. *Journal of Sport and Exercise Psychology*, **10**, 151-166.

Feltz, D.L. (1988b). Self-confidence and sports performance. *Exercise and Sports Science Reviews*, **16**, 423-458.

Feltz, D.L., Bandura, A., Albrecht, R.R., & Corcoran, J.P. (1988, June). *Perceived team efficacy in collegiate hockey*. Paper presented at the meeting of the North American Society for the Psychology of Sport and Physical Activity, Knoxville, TN.

Feltz, D.L., Corcoran, J.P., & Lirgg, C.D. (1989, June). *Relationships among team confidence, sport confidence, and hockey performance*. Paper presented at the meeting of the North American Society for the Psychology of Sport and Physical Activity, Kent, OH.

Feltz, D.L., Landers, D.M., & Raeder, U. (1979). Enhancing self-efficacy in high avoidance motor tasks: A comparison of modeling techniques. *Journal of Sport and Exercise Psychology*, **1**, 112-122.

Feltz, D.L., & Mugno, D.A. (1983). A replication of the path analysis of the causal elements in Bandura's theory of self-efficacy and the influence of autonomic perception. *Journal of Sport Psychology*, **5**, 263-277.

Fielstein, E., Klein, M.S., Fischer, M., Hanan, C., Koburger, P., Schneider, M.J., & Leitenberg, H. (1985). Self-esteem and causal attributions for success and failure in children. *Cognitive Therapy and Research*, **9**, 381-398.

Forsyth, D.R., & McMillan, J.H. (1981). Attributions, affect, and expectations: A test of Weiner's three-dimensional model. *Journal of Educational Psychology*, **73**, 393-403.

Gayton, W.F., Matthews, G.R., & Burchstead, G.N. (1986). An investigation of the validity of the physical self-efficacy scale in predicting marathon performance. *Perceptual and Motor Skills*, **63**, 752-754.

Gould, D., & Weiss, M. (1981). Effect of model similarity and model self-talk on self-efficacy in muscular endurance. *Journal of Sport Psychology*, **3**, 17-29.

Hall, H.K., & Byrne, A.T.J. (1988). Goal-setting in sport: Clarifying recent anomalies. *Journal of Sport and Exercise Psychology*, **10**, 184-198.

Hall, H.K., Weinberg, R.S., & Jackson, A. (1987). Effects of goal specificity, goal difficulty, and information feedback on endurance performance. *Journal of Sport Psychology*, **9**, 43-54.

Hardy, C.J., & Rejeski, W.J. (1989). Not what, but how one feels: The measurement of affect during exercise. *Journal of Sport and Exercise Psychology*, **11**, 281-289.

Harvey, J.H., Arkin, R.M., Gleason, J.M., & Johnson, S. (1974). Effects of expected and observed outcome of an action on the differential causal attributions of actor and observer. *Journal of Personality*, **42**, 62-77.

Heider, F. (1958). *The psychology of interpersonal relations*. New York: John Wiley & Sons.

Hogan, P.I., & Santomeier, J.P. (1984). Effects of mastering swim skills on older adults' self-efficacy. *Research Quarterly for Exercise and Sport*, **56**, 284-296.

Holloway, J.B., Beuter, A., & Duda, J.L. (1988). Self-efficacy and training for strength in adolescent girls. *Journal of Applied Social Psychology*, **18**, 699-719.

Jones, E.E., & Davis, K.E. (1965). From acts to dispositions: The attribution process in person perception. In L. Berkowitz (Ed.), *Advances in experimental social psychology* (Vol. 2, pp. 219-266). New York: Academic.

Kavanagh, D., & Hausfeld, S. (1986). Physical performance and self-efficacy under happy and sad moods. *Journal of Sport Psychology*, **8**, 112-123.

Kelley, H.H. (1973). The process of causal attribution. *American Psychologist*, **28**, 107-128.

Klug, G.A., McAuley, E., & Clarke, S. (1990). Factors influencing the development and maintenance of aerobic fitness: Lessons applicable to the fibrositis syndrome. *Journal of Rheumatology*, **16**, 41-50.

Landers, D.L. (1983). Whatever happened to theory testing in sport psychology? *Journal of Sport Psychology*, **5**, 135-151.

Maehr, M.L., & Nicholls, J.G. (1980). Culture and achievement motivation: A second look. In N. Warren (Ed.), *Studies in cross-cultural psychology* (pp. 221-267). New York: Academic.

Mark, M.M., Mutrie, N., Brooks, D.R., & Harris, D.V. (1984). Causal attributions of winners and losers in individual competitive sports: Toward a reformulation of the self-serving bias. *Journal of Sport Psychology*, **6**, 184-196.

Martin, D.S., & Huang, M. (1984). Effects of time and perceptual orientation on actors' and observers' attributions. *Perceptual and Motor Skills*, **58**, 23-30.

McAuley, E. (1985a). Modeling and self-efficacy: A test of Bandura's model. *Journal of Sport Psychology*, **7**, 283-295.

McAuley, E. (1985b). Success and causality in sport: The influence of perception. *Journal of Sport Psychology*, **7**, 283-295.

McAuley, E. (1989). *Efficacy cognitions and exercise behavior in young females*. Unpublished manuscript, University of Illinois, Department of Kinesiology.

McAuley, E. (1990, June). *Attributions, affect, and self-efficacy: Predicting exercise behavior in aging adults*. Paper presented at the meeting of the American Psychological Society, Dallas.

McAuley, E. (1991a). Efficacy and attributional determinants of affective reactions to exercise participation. *Journal of Sport and Exercise Psychology,* **13**, 382-394.

McAuley, E. (1991b, June). *Self-referent processes in exercise and human movement*. Early Career Distinguished Scholar Lecture delivered at the annual meeting of the North American Society for the Psychology of Sport and Physical Activity, Monterey, CA.

McAuley, E. (1992a). Understanding exercise behavior: A self-efficacy perspective. In G.C. Roberts (Ed.), *Motivation in sport and exercise* (pp. 107-127). Champaign, IL: Human Kinetics.

McAuley, E. (1992b). The role of efficacy cognitions in the prediction of exercise behavior in middle-aged adults. *Journal of Behavioral Medicine*, **15**, 65-88.

McAuley, E., Courneya, K.S., & Lettunich, J. (1991). Effects of acute and long-term exercise responses in sedentary, middle-aged males and females. *The Gerontologist*, **31**, 534-542.

McAuley, E., & Duncan, T.E. (1989). Causal attributions and affective reactions to disconfirming outcomes in motor performance. *Journal of Exercise and Sport Psychology*, **11**, 187-200.

McAuley, E., & Duncan, T.E. (1990a). Cognitive appraisal and affective reactions to following physical achievement outcomes. *Journal of Sport and Exercise Psychology*, **12**, 415-426.

McAuley, E., & Duncan, T.E. (1990b). The causal attribution process in sport and physical activity. In S. Graham & V. Folkes (Eds.), *Attribution theory: Applications to achievement, mental health, and interpersonal conflict* (pp. 37-52). Hillsdale, NJ: Lawrence Erlbaum.

McAuley, E., Duncan, T.E., & McElroy, M. (1989). Self-efficacy cognitions and causal attributions for children's motor performance: An exploratory investigation. *Journal of Genetic Psychology*, **150**, 65-73.

McAuley, E., Duncan, T.E., & Russell, D. (in press). *Measuring causal attributions: The revised Causal Dimension Scale (CDSII). Personality and Social Psychology Bulletin.*

McAuley, E., & Gill, D.L. (1983). Reliability and validity of the physical self-efficacy scale in a competitive sport setting. *Journal of Sport Psychology*, **5**, 410-418.

McAuley, E., & Gross, J.B. (1983). Perceptions of causality in sport: An application of the Causal Dimension Scale. *Journal of Sport Psychology*, **5**, 72-76.

McAuley, E., & Jacobson, L.B. (1991). Self-efficacy and exercise participation in sedentary adult females. *American Journal of Health Promotion*, **5**, 185-191.

McAuley, E., Poag, K., Gleason, A., Wraith, S. (1990). Attrition from exercise programs: Attributional and affective perspectives. *Journal of Social Behavior and Personality*, **5**, 591-602.

McAuley, E., & Rowney, T. (1990). The role of efficacy cognitions in adherence and intent to exercise. In *Psychology and Sociology of Sport: Current Selected Research* (Vol. 2, pp. 3-15). New York: AMS.

McAuley, E., Russell, R., & Gross, J.B. (1983). Affective consequences of winning and losing: An attributional analysis. *Journal of Sport Psychology*, **5**, 2278-2287.

McAuley, E., Wraith, S., & Duncan, T.E. (1991). Self-efficacy, perceptions of success and intrinsic motivation for exercise. *Journal of Applied Social Psychology*, **21**, 139-155.

Meyer, J.P., & Koelbl, S.L.M. (1982). Students' test performances: Dimensionality of causal attributions. *Personality and Social Psychology Bulletin*, **8**, 31-36.

Michela, J.L., & Wood, J.V. (1986). Causal attributions in health and illness. In P.C. Kendall (Ed.), *Advances in cognitive behavioral research and therapy* (Vol. 5, pp. 179-235). New York: Academic.

Miller, D.T., & Ross, M. (1975). Self-serving biases in the attribution of causality: Fact or fiction? *Psychological Bulletin*, **82**, 213-225.

Miller, J.T., & McAuley, E. (1987). Effects of a goal-setting training program on basketball free-throw self-efficacy and performance. *The Sport Psychologist*, **1**, 103-113.

Mullin, B., & Riordan, C.A. (1988). Self-serving attributions in naturalistic settings: A meta-analytic review. *Journal of Applied Social Psychology*, **18**, 3-22.

Oldridge, N.B. (1982). Compliance and exericise in primary and secondary prevention of coronary heart disease: A review. *Preventive Medicine*, **11**, 56-70.

O'Leary, A. (1985). Self-efficacy and health. *Behavior and Research Therapy*, **23**, 437-451.

Passer, M.W. (1977). *Perceiving the causes of success and failure revisited: A multidimensional scaling approach.* Unpublished doctoral dissertation, University of California, Los Angeles.

Rejeski, W.J., & Brawley, L. (1983). Attribution theory in sport: Current status and new perspective. *Journal of Sport Psychology*, **5**, 77-99.

Rejeski, W.J., & Sanford, B. (1984). Feminine-typed females: The role of affective schema in the perception of exercise intensity. *Journal of Sport Psychology*, **6**, 197-207.

Riordan, C.A., Thomas, J.S., & James, M.K. (1985). Attributions in a one-on-one sports competition: Evidence for self-serving biases and gender differences. *Journal of Sport Behavior*, **8**, 42-53.

Roberts, G.C. (1978). Children's assignment of responsibility for winning and losing, In F. Smoll & R. Smith (Eds.), *Psychological perspectives in youth sports*. Washington, DC: Hemisphere.

Roberts, G.C., & Pascuzzi, D. (1979). Causal attributions in sport: Some theoretical implications. *Journal of Sport Psychology*, **1**, 203-211.

Robinson, D.W., & Howe, B.L. (1989). Appraisal variable/affect relationships in youth sports: A test of Weiner's attributional model. *Journal of Sport and Exercise Psychology*, **11**, 431-443.

Russell, D. (1982). The Causal Dimension Scale: A measure of how individuals perceive causes. *Journal of Personality and Social Psychology*, **42**, 1137-1145.

Russell, D., McAuley, E., & Tarico, V. (1987). Measuring causal attributions for success and failure: A comparison of methodologies for assessing causal dimensions. *Journal of Personality and Social Psychology*, **52**, 1248-1257.

Ryckman, R.M., Robbins, M.A., Thornton, B., & Cantrell, P. (1982). Development and validation of a physical self-efficacy scale. *Journal of Personality and Social Psychology*, **42**, 891-900.

Sallis, J.F., Haskell, W.L., Fortnam, S.P., Vranizan, M.S., Taylor, C.B., & Solomon, D.S. (1986). Predictors of adoption and maintenance of physical activity in a community sample. *Preventive Medicine*, **15**, 331-341.

Scanlan, T.K., & Passer, M.W. (1981). Factors influencing the competitive performance expectancies of young female athletes. *Journal of Personality*, **49**, 60-74.

Schoeneman, T.J., & Curry, S. (1990). Attributions for successful and unsuccessful health behavior change. *Basic and Applied Social Psychology*, **11**, 421-431.

Schunk, D.H. (1984). Self-efficacy perspective on achievement behavior. *Educational Psychologist*, **19**, 48-58.

Schunk, D.H., & Cox, P.D. (1986). Strategy training feedback with learning disabled students. *Journal of Educational Psychology*, **78**, 201-209.

Schunk, D.H., & Gunn, T.P. (1986). Self-efficacy and skill development: Influence on task strategy and attributions. *Journal of Educational Research*, **79**, 238-244.

Silva, J.M., & Hardy, C.S. (1984). Precompetitive affect and athletic performance. In W.F. Straub & J.M. Williams (Eds.), *Cognitive sport psychology*. Lansing, NY: Sport Science Associates.

Sonstroem, R.J., & Morgan, W.P. (1989). Exercise and self-esteem: Rationale and model. *Medicine and Science in Sports and Exercise*, **21**, 329-337.

Spink, K.S., & Roberts, G.C. (1980). Ambiguity of outcome and causal attributions. *Journal of Sport Psychology*, **2**, 237-244.

Taylor, C.B., Bandura, A., Ewart, C.K., Miller, N.H., & DeBusk, R.T. (1985). Exercise testing to enhance wives' confidence in their husbands' cardiac capabilities soon after clinically uncomplicated acute myocardial infarction. *American Journal of Cardiology*, **55**, 6335-6638.

Vallerand, R.J. (1983). On emotion in sport: Theoretical and social psychological perspectives. *Journal of Sport Psychology*, **5**, 197-215.

Vallerand, R.J. (1987). Antecedents of self-related affects in sport: Preliminary evidence on the intuitive–reflective appraisal model. *Journal of Sport Psychology*, **9**, 161-182.

Vallerand, R.J., & Richer, F. (1988). On the use of the causal dimension scale in a field setting: A test with confirmatory factor analysis in success and failure situations. *Journal of Personality and Social Psychology*, **54**, 704-712.

Vealey, R. (1986). Conceptualization of sport confidence and competitive orientation: Preliminary investigation and instrument development. *Journal of Sport Psychology*, **8**, 221-246.

Weinberg, R.S., Bruya, L.D., & Jackson, A. (1985). The effects of goal proximity and goal specificity on endurance performance. *Journal of Sport Psychology*, **7**, 296-305.

Weinberg, R.S., Gould, D., & Jackson, A. (1979). Expectations and performance: An empirical test of Bandura's self-efficacy theory. *Journal of Sport Psychology*, **1**, 320-331.

Weiner, B. (1972). *Theories of motivation: From mechanism to cognition*. Chicago: Rand-McNally.

Weiner, B. (1979). A theory of motivation for some classroom experience. *Journal of Educational Psychology*, **71**, 3-25.

Weiner, B. (1983). Some methodological pitfalls in attribution research. *Journal of Educational Psychology*, **75**, 530-543.

Weiner, B. (1985). An attributional theory of achievement motivation and emotion. *Psychological Review*, **92**, 548-573.

Weiner, B. (1986). *An attributional theory of motivation and emotion*. New York: Springer-Verlag.

Weiner, B., Frieze, I., Kukla, A., Reed, L., Rest, S., & Rosenbaum, R.M. (1972). Perceiving the causes of success and failure. In E.E. Jones, D.E. Kanouse, H.H. Kelley, R.E. Nisbett, S. Valins, & B. Weiner (Eds.), *Attribution: Perceiving the causes of behavior*. Morristown, NJ: General Learning.

Weiner, B., Russell, D., & Lerman, D. (1979). The cognition–emotion process in achievement-related contexts. *Journal of Personality and Social Psychology*, **37**, 1211-1220.

Weiss, M.R., McAuley, E., Ebbeck, V., & Wiese, D.M. (1990). Self-esteem and causal attribution for children's physical and social competence in sport. *Journal of Sport and Exercise Psychology*, **12**, 21-36.

Wilkes, R.L., & Summers, J.J. (1984). Cognitions, mediating variables, and strength performance. *Journal of Sport Psychology*, **6**, 351-359.

Zuckerman, M. (1979). Attribution of success and failure revisited; or The motivational bias is alive and well in attribution theory. *Journal of Personality*, **47**, 245-287.

Chapter 6

The Arousal–Athletic Performance Relationship: Current Status and Future Directions

Daniel Gould
University of North Carolina at Greensboro

Vikki Krane
Bowling Green State University

The relationship between emotional arousal and athletic performance, as well as the related topics of stress and anxiety, has been of central importance throughout the history of sport psychology. As early as 1932, Coleman Griffith, the father of North American sport psychology, referred to the arousal–performance relationship

when he discussed the advisability of "keying up teams" and identifying strategies for dealing with athletes' "anxiety and fright" states. More recently, in a content analysis of applied sport psychology texts, Vealey (1988) found that arousal control was discussed by 70% of the authors whereas the method of relaxation training

Note. The authors would like to thank Thelma Horn and Graham Jones for their helpful comments on an earlier draft of this manuscript.

was discussed by 93% of the authors. Finally, virtually every contemporary academic sport psychology text (e.g., Bird & Cripe, 1986; Cox, 1990; Gill, 1986; Silva & Weinberg, 1984; Williams, 1986) has devoted considerable attention to the interrelated topics of arousal, anxiety, and stress.

Since the later 1960s, most sport psychology writers (e.g., Cox, 1990; Landers & Boutcher, 1986; Sonstroem, 1984) have emphasized the notion that an optimal level of arousal is associated with best performance, whereas arousal levels above or below optimal level are related to inferior performance. Indeed, the inverted-U hypothesis has become a stable principle in both the academic and professional sport psychology literature (see p. 125). In recent years, however, a number of European sport psychologists (Hardy & Fazey, 1987; Jones & Hardy, 1989; Kerr, 1985, 1987) have critically examined the inverted-U hypothesis and have questioned both its conceptual and practical utility. These same criticisms have also begun to emerge in the North American sport psychology literature (Martens, 1987a; Neiss, 1988; Weinberg, 1990). From a different but certainly related perspective, a number of sport psychology investigators (Burton, 1988; Gould, Petlichkoff, Simons & Vevera, 1987; Martens, Vealey & Burton, 1990) have begun advocating the view that anxiety is a multidimensional rather than a unitary phenomenon. Furthermore, these researchers have demonstrated that the two different dimensions of anxiety (i.e., somatic and cognitive anxiety states) have differential effects on athletic performance.

Given the number of conceptual and methodological changes proposed in the arousal–performance relationship area, a need exists to provide an in-depth examination of the current status of research on the topic. The intent of this chapter is to provide such an examination. In addition, this chapter will examine conceptual systems for providing future research directions, identify central research issues, and recognize methodological refinements and needs.

First, the relationship among anxiety, stress, arousal, and related terms will be discussed. This is an important issue because major interpretive problems have beset the literature due to the fact that these terms are often used interchangeably even though they are conceptually distinct. Second, arousal–performance relationship hypotheses and theories will be examined and discussed, including drive theory, the inverted-U hypothesis, Hanin's (1989) optimal zones of arousal hypothesis, multidimensional anxiety theory, Hardy and Fazey's (1987) application of catastrophe theory, and Kerr's (1985, 1987) reversal theory interpretation. Finally, future directions for

conceptual and methodological arousal–performance relationship research will be offered, as well as critical research questions in need of study.

Defining Anxiety, Stress, Arousal, and Related Terms

A long-standing problem in the study of the arousal–performance relationship has been the inconsistent use of terms such as *arousal, stress*, and *anxiety*. These terms have been used interchangeably (e.g., Gould, Petlichkoff & Weinberg, 1984; Landers, Wang & Courtet, 1985), although numerous theoretical distinctions have been made among them. The first step in eliminating this semantic confusion is to provide concise operational definitions of the various anxiety-related constructs. Therefore, the constructs of arousal, state anxiety, trait anxiety, cognitive anxiety, somatic anxiety, interpersonal state anxiety, and group state anxiety will be discussed and operational definitions for these terms will be provided.

Arousal

Arousal has typically been referred to as physiological activation or autonomic reactivity. Landers defined arousal as "a motivational construct" that represents "the intensity level of behavior" (1980, p. 77). Arousal is typically seen as varying along a continuum from deep sleep to extreme excitement (Malmo, 1959). Landers and Boutcher viewed arousal as "an energizing function that is responsible for harnessing of the body's resources for intense and vigorous activity" (1986, p. 164).

Measurements of physiological arousal can be classified as electrophysiological, respiratory and cardiovascular, or biochemical (Hackfort & Schwenkmezger, 1989). Typical measures of arousal include heart rate, blood pressure, respiration rate, electrocortical activity (electroencephalograph), electromyograph, biomechanical indicants such as epinephrin or adrenalin, and galvanic skin response. Arousal has also been assessed through self-report scales such as the Thayer (1967) Activation–Deactivation Checklist.

Martens (1987a), writing in an *applied forum*, has recently forwarded a view of arousal that differs somewhat from that of traditional arousal theorists. Specifically, Martens viewed arousal—or what he labeled *psychic energy*—as "the vigor, vitality and intensity with which the mind functions" (p. 92). Hence, arousal is viewed by Martens as being more than physiological activation of the organism. It involves mental activation as well.

Given a composite of these views, *arousal* is best defined as general physiological and psychological activation of the organism that varies on a continuum from deep sleep to intense excitement. Although arousal has traditionally been inferred through physiological indexes such as heart rate and respiration, some investigators feel that it also represents a cognitive or mental intensity of behavior.

Anxiety

Anxiety can be considered the emotional impact or cognitive dimension of arousal. Landers (1980; Landers & Boutcher, 1986) suggested that unpleasant emotional reactions may accompany arousal of the autonomic nervous system and that this maladaptive emotional condition has been labeled *anxiety*. Martens (1977) suggested that anxiety reactions would result from an objective environmental demand interpreted as threatening (a perceived imbalance between the demand and one's response capabilities) by an individual. Hence, *anxiety* has been viewed as feelings of nervousness and tension associated with activation or arousal of the organism.

Spielberger (1966, 1972) has further noted that for a theory of anxiety to be adequate, it must differentiate between anxiety as a mood state and as a personality trait. Additionally, it must differentiate among the stimulus conditions antecedent to these forms of anxiety. Based on this argument, Spielberger (1966) proposed the state-trait theory of anxiety, which differentiates between state and trait anxiety. *State anxiety* is defined as an emotional state "characterized by subjective, consciously perceived feelings of apprehension and tension, accompanied by or associated with activation or arousal of the autonomic nervous system" (Spielberger, 1966, p. 17). This condition varies from moment to moment and fluctuates proportional to the perceived threat in the immediate situation. *Trait anxiety*, on the other hand, is "a motive or acquired behavioral disposition that predisposes an individual to perceive a wide range of objectively nondangerous circumstances as threatening and to respond to these with state anxiety reactions disproportionate in intensity to the magnitude of the objective danger" (Spielberger, 1966, p. 17). The state-trait theory of anxiety predicts that high-trait-anxious individuals will perceive more situations as threatening and react with greater state anxiety in a greater variety of situations than low-trait-anxious individuals.

Anxiety has typically been measured with self-report questionnaires. Although there are many criticisms of self-report measures, especially in regard to their susceptibility to social desirability bias (Hackfort & Schwenkmezger, 1989; Neiss, 1988; Williams & Krane, 1989), psychological inventories have become the more popular measure of anxiety because of the ease of administration, especially in field settings. Martens defended their use by stating that "the assessment of A-state through self-report measures tells us more about the subject's general state of arousal than any single or composite index of physiological measures" (1977, p. 115).

Still, as cautioned by Martens et al. (1990) and Williams and Krane (1989), researchers need to be aware of the potential for social desirability bias and take steps to minimize it. This can be accomplished by developing a good rapport with athletes, using anti-social desirability instructions with questionnaires, and using a social desirability scale to identify athletes likely to repress their true feelings.

There are several self-report anxiety inventories commonly used in sport psychology. Consistent with his state-trait theory of anxiety, Spielberger and his colleagues (Spielberger, Gorsuch & Lushene, 1970a, 1970b) developed the State-Trait Anxiety Inventory (STAI), which differentiated between state and trait anxiety. This became a popular tool in sport psychology and is still being used by a number of sport and exercise psychology anxiety researchers. As the investigation of anxiety in sport psychology progressed, Martens (1977) expressed the need for sport-specific measures of anxiety and developed the Sport Competition Anxiety Test (SCAT) to measure competitive trait anxiety. Competitive trait anxiety was defined as the "tendency to perceive competitive sport situations as threatening and to respond to these situations with feelings of apprehension and tension" (Martens, 1977, p. 23). Martens also noted the need for a sport-specific measure of state anxiety. His modification of the state scale of Spielberger's STAI resulted in the Competitive State Anxiety Inventory (CSAI).

In summary, state anxiety is associated with depressed or heightened arousal and is defined as a transitory state, or a "right now" feeling of apprehension and tension in a given specific situation. Trait anxiety is defined as how one generally feels, or a relatively stable predisposition to perceive a wide range of situations as threatening and to respond to these with state anxiety. Both forms of anxiety are typically assessed via psychological inventories.

Differentiating Between Cognitive and Somatic Anxiety

Recent anxiety literature in sport psychology has focused on the multidimensional nature of anxiety (e.g., Burton, 1988; Gould, Petlichkoff, Simons & Vevera, 1987; Krane & Williams, 1987; Martens et al., 1990). This line of research stems from the work of Borkovek (1976) and Davidson and Schwartz (1976), who differentiated between cognitive and somatic anxiety. Borkovek noted that there are "three separate but interacting" response components of anxiety: cognitive, physiological, and overt behavioral. *Cognitive anxiety* was operationalized as negative concerns about performance, inability to concentrate, and disrupted attention, whereas *somatic anxiety* was operationalized as perceptions of bodily symptoms of autonomic reactivity such as butterflies in the stomach, sweating, shakiness, and increased heart rate (Davidson & Schwartz, 1976; Kauss, 1980; Martens et al., 1990). Behavioral components of anxiety focus on such indicants as facial expressions, changes in communication patterns, and restlessness (Hanson & Gould, 1988).

Although previous research in general psychology and test anxiety had differentiated between cognitive and somatic anxiety, Martens, Burton, Vealey, Bump, and Smith (1990) stimulated this line of research in sport psychology with the development of the CSAI–2, which consisted of separate measures of cognitive and somatic anxiety. (The CSAI–2 also consists of a self-confidence subscale, but the present discussion will examine the scale only as it directly relates to anxiety research.) This is the most commonly used multidimensional anxiety measure in sport psychology, although the Cognitive–Somatic Anxiety Questionnaire (Schwartz, Davidson & Goleman, 1978) has also been utilized.

Recently, a multidimensional measure of trait anxiety has been developed by Smith, Smoll, and Schutz (1990). The Sport Anxiety Scale (SAS) was developed as a sport-specific measure of somatic reactions, cognitive worry, and concentration disruption. Whereas univariate competitive trait anxiety has been found to be highly correlated with cognitive and somatic anxiety (Gould et al., 1984; Martens et al., 1983), because of the newness of the SAS, these findings have not yet been replicated within the multidimensional theory of anxiety. It would be predicted, however, that trait cognitive anxiety and trait somatic anxiety would be strong predictors of state cognitive anxiety and state somatic anxiety, respectively.

Intrapersonal and Group State–Trait Anxiety

Hanin (1989) approached the study of anxiety from a social-psychological perspective. Thus, he incorporated emotional reactions and the social environment into his conceptualization of state anxiety. Anxiety was studied as an interaction between the person and the environment. This innovative approach is holistic and does not separate behavior into separate entities; that is, anxiety is examined within the context of relationships with other people and specific qualities of the environment.

Performance anxiety, an emotional reaction experienced while working on a specific task, was further divided into *interpersonal state anxiety* ($S=A_{int}$) and *intragroup state anxiety* ($S=A_{gr}$): "Both constructs refer to the emotional reactions experienced by a person at a given moment in time as a function of *his/her involvement with a particular partner* ($S=A_{int}$), and/or *as a member of a group or team* ($S=A_{gr}$)" (Hanin, 1989, p. 21). Hanin further differentiated between performance anxiety and optimal state anxiety. *Optimal state anxiety* is defined as "the level of performance State=Anxiety that enables a particular athlete to perform at his/her personal best" (Hanin, 1989, p. 22), whereas *performance anxiety* is his or her specific level of state anxiety in a particular competitive situation.

Interpersonal and intragroup state anxiety have been assessed with the Russian adaptation of Spielberger's STAI (STAI–R; Hanin & Spielberger, 1983). The only difference between the English and Russian measures were the instructions. When measuring interpersonal state anxiety, athletes were asked to complete the questionnaire according to "how he/she felt at a particular moment while in actual or anticipated contact with a particular person (partner, coach, trainer, sports administrator, rival, referee, etc.)" (p. 22). When measuring intragroup state anxiety, athletes were asked "to evaluate how he/she feels at a particular moment as a team member" (p. 22). Hanin also utilized the Psychological Discomfort/Comfort Scale, a visual analogue state anxiety measure, to assess immediate changes in state anxiety while performing a task.

Metamotivational States and Positive Psychic Energy

Traditionally, state anxiety has been viewed as the mental intensity dimension of arousal. Recently, however, Kerr (1985, 1987) has advocated the use of Apter's (1976, 1984) theory of psychological reversals, which suggested that high arousal can at times be both positive and negative. Specifically, Apter's theory of psychological reversals holds that increased arousal may be interpreted as anxiety or excitement depending on one's *metamotivational state*. In a *telic* metamotivational state, the subject is goal-directed and serious and high arousal is perceived as negative affect, much like (in our view synonymous with) high state anxiety. In a *paratelic*, high-arousal metamotivational state, however, the subject (in our case, athlete) is in an activity-oriented, playful, positive affect state that is very enjoyable. In fact, Martens (1987a) has labeled this state as *positive psychic energy*.

Unfortunately, a valid telic metamotivational state measure has not been developed. However, later in this review it will be shown that viewing the cognitive component of arousal as more than the negative state anxiety affective response is intuitively appealing and may assist investigators in better unraveling the arousal–athletic performance relationship.

Stress and the Stress Process

The term *stress* has often been utilized as if it were synonymous with *anxiety*. Martens (1977) noted the inconsistencies in using *stress* in this manner and pointed out that it has at times been defined in three different ways—as a stimulus variable, an intervening variable, and/or a response variable. Stress has also been described as both an environmental variable and an emotional response to a specific situation (Gould & Petlichkoff, 1987). Smith and Smoll (1982) suggested that these are two distinct entities and noted that it is important to distinguish between an athlete's perception of stress and potential environmental stressors. Selye (1974) further differentiated among *eustress*, or good stress, and *distress*, or bad stress, suggesting that not all stressors should be perceived as negative.

In order to address the inconsistencies in the use of the term *stress*, a process definition has been adapted by many sport psychologists (e.g., Gould, 1987; Gould & Petlichkoff, 1987; Martens, 1977; Passer, 1982). This type of definition is based on McGrath's (1970) process model of stress (see Figure 6.1). In this model, *stress* was defined as "a substantial imbalance between (environmental) demand and response capability, under conditions where failure to meet the demand has important consequences" (p. 20).

McGrath's (1970) model is comprised of four interrelated stages that can readily be applied to the athletic environment. The first stage consists

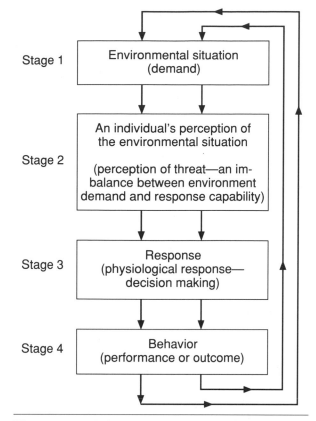

Figure 6.1   McGrath's (1970) stress process.
Note. From "Psychological Stress and the Age-Group Wrestler" by D. Gould and L. Petlichkoff. In *Competitive Sports for Children and Youth* (p. 65) by E.W. Brown and C.F. Branta (Ed.), 1988. Copyright 1988 by Human Kinetics Publishers, Inc. Reprinted by permission.

of an environmental situation or demand placed upon an athlete that may be perceived differently by different athletes. For example, one tennis player may look forward to a competitive match against a strong opponent, whereas another may perceive the situation as demanding or intimidating. Thus, the second stage is the individual's perception of the environmental demand. Martens (1977) elaborated by indicating that an athlete will feel threatened if he or she perceives an imbalance between the demands of the situation and his or her response capabilities. For instance, the first tennis player in the example may perceive the situation as a challenge (i.e., positive) while the second player may perceive it as threatening (i.e., negative) because of the high probability of losing. The third stage in McGrath's (1970) model is the response of the individual that consists of increased physiological arousal, as well as increases in A-state, telic, and paratelic states. The last stage in the model is the performance or outcome of behavior.

Martens summarized this whole process by stating, "Stress is the process that involves the perception of substantial imbalance between environmental demand and response capability, under conditions where failure to meet demand is perceived as having important consequences and is responded to with increased levels of A-state" (1977, p. 9). This statement delineated between stress as an environmental influence mediated by one's perceptions and anxiety as the cognitive manifestation of stress.

There are four advantages to viewing stress as a process:

- Stress is defined as a sequence of events leading to a specific behavior and not in an emotional context.
- Stress is viewed in a cyclical fashion.
- Stress may be viewed as positive or negative, as opposed to negative only.
- The emphasis is placed not merely on the situation but on the athlete's perception of the situation.

Bridging the Gaps Among Stress, Arousal, and Anxiety Terms

Sport psychologists need to resolve the inconsistent use of arousal-and-anxiety-related terminology. It has been shown in this section that these concepts have distinct meanings. Hence, using them interchangeably or assuming that the measures used to assess one concept (e.g., heart rate, cognitive state anxiety) will adequately reflect the total arousal construct has only clouded the arousal–performance relationship from both theoretical and empirical perspectives. It is imperative that future investigators clarify how they are using these terms conceptually and then link their specific arousal and anxiety measures to these conceptual distinctions. Later a conceptual model for integrating arousal construct terminology will be provided. It is hoped that this model will be used by future researchers in identifying the aspect of arousal or anxiety they wish to examine and in developing appropriate measures of that construct.

Arousal–Performance Relationship Hypotheses and Theories

A number of theories and hypotheses have been proposed to account for the relationship between arousal and athletic performance or anxiety and athletic performance. Many of the earlier theories have examined the arousal construct, whereas more recent theories were developed based on the anxiety construct. Two relatively early theories that were proposed and tested in the sport and motor performance context were the drive theory and the inverted-U hypothesis. More recently, additional theories have been advanced. These include Hanin's optimal zones of arousal hypothesis, multidimensional theory of anxiety, catastrophe theory, and reversal theory.

The Drive Theory

The drive theory, originally proposed by Hull (1943) and subsequently modified by J. and K. Spence (1966), suggested that performance is a product of *drive* and *habit strength*. *Drive* is considered synonymous with *arousal* and habit strength is the dominance of the correct or incorrect response (whether the skill is well learned or novel). Thus, the arousal–performance relationship can be expressed as the linear relationship $P = H \times D$, with increased arousal causing an increase in the frequency of the concomitant response. In the early stages of learning, the dominant response would be the incorrect one. So the theory predicts that increased arousal would be detrimental during skill acquisition. However, later in the learning process (i.e., when a skill is well learned) arousal, or drive, would increase the probability of the dominant "correct" response and performance would thus improve (see Figure 6.2).

In an early review of the research on arousal and performance, Taylor (1956) cited a series of studies using a serial-verbal-maze-learning task that supported the drive theory. In these studies,

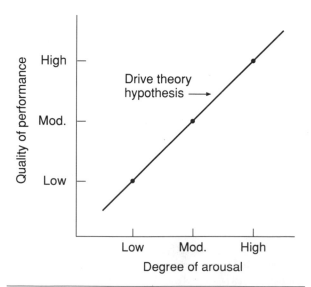

Figure 6.2 The arousal/performance relationship according to drive theory.
Note. From "Arousal and Sport Performance" in *Psychological Dynamics of Sport* (p. 118) by D. Gill, 1986, Champaign, IL: Human Kinetics. Copyright 1986 by Diane L. Gill. Reprinted by permission.

as anxiety increased, subjects committed more errors during learning of this task. These errors, according to Taylor, were due to interfering response tendencies. A decade later, J. and K. Spence (1966) reviewed 25 studies investigating the arousal–performance relationship and found that all but four supported the hypothesis that arousal was positively correlated to performance.

Despite early support for the drive theory, a number of criticisms were levied against this theory during the 1970s. For example, Martens (1971, 1974), conducted an extensive review of the drive theory literature and reported that an equal number of studies supported and rejected the predicted relationships between anxiety and performance. It is important to note that early studies supporting the drive theory employed very simple tasks. More specifically, the drive theory does not appear to be sufficiently applicable to complex motor tasks (Martens, 1971, 1974; Tobias, 1980; Weinberg, 1979) and thus is considered too simplistic to explain complex athletic performance (Fisher, 1976). Another criticism of the drive theory is that it is very difficult to determine the habit hierarchy of correct and incorrect responses in most motor skill tasks and thus difficult to test the theory adequately. Hence, Martens (1971, 1974) and others (Neiss, 1988; Weinberg, 1990) have strongly rejected the use of the drive theory in motor behavior contexts.

The Inverted-U Hypothesis

In 1908 Yerkes and Dodson proposed the inverted-U hypothesis, which also attempted to explain the relationship between arousal and performance. They suggested that heightened arousal enhanced performance to a certain point, after which continued increases in arousal would lead to a detriment in performance. Thus, the predicted relationship between arousal and performance was curvilinear, taking the shape of an inverted-U (see Figure 6.3). In support of such a relationship, Duffy (1932) noted that increased muscular tension leads to poorer performance of a muscular activity and that high tension would decrease response flexibility. Thus, Duffy concluded that "a moderate degree of tension offers the greatest advantages, since very high tension tends to be disruptive and very low tension involves lack of alertness of effort" (p. 545). Hebb (1957) developed the theory further when he suggested that there was an optimal level of arousal, that is, a level of arousal at which an individual would perform to his or her maximum potential, neither overaroused or underaroused.

The inverted-U hypothesis has been examined by a number of researchers in sport psychology

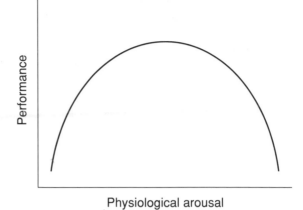

Figure 6.3 Inverted-U model predictions.
Note. From "The Inverted-U Hypothesis: A Catastrophe for Sport Psychology" by J. Fazey and L. Hardy. In *Bass Monograph No. 1* (p. 20), 1988, Leeds, U.K.: British Association of Sports Sciences and National Coaching Foundation. Adapted by permission.

and has received fairly consistent support. Martens and Landers (1970), for example, tested this hypothesis using a tracing task involving arm steadiness. Subjects who performed the task under a moderately stressful situation performed the task better than those performing under the low-stress or high-stress conditions. Klavora (1977) also found support for the inverted-U hypothesis in his study with male high school basketball players. This study found a range of optimal state anxiety where the best athletic performances were observed. Furthermore, separate inverted-U curves were found for low- and high-trait-anxious athletes. Performance of female collegiate basketball players was also shown to follow an inverted-U pattern (Sonstroem & Bernardo, 1982). Athletes with moderate levels of trait and state anxiety scored the most points and displayed the best overall performance. The worst performances were exhibited by the high-anxious players. Support for the inverted-U hypothesis was also found in a study of hitting performance in Little League baseball players (Lowe, 1973), with best performances occurring when players were under moderate stress.

Despite receiving some empirical support from sport psychology researchers, the inverted-U hypothesis has also received much criticism. Landers (1980) contended that the inverted-U hypothesis does not *explain* the relationship between arousal and performance but merely noted that the relationship is curvilinear. Landers suggested that a theory was needed that would allow for explanation and prediction concerning the relationship between arousal and performance.

Landers and Boutcher (1986) have offered possible attentional explanations (focusing on Easterbrook's, 1959, cue utilization theory and Bacon's, 1974, attentional selectivity notions) for why and how arousal influences performance in an inverted-U fashion. However, a full test of these predictions has never been made. Hence, the inverted-U is merely a general prediction, not a theory that explains how, why, or precisely when arousal affects performance. The inverted-U has also been criticized for "an apparent lack of predictive validity in practical situations" (Hardy & Fazey, 1987, p. 4). Specifically, experiential knowledge suggests that after an athlete's anxiety level increases beyond the optimal point (e.g., when an athlete "chokes"), slight decreases in anxiety will not result in slightly improved performance, as the inverted-U hypothesis predicts it will (Hardy & Fazey, 1987). Rather, performance deteriorates in a drastic and catastrophic fashion. Hardy and Fazey suggest that the relationship between anxiety and performance does not follow the symmetrical inverted-U curve because the two halves of the inverted-U curve match only in theory, not in reality.

Other criticisms of the inverted-U hypothesis are based on the methodological, interpretive, conceptual, and statistical problems evident in previous studies purporting to support this hypothesis (Hardy & Fazey, 1987; Neiss, 1988; Weinberg, 1990). Equivocal findings in these studies are often explained by citing individual differences, task characteristics, or imprecise measurement of performance (Weinberg, 1990). Another criticism of the inverted-U hypothesis is the failure to recognize the multidimensional nature of arousal/anxiety (Hardy & Fazey, 1987; Jones & Hardy, 1989). Finally, Neiss (1988) faulted the hypothesis for being by nature not subject to refutation: The proposed variability of optimal arousal and the influence of task complexity allow researchers to fit most data to the inverted-U curve. This is evidenced by the number of studies that apply the inverted-U hypothesis retrospectively (Kerr, 1985). Any evidence contrary to the inverted-U hypothesis can be explained by suggestions that the subjects were not sufficiently aroused or that the task was too simple or complex (Neiss, 1988). These criticisms lead Neiss to claim that "the inverted-U hypothesis has not received clear support from a single study" (p. 355).

Optimal Zones of Arousal Hypothesis

As an alternative to the inverted-U hypothesis, Soviet sport psychologist Yuri Hanin (1980) has proposed the zone of optimal functioning (ZOF) state anxiety–performance relationship. It is Hanin's contention that the large variability in state anxiety scores typically found in field studies with different athletic subsamples make it unlikely that one specific optimal level of state anxiety exists that leads to best performance. Rather, Hanin suggests that through retrospective and systematic multiple observations of athletes' state anxiety and performance levels, a ZOF can be identified. Specifically, this zone consists of an athlete's mean precompetitive state anxiety score on Spielberger and his colleagues' (1970a, 1970b) STAI plus or minus 4 points (approximately one-half a standard deviation). Figure 6.4 compares two swimmers' ZOFs.

The zone-of-optimal-arousal hypothesis was designed as a practical tool that could provide reference points and criteria for diagnosis and evaluation of precompetitive state anxiety in athletes (Hanin, 1980). Athletes whose state anxiety fell within their ZOF would be expected to perform better than athletes whose state anxiety was outside of their ZOF. Moreover, some empirical support has been generated for Hanin's contentions, because weight lifters whose state anxiety was outside of their ZOF three days prior to competition were less successful than weight lifters who remained within their ZOF (Hanin, 1980). Similarly, Morgan and his associates (Morgan, O'Connor, Ellickson & Bradley, 1988; Morgan, O'Connor, Sparling & Pate, 1987) found

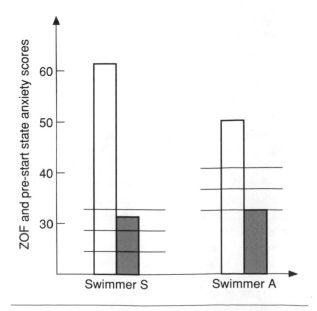

Figure 6.4 Zones of optimal functioning (ZOFs) and state anxiety levels for two swimmers prior to poor and good performances in competition. Shaded regions refer to successful performance; white regions indicate unsuccessful performance.

Note. From Speilberger and Diaz-Guerrero, eds.: *Cross-Cultural Anxiety: Vol. 3,* 1986, Hemisphere Publishing Corp., NY.

that optimal zones of functioning existed for elite male and female distance runners even though the Body Awareness Scale (a measure of self-report somatic activation) was utilized in the investigations, instead of the STAI.

Several aspects of Hanin's (1980) ZOF make it attractive. First, it is intuitively appealing and appears to be very realistic. The ZOF also has the strength of precisely predicting at what state anxiety levels optimal athlete performance will result. However, more independent tests of its contentions are needed before it can be empirically accepted. Like the inverted-U, it is also conceptually limited to hypothesis status, because no explanation has been forwarded to explain why state anxiety influences performance in and out of the ZOF. Additionally, the ZOF is based on a unidimensional conception of anxiety, although a multidimensional approach may yield more information and add to its predictive potential.

Multidimensional Anxiety Theory

As noted earlier, anxiety may not be a unidimensional phenomenon but may be comprised of at least two distinct subcomponents. Liebert and Morris (1967), in the test anxiety literature, labeled these two subcomponents *worry* and *emotionality*, whereas Davidson and Schwartz (1986), in the general psychology literature, used the terms *cognitive* and *somatic* anxiety. Despite the differences in the labels given the subcomponents, the meaning is similar. Worry, or cognitive anxiety, is considered the conscious awareness of unpleasant feelings (Morris, Davis & Hutchings, 1981), whereas emotionality, or somatic anxiety, is defined as perceived physiological arousal. The distinction between these two anxiety subcomponents is important because they have been found to relate to test-taking performance differentially (Libert & Morris, 1967).

One reason for differentiating between cognitive and somatic anxiety is the implication that they have differing antecedent conditions and hence are hypothesized to affect performance differentially (Davidson & Schwartz, 1976; Gould et al., 1984; Krane, 1985; Martens et al., 1983). It was suggested that somatic anxiety is a conditioned response to competitive situations and that cognitive anxiety would be reflective of negative expectations, which have been found to have a powerful influence on performance (Bandura, 1977). Cognitive anxiety has been hypothesized to interfere with performance because of its distracting properties; that is, the performer's attention will be diverted away from his or her performance to task-irrelevant anxiety cognitions.

The concept of cognitive anxiety as negative concerns about performance, inability to concentrate, and disrupted attention (Davidson & Schwartz, 1976) is consistent with previous studies noting the detrimental effects of worry. In the text anxiety literature, for example, the direction–attention hypothesis stated that differences in the performance of high- and low-test-anxious individuals under conditions of evaluative stress will be due to different attentional focuses (Wine, 1980). Low-test-anxious people will remain focused on task relevant cues, whereas the high-test-anxious person's attention will be diverted by self-preoccupied worry. This concept of the distracting nature of cognitive anxiety can also be found in Easterbrook's (1959) cue utilization theory, which suggests that high anxiety will limit the range of task-relevant cues to which one could attend, thus hindering performance.

When applied to sport, multidimensional anxiety theory predicts that cognitive and somatic anxiety will differentially influence athletic performance (Burton, 1988; Martens et al., 1990). Specifically, it predicts a powerful negative linear relationship between cognitive state anxiety and performance and a less powerful, inverted-U relationship between somatic anxiety and performance. Two studies have been conducted (Burton, 1988; Gould et al., 1987) to test multidimensional anxiety theory predictions. Gould and colleagues (1987) found somatic anxiety to have a curvilinear relationship with pistol-shooting performance, supporting the inverted-U hypothesis, whereas cognitive anxiety was unrelated to performance. Burton (1988) also found a curvilinear relationship between somatic anxiety and swimming performance but (unlike Gould and his colleagues) only a negative linear relationship between cognitive anxiety and performance. Increased cognitive anxiety was associated with a detriment in performance.

In summary, while multidimensional anxiety theory has only recently been tested in the sport context, initial results are encouraging. The strength of the theory is its distinction between anxiety subcomponents and initial evidence showing that these anxiety components differentially influence performance. Current limitations include a lack of *consistent* empirical support for its precise predictions and a lack of investigations verifying that cognitive anxiety negatively influences performance via attentional distraction. Explanations for why and when somatic anxiety influences performance must also be developed.

Catastrophe Theory

Another recently proposed alternative to the inverted-U hypothesis is the behavioral application of catastrophe theory (Hardy & Fazey, 1987). The inverted-U hypothesis and the catastrophe

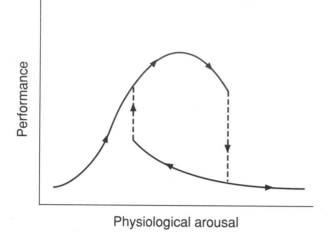

Figure 6.5 Catastrophe model predictions.
Note. From "The Inverted-U Hypothesis: A Catastrophe for Sport Psychology" by J. Fazey and L. Hardy. In *Bass Monograph No. 1* (p. 21), 1988, Leeds, U.K.: British Association of Sports Sciences and National Coaching Foundation. Adapted by permission.

theory are similar in that both predict that increases in state anxiety will facilitate performance up to an optimal level (see Figure 6.5). However, the two theories differ in what occurs next. The inverted-U hypothesis (Figure 6.3) suggests that with further increases in anxiety, performance will decline in a symmetrical, orderly, curvilinear manner. Thus, slight overanxiousness will result in slightly hindered performance. In contrast, the catastrophe theory proposes that when an athlete "goes over the top," there will be a large and dramatic decline in performance. Hence, it would be very difficult for athletes to recover from this "catastrophe" even to a mediocre level of performance.

The catastrophe theory was derived by Rene Thom (1975) as a mathematical model for describing discontinuities that occur in the physical world; that is, Thom believed that few naturally occurring phenomena are symmetrically related in a well-ordered and predictable fashion. Rather, natural phenomena are characterized by sudden transformations and discontinuities. Thus, multivariate mathematical models like catastrophe theory need to be developed to explain such sudden transformations. Although Thom (1972) developed catastrophe theory, it was Zeeman (1976) who popularized it when he demonstrated that the model could be applied to a wide range of social science phenomena. While several catastrophe models have been developed, the most commonly applied model and the one most easily understood is the *cusp* catastrophe model.

The cusp catastrophe model is 3-dimensional and consists of a normal factor, a splitting factor,

and a dependent variable (Zeeman, 1976). The normal factor is associated with changes in the dependent variable. As the normal factor increases, the dependent variable will also increase. The splitting factor at least partially determines the effect of the normal factor on the dependent variable. The bifurcation set is the area in which there are two possible values of the dependent variable (Hardy, 1990); that is, depending on whether the normal factor is increasing or decreasing, there will be two different predicted values for the dependent variable.

When used to explain the arousal–performance relationship, the catastrophe model, as described by Hardy and Fazey (1987), assumes that there are two subcomponents to anxiety: cognitive anxiety and physiological arousal. Physiological arousal (the normal factor) is characterized by a sympathetic physiological arousal response and may "be reflected at least partially by somatic anxiety" (Hardy & Fazey, 1987, p. 9). Cognitive anxiety (the splitting factor) mediates the effects of physiological arousal and can directly influence performance (the dependent variable). Hence, as can be seen in the 3-dimensional cusp model contained in Figure 6.6, athletic performance (the dependent variable) is predicted to be associated with increases in physiological arousal (the normal factor). However, the effects of physiological arousal on performance is mediated by cognitive anxiety (the splitting factor). Thus, the relationship between physiological arousal and performance will differ depending on one's level of cognitive anxiety with catastrophic performance effects occurring *only* when cognitive anxiety is high.

It should be noted that whereas various theorists propose that the normal factor should be *physiological arousal* (e.g., Hardy, 1990; Hardy & Fazey, 1987; Hardy & Parfitt, 1991), others hypothesize that it should be *somatic anxiety* (Jones, personal communication, May, 1989; Krane, 1990). At this time, it is unclear which arousal construct is most appropriate for use with catastrophe theory. Future researchers need to address this important issue.

What is innovative about catastrophe theory is that it does not assume that cognitive anxiety and physiological arousal always interact in a well-ordered fashion when influencing performance. Rather, they interact in a systematic, orderly fashion at times; but when these variables reach certain levels (high physiological arousal combined with high cognition anxiety), large and drastic catastrophic changes in performance occur.

Because the application of the catastrophe theory to the anxiety–performance relationship is

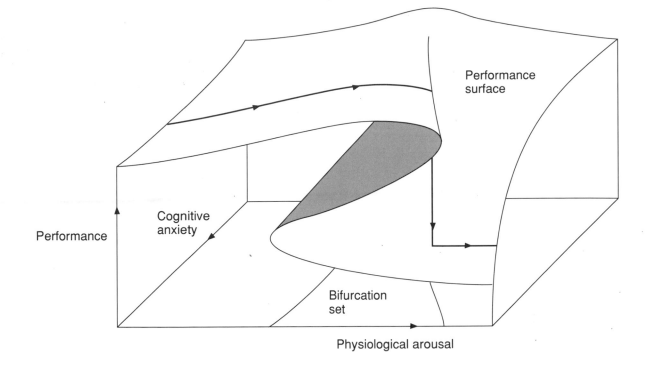

Figure 6.6 A three-dimensional catastrophe theory arousal–performanced relationship. Although the normal factor is labeled *psychological arousal*, some researchers may label it *somatic anxiety* (e.g., G. Jones, personal communication, May, 1989; Krane, 1990).

Note. From "The Inverted-U Hypothesis: A Catastrophe for Sport Psychology" by J. Fazey and L. Hardy. In *Bass Monograph No. 1* (p. 25), 1988, Leeds, U.K.: British Association of Sports Sciences and National Coaching Foundation. Adapted by permission.

such a recent development, there is no direct evidence to support it. However, Hardy and Parfitt (1991) found that increases in physiological arousal, as measured by heart rate, differentially related to performance depending on whether cognitive anxiety was high or low.

The strengths of catastrophe theory are that it jointly looks at the effects of physiological arousal and cognitive anxiety (two dimensions of arousal) on performance and that it has an innovative appeal in recognizing that phenomena in the real-world athletic settings do not always function in perfectly symmetrical ways. Limitations include its complexity and the need to obtain a large number of assessments on the same athletes over time to test it. These limitations, however, should not discourage future researchers from examining it, because its potential as a viable explanation for the arousal performance relationship far outweighs the efforts needed to test it.

Reversal Theory

Another exciting development applicable to the anxiety–performance literature is the reversal theory proposed by Smith and Apter (1975) and popularized in the European sport psychology literature by Kerr (1985, 1987). Reversal theory, however,

was not originally developed to explain the arousal-–performance relationship. Rather, it focused on the relationship between arousal and emotional affect and was forwarded as a general framework for explaining personality and motivation (Apter, 1984). In particular, the basic contention of reversal theory is that the relationship between arousal and affect is dependent upon one's cognitive interpretation of one's arousal level. High arousal may be interpreted as excitement (pleasant) or anxiety (unpleasant), and low arousal may be interpreted as relaxation (pleasant) or boredom (unpleasant). One's interpretation of affect as pleasant or unpleasant is also known as *hedonic tone*. Furthermore, because both arousal and affect vary on continua, reversal theory predicts that two curves depict the relationship between arousal and affective pleasure (see Figure 6.7).

Because there are two curves on the arousal–pleasure graph, "another dimension of change has been introduced: that of sudden discontinuous switching from one curve to the another. Since these are opposite ways of interpreting arousal the switch can be regarded as constituting a *reversal*" (Apter, 1984, p. 268). Apter further explains that each curve represents a different metamotivational state or mode (see p. 122). A metamotivational state has been defined

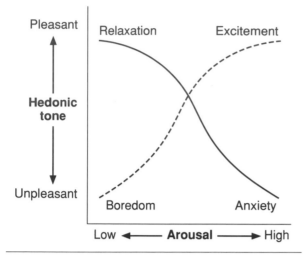

Figure 6.7 The relationship between arousal and affect in the reversal theory.
Note. From "The Experience of Arousal: The New Basis for Studying Arousal Effects in Sport" by J.H. Kerr, 1985, *Journal of Sports Sciences*, **3**, p. 172. Reprinted by permission of E & FN Spon.

as a "phenomenological state characterized by a certain way of interpreting some aspect(s) of one's motivation. Metamotivational states go in pairs of opposites, only one member of each pair being operative at a given time" (Kerr, 1985, p. 173). The telic mode is characterized by its seriousness or orientation toward a goal, whereas the paratelic mode is characterized by playfulness or an activity orientation (Apter, 1984; Svebak & Stoyva, 1980). The telic mode can also be thought of as arousal-seeking, and the paratelic as arousal-avoiding (see telic and paratelic curves on Figure 6.7). More simply, changes from one metamotivational state to the other are reversals (Kerr, 1985). Apter (1984) used the example of risk-taking sports such as rock climbing or parachuting to illustrate his concept of psychological reversals. The danger involved induces a high level of arousal, deemed *anxiety* in the telic mode; and then when the danger is mastered, the anxiety suddenly reverses and becomes *excitement* in the paratelic mode. Hence, psychological reversals can and do take place and result in striking changes in emotional states.

Kerr (1985), in his application of reversal theory to studying arousal effects in sport, suggests that arousal and stress continua must be viewed jointly and are together related to reversal theory. This results in four quadrants: *anxiety, excitement, boredom*, and *relaxation* (see Figure 6.8). The horizontal arousal continuum ranges from high to low, and the vertical axis also ranges from high to low. When arousal and stress (the imbalance between environmental demands and performer response capabilities) are high,

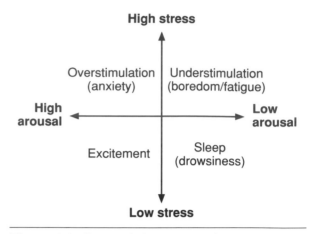

Figure 6.8 Reversal theory arousal-stress continuum.
Note. From "The Experience of Arousal: A New Basis for Studying Arousal Effects in Sport" by J.H. Kerr, 1985, *Journal of Sports Sciences*, **3**, p.175. Reprinted by permission of E & FN Spon.

anxiety, or overstimulation, results. Boredom, or understimulation, occurs when stress is high and arousal is low. Conversely, when stress is low and arousal is high, excitement occurs. When both arousal and stress are low, the result is sleep. Reversal theory, then, has the potential to integrate both stress and arousal notions nicely into its theoretical framework.

A basic interpretation from reversal theory is that arousal is not necessarily pleasant or unpleasant. Rather, depending on one's metamotivational state it can be perceived as a positive (paratelic) or negative (telic) state. Moreover, Martens (1987a) has recently suggested that this distinction is fundamental to understanding the relationship between arousal and performance. In particular, Martens indicates that there is a positive linear relationship between an athlete's paratelic (positive psychic energy) state and performance, whereas telic (negative psychic energy) states are associated with performance in a negative linear fashion. Additionally, Martens has indicated that athletes typically experience both positive and negative psychic energy while performing but that sport psychologists have mistakenly interpreted these two metamotivational states as arousal. The inverted-U principle, then, has been incorrectly labeled and interpreted and in the future should be viewed as depicted in Figure 6.9, where an athlete performs best when he or she has high positive psychic energy and low negative psychic energy. Poor performances result when an athlete exhibits lower levels of positive psychic energy or increased levels of negative psychic energy.

Unfortunately, Martens's (1987a) interpretation of the reversal theory–sport performance

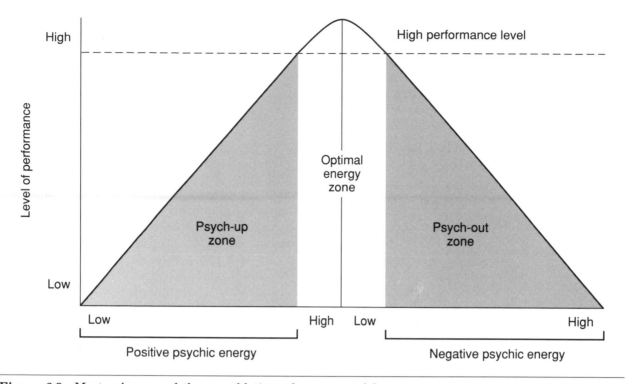

Figure 6.9 Martens's reversal theory–athletic performance model.
Note. From *Coaches Guide to Sport Psychology* (p. 100) by R. Martens, 1987, Champaign, IL: Human Kinetics. Copyright 1987 by Rainer Martens. Adapted by permission.

relationship is based totally on his own tacit knowledge and the intuitive appeal of this approach. No empirical evidence exists to support its predictions. In fact, it has never been empirically examined. It is also important to note that what Martens predicts are not true reversals, because positive and negative psychic energy are thought to be present at the same time (as opposed to switching from a telic to paratelic state). While no evidence exists to link reversal theory to athletic performance, components of the general theory have received support in the literature. In a review of the literature, Apter (1984) cited several studies supporting reversal theory predictions. Specifically, he noted, "The telic–paratelic dimension would appear to have a tangible 'reality' over and above its status as a phenomenological description or an explanatory construct" (p. 283). Apter cited the work of Svebak and colleagues (Svebak, 1982, 1983; Svebak, Storfjell & Dalen, 1982), finding that telic-dominant subjects exhibit increased muscular tension, task-irrelevant muscular tension, greater skin conductance, and greater heart rate in threat conditions compared to paratelic-dominant subjects.

In summary, then, reversal theory and its derivatives offer exciting alternatives to the inverted-U hypothesis. The strengths of reversal theory are its intuitive appeal and the important

distinction it places on the athlete's interpretation of arousal states. Current limitations include the lack of a paratelic positive psychic energy measure (assuming that state anxiety is synonymous with the telic state) and the lack of any investigations designed to test its predictions. It is certainly a theory that holds tremendous potential for increasing our understanding of the arousal–performance relationship.

Future Directions in Examining the Arousal–Performance Relationship

This review has clearly shown that the time has come to reexamine the arousal–athletic performance relationship by testing a number of conceptual systems that might better explain this complex phenomenon. To provide adequate tests of these theoretical frameworks, however, will require a number of methodological, conceptual, and empirical changes in our research approaches. These changes include

- eradication of ambiguities in the use of arousal terminology,
- development of conditions necessary to test arousal–performance relationship theories adequately, and

- incorporation of a number of methodological refinements in future investigations.

Additionally, a need exists for investigators to consider alternative methodological paradigms, research questions, and approaches when designing future studies.

Alleviating Ambiguities in the Use of Arousal Terminology

As noted earlier, there has been considerable inconsistency in the sport psychology literature in the use of arousal-related terminology. This is an extremely important issue because the various terms that pertain to arousal may be related to performance in different ways. Moreover, because many of these concepts and subsequent measures of them have been used interchangeably, it is difficult if not impossible to determine what particular aspects of the arousal construct are being studied, what overlap exists between measures of each construct, and what links exist between specific concepts and performance.

To eliminate the confusion caused by the inconsistent usage of arousal-related terminology, Figure 6.10 contains a conceptual model for integrating arousal construct terminology. An inspection of this figure reveals that arousal is the central construct in this model (Level 1) and is operationally defined as a general *physiological* and *psychological* activation of the organism, which varies on a continuum from deep sleep to intense excitement. It is this psychobiological construct that has for years been the focus of study for sport psychologists attempting to link various psychophysiological and emotional states to performance.

Level 2 of the model differentiates between a physiological arousal component (Level 2.A) and a cognitive interpretation–appraisal arousal component (Level 2.B). The physiological component is assessed via measures such as heart rate, respiration, and skin conductance. The cognitive interpretation–appraisal component is further subdivided into three subcomponents including somatic state anxiety (Level 2.B-1), cognitive state anxiety or telic state (Level 2.B-2), and a paratelic state (Level 2.B-3). The somatic state anxiety can be defined as the athlete's perception of his or her level of physiological arousal and is assessed via the CSAI–2 somatic anxiety subscale or the emotionality subscale of the Worry–Emotionality Inventory. The cognitive state anxiety, or telic state, component is the athlete's "negative affect" (worry) appraisal of arousal and can be measured via the CSAI–2 cognitive anxiety subscale or the worry subscale of the Worry–

Emotionality Inventory. The paratelic state, or positive affect appraisal, component of the model is the athlete's positive affect appraisal, which although hypothesized to exist in reversal theory, has not been operationalized through any valid assessment instrument. Lastly, Level 2.B-2.1 and 2.B-2.2 further subdivide the cognitive anxiety, or telic state, subcomponent into interpersonal and intragroup state anxiety according to Hanin's (1980) conceptualization. Finally, the right side of the model depicts trait anxiety, which influences the athlete's cognitive interpretation–appraisal of arousal (Level 2.B) and which, in turn, affects actual physiological arousal (Level 2.A). Sport-specific global trait anxiety is measured by the SCAT; whereas the SAS has been developed by Smith, Smoll, and Schutz (1990) to measure multidimensional trait anxiety.

It is important to note that Level 2 of the model makes a critical distinction between physiological and psychological arousal. Specifically, physiological arousal manifestations are hypothesized to be related to, but conceptually distinct from, one's cognitive interpretation of the arousal construct. This is not to say that physiological arousal and cognitive appraisal of arousal components do not share common variance. In fact, they would be expected to be correlated. It is our contention, however, that although they are correlated to some degree, they are in many ways unique. Hence, by differentiating between levels 2.A and 2.B of the model, researchers will not fall prey to the conceptual trap of viewing *physiological arousal* and *state anxiety assessment* as synonymous. However, future studies should be conducted to identify common variance between these components, while at the same time determining how and/or whether these components differentially relate to performance.

To further clarify the theoretical distinctions between arousal-related terminology, the conceptual model for integrating arousal terms can be easily placed within current process models of stress (e.g., McGrath, 1970). In particular, Figure 6.11 integrates these two models. An inspection of this figure reveals that the previously discussed four stages of the stress process are included. Hence, the athlete is placed under environmental demand (Stage 1), perceives that environment as more or less threatening (Stage 2), and has a response to that demand (Stage 3), which leads in turn to specific performance outcomes and various consequences (Stage 4). It can be further seen that it is at Stage 3 in McGrath's model that the conceptual clarification of the arousal terminology has the greatest impact; that is, the athlete has a physiological *and*

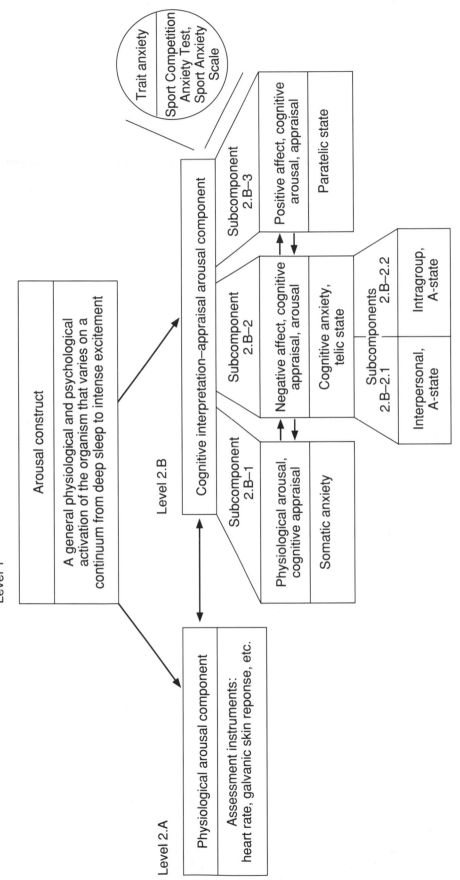

Figure 6.10   A conceptual model for integrating arousal construct terminology.

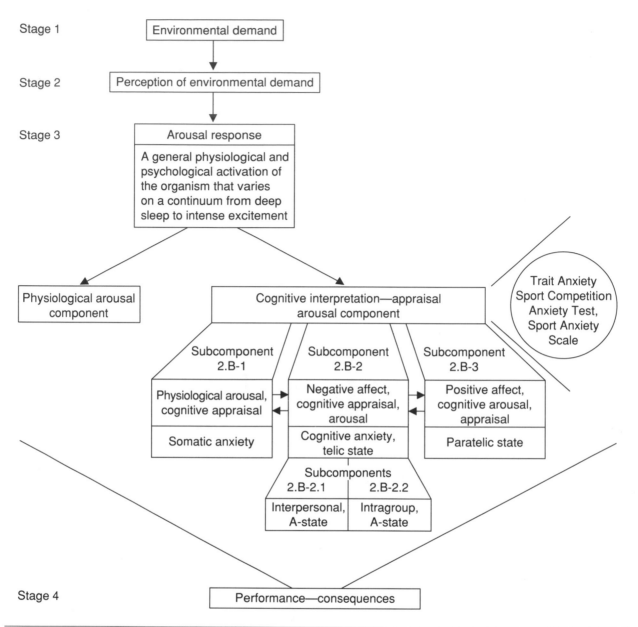

Figure 6.11 The relationship between the stress process and arousal terminology.

psychological response comprising an arousal component and a cognitive interpretation–appraisal component. These result in varying levels of somatic state anxiety, cognitive state anxiety, and paratelic state responses. These physiological and psychological responses, in turn, influence performance. Stages 3 and 4 of the stress process have been our major focus.

Testing Arousal–Performance Relationship Theories

If adequate tests of alternative theoretical frameworks for explaining the arousal–performance relationship are to be conducted, investigators must

- adequately assess arousal and related states,
- utilize more sensitive measures of athletic performance,
- employ intra-individual anxiety analyses, and
- create at least three distinct levels of arousal when testing nonlinear predictions.

Each of these conditional requirements is discussed below.

Assessing Arousal and Related States

One of the most difficult issues that must be reconciled if our understanding of the arousal–performance relationship is to improve, is to develop better assessments of the arousal construct. This is required at both the conceptual and empirical level.

From a conceptual perspective, it has been shown that *arousal, stress, cognitive state anxiety, somatic state anxiety, telic state, and paratelic state* have precise meanings. However, researchers in the past (e.g., Gould et al., 1987; Weinberg & Genuchi, 1980) have often used these terms interchangeably. This has caused a great deal of confusion in the literature because it was assumed that these concepts measured the same underlying construct. However, as previously noted, these concepts may not be related to performance in the same manner. For example, *physiological arousal* and *somatic anxiety* are often viewed as synonymous. However, as Deffenbacher (1980) has noted, somatic anxiety is a subject's cognitive interpretation of his or her physiological arousal, not arousal per se. Thus, a portion of the variance between physiological arousal and somatic anxiety may be common and related to performance in the same manner. Alternatively, another portion of the physiological arousal or somatic anxiety variances may be unique and related to performance in a different way.

In a similar vein, reversal theory emphasizes that one's physiological arousal is not directly linked to performance but that the arousal–performance relationship is mediated by one's metamotivational state (i.e., whether one is in a telic or paratelic state). Hence, it is imperative that the link between physiological arousal and cognitive interpretations of physiological arousal be examined.

Finally, some theorists have made distinctions between arousal types in the brain itself (Pribram & McGuinness, 1975; Tucker & Williams, 1984). For instance, Pribram and McGuinness hypothesize that three separate neural systems interact, one regulating input arousal, another regulating response activation, and a third coordinating activation and arousal into effort. Thus, physiological arousal may be more complicated than was once thought.

Unfortunately, no one conceptual system for viewing arousal and related concepts has been accepted by sport psychology researchers. It is hoped that our model will help rectify this situation. However, even if future investigators do not accept this particular model, they can help alleviate the situation by clearly defining, in both a theoretical and empirical/operational fashion, the arousal variables that they employ and by utilizing both physiological and psychological measures of arousal whenever possible. This will allow investigators to search for causal links between these concepts and their relationship to performance. Further, efforts must be made to determine theoretical and empirical differences between physiological and cognitive anxiety/arousal states. For example, while cognitive state anxiety may provide an important measure of negative affect associated with heightened physiological arousal, no measure of paratelic, or positive, psychological arousal exists. Hence, a need exists to develop a valid measure of the paratelic state, or what Martens (1987a) has labeled *positive psychic energy*. Finally, future research studies are needed that will simultaneously utilize measures of such states as physiological arousal, somatic anxiety, and cognitive anxiety so that the interrelationships between these states can be compared and contrasted.

Another major measurement issue focuses on the need to use multidimensional arousal/anxiety approaches when examining the arousal–performance relationship. For instance, multidimensional anxiety theory (Wine, 1980) and recent empirical evidence (Burton, 1988; Gould et al., 1987) suggest that cognitive and somatic state anxiety differentially influence performance. Similarly, Doctor and Altman (1969) and Gould and colleagues (1987) have found evidence that somatic anxiety was only related to performance within lower strata of worry, or cognitive anxiety. In a similar vein, Hardy and Parfitt (1991) found initial support for the catastrophe theory prediction that physiological arousal and associated somatic anxiety are negatively related to performance when cognitive anxiety is high, but not when it is low. Finally, Svebak and Murgatroyd (1985) have shown that telic-dominant subjects showed higher task-irrelevant muscle tension during performance than did paratelic dominant subjects. Taken together, then, these results suggest that arousal/anxiety must be viewed and assessed as multidimensional phenomena and that investigators must begin to determine the links between separate arousal–anxiety states and performance, regardless of the theoretical framework employed.

Measuring Athletic Performance

Not only must future investigators better conceptualize and assess arousal and arousal-related constructs, but efforts to assess athletic performance more accurately and precisely are needed. Too often in the past, researchers attempting to assess the arousal–performance relationship have failed to utilize standardized performance measures. In an investigation conducted by Gould, Petlichkoff, and Weinberg (1984), for example, performance was assessed by outcome (win–loss) across wrestling matches. Because different opponents competed in each match of the tournament, performance was not standardized; rather, it changed as a function of the opponent. Similarly, in golf studies conducted by Martens and colleagues (1990) and McAuley (1985), performance was compared on the front versus the back nine holes of the golf course or across different courses. Thus, in these studies, changing and nonstandardized task demands may have confounded and/or masked relationships between state anxiety and performance. A better test of the arousal–performance relationship can be obtained when task demands are held constant from one arousal or state anxiety assessment to another. Such was the case with a study conducted by Gould and colleagues (1987) where pistol shooters were required to perform on five separate occasions under identical performance conditions (e.g., identical targets, distance from target, weapon, and range). Hence, only when performance environments are standardized will investigators be able to obtain an accurate and reliable test of the arousal–performance relationship.

Weinberg (1990) has suggested that the use of outcome or win–loss performance measures in arousal–performance studies is also a major concern because of the lack of sensitivity and precision often associated with such measures. Specifically, he questions norm-referenced measures that compare performances of competitors (e.g., 10th-place finish in a road race, 1st-place in a bowling tournament). For example, a person could win a contest and not approach a personal best or, conversely, could be labeled as an inferior performer (e.g., last-place finish) yet achieve a personal best. Similarly, he indicates that comparing game scores may be inaccurate because losing a basketball game 100 to 65 to a top-ranked team might be quite different from losing 100 to 65 to an inferior team. To alleviate these problems, it is recommended that field researchers employ performance measures similar to those used by Burton (1988), where swimmers' best times in an event were assessed relative to their own previous times in that event.

In addition to using standardized and more precise athletic performance measures, the need for employing process measures of performance has also been recently advocated (Gould, 1988; Hackfort & Schwenkmezger, 1989; Weinberg, 1990). Instead of focusing attention on the outcome or end result of task performance, process measures focus attention on how the skill is executed or the quality of movement per se. In essence, the process approach "is centrally concerned with how individuals organize and integrate their energies in the execution of motor skills" (Weinberg, 1990, p. 237). Thus, electromyographic and/or kinematic measures of the movements employed during task performance itself are recommended.

Excellent examples of the utility of using process measures of task performance in arousal–performance relationship studies were provided in several investigations (Beuter & Duda, 1985; Beuter, Duda & Widule, 1989; Weinberg, 1978; Weinberg & Hunt, 1976). In the Weinberg and Hunt study, electromyograph assessments were used to examine electrical activity in muscles occurring before, during, and after performance of a throwing accuracy task. Results revealed that as compared to low-trait-anxious subjects who received failure feedback, high-trait-anxious subjects who received failure feedback not only demonstrated inferior performance but displayed more electrical activity in relevant muscles before, during, and after throwing. These individuals also exhibited cocontraction of relevant muscle groups. Similar results were found in a replication and extension of the original work conducted two years later (Weinberg, 1978).

A different but equally useful approach was employed by Beuter and her colleagues (Beuter & Duda, 1985; Beuter et al., 1989). In particular, movement efficiency was assessed via measures of kinematic characteristics of movement (spatica-temporal organization of the ankle, knee, and hip energies as assessed via biomechanical high-speed filming) in children performing a stepping motion under high- and low-arousal conditions. Results reveal a significant increase in the kinetic energy ratios under increased arousal. These results suggest that under high-arousal states, automatic–smooth movements become less smooth and less efficient as a result of volitional control.

In summary, many advantages can be obtained from utilizing more precise and standardized performance measures when examining arousal–performance relationships. In addition, the utilization of process measures provides investigators with an entirely different perspective on the arousal–performance relationship by identifying what happens during the movement per se. For this reason, process measure studies hold tremendous potential for facilitating arousal–performance relationship theory, because they provide data as to *why* performance may change under conditions of high arousal or anxiety.

Utilizing Intra-Individual Analyses

An important recent development in arousal–performance relationship methodology has been the use of intra-individual analyses. Intra-individual analyses were first advocated by Sonstroem and Bernardo (1982). Use of intra-individual analyses involves taking multiple state anxiety assessments on the same athlete and then relating the individual's anxiety deviations around his or her own norms to performance. This method differs from previous analyses, which compared state anxiety scores between subjects and then linked these scores to performance. For example, in the Sonstroem and Bernardo investigation, female intercollegiate basketball players completed state anxiety assessments prior to at least three games. State anxiety scores of each subject were standardized relative to that subject's own range and median for the three scores and were then linked to performance. Using this procedure, an inverted-U relationship was found between state anxiety and performance across all subjects. Similarly, recent investigations by Gould and colleagues (1987) and Burton (1988) have also demonstrated the value of using intra-individual analyses in testing multidimensional state anxiety–performance relationships in pistol shooting and swimming. Lastly, Neiss (1988) and Landers (1980) have both advocated that arousal researchers employing physiological assessments consider Lacey and Lacey's (1958) notions of interresponse stereotypy and intraresponse stereotypy, which emphasize the identification of specific arousal measures (e.g., heart rate vs. galvanic skin response) that typify specific individual's stress responses. It was also suggested that there is a need to look for intra-individual changes in these specific arousal measures when relating them to performance.

In summary, it is becoming increasingly evident that it is more useful for investigators to examine relative changes in state anxiety/arousal assessments around individual subjects' own previous scores than absolute anxiety/arousal measure changes. The use of between-subjects analyses to test the relationship between anxiety/arousal and performance may not be appropriate. Hence, intra-individual analyses should be conducted in the future.

Testing Nonlinear Arousal–Performance Relationship Predictions

An often overlooked but very important recommendation advocated by Martens (1977) is that when designing tests of the inverted-U hypothesis, investigators must create or assess three distinct levels of arousal; that is, since the inverted-U hypothesis predicts performance differences between low-, moderate-, and high-anxiety levels, to adequately test this hypothesis researchers must obtain at least three significantly different anxiety score measures. Moreover, although these scores must be significantly different, they should be theoretically distinct as well.

For example, the scores on the CSAI–2 (Martens et al., 1983) can range from a low of 9 to a high of 36. It is possible and highly probable in laboratory research that an investigator will obtain three significantly different anxiety levels on this scale (e.g., 13, 16, 19). However, from a theoretical perspective, the highest score only approaches the midpoint of the scale, with none of the scores being classified as high-anxiety in an absolute sense. Hence, an adequate test of the inverted-U hypothesis cannot be achieved with this set of scores, because high anxiety was never assessed or induced.

Although the previously discussed intra-individual anxiety analyses may help alleviate this problem (because high anxiety is determined relative to a subject's typical level of state anxiety as opposed to an absolute scale level), it is still imperative that researchers create at least three distinct levels of state anxiety within subjects when testing the inverted-U or other nonlinear models (e.g., catastrophe theory). Moreover, recognizing whether significantly different scores fall within low, moderate, or high scale levels in an absolute sense is important because multidimensional anxiety investigators (Doctor & Altman, 1969; Gould et al., 1987) have found or predicted that different anxiety–performance relationships occur depending on whether subjects perform under high-somatic-anxiety or low-somatic-anxiety levels.

Critical Research Approaches and Questions

Although it is extremely important for investigators to construct conditions to adequately test arousal–performance relationship hypotheses, other paradigmatic issues must also be considered. Chief among these are decisions relative to the types of research approaches to be taken and specific classes of questions to be posed. In particular, a need exists for future investigators to

- conduct idiographic investigations,
- utilize qualitative methodologies,
- conduct time series analyses,
- move from correlational to causal designs through arousal control investigations, and
- simultaneously test multiple theories.

Idiographic Investigations

The traditional sport psychology arousal–performance relationship study has employed a nomothetic approach, in that hypothesized relationships among constructs are examined across large groups of individuals. By its very nature this approach requires that the investigator assume a reductionistic orientation, because it is not logistically possible to study large groups of athletes in a holistic fashion. However, Martens (1987b) has argued that sport psychologists should also utilize such idiographic approaches as case studies, in-depth interviews, and participant observations if real gains in knowledge about athletes are to be derived. Given the multivariate nature and complexity of the arousal–performance relationship, employing such in-depth approaches would better allow investigators to understand how anxiety affects the athlete as a whole and what systems influence performance over time. It would provide a richness and depth of knowledge about anxiety and performance that has not been generated through the exclusive use of nomothetic methods.

While the utilization of idiographic approaches is advocated here, the weakness of such approaches must be recognized. The gains made in the depth and richness of knowledge are offset by a weakening in the reliability of the knowledge gained. Hence, it would be foolish for investigators to totally abandon the nomothetic approach for an idiographic orientation. Rather, we agree with Hackfort and Schwenkmezgers' (1989) recommendation that anxiety investigators need to utilize both orientations of study. For example, given the current lack of research support for reversal theory, investigators might do well to conduct in-depth case studies to determine if telic and paratelic states exist, whether reversals take place, and under what conditions reversals occur. Once these concepts are better understood in individual athletes, reliable and valid telic–paratelic state measures could be developed and large-group studies could be conducted to determine the generalizability and reliability of any identified relationships. Similarly, a better understanding of catastrophe theory could be obtained if investigators studied its predictions across groups of athletes while simultaneously conducting in-depth case studies with specific individuals or subgroups. The nomothetic portion of the investigation would determine whether reliable and stable relationships existed in key variables, whereas the idiographic portion would generate important information relative to such issues as what cognitions and emotions occur when an athlete "goes over the top" and experiences a catastrophe.

In summary, it is strongly recommended that future arousal–performance relationship investigators use idiographic, as well as nomothetic research methodologies in their investigations. Only by combining the two approaches will we maximize our understanding of this complex relationship.

Qualitative Investigations

Closely paralleling the need for more idiographic approaches to the study of the arousal–performance relationship is the need for qualitative investigations. Although few, if any, qualitative investigations have been conducted in the arousal–performance area, an excellent example of the depth, detail, and richness that can be gained by studying athletes in a qualitative manner was provided in a recent investigation by Scanlan and her colleagues (Scanlan, Ravizza & Stein, 1989; Scanlan, Stein & Ravizza, 1989, 1990). In this investigation, a variety of very specific sources of enjoyment and stress were identified in former elite figure skaters. Similarly, Orlick and Partington (1987) conducted a large-scale qualitative investigation of mental links to excellence in Canadian Olympians. This study identified a number of previously undetected mental factors associated with exceptional athletic achievement.

The strength of the qualitative approach is that it allows the subject to describe in his or her own detailed words the naturally occurring events that surround the phenomena of interest. The qualitative approach may be especially useful in identifying new variables and relationships in unexplored areas or in obtaining in-depth assessments of athlete's emotions and cognitions. Hence, anxiety–performance investigators would do well to utilize such an approach.

Time Series Analyses

A third means of advancing our understanding of the anxiety–performance relationship is for investigators to study relationships between anxiety concepts like telic states, somatic anxiety, and arousal *over time*. Too often in the past, the difficulty of collecting data across time has prevented investigators from conducting such studies. However, time series analyses are essential in order to test newer anxiety–performance conceptualizations like catastrophe theory. Moreover, many of the difficulties in conducting time series analyses have been alleviated with the advent of highly reliable, portable psychophysiological testing instruments.

Finally, investigators must remember that the varied arousal constructs depicted in Figure 6.10 are not independent entities. Rather, they are interrelated and will most likely interact with each other over varying sequences of time. For instance, increased physiological arousal may increase perceived threat in an athlete, which increases that athlete's state anxiety and thus hinders performance. This sequence of events, in turn, is perceived as more threatening by the athlete and causes even more physiological arousal. Taking assessments at only one point in time would not reveal the complex interrelationships between these variables. Only through time series analyses will investigators be able to truly understand these time-linked relationships.

Moving From Correlational to Causal Designs

A major interpretative problem inherent in the vast majority of previous studies on the arousal–performance relationship is the correlational nature of their design; that is, arousal or anxiety is typically assessed on a number of occasions and related to performance measures taken on those same occasions. Seldom, however, is the arousal or anxiety level of the athlete manipulated in an effort to assess its hypothesized effects on performance. While it is true that arousal levels have been successfully manipulated in laboratory investigations (e.g., Martens & Landers, 1970), accomplishing this objective is very difficult. It is difficult to produce the highly stressful conditions inherent in actual competitive environments in laboratory settings. This situation is further compounded by the ethical dilemmas that arise in field settings, where it is often considered unethical to elevate an athlete's arousal level to an extremely high level.

While it is not possible to manipulate arousal in ecologically valid settings, investigators could move toward functional or causal designs by teaching athletes to use arousal management strategies and then having them employ these strategies on a systematic basis. It must be recognized that this approach will be effective in facilitating our understanding of arousal–performance relationships only if time series analyses are utilized where relationships are established between arousal concepts and performance. Then, interventions could be introduced to modify these relationships. For instance, investigators might test the efficacy of catastrophe theory by assessing athletes' somatic anxiety, cognitive anxiety, and performance over a period of time. The covariation of these variables would then be measured. Later, a subgroup of these athletes could receive a stress management intervention like Smith's (1980) Stress Management Training, with other athletes serving as controls. If the intervention athletes were able to prevent catastrophes through their management of cognitive and somatic anxiety levels and the controls experienced catastrophes, some degree of causation would be demonstrated facilitating our understanding of the arousal–performance relationship.

Multitheory Tests

A problem that has plagued sport psychology research in general and arousal–performance relationship research in particular has been investigators' tendency to rely on one theory; that is, most studies have been designed to test specifically only the inverted-U hypothesis or the multidimensional anxiety theory predictions. It must be recognized, however, that supporting one theory in isolation of other existing views does not advance science as fast as when two theories are pitted against one another in the same investigation. The need for multitheory tests may be especially appropriate in the arousal–performance area because a number of multiple theories exist and because the various constructs forming the basis of these theories seem to be so interwoven. For this reason, future arousal–performance relationship investigators should design experiments and studies that simultaneously test multiple theoretical contentions. For instance, an investigator who uses the CSAI–2 to test multidimensional anxiety theory could first examine the predicted linear relationship between cognitive anxiety and performance as well as the predicted curvilinear relationship between somatic anxiety and performance. Following those analyses, the researcher could then use the same data to test catastrophe theory by examining the joint effects of these two variables on performance. Such an approach would provide maximum theoretical payoff.

Conclusion

When considering future directions, it is easy to focus on what we do not know and forget how much progress *has* been made. In terms of the arousal–performance relationship, considerable progress has been made through our research efforts. A number of advances have been made relative to the measurement of state and trait anxiety and methodological procedures needed for testing arousal–performance relationship issues. We also know that the drive theory has little support and that the relationship between arousal and performance is best described by more complex relationships, many of which are thought to be curvilinear in nature.

Especially exciting are the recent theories and hypotheses that have been forwarded to take us beyond the inverted-U hypothesis. These more recent theories include reversal and catastrophe theories. Viewing state anxiety as a multidimensional phenomenon has already advanced and should continue to further advance our understanding of the arousal–performance relationship. To maintain this momentum, however, more research is needed, especially lines of systematic studies designed to tackle the complex relationships between various arousal-related constructs and performance. Additionally, investigators interested in this area must not be afraid to venture into previously unexplored areas by testing fledgling theories and utilizing new innovative methodologies such as time series analyses and qualitative assessments. After all, it has only been through innovative, systematic, and well-thought-out research that our current understanding of the arousal–performance relationship has evolved. Hence, we challenge future investigators to utilize the ideas presented here to guide future research efforts and in so doing advance our understanding of the arousal–performance relationship.

References

Apter, M.J. (1976). Some data inconsistent with the optimal arousal theory of motivation. *Perceptual and Motor Skills, 43*, 1209-1210.

Apter, M.J. (1984). Reversal theory and personality: A review. *Journal of Research in Personality, 18*, 265-288.

Bacon, S.J. (1974). Arousal and the range of cue utilization. *Journal of Experimental Psychology, 103*, 81-87.

Bandura, A. (1977). Self-efficacy: Toward a unifying theory of behavior change. *Psychological Review, 84*(2), 191-215.

Beuter, A., & Duda, D.L. (1985). Analysis of the arousal/motor performance relationship in children using movement kinematics. *Journal of Sport Psychology, 7*, 229-243.

Beuter, A., Duda, D.L., & Widule, C.J. (1989). The effect of arousal on joint kinematics and kinetics in children. *Research Quarterly for Exercise and Sport, 60*, 109-116.

Bird, A.M., & Cripe, B.K. (1986). *Psychology and sport behavior*. St. Louis: Times/Mirror/Mosby College.

Borkovek, T.D. (1976). Physiological and cognitive processes in the regulation of arousal. In G.E. Schwartz & D. Shapiro (Eds.), *Consciousness and self-regulation: Advances in research* (Vol. 1, pp. 261-312). New York: Plenum.

Burton, D. (1988). Do anxious swimmers swim slower? Reexamining the elusive anxiety–performance relationship. *Journal of Sport and Exercise Psychology, 10*(1), 45-61.

Cox, R. (1990). *Sport psychology: Concepts and applications* (2nd ed). Dubuque, IA: William C. Brown.

Davidson, R.J., & Schwartz, G.E. (1976). The psychobiology of relaxation and related states: A multi-process theory. In D.I. Mostofsky (Ed.), *Behavior control and modification of physiological activity* (pp. 399-442). Englewood Cliffs, NJ: Prentice-Hall.

Deffenbacher, J.L. (1980). Worry and emotionality in test anxiety. In I.G. Sarason (Ed.), *Test anxiety: Theory, research, and application* (pp. 111-128). Hillsdale, NJ: Lawrence Erlbaum.

Doctor, R.M., & Altman, F. (1969). Worry and emotionality as components of test anxiety: Replication and further data. *Psychological Reports, 24*, 563-568.

Duffy, E. (1932). The relationship between muscular tension and quality of performance. *American Journal of Psychology, 44*, 535-546.

Duffy, E. (1957). The psychological significance of the concept "arousal" or "activation." *Psychological Review, 64*, 265-275.

Easterbrook, J.A. (1959). The effect of emotion on cue utilization and the organization of behavior. *Psychological Review, 66*, 183-201.

Fisher, A.C. (1976). Psych up, psych out: Relationship of arousal to sport performance. In A.C. Fischer (Ed.), *Psychology of sport: Issues and insights* (pp. 136-144). Mountainview, CA: Mayfield.

Gill, D.L. (1986). *Psychological dynamics of sport*. Champaign, IL: Human Kinetics.

Gould, D. (1987). Promoting positive sport experiences for children. In J.R. May & M.J. Asken (Eds.), *Sport psychology: The psychological health of the athlete* (pp. 77-98). New York: PMA.

Gould, D. (1988, June). *New directions in theory, research, and measurement in competitive anxiety*. Paper presented at the meeting of the North American Society for the Psychology of Sport and Physical Activity, Knoxville, TN.

Gould, D., & Petlichkoff, L. (1988). Psychological stress and the age-group wrestler. In E.W. Brown & C.F. Branta (Eds.), *Competitive sports for children and youth: An overview of research and issues* (pp. 63-73). Champaign, IL: Human Kinetics.

Gould, D., Petlichkoff, L., Simons, H., & Vevera, M. (1987). The relationship between Competitive State Anxiety Inventory–2 subscale scores and pistol shooting performance. *Journal of Sport and Exercise Psychology, 9*, 33-42.

Gould, D., Petlichkoff, L., & Weinberg, R.S. (1984). Antecedents of, temporal changes in, and relationships between CSAI–2 subcomponents. *Journal of Sport Psychology, 6*, 289-304.

Griffith, C.R. (1932). *Psychology of coaching*. New York: Scribner's.

Hackfort, D., & Schwenkmezger, P. (1989). Measuring anxiety in sports: Perspectives and problems. In D. Hackfort & C.D. Spielberger (Eds.), *Anxiety in sports: An international perspective* (pp. 55-76). New York: Hemisphere.

Hanin, Y.L. (1980). A study of anxiety in sports. In W.F. Straub (Ed.), *Sport psychology: An analysis of athlete behavior* (pp. 236-249). Ithaca, NY: Mouvement.

Hanin, Y.L. (1986). State trait anxiety research on sports in the USSR. In C.D. Spielberger & R. Diaz-Guerrero (Eds.), *Cross-cultural anxiety* (Vol. 3, pp. 45-64). Washington, DC: Hemisphere.

Hanin, Y.L. (1989). Interpersonal and intragroup anxiety in sports. In D. Hackfort & C.D. Spielberger (Eds.), *Anxiety in sports: An international perspective* (pp. 19-28). New York: Hemisphere.

Hanin, Y.L., & Spielberger, C.D. (1983). The development and validation of the Russian form of the State Trait Anxiety Inventory. In C.D. Spielberger & R. Diaz-Guerrero (Eds.), *Cross-cultural anxiety* (Vol. 2, pp. 15-26). Washington, DC: Hemisphere.

Hanson, T.W., & Gould, D. (1988). Factors affecting the ability of coaches to estimate their athletes' trait and state anxiety levels. *Sport Psychologist, 2*, 298-313.

Hardy, L. (1990). A catastrophe model of performance in sport. In J.G. Jones & L. Hardy (Eds.), *Stress and performance in sport* (pp. 81-106). Chichester, England: Wiley.

Hardy, L., & Fazey, J. (1987, June). *The inverted-U hypothesis: A catastrophe for sport psychology*. Paper presented at the meeting of the North American Society for the Psychology of Sport and Physical Activity, Vancouver, BC.

Hardy, L., & Parfitt, G. (1991). A catastrophe model of anxiety and performance. *British Journal of Psychology, 82*, 163-178.

Hebb, D.O. (1955). Drives in the C.N.S. (Conceptual Nervous System). *Psychological Review, 62*, 243-254.

Hull, C.L. (1943). *Principles of behavior*. New York: Appleton-Century.

Jones, J.G., & Hardy, L. (1989). Stress and cognitive functioning in sport. *Journal of Sport Sciences, 7*, 41-63.

Kause, D.R. (1980). *Peak performance: Mental game plans for maximizing your athletic potential*. Englewood Cliffs, NJ: Prentice-Hall.

Kerr, J.H. (1985). The experience of arousal: A new basis for studying arousal effects in sport. *Journal of Sport Sciences, 3*, 169-179.

Kerr, J.H. (1987). Structural phenomenology and performance. *Journal of Human Movement Studies, 13*, 211-229.

Klavora, P. (1977). An attempt to derive inverted-U curves based on the relationship between anxiety and athletic performance. In D.M. Landers & R.W. Christina (Eds.), *Psychology of motor behavior and sport—1977* (pp. 369-377). Champaign, IL: Human Kinetics.

Krane, V. (1985). *The relationships between CSAI–2 subcomponents and performance during collegiate golf competition*. Unpublished Master's thesis, University of Arizona, Tucson, AZ.

Krane, V. (1990). *Anxiety and athletic performance: A test of the multidimensional anxiety and catastrophe theories*. Unpublished doctoral dissertation, University of North Carolina at Greensboro.

Krane, V., & Williams, J. (1987). Performance and somatic anxiety, cognitive anxiety, and confidence changes prior to competition. *Journal of Sport Behavior, 10*(1), 47-56.

Lacey, J., & Lacey, B. (1958). Verification and extension of the principle of autonomic response-stereotypy. *American Journal of Psychology, 71*, 50-73.

Landers, D.M. (1980). The arousal-performance relationship revisited. *Research Quarterly for Exercise and Sport, 51*, 77-90.

Landers, D.M., & Boutcher, S.H. (1986). Arousal-performance relationships. In J.M. Williams (Ed.), *Applied sport psychology: Personal growth to peak performance* (pp. 163-184). Palo Alto, CA: Mayfield.

Landers, D.M., Wang, M.Q., & Courtet, P. (1985). Periferal narrowing among experienced and inexperienced rifle shooters under low- and high-stress conditions. *Research Quarterly, 56*, 122-130.

Liebert, R.M., & Morris, L.W. (1967). Cognitive and emotional components of test anxiety: A distinction and some initial data. *Psychological Reports, 20*, 975-987.

Lowe, R. (1973). *Stress, arousal, and task performance of Little League baseball players*. Unpublished doctoral dissertation, University of Illinois, Urbana.

Malmo, R.B. (1959). Activation: A neuropsychological dimension. *Psychological Review, 66*, 367-386.

Martens, R. (1971). Anxiety and motor behavior: A review. *Journal of Motor Behavior, 2*(2), 151-179.

Martens, R. (1974). Arousal and motor performance. In J.H. Wilmore (Ed.), *Exercise and sport science reviews* (Vol. 2, pp. 155-188). New York: Academic.

Martens, R. (1977). *Sport Competition Anxiety Test*. Champaign, IL: Human Kinetics.

Martens, R. (1987a). *Coaches guide to sport psychology*. Champaign, IL: Human Kinetics.

Martens, R. (1987b). Science, knowledge and sport psychology. *Sport Psychologist, 1*, 29-55.

Martens, R., Burton, D., Vealey, R., Bump, L., & Smith, D. (1990). The development of the Competitive State Anxiety Inventory–2 (CSAI–2). In R. Martens, R.S. Vealey, & D. Burton (Eds.), *Competitive anxiety in sport* (pp. 117-190). Champaign, IL: Human Kinetics.

Martens, R., & Landers, D.M. (1970). Motor performance under stress: A test of the inverted-U hypothesis. *Journal of Personality and Social Psychology, 16*, 29-37.

Martens, R., Vealey, R.S., & Burton, D. (Eds.) (1990). *Competitive anxiety in sport*. Champaign, IL: Human Kinetics.

McAuley, E. (1985). State anxiety: Antecedent or result of sport performance. *Journal of Sport Behavior, 8*(2), 71-77.

McGrath, J.E. (1970). Major methodological issues. In J.E. McGrath (Ed.), *Social and psychological factors in stress* (pp. 19-49). New York: Holt, Rinehart, & Winston.

Morgan, W.P., O'Connor, P.J.O., Ellickson, K.A., & Bradley, P.W. (1988). Personality structure, mood states, and performance in elite male distance runners. *International Journal of Sport Psychology, 19*, 247-263.

Morgan, W.P., O'Connor, P.J.O., & Pate, R.R. (1987). Psychological characterization of elite female distance runners. *International Journal of Sports Medicine, 8*, 124-131.

Morris, L.W., Davis, D., & Hutchings, C. (1981). Cognitive and emotional components of anxiety: Literature review and revised worry–emotionality scale. *Journal of Educational Psychology, 73*, 541-555.

Neiss, R. (1988). Reconceptualizing arousal: Psychobiological states in motor performance. *Psychological Bulletin, 103*(3), 345-366.

Orlick, T., & Partington, J. (1988). Mental links to excellence. *The Sport Psychologist, 2*, 105-130.

Passer, M.W. (1982). Psychological stress in youth sports. In R.A. Magill, M.J. Ash, & F.L. Smoll (Eds.), *Children in sport* (2nd ed., pp. 153-177). Champaign, IL: Human Kinetics.

Pribram, K.H., & McGuinness, D. (1975). Arousal, activation, and effort in control of attention. *Psychological Review, 82*, 116-149.

Scanlan, T.K., Ravizza, K., & Stein, G.L. (1989). An in-depth study of former elite figure skaters: Part 1. Introduction to the project. *Journal of Exercise and Sport Psychology, 11*, 54-64.

Scanlan, T.K., Stein, G.L., & Ravizza, K. (1989). An in-depth study of former elite figure skaters: Part 2. Sources of enjoyment. *Journal of Exercise and Sport Psychology, 11*, 65-83.

Scanlan, T.K., Stein, G.L., & Ravizza, K. (1990). An in-depth study of former elite figure skaters Part 3. Sources of stress. *Journal of Exercise and Sport Psychology, 13*(2), 103-120.

Schwartz, G.E., Davidson, R.J., & Goleman, D.J. (1978). Patterning of cognitive and somatic processes in the self-regulation of anxiety: Effects of meditation versus exercise. *Psychosomatic Medicine, 40*, 321-328.

Seyle, H. (1974). *Stress without distress*. New York: New American Library.

Silva, J.M., & Weinberg, R.S. (Eds.) (1984). *Psychological foundations of sport*. Champaign, IL: Human Kinetics.

Smith, K.C.P., & Apter, M.J. (1975). *A theory of psychological reversals*. Chippenham, Wilts, U.K.: Picton Press.

Smith, R.E. (1980). A cognitive–affective approach to stress management training for athletes. In C. Nadeau, W. Halliwell, K. Newell, & G. Roberts (Eds.), *Psychology of motor behavior and sport—1979* (pp. 54-73). Champaign, IL: Human Kinetics.

Smith, R.E., & Smoll, F.L. (1982). Psychological stress: A conceptual model and some intervention strategies in youth sports. In R.A. Magill, M.J. Ash, & F.L. Smoll (Eds.), *Children in sport* (pp. 178-195). Champaign, IL: Human Kinetics.

Smith, R.E., Smoll, F.L., & Schutz, R.W. (1990). Measurement and correlates of sport-specific cognitive and somatic trait anxiety: The sport anxiety scale. *Anxiety Research, 2*, 263-280.

Sonstroem, R.J. (1984). An overview of anxiety and sport. In J.M. Silva & R.S. Weinberg (Eds.), *Psychological foundations of sport* (pp. 104-117). Champaign, IL: Human Kinetics.

Sonstroem, R.J., & Bernardo, P. (1982). Intraindividual pregame state anxiety and basketball performance: A reexamination of the inverted-U curve. *Journal of Sport Psychology, 4*, 235-245.

Spence, J.T., & Spence, K.A. (1966). The motivational components of manifest anxiety: Drive and drive stimuli. In C.D. Spielberger (Ed.), *Anxiety and behavior* (pp. 291-326). New York: Academic.

Spielberger, C.D. (1966). Theory and research on anxiety. In C.D. Spielberger (Ed.), *Anxiety and behavior* (pp. 3-22). New York: Academic.

Spielberger, C.D. (1972). Anxiety as an emotional state. In C.D. Spielberger (Ed.), *Anxiety: Current trends in theory and research* (Vol. 1, pp. 24-54). New York: Academic.

Spielberger, C.D., Gorsuch, R.L., & Lushene, R.E. (1970a). *Manual for the state-trait anxiety inventory*. Palo Alto, CA: Consulting Psychologists.

Spielberger, C.D., Gorsuch, R.L., & Lushene, R.E. (1970b). *STAI manual for the state–trait inventory ("self-evaluation questionnaire")*. Palo Alto, CA: Consulting Psychologists.

Svebak, S. (1982). *The significance of motivation for task-induced tonic physiological changes*. Unpublished doctoral dissertation, University of Bergen, Norway.

Svebak, S. (1983). The effect of information load, emotional load, and motivational state upon tonic physiological activation. In H. Ursin & R. Murison (Eds.), *Biological and psychological basis of psychosomatic disease. Advances in the biosciences* (Vol. 42, pp. 61-73). Oxford: Pergamon.

Svebak, S., & Murgatroyd, S. (1985). Metamotivational dominance: A multimethod validation of reversal theory constructs. *Journal of Personality and Social Psychology, 48*(1), 107-116.

Svebak, S., Storfjell, O., & Dalen, K. (1982). The effect of a threatening context upon motivation and task-induced physiological changes. *British Journal of Psychology, 73*, 505-512.

Svebak, S., & Stoyva, J. (1980). High arousal can be pleasant and exciting: The theory of psychological reversals. *Biofeedback and Self-Regulation, 5*(4), 439-444.

Taylor, J.A. (1956). Drive theory and manifest anxiety. *Psychological Bulletin, 53*, 303-320.

Thayer, R.E. (1967). Measurement of activation through self-report. *Psychological Reports, 20*, 663-678.

Thom, R. (1975). *Structural stability and morphogenesis* (D.H. Fowler, Trans.). New York: Benjamin–Addison Wesley. (Original work published 1972)

Tobias, S. (1980). Anxiety and instruction. In I.G. Sarason (Ed.), *Test anxiety: Theory, research, and applications* (pp. 289-310). Hillsdale, NJ: Lawrence Erlbaum.

Tucker, D.M., & Williams, P.A. (1984). Asymmetric neural control in human self-regulation. *Psychological Review, 91*, 185-215.

Vealey, R.S. (1988). Future directions in psychological skills training. *Sport Psycholoigst, 2*(4), 318-336.

Weinberg, R.S. (1978). The effects of success and failure on the patterning of neuromuscular energy. *Journal of Motor Behavior, 10*, 53-61.

Weinberg, R.S. (1979). Anxiety and motor performance: Drive theory vs. cognitive theory. *International Journal of Sport Psychology, 10*(2), 112-121.

Weinberg, R.S. (1990). Anxiety and motor performance: Where to go from here? *Anxiety Research, 2*(4), 227-242.

Weinberg, R.S., & Genuchi, M. (1980). Relationship between competitive trait anxiety, state anxiety, and golf performance: A field study. *Journal of Sport Psychology, 2*, 148-154.

Weinberg, R.S., & Hunt, V.V. (1976). The interrelationships between anxiety, motor performance, and electromyography. *Journal of Motor Behavior, 8*(3), 219-224.

Williams, J.M. (Ed.) (1986). *Applied sport psychology: Personal growth to peak performance*. Palo Alto, CA: Mayfield.

Williams, J.M., & Krane, V. (1989). Response distortion on self-report questionnaires with female collegiate golfers. *Sport Psychologist, 3*(3), 212-218.

Wine, J.D. (1980). Cognitive-attentional theory of test anxiety. In I.G. Sarason (Ed.), *Test anxiety: Theory, research, and application* (pp. 349-385). Hillsdale, NJ: Lawrence Erlbaum.

Yerkes, R.M., & Dodson, J.D. (1908). The relation of strength of stimulus to rapidity of habit formation. *Journal of Comparative Neurology and Psychology, 18*, 459-482.

Zeeman, E.C. (1976, April). Catastrophe theory. *Scientific American, 234*, 65-83.

Chapter 7

Gender and Sport Behavior

Diane L. Gill
University of North Carolina at Greensboro

Clearly, girls and women are active sport participants today. Ten-year-old girls play in soccer leagues alongside 10-year-old boys. Universities sponsor parallel intercollegiate basketball teams for women and men, and both men and women jog through the streets of our neighborhoods. Just as clearly, gender influences our sport behavior. Gender influences adults' expectations and responses to 10-year-old girl and boy soccer players. Similarly, men and women basketball players face different pressures; and gender influences the exerciser's options (such as time and place of exercise), attire, and activities.

Despite the pervasiveness of gender influences in sport and the seemingly infinite number of psychological questions that one could ask, sport psychology research on gender is incredibly limited in both scope and depth. Moreover, the lack of guiding conceptual frameworks limits our ability to understand gender as a complex, multifaceted phenomenon in sport and exercise settings. Correspondingly, researchers in the larger

discipline of psychology have also been slow to move beyond isolated studies of sex differences toward the examination of gender as a social–psychological phenomenon within a conceptual framework. Given the absence of guiding models in psychology and the complexity of the issues, the lack of systematic, theoretically based sport psychology work on gender is understandable—but still regrettable.

Despite the general lack of scholarly work on gender issues, there is some sport psychology research in this area and many provocative questions. Research on gender, in both the general psychology and sport psychology literatures, is largely a product of the 1980s (and I hope will continue into the 1990s and beyond). The sociopolitical climate of the 1970s, and particularly the passage of Title IX of the Civil Rights Act in 1972, highlighted the importance of gender issues in sport. Although Title IX addressed the scope of educational discrimination and equity, the implications for athletics and sport caught the public's attention and prompted sport and exercise professionals to consider the issues. Clearly, many of the legal barriers to female sport participation are gone (or at least reduced to speed bumps). However, laws do not immediately change thoughts, feelings, and behaviors; and these are the primary concerns of sport psychology. In fact, equity in educational sport programs has been implemented slowly and is not yet fully achieved. Furthermore, although we are moving toward equity in high school and college sport programs, similar trends are not found in all areas of sport and exercise. The clearest example is the dramatic decline in the number of women coaches and administrators over the last 15 years (Acosta & Carpenter, 1987; Hasbrook, 1988).

This cursory look at recent sport history, along with a casual glance at our gymnasiums and exercise centers, suggests that gender continues to exert a pervasive influence on sport and exercise behavior. Furthermore, gender influence likely varies with the situations, activities, and individuals involved. This chapter will review the existing research on the role of gender in sport and exercise behavior and discuss existing and emerging theoretical models that may help explain the complex, multifaceted role of gender within the sport context. The chapter will begin with the early work on sex differences and progress by reviewing the research on individual differences in gender roles that dominates sport psychology research on gender. Then the current work on achievement and gender beliefs that takes a more cognitive approach will be considered. Finally, the last section will discuss the promising work that considers the social context, as well as the individual, and offer suggestions for research directions.

Sex Differences Approach

Within both psychology and sport psychology, research on gender issues began with an examination of sex differences in characteristics and behavior. Before discussing that work, I should clarify my terminology, which follows the current terminology in gender research. *Sex differences* refers to biologically based differences between males and females, whereas *gender* refers to social and psychological characteristics and behaviors associated with females and males. Because this early work assumed dichotomous psychological differences that paralleled—and indeed stemmed from—biological male and female differences, *sex differences* is the appropriate term. The study and discussion of sex differences has a long and colorful history, often

with sociopolitical overtones. For our purposes, though, we can start with the most notable recent work on sex differences, by Maccoby and Jacklin (1974). Maccoby and Jacklin surveyed the vast existing literature on psychological sex differences. Their main finding, which is often ignored, was that few conclusions concerning sex differences could be drawn from the diverse literature on this topic. They did note, however, that the literature suggested the possibility of sex differences in four specific areas: math ability, visual–spatial ability, verbal ability, and aggressive behavior.

Subsequent work casts doubt on even these differences. Several reviews, particularly the meta-analytic reviews of Eagley (1987) and Hyde and Linn (1986), suggest that sex differences in these areas are minimal and not biologically based. Meta-analyses consistently indicate that less than 5% of the behavioral variance in these areas is accounted for by sex. Moreover, sex differences are inconsistent, and interactions are common. For example, sex differences might show up with one task or one type of behavior but not with another. In general, then, overlap and similarities are much more apparent than differences when comparing males and females. Frodi, Macauley, and Thome (1977), in a review of the aggression research concluded that the literature does not support the belief that males are more aggressive than females or that females display more indirect or displaced aggression. Rather, gender differences in aggression are inconsistent and seem to be a function of other factors, such as justification, sex of the instigator, and situational cues. In a more recent meta-analysis, Eagley and Steffin (1986) concluded that on average, males are somewhat more aggressive than females but that sex differences are inconsistent and related to attributes of the studies such as type of aggressive behavior and perceived consequences. Recent reviews and meta-analyses of other cognitive skills and social behaviors, including conformity and nonverbal behavior, lead to similar conclusions. Clear sex differences do not emerge. Rather, overlap and similarity are more apparent; and many interactions qualify the differences that are observed (see Deaux, 1985, for an overview).

Jacklin (1989), who coauthored the most cited work on sex differences, now concludes that despite our preoccupation with the search for gender differences, even the original conclusions on sex differences cannot be supported. She concludes that despite much data, gender is *not* an important variable for explaining individual variation in intellectual abilities. Jacklin continues to actively pursue research on biological factors, particularly hormonal influences; but she suggests that even though some biologically based gender differences may exist, their implications for behavioral development are not known. Finally, Jacklin notes that the rich theoretical and empirical literature on socialization processes yields so many contradictions, revisions, and new hypotheses that gender socialization may be a moving target; that is, gender changes as society changes. Just as we are beginning to explain the processes and relationships, they change. Certainly, this seems true in the sport world as well as in the larger society. Moving targets are difficult to hit (as any sport scientist should know). The task is challenging and demands unique skills and approaches.

Jacklin's point on gender socialization illustrates a major problem with the work on sex differences. Such an approach assumes an underlying, unidimensional cause (i.e., biological sex) and ignores the complexity and variations in gender-related behavior.

Criticisms of the sex differences approach and its failure to shed any light on gender-related behavior prompted some psychologists to try other avenues. The major shift in psychology research was a shift away from biologically based sex differences to psychosocially based gender differences. Specifically, psychologists interested in gender-related behavior began to focus on individual differences in gender role orientation as a personality construct.

Gender Role Orientation (Masculinity, Femininity, and Androgyny)

Sandra Bem's (1974, 1978) theoretical discussion of masculinity, femininity, and androgyny and her development of the Bem Sex Role Inventory (BSRI) to measure individual differences in gender role orientation was the major impetus for the large body of subsequent work on gender role personality characteristics. At the same time that Bem began her work, Janet Spence and Bob Helmreich (1978) also began investigating gender role orientation and also developed a measure of masculinity and femininity, the Personality Attributes Questionnaire (PAQ; Spence, Helmreich & Stapp, 1974). This initial work by Bem, Spence, and Helmreich not only led to considerable research on gender role orientation in the psychology literature but also stimulated a number of researchers to examine these issues in the sport context. In fact, most of the existing sport psychology research on gender is based

on the ideas developed by Bem, Spence, and Helmreich.

In developing her gender role orientation perspective, Bem dismissed the traditional, unidimensional models of gender roles and advocated a new approach to gender-related personality characteristics and behavior. In doing so, Bem built upon earlier multidimensional approaches to gender (Bakan, 1966; Constantinople, 1973) and suggested that the personality characteristics of masculinity and femininity are not necessarily linked to biological sex or sexual orientation. Moreover, masculinity and femininity are not opposite ends of the same personality dimension, as assessed with more traditional measures such as the masculinity/femininity scale of the Minnesota Multiphasic Personality Inventory (MMPI). Instead, masculinity and femininity are separate clusters of desirable personality characteristics. Masculine characteristics are typically perceived as more desirable for men than for women, and feminine characteristics typically are perceived as more desirable for women than for men. According to Bem, there is no reason why males should possess only masculine characteristics or females only feminine characteristics. Indeed, Bem argues that people who are extremely sex-typed (only masculine or only feminine) are inflexible and have limited behavioral options. In contrast, the most mentally healthy and adaptable individuals possess both feminine and masculine characteristics.

The BSRI (Bem, 1974) includes 20 stereotypically feminine items (e.g., affectionate, sensitive to the needs of others) to assess femininity, 20 stereotypically masculine items (e.g., independent, willing to take risks) to assess masculinity, and 20 filler items (e.g., truthful, happy). In her early work Bem emphasized the construct of androgyny and suggested that androgynous individuals, who score high on both the masculine and feminine subscales of the BSRI, are more flexible and adaptable and generally better-off than individuals who possess only masculine or only feminine characteristics. Similarly, the PAQ assesses separate clusters of desirable feminine and masculine characteristics, although the authors (Spence & Helmreich, 1980; Helmreich, Spence & Holohan, 1979) now suggest that the personality clusters are more appropriately labeled *instrumental* (masculine) and *expressive* (feminine).

Bem, Spence, and Helmreich's views—and, perhaps more importantly, their inventories— spurred considerable research. Typically, investigators assessed individuals on the separate masculine and feminine scales and then used median splits to classify people as high or low.

Those scoring high on both scales were classified as androgynous, those high on femininity and low on masculinity as feminine, those high on masculinity and low on femininity as masculine, and those unfortunate enough to be low on both as undifferentiated (see Figure 7.1). Although the median splits and 2 × 2 classification have been criticized (e.g., Taylor & Hall, 1982), that approach is the most common one in the sport psychology literature.

Shortly after their development, both the BSRI and PAQ were used with sport participants. Indeed, Helmreich and Spence (1977) sampled intercollegiate athletes in their early work and reported that most female athletes were either androgynous or masculine. These athletes were similar to high-achieving female scientists in Helmreich and Spence's samples but different from female college students, who were most often classified as feminine.

Several other studies with female athletes yield similar findings. Harris and Jennings (1977) surveyed female distance runners and, replicating Helmreich and Spence, reported that most were androgynous or masculine. Del Rey and Sheppard (1981) and Colker and Widom (1980) used the PAQ with intercollegiate athletes and found most classified as androgynous or masculine. Myers and Lips (1978) used the BSRI with female and male racquet sports participants. In their first study most female raquetball players were androgynous, whereas most males were masculine. In a second study players were classified as competitive or noncompetitive based on their reasons for entering a tournament. All males were competitive and also either androgynous or masculine. Competitive females were either androgynous or masculine, but noncompetitive females had lower masculinity scores and were mainly feminine or undifferentiated.

Although the use of the 2 × 2 classification has waned in the sport psychology literature, it has not disappeared. Wrisberg, Draper, and Everett (1988), for example, reported that both female and male team sport athletes were mainly masculine or androgynous. However, male and female individual sport athletes differed; most females were feminine whereas males were equally distributed across the classifications. Henderson, Stalnaker, and Taylor (1988) extended the gender role approach to leisure settings and explored the relationship between gender role orientation and perceived barriers to recreation. Females classified as masculine perceived the fewest leisure constraints, followed by androgynous women—paralleling the findings with athletes.

I have cited only a few studies. Many more, including many unpublished theses, have used the BSRI or PAQ and classified sport participants in the 2 × 2 model. Generally the results of these studies suggest that female athletes and sport participants are more likely to be masculine or androgynous than are female nonparticipants. Unfortunately, both the methodology and the underlying assumptions of this line of research have been widely criticized. At the bottom line, these numerous studies have little value; they tell us nothing about gender-related behavior in sport and exercise, and they do not lead us toward better explanatory models. Specific criticisms of this research will be discussed and then some promising alternate approaches that may tell us more about gender and sport behavior will be considered.

First, the BSRI and PAQ have been criticized on both psychometric and conceptual grounds (e.g., Locksley & Colten, 1979; Pedhazur & Tetenbaum, 1979). The androgyny construct is of little conceptual or empirical value in gender role research, and the 2 × 2 classification procedure is particularly problematic. As Taylor and Hall (1982) conclude in their review, there is no evidence that an androgyny construct or the interaction of masculinity and femininity adds anything. Instead, a regression approach using the full range of masculine and feminine scores rather than arbitrary categories seems best suited to the questions and purposes of those interested in gender role orientation.

Most gender role researchers accept the separate dimensions of the BSRI and PAQ personality measures; but the meaning of the constructs and their implications for other gender-related constructs and behaviors are questionable. In her review, Deaux (1985) noted that the scales of the BSRI and PAQ do seem to reflect measures of self-assertion and nurturance and do predict specific assertive and nurturant behaviors. However, the personality measures do not relate so well to other gender-related attributes and behaviors.

| | Masculinity | |
	Above median	Below median
Femininity — Above median	Androgynous	Feminine
Femininity — Below median	Masculine	Undifferentiated

Figure 7.1　2 × 2 classification of individuals on BRSI and PAQ masculinity and femininity measures.
Note. From *Psychological Dynamics of Sport* (p. 84), by D.L. Gill, 1986, Champaign, IL: Human Kinetics. Copyright 1986 by Diane L. Gill. Reprinted by permission.

Overall, the sport psychology research on gender role orientation suggests that female athletes possess more masculine/instrumental personality characteristics than female nonathletes. This is not particularly enlightening or far-reaching. Sport, especially competitive athletics, which has been the main setting for most of the research, is an achievement activity that demands instrumental, assertive behavior. Indeed, both the BSRI and PAQ include "competitive" as one of the masculine/instrumental items. The higher masculine scores of female athletes probably reflect an overlap with competitiveness or sport achievement orientation. Competitive orientation can be measured directly (e.g., Gill & Deeter, 1988); and the more indirect, controversial measures of the BSRI and PAQ are not likely to add information.

Indeed, this is just what I found in my work on competitive orientation. In one study with male and female intercollegiate athletes and nonathletes, Dzewaltowski and I (Gill & Dzewaltowski, 1988) found that competitiveness clearly differentiated athletes and nonathletes; and this difference held for both females and males. In collecting that data we also administered both the BSRI and PAQ, although we did not report that information. Our analyses of these data showed that athletes scored higher than nonathletes on masculinity/instrumentality. However, stepwise analyses indicated that competitiveness was the only discriminator between athletes and nonathletes, with BSRI and PAQ scores adding nothing at all.

So participation in sport, particularly highly competitive sport activities, is an instrumental behavior; and participants probably have higher scores than nonparticipants. However, we can use more direct and powerful measures of competitive sport orientation as predictors without invoking gender role connotations.

Furthermore, sport participation or athlete/nonathlete status is an indirect and nonspecific measure of behavior. If instrumental and expressive personality characteristics predict instrumental and expressive behaviors, we might examine specific instrumental and expressive sport behaviors. The tendency simply to classify sport as an instrumental or masculine activity ignores the fact that many different instrumental *and* expressive behaviors occur in sport and exercise settings. Even within highly competitive sports, expressive behaviors may be advantageous. Creative, expressive actions may be the key to success for a gymnast; supportive behaviors of teammates may be critical on a soccer team; and sensitivity to others should help an Olympic coach communicate with each athlete.

I am citing instrumental and expressive *behaviors* as examples. We assume that instrumental and expressive personality *dispositions* relate to these behaviors, but we should not assume an absolute, direct prediction. Sport psychologists have recognized the limits of this trait approach for some time and criticized such work on sport personality (see chapter 3), but we have not progressed beyond this approach with gender role orientation. Helmreich, Spence, and Holohan (1979) recognized the limits of their measure and cautioned that the measures have only weak relationships to gender role behavior. They explicitly emphasized the importance of situational factors. For example, in figure skating expressive behaviors are more appropriate in a free skating program than when doing the prescribed school figures. By considering the joint influence of instrumental and expressive personality characteristics along with situational constraints, incentives, and interaction processes, we move closer to understanding gender-related behavior in sport and exercise.

Even if we recognize the limits of the measures and adopt an interactionist approach, research on gender role orientation raises concerns. M. Ann Hall (1988), a sport sociologist with a track record of feminist scholarship, criticizes the measures and research on gender role orientation. Specifically, Hall cautions that using the gender role constructs and measures reifies the masculine–feminine dichotomy and constructs that do not really exist in concrete terms. The 2 × 2 classification approach highlights this bias. Even with the range of instrumental and expressive scores, Hall suggests that focusing on these particular gender role constructs leads us away from consideration of behaviors and the wider range of characteristics and social psychological processes that influence sport and exercise behavior. Overall, then, the sport psychology research on gender role orientation has all the drawbacks of our early sport personality research wrapped up with limiting gender stereotypes and biases.

Researchers interested in gender and behavior usually recognize the limits of the early gender role approach. Most look beyond the simple male/female or masculine/feminine dichotomy. Even Bem, Spence, and Helmreich have moved beyond their earlier methods to look at gender constructs and behaviors in more complex ways.

Unfortunately, we do not always recognize the same limits in more recent discussions of gender. For example, Carol Gilligan's (1982) work on moral reasoning and moral development brought a needed consideration of women's experiences to that literature. Gilligan questioned the assumed moral reasoning hierarchy with its male biases and introduced alternative methods and analyses that highlighted women's perspectives. That was groundbreaking work. However, if we take Gilligan's work and contrast the "female" model of moral reasoning with a traditional "male" model, we are perpetuating a stereotyped dichotomy. The provocative work of Belenky, Clinchy, Goldberger, and Tarule (1986) on women's ways of knowing could lead us to similar problems. Their focus on women's experiences and their use of nontraditional methods and interviews with diverse women introduced important alternative ideas, methods, and indeed, ways of knowing to our research. However, on the surface, the work leads us to assume a stereotypical dichotomy and a focus on unidimensional gender differences.

Classifying moral reasoning or ways of knowing into feminine and masculine forms (even if we acknowledge that both females and males could use either) focuses on a stereotypical dichotomy and tends to reduce a complex phenomenon to a unidimensional explanation. Instead, we should move beyond simplistic models to consider gender within the context of sociocultural history and the current social environment rather than merely as a characteristic of individuals.

Gender and Sport Achievement

One research area that has progressed from early sex differences research through gender role research to more current models, including social cognitions and social context, is the work on *achievement*. Achievement is a prominent topic in the research on gender, and achievement is particularly relevant to sport psychology. Most sport and exercise activities involve achievement; and competitive behavior is particularly relevant.

Gender differences were recognized in the early achievement research when McClelland, Atkinson, Clark, and Lowell (1953) noted that women did not respond to achievement instructions as men did. Actually, gender differences were ignored at that point, and the theories and findings on achievement motivation became theories and findings on men's achievement motivation. It was not until the 1970s that gender differences in achievement were explicitly considered. Since that time, two particular areas within the broader achievement literature have been related to sport achievement. The early work emphasized gender differences in achievement motivation, specifically, the *fear of success*

motive. More recent work has turned to gender differences in achievement cognitions.

Gender and Achievement Orientations

Martina Horner's (1972) doctoral work was one of the first studies to focus attention on the role of gender in achievement behavior. Horner adopted an individual differences approach and specifically proposed a *motive to avoid success* to explain gender differences in achievement behavior. Horner asserted that the motive to avoid success, more popularly termed *fear of success* (FOS), influences achievement behavior just as the motives to approach success and avoid failure influence achievement behavior within the Atkinson model. Horner suggested that success has negative consequences for women because success requires competitive, achievement behaviors that conflict with the traditional feminine image. This conflict arouses the FOS motive and leads to anxiety and avoidance. Because gender role socialization does not lead to similar conflicts and negative consequences for men, they are less likely to exhibit FOS. Thus, FOS is a negative or inhibitory motive that is more common in women than in men. Horner provided some evidence for the FOS motive and observed that females high in FOS did not perform as well as females low in FOS in a competitive achievement situation. Horner's work was widely publicized in the popular media and inspired much debate and continued research in the psychology literature. However, subsequent research cast doubt on Horner's construct and measure (e.g., Condry & Dyer, 1976; Tresemer, 1977). McElroy and Willis (1979), when considering women's achievement conflicts in sport contexts, concluded that no evidence supports an FOS in female athletes and that the achievement attitudes of female athletes are similar to those of male athletes.

Although Horner's FOS motive and measure have lost their initial appeal, gender differences remain prominent in the achievement literature. The early achievement models emphasizing general achievement motives have been replaced with multidimensional constructs and an emphasis on cognitions as mediators of achievement behavior. For example, Helmreich and Spence (1978) developed a multidimensional Work and Family Orientation questionnaire (WOFO) that assesses the separate achievement dimensions of mastery, work, and competitiveness. Their research (Spence & Helmreich, 1983) indicates that gender differences vary across the dimensions and across samples. Generally, males score higher than females on mastery and competitiveness, whereas females score higher on work. In high-achieving samples of scientists, businesspersons, and athletes, gender differences on mastery and work diminish, but males remain higher than females on competitiveness. Spence and Helmreich also report that masculinity/instrumentality scores on the PAQ relate to all three achievement dimensions, whereas femininity/expressiveness scores relate slightly positively to work and negatively to competitiveness. Generally, gender influence is strongest and most consistent for competitiveness.

My work on sport-specific achievement orientation (Gill, 1988) also suggests that gender influence varies across dimensions. Although we might assume that the gender differences in competitiveness reported by Spence and Helmreich would also be found in sport, the research on sport achievement orientation suggests a more complex picture. Following the lead of Martens (1977) and other sport psychologists who have developed sport-specific psychological measures and demonstrated their value for understanding sport behavior, Gill & Deeter, (1988) developed a sport-specific measure of achievement orientation known as the Sport Orientation Questionnaire (SOQ). Gill and colleagues provided reliability and validity evidence through a series of studies (Gill, 1986; Gill & Deeter, 1988; Gill & Dzewaltowski, 1988; Gill, Dzewaltowski & Deeter, 1988). The SOQ is multidimensional as well as sport-specific, yielding scores for

- competitiveness, an achievement orientation to enter, and strive for success in, competitive sport;
- win orientation, a desire to win and avoid losing in competitive sport; and
- goal orientation, an emphasis on achieving personal goals in competitive sport.

Use of a multidimensional, sport-specific measure permits insights into gender and sport achievement not possible with unidimensional or general achievement measures. During the development of the SOQ we found consistent gender differences in sport orientation. Specifically, males scored higher than females on competitiveness and win orientation, whereas females typically scored slightly higher than males on the goal orientation scale. My subsequent study (1988), focusing specially on gender differences, examined WOFO general achievement scores along with the SOQ in females and males who participated in competitive sport, noncompetitive sport, and nonsport achievement activities. Overall, analyses revealed that males consistently scored higher than females on sport competitiveness and win orientation

and that males reported more competitive sport activity and experience. However, females were just as high as males, and sometimes higher, on sport goal orientation and on all general achievement scores except competitiveness. Also, females were just as likely as males to participate in noncompetitive sport and to report nonsport achievement activities and interests. Generally, then, the gender differences in competitive orientation and sport participation do not seem to reflect either general achievement orientation or interest in sport and exercise activities per se. Instead, gender may influence the individual's emphasis on social comparison and winning within sport.

Other researchers have reported similar gender influences on reactions to competitive sport. When McNally and Orlick (1975) introduced a cooperative broomball game to children in urban Canada and the Northern Territories, they found that the girls were more receptive than the boys. Duda (1986) reported both gender and cultural influences on competitiveness in Anglo and Navajo children. Male Anglo children were the most win-oriented and placed the most emphasis on athletic ability. Weinberg and Jackson (1979) found males were more affected by success/failure than females, who reacted more consistently. Weinberg and Ragan (1979) found males were more interested in a competitive activity, whereas females preferred a noncompetitive activity. Some of the research on intrinsic motivation (e.g., Deci, Betley, Kahle, Abrams & Porac, 1981) suggested that competition and a focus on winning may act as extrinsic motivating forces to decrease intrinsic motivation and that the undermining of intrinsic motivation is especially likely for females.

Although several lines of research suggest a gender influence on sport achievement, particularly on competitive sport behaviors, the research does not point to any unique gender-related personality construct as an explanation. Most investigators attempting to understand gender and sport achievement are turning to socialization factors, societal influences, and a broader range of social cognitive constructs and models for explanations.

Gender and Achievement Cognitions

Cognitive approaches that emphasize interpretations and perceptions and deemphasize personality constructs currently dominate sport psychology research on achievement. Within both sport psychology and general psychology, most cognitive approaches to motivation focus on expectations. Although the currently popular cognitive motivation theories vary in specific constructs and proposed relationships, nearly all of them highlight expectations as key predictors of behavior (see chapters 4 and 5). Expectations may be discussed as generalized expectations, confidence, self-efficacy, challenge, or perceived ability; but all reflect some type of expectation for success. Regardless of the specific expectation construct and theoretical framework, research consistently indicates that expectations are good predictors of achievement behavior and performance (e.g., Bandura, 1977, 1986; Crandall, 1969; Eccles et al., 1983; Feltz, 1988; Roberts, 1984). Research also suggests gender influences on expectations (Crandall, 1969; Eccles, 1985, 1987; Lenney, 1977). Typically, females report lower expectations of success than do males, and this difference may explain gender differences in achievement behavior.

Although females typically report lower expectations and take less responsibility for success than do males, gender differences in expectancy cognitive patterns are not completely consistent but may vary with the situation. In her review of the self-confidence literature, Lenney (1977) concluded that gender differences in confidence are more likely to occur in achievement situations that

- involve tasks perceived as masculine,
- provide only ambiguous feedback or ability information, and
- emphasize social comparison evaluation.

I have discussed how task characteristics may mediate gender differences. Most of the earlier research used tasks likely to be seen as masculine. When tasks or activities that are considered appropriate for females are used, gender differences typically disappear. For example, research by Deaux and Farris (1977) and Stein, Pohly, and

Mueller (1971) indicates that gender differences in achievement cognitions vary with the sex-linked nature of the task. Lenney's own research (Lenney, Browning & Mitchell, 1980) confirmed that clear evaluation guidelines reduced gender differences in self-confidence.

Within sport psychology, Corbin and his colleagues (Corbin, 1981; Corbin, Landers, Feltz & Senior, 1983; Corbin & Nix, 1979; Corbin, Stewart & Blair, 1981; Petruzzello & Corbin, 1988; Stewart & Corbin, 1988) have conducted a series of experimental studies with motor tasks that confirm Lenney's propositions. Specifically, Corbin and his colleagues demonstrated that females did not lack confidence with a gender-neutral, non-socially-evaluative task and that performance feedback could improve the confidence of low-confidence females. Moreover, Petruzzello and Corbin found that feedback-enhanced confidence did not generalize beyond the experimental task and suggested lack of experience as an additional factor affecting female self-confidence. In our lab my colleagues and I (Gill, Gross, Huddleston & Shifflett, 1984) matched male and female competitors of similar ability on a pegboard task. Males were slightly more likely than females to predict a win, perhaps suggesting that the gender influence on competitive win orientation remains. However, performance expectations were similar, females performed slightly better in competition than males did, and females generally had more positive achievement cognitions (higher perceived ability, more effort attributions).

So these studies suggest that when tasks are appropriate for females, when females and males have similar experiences and capabilities, and when clear evaluation criteria and feedback are present, females and males display similar levels of confidence. Importantly, though, these are experimental studies in controlled settings. We cannot so easily equate task appropriateness,

experience, and social influences in the real world of sport and exercise. To understand the influence of gender on achievement cognitions and behavior we must consider these socialization and social context variables.

Eccles (1985, 1987; Eccles et al., 1983) has developed one of the most complete models of achievement, one that incorporates sociocultural factors along with achievement cognitions. Moreover, she considers gender differences and gender influences throughout the model. Recently she (Eccles & Harold, 1991) has extended her research on school achievement and applied the model to explain gender differences in sport achievement.

Like most traditional models of achievement motivation and behavior, Eccles's model adopts an Expectancy × Value framework. Eccles incorporates the work on expectations and recognizes that expectations are key determinants of achievement choices and behaviors. In a somewhat more unique approach, Eccles also gives importance, or value, a direct role in determining achievement choices. Both expectations and value are subjective interpretations or perceptions. Moreover, Eccles does not simply assume expectations and value as the starting point. Instead, she includes a complex system of sociocultural factors; primary socializers; and individual needs, schemata, and experiences as determinants of achievement perceptions. Gender exerts an influence at all stages of the model. As discussed previously, gender differences in expectations are common in most achievement domains, including sport. Also, gender probably influences the importance or value of sport achievement. Eccles's model goes beyond this information to point out that gender differences in expectations and value do not suddenly appear in a particular setting. Rather, they develop over time and are influenced by gender role socialization, stereotyped expectations of others, and sociocultural norms, as well as individual characteristics and experiences. To understand gender and achievement, we must take this broader look at early socialization and the social context.

In their recent work on gender and sport achievement, Eccles and Harold (1991) provide evidence showing that the model holds for sport at least as well as for academic achievement, that gender influences children's sport achievement perceptions and behaviors at a very young age, and that these gender differences seem to be a product of gender role socialization. Specifically, in research with adolescents Eccles and Harold found that boys, more than girls, saw value in sport and themselves as able in sport and that these gender differences were stronger than those for expectations and value English and math. Path analyses revealed that the gender difference in free time spent in sport (achievement choice) was mediated or explained entirely by these perceptions, supporting the model's link from expectations and value to achievement choice. In another study, with younger elementary children, Eccles and Harold found similar gender differences on self-perceptions of sport value and ability. These children also completed a motor proficiency test. Although boys scored slightly better than girls, gender accounted for only 2% of the variance in motor proficiency but 14% of the variance in perceived sport ability. Given these gender differences in perceptions and values, Eccles and Harold then turned to sociocultural and socialization components of the model for an explanation. Teachers rated boys' sport ability higher than girls' sport ability, although no gender differences were found for ratings of math and reading ability, suggesting a potential school socializing influence. Children rated gender stereotypes by indicating how important the abilities were for girls and boys. Sport was rated much more sex-typed than math or reading, and these ratings of sex typing correlated with children's ratings of their own sport ability. These results suggest that gender role stereotypes influence sport confidence even at this young age. Finally, children rated how important it was to their parents that they did well in sports. Not surprisingly, boys gave higher ratings, suggesting a further parental influence on sport achievement perceptions and choices.

Although Eccles's work does not offer a final answer, her model and research findings do provide a framework that can be used to develop relevant and important questions concerning gender and sport achievement. First, Eccles's research indicates that gender differences in sport achievement choices and behaviors do exist. Second, as predicted within the Eccles model, gender apparently influences sport achievement through self-perceptions of value and expectations. Although physical characteristics and aptitude have some influence, the sociocultural context and socialization process seem to be the primary source of gender differences in self-perceptions. These sociocultural processes encompass many specific factors (e.g., parental influence, school influence, sociocultural stereotypes) that are interrelated in complex ways. Although we may not be able to pinpoint precise predictors and lines of influence, we must consider the sociocultural milieu and socialization processes if we are to understand gender and sport achievement.

Gender Belief Systems

As Deaux (1984) reports in an analysis of the research on gender, psychologists have moved away from the sex differences and individual differences approaches to an emphasis on gender as a social category. As with the Eccles achievement model, an emphasis on gender belief systems extends beyond the investigation of individual personality characteristics, cognitions, and behaviors to focus on social context, socialization, and socially developed cognitive frameworks. As described by Deaux (1984; Deaux & Kite, 1987) gender belief systems encompass diverse gender stereotypes and attitudes about appropriate characteristics, roles, and behaviors. Such an approach necessitates moving beyond simple research designs and univariate relationships to consider a complex network of gender beliefs, interrelated factors, and processes. Attempts to explain gender-related behaviors on the basis of sex differences or individual characteristics and immediate cognitions are clearly inadequate. Both Bem, who focused on individual differences in personality in her early work, and Deaux, who conducted research on individual differences in attributions, have moved beyond individual differences to consider broader social belief systems.

Bem's Gender Schema Theory

Even Bem, who initiated much of the research on gender role orientation, has moved away from her early focus on personality to a broader, more social gender schema theory (Bem, 1981, 1983, 1985). Rather than classifying individuals as masculine, feminine, or androgynous, Bem now focuses on sex-typing as an indicant of gender-schematic processing. Persons who are sex-typed (high-masculine males and high-feminine females) are *gender-schematic*, whereas non-sex-typed persons are *gender-aschematic*. Gender-schematic individuals tend to interpret situations and process information according to gender stereotypes and rely on gender schema to explain and guide actions when other schema are more appropriate. Thus, sex-typed individuals see situations in gender terms, stereotype others, and restrict their activities to conform to gender stereotypes. In contrast, gender-aschematic individuals are not restricted by gender schema but use other more appropriate and relevant schema.

Gender schema theory suggests that sex-typed individuals are more likely than non-sex-typed individuals to classify sports as gender-appropriate and to restrict their participation to what they perceive as gender-appropriate sport and exercise activities. Matteo (1986, 1988) applied a gender schema approach to sport and confirmed these suggestions. Csizma, Wittig, and Schurr (1988), along with Matteo, confirmed that sports are indeed sex-typed as masculine or feminine (mostly masculine). Matteo further reported that sex-typing influenced sport choice, and that sex-typed individuals did not participate in what they considered gender-inappropriate sports.

In a recent investigation, Frable (1989) confirmed some predictions of gender schema theory and provided evidence suggesting that gender ideology may have subtle influences even with situational constraints on behavior. Frable found that sex-typing, or gender ideology, predicted *gender* attitudes, rules, and discriminatory behaviors (e.g., devaluing female performance) but not more general rules and attitudes. Frable also noted that sex-typed participants indicated that sex should *not* be a criterion even though they were actually using gender processing. Frable's study did not involve sport attitudes or behaviors; but the finding that sex-typed individuals see the world in gendered terms and behave in line with those perceptions (even without intentional discrimination) may have implications for sport. Gender-schematic processing by teachers, parents, coaches, and others within the social context of sport may influence sport behaviors, just as the participant's own gender schema affects behavior.

Bem's gender schema theory emphasizes social stereotypes and social processes. Indeed, Bem (1985) states that she no longer advocates that individuals should be androgynous; instead, society should be gender-aschematic. However, gender schema theory still relies on the BSRI measure and an individual difference classification and is subject to many of the criticisms that marked the earlier work on gender role orientation.

Deaux's Work on Gender Belief Systems

Deaux (1984) has moved away from both sex difference and individual difference approaches to focus more clearly on social categories and social context in her recent work on gender belief systems. Gender influence depends not only on the gender constructs of the individual but also on the gender beliefs of others and the gender context of the situation. Indeed, Deaux (1984; Deaux & Kite, 1987) emphasizes the social component and proposes that how people *think* males and females differ is more important than how they actually differ. As discussed earlier, actual differences between females and males on psychological and behavioral measures are small and inconsistent. Nevertheless, we (all of us in society) maintain our beliefs in gender differences.

For example, gender differences in individuals' attributions and evaluations of their own performance are small. Moreover, gender differences in attributions and evaluations have only a limited influence on subsequent achievement behaviors, and that influence is mediated by expectations (Deaux, 1976, 1984, 1985). As discussed earlier, gender differences in expectations, although common, diminish with gender-appropriate tasks, clear information, experience, and reduced social evaluation. In contrast, gender influence is clearer for observers' evaluations of males and females, and this gender bias seems to stem from gender-stereotyped beliefs and expectations (Deaux, 1984, 1985; Deaux & Kite, 1987).

Deaux (1984, 1985; Deaux & Kite, 1987) proposes that our gender stereotypes are pervasive and that they exert a major influence on social interactions. Considerable evidence supports the existence of gender stereotypes. The often-cited studies of Rosenkrantz and I. and D. Broverman (Broverman, Vogel, Broverman, Clarkson & Rosenkrantz, 1972; Rosenkrantz, Vogel, Bee, Broverman & Broverman, 1968) identify clusters of personality traits associated with the typical man (competence) and typical woman (warmth–expressiveness). The BSRI and PAQ gender role orientation measures are based on similar stereotypical profiles of ideal or typical women and men.

More recent work (Deaux & Kite, 1987; Deaux & Lewis, 1984; Eagley & Kite, 1987) suggests that bipolar stereotypes continue to exist, and also that gender stereotypes have multiple components. We often recognize gender stereotypes in personality traits, as evidenced in the work of Rosenkrantz and Broverman and with masculinity/femininity measures. However, as Deaux (1984; Deaux & Kite, 1987; Deaux & Lewis, 1984) emphasizes, gender stereotypes have multiple components; we hold gender stereotypes or gender beliefs about role behaviors, occupations, physical appearance, and sexuality, as well as about traits. Research on multidimensional stereotypes is just beginning; but Deaux suggests that these multiple components are interrelated and that the relationships and implications for gender-related behavior may vary with the social context. For example, Deaux and Lewis (1984) found that people weigh physical appearance heavily and infer other gender-related traits and behaviors (e.g., personality, sexuality) from physical characteristics.

Such gender stereotypes are of interest themselves, but they are of even more interest because they influence a wide range of attitudes and behaviors. Considerable research suggests a gender bias in the evaluation of male and female performance and achievement and that bias has implications for sport and exercise.

In a provocative, widely cited study, Goldberg (1968) reported a bias favoring male authors when women judged articles that were equivalent except for sex of author. Many similar studies followed Goldberg's initial work. Most confirmed a male bias in evaluations of females and males, although the findings are not completely consistent and suggest that the bias varies with information and situational characteristics (Deaux & Taynor, 1973; Pheterson, Kiesler & Goldberg, 1971; Wallston & O'Leary, 1981).

Although sport psychologists have not examined multidimensional gender stereotypes and interrelationships, we do have evidence suggesting gender stereotypes and gender bias in evaluations within sport. Gender is a salient social category in sport and exercise settings. Our gender stereotypes have not all disappeared with the implementation of Title IX. Deaux (1985) notes that research documents a shift toward more egalitarian attitudes in the general society, and sport attitudes certainly are moving in that direction. *The Miller Lite Report* (Miller Brewing Company, 1983), for example, suggests that males and females hold similar attitudes, that parents are equally positive toward sport participation of daughters and sons, and that the trend is toward increasing egalitarian attitudes.

Gender stereotypes persist, however. As noted earlier, sports activities are gender-stereotyped (Csizma, Wittig & Schurr, 1988; Matteo, 1986, 1988). Indeed, gender stereotypes in sport were identified in Metheny's (1965) classic work on the social acceptability of various sports. According to Metheny, acceptable sports for women (e.g., gymnastics, swimming, tennis) emphasize aesthetic qualities and are often individual activities in contrast to direct competition and team sports. More recently, Kane and Snyder (1989) confirmed gender stereotyping of sports and, more explicitly, identified physicality as the central feature in gender stereotyping of sport.

Ostrow and colleagues (Ostrow, 1981; Ostrow, Jones & Spiker, 1981) reported both gender and age biases in ratings of the appropriateness of various sport activities for females and males of different ages. Most activities were rated more appropriate for males (in line with Metheny's suggestions), and most activities were seen as less appropriate for older people.

Griffin (1973) reported that undergraduates rated female athletes and female professors as furthest from the image of the ideal woman, whereas the roles of girlfriend and mother were rated much closer. Selby and Lewko (1976) found gender influences on children's attitudes toward women in sport. Girls were more positive toward women in sport than were boys. Moreover, girls who participated in sport were more positive than nonparticipants, but boys who participated were more negative than nonparticipants.

Brawley, Landers, Miller, and Kearns (1979) asked male and female observers to rate the performance of a male and a female on a muscular endurance task. Although the performances were identical, both male and female observers rated the male performer higher. In a subsequent study, Brawley, Powers, and Phillips (1980) failed to replicate the male bias with an accuracy task, suggesting (as with many other gender research areas) that the task mediates gender influence.

Several studies within sport have adopted the Goldberg model and examined gender bias in evaluating performance. A series of studies on male and female attitudes toward hypothetical male and female coaches (Parkhouse & Williams, 1986; Weinberg, Reveles & Jackson, 1984; Williams & Parkhouse, 1988) found a bias favoring male coaches. Williams and Parkhouse (1988) reported that female basketball players who were coached by a successful female did not exhibit the male bias when rating hypothetical coaches but actually exhibited a female bias, suggesting a more complex influence on the formation and consequences of our gender stereotypes.

Not only do gender beliefs persist in sport and exercise, but socialization pressures toward such gender beliefs are pervasive and strong (although often subtle) and begin early. Greendorfer (1987) has contributed a great deal to our understanding of sport socialization and particularly to gender socialization in sport (see chapter 10). For my purposes, I simply note that gender beliefs and behaviors are apparent even in infants and that parents, schools, and other socializers convey gender beliefs in many direct and indirect ways. Some of those influences are apparent in the Eccles work discussed earlier. Any sport psychologist interested in gender beliefs and behaviors should be familiar with this work because an understanding of gender socialization provides the basis for understanding individual gender-related behavior within sport and exercise contexts.

Overall, gender belief systems seem alive and well in the world of sport and exercise. Sport activities are gender-stereotyped, and the sex-typing of sport activities seems linked with other gender beliefs (e.g., physicality). Gender beliefs influence social processes, particularly social evaluation; and the research on gender bias in evaluation of coaches suggests that influence is at least as likely in sport as in other social interactions. Overt discrimination is unlikely, and participants may not recognize the influence of gender belief systems in themselves or others. For example, many sport administrators and participants fail to recognize gender beliefs operating when athletic systems developed for men, stressing male-linked values and characteristics, are opened to girls and women.

Sport psychologists could advance our understanding of gender and sport by investigating gender belief systems in sport and exercise. We have some limited work on sport stereotypes, but that research has not begun to consider multiple components and interrelationships. For example, how do gender beliefs about physical appearance or sexuality relate to beliefs about sport-appropriateness? More important, how do varied gender belief systems in sport relate to evaluations of others, communication, and other social interactions and processes? Quite likely, many aspects of gender belief systems and their relationships to behavior are unique to sport and exercise. Nevertheless, Deaux's initial work and suggestions could provide a good starting point.

Gender and Social Context

Consideration of gender stereotypes and beliefs is critical for understanding gender-related behavior. However, as Deaux and Major (1987) state, we must consider the immediate expectations, self-perceptions, and situational cues—the social context—to understand gender-related behavior in a given situation. Certainly, gender socialization and gender belief systems are major influences on social context. Just as clearly, though, gender-related behaviors vary tremendously from situation to situation. Application of an interactive model that considers direct and subtle aspects of social context should permit greater insight into gender-related behavior.

Deaux and Major's interaction model parallels the interactive models that have replaced early trait approaches to personality and sport behavior. Deaux and Major emphasize that gender-linked behaviors are multiply determined, highly flexible, and context-dependent. Individual characteristics and cognitions, as well as other people's characteristics and cognitions, are important, but the salience and influence of others' expectations, self-perceptions, and situational cues vary tremendously. Although this sounds like the typical Personality × Situation model, Deaux and Major's model is clearly much more social and places more emphasis on socialization, social norms, and belief systems.

This emphasis on *social* context is especially critical for understanding gender-related behavior (although I also suggest that nearly every behavior of interest in sport and exercise psychology is social and would benefit from greater attention to social context and process). Deaux and Major are not the first to advocate consideration of social context in gender research. In her book, *The Female World*, prominent sociologist Jessie Bernard (1981) points out that social experiences and contexts for females and males are quite different, even when they appear similar. Males and females do not just experience the world differently, the worlds are different. In the early days of organized sport (the 1920s–Title IX) we clearly established separate sport worlds for females and males. The different social worlds have not disappeared with our organizational changes. The social world differs for female and male members of a volleyball class, for male and female joggers, and for the girl and boy pitching in a Little League game.

Carolyn Sherif (1972, 1976, 1982) persistently advocated the consideration of social context in psychological research, and she emphasized social context and process when considering gender influences on behavior. Moreover, Sherif often spoke to sport psychology groups and pointed out strategies for incorporating social context and gender into our research on competition and sport behavior. Unfortunately, sport psychologists have not adopted Sherif's suggestions or other current *social*–psychological approaches.

Indeed, our research and practice seems narrower and more oblivious to social context and process than ever before. Such isolation cannot advance our understanding of such an obviously social issue and process as gender.

Actually, I believe that sport psychologists interested in gender should place even more emphasis on social context and social process than Deaux and Major suggest. Within sport and exercise science the most prominent and innovative work on gender is being done by sport sociologists. Moreover, sport sociologists are incorporating feminist theoretical frameworks and alternative approaches (e.g., critical theory, social construction) in their work.

M. Ann Hall (1988) has been an influential leader in feminist sport scholarship for some time. She has criticized sport psychology's limited focus on masculinity and femininity and advocated a more thoughtful consideration of gender as a pervasive social influence. Several other sport scholars have recently devoted systematic attention to gender and have developed varied feminist frameworks. For example, Nancy Theberge (1987) writes extensively on gender issues. Her discussion of the relationship of gender to power and empowerment in sport is particularly relevant. Helen Lenskyj (1987) presents a coherent and provocative analysis of sexuality and gender in sport. Lenskyj emphasizes the historical and sociocultural pressures toward compulsory heterosexuality that influence women's sport participation and behaviors within sport and exercise settings. Like these other feminist scholars, Alison Dewar (1987) examines the role of gender in sport and exercise from a social constructionist perspective. Moreover, Dewar

has moved beyond the typical focus on elite sport to a critical analysis of gender in the physical education curriculum and educational practice. Susan Birrell (1988), in an excellent review of the research on gender and sport, traces the progression from sex differences research, through gender roles, to current considerations of gender relations in a dynamic, sociocultural context.

The work of these feminist sport scholars suggests that gender is pervasive in society, specifically in sport society; that gender beliefs, relations, and processes are multifaceted; and that an understanding of the historical–cultural context and immediate social context is necessary to understand gender and sport. A thorough discussion of feminist scholarship in sport and these varied conceptual approaches is well beyond my scope here. I do not advocate that sport psychologists become sociologists to study gender. Sport psychologists have unique contributions and insights to offer to the study of gender and sport. Sound sport psychology research on gender beliefs and processes within the social context of sport and exercise could advance our overall understanding of gender and sport. Nevertheless, any sport psychologist who seriously intends to pursue gender issues should be familiar with the works of our feminist sport scholars and with feminist theories and approaches from varied social and behavioral sciences.

Status and Future Directions

Adopting a true *social*–psychological perspective is critical for current and future sport psychology research on gender. Gender-related behavior in sport and exercise is not isolated from socialization history, immediate social context, and the broader sociohistorical and cultural context. Indeed, most sport and exercise behavior is interpretable only when considering social context. As Deaux suggests, components of social context vary tremendously; and we should consider the variations in our research on gender. Moreover, as Jacklin (1989) noted, social context changes in a larger sense. The social norms and gender beliefs about sport and exercise may be quite different today from what they were 10 years ago. As society changes, gender socialization, beliefs, and behaviors change. Thus, both the immediate social context and historical–cultural context are dynamic, and we should interpret findings accordingly. With the multifaceted and dynamic nature of the phenomenon, we will not reach clear, absolute conclusions. Still, we should gain greater insight into gender and sport with a broader, more social approach.

Not only should we adopt more encompassing conceptual frameworks, but we should look to a wider range of issues and behaviors. Sport psychology research on gender is remarkably limited in topic as well as perspective. Generally, the research focuses on individual characteristics related to participation in competitive athletics. Focusing our research efforts on one of the most established, limited, inflexible, and, moreover, elite and male-dominated sport systems is far too restrictive an approach for the study of gender. Certainly, gender issues are just as prominent in youth sports, physical education classes, and exercise settings. Indeed, we probably would find more varied gender beliefs, behaviors, and relations and more varied social contexts in such settings.

Just as we should consider gender influences across a wider range of sport and exercise activities, we should consider diversity of sport participants. Most notably, research on racial, ethnic, and cultural influence is virtually nonexistent in sport psychology. Duda and Allison (1990), who have conducted some of the few studies that we do have, point out the striking void in our field on race and ethnicity. Most of the points discussed for gender also could be made for race and ethnicity—that is, stereotypes and belief systems are pervasive and multifaceted; racial and ethnic socialization, self-perceptions, and social context influence sport and exercise behavior; and a grounding in sociocultural history would enhance our understanding of race and ethnicity in sport. Unfortunately, we do not even have the limited work on stereotypes and individual characteristics for race and ethnicity to parallel the gender research in sport. More important for my present purpose, gender belief systems and contexts likely interact with race and ethnicity systems in many complex ways. For example, the experiences of a black female tennis player are not simply a combination of the experiences of white female and black male players. The belief systems, self-perceptions, and social context probably have unique characteristics and relationships. We can extend considerations further to incorporate such other social categories as class, age, and skill level. Quite likely, the social systems and behaviors related to gender vary across combinations of social categories. The lack of sport research on any social category other than gender—and the limited gender research—precludes predictions. At this point, the most logical research questions have not even been identified. Clearly, though, we should move in the direction of considering diversity within gender in our gender research.

Not only should we consider diversity within gender, we should consider diversity across gender. More simply, we need to consider gender for both men and women in sport. Although some sport psychology research on gender includes both males and females, the typical focus is on understanding women in sport. Given that most sport psychology research (like most other research) focuses on male behavior, research aimed at understanding women in sport is important. However, if we hope to understand gender as a social category and process, we must consider the role of gender for both men and women. Certainly, gender belief systems operate for men in sport. Gender may well play a greater role in male sport behavior than in female sport behavior; certainly gender plays different roles for female and male sport behavior. Research on gender as it pertains to men in sport and exercise is limited. Sabo and Runfola (1980) pulled together articles on sports and male identity in their edited volume. Recently, Messner (1987) has written on sport and male identity, offering analyses similar to those of the feminist sport scholars mentioned earlier. Other than the work of Sabo and Messner, who recently edited an important new volume on sport, men, and gender (Messner & Sabo, 1990), gender issues in sport for men and boys are largely ignored.

Finally, sport psychologists interested in gender should not dismiss biological factors. Consideration of physical or biological characteristics and capabilities seems crucial for sport and exercise. Many scholars in varied disciplines have called for stronger feminist theories, consideration of the diversity among women, and the study of gender influences for males as well as females. Most do not discuss biological factors except (justifiably) to dismiss the biological determinism argument. Sport and exercise are physical activities, and we should not ignore biological factors. Instead, we should incorporate physical characteristics and capabilities into our *social*–psychological models. We should not consider physical characteristics as unidirectional determinants of sport and exercise behavior. Rather, we should consider biological factors as part of the dynamic, social process within sport. As Birke and Vines (1987) suggest, biological factors are not static and absolute but dynamic processes that may interact with sociopsychological factors in varied ways.

Eccles's work, for example, suggested that physical capabilities have an influence (although a small one) on gender differences in sport achievement. By incorporating physical measures, Eccles more clearly illustrated social processes that lead to gender differences in sport achievement. Sport psychology might well consider how we take such minimal—and clearly nondichotomous—physical differences and turn them into dichotomous gender influences in sport. Consideration of physical characteristics along with related social beliefs, self-perceptions, and social processes may add insight to research on body image, exercise behavior, youth sport, and health behavior, as well as to competitive sport behavior.

In sum, we have many intriguing questions about gender and sport. Sound sport psychology research on gender could offer practical guidance and advance our knowledge of sport behavior. At present our research is too limited to make important contributions. If we are to contribute to the emerging body of research on gender and sport, we must expand our research. We should expand our research to include varied activities and settings. We should extend our research to encompass diverse women and men, and we should make a special effort to include racially and culturally diverse participants. Most important, we should familiarize ourselves with feminist scholarship on socialization, social dynamics, and the historical–cultural basis of gender to develop a true *social*–psychological approach to gender and sport.

References

Acosta, R.V., & Carpenter, L.J. (1987, April). *Women in intercollegiate sport: A longitudinal study—nine-year update: 1977–1986.* Paper presented at the American Alliance for Health, Physical Education, Recreation and Dance Convention, Las Vegas, NV.

Bakan, D. (1966). *The duality of human existence.* Chicago: Rand McNally.

Bandura, A. (1977). Self-efficacy: Toward a unifying theory of behavior change. *Psychological Review,* **84**, 191-215.

Bandura, A. (1986). *Social foundations of thought and action.* Englewood Cliffs, NJ: Prentice-Hall.

Belenky, M., Clinchy, B., Goldberger, N., & Tarule, J. (1986). *Women's ways of knowing: The development of self, voice, and mind.* New York: Basic Books.

Bem, S.L. (1974). The measurement of psychological androgyny. *Journal of Consulting and Clinical Psychology,* **42**, 155-162.

Bem, S.L. (1978). Beyond androgyny: Some presumptuous prescriptions for a liberated sexual identity. In J. Sherman & F. Denmark (Eds.), *Psychology of women: Future directions for research* (pp. 1-23). New York: Psychological Dimensions.

Bem, S.L. (1981). Gender schema theory: A cognitive account of sex typing. *Psychological Review,* **88**, 354-364.

Bem, S.L. (1983). Gender schema theory and its implications for child development: Raising gender-aschematic children in a gender-schematic society. *Signs: Journal of Women in Culture and Society,* **8**, 598-616.

Bem, S.L. (1985). Androgyny and gender schema theory: A conceptual and empirical integration. In T.B. Sonderegger (Ed.), *Nebraska symposium on motivation, 1984: Psychology and gender* (pp. 179-226). Lincoln, NB: University of Nebraska Press.

Bernard, J. (1981). *The female world.* New York: Free Press.

Birke, L.I.A., & Vines, G. (1987). A sporting chance: The anatomy of destiny. *Women's Studies International Forum, 10,* 337-347.

Birrell, S.J. (1988). Discourses on the gender/sport relationship: From women in sport to gender relations. In K. Pandolf (Ed.), *Exercise and sport sciences reviews* (Vol. 16, pp. 459-502). New York: Macmillan.

Brawley, L.R., Landers, D.M., Miller, L., & Kearns, K.M. (1979). Sex bias in evaluating motor performance. *Journal of Sport Psychology, 1,* 15-24.

Brawley, L.R., Powers, R.C., & Phillips, K.A. (1980). Sex bias in evaluating motor performance: General or task-specific expectancy? *Journal of Sport Psychology, 2,* 279-287.

Broverman, I.K., Vogel, S.R., Broverman, D.M., Clarkson, F.E., & Rosenkrantz, P.S. (1972). Sex role stereotypes: A current appraisal. *Journal of Social Issues, 28,* 59-78.

Colker, R., & Widom, C.S. (1980). Correlates of female athletic participation. *Sex Roles, 6,* 47-53.

Condry, J., & Dyer, S. (1976). Fear of success: Attribution of cause to the victim. *Journal of Social Issues, 32,* 63-83.

Constantinople, A. (1973). Masculinity–femininity: An exception to a famous dictum? *Psychological Bulletin, 80,* 389-407.

Corbin, C.B. (1981). Sex of subject, sex of opponent, and opponent ability as factors affecting self-confidence in a competitive situation. *Journal of Sport Psychology, 3,* 265-270.

Corbin, C.B., Landers, D.M., Feltz, D.L., & Senior, K. (1983). Sex differences in performance estimates: Female lack of confidence versus male boastfulness. *Research Quarterly for Exercise and Sport, 54,* 407-410.

Corbin, C.B., & Nix, C. (1979). Sex-typing of physical activities and success predictions of children before and after cross-sex competition. *Journal of Sport Psychology, 1,* 43-52.

Corbin, C.B., Stewart, M.J., & Blair, W.O. (1981). Self-confidence and motor performance of preadolescent boys and girls in different feedback situations. *Journal of Sport Psychology, 3,* 30-34.

Crandall, V.C. (1969). Sex differences in expectancy of intellectual and academic reinforcement. In C.P. Smith (Ed.), *Achievement-related motives in children* (pp. 11-45). New York: Russell Sage.

Csizma, K.A., Wittig, A.F., & Schurr, K.T. (1988). Sport stereotypes and gender. *Journal of Sport and Exercise Psychology, 10,* 62-74.

Deaux, K. (1976). Sex: A perspective on the attribution process. In J.H. Harvey, W.J. Ickes, & R.F. Kidd (Eds.), *New directions in attribution research,* (Vol. 1, pp. 335-352). Hillsdale, NJ: Erlbaum.

Deaux, K. (1984). From individual differences to social categories: Analysis of a decade's research on gender. *American Psychologist, 39,* 105-116.

Deaux, K. (1985). Sex and gender. *Annual Review of Psychology, 36,* 49-81.

Deaux, K., & Farris, E. (1977). Attributing causes for one's own performance: The effects of sex, norms, and outcome. *Journal of Research in Personality, 11,* 59-72.

Deaux, K., & Kite, M.E. (1987). Thinking about gender. In B.B. Hess & M.M. Ferree (Eds.), *Analyzing gender* (pp. 92-117). Beverly Hills, CA: Sage.

Deaux, K., & Lewis, L.L. (1984). The structure of gender stereotypes: Interrelationships among components and gender label. *Journal of Personality and Social Psychology, 46,* 991-1004.

Deaux, K., & Major, B. (1987). Putting gender into context: An interactive model of gender-related behavior. *Psychological Review, 94,* 369-389.

Deaux, K., & Taynor, J. (1973). Evaluation of male and female ability: Bias works two ways. *Psychological Reports, 32,* 261-262.

Deci, E.L., Betley, G., Kahle, J., Abrams, L., & Porac, J. (1981). When trying to win: Competition and intrinsic motivation. *Personality and Social Psychology Bulletin, 7,* 79-83.

Del Rey, P., & Sheppard, S. (1981). Relationship of psychological androgyny in female athletes to self-esteem. *International Journal of Sport Psychology, 12,* 165-175.

Dewar, A.M. (1987). The social construction of gender in physical education. *Women's Studies International Forum, 10,* 453-465.

Duda, J.L. (1986). A cross-cultural analysis of achievement motivation in sport and the classroom. In L. VanderVelden & J. Humphrey (Eds.), *Current selected research in the psychology and sociology of sport* (pp. 115-132). New York: AMS Press.

Duda, J.L., & Allison, M.T. (1990). Cross-cultural analysis in exercise and sport psychology: A void in the field. *Journal of Sport and Exercise Psychology, 12,* 114-131.

Eagley, A.H. (1987). *Sex differences in social behavior: A social-role interpretation.* Hillsdale, NJ: Erlbaum.

Eagley, A.H., & Kite, M.E. (1987). Are stereotypes of nationalities applied to both women and men? *Journal of Personality and Social Psychology, 53,* 451-462.

Eagley, A.H., & Steffin, V.J. (1986). Gender and aggressive behavior: A meta-analytic review of the social psychological literature. *Psychological Bulletin, 100,* 309-330.

Eccles, J.S. (1985). Sex differences in achievement patterns. In T. Sonderegger (Ed.), *Nebraska symposium on motivation. 1984: psychology and gender* (pp. 97-132). Lincoln, NB: University of Nebraska Press.

Eccles, J.S. (1987). Gender roles and women's achievement-related decisions. *Psychology of Women Quarterly, 11,* 135-172.

Eccles, J.S., Adler, T.F., Futterman, R., Goff, S.B., Kaczala, C.M., Meece, J.L., & Midgley, C. (1983). Expectations, values, and academic behaviors. In J. Spence (Ed.), *Achievement and achievement motives* (pp. 75-146). San Francisco: Freeman.

Eccles, J.S., & Harold, R.D. (1991). Gender differences in sport involvement: applying the Eccles' expectancy-value model. *Journal of Applied Sport Psychology, 3,* 7-35.

Feltz, D.L. (1988). Self-confidence and sports performance. In K. Pandolf (Ed.), *Exercise and sport sciences reviews* (Vol. 16, pp. 423-457). New York: Macmillan.

Frable, D.E.S. (1989). Sex typing and gender ideology: Two facets of an individual's gender psychology that go together. *Journal of Personality and Social Psychology, 56,* 95-108.

Frodi, A., Macauley, J., & Thome, P.R. (1977). Are women always less aggressive than men? A review of the experimental literature. *Psychological Bulletin, 84,* 638-660.

Gill, D.L. (1986). Competitiveness among females and males in physical activity classes. *Sex Roles, 15,* 233-247.

Gill, D.L. (1988). Gender differences in competitive orientation and sport participation. *International Journal of Sport Psychology, 19,* 145-159.

Gill, D.L., & Deeter, T.E. (1988). Development of the Sport Orientation Questionnaire. *Research Quarterly for Exercise and Sport, 59,* 191-202.

Gill, D.L., & Dzewaltowski, D.A. (1988). Competitive orientations among intercollegiate athletes: Is winning the only thing? *The Sport Psychologist, 2,* 212-221.

Gill, D.L., Dzewaltowski, D.A., & Deeter, T.E. (1988). The relationship of competitiveness and achievement orientation to participation in sport and nonsport activities. *Journal of Sport and Exercise Psychology, 10,* 139-150.

Gill, D.L., Gross, J.B., Huddleston, S., & Shifflett, B. (1984). Sex differences in achievement cognitions and performance in competition. *Research Quarterly for Exercise and Sport, 55,* 340-346.

Gilligan, C. (1982). *In a different voice.* Cambridge, MA: Harvard University Press.

Goldberg, P. (1968). Are women prejudiced against women? *Transaction, 5,* 28-30.

Greendorfer, S.L. (1987). Gender bias in theoretical perspectives: The case of female socialization into sport. *Psychology of Women Quarterly, 11,* 327-340.

Griffin, P.S. (1973). What's a nice girl like you doing in a profession like this? *Quest, 19,* 96-101.

Hall, M.A. (1988). The discourse of gender and sport: From femininity to feminism. *Sociology of Sport Journal, 5,* 330-340.

Harris, D.V., & Jenning, S.E. (1977). Self-perceptions of female distance runners. *Annals of the New York Academy of Sciences, 301,* 808-815.

Hasbrook, C.A. (1988, August). Female coaches—Why the declining numbers and percentages? *Journal of Physical Education, Recreation and Dance, 59*(6) pp. 59-63.

Helmreich, R.L., & Spence, J.T. (1977). Sex roles and achievement. In R.W. Christina & D.M. Landers (Eds.), *Psychology of motor behavior and sport—1976* (Vol. 2, pp. 33-46). Champaign, IL: Human Kinetics.

Helmreich, R.L., & Spence, J.T. (1978). The Work and Family Orientation Questionnaire: An objective instrument to assess components of achievement motivation and attitudes toward family and career. *Catalog of Selected Documents in Psychology, 8,* 35.

Helmreich, R.L., Spence, J.T., & Holohan, C.K. (1979). Psychological androgyny and sex role flexibility: A test of two hypotheses. *Journal of Personality and Social Psychology, 37,* 1631-1644.

Henderson, K.A., Stalnaker, D., & Taylor, G. (1988). The relationship between barriers to recreation and gender-role personality traits for women. *Journal of Leisure Research, 20,* 69-80.

Horner, M.S. (1972). Toward an understanding of achievement-related conflicts in women. *Journal of Social Issues, 28,* 157-176.

Hyde, J.S., & Linn, M.C. (Eds.) (1986). *The psychology of gender: Advances through meta-analysis.* Baltimore: Johns Hopkins University Press.

Jacklin, C.N. (1989). Female and male: Issues of gender. *American Psychologist, 44,* 127-133.

Kane, M.J., & Snyder, E. (1989). Sport typing: The social "containment" of women. *Arena Review, 13,* 77-96.

Lenney, E. (1977). Women's self-confidence in achievement settings. *Psychological Bulletin, 84,* 1-13.

Lenney, E., Browning, C., & Mitchell, L. (1980). What you don't know *can* hurt you: The effects of performance criteria ambiguity on sex differences in self-confidence. *Journal of Personality, 48,* 306-322.

Lenskyj, H. (1987). *Out of bounds: Women, sport, and sexuality.* Toronto: Women's Press.

Locksley, A., & Colten, M.E. (1979). Psychological androgyny: A case of mistaken identity? *Journal of Personality and Social Psychology, 37,* 1017-1031.

Maccoby, E., & Jacklin, C. (1974). *The psychology of sex differences.* Stanford, CA: Stanford University Press.

Martens, R. (1977). *Sport Competition Anxiety Test.* Champaign, IL: Human Kinetics.

Matteo, S. (1986). The effect of sex and gender-schematic processing on sport participation. *Sex Roles, 15,* 417-32.

Matteo, S. (1988). The effect of gender-schematic processing on decisions about sex-inappropriate sport behavior. *Sex Roles, 18,* 41-58.

McClelland, D.C., Atkinson, J.W., Clark, R.A., & Lowell, E.C. (1953). *The achievement motive.* New York: Appleton–Century–Crofts.

McElroy, M.A., & Willis, J.D. (1979). Women and the achievement conflict in sport: A preliminary study. *Journal of Sport Psychology, 1,* 241-247.

McNally, J., & Orlick, T. (1975). Cooperative sport structures: A preliminary analysis. *Mouvement, 7,* 267-271.

Messner, M.A. (1987). The life of a man's seasons: Male identity in the life course of the jock. In M.S. Kimmel (Ed.), *Changing men: New directions in research on men and masculinity* (pp. 53-67). Newbury Park, CA: Sage.

Messner, M.A., & Sabo, D.F. (1990). *Sport, men, and the gender order.* Champaign, IL: Human Kinetics.

Metheny, E. (1965). *Connotations of movement in sport and dance.* Dubuque, IA: William C. Brown.

Miller Brewing Company. (1983). *The Miller Lite report on American attitudes toward sports.* Milwaukee, WI: Author.

Myers, A.E., & Lips, H.M. (1978). Participation in competitive amateur sports as a function of psychological androgyny. *Sex Roles, 4,* 571-578.

Ostrow, A.C. (1981). Age grading: Implications for physical activity participation among older adults. *Quest, 33,* 112-123.

Ostrow, A.C., Jones, D.C., & Spiker, D.A. (1981). Age role expectations and sex role expectations for selected sport activities. *Research Quarterly for Exercise and Sport, 52,* 216-227.

Parkhouse, B.L., & Williams, J.M. (1986). Differential effects of sex and status on evaluation of coaching ability. *Research Quarterly for Exercise and Sport, 57,* 53-59.

Pedhazur, E.J., & Tetenbaum, T.J. (1979). BSRI: A theoretical and methodological critique. *Journal of Personality and Social Psychology, 37,* 996-1016.

Petruzzello, S.J., & Corbin, C.B. (1988). The effects of performance feedback on female self-confidence. *Journal of Sport and Exercise Psychology, 10,* 174-183.

Pheterson, G.I., Kiesler, S.B., & Goldberg, P.A. (1971). Evaluation of the performance of women as a function of their sex, achievement, and personal history. *Journal of Personality and Social Psychology, 19,* 114-118.

Roberts, G.C. (1984). Toward a new theory of motivation in sport: The role of perceived ability. In J.M. Silva & R.S. Weinberg (Eds.), *Psychological foundations of sport* (pp. 214-228). Champaign, IL: Human Kinetics.

Rosenkrantz, P., Vogel, S., Bee, H., Broverman, I., & Broverman, D.M. (1968). Sex-role stereotypes and self-concepts in college students. *Journal of Consulting and Clinical Psychology, 32,* 286-295.

Sabo, D.F., & Runfola, R. (1980). *Jock: Sports and male identity.* Englewood Cliffs, NJ: Prentice-Hall.

Selby, R., & Lewko, J. (1976). Children's attitudes toward females' participation in sports. *Research Quarterly, 47,* 453-463.

Sherif, C.W. (1972). Females and the competitive process. In D. Harris (Ed.), *Women and sport: A national research conference* (pp. 115-139). University Park, PA: Pennsylvania State University.

Sherif, C.W. (1976). The social context of competition. In D. Landers (Ed.), *Social problems in athletics* (pp. 18-36). Champaign, IL: University of Illinois Press.

Sherif, C.W. (1982). Needed concepts in the study of gender identity. *Psychology of Women Quarterly, 6,* 375-398.

Spence, J.T., & Helmreich, R.L. (1978). *Masculinity and femininity.* Austin, TX: University of Texas Press.

Spence, J.T., & Helmreich, R.L. (1980). Masculine instrumentality and feminine expressiveness: Their relationships with sex role attitudes and behaviors. *Psychology of Women Quarterly, 5,* 147-163.

Spence, J.T., & Helmreich, R.L. (1983). Achievement-related motives and behaviors. In J.T. Spence (Ed.), *Achievement and achievement motives: Psychological and sociological approaches* (pp. 7-74). San Francisco: W.H. Freeman.

Spence, J.T., Helmreich, R.L., & Stapp, J. (1974). The Personality Attributes Questionnaire: A measure of sex role stereotypes and masculinity–femininity. *JSAS Catalog of Selected Documents in Psychology, 4*, 127.

Stein, A.H., Pohly, S.R., & Mueller, E. (1971). The influence of masculine, feminine, and neutral tasks on children's achievement behavior, expectancies of success, and attainment values. *Child Development, 42*, 195-207.

Stewart, M.J., & Corbin, C.B. (1988). Feedback dependence among low confidence preadolescent boys and girls. *Research Quarterly for Exercise and Sport, 59*, 160-164.

Taylor, M.C., & Hall, J.A. (1982). Psychological androgyny: Theories, methods, and conclusions. *Psychological Bulletin, 92*, 347-366.

Theberge, N. (1987). Sport and women's empowerment. *Women's Studies International Forum, 10*, 387-393.

Tresemer, D.W. (1977). *Fear of success*. New York: Plenum.

Wallston, B.S., & O'Leary, V.E. (1981). Sex and gender make a difference: The differential perceptions of women and men. *Review of Personality and Social Psychology, 2*, 9-41.

Weinberg, R.S., & Jackson, A. (1979). Competition and extrinsic rewards: Effect on intrinsic motivation. *Research Quarterly, 50*, 494-502.

Weinberg, R.S., & Ragan, J. (1979). Effects of competition, success/failure, and sex on intrinsic motivation. *Research Quarterly, 50*, 503-510.

Weinberg, R.S., Reveles, M., & Jackson, A. (1984). Attitudes of male and female athletes toward male and female coaches. *Journal of Sport Psychology, 6*, 448-453.

Williams, J.M., & Parkhouse, B.L. (1988). Social learning theory as a foundation for examining sex bias in evaluation of coaches. *Journal of Sport and Exercise Psychology, 10*, 322-333.

Wrisberg, C.A., Draper, M.V., & Everett, J.J. (1988). Sex role orientations of male and female collegiate athletes from selected individual and team sports. *Sex Roles, 19*, 81-90.

Part III

Social–Environmental Influences and Sport Behavior

Part II identified and discussed the relationship between selected individual difference factors and sport behavior. The collective research and theory reviewed there have very clearly shown that selected characteristics of individual performers can be used to explain and predict how they will behave in sport and physical activity contexts. However, as Gill argued in chapter 7, the individual's behavior in sport and exercise settings is not isolated from his or her socialization history, the immediate social context, or the broader sociohistorical and cultural contexts. Thus, sport behavior will be more accurately and completely interpreted if social-environmental influences are also taken into account.

Part III will look specifically at various aspects of the sport and social environment that interact with individual difference factors to determine the behavior of individuals in the sport or physical activity context. Part III will begin with chapter 8, by W. Neil Widmeyer, Lawrence Brawley, and Albert Carron, which examines the influence of the group. They begin their chapter with an overview of the major theoretical approaches to the study of sport and exercise groups. They then review the empirical research on three selected aspects or characteristics of groups: size, composition, and cohesion. Finally, they identify a number of problems associated with the study of group dynamics and conclude by outlining two approaches for future research in sport group dynamics.

I wrote chapter 9 to focus on a more specific aspect of the sport group environment—the be-havior of the coach or group leader. The chapter provides a review of the research and theory that has been conducted to test the general hypothesis that the type of leadership behavior exhibited by a group leader will have a significant impact on the performance and psychological well-being of the group members. Despite consistent empirical support for this hypothesized connection, much work still remains to be completed in this area. Thus, this chapter concludes by outlining a number of methodological and conceptual approaches that should characterize future research on leadership effectiveness in the sport domain.

In chapter 10, Susan Greendorfer examines the broad issue of sport socialization. In contrast to the topical approach used in other chapters in this volume, Greendorfer takes a more inclusive perspective by introducing the socialization process as a general framework that can be used to understand many aspects of sport behavior that are currently of interest to sport psychologists (e.g., achievement motivation, attrition in sport, competitive stress). Greendorfer begins with a theoretical and conceptual discussion of the socialization process and then provides a critical review of the existing research on socialization into and through sport participation. She concludes by providing suggestions as to how sport psychologists can use an understanding of the socialization process to examine individuals' sport behavior from a more integrated and holistic perspective.

Chapter 8

Group Dynamics in Sport

W. Neil Widmeyer and Lawrence R. Brawley
University of Waterloo

Albert V. Carron
University of Western Ontario

Since the beginning of social psychology, group dynamics has been recognized as a major branch of the discipline. The term *group dynamics* has been used in two major ways. First, it has been used to depict the vitality and changing nature of groups. Second, it has been seen as a field of study that focuses on the behavior of groups. Although Kurt Lewin (1943) is given credit for coining and popularizing the term, Dorwin Cartwright and Alvin Zander (1968) are recognized as two of the most prolific researchers in this area (see Forsyth, 1983). In their classic text, *Group Dynamics*, they stated that this field of inquiry is "dedicated to advancing knowledge about the nature of groups, the laws of their development, and their interrelationships with individuals, other groups, and larger institutions" (1968, p. 7). Group dynamics is not normally recognized as a discipline unto itself but, instead, as an area of study within social psychology and sociology. In the present chapter, it is

accepted both that groups are not static and that group dynamics refers to the scientific study of these changing entities.

The importance of group dynamics stems primarily from the importance of groups. Groups are important because of the large number of groups that each individual encounters and because of the impact that such groups can have on one's life. In addition to a family, most individuals simultaneously belong to a variety of recreational, social, and work groups, all of which can influence, and be influenced by, the person's thoughts, feelings, and actions. Thus, it is not surprising that group dynamics has been a major interest area for social psychologists. Because groups can be seen as microcosms of larger societies, they represent a convenient place for sociologists to study broader social systems. In addition, Forsyth (1983) identified anthropology, political science, education, business/industry, speech/communication, social work, criminal justice, and sports/recreation as the other fields that recognize the importance of understanding group dynamics.

Sport is a particularly important and interesting environment for the study of group dynamics. In North America today, the team sports of baseball, basketball, football, and, more recently, hockey, soccer, and volleyball attract not only millions of competitors but also countless spectators. Next to the family, the sport team may be the most influential group to which an individual belongs. Teams are organized for children of both sexes as young as age 7 and for adults as old as 90. "Old-timers" leagues in sports such as hockey and softball typically begin at age 30, and individuals often participate into their sixties and seventies. Team sports are especially prevalent in high school, where students participate in interscholastic, intramural, and recreational groups. As well, many businesses not only adopt a team approach for work but also encourage play on company softball teams. Because the team can be a major social group for the individual for 10 to 30 years, it has the potential to have a socializing impact of a similar magnitude to that of the church or school. In spite of the prevalence of sport teams and the potential impact such groups may have on individuals, most research conducted within sport has focused on *individual* participants (i.e., their performance, enjoyment, adherence, etc.). Rarely has the *team* been studied either as an entity unto itself or as a factor that influences individuals, other teams, or larger organizations.

From an academic perspective, since the sport team is a small group, the sociological and social psychological reasons for studying any group apply. As Loy, McPherson, and Kenyon (1978) pointed out, "Sport groups possess unique structural features that offer special advantages with respect to small group research." Schafer (1966) identified four such advantages. First, since the sport group is a natural, rather than a laboratory, group, it can provide information about group development and group relationships with other groups and the broader social environment. Second, sport research can control a number of confounding variables such as group size and rules of conduct by automatically holding them constant. Third, because sport groups typically pursue zero-sum (i.e., win-or-lose) goals, they provide an ideal context for the study of cooperation, competition, and conflict. Finally, sport offers objective measures of group effectiveness (e.g., number of errors made, points scored, and percentage of games won). Thus, the sport team offers an excellent setting for research on group dynamics.

According to Cartwright and Zander's (1968) definition, the study of group dynamics in any context should deal with

- the nature of groups,
- group development,
- interrelationships within groups,
- interrelationships between groups,
- interrelationships between groups and individuals, and
- interrelationships between groups and larger institutions.

Although each of these areas has been examined to some extent, group dynamics has focused primarily on interrelationships *within* groups. An examination of group dynamics texts reveals that the topics most often covered are

- group formation,
- group tasks,
- group development,
- group composition,
- group size,
- group structure,
- group cohesion,
- group motivation,
- group leadership,
- group conformity,
- intergroup relations, and
- group decision making.

Thus, even though the study of groups has not been as broad as the definition of group dynamics would suggest, a wide range of topics and numerous relationships have been examined.

For the most part, the same variables that have been studied in nonsport settings have also been investigated in sport. However, an examination of Figure 8.1 indicates that the emphasis on various topics is not the same in both areas. In sport the topics of cohesion and leadership are overrepresented; whereas size, one of the most-examined small-group variables, has hardly ever been investigated in sport. It should be emphasized that the paucity of research into certain small group topics in sport does not necessarily mean that these topics are not important or of interest to sport practitioners and/or researchers. It may simply be that these topics are difficult to examine in sport and/or that other topics have been seen as more central to the functioning of athletic teams.

In summary, group dynamics, the scientific study of groups, is a worthwhile endeavor because of the prevalence of groups and the impact they have on individuals. Likewise, the study of the dynamics of sport groups is equally significant, given the important roles that athletic

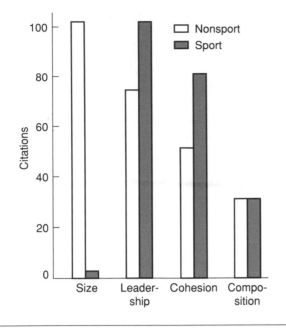

Figure 8.1   Small group topic citations: 1978-1988.

teams play in the lives of many humans. Although numerous relationships could be examined between groups, between groups and individuals, and between groups and larger institutions, group dynamics has primarily focused on interrelationships *within* groups. In this chapter, theoretical approaches to the study of groups are outlined; findings from three of the most-researched topics within sport groups, namely, group size, group composition, and group cohesion, are presented; problems associated with the study of group dynamics are delineated; and finally, suggestions for avoiding or minimizing these "pitfalls" are advanced. Although our primary focus is on group dynamics in sport and exercise, relevant information from other contexts is also included.

Theoretical Approaches

The importance of theoretical perspectives has been espoused by scholars in a wide variety of disciplines. In discussing group dynamics, McGrath (1984, p. 27) emphasized that theory is as important as data. Specifically, he stated:

> Theory strengthens a data-based science in several ways: (a) as a means for identifying problems worthy of study; (b) as a means for connecting one problem or one piece of evidence with another, even when they have been given different labels; (c) as a means for estimating (hypothesizing/predicting) the pattern of data likely to be found in a yet-unstudied area; (d) as a means for

anticipating what aspects of a problem are most likely to be important.

Thus, theory is necessary in order to understand previous research findings and to serve as a guide for future research.

In categorizing theoretical approaches to the study of group dynamics, Shaw (1981) first distinguished between *theoretical orientations* (e.g., field theory), which apply to a broad range of social contexts, not just groups, and *limited theories* (e.g., leadership theory), which apply to very specific phenomena within groups. Between these two extremes lie *middle-range theories* (e.g., exchange theory), which explain more than one, but not all, aspects of group life (see Shaw & Costanzo, 1982).

After listing a number of *theoretical approaches*, most authors conclude that no one theory explains all of group behavior but that each adds something to the understanding of groups. In contrast to such optimistic statements, Zander proposes:

> There are few well-developed theories about behavior in groups. The theories that do exist, moreover, seldom aid in understanding groups as such, or even the behavior of members on behalf of their groups, because the theories often are based on ideas taken from individual psychology, and these are primarily concerned with the actions of individuals for the good of those individuals. (1979, p. 423)

Theoretical Approaches to the Study of Sport Groups

Based on an extensive review of the research on group dynamics in sport, it appears that none of the general theoretical orientations identified by Shaw have been tested or used as a guide in the study of athletic teams. Likewise, rarely have any middle-range theories been employed in sport. One exception has been Schutz's (1958) Fundamental Interpersonal Relations Orientations Theory, which has been utilized to examine coach–athlete compatibility (e.g., Carron & Bennett, 1977). Thus, when theoretical approaches have been used to study athletic teams, they have been what Shaw referred to as *limited theories*. These theories have focused on such specific aspects of groups as leadership (e.g., Chelladurai, 1978), structure (Grusky, 1963), motivation (Zander, 1971), cohesion (Carron, Widmeyer & Brawley, 1985), and effectiveness (Steiner, 1972).

While the theory and research on cohesion are presented later and leadership is dealt with in chapter 9, theories of structure and motivation are not discussed in this book. Grusky's theory of formal structure, employed primarily by sport sociologists to explain both racial discrimination and ascendancy to leadership, is described in detail by Loy, McPherson, and Kenyon (1978). Although Zander (1971) has shown a great interest in athletes, others have not tested his concepts in sport. One limited theory—Steiner's (1972) theory of group productivity, has been utilized by sport researchers. This is not surprising given that sport is so performance-oriented. Hence, we shall outline Steiner's theory in some depth.

Steiner's Theory of Group Productivity

According to Steiner (1972), a group's actual productivity is equal to its potential productivity minus "process losses." Process losses are considered to be the result of either faulty coordination of member resources and/or less-than-optimal motivation by members. Thus, a group of physical education students might not move a wrestling mat as effectively as they potentially could because they did not all lift and move simultaneously and/or because some of them did not give a maximum effort. Potential productivity is determined by the amount of *relevant* resources (e.g., sewing ability is not a *relevant* resource for moving a wrestling mat). Similarly, communication is more relevant for a football team than for a bowling team because coordination of efforts is more crucial in the former.

Based on Steiner's theory, it is predicted that Team A will perform better than Team B if

- A possesses greater relevant resources than B while experiencing equal process losses, or
- A possesses equal relevant resources but experiences fewer process losses than B, or

- A possesses greater relevant resources and experiences fewer process losses than B.

This prediction suggests that the role of any coach is to increase relevant resources (through instruction, training, and recruiting) and to reduce process losses (through strategies for combining players' contributions and motivating them). Because sport is so performance-oriented, Steiner's theory has innumerable applications. For example, it has been utilized to determine the relative contributions of ability and cohesion to performance outcome (Gossett & Widmeyer, 1978) and to look at social loafing in rowing performance (Ingham, Levinger, Graves & Peckham, 1974).

Beginnings to an Overall Theory of Group Dynamics

It has already been noted that there is no overall theory that explains the dynamics of sport teams or even of groups in general. However, certain models, or conceptual frameworks, have been advanced that identify and organize the categories of variables operating within groups. In one recent framework advanced by McGrath (1984), member interaction is hypothesized to be the central factor in group life. McGrath then identified a number of factors that influence, and are influenced by, interaction processes. Specifically, he proposed that interaction is influenced by member characteristics, group structure, environmental properties, and processes internal to interaction itself. In turn, interaction can influence group members, the environment, and group relationships.

No one researcher has identified all of these relationships within a sport team. However, in a recent text devoted solely to group dynamics in sport, one of us (Carron, 1988) presented a linear model (see Figure 8.2) that depicts the majority of inputs, "throughputs," and outputs operating within athletic groups. The inputs that he identifies are member attributes (social, psychological, and physical characteristics) and group environment (the location and task of the group).

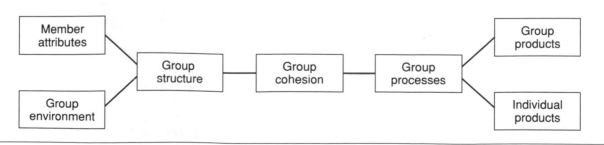

Figure 8.2   A conceptual framework for examining the sport team as a group.
Note. From *Group Dynamics in Sport: Theoretical and Practical Issues* (p. 10) by A.V. Carron, 1988, Eastbourne, U.K.: Spodym Publishers, Copyright 1988 by Spodym Publishers. Reprinted by permission.

"Throughputs" include group structure (positions, roles, and status of members), group cohesion (group unity), and group processes (e.g., motivation, communication, decision making). Finally, group outputs are consequences both for the individual members (e.g., satisfaction, adherence) and for the group (e.g., performance, stability). This comprehensive model can be used to determine (a) relationships that could exist, (b) what *is* actually known to date, and (c) what should be studied in sport groups.

The limited use of theory in group dynamics has undoubtedly restricted the advancement of knowledge in this area. Nevertheless, a considerable amount of research has been conducted. This research has been presented in such classic works as *Group Dynamics: Research and Theory* (Cartwright & Zander, 1968), *The Sociology of Small Groups* (Mills, 1984), *Group Performance* (Davis, 1969), *Group Process and Productivity* (Steiner, 1972), *Group Dynamics: The Psychology of Small Group Behavior* (Shaw, 1981), and *Groups: Interaction and Performance* (McGrath, 1984). In contrast, very little has been written about the small group in sport. Brawley (1989) reported that a content analysis of recent (1984-1989) texts in sport psychology revealed that only 13% of the material was devoted to group dynamics. Similarly, Landers, Boutcher, and Wang (1986) noted that only 9% of the articles appearing in the *Journal of Sport Psychology* from 1979 to 1986 dealt with the sport group. Although some sport psychology texts (e.g., Gill, 1986) do contain excellent sections on the sport group, rarely have there been entire texts devoted to the topic. One recent exception is Carron's (1988) *Group Dynamics in Sport*.

The purpose of this section is to present research conducted in group dynamics. Although the primary emphasis is on sport and/or other physical activity settings, relevant research undertaken with other small groups is also discussed. Because the field of group dynamics encompasses many areas of research, we shall restrict ourselves to the examination of three major topics: group size, group composition, and group cohesion. These topics were selected either because of the amount of research conducted in that area and/or because of the importance the topic has for sport practitioners. Although we recognize that there have been investigations conducted within sport dealing with such additional topics as group structure and selected group processes (e.g., motivation and attribution), space limitations prohibit discussing such topics here. In addition, other important aspects of groups have been examined extensively but not in conjunction with sport teams. For now,

information on such group topics as development, communication, and decision making must be gleaned from nonsport research.

Group Size

Historically, one of the most frequently examined variables in nonsport research on group dynamics has been *size*. Research on this topic has been stimulated by an interest among researchers and practitioners in determining what number of individuals constitute the ideal for group productivity, morale, cohesion, satisfaction, and other outcomes. Specific examples of this research include determining what unit size is optimal for a work group carrying out a manual labor project, for an army platoon entering combat, for a number of friends going on a social outing, and for a secretarial pool within a large corporation.

Popular wisdom says, "The more the merrier," "Two heads are better than one," and "Many hands make the work lighter." However, as Ivan Steiner (1972) pointed out, popular wisdom also says, "Three is a crowd," "Too many cooks spoil the broth," and "A chain is as strong as the weakest link." Scientists, of course, attempt to resolve these conflicting notions.

Much of the research on group size has been guided by Steiner's theory of group productivity. This conceptual framework can be used to explain the impact of group size on a variety of factors related to group effectiveness. The graph presented in Figure 8.3 illustrates how Steiner's framework explains effects of group size on group productivity. Examination of this graph shows that as the number of members in a group increases, the potential for the group to be more productive also increases. The reason for this is quite simple: There are more available resources. It should be apparent, however, that the curve for potential productivity eventually plateaus. This reflects the fact that at some point, all of the expertise necessary for a group to complete its mission is available. Adding new members beyond this point does not increase productivity.

When group size increases beyond the optimal point, it becomes more difficult for each member to interact and communicate in relation to either task or social concerns. It also becomes more difficult to plan and coordinate each group member's activities to ensure minimal duplication and maximal individual involvement. These are examples of group processes. As Figure 8.3 illustrates, when group size increases, group processes decrease.

The final relationship depicted in Figure 8.3 is between group size and the relative productivity

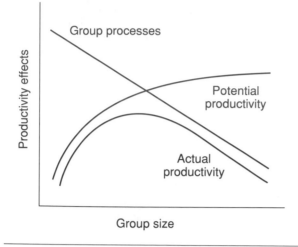

Figure 8.3 The relationship between group size and group productivity.

of each member in the group. There is a decline in relative individual productivity with increasing group size. This is considered to be a result of two factors. First, because of the coordination problems already discussed, the efficiency of the group suffers. Also, in larger groups, each individual member does not give his or her maximum effort. This motivation loss, known as *social loafing*, will be discussed later.

Steiner's predictions regarding group size effects are based primarily on research with nonsport groups. Recently, however, several sets of researchers have examined the effects of group size in both sport and exercise contexts.

Group Size in Sport Teams

Recently, we conducted two studies of the impact of group size in sport teams (Widmeyer, Brawley & Carron, 1990). In designing these studies, different functional definitions of group size, including the number of players "carried" on the overall roster of the team and the number on the field of action at one time, were considered and used. In Study 1, the rosters of three-on-three recreational basketball teams were manipulated to produce teams that carried three, six, and nine members. Each team played two games per week for a 10-week period. The results revealed that in the smallest teams, task cohesiveness was highest; that is, it was easiest to obtain consensus and commitment to the group's goals and objectives in the three-person groups. However, because of the relatively limited number of resources available, it was more difficult for the three-person teams to compete successfully. As well, social cohesion (i.e., closeness among players) was lowest in these small teams either because athletes were constantly competing or

because of the relatively limited number of attractive others with whom to interact. In the largest teams, it was more difficult to obtain consensus and commitment to the group's goals and objectives (i.e., task cohesion was lowest) and to develop a strong sense of social cohesion. The intermediate size groups—the six-person teams—were the highest in social cohesion and also were the most successful in terms of win–loss outcomes.

In Study 2, the number of athletes on the field of action was varied in recreational volleyball teams to produce 3-on-3, 6-on-6, and 12-on-12 competitions. When the participants evaluated these three different situations, they indicated that their sense of enjoyment, their perceptions of cohesiveness, their feelings of having obtained exercise and being fatigued, of having had influence and responsibility on the team, and of being organized and using strategies were greatest in the 3-on-3 teams and least in the 12-on-12 teams. At the same time, feelings of being crowded increased with increasing team size. The smallest teams were associated with the most positive experiences for the participants. The results from the two studies on sport teams clearly show that size has an impact on productivity, the nature and amount of cohesiveness that develops, and individual perceptions about the attractiveness of the group.

Group Size in Exercise Groups

We also recently completed two studies of the impact of group size in exercise classes (Carron, Brawley & Widmeyer, 1990). In Study 1, the relationship between the size of fitness classes and the adherence of members was examined. Archival data from 47 fitness classes varying in size from 5 to 46 members were used to form four categories of groups: small (5-17 members), medium (18-26 members), moderately large (27-31), and large (32-46 members). As the results in Figure 8.4 show, both the attendance and retention of participants were highest in the very small and very large fitness classes and were lowest in the medium and moderately large classes.

The purpose of Study 2 was to examine the nature of the relationship between the size of fitness classes and the social–psychological perceptions of group members. Participants in *small classes* (6-13 members), *medium classes* (25-39 members), and a *large class* (73 members) evaluated their feelings of conspicuousness, the quality and quantity of interactions with their leader, their opportunities for social interaction with other members, the level of crowding and density

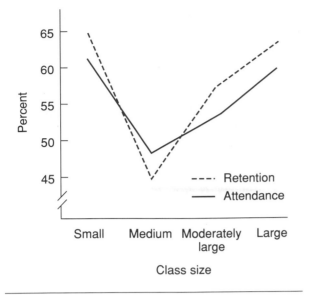

Figure 8.4 Size-adherence relationships in exercise classes.

they experienced, and their feelings of satisfaction. There was a curvilinear relationship between fitness class size and participants' perceptions of the opportunities available for social interaction and also between class size and feelings of crowding and density. Both the small and large classes were perceived more favorably than the medium classes. Perceptions of the instructor and the level of satisfaction experienced varied in a linear way with group size; that is, positive perceptions decreased systematically as class size increased. Finally, there was no difference among the groups in perceptions of conspicuousness. While it is unwise to overgeneralize from the results of two studies, it does seem that smaller is better in fitness class settings. Certainly, further research in the area is recommended.

Group Size and the Phenomenon of Social Loafing

Research on the productivity of groups has identified a phenomenon referred to as social loafing—a reduction in individual effort that occurs when people work collectively on a problem (Latane, Williams & Harkins, 1979). One of the earliest studies to report this was conducted by Ringelmann in the late 19th century (cited in Ingham, Levinger, Graves & Peckham, 1974). Using a tug-of-war task, Ringelmann found that the average male exerted 63 kg of tension when working by himself (cited in Moede, 1927). Thus, potential productivity for a group could be predicted by multiplying the size of the group by 63

kg. However, Ringlemann found that in actuality, for groups of 2, 3, 4, 5, 6, 7, and 8, the average individual in the group produced, respectively, only 93%, 85%, 77%, 70%, 63%, 58%, and 49% of his potential.

Using Steiner's (1972) model of group productivity, Ingham and colleagues (1974) hypothesized that two factors might account for this decrease in individual productivity: *poor coordination*, resulting from the inability of individuals in groups to exert maximal tension simultaneously, and *decreased motivation*, resulting from the fact that individual performances cannot be directly assessed in groups. In order to determine which of these was the more important, Ingham and his colleagues replicated the Ringelmann study. Ringelmann proposed that the major source of the difference between a group's potential productivity and its actual productivity was faulty coordination. Ingham et al. found that it was lower motivation—social loafing. A considerable amount of research has subsequently demonstrated the presence of social loafing in laboratory and nonlaboratory situations (see Hardy, 1989).

Numerous explanations have been proposed to account for the social loafing phenomenon (Harkins, Latane & Williams, 1980). The *allocation strategy* proposal is based on the assumption that people are motivated to work hard in groups but save their best efforts for when they work alone because it is personally most beneficial. In the *minimizing strategy* proposal, it is assumed that people are motivated to get by with as little effort as possible. Because there is minimal personal accountability, groups provide an optimal environment in which to loaf. In the *free rider* proposal, it is assumed that people in groups reduce their personal efforts and go for a free ride because they feel their efforts are not essential to the outcome. Finally, the basis for the *sucker effect* proposal is the assumption that individuals in groups reduce their personal efforts because they do not want to provide a free ride to lessproductive individuals.

Research conducted to test these explanations has shown that the losses in individual productivity that are due to social loafing are greatest when individual contributions are not identifiable, are dispensable, or are in disproportion to the contributions of other group members (Carron, 1988). Thus, when individual inputs to the group product are monitored directly, social loafing is reduced. Also, when individuals perceive that their inputs are essential to the group's productivity, social loafing is reduced. Finally, when individuals consider that their inputs are appropriate to the inputs of other group members, social loafing is reduced. The social loafing phenomenon has been demonstrated primarily in laboratory experiments, but a few researchers have also found the phenomenon in field settings with such subjects as cheerleaders (Hardy & Latane, 1988), swimmers (Harkins et al., 1980), and sprint relay participants (Huddleston, Doody & Ruder, 1985). But as Hardy (1989) recently concluded, more research is necessary to understand the generalizability of the social loafing phenomenon to other field settings in sport.

Group Composition

Group composition refers to the properties possessed by group members. These properties include physical characteristics, mental and motor abilities, attitudes, motives, personality traits, and such social identities as age, education, religion, occupation, race, sex, and social status. The effects of group composition can be examined from the perspectives of

- quantity,
- degree of variation, and
- complementarity of properties among members.

Although each of these manifestations can influence other group inputs and various group processes, the majority of sport research has focused on the impact of group composition on group productivity.

Quantity of Group Resources

The quantity of a group's resources can be represented by either the average or the sum of member attributes. One intuitively expects that groups possessing more relevant resources will perform better. Examinations of the quantity of resources have sought to determine which resources are "relevant" and how much impact group resources have on group performance. The first area of this research has dealt primarily with psychological and social properties, whereas the second has focused on the abilities of group members.

How does the quantity of social–psychological resources in the group influence its productivity? Cooper and Payne (1967) assessed an aspect of the personality of the soccer players and coaches—the extent to which these individuals were task-, self-, and affiliation-oriented when approaching activities. They found that the success of soccer teams was positively related to the task orientations of their coaches/trainers ($r =$

.72). Later, the same researchers reported that high task orientation, low self-orientation, and low affiliation orientations of soccer players were positively linked to team success (Cooper & Payne, 1972). Examining 144 intramural basketball teams, Martens (1970) discovered that teams that were most successful possessed high task and low affiliation motivation. Also, it has been shown that basketball teams possessing high achievement motivation were very successful (Klein & Christiansen, 1969). In contrast, one of us (Widmeyer & Martens, 1978) demonstrated that task motivation, affiliation motivation, and self-motivation, considered singly or in combination, did not predict winning in 3-on-3 basketball teams. However, these variables, when combined with group cohesion, increased cohesion's prediction of performance outcome significantly. These results suggest that multivariate approaches should be taken when examining the impact of the quantity of group resources.

Anthropologists Sutton-Smith and Roberts (1984) identified a personality variable known as "action style." They labeled individuals who approached life as if they were playing a game of physical skill *potents*, those as if playing a game of strategy *strategists*, and those as if playing a game of chance *fortunists*. Members' potent style was positively related to doubles success in men's tennis, whereas negative relationships existed between team success and each of the styles of pure strategy, strategy/fortunism, and pure fortunism (Widmeyer, Loy, & Roberts, 1980). A subsequent study of 28 female tennis teams (Widmeyer & Loy, 1989) found that members' styles of potent/strategy and pure strategy were significantly related to team success ($r = .70$ and $-.41$, respectively). It should be noted that although a number of studies have shown that the quantity of psychological variables has an impact on team performance, no attempt has been made to explain *why* such relationships exist.

Intuitively, one expects that the more ability resources members possess, the better the group's performance should be. In two experiments, Gill (1979) found moderate relationships ($r = .49–.53$) between average member ability and group performance on a motor maze. Jones (1974) reported that the correlation between individual performance and team performance at the professional level was .70 in men's tennis, .80 in women's tennis, .91 in football, .94 in baseball, and .60 in basketball. The different values might reflect differences in the amount of coordination of abilities required in certain sports. For example, basketball requires more coordination than baseball. Therefore, it is possible to have greater productivity losses in the former due to faulty coordination; and therefore, there is likely to be a weaker relationship between ability and performance. Player ability correlated .73 with team performance in men's intramural basketball (Gossett & Widmeyer, 1978) whereas Spense (1980) found the correlation to be .78 in female intramural teams. The reason why member ability was a better predictor of team success in doubles tennis among females (r = .77) than males (r = .54) may be that there were greater ability discrepancies among the females (Widmeyer & Loy, 1989). This rationale was extended to explain why females' backhand ability was more closely related to performance (r = .79) than forehand ability (r = .30); that is, the female players differed little in forehand but greatly in backhand ability.

The studies reported here indicate that only a very few social–psychological variables have been examined when studying the effects of the quantity of member resources. Also, it was shown that the strength of the player ability–team performance relationship varies considerably depending upon the sport, the specific skill, and the level of play.

Variability of Group Resources

The variability of group resources focuses on the impact of the heterogeneity of member characteristics and abilities. Klein and Christiansen (1969) reported that three-person basketball teams whose members were very heterogeneous in achievement motivation were more successful than their homogeneous counterparts. Carron (1988) suggested a "spillover effect" to explain why heterogeneous groups might perform better than homogeneous groups. According to this hypothesis, a stronger member can have a positive influence on a weaker individual by improving his or her learning and motivation. Nevertheless, in Gill's (1979) experiments, there were no significant relationships between the ability discrepancies of members and group performance on a motor task. As to why women's tennis teams with very homogeneous ability performed better than heterogeneous teams,

Many would predict the opposite findings arguing that the heterogeneous teams should do better because they have a high ability person who can play the majority of shots. The results suggest that these female tennis players adopt a very egalitarian strategy when playing with their partners and thus their game was not marked by 'poaching' or any other form of overplaying by

the better players. It could also be that the homogeneous teams were directing the majority of their shots to the weaker player on heterogenerous teams. Support for these two assumptions lies in the fact that the total ability to the weakest player was more positively related to team performance outcome (r = .74) than was the total ability of the best player (r = .49). (Widmeyer & Loy, 1989, p. 27)

Again, it can be seen that only a very limited number of social–psychological variables have been examined when studying the variability of resources-team performance relationship. Also, it was shown that the strength of the effect of the variability of players' ability resources on team performance depended upon how the game was played.

Complementarity of Group Resources

The relationship between complementarity of group resources and group performance is suggested by the ancient rhyme "Jack Sprat could eat no fat, his wife could eat no lean; so between the two of them, they licked the platter clean." Complementarity of group members' action styles has been shown to relate to performance in management games (Roberts, Meeker & Aller, 1972), sport car rallies (Roberts & Kundrat, 1978), deep-sea fishing crews, navy flight crews, and duplicate bridge teams (J. Roberts, personal communication, October 1980). In tennis, serve/ volley complementarity was more important for male tennis teams while forehand/backhand complementarity was more important for female teams. These differences were related to differences in the style of play of the two sexes (Widmeyer & Loy, 1989). At the club level studied, the women engaged in lengthy baseline rallies, whereas in men's games, a serve-and-volley style predominated.

In summarizing the research on group composition in sport, it can be said that researchers have

- focused on the effects of either social–psychological attributes or ability resources of members on team *performance*;
- found that ability composition is more strongly related to team performance in coacting, than in interacting, sports;
- ignored process variables that might explain or mediate composition–performance relationships; and

- focused primarily on the quantity or variability of resources but rarely studied the complementarity of resources and, with only one exception, have never researched all three of these manifestations simultaneously.

Group Cohesion

Group cohesion is one of the most frequently examined group concepts in sport science. A number of reviews provide extensive reports on what the state of the art is, regarding the current level of cohesion knowledge (e.g., Carron, 1988; Gill, 1977; Widmeyer, Brawley & Carron, 1985). In this section of the chapter, the available research captured by these reviews is summarized to give the reader a brief glimpse of the state of knowledge. This summary is necessary in order to understand the problems associated with the research about cohesion in sport. Major problems are discussed following the summary, and more recent conceptual and measurement approaches are presented.

A summary of the cohesion research in sport is best presented within an antecedent–cohesion–consequence framework. Carron (1982) proposed such a framework to help investigators systematically organize the research. The results of the research studies concerning antecedent factors and those concerning consequence factors are summarized and each is illustrated with an example. Greater detail about studies concerning these factors can be found in the reviews mentioned.

Antecedents of Cohesion

Carron's (1982) frame of reference proposes four categories of antecedents: situational, personal, leadership, and team. Specific results drawn from the sport research will exemplify each of the four categories.

Situational Determinants

Group size is a situational variable that differentially impinges on different aspects of cohesion. For example, as indicated previously, we (Widmeyer et al., 1990) found that recreational basketball players assigned to teams of varying size playing in a 10-week season expressed greatest task cohesion in small teams while least cohesion was expressed in large teams.

Personal Determinants

The team member's personal characteristics can influence the amount of cohesion developed. For example, Eitzen (1975) suggested that cohesion is facilitated when team members are from similar social backgrounds. Also, we (Widmeyer et al., 1985) noted gender differences in the social cohesion of team sport athletes, with male team sport athletes expressing greater social cohesiveness than female team sport athletes.

Leadership Determinants

The complex interaction between coach and players may influence cohesion development. For example, an examination of leader decision styles found that a participative style evoked greatest team cohesion (Carron & Chelladurai, 1981).

Team Determinants

Shared team experience may also be a cohesion antecedent. A series of successes or failures has

been known to bring group members together (Carron & Ball, 1977). Ruder and Gill (1982) found that cohesion was also enhanced by immediate success in intramural teams but not in stable, well-established athletic teams. Presumably, cohesion in the latter teams is less transitory. By contrast, there is an immediate but potentially short-lived camaraderie resulting from success in intramurals.

Consequences of Cohesion

The two consequence factors described in Carron's (1982) frame of reference are group outcomes and individual outcomes. Considerably more sport-related research has been conducted on the consequences of team cohesion than on the antecedents of this variable (see Carron, 1988; Widmeyer et al., 1985).

Group Outcomes

One of us (Carron, 1988) has pointed out that the existing research examining the effects of team cohesion on performance has resulted in three general results: Some studies have found that teams with more cohesion have more success, some that cohesion is unrelated to performance, and some that teams with lower cohesion have better performance. Therefore, the results of this research are mixed. However, Carron has also noted that there tend to be more studies supporting a positive relationship between these variables. Furthermore, the results supporting a negative relationship have typically been found in individually oriented sports where team member rivalry may provoke lower cohesion but stimulate better performance.

Performance success is not the only group outcome that has been associated with cohesion. With higher cohesion, there is greater effort toward the achievement of group goals (e.g., Ball & Carron, 1976). Also, lower absenteeism/dropout and greater punctuality have been found for both team athletes and exercise group members who perceived high levels of group cohesion (e.g., Carron, Widmeyer & Brawley, 1988).

Individual Outcomes

Cohesion also impacts on an individual member's psychological state. While there is less sport research about these outcomes, the results are clear. For example, individual satisfaction with the competitive experience is greater (Williams & Hacker, 1982). As well, with increased cohesion comes a more stable group organization and structure (Grand & Carron, 1982).

Problems with the Research on Cohesion

A major problem with the cohesion research in sport is the failure to define and measure sport cohesion in more than a unidimensional manner. This problem is not unique to the sport research but is also characteristic of social science in general. In the sport sciences, the practice has been to borrow concepts and measures from the social sciences. Concepts such as fields of forces, resistance to disruption, and attraction to group were borrowed and have guided all but the most contemporary sport studies. However, in a recent review of the research concerning the definition of group cohesion in general, Mudrack (1989) notes that researchers have not only defined cohesion poorly but also failed to link cohesion measures to the various definitions of cohesion. In sport science, little thought has been given to the limitations of borrowing definitions or measures. This same error has been committed by the larger group of social scientists interested in cohesion. The result, in either case, is inappropriate use of definitions and measures because all operational definitions of cohesion do not have universal application to all settings. The overall consequence for social science and sport is invalid or limited measurement (e.g., unidimensional measure) in many sport investigations.

At the root of the definition problem is one of a still more global dimension, again characteristic of both the social science and sport literature. The global problem is that there is no conceptual or theoretical model that could be used as the basis for the definition of cohesion and its measurement. Without some common foundation to guide research efforts, the variety of cohesion definitions and measures that currently exist in the literature was bound to develop. Subsequent comparisons between studies (e.g., comparing cohesion–performance relationships) may well be inappropriate when the definitions and measures used are not directly comparable. Obviously, when the problems of lack of a conceptual foundation, poor cohesion definition, and poor operational definition to measurement link are considered together, a kind of research error "domino effect" is created. Research problems of measurement cannot be solved without correcting the more basic problem of lack of a theory or model (Widmeyer et al., 1985). What implications do these problems have for the cohesion research in sport?

After considering the sport-related cohesion research conducted between 1969 and 1984, a nagging question arises. If the concerns about the definition, theory, and measurement of cohesion went unresolved, can investigators have confidence in previous sport research? Results have been obtained using cohesion measures that are conceptually and psychometrically inadequate. Results are not comparable because no common measures were used across studies. These deficiencies are of sufficient magnitude that the majority of early studies must be viewed with caution. Much of this research concerns a variety of descriptive and correlational findings. While Carron's (1982) frame of reference offers a means of organizing these results in a causal order, he stressed the need for a conceptual model as a basis for planning future sport cohesion research.

We (Widmeyer et al., 1985) subsequently described the related problems of theory, definition, and measurement and recently developed a conceptual model to address these research problems. The next section describes such new developments in response to the problems in sport cohesion research.

Recent Theoretical and Assessment Developments

The dissatisfaction with operational definitions and unidimensional measurement approaches described recently motivated sport scientists to develop new cohesion ideas and related measures. We (Carron, Widmeyer, & Brawley, 1985) and Yukelson, Weinberg, and Jackson (1984) independently developed instruments to measure group cohesion in the sport context. However, the two research approaches were quite different. Yukelson and his colleagues used a *data-driven* approach, in which data were explored in search of an understandable measure. The result was the Multidimensional Sport Cohesion Instrument (MSCI). Yukelson and his colleagues' new measure recognizes the multidimensionality of cohesion; however, their definition of cohesion was not clearly linked to its measurement. As Mudrack (1989) noted, this type of flaw is characteristic of previous social science cohesion research. The interested reader is referred to Yukelson and his colleagues' report for more detail about the advantages and disadvantages of using the MSCI.

Using a *theory-driven* approach, we developed the Group Environmental Questionnaire (GEQ) (Carron et al., 1985). Our plan was to proceed from Carron's (1982) definition of cohesion—"a dynamic process that is reflected in the tendency for a group to stick together and remain united in pursuit of its goals and objectives" (p. 124)—and to develop a conceptual model. The model then served as the basis for instrument development and validation.

For the development of the model and the GEQ, the group dynamics literature was extensively reviewed focusing particularly on the nature of the group and group cohesiveness. Throughout the literature, two major distinctions are consistently discussed by various authors: the distinction between individual and group aspects of group involvement and the distinction between the task and social aspects of cohesiveness (e.g., Mikalachki, 1969; Van Bergen & Koekebakker, 1959). An example of the former distinction is that group involvement has been examined with respect to the motives of individual members for belonging to their group. By contrast, group involvement has also been considered relative to decisions or perceptions the entire group has about the group's behavior. Thus, the group as a whole may set goals for performance or for a season or may decide why they should keep training together at season's end.

An example of the latter (task–social) distinction arises in examining the reasons groups stay together. Work and competitive sport groups form and pursue task-related activities relative to their goals and objectives, and stay together primarily for task reasons. By contrast, leisure and recreational sport groups may form, set social goals and objectives, and stay together primarily to socialize regularly. Historically, cohesion has been considered to be composed of task and social elements (see Carron, 1988).

Based upon the conclusions and distinctions drawn from their literature review, we proposed a conceptual model of cohesion incorporating the group–individual and the task–social distinctions (Carron et al., 1985; see Figure 8.5).

In our model, cohesiveness is assumed to be perceived in multiple ways by individual group members. There are two major categories of perceptions. The first, referred to as *Group Integration*, represents members' perceptions of the group as a totality. The second, *Individual Attractions to the Group*, represents each member's personal attractions to the group. Both categories of perceptions are further divided into *task* and *social* orientations. Thus, there are four related dimensions in the conceptual model: Group Integration–Task, Group Integration–Social, Individual Attractions to the Group–Task, and Individual Attractions to the Group–Social. Each is potentially sufficient to bind people to their group. It is not assumed that these aspects are traits or a list of all-inclusive cohesive factors. Other forces may also contribute to cohesion. Using this conceptual model as a foundation, we developed the GEQ, a measure of the four dimensions of cohesion specified in the model.

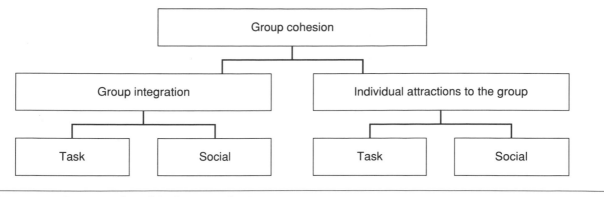

Figure 8.5 Conceptual model of group cohesion.
Note. From *The measurement of Cohesion in Sport Teams: The Group Environment Questionnaire* (p. 18) by W.N. Widmeyer, L.R. Brawley, and A.V. Carron, 1985, Eastbourne, U.K.: Spodym Publishers. Copyright 1985 by Spodym Publishers. Reprinted by permission.

The GEQ is an 18-item, 4-scale instrument and has been shown to be reliable and valid in numerous ways. The validation process for the GEQ consisted of four development projects and 10 studies to date. These are described in detail elsewhere (Brawley et al., 1987, 1988; Carron, Widmeyer & Brawley, 1988; Carron et al., 1985, 1988; Widmeyer et al., 1985, 1990).

In sport and fitness, the aspects of cohesion assessed by the GEQ have been related to

- the task interdependence of group members,
- the duration of team membership, and
- attributions for responsibility (Brawley et al., 1987; Widmeyer et al., 1985),
- team performance (Shangi & Carron, 1987; Widmeyer et al., 1990),
- increased adherence and reduced absenteeism (Carron et al., 1988), and
- the team's resistance to disruption (Brawley et al., 1988).

These relationships are positive, with the exception of reduced absenteeism.

In summarizing the results of the sport-related research concerning recent developments in the study of cohesion, there are five points to be made:

- Two new instruments exist that measure cohesion as more than a unidimensional concept (the GEQ and the MSCI).
- The GEQ instrument is based upon a 4-dimensional conceptual model and has been validated in numerous studies.
- The development of a conceptual model of cohesion fills a void in the otherwise atheoretical area of cohesion in sport.
- Use of the 4-dimensional model and the related GEQ instrument avoids the common research error of not linking conceptual operational definitions of cohesion to its measurement.

- The four aspects of group cohesion specified by the conceptual model are related to both the antecedents (e.g., gender) and the consequences (e.g., attribution of outcome responsibility) of cohesiveness in sport.

Current Problems and Future Directions

It is important to alert those who aspire to investigate sport groups to the problems characteristic of the research in this area. If these problems are identified and then remedied, the quality and quantity of research in sport group dynamics will improve.

Brawley (1989), Carron (1988), and Widmeyer (1989) have noted that while sport groups represent a major social structure across cultures and are the context in which much of participation and competition occurs, group research is surprisingly limited. Figure 8.1 was used to illustrate the limited amount of research attention given groups in the sport science literature. There is little doubt that there is limited knowledge about sport group dynamics. In his recent book on this topic, Carron emphasized this point by noting, "Despite the presence of sufficient content to fill eighteen chapters in this book, it is safe to say we know very little about sport groups" (1988, p. 219). Hopefully, sport researchers will rush to fill this gap.

However, a related problem is that the area of sport psychology has its momentum in the study of individuals and their performance. What sport psychologists often fail to recognize, however, is that the group has a major influence on individual behavior and performance (e.g., motivation, goal setting, performance attributions; Carron, 1988). Ignoring this influence may be a major conceptual and methodological error. The failure to examine the influence of the group on the individual excludes a major source of variance in the sport behavior prediction equation. This exclusion has implications for the accuracy of many of the interpretations in research studies as to *what* influenced behavior. Was it an individual trait or was it the group? If progress is to be made in understanding individual sport behavior, we cannot continue to examine individuals as if they exist in a social vacuum. Both the lack of group research *and* its impact on individual behavior are major reasons for sport psychologists to increase their research efforts in this area.

The plea for more research in the area of sport group dynamics may motivate some sport scientists to increase their research efforts in that direction. However, just doing more of this research is not the solution that will advance our knowledge. What is needed is a simultaneous attempt to avoid the four global research pitfalls of the past while pursuing strategically chosen future research directions. The next section of the chapter will identify these global research pitfalls and conclude with recommendations about future group dynamics research directions in sport.

Global Pitfalls

In sport group research, the scientist can function as an architect or as a laborer. The architect establishes a plan and works toward it, whereas the laborer makes single bricks not necessarily destined for a particular building. Avoiding global research pitfalls prevents the development of an undesirable knowledge base that is simply a collection of unrelated "bricks" of fact about the dynamics of sport groups. What are the four pitfalls to avoid?

The greatest general pitfall in the study of group dynamics in both the sport and general social sciences areas has been the failure to develop and use theory in a systematic way. Both McGrath (1984) and Zander (1979) noted that group research has been highly fragmented with the collection of many "bricks" or data sets but no theory to systematically guide the collection, ordering, and interpretation of the results. Sport scientists must avoid this pitfall so that they do not perpetuate this problem. With so much atheoretical data collection, consistencies in group behavior are difficult to find. Attending to recent theoretical frameworks advanced by authors such as Carron (1988) or McGrath (1984) will guide research plans and reduce fragmentation of the knowledge base. There also exist certain "limited" theories about specific aspects of

group dynamics that were mentioned earlier. They may also be useful in developing systematic research.

A second general pitfall for sport scientists is conducting "snapshot" research. This form of investigation, while offering a concise picture of a specific aspect of group life, fails to adequately capture the dynamic nature of groups as they change over time. Most group studies conducted in the sport context fall into the snapshot, with specific games or seasonal time points as their focus. However, to understand the changing and reciprocal relationships among input and output variables, it will be necessary to conduct prospective, longitudinal studies. A few such attempts have been made recently in examining group cohesion (e.g., Carron & Ball, 1977; Williams & Hacker, 1982). Carron (1988) has also described several categories of models concerning the relationships that may occur *over time* in the development of groups. Although these examples and suggestions exist, sport scientists have yet to take up the challenges they offer in research design. The snapshot design must be coupled with the "video" (longitudinal) approach in future research.

The third global pitfall to avoid is reliance on a univariate approach in examining groups. The univariate approach is often characterized by simple, bivariate correlations between one independent and one dependent variable. What is required is a multivariate approach. Multivariate research involves several independent predictors of one dependent variable or multiple dependent variables (e.g., multiple or multivariate multiple regression). This approach takes into account the complexity of group phenomena and acknowledges interrelationships among group variables that occur simultaneously. A major problem associated with, but not the same as, the univariate approach, is the conducting of antecedent–outcome research (e.g., cohesion–performance) while ignoring the group processes that lead to an outcome. A team may be cohesive and, as a result, perform well. However, did their cohesiveness promote the interaction that caused the team to do well? The bivariate correlation between cohesion and performance fails to yield further knowledge in this regard. A multivariable approach that includes process variables affected by cohesion (e.g., communication), *which in turn* affect performance, would be enlightening.

The fourth global pitfall to avoid is the investigating of teams alone as the focus of group physical activity research. Teams have unique rules, properties, and physical structure that are not necessarily comparable to other types of physical activity groups. There are a variety of other groups in physical activity which strongly influence how we exercise (e.g., fitness classes), how we rehabilitate (cardiac and athlete rehabilitation groups), how we learn motor activities (physical skill classes, music classes), and how sports are organized (sport governing bodies, coaching staff, club executive boards, volunteer groups). Furthermore, the potential to examine group dynamics in physical activity occurs across the life span because there are groups for everyone from the very young (play groups) to retired and older adults (master's clubs, fitness for the elderly). The types of groups that influence an individual's physical activity are numerous, complex, and unique. The study of teams alone leads to a narrow view of group dynamics in physical activity.

The suggestions detailed in this section are offered in an attempt to increase the research on physical activity groups in a *strategic* fashion by avoiding the global pitfalls mentioned. Both Carron (1988) and McGrath (1984) offer numerous suggestions on what to research. Carron focuses on sport, while McGrath concentrates on groups in general and offers a methodological chapter discussing research dilemmas and strategies to which aspiring group investigators should attend.

Future Research Directions

A whole chapter could be devoted to discussing a host of specific future directions. Instead, two approaches for future research will be suggested that will help increase both the quantity and quality of research in sport group dynamics. The first approach is to move our research beyond description by attempting to answer related research questions of increasingly greater complexity. The second approach is a suggestion for categorizing the functions of sport groups, so that research is systematically directed at these functions. In the following section, the future research that could be generated within each approach is discussed.

Moving Beyond Description

Although description is an important aspect of science, it unfortunately has become the main source of information in sport group dynamics. We must move beyond basic description to explanation. To provide a guide for future research in this area, a three-generation hierarchy of research questions is suggested (see Carron, 1988; Zanna & Fazio, 1982) as one approach.

The first generation (and simplest) question is, Does a relationship exist between variables x and y? For example, does a relationship exist between cohesion and team performance? What are its strength, direction, and reliability? While the knowledge obtained from investigating this type of question is useful and provokes other research questions, it is unknown whether this relationship occurs for all types of teams or for all types of conditions that might influence the variables studied.

Accordingly, the second-generation question is one that encourages an examination of conditions moderating the relationship: *When* (i.e., under which conditions) does x relate to y? For example, task cohesion might relate to performance in team sports but not in coactive sports. When the answers to these two generations of questions are provided, the boundaries of the phenomenon are better known and may be placed within some potential theoretical framework (see Carron, 1988).

However, explanations for why these boundaries occur are still tentative unless the third-generation question is asked and answered: Why does variable x relate to y under some conditions but not others? What are the causes of these relationships? For example, task cohesion may influence team performance because team members perceive coordination interdependence as a requirement for success and as demanded by their task (e.g., basketball). Conversely, no great influence of cohesion on performance is observed for coactive teams. These athletes do not perceive its necessity, and task completion does not require team member interaction (e.g., bowling). It is only by considering answers to the three generations of research questions that we can gain understanding of the cohesion–performance relationship and make progress toward a theory. This approach to future research can operate in tandem with the second approach, which concerns the investigation of group functions. The second approach of investigating group functions requires expansion of the types of research we attempt to conduct with sport groups.

Expanding Existing Research

The sport group research conducted to date has primarily been concerned with cohesion and leadership and their influence on performance. A host of other issues require examination. For example, a considerable amount of group member participation occurs outside of the competitive event, in preparation for it. Focusing only on the description of the cohesion–performance relationship, for example, tells us nothing about what conditions moderate and/or cause the relationship. The impact of other factors such as member resources (e.g., abilities), group structure (size), processes (decision making), and intergroup relations (cooperation/conflict) require attention at the level of the group and the level of the individual. In addition to performance, outcomes such as adherence, satisfaction, group efficacy, conformity, group attributions, and motivation require examination.

Although there are numerous issues requiring attention, we do not wish to encourage an asystematic approach to their study. Doing so would simply perpetuate the fragmented knowledge base in sport group dynamics. An alternative approach would be to *categorize* sport groups in some way so that systematic research based on theory could be conducted. There are many ways to attempt this categorization. As one example, McGrath (1984) has identified three *broad* categories of group functions. These functions concern groups as

- task performance systems,
- structures organizing social interaction, and
- mechanisms delivering social influence.

Carrying the example further, the research issues previously identified could be examined, as applicable, within the context of these group functions. Thus, hypotheses and interpretations about a future research issue would be stated relative to the group function. Examining a research issue with respect to a functional theme should lead to more systematic research and a less fragmented knowledge base. To illustrate the research questions associated with these functions, the following examples are provided.

If the team is considered as a task performance system, models such as Steiner's (1972) group productivity formula can be used for the multivariable prediction of team effectiveness as a function of relevant resources, effective coordination due to task cohesion, and increased/decreased motivation to pursue a common team outcome. Some early sport research has already focused on this function.

If the team functions as a means of organizing social interaction, how are team member roles and communication organized for a common understanding of task and social team goals among member athletes? Both the role structure and the communication process among athletes may be influenced by intrateam competition with varying effects on within-team interaction. A study of this organization could tell us whether team processes are effective or ineffective. As well, the degree of social interaction that is promoted or inhibited could provide clues about the eventual level and type of cohesiveness developed. Social satisfaction and motivation would be issues related to this function.

Finally, if the team functions as a powerful social influence over, for example, the efforts of members, do its normative rules bias their thinking (a possible negative effect; Carron, 1988)? The issues of conformity and group attributions are obviously related to this function. Does the degree of team unity influence members in the direction of either a realistic or a false sense of team confidence? The notion of group efficacy would be studied as part of this function.

McGrath's (1984) functions are not the only themes around which thinking about sport groups could be organized. What is important is that a theme or theory be used or tested when investigators attempt to expand the research in sport group dynamics.

The future research opportunities that can be found in the dynamics of physical activity groups is challenging. Will future investigators attempt to meet the challenge? The worst answer to this question would be if the next edition of this book is forced simply to repeat our concerns. Just a few attempts by future investigators to follow the suggestions made here would represent a major advancement in the study of group dynamics in physical activity.

References

Ball, J.R., & Carron, A.V. (1976). The influence of team cohesion and participation motivation upon performance success in intercollegiate ice hockey. *Canadian Journal of Applied Sport Sciences*, **1**, 271-275.

Brawley, L.R. (1989, June). Theoretical background and intent. In L. Brawley (Chair), *Group size in physical activity: Psychological and behavioral impacts.* Symposium conducted at the meeting of the North American Society of the Psychology of Sport and Physical Activity, Kent, OH.

Brawley, L.R., Carron, A.V., & Widmeyer, W.N. (1987). Assessing the cohesion of teams: Validity of the Group Environment Questionnaire. *Journal of Sport Psychology*, **9**, 275-294.

Brawley, L.R., Carron, A.V., & Widmeyer, W.N. (1988). Exploring the relationship between cohesion and resistance to disruption. *Journal of Sport and Exercise Psychology*, **10**, 199-213.

Carron, A.V. (1982). Cohesiveness in sport groups: Interpretations and considerations. *Journal of Sport Psychology*, **4**, 123-128.

Carron, A.V. (1988). *Group dynamics in sport.* London, ON: Spodym.

Carron, A.V., & Ball, J.R. (1977). Cause–effect characteristics of cohesiveness and participation in motivation intercollegiate hockey. *International Review of Sport Sociology*, **12**, 49-60.

Carron, A.V., & Bennett, B.B. (1977). Compatibility in the coach–athlete dyad. *Research Quarterly*, **48**, 671-679.

Carron, A.V., Brawley, L.R., & Widmeyer, W.N. (1990). The impact of group size in an exercise setting. *Journal of Sport & Exercise Psychology*, **12**, 376-387.

Carron, A.V., & Chelladurai, P. (1981). Cohesion as a factor in sport performance. *International Review of Sport Sociology*, **16**, 21-41.

Carron, A.V., Widmeyer, W.N., & Brawley, L.R. (1985). The development of an instrument to assess cohesion in sport teams: The Group Environment Questionnaire. *Journal of Sport Psychology*, **7**, 244-266.

Carron, A.V., Widmeyer, W.N., & Brawley, L.R. (1988). Group cohesion and individual adherence to physical activity. *Journal of Sport and Exercise Psychology*, **10**, 127-138.

Cartwright, D., & Zander, A. (1968). *Group dynamics: Research and theory*. New York: Harper & Row.

Chelladurai, P. (1978). *A contingency model of leadership in athletics*. Unpublished doctoral dissertation, University of Waterloo, Waterloo, ON.

Cooper, R., & Payne, R. (1967). *Personality orientations and performance in football teams: Leaders and subordinates' orientations related to team success* (Report No. 1). Liverpool, England: Organizational Psychology Group.

Cooper, R., & Payne, R. (1972). Personality orientations and performance in soccer teams. *British Journal of Social and Clinical Psychology*, **11**, 2-9.

Davis, J. (1969). *Group performance*. Reading, MA: Addison-Wesley.

Eitzen, D.S. (1975). Group structure and group performance. In D.M. Landers, D.V. Harris, & R.W. Christina (Eds.), *Psychology of sport and motor behavior*. University Park, PA: College of Health, Physical Education, and Recreation, Pennsylvania State University.

Forsyth, D.R. (1983). *An introduction to group dynamics*. Belmont, CA: Wadsworth.

Gill, D.L. (1979). The prediction of group motor performance from individual member ability. *Journal of Sport Psychology*, **11**, 113-122.

Gill, D.L. (1986). *Psychological dynamics of sport*. Champaign, IL: Human Kinetics.

Gill, D.L. (1988). Cohesion and performance in sport groups. In R.S. Hutton (Ed.), *Exercise and sport sciences reviews: Vol. 5*. Santa Barbara, CA: Journal Publishing Affiliates.

Gossett, D., & Widmeyer, W.N. (1978, May). *Improving cohesion's prediction of performance outcome in sport*. Paper presented at the meeting of the North American Society for the Psychology of Sport and Physical Activity, Tallahassee, FL.

Grand, R.R., & Carron, A.V. (1982). Development of a team climate questionnaire. In L.M. Wankel & R.B. Wilberg (Eds.), *Psychology of sport and motor behavior: Research and practice* (pp. 217-229). Edmonton, AB: Department of Recreation and Leisure Studies, University of Alberta.

Grusky, O. (1963). The effects of formal structure on managerial recruitment: A study of baseball organization. *Sociometry*, **26**, 345-353.

Hardy, C.J. (1989, June). Social loafing: Economizing individual effort during team performance. In L. Brawley (Chair), *Group size in physical activity: Psychological and behavioral impacts*. Symposium conducted at the meeting of the North American Society for the Psychology of Sport and Physical Activity, Kent, OH.

Hardy, C.J., & Lantane, B. (1988). Social loafing in cheerleaders: Effects of team membership and competition. *Journal of Sport & Exercise Psychology*, **10**, 109-114.

Harkins, S.G., Latane, B., & Williams, K. (1980). Social loafing: Allocating effort or taking it easy? *Journal of Experimental Social Psychology*, **16**, 457-465.

Huddleston, S., Doody, S.G., & Ruder, M.K. (1985). The effect of prior knowledge of the social loafing phenomenon on

performance in a group. *International Journal of Sport Psychology*, **16**, 176-182.

Ingham, A.G., Levinger, G., Graves, J., & Packham, V. (1974). The Ringelmann Effect: Studies of group size and group performance. *Journal of Experimental Social Psychology*, **10**, 371-384.

Jones, M.B. (1974). Regressing group on individual effectiveness. *Organizational Behavior and Human Performance*, **11**, 426-451.

Klein, M., & Christiansen, G. (1969). Group composition, group structure and group effectiveness of basketball teams. In J.W. Loy & G.S. Kenyon (Eds.), *Sport, culture, and society*. New York: Macmillan.

Landers, D.M., Boutcher, S.H., & Wang, M.Q. (1986). The history and status of sport psychology: 1979-1985. *Journal of Sport Psychology*, **8**, 149-163.

Latane, B., Williams, K., & Harkins, S.J. (1979). Many hands make light the work: The cause and consequences of social loafing. *Journal of Experimental Social Psychology*, **37**, 822-832.

Lewin, K. (1943). Forces behind food habits and methods of change. *Bulletin of the National Research Council*, **108**, 35-65.

Loy, J.W., McPherson, B.D., & Kenyon, G. (1978). *Sport and social systems: A guide to the analysis, problems, and literature*. Reading, MA: Addison-Wesley.

McGrath, J.E. (1984). *Groups: Interaction and performance*. Englewood Cliffs, NJ: Prentice-Hall.

Mikalachki, A. (1969). *Group cohesion reconsidered*. London, ON: School of Business Administration, University of Western Ontario.

Mills, T.M. (1984). *The sociology of small groups* (2nd ed.). Englewood Cliffs, NJ: Prentice-Hall.

Moede, W. (1927). Die Richt linien der Leistungs-Psychologie. *Industrielle Psychotechnik*, **4**, 193-207.

Mudrack, P.E. (1989). Defining group cohesiveness: A legacy of confusion? *Small Group Behavior*, **20**, 37-49.

Orbell, J., & Dawes, R. (1981). Social dilemma. In G. Stephanson & J.H. Davis (Eds.), *Progress in applied social psychology* (Vol. 1). Chichester, Endland: Wiley.

Roberts, J., & Kundrat, D. (1978). Variation in expressive balance and competence for sports car rally teams. *Urban Life*, **7**, 231-251, 276-280.

Roberts, J., Meeker, Q., & Aller, J. (1972). Action style and management game performance: An explanatory consideration. *Naval War College Review*, **24**, 65-81.

Ruder, M.K., & Gill, D.L. (1982). Immediate effects of win-loss on perceptions of cohesion in intramural and intercollegiate volleyball teams. *Journal of Sport Psychology*, **4**(3), 227-234.

Schafer, W. (1966, October). *The social structure of sport groups*. Paper presented at the First International Symposium on the Sociology of Sport, Koln, West Germany.

Schutz, W.C. (1958). *FIRO: A three-dimensional theory of interpersonal behavior*. New York: Holt, Rinehart, & Winston.

Shangi, G., & Carron, A.V. (1987). Group cohesion and its relationship with performance and satisfaction among high school basketball players. *Canadian Journal of Sport Sciences*, **12**, 20.

Shaw, M.E. (1981). *Group dynamics: The psychology of small group behavior* (3rd ed.). New York: McGraw-Hill.

Shaw, M.E., & Costanzo, P.R. (1982). *Theories of social psychology* (2nd ed.). New York: McGraw-Hill.

Spense, E. (1980). *The relative contributions of ability, cohesion, and participation motivation to team performance outcome in women's intramural basketball*. Unpublished manuscript, University of Waterloo, Department of Kinesiology, Waterloo, ON.

Steiner, I.D. (1972). *Group process and productivity*. New York: Academic Press.

Sutton-Smith, B., & Roberts, J. (1964). Rubrics of competitive behavior. *Journal of Genetic Psychology, 105*, 13-37.

Van Bergen, A., & Koekebakker, J. (1959). "Group cohesiveness" in laboratory experiments. *Acta Psychologica, 16*, 81-98.

Widmeyer, W.N. (1989, June). The study of group size in sport. In L. Brawley (Chair), *Group size in physical activity: Psychological and behavioral impacts*. Symposium conducted at the meeting of the North American Society for the Psychology of Sport and Physical Activity, Kent, OH.

Widmeyer, W.N., Brawley, L.R., & Carron, A.V. (1985). *The measurement of cohesion in sport teams: The Group Environment Questionnaire*. London, ON: Sports Dynamics.

Widmeyer, W.N., Brawley, L.R., & Carron, A.V. (1990). The effects of group size in sport. *Journal of Sport & Exercise Psychology, 12*, 177-190.

Widmeyer, W.N., & Loy, J.W. (1989). Dynamic duos: An analysis of the relationship between group composition and group performance in women's doubles tennis. In R. Bolton (Ed.), *Studies in Honor of J.M. Roberts* (pp. 77-97). New Haven, CT: HRAF.

Widmeyer, W.N., Loy, J.M., & Roberts, J. (1980). The relative contribution of action styles and ability to the performance outcomes of doubles tennis teams. In C. Nadeau, W. Halliwell, K. Newell, & C. Roberts (Eds.), *Psychology of motor behavior and sport—1979* (pp. 209-218). Champaign, IL: Human Kinetics.

Widmeyer, W.N., & Martens, R. (1978). When cohesion predicts performance outcome in sport. *Research Quarterly, 49*, 372-380.

Williams, J.M., & Hacker, C. (1982). Causal relationships among cohesion, satisfaction, and performance in women's intercollegiate field hockey teams. *Journal of Sport Psychology, 4*, 324-337.

Yukelson, D., Weinberg, R., & Jackson, A. (1984). A multidimensional group cohesion instrument for intercollegiate basketball. *Journal of Sport Psychology, 6*, 103-117.

Zander, A. (1971). *Motives and goals in groups*. New York: Academic.

Zander, A. (1979). The psychology of group processes. *Annual Review of Psychology, 30*, 417-451.

Zanna, M.P., & Fazio, R.H. (1982). The attitude–behavior relation: Moving toward a third generation of research. In M.P. Zanna, E.T. Higgins, & C.P. Herman (Eds.), *Consistency in social behavior: The Ontario symposium* (Vol. 2, pp. 283-301). Hillsdale, NJ: Erlbaum.

Chapter 9

Leadership Effectiveness in the Sport Domain

Thelma S. Horn
Miami University

Research in the sport leadership area has been conducted under the general assumption that the type of leadership behavior exhibited by a coach will have a significant impact on the athletes' performance and/or on their psychological or emotional well-being. In this research context, leadership has been rather generally conceived of as "the behavioral process of influencing individuals and groups toward set goals" (Barrow, 1977, p. 232). Obviously, this is a broad definition that encompasses many dimensions of coaches' leadership behavior, including the processes they use to make decisions, the type and frequency of feedback they give in response to athletes'

performances, the techniques they use to motivate individual athletes, and the type of relationship they establish with athletes.

Virtually all of the research that has been conducted in the sport leadership area within the last two decades has been motivated by a desire to identify the particular leadership style or styles which are most effective. Under this research approach, leadership effectiveness is typically operationalized in terms of outcome scores or measures; that is, an effective leadership style is defined as that which results in either successful performance outcomes (measured either in terms of win–loss percentages or degree of self-perceived performance abilities) and/or in positive psychological responses on the part of the athletes (e.g., personal/team satisfaction, coach–athlete compatibility).

Despite the number of studies that have been conducted recently to examine leadership effectiveness in the sport domain, there is much that remains to be done. Therefore, the dual purpose of this chapter is to review the available research and theory pertaining to leadership behavior in sport and physical activity settings and provide specific directions for future research in this area. Chelladurai's (1980) Multidimensional Model of Leadership will be used as a framework. This particular model was selected for three reasons. First, Chelladurai's model was developed specifically for the sport domain. Considerably more knowledge about athletes' behavior in sport contexts may be obtained when the researcher uses a theoretical model that is clearly grounded in the sport context (see chapter 1). Second, Chelladurai's model was chosen as a framework because various parts of the model have been tested in the sport context, and the results indicate that the model has merit as an approach to the study of leadership effectiveness. Finally, this multidimensional model may be especially useful because it is a very comprehensive one. In contrast to many other theoretical models that have been developed under the general assumption that they will apply indiscriminately to all subjects, Chelladurai's model rests on the assumption that leadership effectiveness is context-specific; that is, the model inherently assumes that effective leader behaviors will vary as a function of the athletes themselves and the particular sport context in which they participate. Thus, this model does not need to be adapted or changed in order to "fit" groups other than that used in the validation sample.

Although the various research studies conducted in the sport leadership area have shared a common purpose or goal (i.e., the identification of effective leadership styles), the studies themselves have varied considerably in the methodologies used to measure leadership variables and in the conceptual basis underlying the study of leadership style. This chapter will begin with a discussion of some conceptual and methodological approaches to the investigation of leadership effectiveness in the sport domain, then the research conducted to date will be reviewed. Finally, considerable space will be devoted to a discussion of future research directions. Although the suggestions offered will be framed in the context of Chelladurai's (1980) model, the suggestions themselves will go considerably beyond the basic model in order to provide clear directions for future research in this area.

Conceptual Approaches

Early researchers assumed either a trait or a behavioral approach to the study of leadership effectiveness. Under these conceptual models, effective leadership behavior was assumed to be a function either of the leader's personality or dominant behavior. The typical research design consisted of assessing various aspects of leaders' personality or behavior and attempting to identify the particular traits or behaviors that would discriminate the successful from the unsuccessful leaders. These traits or behaviors were then identified as "effective leadership factors." Although these research approaches were much more commonly used in the study of effective leadership in industrial, educational, and other formal organizational contexts, a few researchers have used the trait or the behavioral approach to study effective leadership in the sport setting. Penman, Hastad, and Cords (1974), for example, measured the degree of authoritarianism in interscholastic male football and basketball head coaches and then tested the degree of correlation between that particular personality characteristic and coaching success. They reported that more successful coaches (i.e., those with highest win–loss percentages) were more authoritarian than less successful coaches. Subsequent sport researchers examined similar aspects of a coach's personality or behavior (e.g., autocratic vs. democratic decision styles, creativity) in an attempt to identify the most effective leadership traits or behaviors (e.g., Hendry, 1969; Lenk, 1977; Pratt & Eitzen, 1989).

Disillusionment with the rather simplistic trait and behavioral approaches to the study of leadership effectiveness in nonsport settings arose, at least in part, because the combined results of this type of research failed to identify a particular set of traits or behaviors that *consistently* discriminated between effective and noneffective leaders; that is, the set of traits or behaviors identified as effective in one context did not generalize to other contexts. In response to this lack of generalizability, a variety of situationally based theories were developed. These leadership theories included House's path–goal theory (House & Mitchell, 1974), Hersey and Blanchard's (1972) life-cycle theory, and Fiedler's (1967) contingency theory. Although these theoretical models differed from each other considerably in content, all of them were constructed on the premise that leadership effectiveness cannot be determined solely by assessing the leader's traits or behaviors. Rather, leadership effectiveness is assumed to be a function of both situational and individual factors. More specifically, these situational theories specified that the characteristics and behaviors of the leader and the group members will interact with other aspects of the situation (e.g., task type, work environment) to determine the type of leadership behaviors that will be most effective in attaining the organizational goals. Under this research approach, leadership effectiveness is conceived to be context- or situation-specific; that is, the particular traits, decision styles, and behaviors that are characteristic of an effective leader will vary as a function of factors within the environment.

Although research conducted to test these theories in educational and industrial settings resulted in some support for the situational approach to leadership effectiveness, efforts to apply these same theories to the sport context resulted in minimal success (e.g., Bird, 1977; Chelladurai, 1984; Chelladurai & Carron, 1983; Terry, 1984; Terry & Howe, 1984; Vos Strache, 1979). As some writers (e.g., Chelladurai & Carron, 1978; Terry & Howe, 1984) have suggested, sport teams may possess certain unique characteristics that make the general leadership theories inapplicable.

In response to this lack of fit, Chelladurai (1980) developed a theory of leadership effectiveness that was specific to the sport domain. Consistent with the general leadership theories on which his model was based, Chelladurai also posited that leadership effectiveness in the sport domain will be contingent on both situational factors and on the characteristics of the leader/coach and the group members (i.e., the athletes). Thus, effective leadership behavior can and will

vary across specific contexts as the characteristics of the athletes and as the dictates of the situation change. Chelladurai constructed his Multidimensional Model of Leadership (see Figure 9.1) to provide a framework for the specification/identification of effective leadership behavior in specific sport situations. Specifically, Chelladurai proposes that leadership effectiveness can be multidimensionally measured in terms of two consequences: performance outcomes and member satisfaction (Box 7). The particular leadership behaviors that will produce such desired outcomes are a function of three interacting aspects of leader behavior: the actual behavior exhibited by the coach/leader (Box 5); the type of leader behavior preferred by the athletes (Box 6); and the type of leader behavior appropriate to, or required in, that situational context (Box 4). Each of these constructs are, in turn, driven by corresponding antecedent factors or conditions. Specifically, the type of leader behaviors that the athletes prefer their coaches to exhibit (Box 6) will be primarily determined by specific characteristics of the athletes themselves (e.g., age, gender, skill level, psychological characteristics; Box 3). In addition, the actual behavior exhibited by a coach/leader (Box 5) will be a direct function of her or his own personal characteristics (e.g., gender, age, years experience, ability, psychological characteristics; Box 2). Finally, the behaviors required by the situation (Box 4) will be a function of certain aspects/characteristics of the particular sport situation (e.g., type of sport, program structure, organizational goals, sociocultural environment; Box 1). To put the

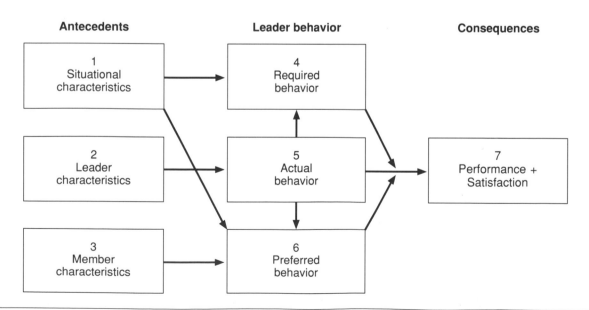

Figure 9.1 Multidimensional model of leadership.
Note. From "Leadership in Sport Organizations" by P. Chelladurai, 1980, *Canadian Journal of Applied Sport Psychology,* **5,** p. 226. Copyright 1980 by the Canadian Association of Sport Science. Reprinted by permission.

model as a whole into perspective, Chelladurai hypothesized that the positive outcomes of optimal performance and group satisfaction on the part of the athletes can be obtained if there is congruence between the three aspects of leader behavior; that is, if the coach exhibits the leadership behaviors dictated for the particular situation and consistent with the preferences or desires of the members, optimal performance and member satisfaction will be achieved.

Methodological Approaches

In order to test both the relationships specified in Chelladurai's multidimensional model and the applicability of the model to the prediction of leadership effectiveness in sport contexts, it is, of course, necessary to develop instrumentation to measure the constructs comprising the model. As Chelladurai and Saleh noted, "The elaboration of any theory entails an obligation to measure its constructs or to specify behavioral manifestations which can be adequately measured. Otherwise, theoretical formulations only yield a proliferation in terminology, instead of fulfilling a promise of empirical advance" (1980, p. 35). To meet this need, two instruments have been developed to measure various aspects of the coach's leadership behavior. The first instrument, entitled the Leadership Scale for Sport (LSS), was developed by Chelladurai and Saleh (1978, 1980) to measure a broad spectrum of leadership behaviors. The LSS consists of five subscales, of which two measure the coach's decision-making style (democratic, autocratic), two measure the coach's motivational tendencies (social support, positive feedback), and one measures the coach's instructional behavior (training and instruction). Coaches who score high on the training and instruction factor exhibit high frequencies of behaviors oriented toward improving the performance of their athletes. These behaviors include

- emphasizing and facilitating hard and strenuous training;
- instructing them in skills, techniques, and tactics;
- clarifying the working relationship among team members; and
- structuring and coordinating the performance activities of the team.

Items on the two decision-making-style factors describe a coach who allows the athletes to participate in decisions relating to group goals, practice methods, and game tactics and strategies (democratic) and/or one who is aloof from the players and stresses personal authority in dealing with them (autocratic). High scores on the positive feedback factor describe a coach who consistently responds to good performance by athletes with praise and/or other rewarding behavior. Finally, items on the social support factor measure a coach's tendency to exhibit a concern for individual athletes and to establish a warm, interpersonal relationship with group members. In contrast to the positive feedback factor, the behaviors described by the social support factor are provided to individual athletes independently of their performance and typically extend outside of the athletic context. Positive feedback, in turn, is contingent on the athletes' performance and is limited to the athletic context.

The total LSS instrument contains 40 items, each of which is scored on a 5-point scale. Due to the fact that Chelladurai's model specifies the need to measure both the actual leadership behaviors exhibited by a coach (Box 5 in Figure 9.1) as well as the leadership behaviors preferred by athletes (Box 6), the LSS can be administered in two versions. To measure perceived (actual) coaching behaviors, individual athletes respond to items prefaced with the words *My coach* (e.g., "My coach expresses appreciation when an athlete performs well"). To measure preferred coaching behaviors, individual items are prefaced with the phrase, *I prefer my coach to* (e.g., "I prefer my coach to ask for the opinion of the athletes on important coaching matters").

The items comprising the LSS were generated by asking 160 male and female physical education university students to respond to a questionnaire containing 99 items adapted from a variety of existing nonsport leadership scales (Chelladurai & Saleh, 1978). The obtained data was then factor-analyzed. Based on these results, the questionnaire was significantly revised and then administered to a second sample (physical education students) and a third set (male university athletes). Independent factor analyses were conducted to establish the stability of a 5-factor solution across different samples. In addition, acceptable measures of internal consistency and test–retest reliability were obtained. Since its development, the LSS has been used in a number of research studies in the sport domain. The researchers who have assessed the statistical properties of the LSS relative to their specific sample of subjects have reported favorable reliability and consistency (e.g., Chelladurai, Imamura, Yamaguchi, Oinuma & Miyauchi, 1988; Chelladurai, Malloy, Imamura & Yamaguchi, 1987). Further comments concerning the reliability and validity of the LSS will be made later.

As discussed earlier, the LSS provides a general measure of leadership style and thus encompasses a fairly wide range of leadership behaviors. A second type of instrument has also been used with some regularity in the sport leadership research to measure a more specific aspect of the coach's leadership behavior. This type of instrument, typically identified as a decision style questionnaire, provides a measure of the coach's decision-making style. At least three different forms of the decision style questionnaire have been developed and used within the past five years (Chelladurai & Arnott, 1985; Chelladurai, Haggerty & Baxter, 1989; Gordon, 1988). These questionnaires were primarily based on a model for decision making in the athletic domain that was proposed by Chelladurai and Haggerty (1978). This model, identified as the Normative Model for Decision Styles in Coaching, was based on Vroom and Yetton's (1973) comprehensive work on leadership and decision making. Consistent with Vroom and Yetton's theories, Chelladurai and Haggerty proposed that the particular decision-making style used by a coach in any situation can vary on a continuum in which the points are defined in terms of the amount of participation that group members (i.e., athletes) are allowed to have in the decision-making process. The continuum can range from an autocratic decision-making style (in which the coach alone makes the decision) to the other end of the spectrum (a delegative style, in which the coach delegates the decision to be made by one or more group members, or athletes). Additional points in between the two ends can consist of a consultative decision-making style (in which the coach consults with one or more team members and then makes the final decision) and a participative style (in which the coach and one or more team members jointly make the decision). Furthermore, the effectiveness of any particular decision-making style can be predicted by assessing certain situational variables. These situational variables include

- the degree of quality inherent in the problem situation (How crucial is the decision?);
- the amount of information relevant to the problem solution available to the coach (Does the coach possess all relevant information?);
- the complexity of the problem (How many factors are there and how do they interrelate?);
- the degree of integration or cohesiveness among group members;
- the presence or absence of time restrictions in regard to the decision-making process;

- the degree to which group acceptance of the decision is necessary or crucial; and
- the amount of status or power the coach holds with regard to team members.

The underlying principle of this theoretical approach to decision-making effectiveness is that coaches do not or should not adhere to only one decision-making style. Rather, the particular style that will be most effective will vary as a function of the situation and the characteristics of the group and its leader. Subsequent research with this type of instrument has verified that the situational factors described do explain a significantly greater amount of the variance in preferred and perceived decision styles than do individual difference factors (Chelladurai & Arnott, 1985; Chelladurai et al., 1989). These results provide consistent support for the situational approach to leadership effectiveness.

To assess the decision-making style used by coaches and/or the decision-making style athletes would prefer their coaches to use, several sets of researchers (Chelladurai & Arnott, 1985; Chelladurai et al., 1989; Gordon, 1988) have developed a decision style questionnaire consisting of a number of problem cases or situations. Each case describes a common sport situation in which a problem must be solved (e.g., substituting for an injured player, selecting a team quarterback, identifying a team manager, making final "cuts"). The particular cases comprising a questionnaire are specifically chosen to represent all possible combinations of the situational factors earlier described (e.g., high in problem complexity, low in group integration). Athletes who complete this questionnaire are variously asked to identify the style they believe their coaches would use in that situation or the style they would prefer their coaches to use. Coaches who complete the questionnaire are typically asked to identify the style they would use in each case.

Although no psychometric test results have been reported for the various versions of the decision style questionnaire, the content, wording, and format of the questionnaires have been carefully constructed and rather extensively reviewed by knowledgeable experts in the leadership field and by the athletes and coaches themselves. Nevertheless, continued psychometric testing of this type of instrumentation is necessary to ensure that a reliable and valid assessment of decision-making styles can be obtained.

The development of these instruments and the publication of Chelladurai's multidimensional model generated a considerable amount of research on sport leadership within the last decade.

In general, these studies were conducted under the aegis of the Chelladurai Multidimensional Model of Leadership and/or the closely related Normative Model for Decision Styles in Coaching. In addition, most of these studies have used one or the other of the instruments just described. The combined results of this research will now be reviewed.

Empirical Research on Leadership Effectiveness

Chelladurai's multidimensional model of leadership effectiveness proposes that optimal performance and satisfaction on the part of the athletes will be achieved if the leadership behaviors exhibited by the coach are congruent with the behaviors preferred by her or his athletes and are appropriate for the particular sport context. A review of the empirical research that has been conducted in the sport leadership area within the last 15 years indicates that these studies can be divided into one of two categories. The first category consists of those research studies that were conducted to identify and/or describe the leadership behaviors which certain groups of athletes prefer their coaches to exhibit. Studies comprising the second category were conducted to test Chelladurai's hypothesis that the congruency between preferred and actual leadership behaviors will result in optimal performance outcomes and high group satisfaction. The two groups of studies will be examined separately.

Identification of Preferred Leadership Styles

Based on both Chelladurai's multidimensional model and on other general situational leadership theories, a number of researchers have hypothesized that the type of leadership behaviors that athletes prefer their coaches to exhibit will vary as a function of certain characteristics of the athletes themselves. This relationship is illustrated in Chelladurai's model (see Figure 9.1) in the arrow that extends from Box 3 to Box 6. To date, researchers have examined the extent to which the athletes' age, skill, gender, and/or nationality may affect preferred leadership styles. In addition, again based on Chelladurai's model, a few research studies have tested the hypothesis that type of sport (Box 1, e.g., open vs. closed, independent vs. interdependent) will also affect preferred leadership styles (Box 6).

Age, Competitive Level, and Years Experience

Although several sets of researchers (e.g., Chelladurai & Carron, 1983; Terry, 1984; Terry & Howe, 1984; Vos Strache, 1979) have used a cross-sectional approach to examine differences between younger and older athletes in preferred leadership styles, the emphasis in these studies has not been on age alone but on age in combination with level of competition and/or years of sport experience. Specifically, these researchers have tested hypotheses inherent in both Hersey and Blanchard's (1972) situational leadership theory and Chelladurai's (1980) model suggesting that the degree of maturity characteristic of group members will affect their need for particular leadership styles or behaviors. In the sport context, *maturity* has been defined as "the relative mastery of skill and knowledge in sport, the development of attitudes appropriate to sport, and experience and the capacity to set high but attainable goals" (Chelladurai & Carron, 1983, p. 372). Due to the structure of sport in which selectivity increases with age, it was assumed in these studies that athletic maturity increases as a function of progression by an individual athlete from elementary school sport, to high school sport, to university sport, and finally to the professional sport level. Thus, maturity was operationalized in these studies in terms of both age and level of competition.

The studies conducted to test the age/maturity hypothesis indicate some support for the notion that increased age and/or athletic maturity affects the type of leadership behaviors preferred by athletes. However, these differences may be evident primarily in the earlier age ranges. Specifically, Terry and Howe (1984) administered the LSS to 160 athletes from a variety of sports ranging from 17 to 40 years of age. They found no age differences in regard to preferred coaching behavior. Similarly, Terry (1984) also found no age differences on the five factors of the LSS in a group of 160 athletes ranging in age from 17 to 28 years. In contrast, Chelladurai and Carron (1983), who used the LSS to measure preferred coaching behaviors among four groups of male basketball players (early high school, high school junior, high school senior, and university level), did find some age differences. Specifically, the preference for coaches who show high levels of socially supportive behavior and who exhibit an autocratic leadership style linearly increased across the four age/competitive levels. In regard to coaching behaviors associated with the training and instruction factor, Chelladurai and Carron reported that preference for this set of coaching behaviors decreased for athletes from early to senior high school level but then increased again at the university level. In an interesting discussion of these results, Chelladurai and Carron suggest that preference for an autocratic coaching style may increase with age and with athletic maturity because sport, as a social system, is generally an autocratic enterprise. Those athletes who remain in sport (i.e., those who progress through the various competitive levels) may become "socialized" into preferring less personal responsibility, thus allocating more control to coaches. Similarly, it may be hypothesized that athletes who prefer to retain personal responsibility for their behavior and who do not adapt to the autocratic coaching style may be selectively deleted from participation at the more elite competitive levels. Thus, the finding that preference for an autocratic coaching style increases with age and/or athletic maturity may not be so much a developmental phenomenon as it is an environmentally induced outcome. Chelladurai and Carron also speculate that the increased preference with age for a socially supportive coaching style may be due to the fact that older athletes who compete at more elite levels spend the greater proportion of their time in the sport context and thus need the social support from individuals in that environment. In contrast, younger athletes, who may spend more of their time outside of the athletic environment, obtain social support from other nonsport individuals and thus have less need to obtain such support from their coaches.

In summary, the results of the research examining age and maturity differences in preference for particular coaching behaviors suggest that these individual characteristics may certainly affect the type of coaching behaviors that will be more effective. However, age in these studies has been confounded with both level of competition (elite vs. novice) and years of sport experience. Thus, an accurate test of any of these factors has probably not yet been obtained.

Gender

Although Terry and Howe (1984) did not find gender differences in preferred coaching style in their sample of 17- to 40-year-old athletes, several other sets of researchers have reported quite consistent variation between male and female sport participants. Chelladurai and Saleh (1978) found that male physical education majors representing a variety of sports exhibited greater preference than their female peers for an autocratic coaching style, whereas the female participants indicated significantly greater performance than

the males for a democratic coaching style. In addition, the male students in this study exceeded their female peers in preference for social support from their coaches. Terry (1984) replicated the finding that male athletes tend to prefer an autocratic coaching style significantly more than do female athletes.

Consistent with the gender differences found in regard to preferred coaching style, two sets of researchers have also found similar gender differences in the type of decision-making style athletes prefer their coaches to use in sport contexts. Chelladurai and Arnott (1985) administered a decision style questionnaire to 144 female and male university-level basketball players to identify the type of decision-making style athletes would prefer their coaches to use in example sport situations. Comparison of male and female responses showed that female athletes were significantly more apt than their male peers to prefer a participatory style in which the coach allows the athletes to participate in the decision-making process. These gender differences were not, however, replicated in a later study by Chelladurai and colleagues (1989) with a similar sample of university-level basketball players. The male and female athletes in this study differed in their preferences for particular decision styles in only one of 32 problem-solving cases.

The results of this research suggest that there are some gender differences in regard to preferred coaching behaviors. Specifically, the male and female athletes differ in degree of preference for an autocratic versus a democratic leadership style. Of course, as Chelladurai and colleagues (1989) and Terry (1984) point out, an alternative perspective with regard to this research is that there are considerably more similarities between male and female athletes than differences in preferred coaching behavior. Although gender differences may occur, they are typically found only in regard to the coach's decision-making style (see chapter 7 for additional information). Certainly, further research is necessary to identify the reasons for such observed differences.

Nationality

According to the Challadurai model, the sociocultural prescriptions that characterize and differentiate between individual cultures may constitute a situational characteristic that will affect the type of leadership behavior that will be most effective. In testing this aspect of the model, three sets of researchers have compared athletes from different cultures in regard to their preferred coaching style. Terry (1984) administered the LSS to 160 elite athletes from 10 different sports and from several different countries.

He reported no differences in preferred coaching style as a function of nationality (United States, Great Britain, and Canada). However, Chelladurai and colleagues (1987, 1988) found significant differences between Japanese and Canadian subjects on several factors from the LSS. Chelladurai and colleagues (1987) administered the LSS to 156 male physical education students from a Canadian university and 106 male students from a Japanese university. The Japanese sample was comprised of students who participated in sports identified as modern (e.g., track-and-field, rugby, wrestling, volleyball, soccer) and those who participated in more traditional sport activities (e.g., judo, kendo, kyudo). The researchers speculated that the attitudes, beliefs, and values of the two disparate cultures would be reflected in the preferences of the subject sample for different types of leader behavior. In addition, however, they expected that *type of sport* (modern vs. traditional) might interact with culture to influence preferred leader behavior. Multivariate and univariate analyses of variance procedures using the five factors of the LSS showed that both groups of Japanese students showed more preference for social support than did the Canadian group. Japanese students engaged in modern sports showed greater preference than did the Canadian sample for a democratic coaching style. Consistent with the researchers' hypotheses, Japanese students from the traditional sports showed greater preference for an autocratic coaching style than did both the Japanese modern group and the Canadian group. Finally, Canadian students exhibited greater preference for positive feedback than did Japanese athletes from traditional sports. In a follow-up study, Chelladurai and colleagues (1988) compared 115 Japanese and 100 Canadian university-level male athletes on preferred coaching behaviors. These results showed that the Japanese athletes preferred a more autocratic coaching style and more social support from their coaches, whereas Canadian athletes preferred significantly more training and instruction.

The results of these studies support the hypothesis that sociocultural prescriptions can be identified and used to predict or explain differences between athletes from different cultures in regard to preferred coaching behaviors. However, as Chelladurai and colleagues (1987) found, the type of sport in which group members are involved may interact with culture to affect preferred coaching styles.

Type of Sport

The particular type of sport in which group members are engaged may also affect the leadership behaviors which will be most effective for that team. Based on concepts from both House's (House & Mitchell, 1974) path–goal theory and on Chelladurai's (1980) Multidimensional Model of Leadership, two particular task attributes have been identified as those which may be the most crucial in determining effective leadership behaviors across sports. These attributes include the degree of task variability inherent in the sport and the extent of cooperation necessary between group members. Task variability describes the environmental conditions under which sport tasks are performed. Sports classified as *open* include those in which the various skills are performed in a constantly changing environment (e.g., soccer, basketball, tennis, volleyball) whereas *closed* sports consist of those which are performed in a relatively stable, static, and unchanging environment (e.g., gymnastics, swimming, track-and-field). Sports can also be classified according to the degree of interdependency among group members that will be necessary for successful performance. Sports classified as interdependent include those in which successful performance outcomes depend on efficient interaction among teammates (e.g., basketball, soccer, hockey). In contrast, independent sports (e.g., tennis, swimming, gymnastics) are those which do not require interaction among team members.

These sport type characteristics have been examined with regard to their influence on preferred coaching behavior. Terry and Howe (1984) found no support for the hypothesis that athletes from open sports would differ in preferred coaching behaviors from their peers who participate in sports classified as closed. However, they did find support for the hypothesis that the degree of interdependency between group members will affect preferred coaching behavior. Specifically, athletes participating in sports that require interaction between group members (i.e., interdependent sports) showed greater preference for an autocratic coaching style and less preference for a democratic coaching style than did their peers who participated in independent (i.e., noninteracting) sports. Terry (1984), in a subsequent study with an additional sample of collegiate athletes, replicated this finding but also found that interdependent sport athletes showed greater preference for high frequencies of training and instruction and rewarding behavior from their coaches and less preference for democratic and social support behavior than did the independent sport athletes.

These results are consistent with the path–goal theory of leadership, which suggests that a highly structured leadership style will be necessary in situations where tasks are varied and interdependency among members is essential. However, in situations where tasks are not varied and where efficient interaction between group members is unnecessary, a highly structure leadership style will be unnecessary and perhaps undesired. Also, as Terry (1984) noted in his discussion, the greater preference of interdependent sport athletes for high frequencies of rewarding behavior may be a function of within-group competition (i.e., the individual athlete wants to be rewarded in front of her or his peers). Alternatively, because good performance by an individual athlete in interdependent sport contexts is not always immediately visible, such athletes may need rewarding behavior from their coaches more than do athletes from independent sports, where an individual's performance is more easily visible.

The results of this research on identification of preferred leadership styles provide very clear support for the situational approach to leadership effectiveness. According to these theories, the type of leadership behaviors that will be most effective will vary as a function of the situation. More specifically, Chelladurai's (1980) sport-oriented model of leadership specifies that the characteristics of the group members (e.g., age, gender), in combination with the dictates of the situation (e.g., sport type, sociocultural factors) will determine the type of leadership behaviors that will be most effective. The results of the research just reviewed provide support for these theories. In the next section, the hypothesized connection between preferred and actual coaching behaviors and various indexes of performance and group satisfaction will be examined.

Relationship Between Leadership Style and Positive Outcomes

According to Chelladurai's model of leadership, optimal performance and satisfaction on the part of athletes will result if the particular leadership behaviors exhibited by the coach are congruent with the leadership behaviors the athletes prefer their coaches to exhibit and with the behaviors required by, or appropriate to, the particular sport situation. In attempting to test this hypothesized connection between actual, preferred, and required leadership behaviors and the positive outcomes of performance and satisfaction, most researchers have followed Chelladurai's (1984) lead in conceiving satisfaction to be a multifaceted construct incorporating satisfaction with a number of aspects of the sport environment, including individual personal performance, team performance, the type of leadership, and overall

team climate. The satisfaction construct has typically been measured by administering a Likert-style questionnaire in which athletes are asked to indicate the degree of satisfaction they feel with regard to each of the facets mentioned. Although fewer researchers have attempted to measure performance as a possible outcome of effective leadership, those who have done so have used

- team win–loss percentage (e.g., Weiss & Friedrichs, 1986),
- amount of playing time/starter status (Garland & Barry, 1988), or
- individualized perceived performance outcomes (e.g., Chelladurai et al., 1988; Horne & Carron, 1985).

The results of the research conducted to test the relationship between satisfaction/performance and leader behavior have provided general support for Chelladurai's model. Chelladurai (1984), for example, who administered both the perceived and preferred versions of the LSS to a sample of 196 university athletes, found that the discrepancy between these two sets of variables (i.e., perceived coaching behaviors subtracted from preferred coaching behaviors) explained a greater percentage of the variance in athletes' satisfaction scores than did either of the two sets of variables alone. In particular, the discrepancy scores representing the leadership behaviors of (a) training and instruction and (b) positive feedback were the two dimensions of coaches' behavior that most affected the athletes' level of satisfaction. Subsequent studies conducted by Schliesman (1987) and Horne and Carron (1985) with university-level athletes demonstrated additional support for the relationship between the discrepancy scores representing training and instruction, positive feedback, and social support and measures of athletes' satisfaction with the coaches' leadership. In contrast, Chelladurai and colleagues (1988), who investigated leadership issues with Japanese and Canadian athletes, reported that the perceived (actual) leadership scores explained a greater amount of the variance in athletes' satisfaction scores than did the discrepancy scores. Nevertheless, the combined results of these studies do suggest some support for the notion that the discrepancy between actual and preferred leadership behaviors can be used to predict the degree of satisfaction athletes will express with regard to their coach's leadership style. More particularly, it appears that the leadership behaviors associated with training and instruction, positive feedback, and social support are most highly correlated with athlete satisfaction.

These studies provided general support for the interactive effects of actual and preferred leader behaviors on the positive outcome measure of group satisfaction. In addition, however, research results reported by Chelladurai and colleagues (Chelladurai, 1984; Chelladurai et al., 1988) provide clear evidence that situational factors must also be taken into account in describing the leader behavior and group satisfaction relationship. Specifically, Chelladurai (1984) found that the relationship between member satisfaction and particular leadership discrepancy scores varied according to sport type (independent vs. interdependent, open vs. closed); that is, the leadership discrepancy scores that were identified as highly predictive for satisfaction among basketball athletes were not necessarily the same as those that were predictive of satisfaction among wrestlers and track-and-field athletes. In addition, Chelladurai and colleagues (1988) reported similar differences between Japanese and Canadian athletes in regard to the relationship between leadership variables and athlete satisfaction. Although a significant overall relationship between preferred leader behaviors and satisfaction scores was found for both groups of athletes, the particular leader behaviors that were most predictive differed somewhat across the groups. Although some of the differences obtained in these two studies can be attributed to clearly identifiable aspects of the situation (i.e., characteristics of the sport tasks and varying sociocultural prescriptions), other differences between sport types and cultures cannot be readily explained. Thus, future research in this area is certainly warranted.

In an expansion of the previous research, Weiss and Friedrichs (1986) incorporated several additional constructs from the Chelladurai model into their study conducted with 251 collegiate male basketball players and their coaches. Specifically, these researchers tested the model's hypothesized connection between coaches' personal characteristics (age at time of hire, previous playing and coaching experience, prior win–loss record), coaches' leadership behaviors (as measured through athletes' perceptions of such behavior), selected situational factors (enrollment size of school, amount of basketball budget, amount of scholarships, prior winning tradition, percent of coach's appointment), and the positive outcomes of member satisfaction and performance. The outcome variables were measured in terms of seasonal win–loss records and athletes' self-reported satisfaction with various dimensions of their sport environment (e.g., playing conditions, teammates, amount of work, school identification, coaches' leadership). Regression analyses indicated some support for the hypothesis that certain coaching behaviors would be linked to member satisfaction. In particular, high frequencies of rewarding behavior, social support, and a democratic decision-making style on the part of coaches were associated with high satisfaction among their athletes. In contrast, only one leader behavior dimension was associated with team win–loss percentage. Specifically, high frequencies of social support were correlated with poorer performance records. In addition, certain coach attributes including age at time of hire, previous win–loss records, and amount of playing experience were related to athlete satisfaction; that is, coaches hired at younger ages and those with better previous win–loss records but less playing experience were associated with higher levels of satisfaction among athletes. These results again provide support for the interacting nature of situational and personal factors in the prediction of leadership effectiveness.

In a somewhat different analysis of leadership effectiveness, Gordon (1988) administered a decision style questionnaire to 161 male intercollegiate soccer athletes and 18 of their coaches. Athletes were asked to identify which decision style (autocratic, consultative, participative, or delegative) they preferred their coach to use in each of 15 different situations and which style they thought their coach would actually use. Coaches were asked to indicate the decision style they would use in each of the 15 situations. Athletes also completed a coaching effectiveness questionnaire, which measured their satisfaction with various aspects of their coach's behavior. Correlational analyses of these sets of data revealed strong support for the hypothesis that discrepancy between actual and preferred decision-making styles will result in decreased satisfaction among athletes. When there was high congruence between a coach's self-reported decision style and that preferred and perceived by athletes, then high ratings of the coach's effectiveness were also reported.

Cumulative Results

In general, the combined results of the empirical research on leadership styles in the sport domain have indicated consistent support for a situational approach to the study of leadership effectiveness. Furthermore, consistent with the tenets proposed in Chelladurai's sport-oriented multidimensional model of leadership, it does appear that situational factors and personal characteristics interact to determine the particular leadership behaviors that will be most effective in specific sport environments. Based on the research conducted to date, it appears that such characteristics of athletes as age, gender, and level of competition will affect both the type of leadership behaviors athletes prefer and the degree to which satisfaction will be attained. Several sets of researchers have also found that preferred leadership behaviors will vary as a function of such situational variables as sport type and sociocultural prescriptions.

Given the complexity of Chelladurai's model of leadership effectiveness and the limited amount of research which has been conducted to this point, considerably more questions remain to be answered. Specific directions for future research in this area will be provided in the following section.

Future Directions in Leadership Research

The review of the empirical research on leadership effectiveness detailed in the previous section has revealed some interesting and fairly consistent results concerning the leadership behaviors that are most effective in the sport domain. However, considerably more research will be needed before a clear picture of the impact of particular leadership styles on athletes can be obtained. The suggestions concerning future directions in leadership research have been divided into five major areas: measurement issues, identification of crucial situational and individual factors, overall model testing, alternative research paradigms, and alternative research contexts.

Measurement Issues

Perhaps no issue is so crucial to theory testing as the measurement of the constructs comprising the model. Very typically, theoretical models from the psychological literature are composed of fairly abstract constructs linked together in some prescribed way. In order to test the predicted or hypothesized linkages between these constructs, the researcher must first operationalize the constructs relative to the research setting and then identify and/or develop the instrumentation that will provide a measure of that construct. Obviously, the quality of the instrumentation will directly affect the researcher's ability to obtain a true test of the theoretical model. In regard to Chelladurai's model of leadership effectiveness, the two constructs that appear to be the most difficult to operationalize and measure are those identified as the multidimensional outcome variables (Figure 9.1, Box 7) and the three measures of coaching behavior (preferred, actual, required; Boxes 4, 5, and 6). Issues relating to the measurement of these constructs will be discussed in the following paragraphs.

Measurement of Coaching Behavior

The two instruments that have been specifically developed to assess the three aspects of coaching behavior incorporated in Chelladurai's model have, in general, been very carefully designed and constructed. In addition, psychometric testing of the LSS across several samples of subjects has consistently indicated stable factor structures, acceptable estimates of reliability over time, and acceptable estimates of internal item consistency. Despite this psychometric work, a couple of reservations remain about the reliability and validity of these measures of leadership behavior. First, it is important to note that the vast majority of the studies just reviewed were conducted with university-level athletes. Thus, it may not be surprising that adequate internal consistency and reliability have been obtained across these samples. Certainly, additional research is necessary to determine the applicability of these scales to other age groups and sport types. Chelladurai and his colleagues have begun work in this direction by examining the psychometric properties of the LSS with high school athletes (Chelladurai & Carron, 1981) and with Japanese university students and athletes (Chelladurai et al., 1987; Chelladurai et al., 1988). Continued work in this area is recommended.

Second, and perhaps more importantly, continued research is necessary to determine whether the various subscales comprising the LSS and the decision style questionnaires really capture the essential elements or dimensions of leadership behavior. It is always possible that the items and subscales comprising any instrument can be highly reliable and valid but not provide a sensitive measure of the crucial behaviors that will distinguish the effective from the noneffective leader/coach. Thus, continued research is necessary to ascertain what leader behaviors need to be incorporated into instruments assessing preferred and actual leader behaviors. To accomplish this objective, interview or open-ended survey studies with athletes and coaches from a wide variety of age groups and sport types will be needed to provide information relative to effective and ineffective leader behaviors. In addition, because the various items comprising the LSS and the decision style questionnaire are written in behavioral terms, observational field studies may be needed to determine whether or not there is an actual observable behavioral correlate for each of the factors comprising the leadership scales. In summary, as with any instrumentation, assessment of the reliability and validity of an instrument should be an ongoing process. Validity, in particular, can best be established only over time and on the basis of a variety of empirical research studies.

In addition to continuing research to determine the reliability and validity of existing instrumentation, it should also be pointed out that there are alternative ways to measure coaching behavior that may provide additional information relative to effective leadership. Specifically, in contrast to the LSS and the decision style questionnaires that measure coaching behavior through the use of a pencil-and-paper format, a variety of instruments have been developed within the last decade to directly measure various aspects of teachers' and/or coaches' behavior

in actual field contexts. These instruments are typically used by trained observers who attend selected class or athletic practice sessions and record the type of behavior exhibited by individual teachers or coaches. The usual format for these observational instruments is to code each coaching or teaching behavior into one or more categories. A compilation of the instrumentation systems that have been developed to measure coaching and teaching behavior has recently been made by Darst, Zakrajsek, and Mancini (1989).

Despite the widespread use of this type of instrumentation in the general educational literature and, to a lesser extent, in the physical education literature to investigate teaching effectiveness, relatively few researchers in the sport psychology literature have employed such behaviorally based scales to assess coaching effectiveness relative to athletes' psychological growth. The few who have done so (e.g., Horn, 1985; Smith, Zane, Smoll & Coppel, 1983; Smoll, Smith, Curtis & Hunt, 1978) have found that these scales can be used to discriminate between the effective and the ineffective coaching behaviors in particular athletic settings. Thus, these scales appear to be of considerable value to researchers who wish to test the theoretical linkages in Chelladurai's model of leadership effectiveness. However, a number of measurement issues will need to be considered if a valid and reliable assessment of coaching behavior is to be obtained. These issues will be briefly summarized in the next several paragraphs.

Frequency and timing of observational sessions. First, in order to obtain an accurate measure of an individual coach's actual behavior, the researcher must carefully schedule observational data collection sessions. Such careful planning is necessitated because coaches' behavior has been found to vary as a function of the context. Lacy and Darst (1985) have found, for example, that coaches' behavior varies as a function of time into the season; that is, a different pattern of feedback has been found for an individual coach depending on whether the measurement is conducted early or late in the athletic season. Similarly, other researchers have demonstrated that coaches' behavior in games differs considerably from their behavior in practices (Horn, 1985; Wandzilak, Ansorge & Potter, 1988). Finally, Lacy and Darst (1985) have shown that observational measures of coaches' behavior varied as a function of the segment of practice (e.g., warm-up activities, conditioning activities, group work, teamwork) that was observed. Given such variability in an individual coach's behavior across both time and context, it is obvious that the reliability of the observational data obtained is dependent upon careful selection of observation sessions.

General-versus-specific referent coding.   To obtain an accurate measure of the relationship between certain types of feedback and players' performance and/or psychological growth, researchers will probably need to record the coach's feedback as provided to individual athletes rather than without reference to the recipient. This recommendation is made based on considerable research demonstrating that coaches do not exhibit the same behaviors or provide the same type of feedback to all athletes on their team. Several studies have found, for example, that coaches give different forms of feedback to their high-ability players than they do to their low-ability athletes (Horn, 1984; Rejeski, Darracott & Hutslar, 1979). Similarly, Markland and Martinek (1988) have found that coaches' feedback differs as a function of starting/nonstarting player status. Certainly other factors such as athletes' gender and/or team position may also affect the type of feedback they receive from their coaches. Researchers who measure a coach's behavior by categorizing or coding feedback without regard to the individual player to whom that feedback statement is directed will get an accurate assessment of the coach's general behavior to her or his team but will not be able to differentiate among the types of feedback received by individual athletes on the team. Certainly, in some cases, measurement of the coach's feedback patterns without reference to the recipient of that feedback may be acceptable research procedure. For research studies, however, where the relationship between coaches' feedback and players' performance and/or psychological responses is being tested, it may be of most value to use the athlete as the unit of coding and data analyses.

Sensitivity of observational system.   In evaluating the quality of the various observational instruments or in selecting the appropriate one to use in any particular research study, most researchers use reported reliability and validity results as the major criteria by which to judge an observational instrument. One other criterion that should also be considered important is the ability of any instrument to adequately measure the aspects of coaches' behavior or feedback patterns that will discriminate between effective and ineffective coaches; that is, any particular observational instrument could be demonstrated to be highly reliable and valid but still not be sensitive enough to measure the aspects of feedback that

will have the most impact on individual athletes. For example, many of the available instruments assess a coach's or teacher's effective use of praise by measuring the frequency with which praise or reinforcement is given as a response to players' performance. Yet, research has consistently shown that it is not the *frequency* of praise/reinforcement that is crucial to an individual's performance and/or psychological growth. Rather, it is the *quality* (e.g., contingency, specificity, appropriateness) of the praise that will have the most impact on a performer's physical and psychological responses (Brophy, 1981; Chaumeton & Duda, 1988; Horn, 1987; Neapolitan, 1988). Thus, researchers who use observational procedures to measure a coach's behavior must be sure that the instrument they use is actually measuring the crucial aspects of coaching behavior. There are at least two potential ways to develop an observational scale or instrument that will be sensitive to the important aspects of coaching behavior. First, the researcher could carefully review the research and theory from such relevant areas as social, developmental, and clinical psychology in an attempt to identify the particular aspects of an adult's behavior that appear to have the most impact on children's performance and psychological growth. Elsewhere (Horn, 1987), I have outlined three such dimensions of adult behavior. Ideally, then, these identified components would be incorporated into an observational scale (e.g., Chaumeton & Duda, 1988). A second possible procedure to identify the essential elements of a coach's behavior would be to interview or survey a large sample of athletes in a particular target group to identify the coaching behaviors they believe have the most impact on their performance and/or psychological growth. Again, this information could then be incorporated into an observational scale. Observational instruments that have not been developed using these or similar procedures may not be sensitive enough to discriminate between effective and ineffective coaches.

In summary, then, the accuracy and reliability of the results obtained from observational studies of coaches' behavior in field contexts are dependent upon

- the type of instrument used to code/record coaches' behavior,
- the procedures used to collect and record the observational data, and
- the ability of the instrument to measure the crucial coaching behaviors.

If these issues are taken into consideration, then observational measures of coaching behavior may provide a unique contribution to the current

Sports File/Scott Smith

research on leadership effectiveness in the sport domain.

Again, consistent with the recommendations offered in chapter 2, it must be emphasized that these observational instruments are not necessarily better or worse than the questionnaire-style instruments developed by Chelladurai and his colleagues. Rather, it is only through the use of diverse measurement systems and research paradigms that a comprehensive understanding of leadership effectiveness can be obtained.

Measurement of Leadership Effectiveness

According to Chelladurai's model of sport leadership, the effectiveness of a coach's behavior or leadership style can be assessed by measuring two multidimensional constructs. These include athletic performance and group satisfaction. More specifically, Chelladurai suggested that high degrees of congruency among the behaviors exhibited by a coach, the leader behaviors preferred by the athletes, and the leader behaviors required for the particular sport situation should result in optimal performance and high group satisfaction on the part of the athletes. Researchers who have attempted to test these hypotheses have typically measured satisfaction through administration of survey or questionnaire forms and performance through either team win–loss percentages (Weiss & Friedrichs, 1986) or perceived relative performance (i.e., perceptions of performance relative to what was expected; Challedurai et al., 1988; Horne & Carron, 1985). The combined results of these studies have indicated quite consistent support for the linkage

between congruency of leader behaviors and satisfaction experienced by the athletes. In contrast, very little support has been found for the linkage from leader behavior to team and individual performance. However, at this point, it cannot yet be concluded that the various measures of leader behavior are unrelated to athletes' performance, because adequate measures of the performance construct may not yet have been obtained. As several writers have noted, team win–loss records may not be an adequate measure to use in the assessment of effective leadership styles because win–loss records are affected by so many factors other than the coach's or the athletes' behaviors (Chelladurai, 1984; Horne & Carron, 1985). Similarly, perceived performance may also not provide an accurate measure of the performance construct. Thus, future researchers will need to develop more sensitive measures of performance outcomes if an adequate test of the connection between leader behavior and athletic performance is to be obtained. Potential solutions may involve measurement of athletes' skill improvement over a season (i.e., pre-season/post-season skill testing) or perhaps the deviation of actual performance outcomes from expected outcomes (see the discussion of performance measurement in chapter 6). Whatever the solution to the problem of performance measurement, however, continued research is needed to test the impact of leader behaviors on athletes' performance in sport contexts.

As noted earlier, the satisfaction construct has typically been measured via self-report questionnaire or survey forms. Although psychometric assessment of some of these questionnaires has indicated some support for the validity and reliability of this type of instrument, further research is certainly necessary to identify the factors that actually underlie athletes' satisfaction with the coach's leadership and the sport environment and to develop the instruments that can provide an adequate measure of such factors.

Finally, although Chelladurai's model specifies only two positive outcomes (performance and satisfaction) of effective leader behavior, there certainly may be additional ways to assess leadership effectiveness. Specifically, based on research and theory from the educational and social psychology literature (e.g., Brophy, 1983; Butler, 1987; Perry & Magnusson, 1989), it can be suggested that various dimensions of the coach's behavior can also affect the athletes' psychological responses; that is, effective leadership behavior may also result in such positive psychological outcomes as high motivation, high self-confidence, an internal locus of control, and optimal levels of anxiety on the part of the athletes.

In the sport setting as well, a few researchers (e.g., Horn, 1985; Smith et al., 1983; Smoll et al., 1978) have found that the type of feedback that coaches give to athletes in response to their performance does affect the athletes' perceptions of themselves and their physical abilities. Similarly, laboratory studies (e.g., Petruzzello & Corbin, 1988; Stewart & Corbin, 1988; Vallerand & Reid, 1984) have also supported the value of adult feedback in facilitating performers' perceptions of competence and confidence at physical activity tasks. Thus, the particular variables used to establish leadership effectiveness may be considerably greater than that hypothesized by Chelladurai and colleagues. Certainly, then, it could be recommended that leadership effectiveness could or perhaps should be operationalized in multidimensional ways in future research studies.

An interesting corollary to this multidimensional perspective of leadership effectiveness is that the interaction of these various outcome measures may be of as much interest as their combined effect; that is, it is possible that the leader behaviors found to be facilitative of athletes' performance in any particular sport context may not be effective leader behaviors with regard to the facilitation of athletes' satisfaction and psychological growth. This possibility is evidenced in the results reported by Weiss and Friedrichs (1986). Their analyses shows that the leadership behavior identified as social support was positively linked to satisfaction but negatively linked to win–loss records. Again, future research is needed either to verify or to dispute the opposing effects of particular leadership behaviors on athletes' performance and satisfaction.

Identification of Crucial Situational and Individual Factors

Previous research has established that such individual factors as the athletes' age and gender and such situational factors as sport type and culture do affect athletes' preferences for particular leadership behaviors. However, continued research is necessary to (a) describe more accurately the contribution of these situational and individual factors to leadership effectiveness and (b) identify additional athlete characteristics and situational factors that contribute to the prediction of effective leadership behaviors.

Although age has been examined in several studies as a potential factor mediating the leadership effectiveness phenomenon, these studies have typically confounded age with years experience and/or competitive level. Thus, it cannot be said with any certainty that the consistently observed increase, with age, in preference for autocratic leader behavior, a socially supportive coaching style, and high emphasis on training and instruction is actually due to developmental changes (i.e., changes associated with cognitive, physical, and emotional maturity). This confounding of age, years experience, increased skill level, and competitive level is very typical in all areas of sport psychology research. Because age is so highly correlated with years of sport experience, level of skill ability, and level of competition (novice vs. elite), what has been identified through either longitudinal or cross-sectional research as age-related changes in any psychological or performance variable may, in fact, be due to the other identified factors. Thus, continued research is necessary to separate out the effects of each of the variables identified. To accomplish this objective, more sophisticated statistical analyses could be used. Alternatively—and perhaps preferably—subject samples could be more carefully selected so that various combinations of groupings could be compared. For example, in large age-group soccer programs, it is typical to find that the athletes in each of the age groups are divided by gender, skill ability, and/or competitive level. For example, the 11- and 12-year-old boys and girls may be divided into teams on the basis of gender, level of skill, and competitive intensity, an organizational practice that results in high ability—high competitive boys and girls teams, and lower ability—low competitive boys and girls teams. Access to such subject samples would facilitate the ability of the researcher to separate out the effects of age, gender, skill level, and competitive level. In addition, since chronological age may not be the best indicator of maturity, it would also be ideal if the variable designated as age could be assessed through more sensitive biologically or cognitively based measures (e.g., skeletal age or cognitive indicators of maturity).

From a different perspective, it is also necessary to test the interaction of the various individual and situational factors (e.g., age, gender, cultural differences, sport type) that have been identified as mediators of preferred leader behavior. Due to relatively small sample sizes, it has been difficult for previous researchers to conduct multiple-factor ANOVAs (or MANOVAs). Thus, the various athlete comparisons (e.g., male vs. female, younger vs. older, team vs. individual sport) have often been conducted separately. In actuality, the interaction of these factors may be of greater research interest. For example, some researchers in the developmental and sport psychology literatures have recently noted that gender differences in regard to various psychological characteristics (e.g., attributional patterns, self-confidence, perceived competence) may not occur until during puberty or even postpuberty (Phillips, 1987; Stevenson & Newman, 1986; Stewart & Corbin, 1988). Thus, few gender differences may be found before the age of 12 or 13 years. In regard to leadership effectiveness, age may also interact with gender to affect preferred leader behaviors. Similarly, sport type may interact with level of competition and/or age; that is, differences between athletes from independent and interdependent sports may be evident only at higher levels of competition (elite) and/or within older age ranges. In support of this interactional perspective, it may be important to note that Chelladurai and colleagues (1987) found that cultural differences in preferred leader behavior interacted with type of sport (traditional vs. modern). Future researchers will need to test for such potential interactions. To identify and/or describe the various interactions, large-scale studies with increased sample sizes will again be needed so that multiple-factor ANOVAs or MANOVAs can be run to test for main as well as interaction effects.

In addition to clarification of the contributions provided by individual and situational factors already identified, continued research is necessary to examine additional factors that may mediate leadership effectiveness. The research conducted to date has only begun to identify the characteristics of athletes and coaches that may impinge on actual and preferred leader behaviors. Application of research and theory from the educational psychology literature—which has demonstrated that certain psychological characteristics of students (e.g., trait anxiety, locus of control, perceived competence) affect what type of teacher behavior will be most effective (e.g., Harpin & Sandler, 1979; Pascarella & Pflaum, 1981; Peterson, 1977; Solomon & Kendall, 1976) —would lead to the hypothesis that the same psychological characteristics may affect leadership effectiveness in the sport domain as well. Horn and Glenn (1988) recently tested this notion and found support for the connection between athletes' psychological characteristics and their preference for particular coach behaviors. Specifically, athletes with an internal perception or locus of control showed strong preference for coaches who excelled in training and instruction behaviors. In contrast, athletes with an external perception of control showed a preference for coaches who exhibited an autocratic leadership style. Interestingly, however, gender interacted with these psychological characteristics, for female athletes who were classified as high-competitive-trait-anxious showed very strong pref-erence for coaches who provided positive, supportive, and informational feedback. In contrast, male athletes' level of trait anxiety did not affect their preference for particular coaching behaviors. These results provide initial support for the notion that athletes' psychological characteristics may affect the type of leadership behavior they will prefer. Further research may identify additional psychological characteristics (e.g., self-confidence, intrinsic/extrinsic motivational orientation, achievement goal orientation) that will affect athletes' preferences for particular leadership behaviors.

Finally, one aspect of Chelladurai's model that has received very little research attention is the hypothesized connection between a coach's personal characteristics and her or his exhibited leadership behavior. According to Chelladurai, the particular leadership styles or behaviors that an individual coach chooses to exhibit in a sport context may actually be a function of certain identifiable personal characteristics of that coach (e.g., age, gender, years experience, locus of control, trait anxiety). General support for this hypothesis can be found in the educational psychology literature where researchers have demonstrated that such teacher characteristics as self-efficacy and locus of control do affect their behavior in the classroom (Gibson & Dembo, 1984; Phillips, Carlisle, Hautala & Larson, 1985; Rose & Medway, 1981; Saklofske, Michayluk & Randhawa, 1988). Comparable research in the sport domain has not been reported. Weiss and Friedrichs (1986) did measure certain personal characteristics in their sample of college basketball coaches (e.g., age at hire, years of coaching and playing experience, prior win–loss record, percent appointment) but assessed the impact of these coach characteristics on athletes' satisfaction rather than on the coach's actual leadership behavior. Although Weiss and Friedrichs did find some significant relationships between the coach's age, degree of playing experience, and prior win–loss record and the satisfaction reported by the athletes, the predictor variables in combination explained only 9.3% of the variation in the satisfaction measures. In all likelihood, a greater percentage of variance in the outcome scores would be explained if additional coach characteristics (e.g., trait anxiety, locus of control) were added to the regression equation and if the intervening variables (i.e., measures of the coach's actual behavior) were also measured. Additional comments concerning the value of research in this area will be provided later.

As was noted at the outset, one of the primary strengths of Chelladurai's model is the underlying notion that leadership effectiveness is context-specific. In other words, the leadership behaviors and/or styles that are identified as effective in one sport context may not be so identified in a different sport context. Furthermore, Chelladurai specifically incorporates into his model specifications for identifying the situational and/or individual characteristics that will interact to determine effective leadership behaviors. In contrast to this notion of context-specificity, previous research in related areas of coaching effectiveness (e.g., feedback patterns) has been conducted under the implicit assumption that there should be one set of coaching behaviors that would be effective across all contexts. As I have argued elsewhere (Horn, 1987), this is an unreasonable assumption, given demonstrated cognitive, behavioral, and motivational differences in subjects as a function of age, gender, skill level, and psychological profiles. Researchers in other areas of exercise science (e.g., exercise physiology, biomechanics, motor control) have recognized the need for specificity of training (i.e., different training techniques for different sport skills). Sport psychologists must also recognize that such situational and interindividual differences will affect the results of our research. Thus, future researchers in the coaching behavior area should not be disappointed when they obtain results inconsistent with those of previous researchers. Rather, they should examine the contexts within which the studies were conducted (i.e., the type of subjects and sport) to identify why such differences occurred. It is only when such factors are taken into account that a clearer understanding of leadership effectiveness can be obtained.

Overall Model Testing

The research conducted to date has provided considerable support for Chelladurai's Multidimensional Model of Leadership, which was adapted from the more general situational leadership theories. However, previous researchers who have examined the applicability of either the general leadership theories or Chelladurai's sport-oriented theory have basically tested only selected aspects of these models. For example, several sets of researchers have tested the link in Chelladurai's model between athlete characteristics and their preferences for particular leadership styles. Other researchers have tested the combined impact of actual and preferred leader behaviors on athletes' performance and satisfaction. To date, a test of Chelladurai's model as a whole has not been reported. It would certainly require a fairly large sample of subjects because the number of variables to be tested

would be extensive. In addition, more sophisticated statistical analyses would need to be used. Specifically, path analysis and/or causal modeling techniques would provide the statistical expertise necessary to test the efficacy of the various paths specified in Chelladurai's model (see Figure 9.1). Because this type of extensive model testing is necessarily dependent upon the identification of an extensive list of crucial situational and personal characteristics, and the development of reliable and valid instrumentation, it will not be an easy task. Nevertheless, due to the complexity of the model and the sequential nature of the proposed linkages, a true test of the model will require such a research effort.

Alternative Research Paradigms

In general, the research studies reviewed, although varying somewhat in conceptual design, instrumentation, and analysis of data, have employed the same basic research methodology. Specifically, these studies have taken a quantitative research approach in which the variables of interest were measured through the administration of questionnaires or through the use of observational analysis of behavior. Although this is certainly a legitimate and ultimately valuable approach to the study of leadership effectiveness, it is not the only way to examine a particular research issue. The application of a variety of research paradigms and methodologies to a single research problem will result in the most complete and rich picture of that particular issue (see chapter 2). Thus, the results of the research obtained to date will be most valuable when combined with additional information about leadership effectiveness that can be acquired through alternative research designs. Such alternative designs could include qualitative data collection methodologies (e.g., participation–observation field studies, case studies), as well as the more experimental laboratory-based study designs. Thus, it is strongly recommended that future researchers consider the use of such alternative research approaches.

Alternative Research Contexts

The discussion in this chapter has focused exclusively on leadership in the sport context. More particularly, the emphasis has been on the leadership behavior of the coach as the primary team leader. Future researchers, however, should be encouraged to expand this area of study to include other physical activity contexts and other types of group leadership. In regard to other types of leaders, for example, Chelladurai's (1980) Multidimensional Model of Leadership could be used to study peer group leadership. In the sport domain, this would include team captains or other peer group leaders. A few researchers (e.g., Glenn, Horn, Dewar & Vealey, 1988; Yukelson, Weinberg, Richardson & Jackson, 1981) have recently begun examining the characteristics of athletes who emerge as team leaders and have found results consistent with the situational approach to leadership effectiveness. However, research in this area is clearly just beginning, and many more questions remain about effective peer group leadership.

Similarly, it would also be of interest to examine leadership effectiveness in such nonsport physical activity contexts as exercise and rehabilitative movement programs. As Franklin (1988) noted in his review of program factors that influence adherence to exercise programs, the behavior of the exercise leader may be the single most important variable affecting exercise compliance. Although a number of general competencies and behavioral strategies have been identified as important for an exercise group leader (see Franklin, 1988), it certainly could be hypothesized that effective leadership in the exercise domain, as in the sport domain, may be situation-specific. Thus, Chelladurai's (1980) model could profitably be applied to the study of effective leadership in exercise, as in many other nonsport physical activity settings.

Conclusion

The review of the research on leadership effectiveness which was provided in this chapter has revealed considerable support for the notion that the type of leadership behavior exhibited by a coach will have a significant impact on the athletes' performance and psychological well-being. From a theoretical perspective, this review has also indicated consistent support for a situationally based approach to the study of leadership effectiveness; that is, the particular leadership behaviors that will be most effective will vary as a function of the characteristics of the coach and her or his athletes and of factors within the sport context.

Given such context specificity with regard to the correlates of leadership effectiveness, it is obvious that the course of future research lies in the identification of the crucial individual and environmental factors that will affect leadership behavior. The research that has been conducted to date has certainly provided some valuable information concerning selected individual and environmental factors. However, much work remains to be done. Given the demonstrated influence of adult behaviors on the performance and psychological growth of athletes, such work appears to be well justified.

References

Barrow, J. (1977). The variables of leadership: A review and conceptual framework. *Academy of Management Review,* **2**, 231-251.

Bird, A.M. (1977). Development of a model for predicting team performance. *Research Quarterly,* **48**, 24-32.

Brophy, J. (1981). Teacher praise: A functional analysis. *Review of Educational Research,* **51**, 5-32.

Brophy, J. (1983). Conceptualizing student motivation. *Educational Psychologist,* **18**, 200-215.

Butler, R. (1987). Task-involving and ego-involving properties of evaluation: Effects of different feedback conditions on motivational perceptions, interest, and performance. *Journal of Educational Psychology,* **79** , 474-482.

Chaumeton, N., & Duda, J. (1988). Is it how you play the game or whether you win or lose? The effect of competitive level and situation on coaching behaviors. *Journal of Sport Behavior,* **11**, 157-174.

Chelladurai, P. (1980). Leadership in sports organizations. *Canadian Journal of Applied Sport Sciences,* **5**, 226-231.

Chelladurai, P. (1984). Discrepancy between preferences and perceptions of leadership behavior and satisfaction of athletes in varying sports. *Journal of Sport Psychology,* **6**, 27-41.

Chelladurai, P., & Arnott, M. (1985). Decision styles in coaching: Preferences of basketball players. *Research Quarterly for Exercise and Sport,* **56**, 15-24.

Chelladurai, P., & Carron, A. (1978). *Leadership.* Canadian Association for Health, Physical Education and Recreation Sociology of Sport Monograph Series A, Calgary, AB: University of Calgary.

Chelladurai, P., & Carron, A. (1981). Applicability to youth sports of the Leadership Scale for Sports. *Perceptual and Motor Skills,* **53**, 361-362.

Chelladurai, P., & Carron, A. (1983). Athletic maturity and preferred leadership. *Journal of Sport Psychology,* **5**, 371-380.

Chelladurai, P., & Haggerty, T. (1978). A normative model of decision-making styles in coaching. *Athletic Administration,* **13**, 6-9.

Chelladurai, P., Haggerty, T., & Baxter, P. (1989). Decision style choices of university basketball coaches and players. *Journal of Sport and Exercise Psychology,* **11**, 201-215.

Chelladurai, P., Imamura, H., Yamaguchi, Y., Oinuma, Y., & Miyauchi, T. (1988). Sport leadership in a cross-national setting: The case of Japanese and Canadian university athletes. *Journal of Sport and Exercise Psychology,* **10**, 374-389.

Chelladurai, P., Malloy, D., Imamura, H., & Yamaguchi, Y. (1987). A cross-cultural study of preferred leadership in sports. *Canadian Journal of Sport Sciences,* **12**, 106-110.

Chelladurai, P., & Saleh, S. (1978). Preferred leadership in sports. *Canadian Journal of Applied Sport Sciences,* **3**, 85-92.

Chelladurai, P., & Saleh, S. (1980). Dimensions of leader behavior in sports: Development of a leadership scale. *Journal of Sport Psychology,* **2**, 34-45.

Darst, D., Zakrajsek, D., & Mancini, V. (1989). *Analyzing physical education and sport instruction* (2nd ed.). Champaign, IL: Human Kinetics.

Fiedler, F. (1967). *A theory of leadership effectiveness.* New York: McGraw-Hill.

Franklin, B. (1988). Program factors that influence exercise adherence: Practical adherence skills for the clinical staff. In R.K. Dishman (Ed.), *Exercise adherence: Its impact on public health* (pp. 237-258). Champaign, IL: Human Kinetics.

Garland, D., & Barry, J. (1988). The effects of personality and perceived leader behaviors on performance in collegiate football. *Psychological Record, 38*, 237-247.

Gibson, S., & Dembo, M. (1984). Teacher efficacy: A construct validation. *Journal of Educational Psychology, 76*, 569-582.

Glenn, S., Horn, T., Dewar, A., & Vealey, R. (1988, June). *Psychological predictors of leadership behavior in female soccer athletes*. Paper presented at the meeting of the North American Society for the Psychology of Sport and Physical Activity, Knoxville, TN.

Gordon, S. (1988). Decision styles and coaching effectiveness in university soccer. *Canadian Journal of Sport Sciences, 13*, 56-65.

Harpin, P., & Sandler, I. (1979). Interaction of sex, locus of control, and teacher control: Toward a student–classroom match. *American Journal of Community Psychology, 7*, 621-632.

Hendry, L. (1969). A personality study of highly successful and "ideal" swimming coaches. *Research Quarterly, 40*, 299-305.

Hersey, P., & Blanchard, K. (1972). *Management of organization behavior*. Englewood Cliffs, NJ: Prentice-Hall.

Horn, T. (1984). Expectancy effects in the interscholastic athletic setting: Methodological considerations. *Journal of Sport Psychology, 6*, 60-76.

Horn, T. (1985). Coaches' feedback and changes in children's perceptions of their physical competence. *Journal of Educational Psychology, 77*, 174-186.

Horn, T. (1987). The influence of teacher–coach behavior on the psychological development of children. In D. Gould & M. Weiss (Eds.), *Advances in pediatric sport sciences* (pp. 121–142). Champaign, IL: Human Kinetics.

Horn, T., & Glenn, S. (1988, June). *The relationship between athletes' psychological characteristics and their preference for particular coaching behaviors*. Paper presented at the meeting of the North American Society for the Psychology of Sport and Physical Activity, Knoxville, TN.

Horne, T., & Carron, A. (1985). Compatibility in coach–athlete relationships. *Journal of Sport Psychology, 7*(2), 137-149.

House, R., & Mitchell, T. (1974). Path–goal theory of leadership. *Journal of Contemporary Business, 3*, 81-97.

Lacy, A., & Darst, P. (1985). Systematic observation of behaviors of winning high school head football coaches. *Journal of Teaching in Physical Education, 4*, 256-270.

Lenk, H. (1977). Authoritarian or democratic styled coaching? In H. Lenk (Ed.), *Team dynamics*. Champaign, IL: Stipes.

Markland, R., & Martinek, T. (1988). Descriptive analysis of coach augmented feedback given to high school varsity female volleyball players. *Journal of Teaching in Physical Education, 7*, 289-301.

Neapolitan, J. (1988). The effects of different types of praise and criticism on performance. *Sociological Focus, 21*, 223-231.

Pascarella, E., & Pflaum, S. (1981). The interaction of children's attribution and level of control over error correction in reading instruction. *Journal of Educational Psychology, 73*, 533-540.

Penman, K., Hastad, D., & Cords, W. (1974). Success of the authoritarian coach. *Journal of Social Psychology, 92*, 155-156.

Perry, R., & Magnusson, J.L. (1989). Causal attributions and perceived performance: Consequences for college students' achievement and perceived control in different instructional conditions. *Journal of Educational Psychology, 81*, 164-172.

Peterson, P. (1977). Interactive effects of student anxiety, achievement orientation, and teacher behavior on student achievement and attitude. *Journal of Educational Psychology, 69*, 779-792.

Petruzzello, S., & Corbin, C. (1988). The effects of performance feedback on female self-confidence. *Journal of Sport and Exercise Psychology, 10*, 174-183.

Phillips, D.A. (1987). Socialization of perceived academic competence among highly competent children. *Child Development, 58*, 1308-1320.

Phillips, D.A., Carlisle, C., Hautala, R., & Larson, R. (1985). Personality traits and teacher–student behaviors in physical education. *Journal of Educational Psychology, 77*, 408-416.

Pratt, S., & Eitzen, D.S. (1989). Contrasting leadership styles and organizational effectiveness: The case of athletic teams. *Social Science Quarterly, 70*, 311-322.

Rejeski, W., Darracott, C., & Hutslar, S. (1979). Pygmalion in youth sports: A field study. *Journal of Sport Psychology, 1*, 311-319.

Rose, J., & Medway, F. (1981). Measurement of teachers' beliefs in their control over student outcomes. *Journal of Educational Research, 74*, 185-190.

Saklofske, D., Michayluk, J., & Randhawa, B. (1988). Teachers' efficacy and teaching behaviors. *Psychological Reports, 63*, 407-414.

Schliesman, E. (1987). Relationship between the congruence of preferred and actual leader behavior and subordinate satisfaction with leadership. *Journal of Sport Behavior, 10*, 157-166.

Smith, R., Zane, N., Smoll, F., & Coppel, D. (1983). Behavioral assessment in youth sports: Coaching behaviors and children's attitudes. *Medicine and Science in Sports and Exercise, 15*, 208-214.

Smoll, F., Smith, R., Curtis, B., & Hunt, E. (1978). Toward a mediational model of coach–player relationships. *Research Quarterly for Exercise and Sport, 49*, 528-541.

Solomon, D., & Kendall, A. (1976). Individual characteristics and children's performance in "open" and "traditional" classroom settings. *Journal of Educational Psychology, 68*, 613-625.

Stevenson, H., & Newman, R. (1986). Long-term prediction of achievement attitudes in mathematics and reading. *Child Development, 57*, 646-659.

Stewart, M., & Corbin, C. (1988). Feedback dependence among low confidence preadolescent boys and girls. *Research Quarterly for Exercise and Sport, 59*, 160-164.

Terry, P. (1984). The coaching preferences of elite athletes competing at Universiade '83. *Canadian Journal of Applied Sport Sciences, 9*, 201-208.

Terry, P., & Howe, B. (1984). Coaching preferences of athletes. *Canadian Journal of Applied Sport Sciences, 9*, 188-193.

Vallerand, R., & Reid, G. (1984). On the causal effects of perceived competence on intrinsic motivation: A test of cognitive evaluation theory. *Journal of Sport Psychology, 6*, 94-102.

Vos Strache, C. (1979). Players' perceptions of leadership qualities for coaches. *Research Quarterly, 50*, 679-686.

Vroom, V., & Yetton, R. (1973). *Leadership and decision-making*. Pittsburgh: University of Pittsburgh Press.

Wandzilak, T., Ansorge, C., & Potter, G. (1988). Comparison between selected practice and game behaviors of youth sport soccer coaches. *Journal of Sport Behavior, 11*, 78-88.

Weiss, M., & Friedrichs, W. (1986). The influence of leader behaviors, coach attributes, and institutional variables on performance and satisfaction of collegiate basketball teams. *Journal of Sport Psychology, 8*, 332-346.

Yukelson, D., Weinberg, R., Richardson, P., & Jackson, A. (1981). Interpersonal attraction and leadership within collegiate sport teams. *Journal of Sport Behavior, 6*, 29-36.

Chapter 10

Sport Socialization

Susan L. Greendorfer
University of Illinois at Urbana-Champaign

Generally speaking, sport psychology has had only a passing interest in sport socialization either as a general or a specific area of research. This neglect is reflected by the literature in the field, which for the most part focuses on cognitive, social, and situational factors that relate to behavior or behavioral outcomes of athletes in sport and competition (Silva & Weinberg, 1984). Thus, instead of acknowledging the process of sport socialization per se, sport psychologists have pursued topical research areas that may have *implications* relative to outcomes or consequences of socialization. Although such research is worthy of attention, a topical approach tends to ignore the underlying significance of a fundamental social process that has been integrally linked (at least theoretically) to play, games, physical activity, and sport for several years (Mead, 1934; Piaget, 1965). In fact considerable writing in both psychology and sociology has been devoted to explanations of how such activities serve as a primary medium for teaching children fundamental concepts, ideas, norms, rules, and expectations of society (Brim & Wheeler, 1966; Clausen, 1968; Goslin, 1969; Mead, 1934; Piaget, 1965; Roberts & Sutton-Smith, 1962).

Despite the fact that such discussion is rare in sport psychology, theoretical perspectives from socialization could be used as viable frameworks when considering such topics as modeling and observational learning (Gould, 1978; Gould & Roberts, 1981; Landers & Landers, 1973), social reinforcement (Roberts & Martens, 1970; Rosenthal, 1973; Wankel, 1975), and motivation and competition (Roberts, 1984, 1986a, 1986b). Unfortunately, however, the trend to consider research findings as social facts contributing to very specific "packages of knowledge" about a specific topic or problem has been carried over to more recent research, because similar examples of this treatment can be found in studies of competitive stress (Smoll, 1986), teacher–coach influences (Horn, 1987), achievement motivation (Roberts, 1984), and attrition in sport (Gould, 1987). Despite occasional reference to the fact that each of these topics is related to some component of sport socialization and that sport may play an important role in the social development of children, sport psychologists have made very few attempts to integrate existing research into a coherent body of knowledge about the process of socialization in general or sport socialization in particular. Interest in sport socialization per se seems to be nonexistent.

In an effort to deal with this neglect, this chapter attempts to close the existing gap by providing the type of information that would make socialization a more appealing topic for sport psychologists. The purpose is to provide a general framework that explains how various social and psychological influences, when considered as aspects of the process of socialization, can lead to a greater understanding of *involvement and performance in physical activity*. Underlying this discussion is the assumption that sport involvement is determined by

- various *influence* processes,
- mechanisms and issues related to concepts of *identity*,
- the nature and quality of *interactions*, and
- *ideological* belief systems.

Each represents a vital consideration relative to the process of socialization. In addition, each of these general concepts relates to specific research topics in sport psychology. Thus, once socialization is described in general and then in reference to sport and physical activity, it could be possible to interpret existing research from a more integrated and holistic perspective.

As a means of moving toward such an objective this chapter first introduces general information about how socialization has been approached theoretically, then offers a general description of the nature of socialization and how it is accomplished. Also included are general definitions and assumptions that researchers have made about the process. Socialization into sport and socialization through sport are considered in separate sections. Although some research findings are summarized, the focus of discussion is on conceptual issues and problems that have facilitated or hindered our understanding of sport socialization. Finally, the chapter concludes with some suggestions as to how sport psychologists might pursue this topic in the future.

What Is Socialization?

Historically, the process of socialization has been systematically examined by three disciplines: psychology, sociology, and anthropology. In the field of psychology primary attention has been given to the development of individual characteristics as they are related to social behavior and the basic processes through which these behavioral tendencies are learned (Goslin, 1969). Although several different psychological approaches to socialization can be found in the literature (i.e., genetic, biological), two of the more popular are the psychoanalytic approach (emphasizing the importance of early life experiences for subsequent personality structure; see Freud, 1924; Miller, 1969) and the cognitive approach (emphasizing the development of children's cognitive structures; see Gerwitz, 1969; Kohlberg, 1966; Piaget, 1951; Zigler & Child, 1969). Regardless of perspective, however, it seems that psychological approaches are behavioristic in nature, focusing on the nature of the learning experience, identification processes, and the compatibility between the individual and her or his social environment (Goslin, 1969). Such considerations clearly draw attention to the relation between individual characteristics and attributes of the learner responding to his or her social environment in the process of acquiring behavioral, cognitive, and social skills.

Although sociologists have also been interested in common social skills acquired by individuals in varying contexts (Goslin, 1969), their primary interest has concentrated on characteristics of specific groups or institutions in which socialization occurs. For example, a good deal of research attention has been given to elements of social structure (Inkeles, 1968; Parsons & Bales, 1955; Rosenberg, 1957; Wheeler, 1966), the acquisition of social roles and role negotiation (Biddle & Thomas, 1966; Goffman, 1959; Mead, 1934; Merton, 1957; Sarbin & Allen, 1968; Stryker, 1959), expectations and interactions that take place between institutionalized settings and individuals and groups (Brim, 1966; Clausen, 1968), theories of learning and social learning (Bandura & Walters, 1963; Clausen, 1968; Miller & Dollard, 1941; Mowrer, 1960), and reference group theory (Kemper, 1968; Merton, 1957).

The field of anthropology, which considers socialization from the broad perspective of culture, focuses on transmission of culture between generations (Levine, 1969), the interaction between cultural beliefs and social experience (Brim, 1957; D'Andrade, 1966; Dornbusch, 1966), and the maintenance of cultural continuity. From this broad perspective the process of socialization is viewed as enculturation—the means by which beliefs, values, and the ways of society are communicated to individuals so that they can become culturally competent.

Whereas each discipline has developed different concepts and emphases (as the previous descriptions suggest), the major difference between them, as well as between perspectives within each discipline, lies in how each conceptualizes characteristics of the learner and how each views consequences of prior experiences. Although these differences in assumptions are basic because they reflect the degree of emphasis that comes from the external environment or from the learner him- or herself (Goslin, 1969), there are also a number of underlying assumptions that are similar. For example, each discipline theoretically assumes that socialization would not be possible without an extraordinary degree of *conformity*. In this sense conformity is considered with respect to commonly held expectations regarding what constitutes appropriate behaviors, attitudes, and values in a wide range of situations (Goslin, 1969). Secondly, each discipline assumes that *learning* takes place in a social setting and takes place in, or is influenced by, the presence of others. Interestingly, despite the fact that each discipline assumes that socialization is a *two-way interaction* in which both the socializing agent and the learner is influenced in the process of *learning roles*, the literature in each discipline fails to consider the reciprocal nature of the process. Virtually ignored in theoretical discussion or research is the potential for mutual influence, interdependence of interaction, and the bidirectional nature of social learning.

Also worth noting is the fact that although each discipline fundamentally differs in some way relative to assumptions pertaining to mechanisms or concepts, there are key theoretical points of agreement relative to consequences and global outcomes of socialization. For example, each discipline would agree theoretically that socialization plays a key role in *social integration*, the aim of which is to establish social ties and to teach individuals to behave in accordance with the expectations of others in the social order (Aberle, 1961; Clausen, 1968; Inkeles, 1968). As such, each would acknowledge that socialization is a social influence process mediated by individuals, groups, institutions, and cultural practices. Such agreement reflects a recognition of the fact that the process involves a rather complex dynamic between psychological, social, and cultural considerations of learning and development.

Although theoretical concepts from psychoanalytic, developmental, cognitive, genetic, maturational, and learning approaches have been applied to the process of socialization, a *social learning* perspective (Bandura, 1969; Bandura & Walters, 1963; McPherson, 1981) has offered some of the most useful contributions in terms of theoretical development and empirical findings. Based on social–psychological concepts of modeling, imitation, and vicarious learning—which assumes the presence, as well as the influence, of others—social learning stands in stark contrast to traditional stimulus–response learning. Instead of immediate practice, feedback, or direct reinforcement, social learning assumes that observed behaviors are assimilated and exhibited in appropriate situations (McPherson, 1981). Thus, an individual is socialized through the mechanisms of modeling, imitation, and vicarious learning. Although *role models* represent an important concept in social learning, such models do not necessarily have to be real (like Steffi Graf or Michael Jordan); they could be symbolic or imagined "characters," (like Wonder Woman, Jack Armstrong, or Batman). Another important consideration pertaining to role models is they need not have direct interaction with the observer; and more often than not, role models are unaware of their impact or influence.

Role theory is another critical component conceptually linked to social learning. This theory attempts to explain how individuals become functioning participants in society by assuming that established patterns of behavior are associated with social positions and social roles and that the content of learning encompasses acquisition of specific role skills that are performed in accordance with expected behaviors associated with social roles (Goslin, 1969; Sarbin & Allen, 1968). Although social learning places primary emphasis on what takes place during childhood, the paradigm assumes that the process impinges on individuals throughout the life cycle. Thus, a social learning orientation views socialization as a *continuous* process that entails the learning of multiple skills to be activated during the performance of a variety of roles (Brim, 1966; Clausen, 1968).

Given this brief description of the content and underlying assumptions of the general socialization process, we can now turn our attention to how the process relates to sport and physical activity.

What Is Sport Socialization?

Sport socialization research was closely linked with the development of sport sociology; during the late 1960s and early 1970s, considerable effort was made to explain various aspects of sport involvement (Kenyon, 1969; Kenyon & McPherson, 1973). Even though this research interest did not extend through the decade of the 1980s, the literature is replete with the numerous attempts to explain the

- *degree* of involvement (frequency, duration, and intensity),
- *kind* of involvement (actual vs. vicarious)
- *type* of involvement (affective, behavioral, or cognitive), and
- *form* of involvement (exercise, dance, physical activity, play, or sport).

Most of this research revolved around one of two issues: *antecedents* of physical activity involvement, that is, how individuals become involved in sport and physical activity (Greendorfer, 1977; Greendorfer & Lewko, 1978a, 1978b; Kenyon, 1970; Kenyon & McPherson, 1973; Laakso, 1978; Lewko & Greendorfer, 1988; McPherson, 1976, 1981; Snyder & Spreitzer, 1973, 1978; Spreitzer & Snyder, 1976) or *consequences* and outcomes of physical activity involvement (Duquin, 1977; Kenyon, 1968; Lever, 1976, 1978; Loy & Ingham, 1973; Roberts & Sutton-Smith, 1962; Snyder, 1970; Stevenson, 1975; Watson, 1977).

For the first topic (becoming involved in physical activity, or socialization *into* sport), researchers employed a social learning framework to examine factors and influences associated with learning various sport roles. Typically, research focused on active sport participation (the dependent variable) at the elite athlete level. Within this framework influence by significant others or reference groups (i.e., peers, teachers, family), as well as opportunity structure (i.e., availability of facilities, programs, equipment), took precedence over considerations of motivational, personality, and cognitive influences (the dependent variables) (Greendorfer, 1977; Greendorfer & Lewko, 1978a, 1978b; Hasbrook, 1986a; Hasbrook, Greendorfer & McMullen, 1981; Kenyon & McPherson, 1973; Lewko & Greendorfer, 1988; Snyder & Spreitzer, 1973).

Although closely connected, outcomes or socialization effects of sport and games (socialization *through* sport) have been consistently treated as if the topic was completely unrelated to the process of becoming involved in physical activity. For the most part, discussion in the literature has revolved around what individuals may or may not learn from their participation in play, games, or sport; and cause and effect relationships have been inferred from correlational studies (Dubois, 1986; Duquin, 1977; Greendorfer, 1987b; Lever, 1976, 1978; Loy & Ingham, 1973; Roberts & Sutton-Smith, 1962; Watson, 1977; Webb, 1969). Few, if any, studies have been concerned with an integral aspect of sport socialization, the dynamic nature of *how* outcomes are

learned; that is, instead of studying when or under what circumstances (i.e., the process by which) game playing may change or affect behavior, researchers have been content merely to cite differences in behavior after game playing and suggest by inference that specific types of games lead to or teach specific social behaviors. For example, based on observed sex differences in play style and organizational structure of games (e.g., role differentiation, interdependence between players, size of play group, explicitness of goals, and number of rules), some researchers have claimed that males are better prepared for leadership and managerial roles (Lever, 1976, 1978) and for participation in the competitive world of business, bureaucracy, economics, and politics (Webb, 1969). Despite the intuitively attractive appeal of these notions, researchers have not been concerned with the *mechanisms* by which these specific social political or economic skills are learned through game playing.

Another topic rarely considered from a perspective of sport socialization is that of sport withdrawal or sport retirement. Prior to the 1980s most information on sport retirement was anecdotal and based on journalistic accounts (McPherson, 1980), whereas that pertaining to dropouts focused either on descriptive patterns (Sapp & Haubenstricker, 1978) or purely motivational influences (Roberts, Kleiber & Duda, 1981). Recently, however, concepts of socialization have been applied to the process of leaving sport; and disengagement, whether voluntary (dropping out or retirement) or involuntary (being cut, participation-ending injury, or retirement) has been considered an aspect of "desocialization" (Brown, 1985; Greendorfer & Blinde, 1985; Hasbrook & Mingesz, 1987). While such a conceptualization offers promise for future research, at the present time, unfortunately, very few studies have considered retirement or dropping out within the context of socialization.

Given the issues raised thus far, then, if sport socialization were viewed along a continuum, the literature could be organized into considerations of

- becoming involved in physical activity or sport,
- staying involved or maintaining involvement, and
- leaving or disengaging from exercise, sport, or physical activity.

Each relates to consequences or learning outcomes from physical activity involvement. Regardless of the topic pursued or the specific research focus, however, it appears that the majority of research assumes some form of social learning, as well as some continuity in the process. What follows is a brief outline of some research findings and theoretical discussion of the two major categories of this research: socialization into sport and socialization through sport.

Socialization Into Sport

Theoretical and empirical studies pertaining to socialization into sport have attempted to explain how individuals acquire essential skills, knowledges, values, and dispositions to become a (sport) participant. Whether implicitly assumed or directly employed, the majority of studies have applied a general social learning paradigm representing three clusters of independent variables: personal attributes, socializing agents, and socializing situations. According to the theoretical depiction in Figure 10.1, these three clusters are viewed as *determinants*, or *causes*, of active sport participation.

Of the three clusters of independent variables, primary attention has been focused on influence of reference groups and significant others, that is, *agents of socialization* who because of their prestige, proximity, and power to distribute love, rewards, and punishment either consciously or unconsciously influence the sport socialization process (McPherson, 1981). Most studies identify family, peer group, teachers, coaches, and role models as major agents of sport socialization (Dubois, 1981; Greendorfer, 1977; Greendorfer & Lewko, 1978a; Higginson, 1985; Lewko & Ewing, 1981).

The personal attributes cluster has been virtually ignored; and, as previously indicated, with few expectations, neither aspects of personality, achievement motivation, perceptions of skill, nor

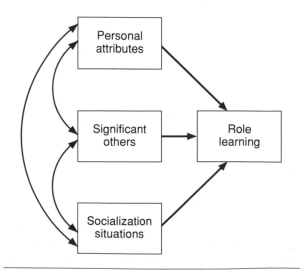

Figure 10.1 The three elements of the social learning paradigm.

the sport experience itself have been examined with any concerted effort toward linking empirical findings or theoretical discussions to a socialization framework. One notable exception is the work of Watson (1976, 1979, 1981, 1984; see also Watson, Blanksby & Bloomfield, 1983), who discussed socialization from a macro perspective, integrating notions of reward, achievement, competence-based models, and social motivation.

Similar to personal attributes influences, the cluster represented by socializing situations has also received very little empirical attention (see Yamaguchi, 1987). Despite the theoretical significance given to settings and situations, the context in which socialization takes place seems to have been ignored in most research studies. When examined, socializing situations seem to have been limited to availability of opportunities (Greendorfer, Blinde & Pellegrini, 1986; Greendorfer & Lewko, 1978b) rather than conceptually expanding the notion to include access to opportunities or ideological beliefs and value structure (Greendorfer & Ewing, 1981; Yamaguchi, 1987). As a consequence, the notion of *socializing situation* has been theoretically and operationally reduced to a collection of specific places, or *opportunity sets*, where participation takes place. In theory, opportunity set should encompass the social and cultural atmosphere as well as physical setting and availability of programs or equipment. Unfortunately, most studies have stripped this cluster of variables of its substantive meaning by decontextualizing it, which totally negates the notion of "lived experience" (i.e., the entire constellation of setting, circumstances, interactions, meanings, and interpretations). Ignored in the treatment of opportunity set is what takes place, when, where, with whom, under what circumstances, and with what consequences. In addition to treating opportunity set rather narrowly, both conceptually and methodologically, researchers have also failed to examine this cluster of variables as a complex and multidimensional *intervening* factor consisting of such structural influences as social class, race, and geographical location (see Greendorfer & Ewing, 1981; Greendorfer & Lewko, 1978b).

During the mid-1970s researchers began to make a slight theoretical shift to a social role–social systems approach, which, similar to the social learning paradigm, also consists of three main elements: significant others or socializing agents who serve as role models, social situations, and role learners (who are characterized by a wide variety of relevant ascribed and achieved personal attributes, such as personality traits, attitudes, motivations, values, motor ability, race, ethnicity, and sex; McPherson, 1981). In contrast to social learning, however, the social role–social systems approach represents a more complex and synthesized model that attempts to combine psychological with sociological parameters. More specifically, each social system (i.e., family, peers, school, and community) with its specific values, norms, sanctions, and situational facilities is viewed as a potential role-learning institution that influences the learning of sport roles (Loy, McPherson & Kenyon, 1978).

Although not a major shift in theoretical perspective, this approach made a conceptual attempt to deal with complexities of human behavior, recognizing that significant others exert influence in social settings that have a system of values and norms. Despite its attempt to capture the dynamic complexities of the sport socialization process, it is questionable whether the social role–social systems approach was appropriately operationalized to do so. Later sections of the chapter consider existing critiques of the research paradigms.

Children's Sport Socialization

One fundamental assumption underlies sport socialization research: Regardless of motor talent, unless exposed to social settings having positive influences that reward physical activity or sport, chances are that the individual is not likely to learn physical skills, become involved in physical activity or sport, or adopt a physically active lifestyle (McPherson, 1976; McPherson & Brown, 1988). Research findings suggest that, regardless of sex, individuals become involved during childhood; that the strongest predictor of adult involvement is childhood involvement (Greendorfer, 1977, 1983; Kenyon & McPherson, 1973, 1974); and that physical activity involvement, particularly in competitive sport is related to *sex*. Given the underlying assumption, as well as this general information, it becomes critical for sport psychologists to understand who learns motor skills and under what circumstances, and who eventually participates in sport and who does not.

Most information about children's physical activity involvement has been derived from two types of research findings: those obtained by applying the social learning framework to retrospective information from elite adult athletes (Kenyon, 1970; Kenyon & McPherson, 1973, 1974) and those obtained from application of the social role–social systems approach to children's sport involvement (Greendorfer & Ewing, 1981; Lewko & Greendorfer, 1978a, 1978b). Studies on adult athletes indicate that active participation begins at an early age (8 or 9); that early participation is associated with a great deal of success;

that young participants receive positive sanctions/support from family, peers, and teachers, each of whom influences participation within a specific setting; and that peer groups and coaches (e.g., the school) appear to be the most influential (McPherson, 1981).

Studies on children that compare family, peer, and school influence suggest that the family is more influential than peers or school; that parents are more influential than siblings; and that the father seems to be the most influential significant other (Greendorfer & Ewing, 1981; Greendorfer & Lewko, 1978a; Lewko & Greendorfer, 1988). While researchers disagree as to who imparts the earliest and most persistent influence on children's sport involvement—some maintain that the family does (McPherson & Brown, 1988) and others feel that peers as well as family play a significant role (Greendorfer & Ewing, 1981; Greendorfer & Lewko, 1978a; Lewko & Greendorfer, 1988)—the important point is that both parents and peers hold the potential for influencing a child's sport involvement.

In terms of general social learning principles, researchers have consistently found a positive relationship between the amount and type of social support from significant others and the degree and type of participation in sport (Lewko & Greendorfer, 1988; McPherson & Brown, 1988). Thus, children who receive positive reinforcement for sport participation are more likely to become involved in sport than those who receive neutral or negative messages (Greendorfer, 1987a; Greendorfer, Blinde & Pellegrini, 1986; McPherson & Brown, 1988; Orlick, 1972, 1974; Watson, 1977).

Although these findings represent a general overview of influences affecting children's sport socialization, these summary statements should also demonstrate how research in sport psychology can be linked to the process of sport socialization, specifically, that pertaining to reinforcement, rewards, and feedback. For example, findings in sport psychology have demonstrated that children positively evaluate coaches who give rewards, technical instruction, and mistake-contingent feedback (Smith et al., 1979). Additional research has found that decisions relating to future participation and expectancies for future success are often related to the various types of rewards and reinforcements children receive (Roberts, 1984, 1986; Smith, Smoll, Hunt, Curtis & Coppel, 1979). When linked to a broad perspective of sport socialization, these findings suggest that the nature and content of information (which are examples of reinforcement, reward, and feedback) are integral aspects that affect children's continued involvement in sport and physical activity.

Another example of sport psychology research that could be linked to sport socialization is the work done on competitive stress, particularly as it may be related to reinforcement from parents and coaches (Roberts, 1986a; Smoll, 1986). As in the previous example, the underlying mechanisms that affect continuing motivation, persistence in sport and physical activity, coaching behaviors, and parental support have also been identified as critical aspects of sport socialization.

Gender Differences in Childhood Sport Socialization

Three specific social learning mechanisms are directly related to reinforcement, rewards, feedback, and content of underlying messages: differential treatment, stereotyping, and labeling. These individually or collectively serve as vehicles for perpetuating existing ideologies and social practices. These mechanisms subtly or overtly convey underlying beliefs about what is, and what is not, appropriate behavior in a physical activity context. When considered as outcomes of social practice, these three mechanisms can be viewed as potent social forces reinforcing existing participation patterns, namely, the overrepresentation of males and the underrepresentation of females in physical activity and sport. However, some attention to this issue is here warranted in order to more fully undertand the ways in which childhood sport socialization is accomplished. (For an indepth consideration of gender issues in regard to physical activity, see chapter 7.)

As previously suggested, child-rearing practices reflect values and beliefs parents and adults hold relative to what is appropriate or inappropriate and what specific learnings are to be imparted to children. In addition, ideological beliefs guide social practice relative to sport socialization. Specific to this notion, evidence suggests that parents (adults) continue to believe that there are inherent differences between the sexes, that girls are weaker, more frail and perhaps less suited for sport and physical activity than are boys (Lewis, 1972; Lewko & Greendorfer, 1980, 1988). Either consciously or unconsciously, it seems that several socialization practices are guided by these underlying beliefs. The information in Table 10.1 outlines various ways in which differential treatment, gender role stereotyping, and labeling of activites impact socialization into physical activity.

Despite the existence of several studies in developmental psychology and sport sociology, there are two critical gaps in the childhood sport socialization literature: (a) the virtual absence of research on younger children and the social and

psychological forces that shape their orientations (Lewko & Greendorfer, 1988) and (b) extended research into the nature and extent to which the family socialization process is reciprocal (Hasbrook, 1982, 1986b; McPherson & Brown, 1988). Relative to the first issue, it could be argued that if, in fact, initial predisposition and entry are shaped prior to adolescence, much of the existing sport socialization research is based on recall of influences rather than on the actual dynamics of influence processes. It could be also argued that socialization studies tell us more about the influences that *maintain* children's involvement than those that get them involved. Relative to the issue of reciprocity, although very little is known about how parents influence the sport behavior of their children, even less is known about how youngsters who become involved subsequently socialize their parents' sport behavior (Hasbrook, 1982, 1986b; McPherson & Brown, 1988).

A close examination of the influence of significant others reveals additional gaps in research, particularly if ability level or skill range is considered. Whereas entry, persistence, or withdrawal could be adapted to an age continuum or some sort of temporal component, sport socialization research—especially on children—has totally ignored the mastery or skill continuum. Nowhere in the literature do researchers deal with the nature and type of influence from significant others with reference to skill development, pursuit of excellence, development of competence, or achievement striving. Further, relatively little attention has been given to socialization influences on degree or extent of involvement. In one study that does take this factor into account, the investigators found no differences in level of involvement due to chronological age (Lewko & Ewing, 1981). More specifically, boys and girls highly active in sports by age 9 remained so through age 11. Similarly, boys and girls low active at age 9 were low active at age 11.

With these limitations, then, the information contained in Table 10.1 suggests that as a result of various social learning practices since early infancy, boys experience a more rewarding and positively rewarding or supportive set of experiences that predispose them toward sport and physical activity. Consequently, they learn basic motor skills, engage in gross physical activity, highly value sport skills and physical ability, and develop a large repertoire of motor skills—all of which are evident by their pervasive participation in competitive team games. In contrast, girls do not receive systematic or consistent encouragement or tutoring in the development of motor skills. Consequently, their engagement in physical activity is problematic. For those who do

Table 10.1   Toy, Play, and Motor Skill Experiences of Males and Females During Childhood

Early infancy and toddler years

Child rearing: Infant girls touched, handled and talked to more by 13 months; girls more dependent, restricted exploratory range of play environment; independence, exploration encouraged in boys (Lewis, 1972; Lewko & Greendorfer, 1980)

Toys: Parents furnish children's rooms with sex-appropriate toys; boys have more toys in number and categories (vehicles, manipulative, instrumental, sports equipment); evidence of rigid sex-typing of toys for boys, not girls (Goodman & Lever, 1974; Rheingold & Cook, 1975)

Play Styles: Girls less exploratory and play more quiet in style; boys play with toys requiring gross motor activity, more vigorous and allowed to bang or break toys (Lewko & Greendorfer, 1980)

Motor Skills: Mothers pick up girls for caretaking but tend to play more with boys; fathers swing and play with boys more vigorously (swing or toss overhead), bounce and roughhouse (Lewis, 1972; Power & Parke, 1983)

Children during first 4–5 years of age

Toys and games: Boys given more sports equipment and instrumental toys; boys' toys more complex, more expensive, with more movable parts, eliciting more motor activity and wider play space; girls given dolls, dishes, housekeeping toys that elicit expression and quiet play, more verbal than physical activity; toys acquire more reinforcement value for both sexes; emotional toning and familiarity reinforces requests for similarly sex-typed toys (Hartley, 1966; Rheingold & Cook, 1975)

Play styles: Boys more active, allowed wider range, physical activity and motor skill development encouraged; more wrestling and roughhousing with boys than girls; boys allowed outdoors more and without supervision (Langlois & Downs, 1980; Lewko & Greendorfer, 1980; Tauber, 1979)

Motor Skills Fathers teach gross motor skills to sons, not daughters; neither parent systematically teaches motor skills to daughters; girls sometimes punished for vigorous physical activity (Fagot, 1978, Langlois & Downs, 1980; Lewko & Greendorfer, 1980; Tasch, 1952; Tauber, 1979)

Children during middle and late childhood (ages 6–10)

Sport and motor skills: Sport skills associated with being male, and more highly valued for boys; associated with achievement for boys, but not for girls; family, peers, and school are important influences of sport socialization for boys; pattern is more diffuse, less predictable for girls (Greendorfer & Lewko, 1978a, 1978b; Lewko & Greendorfer, 1980); expectancies, rewards, reinforcement, and role models are critical social learning mechanisms (Orlick, 1974); differential mechanisms operate for blacks and whites—blacks more influenced by values and opportunities, whites more influenced by significant others (Greendorfer & Ewing, 1981)

Games: Boys play more complex, active, competitive, and team games; girls play less complex, solitary, turn-taking games requiring repetitive tasks (Lever, 1976, 1978; Lewko & Greendorfer, 1980)

---

venture into physical activity the likelihood is that they will gravitate toward sex-typed activities that emphasize qualities associated with being female—rhythmic, graceful movement, emphasizing fluidity of motion (Greendorfer, 1983; Greendorfer & Lewko, 1978b; Metheny, 1965).

Adolescent and Adult Sport Socialization

As previously indicated, research on adolescent and adult socialization into sport consists more of retrospective data relative to influence of significant others and opportunities during previous life-cycle stages. Despite this limitation, however, some patterns are clear. As a child enters adolescence, the influence of the family appears to decline, and the peer group becomes more significant, particularly in the case of same-sex peers who may function as role models

(Brown, 1985; Higginson, 1985; McPherson & Brown, 1988; Patriksson,1981). Thus, studies consistently support the emergent role of the peer group, suggesting that along with parents and teachers peers provide positive environments toward sport experiences (Greendorfer, 1977; Higginson, 1985; Patriksson, 1981; Smith, 1979; Yamaguchi, 1984). These findings further suggest that siblings may not play a major role in sport socialization of males but may reinforce parental input to female sport socialization (Higginson, 1985; Patriksson, 1981; Yamaguchi, 1984). Additional studies have indicated that the school system (i.e., teachers and coaches) may play a more important role in stimulating interest in specific sports (McPherson, 1981; McPherson & Brown, 1988). In contrast, parents seem to generate interest in traditional spectator sports, whereas the peer group provides social support and serves as a source of recognition and acknowledgment (Kenyon & McPherson, 1973,

1974; McPherson, 1981). Although the provision of sport opportunities through the school still appears to be considerably greater for boys (Greendorfer, 1983), it does appear that as sport becomes more acceptable as an activity for adolescent females, the school may provide more opportunities and encouragement for female competitive sport experiences (Higginson, 1985; Weiss & Knoppers, 1982).

Although early research on adult sport socialization focused almost exclusively on college-age athletes (Greendorfer, 1977, 1978, 1987a; Kenyon & McPherson, 1973, 1974; McPherson, 1981) or elite male athletes (Kenyon & Knoop, 1978), some recent studies have applied the process to older adults (Hasbrook & Mingesz, 1987). Such studies seem to be an exception, however, as aspects of the sport socialization process seem to have been completely ignored among older age groups. Consequently, most of what is known about adult sport socialization comes from findings obtained from male and female elite (and college) athletes.

Findings on males suggest that he tends to be first-born, starts young, and experiences early success accompanied by recognition and status. He may be first influenced by the family (with at least one parent actively involved in sport during his childhood); however, from adolescence on he is more influenced by peers and coaches. There appear to be sport differences in the process, and it is clear that influence by significant others differs over time (Kenyon & McPherson, 1973, 1974; McPherson, 1981).

Although there are some differences in female sport socialization, the pattern is quite similar—with two exceptions. Female athletes are *not* the first born (they tend to be a middle or the youngest child), and the school seems *not* to be a major influence in the process but merely reinforces performance and teaches skills previously learned elsewhere. Aside from these differences for the female athlete, one or both parents are actively involved in sport, and introduction to sport or physical activity appears to be a "normal or expected" family activity. In addition she perceives her skill and ability to be well above average at an early age. While peer group influence is consistent through the life cycle, it is not clear (perhaps due to differences in social class background) exactly who in the family influences her (Greendorfer, 1977, 1978, 1979, 1987a).

Criticisms of Definitions, Assumptions, and Approaches

Despite the popularity of sport socialization research during the 1970s and early 1980s, interest in the topic began to wane in the mid-1980s. Although specific factors contributing to this malaise are subject to debate, most scholars agree that a growing dissatisfaction with the relatively simple social learning approach (Theberge, 1984), conceptual disenchantment with the theoretical assumptions (Fishwick & Greendorfer, 1987; McPherson, 1986; Nixon, 1989; Theberge, 1984), and failure to develop a coherent body of knowledge (McPherson, 1986) played a significant role in the demise of this research. While general profiles and patterns provided useful information to some, few researchers used these findings to expand theoretical perspectives. This neglect led some critics to condemn both the social learning and social role–social systems approach because of their technocratic and empiricist roots. As a result, a viable topic that could tremendously contribute to our understanding of sport and physical activity involvement has been virtually ignored in recent years.

This malaise may be due *in part* to the criticisms that questioned the theoretical assumptions of socialization theory in general and sport socialization research in particular (Fishwick & Greendorfer, 1987; Greendorfer, 1987a; McPherson, 1986; Theberge, 1984). Essentially, two different types of critiques have appeared in the literature. One asserts that assumptions of structural functionalism are narrow, normatively biased, deterministic, nonreflexive, and overly behavioristic (Giddens, 1979; Theberge, 1984; Wentworth, 1980) whereas the second criticizes theoretical, as well as methodological, deficiencies specific to sport socialization (Fishwick & Greendorfer, 1987; Greendorfer, 1987a; McPherson, 1986).

As an advocate of the first position, Theberge (1984) challenges the theoretical assumption of social determinism that underlies a social systems approach to socialization. According to this critique, the underlying premise as well as fundamental definition of socialization assumes what the final product of the process "ought" to be. Such a conceptualization suggests that the individual is a willing recipient of society's prescriptions and norms and is "molded" into roles. Thus, this critique holds that the conception of "roles" is deterministic and that social learning conceptualizations fail to deal with notions of reciprocal influence and individualism, that is, either self-determination or individuals who deviate from normative expectations (Giddens, 1979; Hasbrook, 1989; Theberge, 1984; Wentworth, 1980). Proponents of this critique maintain that the focus of existing research is overly behavioristic, that there has been an overemphasis on micro perspectives (i.e., social–psychological variables), and that empiricist assumptions have led to the collection of descriptive social facts without theoretical understanding (McPherson, 1986; Theberge, 1984). They would argue that more consideration should be given to macro concerns, such as power, social conditions, prevailing ideological beliefs, and social structural factors (Greendorfer & Bruce, 1989; Theberge, 1984).

The second criticism is more concerned with methodological issues and research design. This critique argues that the absence of control groups (of nonparticipants), introduction of gender bias in operationalizing theoretical constructs, and the failure to theoretically or methodologically examine normative behavior are more reflective of investigator narrowness than of inherent weaknesses in theoretical conceptualization (Fishwick & Greendorfer, 1987; Greendorfer, 1983, 1987a; Greendorfer & Bruce, 1989; McPherson, 1986). Proponents of this critique argue that most studies purporting to use the social role–social systems approach fail to conceptualize or operationalize its theoretical components adequately and that this failure produces overly descriptive "concrete" facts. Not only do such findings strip social–psychological constructs of context and substantive meaning, but the research itself fails to capture the complexity and dynamic nature of the sport socialization process (Greendorfer, 1983, 1987a). Thus, the criticism is less of underlying theoretical assumptions than it is of an overly simplistic and nonanalytical process. In short, this criticism claims that too much attention was paid to the *who* or *what* rather than to how and under what circumstances, conditions, or constraints the process occurs (Lewko & Greendorfer, 1988). From this perspective critics could argue that the *nature* of sport socialization influences is still not understood and that the lived experiences of socializees as well as the socializing agents, has not been adequately captured.

Apparently motivated by both the malaise and the existing critiques, recent attempts to rejuvenate sport socialization research have suggested alternative theoretical conceptualizations. Rather than advocating traditional functionalist approaches, researchers have suggested more integrated and holistic (i.e., macro) perspectives. They have turned away from social learning or psychologistic approaches and endorsed either

- symbolic and other interactionist approaches that recognize personality and individual behavior, social situations, reactions, and reciprocal adjustments that occur within the broader sociocultural context of society (Nixon, 1989);

- more interactive approaches that avoid the dualism between subject and object, focusing more on how personal characteristics (i.e., psychological and physiological) may shape and interact with social–historical factors (Hasbrook, 1989); or

- cultural studies approaches that attempt to capture social totality by examining how science, history, ideology, and expressions of culture influence the process of becoming involved in sport and physical activity (Greendorfer & Bruce, 1989).

Although each alternative is substantively different, they all share some common features. Each places less emphasis on empiricist or deterministic approaches; each attempts to accommodate macro (societal) as well as micro (individual) concepts; each advocates a more integrated or holistic approach; and each is supportive of interpretive methodologies. Although each has its own inherent conceptual difficulties and only time will tell whether one particular approach or all will offer a greater understanding than currently exists, at the present time these alternatives show great potential for achieving a new level of theoretical, conceptual, and empirical understanding.

Socialization Through Sport

Once individuals have been socialized into sport or physical activity, they find themselves in a social milieu that has the potential to enhance or inhibit their personal growth (McPherson & Brown, 1988). Such a statement reflects an underlying assumption that social learning outcomes are possible through participation in physical activity and sport. Yet, despite the connection, socialization *through* sport has been consistently treated as a topic totally unrelated to socialization *into* sport. Most research on positive or negative outcomes of sport involvement has not considered the extent to which such outcomes (if they actually occur) may be related to the manner, nature, and type of influences that explain what is happening *during* socialization into physical activity. This neglect may have seriously retarded our understanding of the nature of what, as well as how, individuals learn from physical activity participation.

Underlying the entire topic of socialization via sport is the belief that play and games are an essential component of the overall socialization process and are an essential aspect of early-life social experiences. In addition, the assumption that sport is a unique medium or vehicle (compared to other activities) for social learning has not been empirically validated; nor has the assumption that learning will be transferred from a specific sport setting to everyday life experiences. Despite these difficulties, however, the majority of research on socialization through sport implicitly if not explicitly assumes that participation in physical activity teaches children a variety of skills needed to effectively participate socially, politically, and/or economically as an adult.

Whereas early research focused either on the acquisition of *global* behavioral patterns (leadership, character, cooperation), general societal values (achievement, competition, cooperation), or diffuse social roles (good citizen) and skills (Cowell, 1960; Kenyon, 1968), recent studies have focused more on an extensive list of *specific* behavioral outcomes of participation (e.g., achievement values, personality development, moral behavior, social mobility, academic achievement; see Bredemeier & Shields, 1984; Gould, 1984; Greendorfer, 1987b). Because the literature on socialization outcomes can be quite extensive, my discussion will be limited to only three issues, which hardly exhaust the literature on this topic:

- Global values and behavioral outcomes
- Organizational structure and philosophy of sport programs
- Leaving physical activity and sport

Global Values and General Behavioral Outcomes

Three studies serve as representative examples of how researchers have argued that games and play serve as potent vehicles for the transmission of values, behaviors, or general socialization. In a cross-cultural study of games, Roberts and Sutton-Smith (1962) suggested that games provide buffered learning experiences that teach societal values. They found that specific values emphasized during child rearing were linked to specific types of games (achievement training to games of physical skill, obedience training to games of strategy, and responsibility training to games of chance). In addition, their correlational findings between game types and cultural complexity (as well as a link between values transmitted, cultural variation, and sex differences) offered further support of their hypothesis that games are enculturative and expressive models of culture (Roberts & Sutton-Smith, 1962).

In a study that assumed an association between effective socialization and game playing, Webb (1969) argued that how games are played in a society reflects the values emphasized and the dominant ideology. Suggesting that sport is a training ground for occupational, social, and political roles of adult life, Webb found that with increasing age children placed more emphasis on winning than on fairness. The finding of significant differences in orientations according to age, sex, and religion led Webb to conclude that games are vehicles for learning values and that this "professionalization of attitudes" is evidence of how effective the socialization process is (i.e., children were adopting appropriate orientations for success in a competitive, achievement-oriented society).

In a slightly different type of study Lever (1976, 1978) suggested that organizational structure of children's games influenced socialization outcomes. She found that differences between boys' and girls' games in

- size and group composition (i.e., boys play in larger, age-heterogeneous groups),
- types of roles played (i.e., boys' games require more interdependent role skills),
- goals of games (i.e., boys have a set limit or specific goal), and
- rules (i.e., boys' games have more flexible rules that allow for negotiation)

allowed for development of very different skills (Lever, 1978). Because different games had very different outcomes, Lever concluded that girls learned values that did not prepare them for adult participation in occupational, political, and social life.

Despite the intuitive appeal of this research and the clear parallels drawn between game playing and situations in everyday social life, in recent years some rather harsh criticism has been lodged against this line of research. Focusing more on methodological than theoretical issues, the threefold nature of this criticism challenges the validity of the notion of socialization through sport by claiming that

- correlational findings have been interpreted as causal relationships;
- studies comparing athletes and nonathletes have not controlled for initial differences or selection factors; and
- studies fail to explain how transfer occurs, that is, mechanisms through which the process operates have never been identified (Greendorfer, 1987b; Stevenson, 1975).

More recently, researchers have claimed that outcomes related to global behaviors such as leadership, character, and moral development, as well as those relating to diffuse roles such as good citizenship and sportspersonship, are neither automatic nor always in a positive direction (Bredemeier & Shields, 1984; Gould, 1984;

Greendorfer, 1987b; Hodge, 1988). In sum, despite both a narrowing of focus to specific behaviors and changes in research design, sport psychologists and sport sociologists are still unable to explain why or how social learning occurs with some athletes or participants and not with others (Gould, 1984; Stevenson, 1975, 1985).

Organizational Structure and Philosophy of Sport Programs

In recent years sport psychologists and sport sociologists have expanded socialization-through-sport research by considering significant others, as well as organizational structure, as important elements shaping outcomes of the sport experience. As a result, more attention has been given to the social environment in which competitive processes occur (Gould, 1984); and socialization-through-sport considerations have been extended to include coaching behaviors and underlying program philosophy.

Various studies on children and adults have pursued the issue of professionalized orientations, linking such values with sport involvement. In essence, findings that children, preadolescents, and college students who were involved in sport had more professionalized orientations than those who were not involved in sport (Maloney & Petrie, 1972; Mantel & Vander Velden, 1974; Nixon, 1980) suggests that sport involvement and degree of competition are related to greater emphasis on success, winning, and individual performance. Such findings not only cast serious doubts on earlier notions of sport as character building or promoting of sportspersonship, they actually contradict the underlying assumption of positive outcomes of physical activity involvement (Bredemeier & Shields, 1984; Gould, 1984; Hodge, 1988).

Recent empirical findings on program philosophy, organizational structure of programs or athletic leagues, and attitudes of coaches have further challenged existing beliefs. For example, Dubois (1986) finds that children in educational leagues emphasized participation and sportspersonship over winning, whereas those in competitive leagues valued competition, winning, and improving social status over playing. Relative to behaviors and orientations of coaches, Harris (1983, 1984) found that children's conceptualization of their baseball experience was closely related to coaches' characterizations; moreover, this socialization effect was so powerful that orientations of coaches overrode cultural and ethnic value orientations of the children.

Finally, studies on female college athletes suggest that program structure and philosophy, as well as coach's orientations, may also affect the quality of the sport experience and the value orientations of the participants (Blinde & Greendorfer, 1987).

Although implications of these research findings still fall within the purview of socialization through sport and physical activity, it seems that a totally different interpretation or conceptualization of this topic is in order. Rather than accepting the assumption that outcomes of participation are automatic and/or positive, sport psychologists and sport sociologists would do well to consider three pertinent implications of psychosocial outcomes:

- Because competition is a learned social behavior, any outcomes from competitive experiences are learned.
- What will be learned is most likely to be influenced by the type of experiences an individual is exposed to (e.g., how the individual is socialized into sport and physical activity).
- Types of experiences are most likely shaped by the situation (e.g., program philosophy, organizational structure) and influences by significant others (e.g., coaches' orientations and behaviors, parental attitudes).

Leaving Sport: Dropping Out and Retirement

At some stage in the life cycle, involved individuals approach the opposite end of the socialization continuum and leave sport or physical activity. Despite the fact that this process is sometimes referred to as *desocialization*—which encompasses both dropping out (considered by most as a voluntary process) and retirement (considered by most an involuntary and perhaps abrupt or unanticipated termination)—few sport psychologists have considered either of these phenomena as aspects of the socialization process (see Blinde & Greendorfer, 1985; Brown, 1985; Greendorfer & Blinde, 1985). Although withdrawal can occur at any age and for a variety of reasons, for most individuals it occurs during adolescence or early adulthood (McPherson & Brown, 1988). Use of a socialization perspective to understand withdrawal or disengagement would consider the strong possibility that factors influencing involvement could also be related to those influencing withdrawal.

Such a perspective would be fruitful in the interpretation of findings on attrition in youth

sport. To date, most research on dropouts has been based on a motivational framework, with particular attention paid to

- specific reasons for entering, and consequently for leaving, sport programs;
- achievement goals or orientations of athletes; and
- factors related to perceived competence

(Feltz & Petlichkoff, 1983; Gould, 1987; Roberts, 1984; Roberts, Kleiber & Duda, 1981). However, findings from these as well as other studies suggest that dropping out may also be related to *effects of the sport experience* (i.e., socialization through sport). For example, emphasis on competition, lack of fun, not enough playing time, and coaching behavior also contribute to children's dropping out of sport (Gould, 1987; Orlick, 1974; Pooley, 1981).

These findings suggest that decisions to continue or discontinue may also be related to influences from significant others as well as normative expectation sets that shape the social milieu of the sport experience. In short, empirical findings suggest that negative aspects of the sport environment are often introduced by adults who structure the sport setting in accordance with adult value systems and objectives. Ultimately, such organizational structure determines program philosophy and shapes the nature and quality of sport experiences (McPherson & Brown, 1988). Given such dynamics, it would seem that explanations for dropping out should include aspects of the normative value structure, as well as consideration of personal experiences, reinforcement contingencies, and influence of significant others. By considering such general socialization experiences Brown (1985) found that withdrawal from age-group swimming occurred over a period during which individuals gradually divested themselves of commitment, identification, and involvement with their sport role. Critical in this process was the degree of social support received for participation. These findings should suggest that conceptualizing attrition from the perspective of socialization allows for the consideration of a multiplicity of factors; a more complex interpretation of empirical findings; and, ultimately, a broader understanding than currently exists.

Findings pertaining to sport retirement have also been reinterpreted in recent years, due in part to reconceptualizing the process as an aspect of socialization. Prior to the 1980s, existing studies focused on former male athletes in professional spectator sports such as baseball, football, and boxing (Haerle, 1975; Lerch, 1981; Reynolds, 1981; Weinberg & Arond, 1952). In contrast to viewing the process as leading to adjustment difficulties and life disruption (Ball, 1976; Rosenberg, 1981), recent studies on adolescents and college athletes have suggested that sport retirement may be a "rebirth" rather than an ending (Coakley, 1983) and that the process could be viewed as continuity and transition; shifting or reprioritization of interests; mild, rather than severe, adjustment; and continuing participation rather than termination (Greendorfer & Blinde, 1985). These findings suggest that theoretical perspectives leaning more heavily on socialization perspectives might be more fruitful in further explorations of sport retirement.

Future Directions

Given the issues, underlying assumptions of theoretical perspectives, research traditions, empirical findings, and existing criticisms of sport socialization research discussed in this chapter, an important question remains: What does the future hold in store for this topic? First of all, it is clear that sport sociologists who have not abandoned the topic completely seem to be leaning in directions other than those emanating from the social learning and empiricist traditions that stimulated this line of research in the first place. Instead, sociological concern seems to be directed more toward a synthesis of macro considerations that accommodates an integration of historical, cultural, and individual approaches. In addition to this multiple-levels-of-analysis perspective, methodological approaches seem to be more qualitative and interpretive in nature (Greendorfer & Bruce, 1989; Nixon, 1989).

The direction in sport psychology is less clear. It is difficult to predict whether the topical approach with indirect attention toward socialization will continue or whether more direct attention will be devoted to sport socialization per se. Regardless of direction, however, it does seem clear that sport psychologists will continue to focus on cognitive and psychological topics, even with respect to involvement and participation patterns (Branta, Painter & Kiger, 1987; Gould, 1987; Horn, 1987). It is possible, however, that findings and issues touched upon in the existing research could provide insight and guidance for future research on sport socialization. For example, because parents have been found to be an important "source" of children's perceived competence and a predictor of initial involvement and persistence in achievement-oriented activities such as sport (Horn & Hasbrook, 1986, 1987), it would be interesting to explore *how* parents influence the development of perceived competence and how such influences socialize individuals into or away from physical activity. Similarly, since peer interaction is a major source of social acceptance and such acceptance is related to becoming involved and persisting in achievement-oriented activities, more attention could be devoted to the interactive nature and type of reciprocal peer influence.

Thus, instead of measuring the importance of specific significant others (the *who*), research attention could shift to how and why significant others are important and how significant others influence, and are influenced by, the socializee. Rather than asking what personal characteristics or motivational goals influence participation or withdrawal from physical activity, focus could shift to how personal characteristics may shape and interact with the social environment and with expectations of significant others (Hasbrook, 1989). Of course, the entire nature of normative behavior and factors that shape expectations of the socializee as well as significant others represents another direction for sport socialization research.

While these examples tend to focus on becoming involved or persisting in physical activity, additional issues need to be considered, such as explanations as to why some individuals participate and others do not. This issue involves two separate thrusts relating to sport socialization research: persistence and dropping out (Once socialization into physical activity has occurred, why do some individuals continue and others leave?) and the nature of aversive socialization experiences (Why do some individuals not become involved in physical activity? See Hasbrook, 1989).

Although the issue of noninvolvement has been studied in the past relative to attrition (Brown, 1985; Gould, 1987) and retirement from sport (Blinde & Greendorfer, 1985; Coakley, 1983; Greendorfer & Blinde, 1985), future theoretical approaches need to be less narrow and to incorporate notions pertaining to the nature of outcomes and what is learned during participation. More theoretical and empirical understanding is needed relative to how the process of becoming involved incorporates a system of values, behaviors, and predispositions toward future involvement. In other words, why is physical activity incorporated into the lifestyle of some (continued involvement) and not others (dropouts) and what socialization influences lead to aversive experiences and a lifetime of noninvolvement.

The concepts of identity and commitment are also in need of further exploration, particularly as related to issues of persistence and noninvolvement. To date, however, sport socialization research has neglected both theoretical and empirical issues related to these concepts. Yet research findings indicate that both concepts are integrally related to continued participation, withdrawal, and adjustment difficulties associated with desocialization from physical activity (Blinde & Greendorfer, 1985; Brown, 1985; Greendorfer & Blinde, 1985; McPherson & Brown 1988). However, little can be said about how commitment is generated or whether commitment and identification are linked to influence of significant others and environmental situations. The link between these socialization experiences and either identity or commitment may in some way contribute to low value orientations and predispositions that result in the failure of some individuals ever to become involved in physical activity.

As a final consideration, effort should be made to understand the unique factors that create barriers to the sport socialization process— barriers that deter some from entering sport or physical activity and others from persisting in such activities. The meaning and interpretation of such barriers is also a significant aspect of sport socialization, as some may interpret negative or aversive influences as barriers, whereas others will consider such influences as "motivators" to continue. Although gender role stereotyping has been considered as one barrier to sport involvement, particularly for females, other forms of stereotyping based on ideological beliefs and social practice also exist. For example, individuals with disabilities tend to be treated differentially, segregated, and provided with limited opportunities to demonstrate their physical/athletic skills, abilities, and attributes. Because socialization outcomes are products of social practices that are outgrowths of deep-seated ideological beliefs themselves, barriers to the disabled may not be *quite* the same as those faced by females. In the case of the disabled, the barriers may be less visible, created by this group's marginalization from mainstream society and accompanied by the nonconscious belief that the disabled *cannot be*, or simply are not, inclined toward physical activity. While some disabled individuals could interpret the barriers as overwhelming, others could view them as challenges to be overcome.

In conclusion, future research in sport socialization depends on two critical factors: (a) a familiarity with the existing literature and a working knowledge of theoretical and empirical issues raised in previous research and (b) broader theoretical perspectives that attempt to integrate and expand earlier research approaches. Consideration of socialization as a holistic process conceptualized as dynamic, complex, and capable of incorporating micro as well as macro perspectives would seem to be a step in this direction.

References

Aberle, D.F. (1961). Culture and socialization. In F.L.K. Hsu (Ed.), *Psychological anthropology: Approaches to culture and personality* (pp. 381-397). Homewood, IL: Dorsey Press.

Ball, D.W. (1976). Failure in sport. *American Sociological Review, 41*, 726-739.

Bandura, A. (1969). A social learning theory of identificatory process. In D.A. Goslin (Ed.), *Handbook of socialization theory and research* (pp. 213-262). Chicago: Rand McNally.

Bandura, A., & Walters, R. (1963). *Social learning and personality development.* New York: Holt, Rinehart & Winston.

Biddle, B.J., & Thomas, E.J. (Eds.) (1966). *Role theory: Concepts and research.* New York: Wiley.

Blinde, E., & Greendorfer, S.L. (1985). A reconceptualization of the process of leaving the role of competitive athlete. *International Review for Sociology of Sport, 20*, 87-94.

Blinde, E.M., & Greendorfer, S.L. (1987). Structural and philosophical differences in women's intercollegiate sport programs and the sport experience of athletes. *Journal of Sport Behavior, 10*, 59-72.

Branta, C.F., Painter, M., & Kiger, J.E. (1987). Gender differences in play patterns and sport participation of North American youth. In D. Gould & M. Weiss (Eds.), *Advances in pediatric sport sciences* (pp. 25-42). Champaign, IL: Human Kinetics.

Bredemeier, B., & Shields, D. (1984). Divergence in moral reasoning about sport and everyday life. *Sociology of Sport Journal, 1*, 348-357.

Brim, O.G. (1957). The parent–child relation as a social system: Part I. Parent and child roles. *Child Development, 28*, 344-364.

Brim, O.G. (1966). Socialization through the life cycle. In O.G. Brim & S. Wheeler (Eds.), *Socialization after childhood: Two essays* (pp. 1-52). New York: John Wiley & Sons.

Brim, O.G., & Wheeler, S. (Eds.) (1966). *Socialization after childhood: Two essays.* New York: John Wiley & Sons.

Brown, B.A. (1985). Factors influencing the process of withdrawal by female adolescents from the role of competitive age group swimmer. *Sociology of Sport Journal, 2*, 111-129.

Clausen, J.A. (Ed.) (1968). *Socialization and society.* Boston: Little, Brown.

Coakley, J.J. (1983). Leaving competitive sport: Retirement or rebirth? *Quest, 35*, 1-11.

Cowell, C. (1960). The contributions of physical activity to social development. *Research Quarterly, 31*(2), 286-06.

D'Andrade, R. (1966). Sex differences and cultural institutions. In E.E. Maccoby (Ed.), *The development of sex differences* (pp. 174-203). Stanford, CA: Stanford University Press.

Dornbusch, S. (1966). Afterword. In E.E. Maccoby (Ed.), *The develpment of sex differences* (pp. 205-219). Stanford, CA: Stanford University Press.

Dubois, P. (1981). The youth sport coach as an agent of socialization: An exploratory study. *Journal of Sport Behavior, 4*, 95-107.

Dubois, P. (1986). The effect of participation in sport on the value orientations of young athletes. *Sociology of Sport Journal, 3*, 29-42.

Duquin, M. (1977). Differential sex role socialization toward amplitude appropriation. *Research Quarterly, 48*, 288-292.

Fagot, B.I. (1978). The influence of sex of child on parental reaction. *Developmental Psychology, 10*, 554-558.

Feltz, D.L., & Petlichkoff, L. (1983). Perceived competence among interscholastic sport participants and dropouts. *Canadian Journal of Applied Sport Sciences, 8*, 231-235.

Fishwick, L., & Greendorfer, S.L. (1987). Socialization revisited: A critique of the sport related research. *Quest, 39*, 1-8.

Freud, S. (1924). *Character and anal eroticism.* London: Hogarth Press.

Gerwitz, J.L. (1969). Mechanisms of social learning: Some roles of stimulation and behavior in early human development. In D.A. Goslin (Ed.), *Handbook of socialization theory and research* (pp. 57-212). Chicago: Rand McNally.

Giddens, A. (1979). *Central problems in social theory.* Berkeley, CA: University of California Press.

Goffman, E. (1959). *The presentation of self in everyday life.* New York: Doubleday.

Goodman, L.W., & Lever, J. (1974). A report on children's toys. In J. Stacey, S. Bereaud, & J. Daniels (Eds.). *And Jill came tumbling after: Sexism in American education* (pp. 123-125). New York: Dell.

Goslin, D.A. (Ed.) (1969). *Handbook of socialization theory and research.* Chicago: Rand McNally.

Gould, D. (1978). *The influence of motor task types on model effectiveness.* Unpublished doctoral dissertation, University of Illinois, Urbana-Champaign.

Gould, D. (1984). Psychosocial development and children's sport. In J.R. Thomas (Ed.), *Motor development during childhood and adolescence.* Minneapolis: Burgess.

Gould, D. (1987). Understanding attribution in children's sport. In D. Gould & M. Weiss (Eds.), *Advances in pediatric sport sciences: Vol. 2. Behavioral issues* (pp. 61-85). Champaign, IL: Human Kinetics.

Gould, D., & Roberts, G.C. (1981). Modeling and motor skill acquisition. *Quest, 33*(3), 214-230.

Greendorfer, S.L. (1977). The role of socializing agents in female sport involvement. *Research Quarterly, 48,* 304-310.

Greendorfer, S.L. (1978). Social class influence on female sport involvement. *Sex Roles, 4,* 619-625.

Greendorfer, S.L. (1979). Differences in childhood socialization influences of women involved in sport and women not involved in sport. In M.L. Krotee (Ed.), *The dimensions of sport sociology* (pp. 59-72). Champaign, IL: Leisure Press.

Greendorfer, S.L. (1983). Shaping the female athlete: The impact of the family. In M.A. Boutilier & L. San Giovanni, *The sporting woman: Feminist and sociological dilemmas* (pp. 135-155). Champaign, IL: Human Kinetics.

Greendorfer, S.L. (1987a). Gender bias in theoretical perspectives: The case of female socialization into sport. *Psychology of Women Quarterly, 11,* 327-340.

Greendorfer, S.L. (1987b). Psycho-social correlates of organized physical activity. *Journal of Physical Education, Recreation and Dance, 58*(7), 59-64.

Greendorfer, S.L., & Blinde, E.M. (1985). "Retirement from intercollegiate sport: Theoretical and empirical considerations. *Sociology of Sport Journal, 2,* 101-110.

Greendorfer, S.L., Blinde, E.M., & Pellegrini, A.M. (1986). Gender differences in Brazilian children's socialization into sport. *International Review of Sociology of Sport, 21,* 51-64.

Greendorfer, S.L., & Bruce, T. (1989, November). *Rejuvenating sport socialization research.* Paper presented at the meeting of the North American Society for the Sociology of Sport, Washington, DC.

Greendorfer, S.L., & Ewing, M.E. (1981). Race and gender differences in children's socialization into sport. *Research Quarterly for Exercise and Sport, 52,* 301-310.

Greendorfer, S.L., & Lewko, J.H. (1978a). Role of family members in sport socialization of children. *Research Quarterly, 49,* 146-152.

Greendorfer, S.L., & Lewko, J.H. (1978b, August). *Children's socialization into sport: A conceptual and empirical analysis.* Paper presented at the World Congress of Sociology, Uppsala, Sweden.

Haerle, R.K. (1975). Career patterns and career contingencies of professional baseball players: An occupational analysis. In D. Ball & J. Loy (Eds.), *Sport and social order* (pp. 461-520). Reading, MA: Addison-Wesley.

Harris, J.C. (1983). Interpreting youth baseball: Players' understandings of attention, winning, and playing the game. *Research Quarterly for Exercise and Sport, 54,* 330-339.

Harris, J.C. (1984). Interpreting youth baseball: Players' understandings of fun and excitement, danger, and boredom. *Research Quarterly for Exercise and Sport, 55,* 379-382.

Hartley, R.E. (1966). A developmental view of female sex-role identification. In B.J. Biddle & E.J. Thomas (Eds.), *Role theory: Concepts and research* (pp. 354-361). New York: Wiley.

Hasbrook, C.A. (1982). The theoretical notion of reciprocity and childhood socialization into sport. In A.O. Dunleavy, A.W. Miracle, & C.R. Rees (Eds.), *Studies in the sociology of sport* (pp. 139-151). Fort Worth: Texas Christian University Press.

Hasbrook, C.A. (1986a). The sport participation–social class relationship: Some recent youth sport participation data. *Sociology of Sport Journal, 3,* 154-159.

Hasbrook, C.A. (1986b). Reciprocity and childhood socialization into sport. In L. Vander Velden & J.H. Humphrey (Eds.), *Psychology and sociology of sport: Current selected research* (pp. 135-147). New York: AMS Press.

Hasbrook, C.A. (1989, November). *Reconceptualizing socialization.* Paper presented at the meeting of the North American Society for the Sociology of Sport, Washington, DC.

Hasbrook, C.A., Greendorfer, S.L., & McMullen, J.A. (1981). Implications of social class background on female athletes and nonathletes. In S.L. Greendorfer & A. Yiannakis (Eds.), *Sociology of sport: Diverse perspectives* (pp. 139-152). Champaign, IL: Leisure Press.

Hasbrook, C.A., & Mingesz, J.A. (1987, November). *Early socialization into and continuity of involvement in physical activity across the life cycle.* Paper presented at the meeting of the North American Society for the Sociology of Sport, Edmonton, AB.

Higginson, D.C. (1985). The influence of socializing agents in the female sport-participation process. *Adolescence, 20,* 73-82.

Hodge, K.P. (1988). *A conceptual analysis of character development in sport.* Unpublished doctoral dissertation, University of Illinois, Urbana-Champaign.

Horn, T.S. (1987). The influence of teacher–coach behavior on the psychological development of children. In D. Gould & M.R. Weiss (Eds.), *Advances in pediatric sport sciences* (pp. 121-142). Champaign, IL: Human Kinetics.

Horn, T.S., & Hasbrook, C.A. (1986). Information components influencing children's perception of their physical competence. In M.R. Weiss & D. Gould (Eds.), *Sport for children and youth: Proceedings of the 1984 Olympic Scientific Congress* (pp. 81-88). Champaign, IL: Human Kinetics.

Horn, T.S., & Hasbrook, C.A. (1987). Psychological characteristics and the criteria children use for self-evaluation. *Journal of Sport Psychology, 9,* 208-221.

Inkeles, A. (1968). Society, social structure, and child socialization. In J.A. Clausen (Ed.), *Socialization and society* (pp. 73-130). Boston: Little, Brown.

Kemper, T. (1968). Reference groups, socialization, and achievement. *American Sociological Review, 33,* 31-45.

Kenyon, G.S. (1968). Sociological considerations. *Journal of Health Physical Education and Recreation, 39,* 31-33.

Kenyon, G.S. (1969). Sport involvement: A conceptual go and some consequences thereof. In G.S. Kenyon (Ed.), *Sociology of sport* (pp. 77-84). Chicago: Athletic Institute.

Kenyon, G.S. (1970). The use of path analysis in sport sociology. *International Review of Sport Sociology, 5*(1), 191-203.

Kenyon, G.S., & Knoop, J.C. (1978, August). *The viability and cross-cultural invariance of a reduced social system model of sport socialization.* Paper presented at the World Congress of Sociology, Uppsala, Sweden.

Kenyon, G.S., & McPherson, B.D. (1973). Becoming involved in physical activity and sport: A process of socialization. In G.L. Rarick (Ed.), *Physical activity: Human growth and development* (pp. 303-332). New York: Academic Press.

Kenyon, G.S., & McPherson, B.D. (1974). An approach to the study of sport socialization. *International Review of Sport Sociology, 9,* 127-139.

Kohlberg, L. (1966). A cognitive-developmental analysis of children's sex-role concepts and attitudes. In E.E. Maccoby (Ed.), *The development of sex differences* (pp. 82-173). Stanford, CA: Stanford University Press.

Laakso, L. (1978). Characteristics of the socialization environment as the determinants of adults' sport interests in Finland. In F. Landry & W.A.R. Orban (Eds.), *Sociology of sport* (pp. 103-111). Miami, FL: Symposia Specialists.

Landers, D.M., & Landers, D.R. (1973). Teacher versus peer model: Effects of model's presence and performance level on motor behavior. *Journal of Motor Behavior, 5*, 129-140.

Langlois, J.H., & Downs, A.C. (1980). Mothers, fathers, and peers as socialization agents of sex-typed play behaviors in young children. *Child Development, 51*, 1237-1247.

Lerch, S.H. (1981). The adjustment to retirement of professional baseball players. In S. Greendorfer & A. Yiannakis (Eds.), *Sociology of sport: Diverse perspectives* (pp. 138-148). Champaign, IL: Leisure Press.

Lever, J. (1976). Sex differences in the games children play. *Social Problems, 23*, 478-487.

Lever, J. (1978). Sex differences in the complexity of children's play and games. *American Sociological Review, 43*, 471-482.

Levine, R.A. (1969). Culture, personality, and socialization: An evolutionary view. In D.A. Goslin (Ed.), *Handbook of socialization theory and research* (pp. 503-541). Chicago: Rand McNally.

Lewis, M. (1972). State as an infant–environment interaction: An analysis of mother–infant behavior as a function of sex. *Merrill-Palmer Quarterly, 18*, 95-121.

Lewko, J.H., & Ewing, M.E. (1981). Sex differences and parental influence in the sport involvement of children. *Journal of Sport Psychology, 2*, 62-68.

Lewko, J.H., & Greendorfer, S.L. (1980). Family influence and sex differences in children's socialization into sport: A review. In R.A. Magill, M.J. Ash, & F.L. Smoll (Eds.), *Children in sport* (2nd ed., pp. 279-293). Champaign, IL: Human Kinetics.

Lewko, J.H., & Greendorfer, S.L. (1988). Family influences in sport socialization of children and adolescents. In F.L. Smoll, R.A. Magill, & M.J. Ash (Eds.), *Children in sport* (3rd ed., pp. 287-300). Champaign, IL: Human Kinetics.

Loy, J.W., & Ingham, A. (1973). Play, games, and sport in the psychosocial development of children and youth. In G.L. Rarick (Ed.), *Physical activity: Human growth and development* (pp. 257-302). New York: Academic Press.

Loy, J.W., McPherson, B.D., & Kenyon, G.S. (1978). *Sport and social systems*. Reading, MA: Addison-Wesley.

Maloney, T., & Petrie, B. (1972). Professionalization of attitudes toward play among Canadian school pupils as a function of sex, grade, and athletic participation. *Journal of Leisure Research, 4*, 184-195.

Mantel, R., & Vander Velden, L. (1974). The relationship between the professionalization of attitude toward play of preadolescent boys and participation in organized sport. In G. Sage (Ed.), *Sport and American society* (pp. 172-178). Reading, MA: Addison-Wesley.

McPherson, B.D. (1976, April). *The child in competitive sport: Influence of the social milieu*. Paper presented at the Child in Competitive Sport: A symposium on Readiness and Effects, Milwaukee, WI.

McPherson, B.D. (1980). Retirement from professional sport: The process and problems of occupational and psychological adjustment. *Sociological Symposium, 30*, 126-143.

McPherson, B.D. (1981). Socialization into and through sport involvement. In G. Lueschen & G. Sage (Eds.), *Handbook of social science of sport* (pp. 246-273). Champaign, IL: Stipes.

McPherson, B.D. (1986). Socialization theory and research: Toward a "new wave" of scholarly inquiry in a sport context. In C.R. Rees & A.W. Miracle (Eds.), *Sport and social theory* (pp. 111-147). Champaign, IL: Human Kinetics.

McPherson, B.D., & Brown, B.A. (1988). The structure, processes, and consequences of sport for children. In F.L. Smoll, R.A. Magill, & M.J. Ash (Eds.), *Children in sport* (3rd ed., pp. 265-286). Champaign, IL: Human Kinetics.

Mead, G.H. (1934). *Mind, self, and society*. Chicago: University of Chicago Press.

Merton, R.K. (1957). *Social theory and social structure*. New York: Free Press.

Metheny, E. (1965). *Connotations of movement in sport and dance*. Dubuque, IA: William C. Brown.

Miller, D.R. (1969). Psychoanalytic theory of development: A reevaluation. In D.A. Goslin (Ed.), *Handbook of socialization theory and research* (pp. 481-502). Chicago: Rand McNally.

Miller, N.B., & Dollard, J. (1941). *Social learning and imitation*. New Haven, CT: Yale University Press.

Mowrer, O.H. (1960). *Learning theory and symbolic process*. New York: John Wiley & Sons.

Nixon, H. (1980). Orientation toward sports participation among college students. *Journal of Sport Behavior, 3*, 29-45.

Nixon, H.L. (1989, November). *Rethinking socialization and sport*. Paper presented at the meeting of the North American Society for Sociology of Sport, Washington, DC.

Orlick, T.D. (1972, October). *Family sports environment and early sports participation*. Paper presented at the Canadian Psychomotor Learning and Sports Psychology Symposium, University of Waterloo, Waterloo, ON.

Orlick, T. (1974). Sport participation: A process of shaping behavior. *Human Factors, 5*, 558-561.

Parsons, T., & Bales, R.F. (1955). *Family, socialization and interaction process*. Glencoe, IL: Free Press.

Patriksson, G. (1981). Socialization into sports involvement: The influence of family members. *Scandinavian Journal of Sports Sciences, 3*, 27-32.

Piaget, J. (1951). *Play, dreams, and imitation in childhood*. London: Routledge & Kegan Paul.

Piaget, J. (1965). *The moral judgment of the child*. New York: Free Press.

Pooley, J. (1981, April). *Dropouts from sport: A case study of boys' age group soccer*. Paper presented at the American Alliance of Health, Physical Education, Recreation and Dance National Convention, Boston.

Power, T.G., & Parke, R.D. (1982). Play as a context for early learning: Lab and home analyses. In I.E. Siegel & L.M. Asosa (Eds.), *The family as a learning environment*. New York: Plenum.

Reynolds, M.J. (1981). The effects of sport retirement on the job satisfaction of the former football player. In S.L. Greendorfer & A. Yiannakis (Eds.), *Sociology of sport: Diverse perspectives* (pp. 127-137). Champaign, IL: Leisure Press.

Rheingold, H.L., & Cook, K.V. (1975). The contents of boys' and girls' rooms as an index of parents' behavior. *Child Development, 46*, 459-463.

Roberts, G.C. (1984). Toward a new theory of motivation in sport: The role of perceived ability. In J.M. Silva III & R.S. Weinberg (Eds.), *Psychological foundations of sport* (pp. 214-228). Champaign, IL: Human Kinetics.

Roberts, G.C. (1986a). *The growing child and the perception of competitive stress in sport*. Unpublished manuscript, University of Illinois at Urbana-Champaign.

Roberts, G.C. (1986b, October). *Motivation in sport: A theory of personal investment*. Paper presented at the American Association for the Advancement of Applied Sport Psychology, Jekyll Island, GA.

Roberts, G.C., Kleiber, D.A., & Duda, J.L. (1981). An analysis of motivation in children's sport: The role of perceived competence in participation. *Journal of Sport Psychology, 3*, 203-211.

Roberts, G.C., & Martens, R. (1970). Social reinforcement and complex motor performance. *Research Quarterly, 41*, 175-181.

Roberts, J.M., & Sutton-Smith, B. (1962). Child training and game involvement. *Ethnology, 1*, 166-185.

Rosenberg, E. (1981). Gerontological theory and athletic retirement. In S. Greendorfer & A. Yiannakis (Eds.), *Sociology of sport: Diverse perspectives* (pp. 127-137). Champaign, IL: Leisure Press.

Rosenberg, M. (1957). *Occupations and values.* Glencoe, IL: Free Press.

Rosenthal, R. (1973, September). The Pygmalion effect lives. *Psychology Today.*

Sapp, M., & Haubenstricker, J. (1978, April). *Motivation for joining and reasons for not continuing in youth sport programs in Michigan.* Paper presented at the American Alliance for Health, Physical Education, Recreation and Dance National Convention, Kansas City, MO.

Sarbin, T.R., & Allen, V. (1968). Role theory. In G. Lindzey & E. Aronson (Eds.), *Handbook of social psychology* (Vol. 1, pp. 488-567). Reading, MA: Addison-Wesley.

Silva, J.M., & Weinberg, R.S. (Eds.). (1984). *Psychological foundations of sport.* Champaign, IL: Human Kinetics.

Smith, M.D. (1979). Getting involved in sport: Sex differences. *International Review of Sport Sociology, 14*(2), 93-99.

Smith, R.E., Smoll, F.L., Hunt, E., Curtis, B., & Coppel, D.B. (1979). Psychology and the bad news bears. In G. Roberts & K.M. Newell (Eds.), *Psychology of motor behavior and sport—1978* (pp. 109-130). Champaign, IL: Human Kinetics.

Smoll, F.L. (1986). Stress reduction strategies in youth sport. In M.R. Weiss & D. Gould (Eds.), *Sport for children and youths* (pp. 127-136). Champaign, IL: Human Kinetics.

Snyder, E.E. (1970). Aspects of socialization in sports and physical education. *Quest 14*, 1-7.

Snyder, E.E., & Spreitzer, E. (1973). Family influence and involvement in sports. *Research Quarterly, 44*, 249-255.

Snyder, E.E., & Spreitzer, E. (1978). Socialization comparisons of adolescent female athletes and musicians. *Research Quarterly, 49*, 342-350.

Spreitzer, E., & Snyder, E.E. (1976). Socialization into sport: An exploratory path analysis. *Research Quarterly, 47*, 238-245.

Stevenson, C.L. (1975). Socialization effects of participation in sport: A critical review of the research. *Research Quarterly, 46*, 287-301.

Stevenson, C.L. (1985). College athletics and "character": The decline and fall of socialization research. In D. Chu, J. Segrave, & B. Becker (Eds.), *Sport and higher education* (pp. 249-266). Champaign, IL: Human Kinetics.

Stryker, S. (1959). Symbolic interaction as an approach to family research. *Marriage and Family Living, 21*, 111-119.

Tasch, R.G. (1952). The role of the father in the family. *Journal of Experimental Education, 20*, 319-361.

Tauber, M.A. (1979). Parental socialization techniques and sex differences in children's play. *Child Development, 50*, 225-234.

Theberge, N. (1984). On the need for a more adequate theory of sport participation. *Sociology of Sport Journal, 1*, 26-35.

Wankel, L.M. (1975). The effects of social reinforcement and audience presence upon the motor performance of boys with different levels of initial ability. *Journal of Motor Behavior, 7*, 207-216.

Watson, G. (1976). Reward systems in children's games. *Review of Sport and Leisure, 1*, 93-121.

Watson, G. (1977). Games, socialization, and parental values: Social class differences in parental evaluation of Little League baseball. *International Review of Sport Sociology, 12*, 17-48.

Watson, G. (1979, January). A competence-based model of children's play and game involvement. *Proceedings of the Australian Council for Health, Physical Education, and Recreation Conference*, Adelaide, Australia.

Watson, G. (1981). *Introducing children to attractive, competitive situations.* Perth, Australia: Department for Youth, Sport and Recreation.

Watson, G. (1984). Social motivation in games: Toward a conceptual framework of game attraction. *Journal of Human Movement Studies, 10*, 1-19.

Watson, G., Blanksby, B.A., & Bloomfield, J. (1983, July). *Childhood socialization and competitive swimming: A sociological analysis of Australian elite junior swimmers.* Paper presented at 8th Symposium "Sport and Contemporary Society," International Committee for the Sociology of Sport, Paris.

Webb, H. (1969). Professionalization of attitudes toward play among adolescents. In G.S. Kenyon (Ed.), *Aspects of contemporary sport sociology* (pp. 161-180). Chicago: Athletic Institute.

Weinberg, S.K., & Arond, H. (1952). The occupational culture of the boxer. *American Journal of Sociology, 57*, 460-469.

Weiss, M., & Knoppers, A. (1982). The influence of socializing agents on female collegiate volleyball players. *Journal of Sport Psychology, 4*, 267-279.

Wentworth, W. (1980). *Context and understanding.* NY: Elsevier.

Wheeler, S. (1966). The structure of formally organized socialization settings. In O.G. Brim & S. Wheeler (Eds.), *Socialization after childhood* (pp. 53-116). New York: John Wiley & Sons.

Yamaguchi, Y. (1984). A comparative study of adolescent socialization into sport: The case of Japan and Canada. *International Review for Sociology of Sport, 19*, 63-82.

Yamaguchi, Y. (1987). A cross-national study of socialization into physical activity in corporate settings: The case of Japan and Canada. *Sociology of Sport Journal, 4*, 61-77.

Zigler, E., & Child, L.L. (1969). Socialization. In G. Lindzey & E. Aronson (Eds.), *A handbook of social psychology* (Vol. 3, pp. 450-589). Reading, MA: Addison-Wesley.

Part IV

Intervention Techniques and Sport Behavior

As Deborah Feltz and Robin Vealey noted in chapters 1 and 3, there has been increased interest over the last couple of decades in the application of sport psychology research to athletes and other physical activity participants. More specifically, within the last 10 years, a variety of intervention techniques have been developed and promoted as effective means to enhance athletes' performance and to modify their behavior in sport and physical activity contexts. In line with this more clinical perspective of sport psychology, Part IV examines the extent to which selected intervention techniques can be used for performance enhancement and behavioral change.

Although there has been considerable controversy in the field concerning the validity of the intervention techniques that are used by practicing sport psychologists, Part IV is presented under the assumption that researchers and practitioners can and must work together toward the common goal of understanding sport behavior. It is therefore written from the perspective that (a) intervention techniques should be based as much as possible on research and theory and (b) applied practices may provide researchers with valuable information that can then be used to design research studies and to develop theoretical models of sport behavior. Given this overall perspective, Part IV not only discusses the efficacy of selected intervention techniques but also examines potential mechanisms that may explain why and how these intervention strategies effect performance and behavioral change.

Chapter 11 is a comprehensive chapter by Shane Murphy and Douglas Jowdy on the topic of imagery and mental practice. They begin with a review of the research that has been conducted to examine the effects of imagery and mental practice on performance, then review the theoretical models that have been proposed to explain the mechanisms underlying the imagery effect. The information obtained from this review of the research and theory is then used to discuss the practical use of imagery by athletes and other physical activity participants and to suggest directions concerning future research activities.

In chapter 12, Stephen Boutcher examines the complex relationship between attention and athletic performance. He begins with a review of the attention–performance link as it has been studied from three different research perspectives, including information processing, social psychology, and psychophysiology. Boutcher uses these disparate views of the attentional process to develop an integrated model of attention in sport. He concludes with an examination of issues related to attentional training in athletes and other physical activity participants.

Finally, Damon Burton reviews the research and theory on goal setting. He begins with an illustration showing that goal setting can have both positive and negative effects on athletes' performance and motivation. To explain the dual nature of goal setting and to integrate the various theoretical approaches to this topic, Burton develops a competitive goal-setting model. He then uses this model as a framework for reviewing the empirical research on goal setting in sport and other achievement contexts. Burton concludes by outlining two major questions that must be addressed by future researchers.

Chapter 11

Sports File/Tim Hancock

Imagery and Mental Practice

Shane M. Murphy and Douglas P. Jowdy
United States Olympic Committee

The camera zooms in on a figure clad from head to toe in space-age synthetic materials, racing helmet in place, poles gripped firmly in each hand. As the camera brings us closer, we see that her eyes are closed; her body is swaying from side to side; and although she is standing in one spot, her movements suggest that she is skiing down a steep, snow-covered slope, her body twisting and her arms moving as if reacting to dangerous turns and icy patches. The announcer's voice interrupts, saying, "And there is the favorite, waiting her turn in the starting order. You can see her mentally picturing her entire run now,

from the starting gate to the finish line. Look at her concentration!"

Scenes such as this have become increasingly common on television screens during the past decade. The reported use of imagery in sports has become ubiquitous. Athletes from Jack Nicklaus to Greg Louganis have publicly acknowledged the role that imagery has played in helping them attain consistently excellent athletic performance. But what is imagery? How does imagery affect the body during sport? How can something that takes place in the "mind" affect an athlete's physical efforts in competition

Note. The second author is now a graduate student in the doctoral counseling psychology program at Virginia Commonwealth University.

and in training? Is imagery something that only elite athletes can use to enhance performance, or can anybody benefit from using it?

The purpose of this chapter is to review existing imagery research as it relates to sport performance and behavior. Much of the relevant imagery research can be found in the sport psychology literature. In this literature there has been a great deal of concern with evaluating the effects on performance of the use of imagery and mental practice. In contrast, the development of theoretical models to explain the mechanisms underlying the imagery effect has progressed slowly. In addition to examining the sport psychology literature, this chapter will also review the research from related fields that has dealt with the theoretical understanding of the nature and function of imagery. This literature is truly voluminous, and encompasses such fields as cognitive psychology, psychophysiology, psychotherapy, psychometrics, and more. Furthermore, practical suggestions will be offered as to how sport psychologists interested in imagery research can utilize the theories, models, and methods that have been developed in other disciplines and areas.

This chapter will focus on issues that are currently of interest to researchers and practitioners. It begins with a discussion of definitional issues and clarifies the meaning of the terms *mental practice* and *imagery*. Next, a review of existing research is presented, covering four major areas: mental practice studies, the literature on precompetition imagery interventions, psychological comparisons of successful and unsuccessful competitors, and research into variables that mediate imagery effects. Following the review of research, an exposition of major theories in the field is presented, focusing on the psychoneuromuscular theory, symbolic learning theories, and integrative theories. In the next section, applied issues concerning imagery and sport are discussed, and research pertaining to these applied issues is examined. Finally, the chapter concludes with a summary of major research weaknesses and suggestions for future research.

Definitions

First, the term *imagery* itself must be defined. Although several definitions of *imagery* have been advanced, the one offered by Richardson is still without peer and will be utilized here. According to Richardson, "Mental imagery refers to all those quasi-sensory and quasi-perceptual experiences of which we are self-consciously

aware and which exists for us in the absence of those stimulus conditions that are known to produce their genuine sensory or perceptual counterparts" (1969, pp. 2–3). This definition addresses several key issues concerning the nature of imagery. First, imagery experiences mimic sensory or perceptual experience. The individual talks of "seeing" an image, or "feeling" the movements associated with mental rehearsal. Second, the individual is consciously aware of these experiences. Imagery is therefore differentiated from dreaming or daydreaming, since these experiences are not the conscious focus of awareness. (This does not imply that imagery and dreaming or daydreaming may not be related processes. However, the literature in both these areas is large, and is beyond our scope here; see Singer & Antrobus, 1972.) Third, imagery takes place without known stimulus antecedents. No mountain or snow need be present, but the skier can close her eyes and imagine the experience of skiing. Any experience that satisfies these conditions can be called imagery.

An incomplete list of some of the terms related to imagery use in sport includes *symbolic rehearsal, visualization, modeling, covert practice, cognitive rehearsal, imaginal practice, dreams, hallucinations, hypnosis, visuomotor training, introspective rehearsal, implicit practice, ideomotor training*, and even *sofa training*. In the field of sport psychology the terms *imagery* and *mental practice* have been used interchangeably across a variety of contexts. We shall argue that imagery and mental practice should be carefully distinguished. *Imagery* refers to a *mental process*. Some have called it a "mode of thought" (Heil, 1985). Cognitive psychologists have fiercely debated the nature of this mental process, but there is general agreement that this cognitive function does exist. *Mental practice*, on the other hand, is a descriptive term for a particular *technique* used by athletes and many other individuals. In fact, the bulk of studies we shall discuss concern mental practice. Oxendine defines *mental practice* as "the introspective or covert rehearsal that takes place within the individual" (1984, p. 280). Many different kinds of processes can underlie this technique. As Suinn (1983) has pointed out, for example, "mentally practicing" a tennis serve could involve thinking about serving, talking yourself through the steps in a serve, imagining John Newcombe hitting a perfect serve, or visualizing a perfect serve you once hit. For the sake of clarity, therefore, it should not be assumed that asking a subject to practice mentally implies that they will engage in imagery.

For this reason, Suinn (1983) distinguishes between *mental practice* and *imagery rehearsal*.

Only in imagery rehearsal can we definitely conclude that imagery was utilized to achieve the covert practice. Imagery rehearsal usually involves the subject imagining him- or herself successfully completing the sport skill that is the focus of attention. For example, a tennis player learning a new serve may imagine the feel and look of the new skill every night before she goes to bed. Or an elite diver may pause for a moment on the springboard, imagine himself completing the dive he is about to attempt, and then initiate the dive. In both cases, the sport skill is imaginally rehearsed in the absence of actual movement or activity. Only the timing of the act of imagery changes between these two examples. The first example is the typical mental practice example, and its goal is usually to strengthen the learning of a new response or skill. The second example is most commonly called *psyching up*, and its goal is to enhance the upcoming performance of an already-learned skill. Both the relevant psyching up and mental practice research will be discussed.

Imagery processes have also been utilized in the sports context as components of other interventions (e.g., relaxation, meditation, and mood control). Thus, imagery is not used only in mental practice situations. Such alternative uses of imagery have rarely been discussed in the sport psychology literature (see Heil, 1984, 1985), where imagery often seems to be narrowly defined as visual mental rehearsal. A section of this chapter will be devoted to examining several other imagery-based techniques commonly used in sport psychology.

Not only can sport psychology fruitfully employ concepts generated in other areas of psychology, but the study of the relationship between imagery and human performance will enhance our general understanding of imagery and cognitive processes. Many of the major cognitive imagery theorists (e.g., Z.W. Pylyshyn, S.M. Kosslyn, and A. Paivio) have been criticized for not addressing the issue of somatic experiences during imagery (Ahsen, 1984). Sport psychology researchers, with their primary focus on the image–body relationship, can help address this lacuna.

Empirical Research on Imagery and Mental Practice

Many hundreds of studies have been conducted examining the utilization of imaginal strategies in motor and sports performance. A review of these studies indicates that they can be grouped into five major categories:

- Mental practice studies

- Precompetition imagery intervention research
- Studies comparing the psychological characteristics of successful and unsuccessful competitors
- Research into variables that mediate the effects of mental practice
- Research investigating the effectiveness of stress management techniques on sports performance

The studies falling into this last category will not be included in the present review, because all these studies employ a variety of interventions (such as relaxation training and cognitive restructuring) in addition to imagery rehearsal, so that it is not possible to ascertain the effects of the imagery interventions alone (Barling & Bresgi, 1982; Bennett & Stothart, 1978; Decaria, 1977; DeWitt, 1980; Gravel, Lemieux & Ladouceur, 1980; Hall & Erffmeyer, 1983; Kirschenbaum & Bale, 1980; Meyers & Schleser, 1980; Meyers, Schleser & Okwamabua, 1982; Naruse, 1965; Nelson, 1980; Noel, 1980; Silva, 1982; Suinn, 1972, 1976; Weinberg, Seabourne & Jackson, 1981, 1982). Nevertheless, in a recent review of intervention studies in sport psychology, Greenspan and Feltz (1989) concluded that these studies demonstrate that cognitive–behavioral methods, including imagery rehearsal, can be effective in changing sports behavior, particularly in situations in which a problem behavior exists.

Mental Practice Studies

A traditional belief in the sports world is that the only way to learn a motor skill is to spend long, hard hours physically practicing. But reading about a skill, watching a video, or simulating the movements to be executed may also be effective strategies when the objective is motor skill acquisition. These strategies involve some type of cognitive processing and may be mediated by the formation of images or verbal labels. The focus of this section is to review the research examining the effectiveness of using mental practice as a skill acquisition and maintenance strategy. This section will

- discuss the past research in general,
- make reference to comprehensive reviews in the field, and
- review recent research on the effects of mental practice on the learning and performance of motor skills.

Mental practice has been examined extensively by researchers. As early as the 1890s attention was given to muscular activity during mental operations (Jastrow, 1892). Formal investigations examining the use of mental practice began during the 1930s (Jacobson, 1932; Perry, 1939; Sackett, 1934, 1935). A large majority of the studies until the 1980s were concerned with the effects of mental practice on the learning and performance of motor skills and were nearly all based in the laboratory, rather than using field research methodology. The standard methodology involved a between-subjects, pretest/posttest design with four groups: physical practice, mental practice, a combination of physical and mental practice, and no practice. To analyze mental practice effects, researchers usually looked at the changes in performance of each group from preintervention to postintervention. The majority of the studies were not concerned with the mechanisms underlying the "mental practice effect."

A simple review of all published studies indicates equivocal results with respect to the efficacy of mental practice. Although many research studies have revealed support for the relationship between mental practice and performance, a second set of studies (Corbin, 1967b; Ryan and Simons, 1981; Shick, 1970; Steel, 1952; Symth, 1975) failed to find support for the effectiveness of mental practice. Within the last decade, two reviews of the literature have helped clarify the situation. Feltz and Landers (1983) assumed a statistical approach to the mental practice efficacy problem and use a technique known as meta-analysis in order to estimate the average effect size for mental practice. They located 98 studies that used mental practice and a control group or pretest measure and were able to use the meta-analytic procedure on 60 of these studies, yielding 146 effect sizes. They found an overall average effect size of .48. This suggested that mental practice is better than no practice at all. Their analyses also revealed larger average effect sizes for cognitive tasks than for motor or strength tasks.

Weinberg's (1981) content-based review of the literature produced equivocal results. Weinberg states, however, that certain findings do continue to emerge in the literature. Among the conclusions drawn by Weinberg is that mental practice combined and alternated with physical practice is more effective than either alone. This suggests that imagining oneself playing golf, for example, is better than not practicing at all. Imagining playing golf, however, is not as effective as going to the course or driving range and actually practicing. Moreover, to produce the greatest effects, one should physically practice at the driving range or course as well as incorporate mental practice. For more detailed discussions of the past research there exist several other

comprehensive reviews of the mental practice literature (Corbin, 1972; Richardson, 1967a, 1967b; Silva, 1983).

Studies conducted since these reviews have continued to examine the effects of mental practice on learning and performance of motor skills using the same methodology as in previous research studies but have introduced new and different conditions. Meacci and Price (1985), for example, used a golf-putting task to compare the performance of four groups:

- A relaxation, visualization, and body rehearsal group
- A repetition (physical practice) group
- A relaxation, visualization, body rehearsal intervention, and repetition (combined) group
- A control group

The interesting methodological addition to this study was the utilization of simulation, or body rehearsal. In this study, body rehearsal involved performing the putting movement without actually hitting the ball. Results revealed a significant difference in performance from pretest to posttest between the combined group and the other three interventions. When tested on retention, all experimental groups differed significantly from the control group. This study indicates that a combination of physical practice and cognitive methods leads to better skill acquisition than physical practice alone and that all three learning methods significantly enhance retention.

Outside the sport literature, Ross (1985) investigated the use of mental practice to enhance music performance of college trombonists. Similar to the Meacci and Price (1985) study, Ross employed a group that physically simulated the movements while mentally rehearsing. The five conditions were as follows: physical practice, mental practice, combined physical and mental practice, mental practice with simulated slide movements, and a no-practice control. Methodologically, a weakness did exist in this study, in that the groups were not equal on skill level prior to treatment. Analyses were used, however, that controlled for these pretest differences. Based upon the mean gain scores for each condition, the order of performance improvement from best to worst was the following: combined, physical practice, simulation, mental practice, and control. Statistically significant differences existed between the combined and the mental practice and control groups and also between the physical practice and control groups. The Ross (1985) and Meacci and Price (1985) studies suggest that it may be possible to potentiate the effects of mental practice by using body movement rehearsal techniques.

Another variable has been investigated by Andre and Means (1986), who manipulated the rate of the imagery used in mental practice. Andre and Means hypothesized that the speed of imagery rehearsal will influence the efficacy of mental practice, such that slow motion rehearsal might enhance the effectiveness of the practice by enriching the subject's imaginal experience. Contrary to their hypothesis, the regular mental practice group performed better on the posttest than the slow-motion mental practice group.

A well-designed study by Hird, Landers, Thomas, and Horan (1991) examined different combinations in mental and physical practice in their effect on a pegboard (cognitive) and a pursuit rotor (motor) task. Greater task gains were noted as the relative proportion of physical practice increased, although the mental-practice-only group still improved significantly compared to the control group. Also, the effect sizes were greater for all treatment groups on the cognitive task than the motor task.

The results of the recent mental practice research seem to be very consistent with the results of past research. Mental practice appears to be better than no practice, and a combination of mental and physical practice is better than or at least equal to physical practice only. The use of simulation (Ross, 1985) or body rehearsal (Meacci & Price, 1985) is a new variable that may enhance the mental practice effect and deserves further study.

Despite the long history of research into mental practice, it remains an open question just how effective mental practice can be in skill acquisition and retention. The strongest evidence for mental practice appears to be when it is combined with physical practice, but the literature contains no studies utilizing an appropriate control group that intersperses physical practice with rest periods. The need for such a control group is based on the motor learning literature, which consistently demonstrates that distributed practice (i.e., a practice schedule in which individual trials are interspersed with rest periods) is superior to massed practice (Fitts & Posner, 1967). It is possible that pratice groups using mental practice periods interspersed with physical practice periods are improving because the mental practice merely serves as a rest interval. Therefore, mental practice studies that utilize an approrpiate control group must be conducted. Interestingly, Richardson made this suggestion over 20 years ago (Richardson, 1967b, p. 270).

Precompetition Imagery Interventions

The studies of precompetition imagery interventions differ in their design from the mental practice studies because they employ the use of imagery rehearsal immediately prior to performance. Athletes call the use of cognitive strategies prior to competition psyching up, and this term has been adopted to describe this research area. Because psyching-up research studies typically investigate a number of mental preparation strategies besides imagery (e.g., attentional focus, preparatory arousal, and self-confidence manipulations), this section will highlight only the studies that have examined the use of imagery.

The first published study in this area was conducted by Shelton and Mahoney (1978). Employing a test of hand strength, they found that 15 male weight lifters, told to employ their favorite psyching-up strategy, improved their performance significantly more over baseline than 15 lifters urged to improve their performance when given a distracting cognitive task during preperformance. When asked to report the psyching-up strategies they had used, the weight lifters most frequently mentioned positive self-talk, control of attention, preparatory arousal, and imagery. Fifty-four percent of all subjects reported that they used a combination of these techniques. A similar research design has been used in several subsequent investigations (Caudill, Weinberg & Jackson, 1983; Weinberg, Gould & Jackson, 1980, 1981). A problem of interpretation posed by this research design is that it leaves the choice of the psyching-up intervention to the individual athlete. Such a design can provide evidence that some form of mental preparation facilitates performance, but these studies do not clarify the process by which this facilitation takes place. Allowing the individual to define the cognitive strategy can also cause confusion, in that when an athlete says he or she used "imagery," this tells us nothing about the type of process actually engaged in.

To overcome these design problems, several investigators have asked subjects to employ a particular imagery strategy prior to attempting a task. In nearly all these studies subjects are asked to engage in imagery rehearsal of the task prior to actual task performance. Subjects are typically asked to close their eyes, imagine themselves successfully completing the upcoming task, and then attempt the task. Rarely is a check of the imagery experience reported, so that it is often difficult to know what subjects actually imagined during imagery time or whether covert verbal strategies were used in conjunction with imagery. These studies are briefly reviewed next.

Gould, Weinberg, and Jackson (1980) found that asking subjects to use imagery and preparatory arousal as psyching-up techniques produced positive effects on performance of a leg-kick task. Three other preparatory strategies (attentional focus, control rest, and a counting-backward cognitive distraction) produced no performance changes. When these researchers compared preparatory arousal, imagery, and a resting control condition in a between-subjects design, however, only the preparatory arousal group produced significantly higher performance than the control group. Weinberg, Gould, Jackson, and Barnes (1980) examined the effects upon a tennis serve task of four conditions: using imagery to prepare for serving, making positive self-efficacy statements, using attentional focus, and preparing as they normally would (the control). None of the cognitive strategies resulted in better performance than that of the control group. Similarly Epstein (1980) had subjects employ imagery directly before the dart throwing. No significant differences in performance were found between any of three groups (internal imagery, external imagery, or a control condition). Wilkes and Summers (1984) studied the effectiveness of five mental preparation strategies on a leg-kick task measuring strength. Preparatory arousal and self-efficacy techniques produced significantly greater posttest strength performance than did a control group, while attention and imagery groups did not differ from the control group.

Several studies, however, have demonstrated how imaginal rehearsal can improve performance. Lutkus (1975) employed four groups of 16 subjects each in a 2×2 design—Standard or Imagery Instructions × Zigzag or Diamond Drawing. Imaging led to significantly faster times and fewer errors than did the standard instructions. In a study briefly cited by Richardson (1967a), Waterland (1956) compared two groups on a tenpin bowling task. Members of an imaginal rehearsal group were encouraged to recapture the kinesthetic feel of the bowling action before delivering the ball down the alley. This condition was found to produce a smoother action, greater speed of delivery, and a higher score than the standard bowling condition. Woolfolk, Parrish, and Murphy (1985) found that a group which used positive imagery rehearsal improved putting performance significantly more than a control group that utilized physical practice—only for six days. In a follow-up study, however, Woolfolk, Murphy, Gottesfeld, & Aitken (1985) did not find that positive imagery rehearsal resulted in performance increments.

Tynes and McFatter (1987) employed a weight-lifting task and found that subjects in an imagery condition produced superior performance to a cognitive distraction condition but not to a self-selected psyching-up strategy. Burhans, Richman, and Bergey (1988) found that asking subjects to imagine successful running skills from an external perspective prior to a race led to faster times after 4 weeks of training. After 12 weeks of training, however, there were no significant differences in race times between a control group and three imagery conditions.

The studies of imagery as a psyching-up strategy have generated many more questions than they have answered. Although there is a body of evidence to indicate that using imagery rehearsal prior to performance can benefit performance on some tasks compared to a condition where no cognitive intervention is employed, little is known about how this strategy influences performance. Also, several studies have failed to find a positive imagery–performance relationship, and the reasons for this are not clear. Task variables may be critical. As in the mental practice literature, psyching-up research indicates that imaginal rehearsal may be a more effective strategy for predominantly cognitive tasks (Lutkus, 1975) than for tasks requiring gross muscular efforts (Gould, Weinberg & Jackson, 1980; Wilkes & Summers, 1984). However, imagery rehearsal effects have also been found on some predominantly motor tasks (Waterland, 1956; Woolfolk, Parrish & Murphy, 1985). Studies utilizing between-task comparisons and examining the impact of individual difference variables should be a priority of researchers in this area. Also, examining the retention of these psyching-up strategies by subjects may provide more understanding of these techniques.

Overall, the psyching-up research to date has been methodologically poor, especially in terms of intervention descriptions and manipulation checks. In view of the tremendous popularity of this technique among athletes, better research is needed to understand the processes involved. In the next section, an area of investigation that has used a very different research methodology will be discussed.

Psychological Comparisons of Successful and Unsuccessful Competitors

A number of studies have been conducted over the last 15 years that have sought to compare the psychological characteristics of athletes defined as successful with those categorized as unsuccessful. Interest has focused on possible differences in psychological characteristics such as anxiety, personality traits, and cognitive style. A person's *cognitive style* encompasses such areas as thoughts, dreams, attributions, attentional focus, use of imagery, and self-talk. The first such study was conducted by Mahoney and Avener (1977). They administered questionnaires to 13 male gymnasts who were the final candidates for selection in the U.S. Olympic team in 1976. Only 6 gymnasts could be chosen for the team, and the questionnaire responses of the successful candidates were compared to those of the remaining 7 athletes who were not selected. Results indicated that qualifiers were more self-confident than nonqualifiers, reported a higher frequency of gymnastics dreams, thought more about gymnastics in everyday situations, and reported a higher frequency of internal performance imagery than external imagery.

Several other studies, many using modified versions of the Mahoney and Avener questionnaire, were subsequently conducted. Some of these studies examined differences between team qualifiers and nonqualifiers, others attempted to identify predictors of success over the course of a competitive season, and still others looked at correlations between psychological test scores and various performance measures, such as coach ratings (Carpinter & Cratty, 1983; Gould, Weiss & Weinberg, 1981; Highlen & Bennett, 1979, 1983; Meyers, Cooke, Cullen & Liles, 1979; Rotella, Gansneder, Ojala & Billing, 1980). In general, these studies have indicated that successful athletes may be more likely than their unsuccessful counterparts to engage in such mental processes as dreaming successfully about their events, using internal imagery, and using imagery as a problem-solving strategy. In several instances, however, the results obtained across studies were contradictory, and clear-cut patterns were difficult to distinguish. For example, some research studies indicate that more successful athletes reported clearer imagery than less successful athletes (Highlen & Bennett, 1983; Meyers et al., 1979), whereas other studies found no such relationship (Gould et al., 1981; Mahoney & Avener, 1977).

In evaluating this body of research, it is apparent that the correlational type of design comparing successful and unsuccessful competitors is one of the weakest used in the investigation of imagery in sport. Heyman (1982) has pointed out several problems with the research design and methodology of these studies. A central problem is that causality between certain cognitive strategies and performance is implied where none may exist. For example, based on this research it might be suggested that the use of internal imagery leads to improved performance. The methodological limitations of these designs, however, prohibit a causal relationship between imagery perspective and performance from being inferred. Also, this type of research has little to say about *how* imagery processes might affect performances. This area needs more research of an *explanatory* nature.

There is still much that is not known about how athletes utilize imagery in their sporting performance. Because most of the research to date has focused on elite athletes only, it is unclear whether there are large differences between how elite athletes versus recreational-level athletes utilize imagery strategies. Differences among elite athletes at the national level are likely to be much smaller than differences between elite and nonelite athletes. Very few studies have examined psychological differences between elite athletes and appropriate nonelite controls (Morgan, O'Connor, Sparling & Pate, 1987). Both descriptive and explanatory research studies need to be conducted in order for us to understand the types of cognitive processes employed by athletes at all levels.

Mediating Variables

The research evidence suggests that imaginal rehearsal can exert a beneficial effect on performance. However, based on the inconsistencies across studies in regard to the size of the effect, it appears that there may be certain factors that mediate the effectiveness of imaginal rehearsal across various individuals and/or sport contexts. Four classes of mediating variable have received major research attention:

- Individual differences in imagery ability
- The nature of imagery used, with regard to perspective
- The nature of the imagery used, with regard to outcome
- Whether relaxation was used with imaginal rehearsal

The research pertaining to each of these mediating variables will be examined next.

Imagery Ability

It has been suggested by several researchers that mental practice is most effective for individuals who are better imagers. Good imagery ability has been defined by two primary characteristics: vividness and controllability. *Vividness* relates to subject's self-report of clarity and reality in the image. *Controllability* is best illustrated by

Clark's (1960) classic report of a subject asked to imagine making a basketball foul shot, who reported that the ball would not bounce in his imagination, but stuck to the floor instead. This would be described as an uncontrolled image.

The major assessment instruments used in the measurement of imagery ability are the Vividness of Imagery Scale (Sheehan's, 1967, form of Bett's Questionnaire upon Mental Imagery), the Vividness of Visual Imagery Questionnaire (VVIQ; Marks, 1973), and the Gordon Test of Visual Imagery Control (Richardson, 1969). Recently, Hall and colleagues (Hall & Pongrac, 1983; Hall, Pongrac & Buckolz, 1985) have devised an alternative to these measures. Their instrument, identified as the Movement Imagery Questionnaire (MIQ), was designed specifically for the sporting context and was intended to address the issue of kinesthetic imagery in sports more adequately.

Some descriptive evidence that imagery ability plays an important role in sporting performance has been provided by the correlational studies mentioned earlier. Although Mahoney and Avener (1977) did not find a relationship between imagery control and competitive performance, Meyers and colleagues (1979) found that better racquetball players reported having better control of their imagery. Highlen and Bennett (1983), examining the relationship between open- and closed-skill athletes found that divers who qualified for the Pan-American Games rated their imagery as more vivid and controlled than did those divers who did not qualify. More recently, Orlick and Partington (1988) found that in a sample of male Canadian Olympic athletes, use of kinesthetic imagery that was easily controlled was significantly correlated with successful performance at the Olympics.

Imagery ability was also found to be an important variable in several studies examining the effects of mental practice on performance. For example, Start and Richardson (1964) found that a group of subjects who had the most vivid and controlled images exhibited significantly higher gain scores on subsequent performance than groups who had either high vividness and low controllability, low vividness and high controllability, or low vividness and low controllability. Ryan and Simons (1981) found nonsignificant correlations between performance on a stabilometer task (primarily motor) and imagery ability. However, the relationship between imagery ability and performance on a dial-a-maze task (primarily cognitive) revealed that good performers tended to have more vivid imagery. In a follow-up study of 80 subjects asked to learn a novel balancing task, Ryan and Simons (1982) found that those who reported strong visual imagery and those who reported strong kinesthetic imagery performed better than those who did not report strong imagery of either type.

Goss, Hall, Buckolz, & Fishburne (1986) controlled for imagery ability in order to examine effects on the acquisition and retention of movements. Based upon scores on the MIQ, subjects were classified in one of three groups: high-visual, high-kinesthetic; high-visual, low-kinesthetic; and low-visual, low-kinesthetic. Results reveal that there was a significant difference among the three groups on the acquisition of movement patterns. High-visual, high-kinesthetic individuals performed best, whereas low-visual, low-kinesthetic individuals performed worst. However, there was not a significant difference when the groups were tested on retention.

From the psychological literature, Dyckman and Cowan (1978), investigating the role of imagery vividness in the success of a desensitization procedure with snake phobics, found that imagery vividness was significantly correlated with therapeutic success (posttherapy avoidance of snakes). Housner (1984) classified subjects as high- or low-imagers on the Marks (1973) VVIQ and then had both groups of subjects recall movement patterns after viewing a particular sequence on a video. Results revealed that subjects with a high imagery ability reproduced movements with significantly greater accuracy than those with low imagery ability.

Common sense suggests that imagery ability is one of the most critical variables that might influence performance effects of mental practice and psyching up, yet it has not received the amount of serious attention from researchers that would be expected. The combined results of the research described suggest that individual differences in imagery ability must certainly be considered by researchers who are investigating the performance effects of imagery-based strategies.

Imagery Perspective

Imagery perspective was formally recognized and identified with Mahoney and Avener's (1977) study. These researchers reported that gymnasts who qualified for the Olympic team reported using a higher frequency of internal images compared with external images than did the nonqualifying gymnasts. Mahoney and Avener defined *imagery perspective* in the following way: "In external imagery, a person views himself from the perspective of an external observer (much like in home movies). Internal imagery, on the other hand, requires an approximation of the real life phenomenology such that the person actually imagines being inside his/her body and experiencing those sensations which might be expected in the actual situation" (p. 137).

As discussed earlier, a number of studies have attempted to replicate the Mahoney and Avener findings, with mixed results. Meyers and colleagues (1979) found no relationship between perspective and performance in their study of highly skilled racquetball players; but Rotella and colleagues (1980) found that higher skilled skiers visualized the course from an internal perspective, whereas the less successful skiers reported that they visualized their entire body skiing—an external perspective. Mahoney, Gabriel, and Perkins (1987), in a survey study of hundreds of athletes, provided further evidence that elite athletes are more likely than nonelite athletes to adopt an internal imagery perspective—"I imagine what it will feel like in my muscles." Conversely, non-elite athletes reported a higher frequency of use of external imagery—"I see myself performing—just like I was watching a videotape."

A few investigators have examined the relationship between internal/external perspective and performance using an experimental research design. Epstein (1980) did not find a difference in performance between subjects using internal and external imagery on a dart-throwing task. Mumford and Hall (1985) used three different types of imagery (internal kinesthetic, internal visual, and external visual) and found no difference between groups on figure skating performance. Epstein and Mahoney (1979) found that external imagery was associated with shaky confidence and distractibility in track athletes.

Research studies examining the neuromuscular basis of imagery have attempted to control for imagery perspective as a mediating variable. Hale (1982) found that internal imagery resulted in a significant increase in muscle activity during imagery, whereas external imagery did not. Harris and Robinson (1986) also found that internal imagery resulted in significantly more muscle activity than external imagery among the karate athletes they tested. This finding is questionable, however, because Harris and Robinson found that a majority of the subjects switched imagery perspectives during testing. The more highly skilled athletes tested in this study reported that they favored internal imagery to a greater extent than did the lower-skilled athletes.

Imagery perspective has been infrequently addressed in the clinical psychology research literature. However, one study that did control for this variable was conducted by Bauer and Craighead (1979). While measuring skin conductance, heart rate, finger pulse volume, and respiration, they manipulated attentional focus and orientation during imagery. Orientation, or imagery perspective, involved having subjects imagine themselves as a participant (internal imagery) or as an observer (external imagery) of fearful and neutral scenes. Although it was hypothesized that visualizing from a participant orientation would result in greater physiological reaction than visualizing oneself as an observer, only marginal physiological differences between the groups were found. The authors concluded that the data did not support the suggestion that the subjects involved in desensitization should necessarily imagine themselves as a participant (Paul, 1966).

The results of the Bauer and Craighead (1979) study illustrate the inconsistencies in results that exist in the literature with regard to imagery perspective. It is impossible to draw a definitive conclusion concerning the effect of internal/external perspective based on the evidence presently available. It is possible, however, that the influence of imagery perspective may be more powerful in athletic performance than in therapy situations because of the importance of kinesthetic awareness to sports performance. Kinesthetic awareness seems to be experienced more through internal images than through external ones. Studies of highly competitive athletes indicate that imagery techniques are widely used in performance and in training (99% of athletes surveyed by Orlick and Partington, 1988, reported using imagery techniques) and that internal and kinesthetic imagery are highly valued; but such studies also indicate that imagery perspective often fluctuates during imaginal rehearsal (Jowdy, Murphy & Durtschi, 1989). Research that attempts to show that internal imaginal rehearsal is "better" than external imaginal rehearsal or vice versa is probably fruitless. Instead, researchers might be better advised to investigate whether internal and external imagery perspectives have different features associated with them, such as generating more self-confidence, involving the musculature more, making it easier to identify technique mistakes, and so on.

Image outcome

Nearly all the mental practice studies conducted to date have examined the effects of positive imagery or have at least assumed that subjects were imagining successful outcomes. Powell (1973) was one of the first to utilize a negative imagery manipulation, in which subjects were asked to rehearse performing the task but to imagine a failure outcome. For example, a subject would be told to rehearse throwing a dart at a target but would be asked to imagine the dart missing the target. Powell found that negative imagery degraded performance on a dart-throwing task when compared to positive mental practice. In a study mentioned earlier, Woolfolk, Parrish, and Murphy (1985) used a positive image group, a negative image group, and a control group. They found that the negative image group performed significantly worse than both the positive imagery and control groups. Woolfolk, Parrish, and Murphy (1985) compared imagining the outcome only (no imaginal task rehearsal) with imagining task rehearsal and both negative and positive outcomes. Results showed that performance declined significantly for subjects in both the task rehearsal with negative outcome and the negative outcome alone conditions. These studies all suggest, therefore, that negative imagery rehearsal will inhibit performance.

Few explanations have been offered as to how negative rehearsal might degrade performance (Murphy, 1986; Suinn, 1985). It is possible that negative mental practice interferes with the subject's motor program, causing a decline in performance. Also possible is a disturbance in the subject's cognitive representation of task execution caused by negative mental practice. It may be that negative mental practice affects performance through its impact on dynamic properties of the subjects such as confidence, concentration, or motivation. The study of negative imagery rehearsal should be viewed as a valuable adjunct to the general study of imagery and mental practice.

Relaxation

Using relaxation in combination with imagery has a long tradition in psychological research, extending back at least to Wolpe's (1958) seminal work on systematic desensitization. In work with athletes, many writers suggest using relaxation inductions prior to imagery instructions in order to facilitate imagery control (Suinn, 1985; Vealey, 1986). Suinn's visuomotor behavior rehearsal (VMBR) method, in fact, requires beginning each imagery session with a relaxation induction. However, research studies that have examined whether combining relaxation with imagery produces effects significantly different from using imagery alone are strikingly consistent in their findings. None of the studies conducted to date have found any significant benefits to using relaxation in combination with imagery

(Gray, Haring & Banks, 1984; Hamberger & Lohr, 1980; Weinberg, Seabourne & Jackson, 1981, 1987). In addition, many of the studies that have demonstrated strong mental practice effects have not used relaxation procedures in combination with the mental practice (e.g., Clark, 1960; Corbin, 1967a; Woolfolk, Parish, & Murphy, 1985). Research thus suggests that while relaxation may interact with imagery, it is not a critical mediating variable in producing imagery effects upon performance.

In summarizing the literature dealing with the variables that mediate imagery-based techniques, it is apparent that the imagery ability variable has most clearly been identified as mediating the effects of imaginal techniques on performance. Additionally, negative images seem to exert a powerful and consistent debilitating effect on performance. This confirms anecdotal reports from coaches and athletes of the deleterious effects of negative images. One of the functions of positive imagery rehearsal may be to prevent attentional capacity from being devoted to negative images and thereby to maintain consistent performance. Studies of imagery perspective have yielded inconclusive results. Imagery perspective differences may prove to be related to the preferred cognitive styles of the athlete. It is also possible that future research will be able to show that one perspective is better suited than the other for a particular intervention purpose (e.g., internal perspective for promoting the development of "muscle memory" of a skill, external perspective for detecting and analyzing errors in task execution). Finally, relaxation may alter the imagery experience for some subjects, but it does not appear to be a necessary prerequisite for producing imagery rehearsal effects.

Yet it is also apparent that all the relevant dimensions of imagery that may mediate performance effects have not yet been identified. Anderson (1981a), who reviewed the imagery assessment literature, concluded that "the number of specific dimensions of imaginal activity that could be assessed is limited only by the number of hypotheses that could be generated linking different aspects of imaginal activity with behaviors of interest to the investigator" (p. 153).

Several such variables have been suggested by different researchers. Paivio (1985), for example, has suggested that a crucial function of mental practice use by athletes may be that it serves a motivational role when reinforcers are rare. Richardson (1977) adopted an approach that sought to classify persons on the basis of individual differences in habitual modes of processing cognitive events. Based on this approach, he developed the Verbalizer–Visualizer Questionnaire (VVQ), which measures whether individuals typically respond to cognitive demands with greater visualizing or verbalizing responses. Other researchers have investigated individual differences in the ability to become absorbed in the imagery experience (Tellegen & Atkinson, 1974). These examples all suggest that there are many relevant dimensions of imagery experience that have been largely ignored in sport psychology research.

A challenge for researchers interested in the assessment of imagery is to find a satisfactory approach to the assessment issue. A problem for sport psychology researchers is that a lack of theory development in imagery research has led to a corresponding paucity of assessment approaches. After an extensive review of the sport psychology literature, Mahoney and Epstein concluded that "it appears that researchers who are interested in imaginal processes in athletes are left in the unenviable position of facing a potentially important phenomenon that may be elusively dynamic and for which there is no psychometrically adequate assessment" (1981, p. 448). Two approaches to the assessment of self-reported experiences which have good research potential must be noted. Fenker and Cox (1987) have demonstrated how a data analysis technique, multidimensional scaling (MDS), can be successfully utilized to describe the emotional experiences of athletes in sporting situations. It is a useful assessment approach because it allows for both idiographic and nomothetic analyses of self-reported experience. In a series of studies conducted by Murphy (1985), the technique known as magnitude estimation scaling (MES), developed by Stevens (1975), was used in the assessment of imagery experiences. The MES technique allows judgments about an image to be made on a wide variety of dimensions. In these studies, subjects were asked to rate their imagery experience on dimensions such as reality of the image, sharpness, intensity, detailedness, degree of focus, and degree of attention present. Subjects were able to successfully discriminate among different types of images on many of these dimensions. It will be a critical challenge for researchers to incorporate more appropriate and descriptive assessment techniques, such as MDS and MES, in future imagery research.

This concludes the review of existing research into imagery-based techniques and their effects upon performance. In the next section, the theories that have been proposed to account for mental practice effects will be discussed, and the research pertaining to these theories will be examined. Also, theories of imagery from areas other than sport psychology will be briefly discussed, and their relevance for sport psychology examined.

Theoretical Explanations of Mental Practice Effects

The mental practice literature has generated two major approaches to the explanation of why mental practice might benefit performance. These approaches are known as the *psychoneuromuscular hypothesis* and the *symbolic learning hypothesis*. Both approaches were developed in order to explain the mental practice phenomenon, Why does mentally rehearsing a physical activity lead to improved physical performance? Few attempts have been made to apply these explanations to other imagery-based interventions such as psyching up. After examining these two approaches, this section will conclude with a discussion of other theoretical approaches to the imagery question, which, because they are more integrative in nature and less focused on one particular research area, may be of more benefit to researchers. Two prominent theories in the imagery area, developed by Lang and Ahsen, will be examined in some detail.

Psychoneuromuscular Theory

The psychoneuromuscular explanation of mental practice is that the muscles involved in the skill being imagined become slightly innervated during mental practice, sufficiently to provide kinesthetic feedback that can be utilized to make skill adjustments on future trials. Although this explanation has been proposed by a number of researchers (Corbin, 1972; Richardson, 1967b; Schmidt, 1987), it has never been fully developed or stated in sufficient detail to be truly deserving of the description of a "theory." Nevertheless, it has generated a number of research studies and must be examined in detail.

Psychoneuromuscular explanations of mental practice effects have a long tradition. As early as the end of the last century, Jastrow (1892) examined and found involuntary movements occurring during various mental operations. According to the ideomotor principle (Carpenter, 1894), an image will produce muscular activity similar to that during actual movement, but at a lesser magnitude. Washburn, in *Movement and Mental Imagery* (1916), also suggested that "tentative movements" occur during imagery. Furthermore, the tentative movements during imagery were believed to influence subsequent skilled behavior.

Jacobson (1930a, 1930b, 1930c, 1930d, 1931a, 1931b) did an extensive amount of research in the area and found that muscle activity while a subject imagined such activities as bending his or her forearm, lifting (curling) a weight, weeping, or climbing a rope was generally greater than the muscle activity associated with rest. Further, the muscle activity was located in the specific muscles associated with the particular movement being studied. Jacobson argued that this research demonstrated that mental practice must be associated with muscle innervation. While some research has shown that the muscular response to imagery is an indication of generalized arousal (Shaw, 1938), others have shown that the muscle response concomitant with mental practice is indeed localized and specific to the muscles involved in the imaginal scene (Harris & Robinson, 1986).

The most recent statements of the psychoneuromuscular position have tried to specify the actual physiological mechanisms that might be involved in the innervation–feedback loop. Schmidt (1987), for example, has speculated that very small forces (not sufficient to cause movement) are generated by mental practice and that these forces are detected by the very sensitive Golgi tendon organs. Feedback from these Golgi tendon organs goes to the premotor cortex and strengthens the existing motor program or allows for adjustments in the motor program to take place. These changes in the motor program improve subsequent performance. Research in this area utilizing the current sophistication of psychophysiological assessment devices or taking account of recent knowledge concerning neuropsychological substrates remains to be done.

In order to investigate the psychoneuromuscular hypothesis, some researchers have focused attention on whether or not the muscular responses during imagery are similar to muscle activity during actual performance. Jacobson (1930b) provided evidence that records from muscle activity during mental practice of rhythmical activities (e.g., pumping a tire) were similar to records obtained during the physical movements associated with actual performance. Further evidence is provided by Suinn (1980), who found that an electromyographic record for an alpine skier imagining a downhill run contained isolated bursts of activity that matched the skier's description of the particular course he was visualizing. Bird (1984) also found support for Jacobson's hypothesis in a study that measured the amplitude of muscular responses of five athletes at different muscle sites based upon their particular sport. Bird found an increase in the magnitude of muscle activity during mental practice. Moreover, like Suinn, Bird reports that the bursts of muscle activity occurred at the times when they would be expected to occur during actual performance. However, Hale (1981) replicated Jacobson's work in a more controlled study and did not find evidence that muscle activity during actual and imaginary practice resembled each other.

A problem with these studies is that only the amplitude, but not the frequency and duration, of the muscle activity was examined. Wehner, Vogt, and Stadler (1984) utilized a time series analysis to examine the frequency, as well as the amplitude, of muscle activity during mental and physical practice. Although some questions about the study can be raised due to the report of actual movement during the mental training and control conditions, the frequency and amplitude curves of the mental and active training groups resemble each other.

Research in the psychological literature is also extensive and provides results to support the phenomenon of muscle activity during imagery (see Qualls, 1982, for a review). Thus, at this point we may conclude that muscle activity is concomitant with mental practice. However, for the psychoneuromuscular hypothesis to be strongly supported, it must be demonstrated that there is a relationship between muscle activity during imagery and subsequent performance.

In order to examine this relationship with performance, researchers have examined the magnitude of muscle activity in high-skilled and low-skilled performers. Several studies have demonstrated that the magnitude of muscle activity during mental practice is related to skill level (Durall, 1986; Hale, 1982; Harris & Robinson, 1986). However, another recent study found no such relationship (Jowdy, 1987). Ulich (1967) has provided evidence to suggest that in fact a moderate amount of muscular activity during mental practice, rather than high or low amounts of activity, is associated with greater increases in physical performance. Thus, the magnitude of muscle activity responses may not be the significant factor in mediating mental practice effects. Even if a relationship were found between skill level and muscle activity during mental practice, this is not a direct test of the neuromuscular explanation. This type of research design can only demonstrate relationships and is not capable of indicating causality.

From the experimental psychology field, a substantial amount of research has provided evidence that the effects of mental practice cannot be explained by muscular activity during imagery and is more a function of operations within the central nervous system (Johnson, 1982; Kohl & Roenker, 1980, 1983). To date, results from studies examining the neuromuscular basis of mental practice in the psychology literature support the contention that the muscular responses are an effect mechanism rather than causal of performance changes. Evidence to support a relationship between muscular activity during mental practice and subsequent performance in the sport-related literature has yet to be obtained. The failure to demonstrate such a relationship is one of the most significant reasons for the current skepticism regarding the psychoneuromuscular hypothesis. Feltz and Landers (1983), in their review of the mental practice literature, concluded that "it is doubtful that mental practice effects are produced by low-gain innervation of muscles that will be used during actual performance" (p. 48).

Although the psychoneuromuscular hypothesis has received a fair hearing from researchers, there is very little direct evidence to suggest that feedback to the premotor cortex from minute innervations of the peripheral musculature causes mental practice effects. It would seem that we can reject the psychoneuromuscular explanation in its present form. However, our understanding of the relationship between mental activity and physiological responses is still in its infancy, and it may well be that a more sophisticated physiologically based theory of mental practice will prove to be a valuable addition to our understanding of mental practice effects.

The psychoneuromuscular hypothesis has scarcely been considered in the context of the psyching-up research methodology described earlier. Although imaginal psyching up might "prime" the appropriate muscles via some process analogous to that suggested by Mackay (1981), it is even more plausible that imaginal psyching up affects a variety of physiological systems via its impact on the athlete's emotional state. Urgently needed are investigations of the effects of imaginal psyching-up strategies on the body's physiological responses. Might imaginal psyching-up somehow prepare the body physiologically for upcoming performance? For example, might it be possible for a long-distance runner to imagine an upcoming race and thereby trigger the release of endorphins (the putative naturally occurring pain killers) in the body? Such a physiological reaction might benefit subsequent performance. Variables that should be assessed in future research efforts include electromyograph, electroencephalograph, galvanic skin response, heart rate, and measures of those endocrine products postulated to be involved in effective physical performance, such as endorphins, epinephrine, and cortisol. The impressive and growing body of knowledge being gathered in the field of psychoneuroimmunology (Achterberg, Lawlis, Simonton & Mathews-Simonton, 1977; Lloyd, 1987; Locke, 1982; Marx, 1985; Wechsler, 1987) shows that relationships between the mind and body are accessible to empirical investigation, especially in view of some of the advanced research technologies available today. The field of sport, with its great emphasis on the measurement of physical performance, should be especially amenable to testing some of these speculative relationships.

In contrast to psychoneuromuscular explanations, those theorists who propose that a symbolic learning explanation of mental practice effects is most parsimonious with extant research argue that the effects of mental practice are due to operations within the central nervous system.

Symbolic Learning Theory

The symbolic learning hypothesis, sometimes known as the symbolic–perceptual hypothesis (Denis, 1985), is that mental practice benefits performance because it allows participants cognitively to prepare for and plan performance. The sequential aspects of a task can be rehearsed, the spatial characteristics of the skill can be considered, task goals can be clarified, potential problems in performance can be identified, and effective procedures for task execution can be planned. All of these procedures are based in the central nervous system; and, unlike the psychoneuromuscular approach, their execution does not imply the involvement of the peripheral musculature. Symbolic learning approaches to the mental practice phenomenon go back many years, at least to the work of Sackett (1934, 1935) and Perry (1939).

Two major bodies of evidence have been relied upon to support the symbolic learning approach. First, a number of studies have shown that mental practice is more effective for tasks that have a high cognitive (as opposed to a motor) component. Second, theoretical accounts of motor learning arguing that the early stages of learning are primarily cognitive (e.g., Fitts, 1962) are compatible with the notion that mental practice will have its greatest effects during the early stages of learning. Several studies have examined whether mental practice is most effective during the early stages of learning. Additionally, recent research using sophisticated experimental methodologies has shed further light on the symbolic learning explanation controversy.

Effects of Task Characteristics on Mental Practice

This category of research has examined the nature of the task as a variable influencing mental practice effects. In this approach, tasks are classified on a continuum ranging from mainly motor tasks to predominantly cognitive tasks. The symbolic learning hypothesis states that the effects of mental practice should be greatest for those tasks lying more on the cognitive (symbolic) end of the continuum. For example, a stabilometer task would be classified as mostly a motor task, due to the greater involvement of motor components, as opposed to a digit symbol substitution task, which is more symbolic in nature.

Sackett (1934, 1935) used a maze-tracing task—high in symbolic components—and found that imaginary practice led to greater effects on performance than verbal or overt rehearsal. Perry (1939), another proponent of the symbolic learning hypothesis, examined the effects of imaginary practice on five different tasks. Perry found that imaginal practice was most effective in pegboard, symbol digit substitution, and card sorting and relatively less effective in mirror tracing and tapping, tasks that require actual movements. Morrisett (1956) found that on a task high in symbolic components there was a difference between physical practice and mental practice groups and that these groups were significantly different from a control group. On a task high in motor elements, however, Morrisett found no enhancement of performance under a mental practice condition. Wrisberg and Ragsdale (1979) found mental practice to produce

greater effects on the McCloy test of multiple response (high-symbolic-demand task) than on a stabilometer task (low-symbolic-demand task). In one of the most recent studies of this kind, Ryan and Simons (1981) found that on a predominately motor task (stabilometer) there was not a significant difference between mental practice and a control group. On a more symbolic task (dial-a-maze), the mental practice and physical practice groups improved equally, and both groups improved significantly more than the control group.

Although the preponderance of studies have found greater mental practice effects with symbolic, as opposed to motor, tasks, a few studies have yielded contradictory results. Rawlings, Rawlings, Chen, and Yilk (1972), utilizing the pursuit rotor, a task high in motor components, found that both a mental and physical practice group improved performance and were not significantly different from each other. Symth (1975) used the pursuit rotor task as well as a mirror-drawing (symbolic) task to investigate the effects of the task nature on mental practice outcome. Symth found that the mental practice group improved performance very little when attempting the task high in symbolic components. The effects of mental practice were not significant on the pursuit rotor task. Symth concluded that mental practice was not effective on either the symbolic or motor tasks, and that subjects may have benefited from more experience with mental practice.

The most recent evidence addressing the effects of task nature on mental practice effects is the Feltz and Landers (1983) study. Feltz and Landers found that the effects of mental practice on symbolic tasks were greater than the effects on motor or strength tasks. Because this relationship was so clear, even across 60 different studies using many methodologies, Feltz and Landers concluded that the distinction between symbolic and motor aspects of motor skill learning is very robust, therefore providing strong support for the symbolic–perceptual hypothesis. Oslin (1985), in a replication of the Feltz and Landers study, found that the effects of mental practice on symbolic tasks were greater than on motor or strength tasks, consistent with past research.

The weight of evidence clearly favors the position that mental practice produces the greatest effects on tasks that are high in symbolic (or cognitive) components. Although supportive of a symbolic learning explanation of mental practice, this research cannot prove the symbolic learning position.

Relationship of Mental Practice to Stages of Learning

Fitts (1962) identifies the first stage of learning as the cognitive phase. In this phase the learner attends to cognitive (or symbolic) cues regarding the task, spending much time processing information. Mental practice may assist in the organization of such data at the central processing level. Several of the previously mentioned studies have found evidence to support this view. Wrisberg and Ragsdale (1979) found that mental practice was most effective during the early stages of learning of the task high in symbolic demands. Consistent with the Wrisberg and Ragsdale findings, Minas (1980) also concluded that mental practice may be most beneficial before the subject has experience with the task. Minas did find motor improvements on the task in the mental practice condition (speed, balance, and rhythm) but argued that these improvements were likely to be secondary gains resulting from greater attentional capacity once the symbolic planning of the motor task was achieved.

The Wrisberg and Ragsdale (1979) and Minas (1980) studies suggest that the stage of learning interacts with mental practice effects. Evidence that prior experience at the task may not be necessary for mental practice to be effective and that mental practice may be most effective during the early stages of learning are consistent with a symbolic learning explanation of mental practice. Other researchers have found that some prior experience with the task is necessary for mental practice to be effective (Corbin, 1967a, 1967b; Phipps, 1968). Minas proposes that this conflict may be resolved on the basis of how familiar the subject is with the task. Mental practice may be impossible if the subject has no centrally coded information about the constituent movements of the task. But if the task, although unfamiliar, comprises known movements, mental practice may be effective despite lack of prior experience. This consideration suggests that researchers should carefully evaluate and describe the amount of experience their subjects have had with the task or tasks being investigated.

In their meta-analytic review of the literature, Feltz and Landers (1983) found that the average mental practice effect size for experienced subjects (at a later learning stage) was larger than that for novice subjects (at an earlier learning stage), although this difference was not significant. This finding would run counter to the hypothesis that mental practice is most effective during early learning. Oslin (1985) found similar results, showing that although experienced subjects utilized cognitive strategies more often than novice subjects, the difference was not significant.

More research would be necessary before strong conclusions could be drawn about the relationship between the stage of learning of the subject and mental practice effects. It is plausible that mental practice serves an organizational and planning role in the early stages of learning of a task and is therefore beneficial to the novice. For imagery rehearsal to be effective, however, it is highly probable that the learner should have a correct internal representation of the task. This could be gained through experience or modeling. The research suggests that mental practice does not lessen in importance as the learner becomes more experienced. Some theorists have questioned the validity of the notion that symbolic factors become less important to learning as it progresses. They have found evidence that symbolic factors in learning do not become less important over time (Adams, 1981). If this is true, then mental practice should be effective later, as well as earlier, in the learning process, although it might achieve its impact through different processes (e.g., motor program strengthening and diversification, rather than motor program organization).

Research in the stages-of-learning field may currently be more important from a practical viewpoint than a theoretical one. Newer and better methodologies are now being found to examine the symbolic learning question. The stage of learning research provides only an indirect test of the symbolic learning hypothesis.

Recent Research

Bilateral transfer studies have provided evidence consistent with a central processing account of mental practice effects. Kohl and Roenker (1980) showed that when the task was physically performed with the left hand, subjects who had mentally practiced using their right hand performed as well as or better than subjects who had physically practiced with their right hand. To refute the possibility that work decrement in the physical practice group influenced the results, they conducted a second experiment that showed no difference between the physical practice and mental practice groups even after the subjects in the physical practice group were given a 5-minute interpolated rest period. In a third experiment, Kohl and Roenker showed that work decrement can also occur under conditions of mental imagery. These findings are significant, for explanations of work decrement suggest that it is a function of centrally related mechanisms as opposed to peripheral ones (Catalano, 1967; Catalano & Whalen, 1967; McIntyre, Mostowan, Stojak & Humphries, 1972). Kohl and Roenker (1983) continued to provide evidence that presents problems for a psychoneuromuscular position. Results again showed that performance after mental practice was similar between unilateral and bilateral transfer. The authors suggested that the neuromuscular activity concomitant with mental practice is an effect rather than a causal mechanism. They argued that the mechanisms underlying the effects of mental practice are centrally rather than peripherally based.

Johnson (1982) has also provided evidence that the effects of mental practice are due to cognitive processes. He examined the type of bias that visual and motor interference would have on the reproduction of movements on a linear positioning task. He hypothesized that if the motor system was involved during imagery, motor interference during the imagery period would inhibit subsequent performance and visual interference would not. Results from the first experiment showed that imagining incorrect responses produced a biasing effect when subjects were later tested on physical ability to reproduce various movements to an established criterion. The second experiment showed that differential effects in performance occur as a function of the type of interference given during the imagery period. In analysing variable error, Johnson found that visual interference produced more response bias than motor interference, supporting the notion that mechanisms of mental practice are centrally based.

Research investigating the physiological responses of the brain during imagery provide interesting results relevant to the symbolic learning explanation. Davidson and Schwartz (1977) found differences in electroencephalograph activity patterns of subjects during visual and kinesthetic imagery. During visual imagery there was significantly greater occipital activation, while kinesthetic imagery led to greater activation of the sensorimotor region. When subjects engaged in both types of imagery, there was a significant increase in electroencephalograph activity at each respective cortical region. Roland, Larsen, Lassen, and Shinhoj (1980) monitored regional cerebral blood flow during "internal programming." While subjects imagined themselves executing a sequence of finger movements in the absence of overt movement, an activation in both cortical supplementary motor areas occurred. This increase, however, was only 60% of that exhibited during actual execution of the motor sequence test. Although these studies were not designed to look at mental practice effects, their results are clearly relevant to the issue because activation of relevant cortical regions during imagery is consistent with a symbolic learning explanation of imaginal mental practice.

To summarize the research pertaining to symbolic learning explanations of mental practice, it is apparent that a strong body of research exists to support centrally based mechanisms in the effectiveness of mental practice. The weakness of symbolic learning explanations is that they have been poorly explicated by theorists and researchers. As a result, the symbolic learning hypothesis has not been amenable to experimental verification and has not generated much new research. Before moving on to a discussion of more recent integrative theories in the imagery area, a discussion of the theoretical questions that have been left unaddressed by the cognitive model will be presented.

A major issue is the nature of the cognitive processing that takes place during mental practice. How does the cognitive processing of mental practice take place: through visual imagery, through kinesthetic imagery, or through verbal mediation? As far back as 1939, Perry contended that mental practice was not mediated by imaginal processes at all but was primarily mediated by subject verbalizations. This approach suggests that verbal strategies (such as cue labeling) might underlie the mental practice effects found in many studies. A few studies have directly compared imagery strategies, verbal and other strategies. Singer, Goren, and Risdale (1979) found that an imagery strategy produced more accurate responses and fewer errors on a curvilinear repositioning apparatus than a labeling, a kinesthetic, and an informed-choice strategy. In another study, Singer, Risdale, and Korienek (1980) found that imagery and chunking (grouping discrete activities) strategies produced more accurate and consistent performances in a movement-sequencing task than a rhythm strategy and a control condition.

This line of research suggests that verbal mediation alone cannot fully account for the mental practice phenomenon. Especially when tasks involving item information or location information are involved (Housner, 1984; Housner & Hoffman, 1981), visual imagery ability seems to be an important determinant of the effectiveness of mental practice. The literature on observational learning (Bandura, 1971) also supports the notion that cognitive processes beyond verbal mediation are involved when modeling is used to acquire motor skills. According to the modeling account of learning, the learner matches executed movement patterns with a conceptual representation or standard. This conceptual representation provides feedback so that corrections can be made on subsequent movement executions. Several studies support the existence of such a process (Bandura, Jefferey & Bachicha,

1974; Carroll & Bandura, 1982; Shea, 1977). While the nature of the conceptual representation is not yet clear, many theorists believe that imagery is involved in this internal representation (see Denis, 1985; Richardson, 1985). The literature discussing the mental operations involved in the acquisition of motoric movements also makes reference to the role and function of imagery in mental practice (for more detailed discussions, see Keele, 1982; Magill, 1984; Stelmach & Hughes, 1984).

Interdisciplinary research appears to be moving in the direction of trying to determine what the nature of the internal representations generated during imagery rehearsal might be and how they function. Determining the nature of the encoding of imaginal material has been the source of fierce debate in the information-processing literature. A popular view has been that humans encode information in the brain in two ways: pictorially and verbally (Paivio, 1971). Although this approach has been vigorously criticized by theorists who believe that all information is encoded in propositions (verbally; Pylyshyn, 1973, 1981), newer theories in the information-processing realm have returned to various pictorially or spatially based explanations of imagery (see Pinker & Kosslyn, 1983). Various innovative experimental methodologies have been generated in an attempt to determine the "true nature" of imagery (Shepard & Metzler, 1971).

Clearly, the symbolic–perceptual hypothesis has little to say about such issues in its current incarnation. Although the centrally based symbolic learning hypothesis can be clearly differentiated from the peripherally based psychoneuromuscular hypothesis, it is too simplistic in not offering a proposal for explaining *where* the beneficial effects of mental practice occur. Do the "cognitive" effects of mental practice occur in the encoding of the skill, the retrieval of the skill, or the execution of the skill? Without a rigorous explanatory framework, the symbolic learning approach cannot serve as a useful heuristic for future researchers. It is probable that in the future the "symbolic learning hypothesis" will be either ignored as newer and more detailed theories are studied or developed into a more complete theory with the addition of the latest findings from the information-processing realm.

The final theoretical section will deal with the theories and approaches both within and outside sport psychology that have attempted to deal with the theoretical issues involved in positing imagery as a basis for behavior change. These approaches all have in common the characteristic that they have elaborated in some detail how imagery might be effective in changing human behavior.

Integrative Theories

The research addressing the mental practice issue in sport is substantial, as studies such as the Feltz and Landers (1983) meta-analysis indicate. In the area of theory development, however, much needs to be done. As we have indicated, current "theories" of mental practice are really little more than explanations of a limited subset of mental practice findings. The psychoneuromuscular hypothesis, for example, offers a plausible account as to why electromyographic activity is found in relevant muscle groups during mental practice, but it appears to have little validity in explaining the causality of mental practice effects. The symbolic–perceptual hypothesis provides an explanation as to why mental practice effects are usually larger for tasks containing more cognitive demands, but it offers no direction as to what form the conceptual representations developed during mental practice may take. We shall argue that sport psychology researchers can profitably look beyond the field of sport psychology and investigate the relevance to sport of imagery theories developed in other areas.

Researchers and theorists working in the areas of cognitive and clinical psychology have paid special attention to the development of imagery theories. Cognitive theorists have proposed various models that might explain the mental processes underlying imaginal experience. Recently, computer-based models have been popular. Models based on an information-processing account of mental processes have been proposed, such as those of Paivio (1971) and Kosslyn (1981). This approach will not be discussed in detail here, because much of this research seeks to explain a rather sophisticated set of experimental research findings and has been little concerned with direct application issues. (Most of the information-processing literature has been concerned with visual imagery. This approach has been criticized by some theorists, who argue that such an emphasis is overly narrow: "The idea of a body experience involved with the image is notoriously absent in the views of imagery held by Pylyshyn, Kosslyn, and Paivio alike. It appears that this debate was held in some kind of a happily floating ivory tower which had no moorings with the earth," Ahsen, 1984, p. 16. Sport psychology, with its emphasis on bodily experience and kinesthetic imagery, may be able to offer a useful complementary line of research to that of the information-processing researchers.) Clinical theorists have been concerned with explaining how it is that imagery interventions lead to behavior change. In the clinical area, theories of imagery have addressed two important aspects of imagery that have been largely neglected in the mental practice literature: psychophysiology and meaning.

Two influential theories from the clinical area will be examined next. These theories might best be described as *integrative*, because they seek to integrate findings from a diverse set of studies and do not concentrate solely on one research methodology. The work of the most influential pair of imagery theorists, Lang and Ahsen, will be focused upon.

Lang's Psychophysiological Information-Processing Theory

A model of imagery originally developed by Peter Lang for the purpose of understanding a great amount of research into phobia and anxiety disorders deals specifically with the psychophysiology of imagery. Although Lang's model is clinically based, it utilizes an information-processing model of imagery (Lang, 1977, 1979). The model begins with the assumption that an image is a functionally organized, finite set of propositions stored by the brain. The model further states that a description of an image contains two main types of statements: stimulus propositions and response propositions. *Stimulus propositions* are statements that describe the content of the scenario to be imagined. *Response propositions* are statements that describe the imager's response to that scenario.

The image is also believed to contain a motor program containing instructions for the imager on how to respond to the image; it is thus a template for overt responding. It is assumed in Lang's theory that modifying either overt behavior or vivid imagery will result in a change in the other. This relationship, it is argued, explains the therapeutic impact of imagery. Lack of identity between the physiological pattern of the perceptual–affective response in overt behavior and in vivid imagery will lead to therapeutic failure.

The crucial point to emphasize here is that response propositions are a fundamental part of the image structure in Lang's theory. The image is *not* just a stimulus "in the person's head" to which he or she responds. The information-processing model of imagery is therefore very different from the analog representation suggested by phenomenological analysis. Lang and others have demonstrated, in a variety of psychophysiological studies, that imagery is accompanied by an efferent outflow appropriate to the content of the image (Brady & Levitt, 1966; Brown, 1968; Hale, 1982; Jacobson, 1932; Lang, 1979; Shaw, 1940). Lang's studies of phobic patients have indicated that the greater the magnitude of these physiological responses during imagery, the greater will be the accompanying changes in behavior (Lang, Melamed & Hart, 1970). Also, imagery instructions that contain response propositions elicit far more physiological responses than do imagery instructions that contain only stimulus propositions (Lang, Kozak, Miller, Levin & McLean, 1980).

This suggests that the sport psychologist who wishes to help an athlete change behavior by using rehearsal imagery would do well to include many response propositions in the imagery descriptions, enabling the athlete to access the appropriate motor program. To give an example, we present two sets of imagery instructions to imagine oneself running. The first is a script weighted with stimulus propositions:

> *You are engaged in a training run down a street close to your home on a beautiful autumn day. You are wearing a bright red track suit; and as you run, you watch the wind blowing the leaves from the street onto a neighbor's lawn. A girl on a bicycle passes you, and you see that she is delivering newspapers. You swerve to avoid a pothole in the road, and you smile at another runner passing you in the opposite direction.*

The second script is weighted with response propositions:

> *You are engaged in a training run down a street close to your home on a crisp autumn day. You feel the cold bite of the air in your nose and throat as you breathe in large gulps of air. You are running easily and smoothly; but you feel pleasantly tired and can feel your heart pounding in your chest. Your leg muscles are tired, especially the calf and thigh; and you can feel your feet slapping against the pavement. As you run, you can feel a warm sweat on your body.*

The research conducted by Lang and his associates indicates that the second set of imagery instructions is more likely to produce the report of a vivid image than the first set of instructions. It is also more likely to produce accompanying physiological responses, which may make it more likely that this kind of imagery description may be used to effectively alter athletic performance (although these changes may actually be mediated by central processes rather than peripheral ones, as we have seen). These predictions await empirical verification in the field of sport psychology.

An initial study utilizing Lang's theory is that of Hecker and Kaczor (1988). Four imagery scenes were utilized: a neutral scene, an unfamiliar fear scene, a familiar action scene, and a familiar athletic anxiety scene. All scene descriptions contained response propositions except the neutral scene. Heart rate was the only physiological measure. Results showed that physiological response was significantly greater during the familiar action and athletic anxiety scenes (for which subjects presumably had a prototype for overt responding) when compared to the fear scene. Physiological response was also significantly greater during the action scene when compared to the neutral scene. Although somewhat confirmatory of Lang's theory, this study was not designed to investigate whether physiological responses during imagery contribute to subsequent behavior (performance) change. This prediction should be investigated by sport psychology researchers.

Although developed independently of Lang's model, Suinn's visuomotor behavior rehearsal, (VMBR) model is similar in that he proposes that imagery should be a holistic process that involves a total reintegration of experience, including visual, auditory, tactile, kinesthetic, and emotional cues. Suinn's model provides an example of how the physiological and emotional aspects of imagery can be incorporated into imagery-based interventions by sport psychologists. Indeed, Suinn has demonstrated that physiological responses can be obtained from athletes imaginally experiencing athletic participation (Suinn, 1983); and Suinn's VMBR method is one of the psychological intervention approaches in sport that has empirical evidence to support its effectiveness (Seabourne, Weinberg, Jackson & Suinn, 1985). Suinn also suggests that VMBR be carried out when a subject is first able to obtain a state of relaxation (Suinn, 1976), although (as discussed previously) the research literature is equivocal as to whether this is, in fact, a necessary precondition for imagery to successfully impact upon performance (Hamberger & Lohr, 1980).

Ahsen's Triple-Code Theory

Another recently developed model of imagery also recognizes the primary importance of psychophysiological processes in the imagery process but goes a step further in describing another essential aspect of imagery that must be incorporated into theories of imagery—the *meaning* the image has for the individual. Ahsen's triple-code (image–somatic response–meaning [ISM]) model

of imagery (Ahsen, 1984) specifies the three essential parts of imagery that must be described by both theorists and clinician. The first part is the image itself: "The image can be defined as a centrally aroused sensation. It possesses all the attributes of a sensation but it is internal at the same time. It represents the outside world and its objects with a degree of sensory realism which enables us to interact with the image as if we were interacting with a real world" (Ahsen, 1984, p. 34). The second part is the somatic response; that is, as Lang and others (Sheikh & Kunzendorf, 1984) have demonstrated, the act of imagination results in psychophysiological changes in the body. The third aspect of imagery, most ignored by the other models so far discussed, is the meaning of the image. According to Ahsen, every image imparts a definite significance or meaning to the individual. Further, every individual brings his or her unique history into the imaginal process, so that the same set of imagery instructions will never produce the same imagery experience for any two individuals.

The repercussions of ignoring the meaning component of imagery were forcefully brought home to one of us (Murphy) when working with a group of elite young figure skaters as part of a mental training program. Work with another client from the same sport had indicated that a powerful image used by the athlete to relax and concentrate prior to beginning his program involved imagining "a bright ball of energy, glowing golden, floating in front of me, which I inhale and take down to the center of my body. There I feel the energy radiate to all parts of my body, golden and warm, bringing me a peaceful attitude and providing me with the energy I need for my program." Almost the same imagery description was therefore used with the group of young skaters, followed by a description of a perfect skating program. The skaters were then asked to describe their imagery experience. The results were surprising. One skater reported that he had imagined the glowing energy ball "exploding in my stomach, leaving a gaping hole in my body, so that I was crippled and unable to compete." Another skater said that the image of the ball of energy "blinded me, so that when I began skating I could not see where I was going, and I crashed into the wall of the rink and lay there, unmoving." A third athlete reported imagining inhaling a helium-filled balloon, leaving her speaking in a squeaky voice, at which point she began giggling uncontrollably and was unable to skate. And so it went, with every athlete reporting a different experience. Clearly, these young skaters were bringing their own fears, anxieties, and preconceptions into the imagery process, with the result that they brought their own meanings to the imagery, different from the meaning intended by the sport psychologist. This example illustrates how important it is to attend to the meaning the athlete attaches to the image that is being employed in imaginal rehearsal or any other imagery technique. Ahsen's triple-code model recognizes the powerful reality of imagery for the individual and also reminds sports psychologists to pay attention to the meaning of the images they employ and their clients report.

Ahsen's ISM triple-code model suggests three important areas to which researchers should give attention. Adopting the ISM approach would suggest that the image script employed should be described completely and that the imaginal experience (I component) of the subject should be obtained (e.g., by the content analysis method, Anderson, 1981b). Psychophysiological measures should be employed more frequently, and imagery scripts should contain response propositions in addition to stimulus propositions (assessing the S component of imagery). Finally, the meaning of the image for the subject should be evaluated by the experimenter (measuring the M component of imagery).

Clearly, no one model of imagery is sufficiently developed as yet to be deserving of recommendation for use by all sport psychology researchers. An appropriate recommendation at the present time would be that researchers utilize some version of an information-processing model of imagery. Information-processing models have much to recommend them:

- They have generated a great deal of useful research.
- They are sufficiently detailed to be of great help in designing both imagery interventions and imagery research.
- They have already been adapted to the applied area (e.g., Lang's work).

Information-processing models are sufficiently broad to incorporate the study of many related areas within the imagery field, such as the effect of imagery on performance, attention, emotional state, physiological arousal, and self-efficacy. Although they are "cognitive," information-processing models go far beyond the simple symbolic–perceptual hypothesis of the mental practice literature. The use of rigorous imagery models in sport psychology will bring many benefits to researchers. As theory development becomes a more integral part of the research process, the study of imagery in sport psychology may be entering its most productive and exciting stage.

Before concluding this chapter with a summary of recommendations for future research in the imagery and sport area, current areas of interest to applied sport psychologists will be explored. Many imagery-based techniques have recently been described by various writers in the applied sport psychology area.

Current Applied Issues in Imagery and Sport

As well as having been extensively studied by researchers, imagery interventions are very popular among applied sport psychologists. Various books have been published recently describing the application of psychological interventions to sport, and all of them contain at least one chapter on imagery interventions (Bennett & Pravitz, 1987; Loehr, 1986; Orlick, 1986, 1990; Porter & Foster, 1986; Williams, 1986; Zaichowsky & Fuchs, 1986). In this section, some of the imagery-based techniques that have been utilized by sport psychologists will be described, and in addition, the research evidence upon which they are based will be delineated. Because so many imagery-based techniques have been described in the literature, in this section the described techniques will be grouped together according to the purpose of the intervention. For example, techniques that have been used for skill acquisition will be discussed first, imagery techniques for arousal regulation later.

Skill Acquisition

Many studies in the mental practice literature suggest that learning a new skill can be assisted by imaginal rehearsal of the skill. The greater the number of cognitive components of the skill, the more assistance to learning is provided by mental practice. In fact, some researchers have suggested that "tasks which emphasize kinesthetic cues may not be mentally rehearsable" (Wrisberg & Ragsdale, 1979, p. 207). While this assertion is challenged by the self-report of many athletes who emphasize the importance of kinesthetic rehearsal, the evidence suggests that tasks that are primarily motoric in nature require a certain level of familiarity with the skill before mental practice can be effective. For cognitive tasks, mental practice appears to assist the learner in developing a conceptual plan for understanding and organizing the task.

Some writers (e.g., Gallwey, 1974; Heil, 1985) have suggested that there are two principal ways of learning new motor skills. One way is primarily verbal and analytical, the other is intuitive and global. According to these writers, the second method has much to recommend it, particularly in overcoming the self-critical anxiety that often accompanies the learning of a new skill. Anyone who has learned a sport skill (e.g., a golf swing) will certainly remember a time when attention needed to be directed to many subcomponents of the total skill for even a poor approximation of the skill to occur (the molecular approach) and another time, often much later, when a feeling of "gestalt" occurred and correct skill execution seemed to occur automatically (the molar approach). It would be interesting to investigate whether imagery techniques can enhance the transfer of attention from the molecular to the molar level and thus hasten skill acquisition. Another area within the skill acquisition domain that deserves attention is research into the use of imagery by children learning new skills. This would appear to be an excellent area of study to further our knowledge of the motor skill acquisition process.

Skill Maintenance

The primary imagery technique used by athletes to maintain a skill is mental practice. Despite the wealth of mental practice studies, surprisingly few have looked at *long-term* retention of the skills studied. Retention tests are much more common in the motor learning area and should be more regularly included in mental practice designs. The few studies that have examined retention (e.g., Meacci and Price, 1985) have found that if a mental practice strategy is used during learning, retention is usually better than that displayed by a no-practice control group. Yet it would be interesting to examine whether a skill, once learned, could be maintained for long periods of time by mental practice alone. It might be possible to establish separate "forgetting" curves for a skill not physically practiced, with and without mental practice. Certainly, there have been several testimonial accounts of athletes who have maintained their sport skills for long periods by mental practice alone. This issue would be extremely relevant for injured athletes. Experimental evidence on this question is sparse. As mentioned previously, psyching-up studies should also include measures of retention in order to evaluate whether the effects of such interventions will be sustained over the long term.

Arousal Regulation

Imagery techniques have long been used in clinical psychology as a relaxation-inducing device. This approach has been adopted in sport psychology as a way of calming the anxious athlete prior to competition. D. and B. Harris (1984), for example, suggest that athletes practice visualizing whatever provides them with a sense of relaxation. This strategy can then be employed when the athlete gets nervous or worried about an upcoming performance in order to restore a sense of calm.

A large body of research has examined the relationship between arousal and performance (Martens, 1974). The inverted-U hypothesis posits that performance is optimal at some moderate arousal level and that arousal levels that are too low or too high inhibit performance. More recently, reversal theory and catastrophe theory have complicated this once-simple picture (see chapter 6). Oxendine (1970) is responsible for the notion that different tasks require different levels of optimal arousal. For example, an athlete who is required to lift a heavy weight may need to be at a much higher level of arousal than one who is attempting to shoot at a distant target with an air pistol. Techniques to increase an athlete's arousal have been called "preparatory arousal" techniques (Shelton & Mahoney, 1978), and a body of research exists to indicate that such techniques can enhance performance on certain tasks (Wilkes & Summers, 1984).

Imagery has been used in research both to increase and decrease arousal. Kavanagh & Hausfeld (1986), for example, studied performance on a hand grip strength task under three mood conditions: happy, sad, and no-mood-manipulation. Moods were induced via the use of personalized images. Kavanagh and Hausfeld found that the happy mood produced significantly greater strength performance than the sad mood, with the no-mood-manipulation condition falling between the two. An examination of the effects of three emotive images on performance on a strength task (Murphy, Woolfolk & Budney, 1988) found that subjects reported increased arousal levels after imagining scenes that made them fearful or angry, but they showed no strength increases. After imagining a scene that made them feel calm, subjects had significantly lower strength performance. In both these studies, images that generated moods thought to be inappropriate to the task (sadness, relaxation) resulted in decreased performance.

Although the research in this area is limited, it suggests that imagery can be an effective tool for arousal regulation. It has been suggested that emotive imagery is most effective when it is used as a cognitive coping strategy and attention is directed toward utilizing the arousal to achieve goals (Murphy et al., 1988). This hypothesis was explored by Lee (1990), who conducted two studies in order to examine whether inducing a positive, confident mood through imagery would affect performance. In both studies, Lee found that imagery which was task relevant resulted in greater performance improvement on a sit-up task than did task-irrelevant imagery. No relationship was found between mood state and subsequent performance. This research suggests that psyching-up imagery may achieve its effects through directing cognitive attention to the task at hand, not through its effects on mood or arousal level alone.

Planning/Event Management

Another popular use of imagery techniques in the applied sport psychology area is to prepare athletes cognitively for upcoming competitions. A good example of this strategy is provided by Rotella and colleagues (1980). In their study, successful skiers developed a visual image of the course after previewing it; and in the time between inspecting the course and reaching the starting gate they concerned themselves with planning effective strategies for skiing the course. Less successful skiers, on the other hand, simply tried to maintain positive thoughts prior to racing.

A three-time Olympian who consulted with one of us (Murphy) provided a succinct account of his utilization of this approach:

It's as if I carry around a set of tapes in my mind. I play them occasionally, rehearsing

different race strategies. Usually I imagine the race going the way I want—I set my pace and stick to it. But I have other tapes as well—situations where someone goes out real fast and I have to catch him, or imagining how I will cope if the weather gets really hot. I even have a "disaster" tape, where everything goes wrong, and I'm hurting badly, and I imagine myself gutting it out.

Terry Orlick, in *Psyching for Sport* (1986), provides a detailed guide for constructing what he calls a "competition focus plan," which can be mentally practiced as often as one wishes, prior to competition. Visualization can be an aid in rehearsing such a plan prior to the actual competition situation.

As with many imagery interventions, this technique has received scant research attention, but mental practice findings regarding the effectiveness of imagery rehearsal in organizing tasks in a conceptual framework suggest that this approach to event planning has merit. A question that has been little addressed in the research literature is whether athletes can be taught to more effectively apply imagery techniques for cognitive planning. Some research suggests that mental preparation strategies such as imagery affect the attentional set or the cognitive preparation of the athlete prior to performance (Feltz & Landers, 1983; Lee, 1990; Mahoney, 1979; Murphy et al., 1988). Applied research has not yet examined whether training in the use of such imagery techniques can enhance the effects upon performance (see George, 1986, for a review of the literature on imagery enhancement training).

Emotional Rescripting (Stress Management)

This approach is similar to event planning; but instead of imaginally rehearsing their rational cognitive strategies, athletes rehearse their emotional response to competitive situations. For example, an athlete might sit down with a sport psychologist and list all the thoughts and feelings he or she typically experiences in a race situation. Then the athlete will go back and identify the emotions that might interfere with performance or prevent him or her from giving maximum effort; for example, feelings such as intense fatigue, panic, or depression (often verbalized via phrases such as "I can't go on" or "I'm not as good as these other competitors"). Next, the athlete and sport psychologist devise strategies to replace these negative emotions with more appropriate cognitive strategies, for example, through the use of thought stopping, positive self-talk, or self-affirmations (Porter & Foster, 1986). Finally, the athlete imaginally rehearses a race and sees himself or herself coping successfully, using the techniques he or she has practiced. The goal of this intervention is for the athlete to develop and become familiar with a set of successful strategies for coping with stress (see Lazarus & Folkman, 1984).

Clinical psychologists would recognize this procedure as a typical variant of stress management training (Ellis, 1973). A variety of studies have shown these techniques to be effective in reducing many types of anxiety, from medical and dental anxiety (Miller & Henrich, 1984) to test anxiety (Wine, 1971). Although stress management interventions have yet to be systematically studied in the sport psychology area, the studies published to date have yielded promising results (Crocker, 1989; Crocker, Alderman & Smith, 1988; Crocker & Gordon, 1986; Mace & Carroll, 1985; Ziegler, Klinzing & Williamson, 1982). Smith (1980) has outlined a comprehensive cognitive–affective approach to stress management training in sport which is a useful guide for researchers as well as practitioners. Imagery interventions are only one component of stress management approaches, so it may not be practical to study the effects of imagery alone in this area.

Self-Image Manipulation

An illustration of the use of imagery to affect self-image is provided from the files of Murphy. A young athlete sought consultation because she felt she had a problem in defeating certain opponents. Analysis revealed that she was rapidly improving in her sport and was meeting stronger opponents in competition. Because they were higher-ranked than she, she lacked confidence against them. Often, however, she possessed the skills necessary to defeat them. An intervention strategy was designed in which the athlete practiced imagining herself defeating specific higher-rated opponents, as well as the consequences of these victories (how others would react, her own emotional response, and so on). Within weeks, she had achieved first-time victories against several of these opponents and attributed her success to a newfound confidence generated by her imaginal rehearsal.

The images we hold of ourselves are one of our major sources of self-esteem. The fact that imagery can impact self-confidence has long been recognized by cognitive–behavioral therapists, who have developed a number of imaginal strategies that encourage behavior change by asking clients to imagine more successful behaviors

than they presently exhibit. These imaginal strategies include systematic desensitization (Wolpe, 1958), flooding (Rachman, 1968), coping imagery (Meichenbaum, 1977), and implosion (Levis & Hare, 1977). Bandura (1977) has developed a theory of human behavior change arguing that many psychological interventions achieve their effects through modifications of an individual's self-efficacy level. Such modifications can be achieved via both actual experience and through vicarious or even imagined experience (Bandura, 1971). Modeling is a well-established treatment intervention based on this theory, and Cautela has developed an imaginally based variant of this procedure known as *covert modeling* (Cautela & Kearney, 1986). Rushall (1988) describes a successful application of covert modeling in a sports setting to deal with lack of confidence. Although several studies have failed to show a relationship between confidence changes and performance changes during imagery interventions (Wilkes & Summers, 1984; Woolfolk, Murphy, Gottesfeld & Aitken, 1985), self-reports from athletes who regularly utilize visualization techniques indicate that confidence changes often accompany imagery rehearsal. Measures of self-efficacy should be routinely included in future mental practice and imagery studies in order to gather more information on this relationship.

Attentional and Pain Control

Imagery-based techniques have been suggested by several authors for use in injury rehabilitation and healing and in controlling pain (Epstein, 1989; Jaffe, 1980; Levine, 1982). The well-known work of Simonton, Mathews-Simonton, and Creighton (1978) has popularized the use of imagery and visualization in assisting the healing process and fighting disease. Some authors have applied this approach to athletes and sports (e.g., Lynch, 1987; Porter & Foster, 1986, 1990), suggesting the use of visualization for healing sports injuries and coping with athletic pain. Utilizing imagery following deep relaxation is similar to hypnosis, so that the extensive literature on hypnosis effects is relevant in this area. Research has consistently demonstrated that hypnosis is effective in treating clinical pain, although only with hypnosis-susceptible patients (Wadden & Anderton, 1982). Surprisingly little research has been conducted on clinical uses of imagery with athletes. A number of authors have described imagery methods that are applicable in helping injured athletes (Rotella, 1984; Wiese & Weiss, 1987; Yukelson, 1986); hopefully, research into such imagery applications will soon follow. Apparently no research investigations have yet been conducted into whether combined imagery-and-relaxation-training interventions can actually help prevent injury and illness in athletic populations. Evidence from other areas of psychology suggests that this might be possible (Lloyd, 1987).

To summarize the state of applied interventions using imagery techniques, it is clear that imagery can be used in many ways that go beyond simple practice of sports skills. In many cases, these new applications have been suggested and utilized before research has been conducted into their efficacy. Hopefully, new research efforts will be directed at understanding these intervention techniques; for this area promises to be an exciting and rewarding one for researchers.

This chapter will conclude with a summary of suggestions meant to guide future research efforts and some proposals for the consideration of researchers interested in the relationships between imagery and sporting performance.

Future Research Directions

Although a great deal of interesting and informative research into imagery use in sport has been accomplished, a number of weaknesses have been noted in the current research base as we have conducted this literature review. Some of the major problems with existing research will be used to provide suggestions for future research. Each of the methodological suggestions offered will be discussed briefly.

Complete Descriptions of Imagery Scripts Used in Research

A problem for investigators wishing to replicate research in this area is that published studies rarely provide detailed descriptions of what subjects were instructed to imagine in the study (Murphy, 1990). This seems to be especially problematic in the psyching-up literature, where brief two-to-three sentence intervention "descriptions" are often all that is provided. Until more information is collected concerning the effects of various imagery variables (e.g., imagery ability, imagery perspective, presence of response propositions, whether covert verbalizations were present, length of time used for imagery, whether imagery practice was allowed, subjects' prior use of imagery, use of relaxation), it seems wise to include a detailed description of all relevant variables within the study. This will be a great boon in allowing comparisons among studies.

It is suggested that *imagery instructions should be classified as an independent variable*

in research. If the actual instructions given by the experimenter as to *what* to imagine and *how* to imagine it are always classified as an independent variable, a data base will quickly be established concerning the effects of the instructions themselves.

Manipulation Checks in All Imagery Interventions

This issue was raised succinctly at the 1989 Canadian Behavioral Sciences Conference, when Richard Suinn asked Terry Orlick, "How do you know what your subjects are really imagining?" This question strikes to the heart of a fundamental concern in imagery research, always complicated by the inherently ephemeral nature of the subject of study. New means of addressing this issue have included the use of psychophysiological measures during imagery and creative task requirements such as those used by Roger Shepard (Shepard & Metzler, 1971). However, there is no substitute for asking the subject to describe his or her imagery experience. Many of those studies that have included such a check have found that the imagery experience reported by some subjects was different from that described by the experimenter (Harris & Robinson, 1986; Jowdy, 1987; Smyth, 1975; Woolfolk, Murphy, Gottesfeld & Aitken, 1985). A deterrent to the widespread use of such checks by researchers may be the lack of availability of quality assessment devices. A recommended solution, at least until we develop more standardized descriptions of imagery experiences, is to use a coding system like that suggested by Anderson (1981a) to check both the experimenter's script and the subject's reported script. Then the match between the two can be assessed. This would allow researchers to ascertain whether subjects are imagining a content consistent with the experimenter's manipulation and also provide a means for systematically examining the nature of the deviations that occur.

Dynamic Properties Associated with Mental Practice

The mental practice literature has been characterized by a lack of adequate assessment of potential imagery dimensions. Researchers must design assessment approaches that better test the theory being investigated. Attempts to incorporate recent psychometric approaches such as multidimensional scaling and magnitude estimation scaling should be encouraged.

Psychophysiological Approaches to the Study of Imagery

We devoted a large amount of space to a review of the psychoneuromuscular hypothesis. This approach to explaining mental practice effects has not proved to be parsimonious or heuristic. Although cognitive explanations may prove to be most parsimonious in explaining the mental practice literature, there is no a priori reason to believe that other uses of imagery are mediated by the same processes. Instead of abandoning the search for a physiological basis for imagery effects, researchers should employ the newly available techniques of biotechnology to explore the many systemic changes (neural, endocrine, and immunological) that are thought to accompany imagery experiences (e.g., Rider & Achterberg, 1989). This will call for greater interdisciplinary research among sport and exercise scientists. Presently, it is difficult to find studies in the sport psychology literature that include physiological measures other than electromyograph and heart rate. This situation is lamentable, given the variety of technologies available today to assess the body's responses to mental stimuli (see Lloyd, 1987).

Training in Imagery Use

Much of the mental practice and psyching-up literature to date relies on analogue research designs, which presents a critical generalizability problem for researchers. Most published studies of mental practice, for example, utilize nonathletic samples, expose them briefly to imaginal rehearsal techniques, and proceed to measure mental practice effects. It is difficult to generalize from such studies to the athletic population, because this is not how imagery rehearsal techniques are typically employed (see the critique of mental practice designs by Silva, 1983). Elite athletes are highly motivated to achieve excellent performance, and are often diligent in the amount of time they give to the practice of the cognitive strategies they employ to manage their performance (Orlick & Partington, 1988). Future research should focus on three critical issues:

- If subjects are trained in imagery use and allowed sufficient time to practice imagery techniques, will this affect the magnitude of mental practice and psyching-up effects?
- Will imagery effects on performance be greater if subjects are actually taught how to apply the techniques to the management of their performance, as has been suggested

by some writers (e.g., Lee, 1990; Murphy et al., 1988)?
- What is the impact of teaching imagery skills to serious and elite athletes? It is apparent that applied sport psychologists have begun to offer imagery training programs to a variety of elite and junior athletes (Gould, Tammen, Murphy & May, 1989; Orlick, 1989), but the effects of such training programs have yet to be evaluated.

Critical Parameters of Mental Practice Use in Skill Acquisition

A number of issues have been touched upon under this heading during the review of the literature. First, what impact does mental practice have at different stages of learning? Can mental practice speed early learning of a skill, or is it more effective when a skill is being consolidated? Or do both effects exist? Second, are there optimal time lengths for mental practice? Can mental practice negatively impinge on performance if carried out for too great a length of time? Third, can the effectiveness of interspersing mental practice with physical practice be demonstrated apart from the benefits accruing due to differences between massed and distributed practice? Finally, what effects does mental practice have on the retention of a learned skill? Although the mental practice literature is extensive, well-controlled studies addressing these issues are lacking.

Conclusion

Many myths and misconceptions have gathered around the use of imagery in sport. Often heard is the question, "Does imagery work?" This is like asking, "Does breathing work?" As demonstrated in this chapter, imagery is a basic cognitive function in humans and is central to motor skill acquisition and execution. The self-report of athletes indicates that visualization and mental practice are techniques they routinely use to master skills and achieve consistently superior performances (Hall, Rodgers & Barr, 1990; Orlick & Partington, 1988). Future research needs to be directed toward a better understanding of the roles that imagery plays in human performance so that we can help all persons to optimally utilize their innate capacities.

References

Achterberg, J., Lawlis, G.F., Simonton, O.C., & Mathews-Simonton, S. (1977). Psychological factors and blood chemistries as disease outcome predictors for cancer patients. *Multivariate Experimental Clinical Research, 3*, 107-122.

Adams, J.A. (1981). Do cognitive factors in motor performance become nonfunctional with practice? *Journal of Motor Behavior, 13*, 262-273.

Ahsen, A. (1984). ISM: The triple code model for imagery and psychophysiology. *Journal of Mental Imagery, 8*, 15-42.

Anderson, M.P. (1981a). Assessment of imaginal processes: Approaches and issues. In T.V. Merluzzi, C.R. Glass, & M. Genest (Eds.), *Cognitive assessment* (pp. 149-187). New York: Guilford.

Anderson, M.P. (1981b). Imagery assessment through content analysis. In E. Klinge (Ed.), *Imagery: Vol. 2. Concepts, results, and applications*. New York: Plenum Press.

Andre, J.C., & Means, J.R. (1986). Rate of imagery in mental practice: An experimental investigation. *Journal of Sport Psychology, 8*, 124-128.

Bandura, A. (Ed.)(1971). *Psychological modeling: Conflicting theories*. Chicago: Aldine-Atherton.

Bandura, A. (1977). Self-efficacy: Toward a unifying theory of behavioral change. *Psychological Review, 84*, 191-215.

Bandura, A., Jeffery, R., & Bachicha, D.L. (1974). Analysis of memory codes and cumulative rehearsal in observational learning. *Journal of Research in Personality, 17*, 295-305.

Barling, J., & Bresgi, I. (1982). Cognitive factors in athletic (swimming) performance: A re-examination. *Journal of General Psychology, 107*, 227-231.

Bauer, R.M., & Craighead, W.E. (1979). Psychophysiology responses to the imagination of fearful and neutral situations: The effects of imagery instructions. *Behavior Therapy, 10*, 389-403.

Bennett, B.K., & Stothart, C.M. (1978). *The effects of a relaxation-based cognitive technique on sports performances.* Paper presented at the meeting of the Canadian Society for Motor Learning and Sport Psychology, Toronto.

Bennett, J.G., & Pravitz, J.E. (1987). *Profile of a winner: Advanced mental training for athletes.* Ithaca, NY: Sport Science International.

Bird, E.I. (1984). EMG quantification of mental practice. *Perceptual and Motor Skills, 59*, 899-906.

Brady, J.P., & Levitt, E.E. (1966). Hypnotically induced visual hallucinations. *Psychosomatic Medicine, 28*, 351-353.

Brown, B.B. (1968). visual recall ability and eye movements. *Psychophysiology, 4*, 300-306.

Burhans, R.S., Richman, C.L., & Bergey, D.B. (1988). Mental imagery training: Effects on running speed performance. *International Journal of Sport Psychology, 19*, 26-37.

Carpenter, W.B. (1984). *Principles of mental physiology.* New York: Appleton.

Carpinter, P.J., & Cratty, B.J. (1983). Mental activity, dreams, and performance in team sport athletes. *International Journal of Sport Psychology, 14*, 186-197.

Carroll, W.R., & Bandura, A. (1982). The role of visual monitoring in observational learning of action patterns: Making the unobservable observable. *Journal of Behavior, 14*, 153-167.

Catalano, J.F. (1967). Arousal as a factor in reminiscence. *Perceptual and Motor Skills, 24*, 1171-1180.

Catalano, J.F., & Whalen, D.M. (1967). Factors in recovery from performance decrement: Activation, inhibition, and warm up. *Perceptual and Motor Skills, 24*, 1223-1231.

Caudill, D., Weinberg, R., & Jackson, A. (1983). Psyching-up and track athletes: A preliminary investigation. *Journal of Sport Psychology, 5*, 231-235.

Cautela, J.R., & Kearney, A.J. (1986). *The correct conditioning handbook.* New York: Springer.

Clark, L.V. (1960). Effect of mental practice on the development of a certain motor skill. *Research Quarterly, 31*, 560-569.

Corbin, C.B. (1967a). Effects of mental practice on skill development after controlled practice. *Research Quarterly, 38*, 534-538.

Corbin, C.B. (1967b). The effects of covert rehearsal on the development of a complex motor skill. *Journal of General Psychology, 76*, 143-150.

Corbin, C.B. (1972). Mental practice. In W.P. Morgan (Ed.), *Ergogenic aids and muscular performance* (pp. 94-118). New York: Academic Press.

Crocker, P.R.E. (1989). A follow-up of cognitive–affective stress management training. *Journal of Sport and Exercise Psychology, 11*, 236-242.

Crocker, P.R.E., Alderman, R.B., & Smith, F.M.R. (1988). Cognitive–affective stress management training with high performance youth volleyball players: Effects on affect, cognition, and performance. *Journal of Sport and Exercise Psychology, 10*, 448-460.

Crocker, P.R.E., & Gordon, S. (1986). Emotional control training for soccer players. In J. Watkins, T. Reilly, & L. Burwitz (Eds.), *Sport Science* (pp. 187-191). New York: E. & F.N. Sfon.

Davidson, R.J., & Schwartz, G.E. (1977). Brain mechanisms subserving self-generated imagery: Electrophysiological specificity and patterning. *Psychophysiology, 14*, 598-602.

Decaria, M.D. (1977). *The effect of cognitive rehearsal training on performance and on self-report of anxiety in novice and intermediate female gymnasts.* Unpublished doctoral dissertation, University of Utah, Salt Lake City.

Denis, M. (1985). Visual imagery and the use of mental practice in the development of motor skills. *Canadian Journal of Applied Sport Science, 10*, 45-165.

DeWitt, D.J. (1980). Cognitive and biofeedback training for stress reduction with university athletes. *Journal of Sport Psychology, 2*, 288-294.

Durall, R.T. (1986). *A comparison between the time of mental practice and the time of physical performance.* Unpublished master's thesis, Pennsylvania State University, University Park, PA.

Dyckman, J.M., & Cowan, P.A. (1978). Imaging vividness and the outcome of in vivo and imagined scene desensitization. *Journal of Consulting and Clinical Psychology, 46*, 1155-1156.

Ellis, A. (1973). *Humanistic psychotherapy: The rational–emotive approach.* New York: Julian Press.

Epstein, G. (1989). *Healing visualizations: Creating health through imagery.* New York: Bantam Books.

Epstein, M.L. (1980). The relationships of mental imagery and mental practice to performance of a motor task. *Journal of Sport Psychology, 2*, 211-220.

Epstein, M.L., & Mahoney, M.J. (1979). *Anxiety in high school female track team participants.* Unpublished study, Dept. of Psychology, Pennsylvania State University, University Park.

Feltz, D.L., & Landers, D.M. (1983). The effects of mental practice on motor skill learning and performance: A meta-analysis. *Journal of Sport Psychology, 5*, 25-57.

Fenker, R.M., & Cox, C. (1987). *The measurement of peak performance states for athletes in four sports: A problem-oriented cognitive mapping technique.* Paper presented at the meeting of the North American Society for the Psychology of Sport and Physical Activity, Vancouver, BC.

Fitts, D.M. (1962). Skill training. In R. Glaser (Ed.), *Training research and education* (pp. 177-199). Pittsburgh: University of Pittsburgh Press.

Fitts, P.M., & Posner, M.J. (1967). *Human performance.* Belmont, CA: Brooks/Cole.

Gallwey, W.T. (1974). *The inner game of tennis.* New York: Random House.

George, L. (1986). Mental imagery enhancement training in behavior theory: Current status and future prospects. *Psychotherapy,* **23,** 81-92.

Goss, S., Hall, C., Buckolz, E., & Fishburne, G. (1986). Imagery ability and the aquisition of retention of movements. *Memory and Cognition,* **14,** 469-477.

Gould, D., Tammen, V., Murphy, S.M., & May, J. (1989). An examination of the U.S. Olympic sport psychology consultants and the services they provide. *The Sport Psychologist,* **3,** 300-312.

Gould, D., Weiss, M., & Weinberg, R.S. (1981). Psychological characteristics of successful and non-successful Big Ten wrestlers. *Journal of Sport Psychology,* **3,** 69-81.

Gould, D., Weinberg, R., & Jackson, A. (1980). Mental preparation strategies, cognitions, and strength performance. *Journal of Sport Psychology,* **2,** 329-339.

Gravel, R., Lemieux, G., & Ladouceur, R. (1980). Effectiveness of a cognitive behavioral treatment package for cross-country ski racers. *Cognitive Therapy and Research,* **4,** 83-89.

Gray, J.J., Haring, M.J., & Banks, N.M. (1984). Mental rehearsal for sport performance: Exploring the relaxation-imagery paradigm. *Journal of Sport Behavior,* **7,** 68-78.

Greenspan, M.J., & Feltz, D.L. (1989). Psychological interventions with athletes in competitive situations: A review. *The Sport Psychologist,* **3,** 219-236.

Hale, B.D. (1981). *The effects of internal and external imagery on muscular and ocular concomitants.* Unpublished doctoral dissertation, Pennsylvania State University, University Park, PA.

Hale, B.D. (1982). The effects of internal and external imagery on muscular and ocular concomitants. *Journal of Sport Psychology,* **4,** 379-387.

Hall, C.R., & Pongrac, J. (1983). *Movement Imagery Questionnaire.* London, ON: University of Western Ontario.

Hall, C.R., Pongrac, J., & Buckolz, E. (1985). The measurement of imagery ability. *Human Movement Science,* **4,** 107-118.

Hall, C.R., Rodgers, W.M., & Barr, K.A. (1990). The use of imagery by athletes in selected sports. *The Sport Psychologist,* **4,** 1-10.

Hall, E.G., & Erffmeyer, E.S. (1983). The effect of visuomotor behavior rehearsal with videotaped modeling on free throw accuracy of intercollegiate female basketball players. *Journal of Sport Psychology,* **5,** 343-346.

Hamberger, K., & Lohr, J. (1980). Relationship of relaxation training to the controllability of imagery. *Perceptual and Motor Skills,* **51,** 103-110.

Harris, D.V., & Harris, B.L. (1984). *The athlete's guide to sports psychology: Mental skills for physical people.* Champaign, IL: Leisure Press.

Harris, D.V., & Robinson, W.J. (1986). The effects of skill level on EMG activity during internal and external imagery. *Journal of Sport Psychology,* **8,** 105-111.

Hecker, J.E., & Kaczor, L.M. (1988). Application of imagery theory to sport psychology: Some preliminary findings. *Journal of Sport Psychology,* **10,** 363-373.

Heil, J. (1984). Imagery for sport: Theory, research, and practice. In W.F. Straub & J.M. Williams (Eds.), *Cognitive sport psychology* (pp. 245-252). Lansing, NY: Sport Science Associates.

Heil, J. (1985). *The role of imagery in sport: As a "training tool" and as a "mode of thought."* Paper presented at the World Congress in Sport Psychology, Copenhagen.

Heyman, S.R. (1982). Comparisons of successful and unsuccessful competitors: A reconsideration of methodological questions and data. *Journal of Sport Psychology,* **4,** 295-300.

Highlen, P.S., & Bennett, B.B. (1979). Psychological characteristics of successful and non-successful elite wrestlers: An exploratory study. *Journal of Sport Psychology,* **1,** 123-137.

Highlen, P.S., & Bennett, B.B. (1983). Elite divers and wrestlers: A comparison between open- and closed-skill athletes. *Journal of Sport Psychology,* **5,** 390-409.

Hird, J.S., Landers, D.M., Thomas, J.R., & Horan, J.J. (1991). Physical practice is superior to mental practice in enhancing cognitive and motor task performance. *Journal of Sport and Exercise Psychology,* **13,** 281-293.

Housner, L.D. (1984). The role of visual imagery in recall of modeled motoric stimuli. *Journal of Sport Psychology,* **6,** 148-158.

Housner, L., & Hoffman, S.J. (1981). Imagery ability in recall of distance and location information. *Journal of Motor Behavior,* **13,** 207-223.

Jacobson, E. (1930a). Electrical measures of neuromuscular states during mental activities (Part I). *American Journal of Physiology,* **91,** 567-608.

Jacobson, E. (1930b). Electrical measures of neuromuscular states during mental activities (Part 2). *American Journal of Physiology,* **94,** 22-34.

Jacobson, E. (1930c). Electrical measures of neuromuscular states during mental activities (Part 3). *American Journal of Physiology,* **95,** 694-702.

Jacobson, E. (1930d). Electrical measures of neuromuscular states during mental activities (Part 4). *American Journal of Physiology,* **95,** 703-712.

Jacobson, E. (1931a). Electrical measures of neuromuscular states during mental activities (Part 5). *American Journal of Physiology,* **96,** 115-121.

Jacobson, E. (1931b). Electrical measures of neuromuscular states during mental activities (Part 6). *American Journal of Physiology,* **96,** 122-125.

Jacobson, E. (1932). Electrophysiology of mental activities. *American Journal of Psychology,* **44,** 677-694.

Jaffe, D.T. (1980). *Healing from within.* New York: Knopf.

Jastrow, J.A. (1892). Study of involuntary movements. *American Journal of Psychology,* **4,** 398-407.

Johnson, R. (1982). The functional equivalence of imagery and movement. *Quarterly Journal of Experimental Psychology,* **34A,** 349-365.

Jowdy, D.P. (1987). *Muscular responses during imagery as a function of motor skill level.* Unpublished master's thesis, Pennsylvania State University, University Park, PA.

Jowdy, D.P., Murphy, S.M., & Durtschi, S. (1989). *An assessment of the use of imagery by elite athletes: Athlete, coach, and psychologist perspectives.* (Report). Colorado Springs, CO: United States Olympic Committee.

Kavanagh, D., & Hausfeld, S. (1986). Physical performance and self-efficacy under happy and sad moods. *Journal of Sport Psychology,* **8,** 112-123.

Keele, S.W. (1982). Learning and control of coordinated motor patterns: The programming perspective. In J.A. Scott-Kelso (Ed.), *Human motor behavior: An introduction* (pp. 161-188). Hillsdale: Lawrence Erlbaum.

Kirschenbaum, D.S., & Bale, R.M. (1980). Cognitive behavioral skills in golf: Brain power golf. In R.M. Suinn (Ed.), *Psychology in sports: Methods and applications* (pp. 334-343). Minneapolis: Burger.

Kosslyn, S.M. (1981). The medium and the message in mental imagery. In N. Block (Ed.), *Imagery* (pp. 207-258). Cambridge, MA: MIT Press.

Kohl, R.M., & Roenker, D.L. (1980). Bilateral transfer as a function of mental imagery. *Journal of Motor Behavior,* **12,** 197-206.

Kohl, R.M., & Roenker, D.L. (1983). Mechanism involvement during skill imagery. *Journal of Motor Behavior,* **15,** 179-190.

Lang, P.J. (1977). Imagery in therapy: An information-processing analysis of fear. *Behavior Therapy, 8,* 862-886.

Lang, P.J. (1979). A bio-informational theory of emotional imagery. *Psychophysiology, 17,* 495-512.

Lang, P.J., Kozak, M., Miller, G.A., Levin, D.N., & McLean, A. (1980). Emotional imagery: Conceptual structure and pattern of somato-visceral response. *Psychophysiology, 17,* 179-192.

Lang, P.J., Melamed, B.G., & Hart, J.A. (1970). A psychophysiological analysis of fear modification using an automated desensitization procedure. *Journal of Abnormal Psychology, 76,* 229-234.

Lazarus, A.S., & Folkman, S. (1984). *Stress, appraisal, and coping.* New York: Springer.

Lee, C. (1990). Psyching up for a muscular endurance task: Effects of image content on performance and mood state. *Journal of Sport and Exercise Psychology, 12,* 66-73.

Levine, S. (1982). *Who dies.* New York: Anchor Books.

Levis, D.J., & Hare, N. (1977). A review of the theoretical rationale and empirical support for the extinction approach of implosive (flooding) therapy. In M. Hersen, R.M. Eisler, & P.M. Miller (Eds.), *Progress in behavior modification* (Vol. 5, pp. 299-376). New York: Academic Press.

Lloyd, R. (1987). *Explorations in psychoneuroimmunology.* Orlando, FL: Crewe & Stratton.

Locke, S.E. (1982). Stress, adaptation, and immunity: Studies in humans. *General Hospital Psychiatry, 4,* 49-58.

Loehr, J. (1986). *Mental toughness training for sports.* Lexington, MA: Stephen Greene.

Lutkus, A.D. (1975). The effect of "imaging" on mirror drawing. *Bulletin of the Psychonomic Society, 5,* 389-390.

Lynch, G. (1987). *The total runner: A complete mind–body guide to optimal performance.* Englewood Cliffs, NJ: Prentice-Hall.

Mace, R.D., & Carroll, D. (1985). The control of anxiety in sport: Stress innoculation training prior to abseiling. *International Journal of Sport Psychology, 16,* 165-175.

Mackay, D.G. (1981). The problem of rehearsal or mental practice. *Journal of Motor Behavior, 13,* 274-285.

Magill, R.A. (1984). Influences on remembering movement information. In W.F. Straub & J.M. Williams (Eds.), *Cognitive sport psychology* (pp. 175-188). New York: Sport Science Associates.

Mahoney, M.J. (1979). Cognitive skills and athletic performance. In P.C. Kendall & S.D. Hollon (Eds.), *Cognitive-behavioral interventions* (pp. 423-443). New York: Academic Press.

Mahoney, M.J., Gabriel, T.J., & Perkins, T.S. (1987). Psychological skills and exceptional athletic performance. *The Sport Psychologist 1,* 181-199.

Mahoney, M.J., & Avener, M. (1977). Psychology of the elite athlete: An exploratory study. *Cognitive Therapy and Resaerch, 3,* 361-366.

Mahoney, M.J., & Epstein, M. (1981). The assessment of cognition in athletes. In T.V. Merluzzi, C.R. Glass, & M. Genest (Eds.) *Cognitive assessment* (pp. 439-451). New York: Guilford Press.

Marks, D.F. (1973). Visual imagery differences in the recall of pictures. *British Journal of Psychology, 64,* 17-24.

Martens, R. (1974). Arousal and motor performance. In J. Wilmore (Ed.), *Exercise and Sport Science Review* (Vol. 2). New York: Academic Press.

Marx, J.L. (1985). The immune system "belongs in the body." *Science, 227,* 1188-1192.

McIntyre, J.S., Mostoway, W., Stojak, R.A., & Humphries, M. (1972). Transfer of work decrement in motor learning. *Journal of Motor Behavior, 4,* 223-229.

Meacci, W.G., & Price, E.E. (1985). Acquisition and retention of golf putting skill through the relaxation, visualization, and body rehearsal intervention. *Research Quarterly for Exercise and Sport, 56,* 176-179.

Meichenbaum, D. (1977). *Cognitive-behavior modification: An integrative approach.* NY: Plenum.

Meyers, A.W., Cooke, C.J., Cullen, J., & Liles, L. (1979). Psychological aspects of athletic competitors: A replication across sports. *Cognitive Therapy and Research, 3,* 361-366.

Meyers, A.W., & Schleser, R. (1980). A cognitive behavioral intervention for improving basketball performance. *Journal of Sport Psychology, 2,* 69-73.

Meyers, A.W., Schleser, R., & Okwamabua, T.M. (1982). A cognitive behavioral intervention for improving basketball performance. *Research Quarterly for Exercise and Sport, 13,* 344-347.

Miller, W.H., & Heinrich, R.L. (1984). *Personal stress management for medical and dental patients.* Los Angeles: PSM Press.

Minas, S.C. (1980). Mental practice of a complex perceptual–motor skill. *Journal of Human Studies, 4,* 102-107.

Morgan, W.P., O'Connor, P.J., Sparling, P.B., & Pate, R.R. (1987). Psychological characterization of the elite female distance runner. *International Journal of Sports Medicine, 8,* 124-131.

Morrisett, L.N. (1956). *The role of implicit practice in learning.* Unpublished doctoral dissertation, Yale University, New Haven, CT.

Mumford, P., & Hall, C. (1985). The effects of internal and external imagery on performing figures in figure skating. *Canadian Journal of Applied Sport Sciences, 10,* 171-177.

Murphy, S.M. (1985). *Emotional imagery and its effects on strength and fine motor skill performance.* Unpublished doctoral dissertation, Rutgers University, NJ.

Murphy, S.M. (1986). Re: Sports psychology. *Behavior Therapist, 9,* 60.

Murphy, S.M. (1990). Models of imagery in sport psychology: A review. *Journal of Mental Imagery, 14,* 153-172.

Murphy, S.M., Woolfolk, R.L., & Budney, A.J. (1988). The effects of emotive imagery on strength performance. *Journal of Sport and Exercise Psychology, 10,* 334-345.

Naruse, G. (1965). The hypnotic treatment of stage fright in champion athletes. *International Journal of Clinical and Experimental Hypnosis, 13,* 63-70.

Nelson, J. (1980). *Investigation of effects of hypnosis, relaxation, and mental practice on the performance moves of golfers and runners.* Unpublished doctoral dissertation, Louisiana State University, Baton Rouge, LA.

Noel, R.C. (1980). The effect of visuo-motor behavior rehearsal on tennis performance. *Journal of Sport Psychology, 2,* 221-226.

Orlick, T. (1986). *Psyching for sport: Mental training for athletes.* Champaign, IL: Human Kinetics/Leisure Press.

Orlick, T. (1989). Reflections on SportPsych consulting with individual and team sport athletes at summer and winter Olympic games. *Sport Psychologist, 3,* 358-365.

Orlick, T. (1990). *In pursuit of excellence* (2nd ed.). Champaign, IL: Human Kinetics.

Orlick, T., & Partington, J. (1988). Mental links to excellence. *Sport Psychologist, 2,* 105-130.

Oslin, J.L. (1985). *A meta-analysis of mental practice research: Differentiation between intent and type of cognitive activity utilized.* Unpublished master's thesis, Kent State University, Kent, OH.

Oxendine, J.B. (1970). Emotional arousal and motor performance. *Quest, 13,* 23-30.

Oxendine, J.B. (1984). *Psychology of motor learning* (2nd ed.). Englewood Cliffs, NJ: Prentice-Hall.

Paivio, A. (1971). *Imagery and verbal processes.* New York: Holt, Rinehart & Winston.

Paivio, A. (1985). Cognitive and motivational functions of imagery in human performance. *Canadian Journal of Applied Sport Sciences, 10,* 22-28.

Paul, G.L. (1966). *Insight versus desensitization in psychotherapy.* Stanford, CA: Stanford University Press.

Perry, H.M. (1939). The relative efficiency of actual and imaginary practice in five selected tasks. *Archives of Psychology, 34,* 5-75.

Phipps, S.J. (1968). *Effect of mental practice on acquisition of motor skills of varying complexity.* Unpublished master's thesis, Pennsylvania State University, University Park, PA.

Pinker, S., & Kosslyn, S.M. (1983). Theories of mental imagery. In A.A. Sheikh (Ed.), *Imagery: Current theory research and application* (pp. 43-71). New York: John Wiley & Sons.

Porter, K., & Foster, J. (1986). *The mental athlete: Inner training for peak performance.* Dubuque, IA: William C. Brown.

Porter, K., & Foster, J. (1990). *Visual athletics.* Dubuque, IA: William C. Brown.

Powell, G.E. (1973). Negative and positive mental practice in motor skill acquisition. *Perceptual and Motor Skills, 37,* 312.

Pylyshyn, Z.W. (1973). What the mind's eye tells the mind's brain: A critique of mental imagery. *Psychological Bulletin, 80,* 1-23.

Pylyshyn, Z. (1981). The imagery debate: Analog media versus tacit knowledge. In N. Block (Ed.), *Imagery* (pp. 151-205). Cambridge, MA: MIT Press.

Qualls, P.J. (1982). The physiological measurement of imagery: An overview. *Imagination, Cognition and Personality, 2,* 89-101.

Rachman, S. (1968). *Phobias: Their nature and control.* Springfield, IL: Thomas.

Rawlings, E.J., Rawlings, J.L., Chen, S.S., & Yilk, M.D. (1972). The facilitating effects of mental practice in the acquisition of rotary pursuit tracking. *Psychonomic Science, 26,* 71-73.

Richardson, A. (1967a). Mental practice: A review and discussion (Part 1). *Research Quarterly, 38,* 95-107.

Richardson, A. (1967b). Mental practice: A review and discussion (Part 2). *Research Quarterly, 38,* 263-273.

Richardson, A. (1969). *Mental imagery.* New York: Springer.

Richardson, A. (1977). Verbalizer–visualizer: A cognitive style dimension. *Journal of Mental Imagery, 1,* 109-126.

Richardson, A. (1985). Imagery: Definition and types. In A.A. Sheikh (Ed.), *Imagery: Current theory research and application* (pp. 3-42). New York: John Wiley & Sons.

Rider, M.S., & Achterberg, J. (1989). Effect of music-assisted imagery on neutrophils and lymphocytes. *Biofeedback and Self-Regulation, 14,* 247-257.

Roland, P.E., Larsen, B., Lassen, N.A., & Shinhoj, E. (1980). Supplementary motor area and other critical areas in organization of voluntary movements in man. *Journal of Neurophysiology, 43,* 118-136.

Ross, S.L. (1985). The effectiveness of mental practice in improving the performance of college trombonists. *Journal of Research in Music Education, 33,* 221-230.

Rotella, R.J. (1984). The psychological care of the injured athlete. In L.K. Bunker, R.O. Rotella, & A.S. Reilly (Eds.), *Sport psychology: Psychological considerations in maximizing sport performance* (pp. 273-287). Ann Arbor, MI: McNaughton & Gunn.

Rotella, R.J., Gansneder, B., Ojala, D., & Billing, J. (1980). Cognitions and coping strategies of elite skiers: An exploratory study of young developing athletes. *Journal of Sport Psychology, 2,* 350-354.

Rushall, B.S. (1988). Covert modeling as a procedure for altering an athlete's psychological state. *Sport Psychologist, 2,* 131-140.

Ryan, E.D., & Simons, J. (1981). Cognitive demand imagery and frequency of mental practice as factors influencing the acquisition of mental skills. *Journal of Sport Psychology, 4,* 35-45.

Ryan, E.D., & Simons, J. (1982). Efficacy of mental imagery in enhancing mental practice of motor skills. *Journal of Sport Psychology, 4,* 41-51.

Sackett, R.S. (1934). The influences of symbolic rehearsal upon the retention of a maze habit. *Journal of General Psychology, 10,* 376-395.

Sackett, R.S. (1935). The relationship between amount of symbolic rehearsal and retention of a maze habit. *Journal of General Psychology, 13,* 113-128.

Schmidt, R.A. (1987). *Motor control and learning* (2nd ed.). Champaign, IL: Human Kinetics.

Seabourne, T.G., Weinberg, R.S., Jackson, A., & Suinn, R.M. (1985). Effect of individualized, nonindividualized, and package intervention strategies on karate performance. *Journal of Sport Psychology, 7,* 40-50.

Shaw, W.A. (1938). The distribution of muscular action potentials during imaging. *Psychological Record, 2,* 195-216.

Shaw, W.A. (1940). The relation of muscular action potentials to imaginal weightlifting. *Archives of Psychology, 247,* 50.

Shea, J.B. (1977). Effects of labelling on motor short-term memory. *Journal of Experimental Psychology: Human Learning and Memory, 3,* 92-99.

Sheehan, P. (1967). A shortened form of Bett's Questionnaire upon mental imagery. *Journal of Clinical Psychology, 23,* 386-389.

Sheikh, A., & Kunzendorf, R. (1984). Imagery, physiology, and somatic illness. In A.A. Sheikh (Ed.), *International review of mental imagery.* New York: Human Sciences.

Shelton, T.O., & Mahoney, M.J. (1978). The content and effect of "psyching-up" strategies in weightlifters. *Cognitive Therapy and Research 2,* 275-284.

Shepard, R.N., & Metzler, J. (1971). Mental rotation of three-dimensional objects. *Science, 171,* 701-703.

Shick, J. (1970). Effects of mental practice on selected volleyball skills for college women. *Research Quarterly, 41,* 88-94.

Silva, J.M., III. (1982). Competitive sport environments: Performance enhancement through cognitive intervention. *Behavior Modification, 6,* 443-464.

Silva, J.M., III. (1983). Covert rehearsal strategies. In M.W. Williams (Ed.), *Ergogenic aids in sport* (pp. 253-274). Champaign, IL: Human Kinetics.

Simonton, O.C., Mathews-Simonton, S., & Creighton, J. (1978). *Getting well again.* Los Angeles: Tarcher.

Singer, J., & Antrobus, J.S. (1972). Daydreaming, imaginal processes, and personality: A normative study. In P. Sheehan (Ed.), *The function and nature of imagery* (pp. 175-202). New York: Academic Press.

Singer, R.N., Goren, R.F., & Risdale, S. (1979). The effect of various strategies on the acquisition, retention, and transfer of a serial positioning task. *U.S. Army Research Institute for the Behavioral and Social Sciences, Jul. Tr. 399,* p. 52.

Singer, R.N., Risdale, S., & Korienek, G.G. (1980). Achievement in a serial positioning task and the role of the learner's strategies. *Perceptual and Motor Skills, 50,* 735-747.

Smith, R.E. (1980). A cognitive effective approach to stress management training for athletes. In C. Nadeau, W. Halliwell, K. Newell, & G. Roberts (Eds.), *Psychology of motor behavior and sport-1979* (pp. 54-73). Champaign, IL: Human Kinetics.

Smyth, M.M. (1975). The role of mental practice in skill acquisition. *Journal of Motor Behavior, 7*, 199-206.

Start, K.B., & Richardson, A. (1964). Imagery and mental practice. *British Journal of Education Psychology, 34*, 280-284.

Steel, W.I. (1952). The effect of mental practice on the acquisition of a motor skill. *Journal of Physical Education, 44*, 101-208.

Stelmach, G.E., & Hughes, B. (1984). Memory cognition and motor behavior. In W.F. Straub & J.M. Williams (Eds.), *Cognitive sport psychology* (pp. 163-174). New York: Sport Science Associates.

Stevens, S.S. (1975). *Psychophysics: Introduction to its perceptual, neural, and social aspects.* New York: Wiley.

Suinn, R.M. (1972). Behavior rehearsal training for ski racers. *Behavior Therapy, 3*, 519-520.

Suinn, R.M. (1976). Visual motor behavior rehearsal for adaptive behavior. In J. Krumboltz & C. Thoresen (Eds.), *Counseling methods.* New York: Holt.

Suinn, R.M. (1980). Psychology and sports performance: Principles and applications. In R. Suinn (Ed.), *Psychology in sports: Methods and applications* (pp. 26-36). Minneapolis: Burgess.

Suinn, R.M. (1983). Imagery and sports. In A.A. Sheikh (Ed.), *Imagery: Current theory research and application* (pp. 507-534). New York: John Wiley & Sons.

Suinn, R.M. (1985). Imagery rehearsal applications to performance enhancement. *Behavior Therapist, 8*, 155-159.

Tellegen, A., & Atkinson, G. (1974). Openness to absorbing and self-altering experiences ("absorption"), a trait related to hypnotic susceptibility. *Journal of Abnormal Psychology, 83*, 268-277.

Tynes, L.L., & McFatter, R.M. (1987). The efficacy of "psyching" strategies on a weightlifting task. *Cognitive Therapy and Research, 11*, 327-336.

Ulich, E. (1967). Some experiments on the functions of mental practice training in the acquisition of motor skills. *Ergonomics, 10*, 411-419.

Vealey, R. (1986). Imagery training for performance enhancement. In J.M. Williams (Ed.), *Applied sport psychology: Personal growth to peak performance* (pp. 209-234). Mountain View, CA: Mayfield.

Wadden, T.A., & Anderson, C.H. (1982). The clinical use of hypnosis. *Psychological Bulletin, 91*, 215-243.

Washburn, M.F. (1916). *Movement and mental imagery.* Boston: Houghton Mifflin.

Waterland, J.C. (1956). *The effect of mental practice combined with kinesthetic perception when practice precedes each overt performance of a motor skill.* Unpublished master's dissertation, University of Wisconsin, Madison, WI.

Wechsler, R. (1987, August). A new prescription: Mind over malady. *Science Periodical on Research in Technology and Sport*, pp. 1-11.

Wehner, T., Vogt, S., & Stadler, M. (1984). Task-specific EMG-characteristics during mental training. *Psychological Research, 46*, 389-401.

Weinberg, R.S. (1981). The relationship between mental preparation strategies and motor performance: A review and critique. *Quest, 33*, 195-213.

Weinberg, R.S., Gould, D., & Jackson, A. (1980). Cognition and motor performance: Effect of psyching-up strategies three motor tasks. *Cognitive Therapy and Reserch, 4*, 239-245.

Weinberg, R.S., Gould, D., & Jackson, A. (1981). Relationship between the duration of the psych-up interval and strength performance. *Journal of Sport Psychology, 3*, 166-170.

Weinberg, R.S., Gould, D., Jackson, A., & Barnes, P. (1980). Influence of cognitive strategies on tennis serves of players of high and low ability. *Perceptual and Motor Skills, 50*, 663-666.

Weinberg, R.S., Seabourne, T.G., & Jackson, A. (1981). Effects of visuo-motor behavioral rehearsal, relaxation, and imagery on karate performance. *Journal of Sport Psychology, 3*, 228-238.

Weinberg, R.S., Seabourne, T.G., & Jackson, A. (1982). Effects of visuo-motor behavior rehearsal on state–trait anxiety and performance: Is practice important? *Journal of Sport Behavior, 5*, 209-219.

Weinberg, R.S., Seabourne, T.G., & Jackson, A. (1987). Arousal and relaxation instructions prior to the use of imagery. *International Journal of Sport Psychology, 18*, 205-214.

Wiese, D.M., & Weiss, M.R. (1987). Psychological rehabilitation and physical injury: Implications for the sportsmedicine team. *Sport Psychologist, 1*, 318-330.

Wilkes, R.L., & Summers, J.J. (1984). Cognitions, mediating variables, and strength performance. *Journal of Sport Psychology, 6*, 351-359.

Williams, J. (Ed.) (1986). *Applied sport psychology.* Palo Alto, CA: Mayfield.

Wine, J. (1971). Test anxiety and direction of attention. *Psychological Bulletin, 76*, 92-104.

Wolpe, J. (1958). *Psychotherapy by reciprocal inhibition.* Stanford, CA: Stanford University Press.

Woolfolk, R.L., Murphy, S.M., Gottesfeld, D., & Aitken, D. (1985). The effects of mental practice of task and mental depiction of task outcome on motor performance. *Journal of Sport Psychology, 7*, 191-197.

Woolfolk, R., Parrish, W., & Murphy, S.M. (1985). The effects of positive and negative imagery on motor skill performance. *Cognitive Therapy and Research, 9*, 335-341.

Wrisberg, C.A., & Ragsdale, M.R. (1979). Cognitive demand and practice level: Factors in the mental practice of motor skills. *Journal of Human Movement Studies, 5*, 201-208.

Yukelson, D. (1986). Psychology of sports and the injured athlete. In D.B. Benhart (Ed.), *Clinics in physical therapy* (pp. 173-175). New York: Churchill Livingston.

Zaichowsky, L.D., & Fuchs, C.Z. (1986). *The Psychology of motor behavior: Development, control, learning, and performance.* Ithaca, NY: Mouvement.

Ziegler, S.G., Klinzing, J., & Williamson, K. (1982). The affects of two stress management training programs on cardiorespiratory efficiency. *Journal of Sport Psychology, 4*, 280-289.

Chapter 12

Attention and Athletic Performance: An Integrated Approach

Stephen H. Boutcher
University of Wollongong

The theme of *attention* has had a rich and varied history. In the late 1800s and early 1900s the laboratories of Wundt, Titchener, and Helmholtz carried out many experiments examining different aspects of attention. Surprisingly, however, interest in attention waned over the next 25 years and was not rekindled until the advent of World War II, which challenged psychologists with many applied problems concerning attention (e.g., How long could a radar operator watch a screen without a decline in attention?). At present, attention is one of the core themes in psychology and is viewed as a complex multidisciplinary field of study. According to Parasuraman (1984), research in attention is being conducted in many areas of the psychological sciences, including cognitive psychology, psychophysiology, neuropsychology, and developmental psychology.

In the sport context, several authors have suggested that attention is a vital aspect of athletic performance (Boutcher, 1990; Nideffer, 1976a).

The research, however, examining the role of attention in sport is underdeveloped. Furthermore, few studies have examined the attentional mechanisms underpinning athletic performance. Thus, a suitable framework to study the influence of attention on sport skills has not been established.

This chapter will review the research and theory pertaining to attention with a view toward synthesizing various perspectives in order to develop a better understanding of the attention–performance relationship. The first part of this chapter will focus on a review of the attention–performance literature as it has been studied from three different perspectives: information processing, social psychology, and psychophysiology. At the conclusion of this section a synthesis of the three perspectives will be provided, and an integrated model of attention in sport will be presented. The last part of this chapter will focus on a more applied perspective, discussing several issues related to attentional training in athletes.

Each of the three research thrusts—information processing, social psychology, and psychophysiology—has emphasized a different but related perspective of the attentional process. Research in information processing has established the existence of two related forms of processing. Control processing requires effort and is slow and cumbersome, whereas automatic processing is effortless, quick, and efficient. Social psychologists have focused on individual differences and environmental influences on attentional processes. The ability of extraneous, inappropriate cues to disrupt performance has been documented. Sport psychophysiologists have attempted to examine the underlying mechanisms of attention by monitoring cortical and cardiac activity. Both cortical and autonomic indicants of attention have been successfully used to assess attentional style in athletes during performance. The following three sections will discuss the relevant aspects of these approaches necessary to develop an integrated model of attention and sport performance.

Information-Processing Perspectives

Cognitive psychologists consider humans to be processors of information. The information-processing approach attempts to understand the stimulus–response relationship, *stimulus* being some kind of information entering the body through the sensory system and *response* being the resulting behavior. This approach assumes that there are a number of processing stages that occur between the stimulus and response initiation. Although the names of the different stages vary, most information-processing models include perceptual, short-term memory, and long-term memory stages (for overviews of different information-processing models, see Marteniuk, 1976, and Schmidt, 1988).

Information-processing models provide a framework for examining the characteristics of perception, memory, decision making, and attention. Attention is conceptualized as the ability to switch focus from one source of information to another and as the amount of information that can be attended to at any one time. Thus, attention is a central concept in the information-processing approach. Researchers working from this perspective have primarily focused on three aspects of attention. These include three interacting processes: selective attention, capacity, and alertness (Posner & Bois, 1971). Because the literature examining these processes is extensive, only those aspects pertinent to the theme of

this chapter will be examined (for more complete overviews, see Parasuraman, 1984; Schmidt, 1988).

Attentional Selectivity

Selective attention refers to the process by which certain information from the internal or external environment enters the information-processing system, whereas other information is screened out or ignored. In any situation the organism is constantly being bombarded with a mass of information from both the internal and external environments and can only assimilate a certain amount at a particular moment. Therefore, selection is necessary so that only a few stimuli are processed. The organism focuses on certain aspects that directly affect behavior, whereas the remaining stimuli serve as background. Selection can be "voluntary" or "involuntary" depending on whether the selection is due to the organism or to the actual stimuli itself. Selection can take place in a large variety of behavioral situations; that is, an individual may choose to focus "inwardly" on certain strategies and past experiences or "outwardly" on a wide range of environmental cues. Thus, selection is multifaceted and appears to be an essential condition for sport performance. William James expressed this quite succinctly in his classical statement that "without selective attention, experience is an utter chaos" (1890, p. 402).

Selective attention is believed to play a central role in both the learning and performing of sport skills. However, the stimuli that are essential for a particular performance change as a function of practice and skill improvement. For example, neophytes first learning to dribble a basketball must devote much attention to watching the ball and are unable to lift their heads to focus on the players around them. With practice, however, dribbling is carried out without watching the ball, and the skill becomes more synchronized and automatic. Eventually, after many years of practice, dribbling can be carried out with either hand, while simultaneously defending the ball from an opposition point guard and monitoring the positions of fellow players. In this latter situation, most of the performer's attention is focused externally on surrounding players rather than on the process of dribbling. In contrast, the player sent to the foul line does not have to attend to the same amount of external information. However, because the foul shot is typically well learned, attention that was previously available to focus on teammates and opponents now has the potential to focus on task-irrelevant cues and internal information such as worry about missing, spectators, and so forth.

It can be seen from the previous basketball example that with practice, attention can be changed from a cumbersome, conscious process to a smooth unconscious process. These two aspects of attention have been called control and automatic processing (Schneider, Dumais & Shiffrin, 1984). *Control processing* is used to process novel or inconsistent information and is slow, effortful, capacity-limited, and controlled by the individual. In sport, control processing would be involved when decisions are required. For example, a golfer taking into consideration distance, wind conditions, and the position of hazards to determine club selection would use control processing. In contrast, *automatic processing*, which is responsible for the performance of well-learned skills, is fast, effortless, and not under direct conscious control. In sport, automatic processing would be found when athletes have developed skills after many years of practice. Thus, the professional golfer swinging the club would use automatic processing. The major differences between automatic and control processing are that automatic processing requires little effort, attention, or awareness, whereas control processing requires high awareness, much attention, and intensive effort. All sports require a combination of automatic and control processing, because athletes need to perform many skills in a reflexive, automatic manner but are also required to make decisions and process inconsistent cues and new information. Closed-skill sports such as golf, archery, and shooting probably require more automatic processing, whereas open-skill sports involve a combination of the two. Thus, control processing and automatic processing have the potential to play important roles in sport performance.

Attentional Capacity

A second aspect of attention that has been examined relative to performance is attentional capacity. This term refers to the fact that control processing is limited in the amount of information that can be processed at one time. Specifically, an individual is limited to performing one complex task at a time and thus would have difficulty focusing attention on two sources of information simultaneously. Consequently, control processing can be viewed as having a limited capacity for processing information from either the internal or external environments. Thus, performing multiple tasks or attempting to focus on more than one source of information may result in reduced performance. An example of control processing overload in the sport context would be two coaches simultaneously giving a basketball player a stream of instructions during a time-out.

The restrictions on attentional capacity are due to both structural and central capacity limitations. Structural interference involves two tasks performed at the same time using the same receptor or effector systems. For example, listening for the sound of a starter's gun while at the same time listening to a voice in the crowd could provoke auditory structural interference. Capacity interference occurs when two tasks compete for limited central information-processing capacity simultaneously. Fixed-capacity and undifferentiated theories represent two different views for explaining how task performance will be affected if capacity for processing is exceeded. Fixed-capacity theories (e.g., Broadbent, 1958; Keele, 1973; Kerr, 1973; Norman, 1969) assume that capacity is fixed in size and remains the same for different tasks. In contrast, theories of undifferentiated capacity (e.g., Kahneman, 1973) view attention as a resource that can be channeled to various processing operations. This approach is a more flexible view of attention and suggests that capacity changes as task requirements change. Multiple resource theory (Navon & Gopher, 1979; Wickens, 1984) is a recent extension of flexible attention capacity and suggests that attention may consist of a set of pools of resources, each with its own capacity to handle information processing. This view suggests that processes requiring attention may be able to handle more than one stimulus at any one time (parallel processing). The ability of the human information-processing system to process multiple sources of information simultaneously would depend on the importance of the tasks involved, task difficulty, and structural considerations. Resource theory is generally viewed as an attractive framework for understanding attention. Critics of the theory, however, have focused on issues regarding practice and divided attention and the number of resources necessary to cover all aspects of attention (see Hirst, 1986).

Whereas control processing is fragmentized; requires much attention, effort, and awareness; and can only handle relatively simple tasks—automatic processing is just the opposite. Automatic processing requires little attention, effort, or awareness; is not serial-dependent; and is holistic rather than fragmentized in nature. The capacity limitations of automatic processing are less restrictive compared to those of control processing. For instance, performance of a golf swing involves a variety of muscles initiated by millions of efferent neural impulses. Presumably, if this process had to be consciously monitored by an individual the task would be overwhelming. Thus, control processing, which may be dominant in the early stages of learning (Shiffrin, 1976), will eventually give way to automatic processing if the skill is to be performed in an effortless, efficient manner. For skill performance, then, the greater attentional capacity limitation of control processing compared to automatic processing is an important factor to be considered.

Attentional Alertness

The third aspect of attention that has been examined in information-processing research concerns the effects of alertness and arousal on the breadth of the attentional field. Easterbrook (1959), in a comprehensive review of the available literature, cites numerous research studies supporting the hypothesis that increases in emotional arousal result in a narrowing of the attentional field due to systematic reduction in the range of cue utilization. More recently, Landers (1980, 1981) has used Easterbrook's work to examine the effects of emotional arousal on the visual field of athletes during performance. Numerous studies have indicated that in stressful situations, performance on a central visual task decreases the ability to respond to peripheral stimuli (Bacon, 1974; Hockey, 1970; Wachtel, 1967). Thus, it appears that arousal can bring about sensitivity loss to the cues that are in the peripheral visual field. In sport, point guard play in basketball provides an example of how overarousal can affect the visual attentional field. If a point guard is looking for teammates outside the key (scanning the periphery of his or her attentional field), overarousal may bring about perceptual narrowing. This narrow focus may result in the point guards failing to detect open players in the periphery. Because many sport skills are performed in aroused states, the attentional-field-narrowing phenomenon may be an important determinant of sport performance.

Researchers using the information perspective have focused primarily on selection, alertness, and capacity aspects of attention. Important aspects of selective attention are control and automatic processing. Control processing is slow, requires effort, and is controlled by the individual. In contrast, automatic processing is fast, effortless, and not under conscious individual control. Control processing is important in the early stages of learning and for dealing with novel and inconsistent information, whereas automatic processing is responsible for skills that are so well learned they require little attention

or effort. Regarding alertness, it has been demonstrated that increases in emotional arousal can result in a narrowing of the attentional field due to systematic reduction in the range of cue utilization. It has also been shown that the capacity limitation of control processing is more restrictive than that of automatic processing.

Social–Psychological Perspectives

Because sport typically requires performance of well-learned skills, it would appear that automatic processing is an important aspect of athletic performance. However, successful performance in the sporting context also requires the use of control processing. For instance, receivers and quarterbacks have to constantly monitor the environment through control processing in order to attend to vital cues. In these performance situations, focusing attention on task-irrelevant information while attempting to perform well-learned skills may be detrimental to performance. This aspect of control processing (i.e., the possibility that task-irrelevant rather than task-relevant stimuli may enter the information-processing system, thus disrupting performance) has largely been studied by social psychologists. Most theories and explanations concerning this phenomenon have evolved from research in test anxiety, self-awareness, and pain. Three areas of this attentional research have pertinence to the role of attentional control and performance of well-learned skills: distraction theories, automatic functioning, and attentional style.

Distraction Theories

Distraction theories focus on the loss of attention caused by factors that attract attention to task-irrelevant cues. Thus, if task-irrelevant cues attract an athlete's attention, performance may be negatively affected. If an archer focuses solely on thoughts of missing the target, it is possible that attention will be disrupted and performance degraded. Similarly, if a batter in baseball does not focus visual attention on the pitcher, it is probable that he or she will not make contact with the ball. Thus, even momentary loss of concentration during the initial flight of the ball may have devastating results.

One factor that may cause attention to be diverted to irrelevant stimuli is *worry*. Sarason (1972) and Wine (1971) have suggested that worry as an emotional state serves as a distractor of attention and can thus explain the negative

to generate increased focus on the self, thus distracting the athlete. Thus, distraction in the form of worry or self-awareness is another attentional factor that can affect skill performance.

Automatic Functioning

The second area of study in the social psychology research literature that has relevance for explaining the disruptive effects of inappropriate attentional focus is the automatic execution of sport skills. This concept relates to the automatic processing idea discussed earlier. Baumeister (1984) has suggested that the effect of competitive pressure is to make individuals want to do so well that they tend to focus on the process of performance. In competitive situations, when individuals realize the importance of correct skill execution, they attempt to ensure success by consciously monitoring the process of performance; that is, they attempt to put the execution of a skill which is typically under automatic processing control, under the control processing mechanism. Unfortunately, consciousness (control processing) does not contain the necessary information regarding the muscle movement and coordination essential for effective performance. Thus, attempting actively or consciously to control the process involved in a skill can result in a degradation of performance (Kimble & Perlmuter, 1970). An example of the effect of consciously controlling well-learned skills is provided by Langer and Imber (1979), who demonstrated that attempting to ensure accuracy by consciously monitoring finger movements during typing was detrimental to performance. Also, focusing attention on hand movements during piano playing has been found to detract from performance (Keele, 1973). Baumeister (1984) has also demonstrated this effect using laboratory tasks when he found that increasing subject's attention to the process of performing a "roll-up" game debilitated performance. Thus, attempting to ensure success by consciously monitoring the process of performance during competition has been established as another inefficient use of attention.

Attentional Style

It is possible that there are individual differences regarding the distraction and automatic processing concepts so far discussed. Thus, in competitive situations certain athletes may tend to use an attentional style that hinders performance. Variations in attentional style and their effect on sport performance has formed the focus

effects that test anxiety can have on performance. According to both Sarason and Wine, anxious individuals typically focus their attention on task-irrelevant thoughts and ignore critical task cues during testing. Thus, individuals who dwell on thoughts such as "I know I'll fail because I'm not as good as the others" are not focusing their attention on task-relevant cues and will not produce performance results reflective of their ability. Acute anxiety, in the form of self-debilitating thoughts, has been associated with competitive athletic situations (Kroll, 1982). Thus, this research on distraction seems to be especially relevant to the study of sport. Processing task-irrelevant information can explain performance decrements in a wide range of athletic settings. In highly competitive situations, for example, performance could be negatively affected because the individual athlete focuses on self-defeating thoughts. In contrast, in nonstimulating, low-arousal environments (e.g., competitions that occur over hours or days), a lack of intensity in attention may result in the missing of important task-relevant cues.

Another source of distraction information is *self-awareness*. Carver and Scheier (1981) have suggested that attending to oneself while performing may take attention away from task cues, thus degrading performance. Other authors (Duval & Wicklund, 1972; Scheier, Fenigstein & Buss, 1974) have suggested that it is impossible to attend to oneself and to the environment at the same time. Because social facilitation generally tends to increase self-awareness (Carver & Scheier, 1978), the presence of spectators and cameras at sporting events has the potential of much of the attentional research in sport psychology. For instance, Nideffer (1976b)—using initial concepts developed by Easterbrook (1959), Wachtel (1967), and Bacon (1974)—suggests that the attentional demands of any sporting situation will vary along two dimensions: width (broad–narrow) and direction (internal–external). A broad, external focus requires individuals to focus on a wide area of the external environment (e.g., a quarterback scanning the width of the field), whereas a broad, internal focus is a style that focuses attention internally on a variety of strategies and past experience. A narrow, external focus would be appropriate for activities that require the individual to focus attention on a narrow aspect of the external environment, such as a golf ball or the ring in foul shooting. A narrow, internal attentional focus is most suited to attending to specific images or cognitive cues.

The challenge for the athlete, according to Nideffer (1976b), is to match the attentional demands of the sporting environment with the appropriate attentional style. Therefore, performance may be impaired when an individual uses an inappropriate style for a particular activity (e.g., a baseball batter who broadly focuses his attention on players and spectators rather than using a narrow focus on the pitcher). Nideffer (1976b) has also used Easterbrook's notion of attentional narrowing to explain the effects of anxiety and arousal on attentional processes. As mentioned, the suggestion is that arousal produces an involuntary narrowing in attention and may interfere with the individual's ability to shift attentional focus.

Nideffer (1976b) has proposed that individuals may possess a particular attentional style. These styles, which are relatively stable across situations and over time, may affect performance in certain situations if the athlete's style is incompatible with the attentional requirements of that situation. For example, a basketball player may consistently focus on thoughts of missing when shooting foul shots. In contrast, the aspects of attention that are state-dependent are situation-specific and thus are amenable to change. Nideffer (1976b) has developed the Test of Attentional and Interpersonal Style (TAIS) to assess the strengths and weaknesses of an individuals' attentional style. The subscales of the TAIS are

- broad–external,
- external overload,
- broad–internal,
- internal overload,
- narrow effective focus, and
- errors of underinclusion.

Although Nideffer has provided preliminary support for the reliability and validity of the TAIS (Nideffer, 1976c), results of more recent research has suggested that the TAIS has limited validity and predictive properties for sport performance. Landers (1981, 1985) has reviewed research examining the TAIS and sport performance and has concluded that the scale seems to measure the narrow–broad dimension but not the internal–external dimension. Furthermore, he found no evidence to suggest that the TAIS is a good predictor of sport performance. Other researchers have developed sport-specific versions of the TAIS for tennis (Van Schoych & Grasha, 1981) and baseball (Albrecht & Feltz, 1987) in an attempt to increase the reliability and validity of questionnaire assessment of attentional style. Although these versions of the TAIS did increase internal consistency and were better predictors of performance, the prediction–performance relationship was still weak.

It appears that any questionnaire assessment of attention is inherently limited in at least two ways. For instance, the assumption underlying questionnaire assessment is that athletes are able to assess their attentional focus accurately across varying situations. The veracity of this assumption has not been established. Second, there are problems with the assumption that attention can be accurately described through self-analysis and language. As discussed earlier, the automatic processing aspect of attention appears to be free of conscious monitoring (Schneider et al., 1984). Thus, a paradox may exist when athletes are asked to assess nonconscious attentional states by way of conscious processing.

A related aspect of attentional style is the association/dissociation attentional strategies used by elite and nonelite marathon runners. Results of exploratory interviews with such athletes (Morgan & Pollack, 1977) have revealed that elite runners compared to nonelite runners were less likely to use dissociative strategies (focusing on distractive thoughts to divert attention away from the discomfiture of running) when running. Rather, elite marathoners reported that they used associative strategies (focusing on bodily sensations such as breathing and feelings in legs) more often than did nonelite runners.

More recently, Schomer (1986) has suggested that postinterview data, post-race questionnaires, and anecdotal reports do not accurately assess the continuous thought flow of runners while they are running. In response to this criticism, Schomer (1986) used a tape recorder to record runners' thoughts while running on a treadmill. The tapes were then content-analyzed by coding thoughts into mental strategies. From this analysis 10 categories emerged as mental strategy subclassifications. Comparison of elite and nonelite runners' use of the 10 categories did not support the results of Morgan and Pollack (1977), who found that elite marathoners used associative mental strategies, whereas non-world-class runners preferred to dissociate. In contrast, the results of the Schomer study suggest that regardless of the marathon runners' status, increased running pace was accompanied by a predominately associative mental strategy. These contrasting results suggest that further research using thought-sampling techniques, interviews, and questionnaires is needed to clarify the association/dissociation phenomenon in continuous activities such as running.

Social psychologists' interest in attention has primarily focused on the disruptive influence of nonrelevant task stimuli such as worry and self-consciousness. In well-learned tasks, inappropriate use of control processing appears to have the potential to detrimentally influence the performance of well-learned skills that are typically under the control of automatic processing. In sport, where many skills are well learned, there is potential for athletes to interfere with automatic nonconscious performance by focusing on distractive information such as worry and fear of failure and by consciously attempting to control movement.

Social psychologists have also been interested in potential individual differences in attentional capabilities. These differences in attentional style of different athletic groups have been assessed through questionnaires. The rationale behind such questionnaires is that assessment of an athlete's attentional style can predict future performance. Unfortunately, no evidence exists to suggest that attentional questionnaires are good predictors of sport performance. Also, because of the nature of automatic processing, the validity of assessing attentional states by retrospective recall may be questioned. Other ways of assessing attentional style include interviews and thought-sampling techniques. The latter strategy may have greater potential for attentional assessment, because it does not rely on retrospective recall.

Psychophysiological Perspectives

In contrast to cognitive psychologists who have attempted to understand attention by studying the whole process (receptor, information processing, and motor output), psychophysiologists have attempted to identify the mechanisms of attention by examining its component parts. In psychophysiological research, electroencephalogram (EEG), evoked response potentials, contingent variation, and heart rate have primarily been used to examine attention and its relationship to performance. For instance, EEG (obtained by monitoring general cortical activity through scalp electrodes) has been studied in relation to a variety of cognitive tasks, including vigilance detection, perceptual structuring, and object recognition and discrimination. Evoked response potentials, which are averaged brain responses to a series of stimuli, have also been examined as indicants of attention, and contingent variations have been found to be sensitive to the level of concentration on a task.

Psychophysiological indicants of attention have also been used in sport research. Hatfield, Landers, and Ray (1984), for example, examined left- and right-brain alpha EEG activity of elite rifle shooters while they were shooting and while they were performing a series of mental tasks. Results indicate that progressive electrocortical lateralization occurred toward right-hemispheric dominance before the trigger pull. Thus, seconds before pulling the trigger, shooters exhibited more alpha activity in their left hemisphere than in their right. The authors suggest that elite marksmen may possess such a high degree of attentional focus that they can effectively reduce conscious mental activities of the left hemisphere, thus reducing cognitions unnecessary to performance of the task.

These data provide support for the notion that there are general processing differences between the left and right cerebral hemispheres of the brain. For example, studies of split-brain patients' (a) performance (Le Doux, Wilson & Gazzaniga, 1977; Sperry, 1968), (b) EEG patterns (McKee, Humphrey & McAdam, 1973), and (c) lateral eye movements (Schwartz, Davidson & Maer, 1975; Tucker, Shearer & Murray, 1977) have demonstrated that for most people verbal and linguistic processing occurs in the left cerebral hemisphere, whereas spatial cognitive processing occurs in the right hemisphere. Also, the left hemisphere appears to process information analytically, breaking down a concept into discrete parts, whereas the right hemisphere processes holistically in a gestaltic fashion (Tucker et al., 1977).

Another variable that has been used to explore attentional states in athletes is cardiac deceleration. For example, Landers, Christina, Hatfield, Daniels, and Doyle (1980) found heart rate deceleration with elite rifle marksmen just prior to the trigger pull. Similar results have been found with archers, who exhibited a progressive deceleration in heart rate seconds before the release of the arrow (Wang & Landers, 1988). Interestingly, both skilled and unskilled archers recorded similar heart rate deceleration patterns during the aiming period. However, skilled archers demonstrated significantly greater heart rate deceleration compared to less accomplished archers. The authors suggest that skilled archers may have been more able to control their concentration while performing.

Boutcher and Zinsser (1990) also found similar deceleration effects with elite and beginning golfers on a putting task. Both groups displayed heart rate deceleration during the performance of 4- and 12-foot putts, although the elite golfers showed significantly greater deceleration. The elite golfers also possessed significantly less variable preshot routines. We suggested that the different heart rate deceleration patterns may reflect the more efficient attentional control of the elite golfers.

Sport psychophysiologists have studied attention by monitoring cortical and autonomic responses during athletic performance. Electroencephalograph studies have indicated that elite marksmen display cortical lateral asymmetry during shooting performance. Also, cardiac deceleration has been associated with attentional states in archery, shooting, and putting.

Summary and Synthesis of Theoretical Perspectives

The attention–performance relationship has been studied from three different viewpoints. Despite the relatively diverse nature of these three perspectives, they actually represent complementary approaches and together provide a unique, integrated perspective on the attention and sport performance relationship. Therefore, it is recommended that future research into the attentional processes underlying athletic performance should take into account the principles outlined for information processing, social psychology, and sport psychophysiological research. Thus, attention should be viewed as a multifaceted, multileveled phenomenon that can be assessed through questionnaires, thought sampling, observation analysis, performance, and psychophysiological measures. The appropriateness of the measure would depend on whether skill performance is carried out in either the control or automatic processing mode. In addition, other factors that need to be considered when investigating the attention–performance relationship

include individual differences, environmental influences, and changes in the performer's level of arousal. A preliminary framework based on this multidimensional approach is illustrated in Figure 12.1. This proposed model integrates relevant aspects of the research and theory on attention from all three perspectives. As the figure shows, enduring disposition (e.g., high trait anxiety), demands of the activity (e.g., putting versus sprinting), and environmental factors (e.g., spectators and television cameras) will initially determine the level of physiological arousal of the individual. During task performance this arousal could be channeled into either control processing, automatic processing, or a combination of the two. The appropriateness of using either control or automatic processing would be determined by the nature of the task. An optimal attentional state, then, would be achieved if the individual reached or attained the exact balance of control and automatic processing essential for that particular task. Obviously, disruption in attentional processes would occur if internal/external factors caused the individual to reach a level of arousal that would cause an imbalance in control and automatic processing.

The arrows linking the ellipses and boxes in Figure 12.1 indicate feedback mechanisms that would allow for factors to interact and influence attention both during and after performance. An example of the interaction of these factors is a golfer attempting to hole an important putt. The perceived importance of the putt (e.g., a putt to win a tournament) could increase physiological arousal and anxiety, which, in turn, could reduce the attentional capacity of the golfer. This anxiety could generate thoughts of missing the putt, which could direct attention away from task-relevant cues. Thus, the golfer's attention could be focused mostly on irrelevant information and be primarily in the control processing mode. This could be detrimental to putting performance, which probably should be performed in the automatic processing mode.

Possible ways to measure either control or automatic processing are illustrated in the end column of Figure 12.1. It should be noted that self-report may be most useful for individuals engaging in control processing, although this does not preclude the use of retrospective recall to assess feelings and emotions associated with automatic processing. Variables such as facial state, eye gaze (discussed later), and psychophysiological variables also appear to have potential for measuring attention during athletic performance.

In summary, it is suggested that researchers in the attention–performance area need to consider integrated models of attention. Viewing

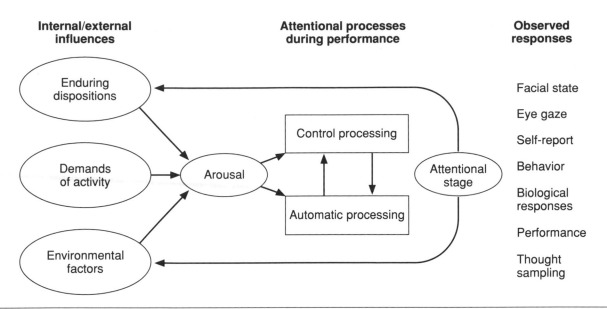

Figure 12.1 Interactions between internal and external factors and attentional processing.

attention from a multidimensional perspective may generate more systematic research and provide a more reliable and valid research paradigm.

As can be seen from this review, attentional theories of sport performance are not well developed. In addition, the empirical research that has been conducted on attention in sport has lacked a unifying model. Consequently, techniques to improve athletes' attentional capabilities have not been developed within a theoretical framework and have largely proceeded by trial and error. Certainly, at this point, it is recommended that applied research be conducted to understand better how athletes' attentional capabilities can be improved. Specifically, qualitative strategies (e.g., single-subject research) should be wedded to the idiographic framework suggested earlier.

Given the current lack of empirical research on attentional training, sport psychologists who want to provide attentional training for individual athletes will need to develop programs based on the research and theory discussed previously. The purpose of this last section will be to outline a preliminary attentional training program. This proposed training program is based on the research and theory already described. These recommendations are consistent with the principles outlined in the integrated model illustrated in Figure 12.1. It should be remembered, however, that considerably more field research is needed to test the suitability and efficacy of these proposed techniques. The program includes

- assessment of athletes' attentional strengths and weaknesses,

- basic attentional training, and
- advanced attentional training.

Assessment of Attentional Strengths and Weaknesses

Before an attentional training program can be designed and conducted with individual athletes, it will be necessary to assess the athlete's attentional strengths and weaknesses. Given the multifaceted nature of attention, one would expect assessment strategies to be most effective if they were also multifaceted. Some possible ways to assess an individual's attentional capabilities include questionnaires, interviews, thought-sampling techniques, observational analysis, performance tests, and psychophysiological measurement. These assessment strategies will now be further examined.

Sport-specific questionnaires seem to be more reliable and predict more variance associated with performance than general measures of attention (Zaichkowsky, 1984). As was mentioned earlier, sport-specific forms of the TAIS have been developed for tennis (Van Schoyck & Grasha, 1981) and baseball (Albrecht & Feltz, 1987). It is recommended, however, that these questionnaires be used with caution and only as one part of a multidimensional assessment of attention, because of their inherent limitations (discussed previously). The thought-sampling technique (Klinger, 1984; Schomer, 1986) appears to be a more valid way of assessing what athletes are focusing their thoughts on during performance. This technique involves recording individuals' thoughts during actual activity (usually by tape recorder). It seems to be especially appropriate for continuous activities such as running but could also be adapted to other sports. For instance, golfers could record on a tape or write on a scorecard (see Boutcher & Rotella, 1987) their thoughts and feelings after shots. One could then perform content analysis and establish an estimate of attentional foci during task performance.

Athletes' attentional strengths could also be measured through laboratory tasks, such as choice reaction time tasks, the Stroop test, and the grid test. For instance, in research with elite and nonelite archers (Landers, Boutcher & Wang, 1986) it was found that the better archers recorded lower reaction times when performing a reaction/anticipation time task than did their less skilled counterparts. The lower reaction times of better archers was due to greater consistency across performance trials and was not because the better archers were innately faster. Thus, it is feasible that these elite athletes' responses were more consistent because they could concentrate more effectively in this testing situation. Whether or not this difference in concentrational capabilities is linked to actual performance differences between elite and nonelite archers has not yet been established.

Another laboratory task that could be used to assess attentional capabilities is the Stroop test (Stroop, 1935). This test involves watching a series of slides flashed on a screen at the rate of one per second. On each slide is a word of a color in a contrasting color. For example, the word red may appear in green letters. Subjects are required to report the color of the letters rather than the word. This task has been used extensively in a variety of research areas and usually produces heart rate increases of approximately 10–20 beats per minute. The task requires individuals to learn to focus attention on the color aspect of the slide while ignoring the letters. Stroop performance could be collected and used both to assess the efficacy of the Stroop as a training strategy and to assess the efficacy of other attentional techniques. The grid test is another task that has been used with athletes (Harris, 1984, p. 98). Basically, this test involves checking off random numbers on a sheet as quickly as possible in a one minute period. This test is easily administered and requires little equipment. As will be discussed in connection with the advanced attentional training, other more sport-specific attentional strategies involving computers and videos could be used after initial experience with these laboratory tasks.

Another form of attentional assessment involves the use of observational behavioral analysis. Crews and I (Crews & Boutcher, 1987) have developed an observational analysis technique that we have used to assess the consistency of professional golfers' preshot routines. In a series of studies, we found that elite golfers possessed more consistent preshot routines than collegiate or beginning golfers (Boutcher & Crews, 1987; Crews & Boutcher, 1986). Thus, behavioral analysis through observation or videotaping would appear to be an effective way of examining the behavioral concomitants of attention during actual performance.

Another potential indicant of attention may be the assessment of facial/eye states. There is a well developed body of literature examining facial reactions as an indicant of affective states (Ekman & Friesan, 1975; Izard, 1977; Tomkins, 1983; Tourangeau & Ellsworth, 1979), although facial reactions associated with attentive states do not appear to have been examined. Similarly, the direction and characteristics of eye gaze have not been tested with regard to athletic performance. However, it is feasible that facial responses and eye gaze may be able to reflect the general control and automatic processing styles discussed earlier. For instance, Tucker and colleagues (1977) have characterized individual's hemispheric usage by observing lateral eye movements. As discussed previously, prior research has established that for most individuals, verbal and linguistic processing occurs in the left hemisphere, whereas spatial cognition and perception are generally processed in the right hemisphere of the brain. Kocel, Galin, Ornstein, and Merrin (1972) have suggested that individuals who are responding to a question will tend to look left if the response requires spatial thinking and right if the question requires verbal thought. Thus, lateral eye movement to different types of questions may indicate primary activation of the contralateral hemisphere. Although this lateral eye movement assessment has not been used in sport, research in cognitive behavioral therapy has suggested that cognitive behavioral methods were most effective if they employed cognition of the subjects' nonpreferred hemisphere (Tucker et al., 1977). Consequently, it may be possible to characterize athletes as to their primary patterns of hemispheric usage based on the frequency of leftward and rightward eye movement when responding to different types of sport-related questions.

Psychophysiological indicants of attention could also be used to assess attention. Equipment to collect indicants of attentional style is becoming cheaper, more portable, and easier to use. Several companies offer relatively inexpensive, user-friendly biofeedback systems that can collect a host of physiological variables. Thus, EEG, heart rate, pulse amplitude, respiration, electromyograph, skin temperature, and other physiological variables can be either used in a biofeedback setting or stored for research or applied purposes. Autonomic indicants of attention such as heart rate are less affected by movement and therefore lend themselves to collection during actual performance. For example, wrist telemetry monitors (Uniq Heart Watch, Model 8799) can record up to four hours of heart rate during actual athletic performance and then be downloaded to a computer and displayed graphically. Because cardiac patterns seem to be associated with attentional style (Boutcher & Zinsser, 1990; Wang & Landers, 1988), this variable would seem to have potential for assessing cognitive activity during performance.

Finally, techniques to assess the attentional demands of sporting situations also need to be developed. As has been pointed out by Nideffer (1976a), athletes need to match the attentional demands of the sporting environmnent with the appropriate attentional style. Thus, it seems important that the attentional strengths and weaknesses of the athlete should be assessed and compared to the attentional demands of the particular sport. Table 12.1 illustrates some of the factors that need to be considered when analyzing the attentional demands of an individual position in a particular sport. Open-skill activities involve continuous and repetitious movement patterns (e.g., swimming, basketball), whereas closed-skill activities are stop–start in nature (e.g., golf, archery). Fine skills are those which require accuracy and generally involve more delicate movements (e.g., putting or dart throwing), whereas gross skills are more dynamic and involve larger muscle groups (e.g., sprinting). Generally, fast, gross, open-skilled sports would be less prone to sources of distraction because of more limited attentional capacity when performing. In contrast, closed-skill activities

Table 12.1   Nature of Sport Skills and External Demands

Nature of the task	External factors	Attentional processing
Slow/fast	Game demands	Control processing
Open/closed	Environmental demands	Automatic processing
Fine/gross	—	Combination of above

may be more susceptible to disruption of attention because of the extra time and capacity available.

Basic Attentional Training

Based on the multidimensional profile that can be obtained from the assessment of an athlete's current attentional capabilities, a training program would be designed around the attentional strengths and weaknesses of the athlete. If basic attentional training is required, the program would start at a basic level and gradually progress to more complex, sophisticated attentional skills. It should be pointed out, however, that it is not clear whether attentional training on laboratory or nonsport tasks will actually transfer to athletic performance. Considerably more research needs to be conducted to assess the generalizability of attentional training as well as that of other forms of training (e.g., relaxation and imagery). Nevertheless, there appears to be potential in viewing attentional skills similarly to motor skills, where the learning environment is most productive if structured in a graduated fashion (Adler, 1981). Thus, attentional training on laboratory tasks such as the Stroop, reaction time, and grid tests could form the first phase of the attention training program, with training on more sport-specific skills conducted in later phases.

In addition to the laboratory training tasks already identified, biofeedback is another technique that can be used to develop basic attentional skills. Biofeedback requires individuals to be able to self-monitor and eventually control autonomic and somatic responses by interacting with some form of feedback loop (usually a computer). Thus, athletes can practice basic attentional control by learning to focus their attention on a variety of biofeedback cues. When athletes are directed to watch the screen or listen to an auditory cue, an assessment of their attentional efficiency could be attained by monitoring the resultant effects on the physiological variables being utilized. Because biofeedback reinforces the subject, this type of training task gives instant feedback to the individual regarding his or her ability to focus and adjust to the appropriate cue.

Thus, basic attentional training programs could be structured around a variety of laboratory tasks and organized so that attentional tasks become progressively more difficult. Through these types of training activities, athletes could attempt to acquire basic control of variables such as heart rate, respiration, and attentional focus.

Advanced Attentional Training

An extension of basic attentional training may take the form of a sport-individualized program. At this advanced phase it should first be verified that the athlete has acquired basic attentional control and is ready to develop sport-specific attentional skills. Also, for closed-skill athletes, much of the initial work at the advanced attentional training level needs to focus on the development of sound, effective preperformance routines (see Boutcher, 1990). Thus, the precursor to successful attentional control during actual performance may be the establishment of a series of behavioral, physiological, and cognitive cues that optimally prime both body and mind for the ensuing skill.

Although an increasing number of researchers are examining preperformance states, little research has explored attentional states during actual athletic performance. This lack of inquiry is probably due to the general reluctance of cognitive psychologists to examine processes that are not readily available to conscious processing. Consequently, unconscious or subconscious processing has largely been confined to psychodynamic theory and has remained relatively unexplored in cognitive psychology (Kissin, 1986). In sport, optimal attentional states have been labeled *peak performance* or *flow* states (Csikszentmihalyi, 1975; Privette, 1982, 1983). Unfortunately, these states have been assessed through retrospective self-report of athletes (Ravizza, 1984). This approach views optimal attentional functioning as an outcome rather than a process and does not tell us much about the underlying process (Hatfield & Landers, 1983). Thus, an outcome approach may not be helpful in designing programs to improve attentional flow during performance.

A tentative hypothesis based on the concepts of control and automatic processing and left- and right-brain functioning discussed earlier may help stimulate research into the process of attentional flow. As noted, previous research has demonstrated that elite shooters exhibit different patterns of left- and right-brain cortical activity than do less elite shooters (Hatfield et al., 1984). Specifically, the elite shooters showed suppressed left-brain and enhanced right-brain activity. It is hypothesized that this particular pattern may represent the optimal attentional state during automatic skill execution. Furthermore, because performing in competitive environments is likely to generate physiological arousal (Nideffer, 1976a), it is possible that attentional flow may be achieved when physiological arousal is channeled into automatic processing rather than control processing. Thus,

focusing attention on the task at hand when physiologically aroused may result in increased attentional flow. Because arousal tends to focus and narrow attention (Easterbrook, 1959), it is plausible that increased arousal and task-appropriate processing may generate positive emotion, focused attention, and oneness with the task that is associated with attentional flow states (Ravizza, 1984). Thus, optimal attentional flow may be created by the athlete who directs arousal away from task-irrelevant information and into the task itself. This relationship is diagrammed in Figure 12.1. Consequently, the challenge for the athlete or any other performer may be to learn how to direct competition-generated arousal into automatic processing of the task at hand while suppressing analytical processing. Thus, actively thinking of "nothing" while allowing skills to be performed reflexively and automatically may be the most efficient attentional style for the athletes who typically perform in competitive challenging situations.

Due to the fact that a large body of research indicates that brain wave activity can be self-regulated, sport-specific EEG biofeedback would seem to be of value in teaching athletes appropriate attentional focus during performance. For instance, research has established that individuals can learn to suppress cortical activity by learning to enhance alpha waves (Bauer, 1976; Elder et al., 1985; Jackson & Eberly, 1982). Furthermore, other studies have demonstrated that subjects can self-regulate EEG activity. For example, Schwartz, Davidson, and Pugwash (1976) have trained subjects to develop both symmetrical and asymmetrical EEG patterns. Suter, Griffin, Smallhouse, and Whitlach (1981) have also shown biofeedback control of EEG asymmetries.

In the sport context, one study has examined the effect of brain wave biofeedback on archery performance. Petruzzello, Landers, Salazar, Kubitz, and Hahn (1989) administered right-hemispheric alpha feedback, left-hemispheric alpha feedback, or no feedback to three groups of archers. Results indicated that the left-hemisphere group improved performance, whereas the right-hemisphere group exhibited significantly worse performance.

Although the efficacy of these EEG biofeedback techniques have yet to be established in sport, the increasing use of biofeedback techniques in a variety of athletic situations (Landers, 1985b) suggests that this technique has potential. For example, it is possible that biofeedback techniques could be combined with sport-specific videos. Thus, the athlete could be trained to produce the appropriate attentional focus while participating in a video experience of the actual sport. A progression from the video to actual sporting situations on the practice ground and then eventually to the actual competitive setting would appear to be logical following steps. However, the efficacy of these techniques relative to the sport domain clearly needs to be established through research.

Applied aspects of attentional control in sport are only beginning to be explored. Many of the ideas and suggestions expressed in this section are speculative and unsubstantiated by empirical research. It was not the intent of this section to provide the reader with untried techniques but rather to provide a broad review of potential strategies that need to be investigated by future researchers. It is hoped that this attempt to synthesize relevant research in attention and applied interests in sport will result in the generation of both basic and applied investigations into the attention phenomenon.

Conclusion

This chapter has attempted to integrate research examining different aspects of attention from the areas of information processing, social psychology, and psychophysiology. Each of these research thrusts has emphasized a different but related perspective of the attentional process. Research in information processing has established the existence of two related forms of processing. Control processing requires effort and is slow and cumbersome, whereas automatic processing is effortless, quick, and efficient. Social psychologists have focused on individual differences and environmental influences on attentional processes. The ability of extraneous, inappropriate cues to disrupt performance has been established. Sport psychophysiologists have attempted to examine the underlying mechanisms of attention by monitoring cortical and cardiac activity. Both cortical and autonomic indicants of attention have been successfully used to assess attentional style in athletes during performance. A preliminary model encapsulating these principles was outlined. This multileveled, multifaceted nature of attention was further developed in the applied section and a variety of assessment and training strategies were described. Assessment strategies included questionnaire, performance, thought-sampling techniques, behavioral analysis, and psychophysiological indicants. A preliminary model of attentional flow during peak performance was outlined. Training strategies to enhance attentional abilities, including performance tests, computer and video tasks, and biofeedback strategies, were then described.

References

Adler, J.D. (1981). Strategies of skill acquisition: A guide for teachers. *Motor Skill: Theory into practice, 5,* 75-80.

Albrecht, R.A., & Feltz, D.L. (1987). Generality and specificity of attention related to competitive anxiety and sport performance. *Journal of Sport and Exercise Psychology, 9,* 231-248.

Bacon, S. (1974). Arousal and the range of cue utilization. *Journal of Experimental Psychology, 102,* 81-87.

Bauer, R.H. (1976). Short-term memory: EEG alpha correlates and the effect of increased alpha. *Behavioral Biology, 17,* 425-433.

Baumeister, R.F. (1984). Choking under pressure: Self-consciousness and paradoxical effects of incentives on skillful performance. *Journal of Personality and Social Psychology, 46,* 610-620.

Boutcher, S.H. (1990). The role of performance routines in sport. In G. Jones & L. Hardy (Eds.), *Stress and performance in sport* (pp. 231-245). London: John Wiley.

Boutcher, S.H., & Crews, D.J. (1987). The effect of a preshot routine on a well-learned skill. *International Journal of Sport Psychology, 18,* 30-39.

Boutcher, S.H., & Rotella, R.J. (1987). A psychological skills educational program for closed-skill performance enhancement. *Sport Psychologist, 1,* 127-137.

Boutcher, S.H., & Zinsser, N. (1990). Cardiac deceleration of elite and beginning golfers during putting. *Journal of Sport and Exercise Psychology, 12,* 37-47.

Broadbent, D.E. (1958). *Perception and communication.* London: Pergamon.

Carver, C.S., & Scheier, M.F. (1978). Self-focusing effects of dispositional self-consciousness, mirror presence, and audience presence. *Journal of Personality and Social Psychology, 36,* 324-332.

Carver, C.S., & Scheier, M.F. (1981). *Attention and self-regulation.* New York: Springer-Verlag.

Crews, D.J., & Boutcher, S.H. (1986). The effects of structured preshot behaviors on beginning golf performance. *Perceptual and Motor Skills, 62,* 291-294.

Crews, D.J., & Boutcher, S.H. (1987). An observational analysis of professional female golfers during tournament play. *Journal of Sport Behavior, 9,* 51-58.

Csikszentmihalyi, M. (1975). Play and intrinsic rewards. *Journal of Humanistic Psychology, 15,* 41-63.

Duval, S., & Wicklund, R.A. (1972). *A theory of objective self-awareness.* New York: Academic.

Easterbrook, J.A. (1959). The effect of emotion on cue utilization and the organization of behavior. *Psychological Review, 66,* 183-201.

Ekman, P., & Friesan, M.V. (1975). *Unmasking the face.* Englewood Cliffs, NJ: Prentice-Hall.

Elder, S.T., Grenier, C., Lashley, J., Martyn, S., Regenbogen, D., & Roundtree, G. (1985). Can subjects be trained to communicate through the use of EEG biofeedback? *Biofeedback and Self-Regulation, 10,* 88-89.

Harris, D., & Harris, L. (1984). *The athlete's guide to sports psychology: Mental skills for physical people.* Champaign, IL: Leisure Press.

Hatfield, B.D., & Landers, D.M. (1983). Psychophysiology—A new direction for sport psychology. *Journal of Sport Psychology, 5,* 243-259.

Hatfield, B.D., Landers, D.M., & Ray, W.J. (1984). Cognitive processes during self-paced motor performance: An electroencephalographic profile of skilled marksmen. *Journal of Sport Psychology, 6,* 42-59.

Hirst, W. (1986). The psychology of attention. In J. LeDoux and W. Hirst (Eds.), *Mind and brain* (p. 105-141). Cambridge: Cambridge University Press.

Hockey, G. (1970). Effects of loud noise on attentional selectivity. *Quarterly Journal of Experimental Psychology, 22,* 28-36.

Izard, C.E. (1977). *Human emotions.* New York: Plenum Press.

Jackson, G.M., & Eberly, D.A. (1982). Facilitation of performance on an arithmetic task as a result of the application of a biofeedback procedure to suppress alpha wave activity. *Biofeedback and Self-Regulation, 7*, 211-221.

James, W. (1890). *Principles of psychology* (Vol. 1). New York: Holt.

Kahneman, D. (1973). *Attention and effort.* Englewood Cliffs, NJ: Prentice-Hall.

Keele, S.W. (1973). *Attention and human performance.* Pacific Palisades, CA: Goodyear.

Kerr, B. (1973). Processing demands during mental operations. *Memory and Cognition, 1*, 401-412.

Kimble, G., & Perlmuter, L. (1970). The problem of volition. *Psychological Review, 77*, 361-384.

Kissin, B. (1986). *Conscious and unconscious programs in the brain.* New York: Plenum Press.

Klinger, E. (1984). A consciousness-sampling analysis of test anxiety and performance. *Journal of Personality and Social Psychology, 47*, 1376-1390.

Kocel, K., Galin, D., Ornstein, R., & Merrin, E.L. (1972). Lateral eye movements and cognitive mode. *Psychonomic Science, 27*, 223-224.

Kroll, W. (1982). Competitive athletic stress factors in athletes and coaches. In L.D. Zaichowsky & W.E. Sime (Eds.), *Stress management for sport* (pp. 1-10). Reston, VA: American Alliance for Health, Physical Education, Recreation and Dance.

Landers, D.M. (1980). Motivation and performance: The role of arousal and attentional factors. In W.F. Straub (Ed.), *Sport psychology: An analysis of athlete behavior* (pp. 91-125). New York: Mouvement.

Landers, D.M. (1981). Arousal, attention, and skilled performance: Further considerations. *Quest, 33*, 271-283.

Landers, D.M. (1985a, May). *Beyond the TAIS: Alternative behavioral and psychophysiological measures for determining an internal vs. external focus of attention.* Paper presented at the North American Society for the Psychology of Sport and Physical Activity Conference, Gulfpark, MS.

Landers, D.M. (1985b). Psychophysiological assessment and biofeedback: Application for athletes in closed-skill sports. In J. Sandweiss & S. Wolf (Eds.), *Biofeedback and sports science* (pp. 65-105). New York: Plenum Press.

Landers, D.M., & Boutcher, S.H. (1986). Optimal arousal/performance relationships. In J. Williams (Ed.), *Applied sport psychology: Personal growth for peak performance* (pp. 163-184). Palo Alto, CA: Mayfield.

Landers, D.M., & Boutcher, S.H., & Wang, M.Q. (1986). A psychobiological study of archery performance. *Research Quarterly for Exercise and Sport, 57*, 236-244.

Landers, D.M., Christina, B.D., Hatfield, L.A., Doyle, L.A., & Daniels, F.S. (1980). Moving competitive shooting into the scientists' lab. *American Rifleman, 128*, 36-37, 76-77.

Langer, E.J., & Imber, L.G. (1979). When practice makes imperfect: Debilitating effects of overlearning. *Journal of Personality and Social Psychology, 37*, 2014-2024.

LeDoux, J.E., Wilson, D.H., & Gazzaniga, M.S. (1977). Manipulo-spatial aspects of cerebral lateralization: Clues to the origin of lateralization: *Neuropsychologica, 15*, 743-750.

Marteniuk, R.G. (1976). *Information processing in motor skills.* New York: Holt, Rhinehart & Winston.

McKee, G., Humphrey, B., & McAdam, N.W. (1973). Scaled lateralization of alpha activity during linguistic and musical tasks. *Psychophysiology, 10*, 441.

Morgan, W.P., & Pollack, M.L. (1977). Psychologic characterization of the elite distance runner. *Annals of the New York Academy of Sciences, 301*, 382-403.

Navon, D., & Gopher, D. (1979). On the economy of the human processing system. *Psychological Review, 86*, 214-255.

Nideffer, R. (1976a). *The inner athlete: Mind plus muscle for winning.* New York: Crowell.

Nideffer, R. (1976b). Test of attentional and interpersonal style. *Journal of Personality and Social Psychology, 34*, 394-404.

Nideffer, R. (1976c). *An interpreters' manual for the test of attentional and interpersonal style.* Rochester, NY: Behavioral Research Applications Group.

Norman, D. (1969). Toward a theory of memory and attention. *Psychological Review, 75*, 522-536.

Parasuraman, R. (1984). Preface. In R. Parasuraman & D. Davies (Eds.), *Varieties of attention* (pp. xi-xvi). Orlando, FL: Academic Press.

Petruzzello, S.J., Landers, D.M., Salazar, W., Kubitz, C.A., & Hahn, M.W. (1989). *Brain wave biofeedback to improve archery performance.* Unpublished manuscript, Arizona State University, Tempe, AZ.

Posner, M.I., & Bois, S.J. (1971). Components of attention. *Psychological Review, 78*, 391-408.

Privette, G. (1982). Peak performance in sports: A factorial topology. *International Journal of Sport Psychology, 13*, 242-249.

Privette, G. (1983). Peak experience, peak performance, and flow: A comparative analysis of positive human experiences. *Journal of Personality and Social Psychology, 43*, 1361-1367.

Ravizza, K. (1984). Qualities of the peak experience in sport. In J. Silva & R. Weinberg (Eds.), *Psychological foundations of sport* (pp. 452-461). Champaign, IL: Human Kinetics.

Sarason, I.G. (1972). Experimental approaches to test anxiety: Attention and the uses of information. In C.D. Spielberger (Ed.), *Anxiety: Current trends in theory and research* (Vol. 2) (pp. 380-403). New York: Academic Press.

Scheier, M.S., Fenigstein, A., & Buss, A.H. (1974). Self-awareness and physical aggression. *Journal of Experimental Social Psychology, 10*, 264-273.

Schmidt, R.A. (1988). *Motor control and learning.* Champaign, IL: Human Kinetics.

Schneider, W., Dumais, S.T., & Shiffrin, R.M. (1984). Automatic and control processing and attention. In R. Parasuraman & R. Davies (Eds.), *Varieties of attention* (pp. 1-27). Orlando, FL: Academic Press.

Schomer, H. (1986). Mental strategies and the perception of effort of marathon runners. *International Journal of Sport Psychology, 17*, 41-59.

Schwartz, G.E., Davidson, R.J., & Maer, F. (1975). Right hemispheric specialization for emotion: Interactions with cognitions. *Science, 190*, 286-290.

Schwartz, G.E., Davidson, R.J., & Pugwash, E. (1976). Voluntary control of patterns of EEG parietal asymmetry: Cognitive concomitants. *Psychophysiology, 13*, 498-504.

Shiffrin, R.M. (1976). Capacity limitations in information processing, attention, and memory. In W.K. Estes (Ed.), *Handbook of learning and cognitive processes* (Vol. 4) (pp. 117-136). Hillsdale, NJ: Erlbaum.

Sperry, R.W. (1968). Hemisphere deconnection and unity in conscious awareness. *American Psychologist, 23*, 723-733.

Stroop, J.P. (1935). Studies of interference in serial verbal reactions. *Journal of Experimental Psychology, 18*, 643-662.

Suter, S., Griffin, G., Smallhouse, P., & Whitlach, S. (1981). Biofeedback regulation of temporal EEG alpha asymmetries. *Biofeedback and Self-Regulation, 6*, 45-56.

Tomkins, S. (1983). Affect theory. In P. Eckman (Ed.), *Emotion in the human face* (2nd ed., pp. 353-395). New York: Cambridge University Press.

Tourangeau, R., & Ellsworth, P.C. (1979). The role of facial response in the experience of emotion. *Journal of Personality and Social Psychology, 37*, 1519-1531.

Tucker, D.M., & Shearer, S.L., & Murray, J.D. (1977). Hemispheric specialization and cognitive behavior therapy. *Cognitive Therapy and Research*, **1**, 263-273.

Van Schoyck, S.R., & Grasha, A.F. (1981). Attentional style variations and athletic ability: The advantage of a sports-specific test. *Journal of Sport Psychology*, **3**, 149-165.

Wachtel, P.L. (1967). Conceptions of broad or narrow attention. *Psychological Bulletin*, **68**, 417-429.

Wang, M.Q., & Landers, D.M. (1988). *Cardiac responses and hemispheric differentiation during archery performance: A psychophysiological investigation of attention.* Unpublished manuscript, Arizona State University, Tempe, AZ.

Wickens, C.D. (1984). Processing resources in attention. In R. Parasuraman & R. Davies (Eds.), *Varieties of attention* (pp. 63-102). Orlando, FL: Academic Press.

Wine, J. (1971). Test anxiety and direction of attention. *Psychological Bulletin,* **76**, 92-104.

Zaichkowsky, L.D. (1984). Attentional styles. In W. Straub & J. Williams (Eds.), *Cognitive sport psychology* (pp. 140-150). New York: Sports Science Associates.

Chapter 13

The Jekyll/Hyde Nature of Goals: Reconceptualizing Goal Setting in Sport

Damon Burton
University of Idaho

My initial revelation that goal setting is not always the simple motivational technique that it is supposed to be came in my final year as a high school basketball coach. Going into the season, expectations in our community were high for the team. "Best basketball team since the state championship club five years ago," the regulars at the drug store told me repeatedly. Not surprisingly, conference coaches made us preseason favorites to win the league title; and I was confident that this team had the potential to bring our community another state title. However, because I was concerned that these lofty expectations would breed overconfidence and complacency, our team set only one goal for the season—to win the Central Prairie League Championship.

During the first four weeks of the season, the team played superbly, better than any team I had ever coached. We had talented, although somewhat undersized, athletes who played well together, understood what we wanted to do offensively and defensively, and executed with tremendous confidence and aggressiveness. Our record at Christmas break was 6-1, with our only loss coming on the road in double overtime to the third-ranked team in the state.

Then a funny thing happened on the way to our "dream" season. Our community was hit by a particularly nasty strain of the Hong Kong flu, decimating the team for over three weeks. During this time we had at least two starters out of every game, and our best player was further hampered by a freak blister on his heel that went all the way to the bone. The kids confronted these adversities head on, seemingly practicing harder and competing more intensely than ever; but we still lost six of the next seven games. Suddenly, the single goal we had established for the season was now *unrealistic*; and the players fixated on this failure. For several weeks, my assistant coach and I did nothing but talk to the players individually and as a team about putting our problems behind us and making the best of the remaining season. We also tried instituting a substitute goal—qualifying for the state tournament—but that goal adjustment was only modestly successful.

Although we lost only four more games the rest of the year—all by small margins—and made a good run at the state tournament, we were just not the same team. We recovered physically and continued to improve our offensive and defensive execution over that final six weeks of the season; but psychologically, the damage was irreparable. We had lost that great confidence that had allowed us to play with such poise, aggressiveness, and mental toughness. Now our play was much less aggressive and punctuated by indecision and mental lapses. The close losses were particularly frustrating because the team that played with great confidence before Christmas almost assuredly would have won those games. Above all, everyone seemed to understand intuitively that like Humpty Dumpty, once our self-confidence was shattered, it was virtually impossible to put the pieces back together.

I tell this story often because it makes the important point about the Jekyll/Hyde nature of goals. Most researchers and practitioners view goal setting as a positive motivational strategy designed to enhance performance by focusing attention and promoting increased intensity and persistence. However, when used improperly, goals can also become a major source of stress because they become the standards by which athletes define failure as well as success. Surprisingly, scant attention has been paid in the psychological literature to the negative aspects of improper goal setting. As my goal-setting story emphasizes, our basketball team's challenging but realistic pre-Christmas goals promoted consistent goal attainment; and that success enhanced our motivation, self-confidence, and performance. Regrettably, when goal attainment became impossible following our team's bout with the flu, our goals now confirmed our failure and prompted anxiety, diffidence, and performance impairment.

Much of the contemporary research on goal setting comes from industrial and organizational psychology, where goals are viewed as motivational tools to enhance performance. The major premise of industrial and organizational psychology research is that a positive linear relationship exists between level of challenge and performance enhancement: The greater the challenge, the better the resulting performance (e.g., Latham & Locke, 1979; Locke & Latham, 1985; Locke, Shaw, Saari & Latham, 1981; Mento, Steel & Karren, 1987). The notion that goals can be stress-producing when set too high has been virtually ignored (see Burton, 1989b). However, contemporary motivation theory suggests that for most individuals motivation is dependent on developing high perceived ability through consistent goal attainment (e.g., Elliott & Dweck, 1988; Maehr, 1984; Maehr & Braskamp, 1986; Maehr & Nicholls, 1980; Nicholls, 1984a, 1984b). Thus, unrealistic goals not only lose their motivational value over time if individuals can't be successful enough to maintain high perceived ability, they also create evaluation stress that impairs performance (e.g., Burton, 1989b). Therefore, the notion that goals are a simple performance enhancement strategy may be somewhat simplistic in sport because unrealistic goals can impair rather than facilitate performance.

Another problem with the existing goal-setting literature is the lack of integration between goal-setting research conducted in different disciplines or using different conceptual models. Industrial and organizational psychologists have extensively researched goal setting, using a primarily mechanistic cognitive framework (e.g., Latham & Locke, 1979; Locke & Latham, 1985; Locke et al., 1981; Mento et al., 1987). Similarly, clinical psychologists (e.g., Bandura & Cervone, 1983; Bandura & Schunk, 1981; Bandura & Simon, 1977; Schunk, 1983) have employed a cognitive behavior modification model to assess the impact of goals on behavioral change. Finally, contemporary motivation theorists (e.g., Elliott & Dweck, 1988; Maehr, 1984; Maehr & Braskamp, 1986; Maehr & Nicholls, 1980; Nicholls, 1984a, 1984b) have utilized the notion of goal orientations to explain motivation and behavior in educational or business settings. Regrettably, existing research and theory has generally failed to integrate these somewhat different conceptions of goals from divergent literatures into a comprehensive and coherent goal-setting model.

Therefore, the primary purpose of this chapter is to review the available research and theory on goal setting with the intent of integrating the various conceptual approaches into a comprehensive framework that can be applied to sport. In the first section, the parameters of goal setting will be defined, including clarification of what goal setting is and its primary psychological functions. Section 2 will outline a competitive-goal-setting model that attempts to integrate all major lines of goal-setting theory and research into a comprehensive conceptual framework highlighting a series of specific model predictions. In the third section, research will be reviewed that tests specific predictions of this competitive-goal-setting model and then the fourth section will focus on critical measurement issues in assessing individual goal-setting styles. In the final section, potential future directions for goal-setting research will be addressed, and both theoretical and application/implementation issues needing empirical investigation will be identified.

William James prefaced his classic definition of *attention* by saying "Every one knows what attention is" (1890, p. 455). It is tempting to define goal setting in a similar way, because it is one of the most commonly used performance enhancement strategies in psychology; and both researchers and practitioners assume that the concept has a straightforward meaning. Indeed, Edwin Locke and his colleagues define a goal simply as "what an individual is trying to accomplish; it is the object or aim of an action" (1981, p. 126). Locke and Latham (1985) also emphasize that every goal includes two basic components: direction and amount or quality of the product. Direction implies choice, specifically the choice about how to direct or focus one's behavior, whereas amount or quality suggests a minimal standard of performance that must be attained.

However, several subdisciplines within psychology are now employing the term *goal* prominently as a major component of motivational theories, prompting confusion about the exact meaning of the term in specific contexts. The notion of goals is used in two major ways by motivational theorists. Industrial and organizational psychologists such as Edwin Locke and his colleagues look at goals as a direct, specific motivational strategy. In this context, goals function primarily like a psychological *state*, providing a specific standard that serves to motivate individuals to take direct action by focusing attention, increasing effort and intensity, prompting development of new problem-solving strategies, and/or encouraging persistence in the face of failure.

Several contemporary motivation theorists (e.g., Dweck, 1980; Elliott & Dweck, 1988; Maehr & Braskamp, 1986; Maehr & Nicholls, 1980; Nicholls, 1984a) use the notion of goals in a second way to suggest a more global purpose for involvement in particular activities. Goals in this context are more like personality *traits*, implying predispositions for participation based on underlying motives for what individuals want to attain or accomplish. Motivation theorists often label these more-global goals *goal orientations* (e.g., Maehr & Braskamp, 1986; Maehr &

Nicholls, 1980; Nicholls, 1984a, 1984b). Inherent in the idea of goal orientations is the premise that success and failure are subjective perceptions, not objective events. Thus, "success" can be attained in any situation in which individuals are able either to infer personally desirable characteristics, qualities, or attributes about themselves or attain personally meaningful objectives (Maehr & Braskamp, 1986). In attempting to integrate these two notions of goals, it can be inferred that individuals may use discrete goals as tools for achieving more global goal orientations. In this chapter I shall present a Competitive-Goal-Setting (CGS) model which incorporates both types of goals.

Existing goal-setting theories depicting goals as discrete (e.g., Locke, 1968) or global processes (e.g., Elliott & Dweck, 1988; Maehr & Braskamp, 1986; Nicholls, 1984a) are quite different in focus but include a significant amount of overlap, both conceptually and pragmatically. Thus, the purpose of presenting the CGS model is not to advance a new theory of goal setting but simply to provide the reader with a heuristic tool for understanding how (a) these two major conceptions of goals can be integrated successfully into a single more comprehensive model that considers both the motivational and stress management functions of goals and how (b) that comprehensive model can further aid our understanding and investigation of the goal-setting process in sport (see Figure 13.1).

Consistent with previous motivation research (Elliott & Dweck, 1988; Locke, 1968; Locke et al., 1981; Maehr, 1984; Nicholls, 1984a, 1984b), the CGS model shown in Figure 13.1 predicts that the motivational function of goals is most evident in the top portion (Links 1-5). First, goal orientations interact with perceived ability to prompt the development of three distinct goal-setting styles: performance-oriented (see Link 1), and success- and failure-oriented (see Link 2). These goal-setting styles, along with situation type (i.e., practice vs. competition) and performance expectancies, then dictate the specific goal set (see Link 3). Next, these discrete goals interact with perceived goal commitment to prompt specific goal responses—task choice, effort/intensity, strategy development, and persistence/continuing motivation (see Link 4)—that ultimately dictate how athletes will perform and their competitive outcome (see Link 5).

Based on perceived ability theory and research (e.g., Elliott & Dweck, 1988; Harter, 1981; Nicholls, 1984a, 1984b), the CGS model further predicts that goals also have an important stress management function because they become the standards against which performance

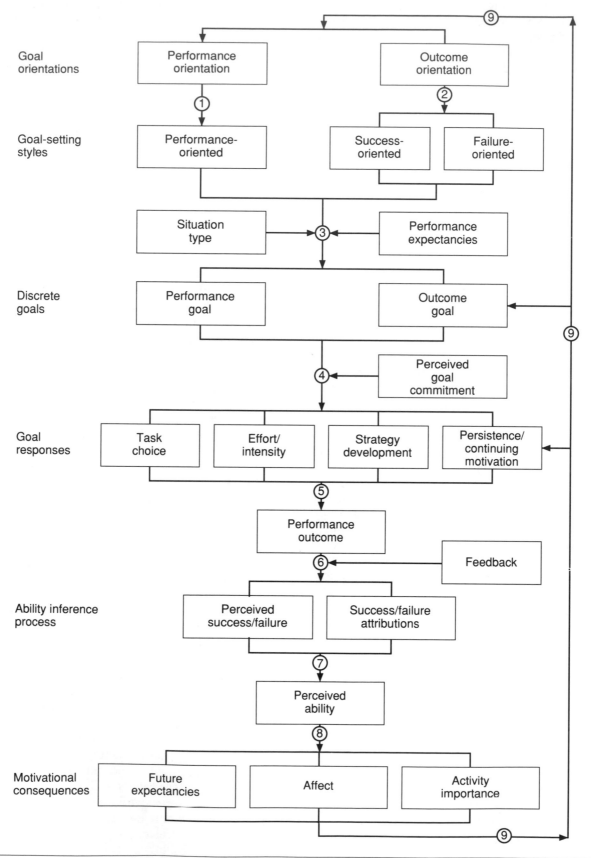

Figure 13.1   Competitive goal-setting model.

and outcome are weighed in order to determine perceived success and failure and to assess specific success/failure attributions (see Link 6), the two primary antecedents of perceived competence or ability (see Link 7). Finally, the CGS model predicts that perceived ability directly influences motivational consequent variables such as future expectancies, affect, and activity importance (see Link 8). Feedback loops then allow motivational consequent variables subsequently to influence goal orientations, specific goals, and goal responses (see Link 9).

Although the CGS model is depicted as a sequential process, this was done as a heuristic tool to facilitate understanding of the separate motivation and stress management functions of goals. In reality, the model is probably much more complex and feedback loops more extensive. Moreover, it is not my intention to venture into the argument about whether cognition precedes affect or vice versa but, rather, to suggest that these variables are related, probably in some reciprocal fashion.

The most innovative aspect of the CGS model is the prediction that athletes who adopt different goal-setting styles can be expected to set different types of practice and competitive goals that will significantly influence their cognitions and performance. In the next section, the conceptual framework for goal-setting styles will be examined and the specific characteristics of athletes adopting performance-oriented, success-oriented, and failure-oriented goal-setting styles will be outlined.

Goal-Setting Styles

The notion of goal-setting styles is based on research in contemporary motivation theory that combines the concept of global goal orientations with personal perceptions of ability. In examining the genesis of the conception of goal-setting styles, it is important first to review the research on goal orientations. Contemporary conceptions of goal orientations are based on two primary theoretical premises (e.g., Elliott & Dweck, 1988; Nicholls, 1984a, 1984b):

- Perceived competence or ability is conceived as the critical underlying construct responsible for mediating motivational behaviors.
- Individuals' goal orientations are hypothesized to mediate how perceived ability develops and what its impact is on achievement behavior.

Nicholls (1984a, 1984b) and Dweck (1975; Diener & Dweck, 1978; Elliott & Dweck, 1988) have also postulated two primary goal orientations in achievement situations. Although these researchers use somewhat different terminology, they define these goal orientations quite similarly. In this chapter the two goal orientations will be labeled *performance* and *outcome*.

Athletes adopting a performance goal orientation are concerned with increasing perceived ability, mastering new tasks, or improving skills. These athletes define success in terms of self-referent standards, striving to demonstrate learning, skill improvement, and/or task mastery. Performance-oriented competitors assume they have the ability to learn and improve if they put forth sufficient effort, thus freeing them from worrying about demonstrating their competence and allowing them to focus on ways to improve competence through skill development. Thus, these athletes focus their attention on the process rather than the final product.

Individuals who adopt an outcome goal orientation seek to "maintain positive judgments of their ability and avoid negative judgments by seeking to prove, validate, or document their ability and not discredit it" (Elliott & Dweck, 1988, p. 5). Outcome goal orientations base success/failure on social comparison processes, thus making winning or positive social comparison essential in order to maintain high perceived ability. For outcome-oriented performers, improvement and task mastery are only seen as a means (i.e., process) of achieving positive social comparison (i.e., product).

The CGS model hypothesizes that goal orientation and level of perceived ability interact to create three distinct goal setting styles: performance-oriented, success-oriented, and failure-oriented. The general focus of each of these goal-setting styles is outlined in column 2 of Table 13.1 and the specific characteristics of each style will be discussed in the following sections.

Performance-Oriented Goal-Setting Style

As noted in columns 2 and 3 the primary goal focus of athletes adopting a performance-oriented goal-setting style is learning and improvement, not demonstrating ability to others. Thus, high- and low-skilled performance-oriented performers should demonstrate very similar motivational patterns in practice and competition. Ability comparison is simply not an issue for performance-oriented competitors; they are only interested in raising perceived ability through learning and skill development. Performance-oriented athletes should view any situation as an opportunity to learn and improve their skills,

Table 13.1 Characteristics of Performance-, Success-, and Failure-Oriented Goal-Setting Styles

Goal-setting style (orientation)	General focus of goals (primary interest)	Level of perceived ability	Success/failure attributions		Role of feedback	
			Success	Failure	Positive	Negative
Performance	Learning performance improvement and *increasing* self-referent ability	High or low	High effort (ability assumed)	No perception of failure	Confirms successful learning or performance improvement	Signal to increase effort and/or try new strategies
Success	Competitive outcome and positive social comparison as a means of demonstrating high ability	High	High ability	Internal–unstable–controllable factors such as low effort or poor mental preparation	Confirms successful social comparison	Signal to increase effort and/or try new strategies
Failure	Avoid competition because of fear that negative social comparison will reveal low ability	Low	External or uncontrollable factors such as luck or an easy opponent	Low ability	Discounted because success attributed to external and/or uncontrollable factors	Confirms unsuccessful social comparisons

thus prompting high levels of intrinsic motivation.

Based on learned helplessness and perceived ability research (e.g., Diener & Dweck, 1978; Dweck, 1975; Elliott & Dweck, 1988; Nicholls, 1984a), the CGS model predicts that performance-oriented athletes assume the ability to learn and improve, prompting them to attribute success primarily to effort (see column 4). Moreover, performance-oriented competitors are not predicted to make failure attributions (see column 5). Because of their learning focus, lack of success is dealt with by increasing effort or developing new problem-solving strategies.

Table 13.2 shows further model predictions. Performers adopting a performance-oriented goal-setting style are predicted to select challenging or difficult goals even at the risk of making mistakes because their primary objective is to increase competence. Performance-oriented athletes should also exert high effort in most situations in order to maximize learning and performance improvement regardless of the level of task difficulty. Moreover, the model also predicts that performance-oriented performers should confront failure constructively, remain focused on the task, and develop more effective problem-solving strategies, thus demonstrating high persistence and continuing motivation for their sport.

The CGS model predicts that performance-oriented athletes should perform consistently better than either success- or failure-oriented performers, both in the short run and over the course of their career, because they set more challenging goals, give consistently higher effort, use more effective problem-solving strategies, and persist longer in the face of failure (see bottom of Table 13.2). Moreover, because athletes maximize their chances of winning by performing their best, performance-oriented athletes should also win more often than success- or failure-oriented competitors of similar ability.

Finally as noted in Table 13.3, the CGS model predicts that performance-oriented athletes should experience positive motivational consequences from goal setting. Their learning focus allows performance-oriented competitors to remain optimistic about their ability to learn and improve despite temporary plateaus or failure. In fact, low current ability in a valued area may actually make skill acquisition more desirable

Table 13.2 Goal Response Predictions for Performance-, Success-, and Failure-Oriented Athletes

	Goal-setting style		
	Performance	Success	Failure
Task choice	Choice of learning opportunities at the risk of displaying mistakes in order to increase competence	Sacrifice of learning opportunities that involve risk of error	Sacrifice of learning for either moderately easy tasks to avoid displaying low ability or extremely difficult tasks to supply a build-in excuse for failure
Effort/intensity	Consistent high effort	Only as high effort as necessary to continue to display positive social comparison	Low effort on *hard tasks* to confuse others about the reason for failure and avoid revealing low ability, very high on effort on *easy tasks* to avoid failure, which would reveal low ability
Strategy development	Quality of problem solving maintained or enhanced under failure	Quality of problem solving maintained or enhanced under failure	Quality of problem solving deteriorates sharply under failure
Persistence/ continuing motivation	Remains high despite extensive failure	Deteriorates only with extensive failure	Deteriorates sharply with minimal failure
Performance	High performance that eventually will closely approach athletes' performance potential	Good enough to win, but long-term potential depends on situational factors that necessitate development of full capabilities	Poor performance that should deteriorate over time with continued failure

for them (Diener & Dweck, 1978). The model also predicts that performance-oriented performers should experience satisfaction and pride from success; and although they should perceive negative affect when unsuccessful, these negative emotions may prompt performance-oriented athletes to demonstrate even higher future motivation. Finally, performance-oriented athletes are predicted to increase their commitment to challenging tasks that help them enhance their perceptions of ability.

Success-Oriented Goal-Setting Style

Competitors with success-oriented goal-setting styles evaluate success based on competitive outcome. However, they demonstrate high perceived ability because they win consistently and socially compare well (see columns 2 & 3 of Table 13.1). A success-oriented performer's primary objective

is to win in order to demonstrate high perceived ability (column 2). Although they view most situations as opportunities to demonstrate competence, success-oriented competitors are optimally motivated, confident, and play their best only when matched against an opponent of similar ability. Otherwise, success-oriented athletes tend to be under- or overconfident, both of which are predicted to lower motivation and performance (Burton, 1989b). Success-oriented athletes are predicted to attribute success to ability, an internal–stable–controllable factor that creates a positive–optimistic outlook toward competition, whereas failure is normally attributed to internal–unstable–controllable factors such as low effort, poor mental preparation, and the need to further develop skills (see column 5). Although success-oriented competitors still worry about failure, they do respond to failure in a constructive way.

The CGS model hypothesizes that competitors with success-oriented goal-setting styles will

Table 13.3 Goal Consequences Predictions for Performance-, Success-, and Failure-Oriented Athletes

	Performance	Goal-setting style Success	Failure
Future expectancies	Positive and optimistic because of high self-confidence in ability to learn and improve	Positive and optimistic because of high self-confidence in talent and ability to win and socially to compare well.	Negative and pessimistic because convinced they lack talent and ability to win and socially to compare well.
Affect	Consistently high self-confidence, enjoyment, and satisfaction	Consistently high self-confidence, enjoyment, and satisfaction	Anxiety, dissatisfaction, and shame
Activity importance	Importance of activity should increase over time	Importance of activity should increase over time	Importance of activity should decrease over time

avoid challenging goals that involve learning opportunities if they perceive a risk of making public mistakes (see Table 13.2). Instead, they are predicted to prefer to set moderately difficult goals on tasks at which they are already reasonably proficient to ensure that low ability is not revealed. Success-oriented competitors' effort expenditure is predicted to fluctuate, depending on task difficulty. For moderately difficult tasks, success-oriented performers should put forth high effort to reach their goals. However, when the task is easy, success-oriented performers will expend as little effort as necessary to win, a strategy that allows them to demonstrate even higher ability. Finally, for very hard tasks where the probability of failure is high, success-oriented competitors will exert high effort until they become convinced that successful social comparison is not possible, and then concentrate their effort on other tasks at which they are more likely to be successful.

The CGS model predicts that the positive social comparison focus of success-oriented athletes should help them approach failure in a positive way and allow them to manifest high confidence, remain task-focused, and develop effective problem-solving strategies (see Table 13.2). However, because of their need to continue to demonstrate high ability, the continuing motivation of success-oriented performers should eventually deteriorate with extensive failure.

The model predicts that success-oriented athletes will generally perform well (see Table 13.2). However, success-oriented athletes are not expected to perform as close to their performance potential as performance-oriented performers because their concern about demonstrating high

ability to others reduces performance two ways. First, the importance of positive social comparison reduces the level of challenge of the goals set and limits how long success-oriented athletes will persist in the face of failure. Second, the desire to maximize demonstration of ability prompts success-oriented competitors to give low effort against weaker opponents and not look for ways to learn and improve unless pushed to do so in order to win. Such motivational patterns ultimately prevent them from developing to the full extent of their performance potential.

As noted in Table 13.3, the CGS model predicts that success-oriented performers should experience positive motivational consequences from the goal-setting process. Success-oriented performers are predicted to maintain optimistic future expectancies because past experience has told them that their normatively high "ability" will allow them to continue to socially compare well. The model also predicts that success-oriented performers should experience satisfaction and pride from success, whereas dissatisfaction over failure coupled with functional attributional patterns should prompt even higher future motivation. Finally, success-oriented performers are predicted to increase activity importance for tasks at which they socially compare well in order to enhance their perceptions of ability.

Failure-Oriented Goal-Setting Style

Performers with failure-oriented goal-setting styles are outcome-oriented, but they have low perceived ability due to their inability to socially compare well (see columns 2 and 3 of Table

13.1). A failure-oriented competitor's primary objective is to prevent others from finding out they have low ability, and they fear competitive situations because of the risk of publicly revealing their incompetence. Thus, failure-oriented performers approach competition with diffidence and anxiety and often perform well below their capabilities. The CGS model hypothesizes that failure-oriented competitors typically attribute failure to lack of ability, thus reinforcing their negative perceptions of ability (column 5). Success, however, is attributed to external and/or uncontrollable factors such as luck or an easy task, thus providing little help in raising their feelings of competence (column 4). Regrettably, goals that foster increased success will not necessarily increase motivation for failure-oriented performers unless they also take responsibility for their success and/or perceive they can do something to turn failure into future success.

The CGS model hypothesizes that performers with failure-oriented goal-setting styles have little interest in learning (see Table 13.2). Because they are concerned with concealing their low ability from others, they should set goals that are moderately easy for tasks at which they are already experienced and/or proficient, or else adopt extremely difficult goals so they have a built-in excuse for failure. The CGS model predicts that the effort expenditure of failure-oriented competitors will fluctuate with the level of task difficulty. The failure-oriented competitor who has not completely given up hope of demonstrating high ability should choose very difficult tasks. Despite the high probability of failure, failure-oriented performers will exert high effort trying to "get lucky" and demonstrate high ability, while secure in the knowlege that they have a good excuse for almost certain failure. If they are resigned to having low ability, they should prefer easy tasks and put forth high effort to ensure that they will not fail. Moderately difficult tasks are predicted to be highly threatening to failure-oriented competitors, prompting them to respond by putting forth low effort as an ego-defense mechanism. Thus, this "token effort" strategy serves the function of preventing the revelation of low ability by creating confusion about whether failure was due to lack of ability or simply low effort.

The CGS model hypothesizes that failure-oriented performers should demonstrate a significant deterioration in problem-solving skills when confronted with failure, probably due to the negative effects of diffidence and anxiety that prompt attentional distraction (see Table 13.2). Finally, failure-oriented athletes are predicted to demonstrate a sharp deterioration in persistence and

continuing motivation, even with minimal failure. Fear of revealing low ability to others should prompt failure-oriented performers to respond to failure by developing high levels of anxiety and self-doubt, focusing internally on their own arousal and self-rumination and demonstrating severe deterioration in their problem-solving skills.

The CGS model predicts that failure-oriented athletes should normally perform poorly (see Table 13.2). Fear of failure due to inability to socially compare well should elicit high levels of anxiety that significantly impair failure-oriented competitors' performance. Moreover, negative competitive cognitions coupled with the most dysfunctional types of goal responses, including easy goals, low effort expenditure, poor strategy development (particularly under failure), and low persistence should ensure that performance deteriorates even further over time.

Finally, the model predicts that failure-oriented athletes should experience generally negative motivational consequences from the goal-setting process (see Table 13.3). Failure-oriented performers are predicted to demonstrate negative future expectancies due to previous unsuccessful social comparison that they attributed to low ability. The model also predicts that failure-oriented competitors will experience minimal satisfaction from success, which they attribute to external–uncontrollable factors, whereas failure should promote extensive negative affect such as anxiety and shame that should impair performance and prompt a desire to drop out of sport. Finally, failure-oriented competitors are predicted to devalue activities that force them to risk the demonstration of low ability as a precursor to changing activities.

Goal Attribute Preferences

Based on the general model predictions for each goal-setting style just reviewed, the next section will specify CGS model predictions for the goal attribute preferences of each goal-setting style for

- goal specificity,
- goal difficulty,
- goal proximity,
- goal collectivity, and
- goal valence.

Preferred Goal Attributes of Performance-Oriented Athletes

The CGS model hypothesizes that performance-oriented athletes' learning orientation should prompt them to prefer self-referenced goals that are specific, difficult, positive, individual, and long-term/short-term (see Table 13.4). Performers adopting performance-oriented goal-setting styles are predicted to prefer goals with these attributes because such goals provide maximum information for developing new strategies to facilitate learning and performance improvement. Performance-oriented competitors are also predicted to set long-term goals and then to achieve them, they develop action plans that focus on attainment of more specific short-term goals. However, because performance-oriented performers are interested in learning as a long-term and ongoing process, they should be able to focus on more long-term goals than either success-oriented or failure-oriented competitors and delay gratification and accept temporary setbacks as the price that must be paid in order to maximize long-term learning and skill development.

Preferred Goal Attributes of Success-Oriented Athletes

Because success-oriented competitors define success in terms of positive social comparison, the CGS model predicts that they should prefer goals that are positive/negative, specific, individual, moderately difficult, and short-term/long-term (see Table 13.4). Success-oriented performers should prefer positively focused goals for new or difficult skills but benefit from more negatively focused goals that emphasize minimizing mistakes for well-learned skills. Model predictions suggest that specific, individual goals should facilitate social comparison, thus allowing success-oriented competitors to demonstrate high ability, whereas moderately difficult goals should maximize the chances of positive social comparison and ensure that success-oriented performers will consistently demonstrate high ability. Athletes with success-oriented goal-setting styles also should set a combination of short- and long-term goals (e.g., "I want to win the race this week as an important step toward my long-term goal of being an Olympic champion."). However, because of their concern with demonstrating high ability to others, success-oriented performers should place more emphasis on short-term goals, sometimes retarding long-term skill development because it would cause a temporary dropoff in performance that might hurt social comparison.

Preferred Goal Attributes of Failure-Oriented Athletes

Finally, the CGS model predicts that failure-oriented athletes should dislike competition because of its threat of revealing their low ability, thus prompting them to prefer goals that are general, team-oriented, extremely difficult or moderately easy, long-term, and positively focused (see Table 13.4). General and team-oriented goals make social comparison more difficult, thus lessening its threat. Extremely difficult goals retain a small chance of demonstrating high ability while providing a built-in excuse for failure, whereas moderately easy goals minimize the chances of failure. Long-term goals delay the threatening evaluation process as long as possible. Finally, because failure-oriented athletes have a strong fear of failure, they are also predicted to prefer positively focused goals that lessen concern about revealing low ability.

Mediating Variables

The CGS model predicts that the influence of the three goal-setting styles is mediated by

- situation type,

Table 13.4   Goal Attribute Preference Predictions for Performance-, Success-, and Failure-Oriented Athletes

	Goal-setting style	
Performance	Success	Failure
Self-referenced	Social-comparative	Social-comparative
Specific	Specific	General
Difficult	Moderately difficult	Moderately easy
Positive	Positive & negative	Positive
Individual	Individual	Team
Long-term/short-term	Short-term/long-term	Long-term

- perceived goal commitment, and
- performance feedback.

The next section will outline specific predictions about how these variables moderate the goal–performance relationship for performance-oriented, success-oriented, and failure-oriented performers.

Situation Type

The CGS model recognizes that goals often have different functions in practice and competition. Because practices are designed to enhance learning and promote skill development, evaluation pressure is normally low and the motivational function of goals is therefore more salient, prompting athletes to adopt a performance-oriented style and practice with purpose and intensity. However, because competition is designed to facilitate social comparison and outcome evaluation, evaluation pressure is often high, prompting athletes to adopt success-oriented and failure-oriented goal-setting styles and making the stress management function of goals more important for developing poise, maintaining mental toughness, and performing optimally. The CGS model is consistent with recent empirical research (e.g., Elliott & Dweck, 1988) suggesting that not only can situational constraints elicit performance-oriented, success-oriented, and failure-oriented goal-setting styles, but goal-setting styles can influence goal responses (e.g., task choice, strategy development, persistence) and motivational consequences (e.g., affect). Thus, the CGS model predicts that practice is more likely to elicit performance-oriented goal-setting styles while competition induces success-oriented and failure-oriented goal-setting styles among competitors. Of course, success-oriented and failure-oriented goal-setting styles may be created in practice if the evaluative or social comparison aspects of the situation are highlighted; and a performance-oriented style can still be elicited in competition but only if athletes focus on salient learning or performance aspects of the situation.

Goal Commitment

The CGS model emphasizes that strong goal commitment is necessary for the goal-setting process to function effectively, but the model makes different goal commitment predictions for each goal-setting style. Specifically, the model suggests that performance-oriented athletes should base their commitment primarily on intrinsic factors, whereas success-oriented and failure-oriented performers should weigh extrinsic factors heavily in determining their level of goal commitment. Thus, performance-oriented competitors are predicted to demonstrate strong commitment to any goal that helps them learn or further develop their skills. Similarly, the commitment of success-oriented competitors is predicted to be high as long as they perceive the opportunity to demonstrate their competence to others through favorable social comparison (i.e., to win consistently) and/or desirable extrinsic rewards are available for winning. Finally, the model predicts that failure-oriented performers will normally have low commitment to any competitive goal because of the threat of publicly revealing low ability. Nevertheless, extrinsic factors (e.g., rewards for winning) may still promote reasonably high goal commitment from failure-oriented performers, even though the threat of negative public evaluation is still salient.

Performance and Outcome Feedback

The CGS model predicts that feedback should facilitate goal setting for performance-oriented and success-oriented athletes but impair goal setting for failure-oriented performers (see columns 6 and 7 of Table 13.1). For performance-oriented athletes, positive feedback should confirm successful learning and performance improvement, whereas negative feedback should signal the need to increase effort and/or try new strategies to ensure future success. Similarly, the model hypothesizes that success-oriented athletes utilize positive feedback to confirm successful social comparison and negative feedback as a signal that future success requires increased effort or the employment of new strategies. Finally, the model predicts that feedback will further impair the performance of failure-oriented athletes because it makes negative social comparison more explicit. Failure-oriented athletes are predicted to discount positive feedback because success is attributed to external and uncontrollable factors, and readily internalize negative feedback about unsuccessful social comparison as indicative of low ability.

Research Testing the Competitive Goal-Setting Model

The previous section outlined a competitive goal-setting model that integrated several different conceptions of goals into a comprehensive conceptual framework. Although the overall CGS model has not been specifically tested in the sport domain, research has been conducted testing selected components of the model, some in sport and some in other achievement domains. In this section, research testing specific components of the CGS model will be reviewed. The first part of this section will summarize research that has been conducted to examine the characteristics associated with the three major goal-setting styles. These characteristics (outlined in Table 13.1) include level of perceived ability, success/failure attributions, and role of feedback. The second part of this section will summarize the research that focuses on the predictions for the four major categories of goal responses (outlined in Table 13.2), including task choice, effort/intensity, strategy development, and persistence/continuing motivation, as well as performance. Next, research will be examined that tests the three major categories of motivation consequent predictions (Table 13.3) for future expectancies, affect, and activity importance. Finally, in the last part of this section research that tests specific goal attribute preferences of the three goal-setting styles will be outlined (Table 13.4), including goal precision, goal difficulty, goal proximity, goal collectivity, and goal valence.

Empirical Support for Performance-, Success-, and Failure-Oriented Goal-Setting Styles

The CGS model hypothesizes that athletes adopt different goal-setting styles that subsequently influence how they perform in sport. In testing the model predictions for the characteristics of each goal-setting style outlined in Table 13.1, it should be noted that the majority of the available support comes from nonsport achievement domains. Nicholls (1984a, 1984b) has marshaled considerable evidence to support the existence of (a) both performance and outcome goal orientations and (b) both success-oriented and failure-oriented goal-setting styles among the outcome-oriented competitors, reflecting their differential levels of perceived ability. Nicholls's review of research on risk taking, achievement motivation, attribution theory, and perceived ability presents a strong case for the prediction that the goals of performance-, success-, and failure-oriented athletes are not only each unique in general focus but also prompt differential definitions of success and failure and characteristic attributional patterns.

Interestingly, empirical evidence documenting different goal-setting styles among 4-, 5-, and 6-grade children who were performing reading and arithmetic tasks has been found dating back more than 50 years (Sears, 1940). Although she didn't find a performance-oriented style, Sears's three goal-setting styles did correspond almost exactly to Nicholls's (1984a) predictions for the task choice preferences of success-oriented and failure-oriented individuals. Group 1 was similar to the success-oriented goal-setting style, whereas Groups 2 and 3 seemed to represent two different types of failure-oriented goal-setting styles, one setting very hard goals and the other very easy ones. Consistent with these findings, Nicholls (1984a) has postulated that failure-oriented performers who have not given up trying to demonstrate high ability normally set very difficult goals that are virtually impossible to achieve. Such goals present little risk to failure-oriented performers' perceived ability because no one expects them to succeed, though they maintain a small chance of achieving success that would allow them to demonstrate high ability. Similarly, Nicholls (1984a) also hypothesized that once failure-oriented competitors have given up trying to demonstrate high ability, they should set very easy goals that virtually assure their success, thereby avoiding demonstrating low ability. Although Sears's (1940) findings demonstrate the existence of multiple goal setting styles, she was unable to demonstrate a causal link between goal-setting styles and academic achievement.

Consistent with the goal-setting style predictions of the CGS model, Locke and his colleagues (1981) have argued that the impact of goals on performance may be moderated by personality variables such as self-esteem, self-efficacy, or self-assurance. For example, Yukl and Latham (1978) found that high-self-esteem subjects worked hard without rewards, whereas low-self-esteem subjects did not. Similarly, Carroll and Tosi (1970) found that subjects high in self-assurance increased their effort congruently with increases in goal difficulty, whereas low-self-assurance subjects decreased their effort as goals became harder. Dossett, Latham, and Mitchell (1979) demonstrated that high-self-esteem word-processing operators who were provided with performance feedback attained their goals significantly more often than did their low-self-esteem counterparts. Finally, Schrauger and Rosenberg (1970) revealed that high-self-esteem subjects improved their performance more than did low-self-esteem performers following positive feedback; whereas following negative feedback, the performance of low-self-esteem subjects decreased more than did that of their high-self-esteem counterparts. The consensus of this research supports goal-setting style predictions of the CGS model by suggesting that differences in goal-setting patterns are related to differential levels of self-esteem.

Frederick, Lee, and Bobko (1984) have recently provided stronger support for CGS model predictions that self-efficacy moderates the goal–performance relationship. Their results confirmed that self-efficacy along with ability and past performance were major predictors of goal choice. Self-efficacy ratings also exhibited a stronger relationship with past performance than future performance; and self-efficacy ratings of moderate to difficult levels of performance were the best predictors of future performance. In summary, these five industrial and organizational psychology studies provide support for the mediating role that competency constructs such as self-esteem or self-efficacy play in determining specific goal-setting style preferences.

Perceptions of Success and Failure

Empirical support is also available to support the CGS model prediction that performance-oriented competitors base their perceptions of success and failure on self-referent standards including learning and performance improvement, whereas success-oriented and failure-oriented performers evaluate success and failure based on social comparison standards such as winning and losing. Nicholls (1984a) has marshaled support for this prediction from several different lines of motivational research including investigations on risk taking, achievement motivation, attribution theory, and perceived ability. Moreover, Elliott and Dweck's (1988) research on learned helplessness demonstrates that experimental manipulations of goal orientation altered perceptions of success and failure that were consistent with performance and outcome orientations. Furthermore, when perceived ability was also manipulated, subjects responded with mastery and helpless responses consistent with model predictions. Duda (1986a, 1986b, 1987) has also confirmed that athletes base success and failure on both performance and outcome standards, although her research did not look at differences in outcome orientation due to differential levels of perceived ability (i.e., success-oriented and failure-oriented goal-setting styles).

Success/Failure Attributions

Consistent with the predictions of the CGS model, Nicholls (1984a, 1984b) demonstrated that goal-setting style influences the attributional patterns that individuals employ to explain success and failure. Similarly, Diener and Dweck (1978) found that to performance-oriented individuals effort is the most critical attribution because they assume that they have the ability to learn and improve. Thus, to them, more effort implies more learning, which, in turn, indicates higher ability. Conversely, because performance-oriented athletes are interested in increasing ability and improving performance, feedback indicating lack of success isn't perceived as failure. Rather, it is viewed as a signal for the need to exert more effort and/or try a different strategy to achieve success (e.g., Diener & Dweck, 1978; Nicholls, 1984a, 1984b). Indeed, Ames and her colleagues (Ames & Ames, 1981; Ames, Ames & Felker, 1977; Ames & McKelvie, 1983) have demonstrated that under noncompetitive conditions likely to elicit a performance-oriented goal-setting style individuals give more effort attributions and use more self-instructional strategies for task completion than they do under competitive conditions.

Similarly, contemporary motivation theory research (e.g., Diener & Dweck, 1978; Dweck, 1975; Elliott & Dweck, 1988; Nicholls, 1984a, 1984b) confirmed CGS model predictions that perceived ability is the primary factor differentiating between success-oriented and failure-oriented goal-setting styles. Conceptual and empirical research on perceived ability (Nicholls, 1984a, 1984b) and learned helplessness (e.g., Diener & Dweck, 1978; Dweck, 1975; Elliott & Dweck, 1988) has demonstrated that success-oriented individuals attribute success to high ability and failure to internal–unstable–controllable factors such as low effort or need for better physical and mental preparation, an optimistic attributional pattern that helps maintain high perceptions of ability and positive future expectancies. On the other hand, this research supported model predictions that failure-oriented performers employ pessimistic attribution patterns, taking little credit for success, which they attribute to external or uncontrollable factors such as luck or an easy opponent, yet accepting the blame for failure, which they attribute to low ability.

In related research, Ames and her colleagues support CGS model predictions by demonstrating a similar link between ability attributions and success-oriented and failure-oriented goal-setting styles. C. and R. Ames and Felker (1977) demonstrate that in competitive situations designed to elicit success-oriented and failure-oriented goal-setting styles performance satisfaction was greatest when attributed to high ability, whereas Ames and McKelvie (1983) found that competition produced primarily ability and task difficulty attributions. Moreover, my reanalysis of data from a study to assess the impact of setting performance versus outcome goals on collegiate swimmers' cognitions and performance (Burton, 1989b) revealed that swimmers who went through a comprehensive goal-setting training program, designed to teach them to emphasize setting performance goals, rated effort attributions higher and ability attributions lower in explaining both success and failure than did non-trained swimmers. Therefore, empirical research in the educational and sport domains provides preliminary support for the existence of three distinct goal-setting styles distinguishable by a combination of goal focus, perceived ability, and attributional patterns.

Role of Feedback

The CGS model hypothesizes that feedback is a critical component in the goal-setting process. Although feedback is implied, it is not explicitly discussed in Nicholls's (1984a, 1984b) motivation theory. Implicitly, goals become the evaluation standards against which athletes adopting performance-oriented, success-oriented, and failure-oriented goal-setting styles assess perceived success or failure. Without intrinsic and extrinsic feedback, evaluation would be virtually impossible. Nicholls (1984a, 1984b) predicts that the motivational benefits of goals are achieved through the cyclical process of developing or demonstrating competence, and feedback is inferred as an essential component of this evaluation process.

Nevertheless, the influence of feedback on goals has been extensively researched in industrial and organizational psychology; and consistent with CGS model predictions, this research suggests that feedback is a necessary condition to ensure goal-setting success. Locke and his colleagues (1981) conclude that goals only enhance performance if they are accompanied by frequent and precise feedback or knowledge of results. Interestingly, the goal-setting literature demonstrates that neither setting goals without providing feedback (e.g., Becker, 1978; Komaki, Barwick, & Scott, 1978; Strang, Lawrence & Fowler, 1978) nor providing feedback without setting goals (e.g., Bandura & Simon, 1977; Latham, Mitchell & Dossett, 1978; Nemeroff & Cosentino, 1979) normally leads to performance improvement. In Locke's (1968) goal-setting model, the role of feedback in the goal-setting process is to provide information that either enhances self-efficacy or perceived ability (e.g., Bandura & Cervone, 1983; Locke et al., 1984) or allows adjustment or improvement of performance strategies (Latham & Baldes, 1975).

Moreover, Mento, Steel, and Karren (1987) have demonstrated through meta-analysis that feedback raised productivity 17% beyond the level of setting goals alone. Overall, this research supports the critical role feedback plays in the goal-setting process and generally supports the predictions of the CGS model.

Empirical Support for Goal Response Predictions

The CGS model predicts that performance-oriented, success-oriented, and failure-oriented athletes will demonstrate differential goal responses. This section will review research that tests the goal response predictions outlined in Table 13.2 for task choice, effort/intensity, strategy development, and persistence/continuing motivation.

Task Choice

Elliott and Dweck (1988) confirmed the CGS model's general task choice predictions directly in an educational setting by experimentally manipulating level of perceived ability and goal orientation. Their results revealed that when the value of outcome goals was highlighted and low ability was perceived (i.e., failure-oriented style), children sacrificed attempts to learn and instead selected moderately easy tasks in order to avoid displaying low ability even though they believed they had the "ability to learn." When outcome goals and high ability were made salient (i.e., success-oriented style), children did not select challenging tasks that provided the opportunity to increase their skills if they entailed enduring public mistakes. Finally, when children were placed in a situation that made performance more salient than outcome regardless of whether they perceived their ability to be high or low (i.e., performance-oriented style), they opted for challenging tasks and did not pass up opportunities to learn new skills, even when errors were made public. This research, then, provides support for the hypothesis that athletes adopting performance-oriented, success-oriented, and failure-oriented goal-setting styles will demonstrate differential task choice preferences. Unfortunately, these predictions have, as yet, not been tested in sport.

Effort/Intensity

Locke and Bryan (1966) confirmed in an early study that goals enhance performance by stimulating greater levels of effort. Consequently, effort was built into Locke's (1968) goal-setting

Success-Oriented Athletes Give Only Enough Effort to Win

The support for the model prediction that success-oriented athletes will give only as much effort as necessary in order to win is more conceptual than empirical. Nicholls (1984a, 1984b) hypothesizes that because social comparison depends on a combination of three factors, performance, task difficulty, and effort expenditure, high effort can imply lower ability or capacity if others require less effort to accomplish the same level of performance or perform better with the same amount of effort. Thus, success-oriented competitors can maximize perceived ability by putting forth as little effort as necessary to win. Empirical support from both sport and nonsport domains is sketchy on this prediction, although anecdotal evidence in the popular sport literature tends to support its validity (Russell & Branch, 1979).

Failure-Oriented Athletes Give Low Effort

Finally, both conceptual and empirical evidence supports the CGS model predictions about the effort expenditure patterns of failure-oriented athletes. Nicholls (1984a, 1984b) emphasized that high effort can imply lower ability if others require less effort to attain the same performance level. Thus, on normatively difficult tasks, if athletes try hard and fail, low ability will be evident. Not surprisingly, failure-oriented competitors often exert only minimal effort on difficult tasks as an ego-protective mechanism to prevent others from finding out they have low ability. Moreover, research has confirmed that failure-oriented individuals eventually develop the belief that increased effort will not be beneficial in attaining success (e.g., Ames, 1984; Diener & Dweck, 1978; Dweck, 1975), which often prompts the use of this low-effort strategy as an ego-defense mechanism (e.g., Frankel & Snyder, 1978; Nicholls, 1976).

Although current sport research (Burton, 1989b; Duda, 1988) has documented that performance-oriented athletes exert more effort than outcome oriented athletes, the research designs employed make it impossible to determine whether these effort expenditure differences are due to

- success-oriented competitors' trying to maximize high perceptions of ability by putting forth only as much effort as necessary to attain favorable social comparison,
- failure-oriented performers' adopting low-effort strategies to avoid revealing low ability, or
- both.

model as a major mediating variable. Subsequent research has also confirmed that goals enhance performance, in part, by eliciting higher levels of effort (e.g., Bassett, 1979; Latham & Locke, 1975; Sales, 1970; Terborg, 1976; Terborg & Miller, 1978). The CGS model hypothesizes that the motivational function of goals prompts increased levels of effort and intensity. However, model predictions confirm that performance-oriented, success-oriented, and failure-oriented goal-setting styles should exert differential levels of effort. The following sections will summarize research supporting these effort expenditure predictions, which are outlined in Table 13.2

Performance-Oriented Athletes Give Consistently High Effort

Consistent with CGS model predictions, educational research (e.g., Ames, 1984), particularly with learned helpless children (e.g., Diener & Dweck, 1978; Dweck, 1975; Elliott & Dweck, 1988) confirmed that performance-oriented individuals' learning focus prompts them to exert high effort in order to attain difficult goals. Evidence supporting this prediction in sport is limited to two investigations. Duda (1988) found that performance-oriented intramural athletes practiced their sport more in their spare time than did outcome-oriented competitors. Moreover, my goal-setting-training study (Burton, 1989b) demonstrated that swimmers who were taught to set performance goals reported giving higher effort and using more effort attributions than did non-trained swimmers, who primarily set outcome goals.

Future research is needed to test these important predictions.

Strategy Development

Research testing CGS model predictions supported the important role of goals in stimulating the development of new performance enhancement strategies (Locke et al., 1981). For example, Latham and Baldes (1975) found that truck drivers attempting to achieve specific-difficult goals to load their trucks to their weight limits made minor modifications to their trucks to help them judge weight more accurately. In another study, Terborg (1976) demonstrated that students with learning goals wrote more notes in the margins than did classmates without goals.

The CGS model emphasizes that strategies are a normal outcome of the problem-solving process and tend to reflect both individual differences and situational constraints. Regrettably, strategies sometimes involve a trade-off, promoting quantity at the expense of quality and vice versa. For example, across three experiments focusing on such tasks as brainstorming and math computation, Bavelas and Lee (1978) found subjects would tend to redefine the task in a way that allowed them to use lower-quality solutions. Similarly, Rosswork (1977) found subjects simply wrote shorter sentences to meet their quota for a number of total sentences written, whereas Sales (1970) demonstrated that subjects given a higher work load made more errors than did those with a lower work load. Finally, Christensen-Szalanski (1980) revealed that under a short deadline, subjects used less complex and less adequate strategies than they did when the time limit was longer.

Strategy development seems particularly important on complex tasks such as sport skills. Recently, Wood, Mento, and Locke (1987) demonstrated that task complexity can significantly moderate goal-setting effects. Their meta-analysis confirmed that the attentional, effort, and persistence benefits of goals have a more direct impact on simple tasks, whereas complex tasks require effective strategy development to occur first before the motivational benefits of goals can enhance performance. The CGS model postulates that goals take longer to enhance performance on complex skills because (a) extensive instruction and feedback is required to develop the correct learning strategy in the first place, and (b) this new strategy must then be practiced extensively to automate the new response. My recent basketball study (Burton, 1989a) found a significant interaction between goal specificity and task complexity. In that eight-week study specific,

difficult goals enhanced performance more than do-your-best goals on two simple basketball skills; but no differences were evident between goal-setting groups on five moderate-to-high-complexity skills. These results, however, cannot determine whether students simply needed more time to develop these complex skills or needed to develop more effective strategies in order to improve performance. Nevertheless, for complex skills, strategy development is necessary in order to first develop a way to execute the technique correctly; then the motivational effects of goals can facilitate performance by focusing attention and increasing effort and persistence.

Similarly, Giannini, Weinberg, and Jackson (1988) found that task complexity mediated the impact of performance, outcome, cooperative, and do-your-best goals on basketball shooting and one-on-one performance. Their results demonstrated that the competitive goal group performed better than did the do-your-best group on the one-on-one competition but not on the shooting task. Although the authors argue that one-on-one competition is the more complex task, new and better strategies can probably be developed to improve one-on-one performance more easily than shooting efficiency, so that the shooting task may actually require a more complex learning process. If this argument is valid, these results are congruent with model predictions. In summary, industrial and organizational psychology and sport research both support CGS model predictions for the role of task complexity and subsequent strategy development as important mediators of the goal–performance relationship, even though these data do not test the strategy development hypotheses in Table 13.2 directly.

Research (e.g., Ames, 1984; Diener & Dweck, 1978; Elliott & Dweck, 1988) in education has tested the strategy development predictions of the CGS model directly. Using a think-aloud format, Diener and Dweck (1978) found that the learning strategies used by learned helpless (failure-oriented) subjects deteriorated under failure, whereas mastery-oriented (performance-oriented and success-oriented) students maintained or improved the quality of the learning strategies they employed when confronted with failure. Subsequently, Ames (1984) demonstrated that competitive situations tend to accentuate the helpless-type deterioration in the quality of solution strategies under failure, whereas an individualistic learning environment prompted a more mastery-oriented maintenance or improvement in the quality of self-instructions, self-monitoring, and problem-solving strategies employed to overcome failure. Finally, Elliott and Dweck (1988) demonstrated that manipulating both goal orientation and level of perceived ability resulted in self-instructional and strategy development behaviors that were consistent with predictions for performance-oriented, success-oriented, and failure-oriented goal-setting styles outlined in Table 13.2

Persistence/Continuing Motivation

The CGS model hypothesizes that another function of goals is to stimulate greater behavioral persistence. Persistence, however, has not been a frequently used dependent variable in goal-setting studies. In fact, the extensive review conducted by Locke and his colleagues (1981) cited only two studies (LaPorte & Nath, 1976; Rothkopf & Billington, 1979) that found that goals stimulated increased behavioral persistence.

However, learned helplessness research (e.g., Diener & Dweck, 1978; Dweck, 1975; Elliott & Dweck, 1988) has supported the CGS model predictions about persistence outlined in Table 13.2, confirming that performance-oriented and success-oriented individuals demonstrate high persistence despite failure, whereas failure-oriented performers display sharp performance deterioration when confronted with failure. Most importantly, Elliott and Dweck (1988) have linked such nonpersistent behaviors to situational factors that stimulate performance-oriented, success-oriented, and failure-oriented goal-setting styles.

Although persistence and its more long-term counterpart, continuing motivation (Maehr, 1984), have been studied extensively in sport, none of these studies tested the persistence predictions of the CGS model specified in Table 13.2 directly. However, numerous empirical studies (e.g., Burton & Martens, 1986; Duda, 1985b, 1988; Ewing, 1981; Feltz & Petlichkoff, 1983; Gould, Feltz, Horn & Weiss, 1982; Roberts, Kleiber & Duda, 1981) have linked perceived ability with the decision to continue participation or to drop out of sport.

Additionally, several sport investigations have tested the influence of goal orientations on persistence and continuing motivation, although they did not directly test CGS model predictions. Ewing (1981) found that sport dropouts tended to be ability-oriented (i.e., failure-oriented), whereas continuing sport participants were more social-approval-oriented. Although these results were a bit surprising, she suggested that among adolescents, peer, coach, and parental approval and status are highly prized goals that are relatively easily attained, thereby promoting continuing motivation. More recently, Duda (1988) confirmed that sport persistence among intramural

athletes was more strongly related to performance orientations than to outcome orientations.

Finally, in a study of over 700 high school students, Duda (1985) assessed the goal orientations of students who were

- involved in both organized and recreational sports,
- involved in organized sports only,
- involved in recreational sports only,
- never regularly involved in sport, and
- sport dropouts.

Her results indicated that sport participants, especially recreational sport performers, were more performance-oriented than were dropouts or students who had never participated in sport. As predicted, dropouts had the least preference for personal, outcome-oriented failure and had a stronger outcome orientation than performance orientation. Overall, although empirical research in sport has not tested all the persistence/continuing motivation predictions of the CGS model directly, available results are generally consistent with model predictions.

Performance

As shown in Table 13.2, the CGS model predicts that goal-setting styles mediate the performance enhancement effects of goals. Industrial and organizational psychology research confirming the performance enhancement benefits of goal setting represents one of the most positive, consistent, and robust empirical literatures in the behavioral sciences (e.g., Locke et al., 1981; Mento et al., 1987). For example, Locke and his colleagues (1981) found that 99 out of 110 studies demonstrated that specific, hard goals elicited better performance than moderate, easy, or do-your-best goals or no goals. More recently, a meta-analysis by Mento and his colleagues (1987) involving over 7,000 subjects and 70 experimental and field studies conducted over a nearly 20-year period yielded effect sizes of .58 for goal difficulty and .44 for goal specificity, which correspond to productivity increases of 11.6% and 8.9%, respectively. Moreover, coupling the benefits of specific, difficult goals with feedback has been shown to raise productivity an additional 17.5% (Mento et al., 1987).

Research on peak or "flow" experiences in both sport settings (e.g., Csikszentmihalyi, 1977; Garfield & Bennett, 1984; Loehr, 1984; Mahoney & Avener, 1977; Ravizza, 1977) and nonsport settings (e.g., Csikszentmihalyi, 1977) suggests that a performance orientation facilitates performance, whereas an outcome orientation impairs flow by creating excess analysis and evaluation that diverts attention away from the task. Finally, in an investigation more directly testing CGS model predictions, my goal-setting-training study (Burton, 1989b) revealed that swimmers trained to set performance goals improved their performance significantly more than non-trained swimmers who set primarily outcome goals. Unfortunately, this investigation did not separate outcome orientation into success-oriented and failure-oriented goal-setting styles, thus preventing direct testing of model predictions.

Empirical Support for Motivational Consequent Predictions

The competitive goal-setting model predicts that goal-setting styles impinge differentially on three motivational consequent variables: future expectancies, affect, and activity importance (see Table 13.3). In this section, research will be reviewed that tests these CGS model predictions.

Future Expectancies

The CGS model hypothesizes that different goal-setting styles should exhibit differential future expectancies. Future expectancies have traditionally been linked to the stability of attributions given for success and failure (e.g., Frieze & Weiner, 1971; Weiner, 1972). Thus, success attributed to stable factors is predicted to prompt positive future expectancies, whereas success attributed to unstable causes should elicit more negative future expectancies. Similarly, failure attributed to unstable but internal–uncontrollable factors is predicted to provide optimism for future success, whereas failure attributed to stable factors such as low ability should create a bleak outlook for the future. Expectancy predictions of the CGS model were based primarily on the attribution patterns expected for the different goal-setting styles; and although conceptually these CGS predictions are consistent with attribution research, empirical support for them is minimal.

Affect

Consistent with Nicholls's (1984a, 1984b) motivational theory, the CGS model predicts that performance-oriented and success-oriented performers should have positive affect under conditions of both success and failure. In fact, Diener

and Dweck (1978) suggest that affect may actually become more positive under failure because of these performers' enjoyment of challenge. However, the model predicts that failure-oriented competitors should experience extensive negative affect, particularly anxiety and shame, that can create negative self-rumination and divert attention from the task (e.g., Lewthwaite, 1988; Martens, Burton, Vealey, Bump & Smith, 1990; Morris, Davis & Hutchings, 1981; Wine, 1980) and motivate escape attempts (e.g., Weiner, 1981, 1982). In support of this notion, Lewthwaite (1988) has presented compelling evidence linking cognitive anxiety to the endangerment of important personal goals. More importantly, Elliott and Dweck's (1988) learned helplessness research confirmed these predictions revealing that performance-oriented and success-oriented subjects reported negative affect in less than 4% of their verbalizations, whereas over 30% of the verbalizations of failure-oriented subjects focused on negative affect.

Empirical support in sport for the CGS model's affective predictions is limited (e.g., Burton, 1989b). In one of the few studies to assess the link between goal orientations and affect, I found that goal-setting-training swimmers trained to adopt a performance-oriented goal-setting style reported significantly lower cognitive anxiety and higher self-confidence prior to an important competition than did non-trained swimmers who adopt traditional outcome goals (Burton, 1989b). Thus, my findings suggest that goals can be set too high for some performers, thereby eliciting negative affective responses such as anxiety. Building on this notion that unrealistic goals can be stress-inducing, Elliott and Dweck's (1988) research has several alarming implications for sport. First, their results demonstrated that individuals' perceived ability on a particular task can be altered drastically in a particular situation, even though high overall perceived ability was maintained. Thus, these findings suggest that a competitor may feel like a failure-oriented performer for a particular race or competition without diminishing his or her overall feelings of competence. Second, if a failure-oriented goal-setting style is elicited for a particular competition, even highly skilled performers may experience significant negative affect (i.e., anxiety) about achieving their goals, which may impair their performance.

Activity Importance

Consistent with Nicholls's (1984a, 1984b) motivation theory, the CGS model hypothesizes that failure-oriented competitors who characteristically lose often, attribute their failure to low ability, and feel anxious and dissatisfied will eventually devalue participation in the activity as an ego-defense mechanism. Although this particular prediction has not received much attention among researchers, Burton and Martens's (1986) sport dropout research supported this contention. Their results demonstrated that although wrestling participants and dropouts did not differ significantly on the overall degree of importance they placed on success in sport and nonsport activities, they did differ on the amount of importance they placed on wrestling. Not only did participants place more importance on wrestling than dropouts did, but trends suggested that dropouts valued success in team sports more than participants did. These findings indicate that dropouts may have rechanneled their achievement energies into activities where the evaluation potential was reduced because responsibility for failure could be distributed among teammates and they would not have to take all the blame for failure themselves, as they would in wrestling.

Empirical Support for Goal Attribute Predictions

According to the CGS model, goal-setting styles are predicted to differentially influence the type of goal attributes that individuals prefer. In particular, performance-oriented, success-oriented, and failure-oriented athletes should demonstrate different goal specificity, goal difficulty, goal proximity, goal valence, and goal collectivity preferences. This section summarizes the extensive goal-setting literature in industrial and organizational, clinical, educational, and sport psychology on goal attribute preference and then reviews support for the CGS model's goal attribute predictions for performance-oriented, success-oriented, and failure-oriented athletes.

Goal Specificity

Several recent reviews of the industrial and organizational psychology goal specificity literature (Chidester & Grigsby, 1984; Latham & Lee, 1986; Locke et al., 1981; Mento et al., 1987; Tubbs, 1986) have confirmed that goal specificity, or precision, enhances performance. Locke and his colleagues (1981) found that 51 of 53 goal specificity studies partially or completely supported the premise that specific goals promote better performance than general or do-your-best goals or no goals. Moreover, Chidester and Grigsby's (1984)

meta-analytic review of 22 studies confirmed that goal specificity consistently improved performance; Latham and Lee (1986) subsequently reviewed 64 studies with almost identical findings. Finally, in a broader-based meta-analysis, Mento and his colleagues (1987) revealed an effect size of .44 for goal specificity across 49 studies and over 5,800 subjects, which translates into a nearly 9% increase in productivity.

Interestingly, goal specificity research in sport has not been quite so consistent. Perhaps because of smaller sample sizes that make significance harder to attain, only two-thirds of the 13 studies in sport have documented that athletes setting specific goals performed significantly better than performers setting general or do-your-best goals or no goals (Anderson, Crowell, Doman & Howard, 1988; Barnett & Stanicek, 1979; Burton, 1989a, 1989b; Giannini, Weinberg & Jackson, 1988; Hall & Byrne, 1988; Hall, Weinberg & Jackson, 1987; Weinberg, Bruya, Longino & Jackson, 1988; Yin, Simons & Callaghan, 1989), whereas the remaining four studies failed to document significant goal-setting effects (Hollingsworth, 1975; Miller & McAuley, 1987; Weinberg, Bruya & Jackson, 1985; Weinberg, Bruya, Jackson & Garland, 1986).

Goal Difficulty

Several recent reviews of the industrial and organizational psychology goal difficulty literature (Chidester & Grigsby, 1984; Latham & Lee, 1986; Locke et al., 1981; Mento et al., 1987; Tubbs, 1986) indicated that difficult but realistic goals enhance performance more than do easy goals. Locke and his colleagues (1981) found that 48 of 57 (i.e., 84%) studies partially or completely supported goal difficulty predictions. More recently, Mento and his colleagues' (1987) meta-analysis of the goal difficulty literature revealed that for quality and quantity of performance in both laboratory and field settings goal difficulty demonstrated an effect size of .58 across 70 studies and over 7,000 subjects, which is comparable to a productivity increase of 11.6%.

Interestingly, sport research (Burton, Williams-Rice, Phillips & Daw, 1989; Hall et al., 1987; Weinberg et al., 1986) has failed to support the CGS model's goal difficulty predictions. Although Weinberg and his colleagues' (1986) first experiment contrasted easy, moderate, and difficult goals, their second experiment as well as the other two difficulty studies (Burton, Williams-Rice, Phillips and Daw, 1989; Hall et al., 1987) compared moderately difficult goals (i.e., 5–15% improvement over initial or previous performance) with unrealistically hard goals (i.e.,

25–30% improvement). Despite the somewhat harder goals used in these sport studies compared to previous industrial and organizational psychology investigations, the reason for these nonsignificant findings was not readily apparent from existing goal-setting theories. However, the CGS model suggests that very difficult goals should not impair the performance of performance-oriented athletes and may actually lead to better long-term performance than more moderately difficult goals. Thus, one explanation for these results is that learning was emphasized in these investigations, prompting athletes to adopt a predominantly performance-oriented goal-setting style.

Goal Valence

Sport practitioners often encourage athletes to set goals in positive terms, focusing on what they want to accomplish (e.g., two hits in four at-bats) rather than what they hope to avoid (e.g., striking out, Gould, 1985). Recently, Kirschenbaum (1984) has suggested that the conventional wisdom of this goal-setting strategy may only be true in certain situations. Kirschenbaum (1984) concluded from extensive self-regulation research that positively focused goals are most effective for new or difficult skills (e.g., Johnston-O'Connor & Kirschenbaum, 1984; Kirschenbaum, Ordman, Tomarken & Holtzbauer, 1982), whereas negatively focused goals that emphasize minimizing mistakes are more effective for well-learned skills (e.g., Kirschenbaum, Wittrock, Smith & Monson, 1984).

Goal Proximity

Research from clinical psychology has demonstrated equivocal results from the goal proximity predictions of the CGS model. Several studies (e.g., Bandura & Schunk, 1981; Bandura & Simon, 1977; Manderlink & Harackiewicz, 1984) suggest that short-term goals will lead to better performance than long-term goals, primarily because they offer the performer more opportunities to assess success and correct effort levels or modify strategies, thereby enhancing self-efficacy and intrinsic motivation. However, self-regulation findings have revealed that moderately specific planning and longer-term goals seem to facilitate behavioral change (Kirschenbaum, Tomarken & Ordman, 1982). Although research conducted in both sport and nonsport settings suggests that long-term goals are important to provide individuals with direction for their achievement strivings, these findings also confirmed that the motivational impact of long-term

goals depends on establishing short-term goals to serve as intermediate steps in the achievement process (Bandura & Simon, 1977; Hall & Byrne, 1988; Locke, Cartledge & Knerr, 1970).

In sport, goal proximity findings are equivocal. Weinberg and his colleagues (Weinberg et al., 1985; Weinberg et al., 1988) failed to find any goal proximity effects on endurance performance. Subjects who set short-term goals only, long-term goals only, or a combination of long-term and short-term goals did not demonstrate significant differences in performance on a 3-minute sit-up task. However, Hall and Byrne (1988) have recently shown that subgoals play an important role in enhancing the effectiveness of long-term goals. Weight-training subjects were assigned to one of four experimental treatments:

- Long-term goals
- Long-term plus intermediate goals set by the experimenter
- Long-term plus intermediate goals set by the subject
- Do-your-best goals

Results revealed that long-term-with-subgoal groups performed significantly better than do-your-best subjects but that the performance of the long-term-goal group only approached significance. These findings suggest that long-term goals can facilitate performance most effectively when subgoals are used to mark progress.

Goal Collectivity

To date, goal-setting research has failed to test CGS model predictions empirically for the impact of team versus individual goals on performance, although Locke & Latham (1985) indicated that they have preliminary data suggesting that both can be effective. However, based on Nicholls's (1984a, 1984b) motivation theory, I have argued that team goals are neither personally flexible nor controllable, thus offering fewer motivational benefits while ensuring more anxiety and diffidence "side effects" compared to individual goals (Burton, 1982). The issue of goal collectivity, just like that of goal proximity, is probably not an either/or propostion. Team goals seemingly offer direction for establishing appropriate types and levels of individual goals, which then are responsible for the specific motivational benefits to individual athletes. I also cautioned that for team or individual goals to be effective, team goals must be broken down into individual goals representing the "roles" that athletes must play in order to maximize overall team effectiveness (Burton, 1982).

The model's goal collectivity predictions are, however, consistent with social loafing research (e.g., Hardy & Latane, 1988; Jackson & Williams, 1985; Latane, 1986; Latane, Williams & Harkins, 1979). Social loafing is a group performance phenomena in which individuals working together on a task tend to exert less individual effort than when they perform the same task individually (Jackson & Williams, 1985). Although not extensively studied in sport settings, social loafing has been shown to occur for a variety of physically effortful tasks such as rope pulling (Ingham, Levinger, Graves & Peckham, 1974), noise production (Latane et al., 1979), and force production (Kerr & Brunn, 1981) for both males and females of all ages (Harkins, Latane & Williams, 1980; Latane, 1986). Interestingly, research has confirmed that social loafing is reduced or eliminated under several conditions:

- When individual efforts are identifiable (Williams, Harkins & Latane, 1981)
- When individuals perceive that they have made a unique contribution to group effort or performed difficult tasks (Harkins & Petty, 1982)
- When individuals performed with friends rather than strangers (Williams, 1981)
- When the task was personally involving (Brickner, Harkins & Ostrom, 1986)

Recently, Hardy and Latane (1988) demonstrated that social loafing effects extended to established cheerleading teams performing an intrinsically motivating competitive noise production task. Although these results confirmed that performing with friends on personally involving tasks did not necessarily reduce loafing, the consensus of previous research seems to support the conclusion that loafing can best be reduced or eliminated by making individual efforts identifiable and convincing individuals that their efforts are indispensible to group success.

The results of social loafing research suggest that athletes setting team goals should be prone to loaf unless (a) they also set individual goals that hold each team member responsible for a specific level of performance and (b) these individual goals are perceived indispensible for team success. Regrettably, research testing the goal collectivity prediction that a combination of team and individual goals should reduce social loafing has not been conducted to date.

Goal Attribute Preferences of Each Goal-Setting Style

The CGS model hypothesizes that athletes with performance-oriented, success-oriented, and failure-oriented goal-setting styles will differ in their goal attribute preferences. Research testing the specific goal attribute preferences of each goal setting style is summarized in the next section.

Performance-Oriented Athletes' Goal Attribute Preferences

According to the CGS model, the learning focus of performance-oriented athletes suggests that they would prefer the higher informational content of specific, difficult, positive, and individual goals that promote the development of new strategies necessary to increase learning. The model predicts that performance-oriented performers should set both short- and long-term goals. However, because performance-oriented athletes' primary concern is learning and improvement,

Elliott and Dweck (1988) emphasize that they should prefer more long-term goals that will allow them to make choices that foster learning such as developing prerequisite skills, modifying strategies, and enduring slumps and plateaus while still maintaining feelings of competence and remaining motivated to improve.

At least two goal-setting studies in sport (Burton, 1989a; Burton, Williams-Rice, Phillips & Daw, 1989) have been conducted under conditions that minimized evaluation, thus making a performance goal-setting style likely. In the first study, college students in a physical education major's basketball class with specific, assigned goals performed better than students with do-your-best goals on two simple basketball tasks in which effort should seemingly have led directly to performance improvement (Burton, 1989a). However, I did not find group differences on five moderate-to-complex tasks predicted to require strategy development before the motivational effects of goals could enhance performance improvement.

Consistent with model predictions, recent research (Burton, Williams-Rice, Phillips & Daw, 1989) demonstrated that under practice-like conditions, players setting unrealistically difficult goals outperformed classmates setting realistic goals, although these differences did not reach statistical significance. Unfortunately, CGS model predictions for goal proximity, goal valence, or goal collectivity of performance-oriented athletes have not yet been tested.

Success-Oriented Athletes' Goal Attribute Preferences

According to the CGS model, success-oriented athletes strive to demonstrate high ability; and the higher informational content of specific, individual, and short-term-long-term goals should make ability evaluations easier (e.g., Elliott & Dweck, 1988; Nicholls, 1984a). As I suggested (Burton, 1989b), specific, individual and short-term goals are all more flexible and controllable, so they should not only allow athletes to achieve more consistent success, but they should more readily internalize credit for that success as indicative of high ability.

Of the 12 goal specificity studies in sport conducted in an evaluative setting conducive to eliciting success-oriented goal-setting styles, 8 demonstrated positive goal-setting effects. However, because perceived ability was not assessed, these studies cannot test model predictions directly. Similarly, the three goal proximity studies in sport failed to assess perceived ability, thus negating the possibility of testing model predictions for success-oriented performers.

The CGS model hypothesizes that success-oriented athletes set moderately difficult goals because they want to demonstrate high ability. Thus, success-oriented performers are predicted to sacrifice learning opportunities that risk public failure. Based on Kirschenbaum's (1984) self-regulation research, success-oriented athletes should also prefer positively focused goals on new or difficult skills, and negatively focused goals that emphasize minimizing mistakes on well-learned tasks. Neither of these model predictions has been tested directly in sport.

Failure-Oriented Athletes' Goal Attribute Preferences

The CGS model predicts that failure-oriented athletes are interested in avoiding the revelation of low ability and therefore goals that prevent evaluation or make evaluation difficult should be prized (e.g., Elliott & Dweck, 1988; Nicholls, 1984a). The lower informational content of general, team, and long-term goals should make such ability evaluations more difficult, thus lessening the possibility of revealing low ability to others. Failure-oriented athletes are also predicted to prefer moderately easy, positively focused goals because they minimize the risk of revealing low ability. Unfortunately, none of these model predictions has yet been tested in sport.

In summary, empirical research from industrial and organizational, clinical, educational, and sport psychology literatures is generally supportive of the overall predictions of the CGS model. However, many predictions have not been tested directly, particularly not in sport settings. Nevertheless, regardless of its ultimate validity, the CGS model has been proposed to provide a number of testable predictions that will, hopefully, prompt increased goal-setting research in sport.

Measurement of Goal-Setting Styles

Just as with most new psychological constructs, the ultimate utility of goal-setting styles will hinge, in part, on researchers' ability to develop effective instruments to measure them. The limited previous research directly testing goal-setting styles was conducted in a lab setting using an academic learned helplessness paradigm (Elliott & Dweck, 1988). In that study, goal orientation and perceived ability were experimentally manipulated to investigate their impact on motivation and performance variables. Although similar lab investigations could be conducted using simulated sport tasks, it also seems desirable to develop instruments that can measure existing goal-setting styles in real sport situations. On the surface, the task of developing reliable and valid instruments to measure performance-, success-, and failure-oriented goal-setting styles seems challenging for three reasons:

- Reliable and valid instruments must be identified or developed to measure both goal orientation and perceived ability.
- Joint scores for goal orientation and perceived ability must be identified that accurately bound each goal-setting style.
- Because goal-setting styles seem to be influenced by powerful situational factors, both state and trait versions of goal-setting style instrumentation must be developed.

In the following sections, existing instruments for measuring goal orientation and perceived ability will be described, and other important measurement issues in assessing goal-setting styles will be addressed.

Measuring Goal Orientation

Several reliable and valid instruments have been developed to measure goal orientation in sport (Gill & Deeter, 1988; Vealey, 1986). Gill and Deeter's Sport Orientation Questionnaire (SOQ) is a 25-item self-report instrument that is comprised of three subscales measuring competitiveness, win orientation, and goal orientation. The 13-item competitiveness subscale represents a basic sport-specific achievement orientation to seek out and strive for excellence in competitive situations. However, the other two 6-item subscales reflect performance and outcome competitive goal orientations, with the win subscale assessing the desire for positive social comparison (i.e., outcome orientation) and the goal subscale measuring the tendency to evaluate competitive success based on the attainment of personal goals (i.e., performance orientation). All SOQ items are rated on a 5-point Likert format from 1 (*strongly disagree*) to 5 (*strongly agree*), yielding win and goal subscale totals ranging from 6 to 30. Gill and her colleagues (Gill, 1986; Gill & Deeter, 1988; Gill, Dzewaltowski, & Deeter, 1988) have marshaled extensive reliability and validity evidence for the SOQ, documenting its appropriateness for measuring competitive goal orientation.

Vealey's (1986) Competitive Orientation Inventory (COI) simultaneously evaluates the relative importance of playing well and winning. Using a unique format, the COI consists of a 16-cell matrix, with each cell representing a situation that is a unique combination of performance quality and type of competitive outcome. Athletes rate their level of satisfaction on a 0-10 scale for 16 different situations that systematically vary four categories of performance (i.e., *very good, above average, below average,* and *very poor*) with four types of game outcomes (i.e., *easy win, close win, close loss,* and *big loss*). Overall scores for both performance and outcome are calculated by computing the sum of the squares for both columns (i.e., performance) and rows (i.e., outcome) and dividing each by the total sum of squares, thus yielding performance and outcome scores betwen 0.00 and 1.00. Although the COI is relatively new, Vealey has shown it to be a reliable and valid measure of competitive goal orientation.

Measuring Perceived Ability in Sport

Several reliable and valid instruments have also been developed to measure perceived ability-related constructs in sport (Fox & Corbin, 1989; Vealey, 1986). Fox and Corbin (1989) have developed the Physical Self-Perception Profile (PSPP) to measure multidimensional self-esteem in the physical domain using methodology borrowed from Harter (1985). Based on Shavelson, Hubner, and Stanton's (1976) hierarchical self-esteem model, the PSPP measures three levels of self-esteem:

- Global self-esteem
- Physical self-worth
- Four physical self-esteem subdomains (sport competence, attractive body, physical strength, and physical condition)

Global self-esteem is measured by the 10-item Rosenberg (1965) Global Self-Esteem Scale, whereas the 30-item PSPP consists of a 6-item Physical Self-Worth Scale and four 6-item subscales measuring sport competence, attractive body, physical strength, and physical condition. A 4-choice alternative format (Harter, 1985) is used to offset social desirability biases, yielding subscale totals ranging from 6 to 24. Initial reliability and validity for the PSPP make it a promising measure of self-esteem in sport.

Vealey (1986) developed the 13-item Trait Sport Confidence Inventory and companion 13-item State Sport Confidence Inventory to measure confidence in sport. Sport confidence is operationalized as "the belief or degree of certainty individuals possess about their ability to be successful in sport," a definition that links this construct closely to perceived ability. Both instruments demonstrate adequate item discrimination, internal consistency, test–retest reliability, content validity, concurrent validity, and construct validity. Items create a frame of reference for respondents by comparing their sport confidence to the "most confident athlete you know." Responses are recorded on a 9-point Likert format resulting in scores from 13 to 177.

Because none of the four instruments described earlier has been used to assess goal-setting styles in sport, the decision on which instruments are most valid must await future research. In the meantime, researchers will have to select instruments to measure goal-setting styles in sport based on theoretical and personal preferences.

Other Measurement Issues in Assessing Goal-Setting Styles

Not only are reliable and valid instruments needed to assess goal orientation and perceived ability in sport, but researchers need to identify the score profile on each instrument that defines each goal-setting style. Moreover, the CGS model views goal-setting styles as both (a) a general predisposition to set certain kinds of goals across most situations (i.e., psychological trait), and (b) momentary goal-setting behavior reflecting the influence of particular situational factors (i.e., psychological states). Thus, an athlete who typically adopts a performance-oriented goal-setting style may be constrained by powerful situational factors to adopt a failure-oriented style in a particularly important competition. In order to assess the influence of goal-setting styles on motivation and performance accurately, researchers need to develop measurement instruments that assess both trait and state goal-setting styles and conduct research to assess the stability of these styles across situations.

Future Directions in Goal-Setting Research in Sport

The CGS model which was proposed in this chapter contains a number of specific predictions for performance-oriented, success-oriented, and failure-oriented goal-setting styles and the goal responses, motivational consequences, and preferred goal attributes of each goal-setting style. However, most of the research that has been cited to support model predictions was conducted in nonsport achievement domains. We need considerably more future research to examine the relevance of the CGS model in sport. In particular, two major questions must be addressed by future researchers:

- Do goal-setting styles exist in sport; and if so, do they impinge on competitive cognitions and performance as predicted by this model?
- How can practitioners create performance-oriented athletes and help them remain focused on performance in practices and games?

These two important questions are discussed in more detail in the following sections.

Goal-Setting Styles and Their Impact on Sport Behavior

Despite its compelling logic, the evidence supporting goal-setting styles in sport and their impact on competitive cognitions and performance must be regarded as promising but preliminary. The empirical data base supporting the efficacy of developing a performance-oriented style is growing both in education (e.g., Ames, 1984; Elliott & Dweck, 1988; Nicholls, 1984a) and sport (e.g., Burton, 1989b). My own experience in conducting the goal-setting-training study with swimmers confirmed theoretical predictions that performance-oriented swimmers would demonstrate lower anxiety, higher self-confidence, and better performance than did non-trained swimmers who typically adopted success-oriented and failure-oriented goal-setting styles. Moreover, the link between the motivation and stress management function of goals and the overall power of goal-setting interventions was evident with both the group and case study data. However, one of the most intriguing questions arising from this study was what factors contributed to the development of a performance-oriented goal-setting style in individual athletes. The goal-setting-training results revealed several interesting differences in commitment to adopting a performance-oriented style, which collectively suggest that a performance-oriented style was easier to adopt in less important competitions, by females, and by less experienced athletes.

The difficulty of maintaining a performance-oriented style as competitive level or importance increases is not surprising. Indeed, Nicholls (1984a) suggests that the likelihood of an outcome orientation being elicited increases if

- the importance of the contest is emphasized or the contest is portrayed as a test of highly valued abilities,

- the competitive or evaluative aspects of a highly ego-involving skill are emphasized, and/or
- evaluation is public and involves audiences, media coverage, and television or video-taping.

Socialization factors are perhaps the best explanation for the unwillingness of males and more experienced athletes to place higher priority on performance than outcome. Although competitive opportunities for women have greatly expanded over the past 15 years, males probably receive earlier and more extensive socialization through parents, coaches, and peers about the importance of sport as an achievement domain. In support of this socialization hypothesis, Chaumeton and Duda (1988) have recently demonstrated that coaches may play an important role in prompting athletes to develop a strong outcome orientation. They observed the positive and negative social reinforcement of elementary, junior high, and high school basketball coaches and classified these coaching behaviors as emphasizing primarily performance or outcome. Their results revealed a strong developmental trend with both players and coaches emphasizing winning more at higher levels of competition. Furthermore, outcome was reinforced more by coaches in games than in practices.

Nevertheless, some coaches, such as former UCLA basketball coach John Wooden, seem to emphasize performance ahead of winning and to utilize feedback primarily to convey instruction and skill correction (Tharp & Gallimore, 1976). Not only did Wooden's coaching approach seem to develop performance-oriented athletes, but his record of 10 national championships in 12 years is nonpareil. The secrets that master coaches such as John Wooden use to develop performance-oriented athletes and keep them performance-oriented in important competitions await empirical elucidation. However, Elliott and Dweck's (1988) research which showed that perceived ability can be manipulated by powerful situational factors, prompting competent performers to adopt failure-oriented goal patterns temporarily, has great significance for sport where athletes may train a dozen or more years for one important competition (e.g., the Olympic Games). If these findings hold in sport, then a great deal of practical goal-setting research is needed to help practitioners discover exactly what goal-setting strategies are going to be most effective in creating performance-oriented athletes and helping them maintain a performance-oriented goal-setting style in important competitions. In the following section, several potential areas of goal-setting implementation research will be suggested that may prove helpful in the development of performance-oriented athletes.

Development and Maintenance of Performance-Oriented Goal-Setting Style in Sport

A paucity of empirical research has focused on implementation issues necessary to maximize the effectiveness of goal-setting programs. A number of recent goal-setting articles (e.g., Botterill, 1978; Burton, 1984; Gould, 1985; Locke & Latham, 1985; Martens, 1987; O'Block & Evans, 1984) have attempted to provide implementation strategies to sport practitioners. These recommendations were based primarily on principles extrapolated from research conducted in industrial and organizational psychology rather than sport. Although this research provides a good starting point, it does not provide conclusive answers to several critical goal-setting implementation issues. The next section will address crucial goal implementation issues such as

- determining optimal goal difficulty,
- developing goal commitment and acceptance,
- assessing the optimal frequency of goal monitoring and evaluation,
- examining the importance of environmental engineering and the development of action plans, and
- investigating factors that influence generalization of goal-setting effects.

Determining Optimal Goal Difficulty

The CGS model predicts that the establishment of goals that are too difficult for success-oriented and failure-oriented athletes can prompt diffidence, anxiety, and attention distraction that impair performance. This prediction suggests that goal-setting styles have an optimal goal difficulty range for best performance. Although several researchers have attempted to provide practitioners with strategies to determine appropriate levels of goal difficulty (e.g., O'Block & Evans, 1984), few goal-setting studies have attempted to operationalize the goal difficulty level that will foster best performance.

Recently, my colleagues and I (Burton, Daw, Williams-Rice & Phillips, 1989) asked students in a physical education major's basketball class to set goals for seven basketball skills twice a week for a semester. Each class period students were given a written record of their previous performance levels on each skill but were free to set goals at whatever difficulty level they preferred. Although performance-, success-, and failure-oriented goal-setting styles were not assessed, results evaluating goal difficulty preferences of high-versus-low-perceived-ability performers revealed that high-perceived-ability performers set more difficult goals across all seven tasks (Ms = 102-111% of previous performance) than did low-perceived-ability classmates (Ms = 94-103% of previous performance). Future research needs to confirm the goal difficulty range that is optimal for each goal-setting style. Additional questions concerning how to optimize goal difficulty need to be addressed:

- How should goal difficulty be adjusted as key situational factors change?
- How does personal goal difficulty influence performance?
- Is the goal difficulty–performance relationship linear or curvilinear?

Goal Commitment/Acceptance

For goals to have motivational value, individuals must have a high degree of commitment to their achievement. Goal commitment is an important component of Locke's (1968) goal-setting model; and he emphasizes that factors such as participation in setting the goal, incentives available for goal achievement, and the level of trust and supportiveness of others in the organization such as coaches, teammates, and parents is important to the development of high commitment. Moreover, Locke and his colleagues (1981) concluded that lack of goal commitment often significantly reduces the effectiveness of goal-setting programs. However, despite the intuitive appeal of goal commitment/acceptance as a moderator of goal-setting effects, research has failed to document this relationship empirically. The CGS model suggests that goal acceptance or commitment should decrease when success-oriented and failure-oriented performers are asked to set goals out of their optimal goal range. Indeed, the results of a recent goal difficulty investigation (Burton, Williams-Rice, Phillips and Daw, 1989) revealed that 80% of the students asked to set unrealistically high goals (i.e., 125-130% of previous performance) reported lowering their goals, suggesting that individuals commonly deal with goal acceptance problems by simply setting different personal goals. Additional goal commitment questions needing further examination include:

- How is commitment related to locus of control?
- How is commitment related to perceived threat?
- How effective is identification as a motivational strategy for enhancing commitment?

Frequency of Goal Monitoring and Evaluation

Kirschenbaum (1984) concluded that self-monitoring and self-evaluation are necessary-but-not-sufficient to maintain effective self-regulation. Based on Carver and Scheier's (1981) self-focused attention model, Kirschenbaum and Tomarken (1982) argued that increasing self-awareness through self-monitoring typically increases attempts to match behavior to goals. However, there seems to be a trade-off inherent in the self-monitoring/evaluation process. If monitoring and evaluation are too infrequent, athletes will have difficulty perceiving improvement in competence, which is necessary to enhance intrinsic motivation (e.g., Deci & Ryan, 1985; Vallerand, Gauvin & Halliwell, 1986). However, if monitoring and evaluation are too frequent, it may be difficult to maintain a performance orientation because extensive evaluation makes outcome concerns more salient (e.g., Nicholls, 1984a) and may prompt individuals to feel like "pawns" because goals are perceived as controlling rather than informational (e.g., deCharms, 1976; Deci & Ryan, 1985; Vallerand et al., 1986). In fact, some self-regulation research (Kirschenbaum, Tomarken & Ordman, 1982) suggests that moderately specific and longer-term plans may facilitate self control to a greater degree than specific, short-term plans because they foster "protracted choice." These results are consistent with the model prediction that too frequent goal evaluation may prompt athletes to become success-oriented or failure-oriented, thus impairing performance. Indeed, anecdotal evidence from a dozen years of practical goal-setting work with athletes confirms that maintaining the same goals for weekly intervals seems to facilitate improvement more than changing goals daily. It is assumed that this technique makes weekly rather than daily evaluation more salient. Additional goal monitoring and evaluation questions needing further research include:

- Does excessive self-evaluation lower perceived ability; and if so, how?
- What is the most effective way to provide feedback to encourage protracted choice?
- Can social support (e.g., the buddy system) be used to facilitate self-monitoring?

Environmental Engineering/ Developing Action Plans

Goal-setting research assessing the moderating effects of task complexity (Mento et al., 1987) suggested that the motivational benefits of goals only work when athletes are practicing skills correctly and have good action plans for long-term skill development (e.g., Hall & Byrne, 1988). Thus, optimal skill development requires first developing a fundamentally sound technique and then practicing that skill until it becomes highly automated. For complex skills, athletes must find competent coaches who can help them develop correct technique. Moreover, coaches must also understand the basic principles of periodization of training so they can develop accurate action plans that help athletes adjust goals appropriately during different portions of the training or skill development cycle (Burton, 1987). Recently, Heckhausen and Strang (1988) demonstrated that performers who were more effective at developing action plans to modify exertion performed better on a simulated basketball task, particularly under stressful conditions, than did less action-oriented performers. One of the most difficult aspects of skill development is understanding when a learning strategy is appropriate and needs only systematic practice to automate skills and when it is limited or ineffectual and a new strategy must be developed in order to reach one's performance potential. Abandoning an effective strategy too soon is undesirable and will only lengthen the time necessary to automate skills. However, practicing an ineffective technique will prevent optimal skill development. Perhaps one of the talents that separates effective from ineffective coaches is the ability to understand the skill development process well enough to know which approach is needed in a particular situation. Future research is needed on a number of environmental engineering/action plan questions:

- Would formal problem-solving training facilitate the development of new strategies necessary to enhance complex skills?
- How does the coach know when to encourage athletes to maintain the same strategy and just practice more diligently?
- How does the coach know when to adopt a new skill development strategy?

Generalization of Goal-Setting Effects

Kirschenbaum (1984) suggests that self-regulatory failure typically occurs because of the inability to generalize relevant behaviors to other settings, times, or conditions. Kirschenbaum (1984) emphasizes that circumventing generalization problems requires an obsessive–compulsive behavior style in which vigilant self-monitoring and self-evaluation lead to appropriate changes in goals or goal levels. Not only do goals need to be set in sport to help athletes develop new skills and strategies, but goals also need to be established that focus on how skills and strategies must be adjusted in different competitions, at different times of the competitive season, and against different opponents. Some goal generalization questions needing further research include:

- What situational cues typically prompt athletes to adopt an outcome-oriented goal-setting style?
- How can athletes be trained to maintain a performance perspective in the face of highly competitive situations?
- How can goal-setting strategies best help failure-oriented athletes become performance-oriented athletes?

Conclusion

This chapter has presented a CGS model as a heuristic tool that integrates the motivational and stress management functions of goals with conceptual goal notions from disciplines such as industrial and organizational, clinical, educational, and sport psychology. The model hypothesizes three distinct goal-setting styles and makes specific predictions for the attributes of each goal-setting style and their impact on goal responses and motivational consequences. Research supporting the CGS model was reviewed, both generally and for each specific prediction, with the consensus of these findings supporting the existence of performance-, success-, and failure-oriented goal-setting styles. These results suggest that goal-setting styles differentially affect goal responses (e.g., task choice, effort/intensity, strategy development, persistence/continuing motivation, and performance), as well as motivational consequences (e.g., future expectancies, affect, and activity importance). Research testing specific goal attribute preferences of performance-, success-, and failure-oriented athletes was also reviewed, although only minimal research has tested these predictions directly. Measurement technology for measuring goal-setting styles was examined, and future measurement needs were identified. Finally, directions for future basic and applied research were highlighted that would expand our knowledge base about implementation strategies to facilitate goal-setting effectiveness.

References

Ames, C. (1984). Achievement attributions and self-instructions under competitive and individualistic goal structures. *Journal of Edcuational Psychology, 78,* 478-487.

Ames, C., & Ames, R. (1981). Competitive versus individualistic goal structures: The salience of past performance information for causal attributions and affect. *Journal of Educational Psychology, 73,* 411-418.

Ames, C., Ames, R., & Felker, D. (1977). Effects of competitive reward structure and valence of outcome on children's achievement attributions. *Journal of Educational Psychology, 69,* 1-8.

Ames, C., & McKelvie, S. (1983, April). *Achievement attributions and self-instructions under competitive and individualistic goal structures.* Paper presented at the meeting of the American Educational Research Association, Montreal.

Anderson, D.C., Crowell, C.R., Doman, M., & Howard, G.S. (1988). Performance posting, goal setting, and activity-contingent praise as applied to a university hockey team. *Journal of Applied Psychology, 73,* 87-95.

Bandura, A., & Cervone, D. (1983). Self-evaluative and self-efficacy mechanisms governing the motivational effects of goal systems. *Journal of Personality and Social Psychology, 45,* 1017-1028.

Bandura, A., & Schunk, D.H. (1981). Cultivating competence, self-efficacy and intrinsic interest through proximal self-motivation. *Journal of Personality and Social Psychology, 41,* 586-598.

Bandura, A., & Simon, K.M. (1977). The role of proximal intentions in self-regulation of refractory behavior. *Cognitive Therapy and Research, 1,* 177-193.

Barnett, M.L., & Stanicek, J.A. (1979). Effects of goal-setting on achievement in archery. *Research Quarterly, 50,* 328-332.

Bassett, G.A. (1979). A study of the effects of task goal and schedule choice on work performance. *Organizational Behavior and Human Performance, 24,* 202-227.

Bavelas, J.B., & Lee, E.S. (1978). Effects of goal level on performance: A trade-off of quantity and quality. *Canadian Journal of Psychology, 32,* 219-240.

Becker, L.J. (1978). Joint effect of feedback and goal setting on performance: A field study of residential energy conservation. *Journal of Applied Psychology, 63,* 428-433.

Botterill, C. (1978). Goal setting with athletes. *Science Periodical on Research and Technology in Sport,* **BV-1**, 1-8.

Brickner, M.A., Harkins, S.G., & Ostrom, T.M. (1986). Effects of personal involvement: Thought-provoking implications for social loafing. *Journal of Personality and Social Psychology, 51,* 763-769.

Burton, D. (1982). *Goal setting training manual for collegiate swimmers.* Unpublished manuscript, University of Illinois at Urbana-Champaign.

Burton, D. (1984, February). Goal setting: A secret to success. *Swimming World,* pp. 25-29.

Burton, D. (1987, September). Integrating psychological skills training (PST) into a periodized training program. In G. Dirkin (Chair), *Periodized training models: Implications for the sport psychologist.* Symposium conducted at the meeting of the Association for the Advancement of Applied Sport Psychology, Newport Beach, CA.

Burton, D. (1989a). The impact of goal specificity and task complexity on basketball skill development. *Sport Psychologist, 3,* 34-47.

Burton, D. (1989b). Winning isn't everything: Examining the impact of performance goals on collegiate swimmers' cognitions and performance. *Sport Psychologist, 3,* 105-132.

Burton, D., Daw, J., Williams-Rice, B.T., & Phillips, D. (1989, October). *Goal setting styles: The influence of self-esteem on goal difficulty preferences.* Paper preented at the meeting of the Canadian Society for Psychomotor Learning and Sport Psychology, Victoria, BC.

Burton, D., & Martens, R. (1986). Pinned by their own goals: An exploratory investigation into why young athletes drop out of wrestling. *Journal of Sport Psychology, 8,* 183-197.

Burton, D., Williams-Rice, B.T., Phillips, D., & Daw, J. (1989, June). *The impact of goal difficulty and task complexity on basketball skill development.* Paper presented at the meeting of the North American Society for the Psychology of Sport and Physical Activity, Kent, OH.

Carroll, S.J., Jr., & Tosi, H.L. (1970). Goal characteristics and personality factors in a management-by-objectives program. *Administrative Science Quarterly, 15,* 295-305.

Carver, C.S., & Scheier, M.F. (1981). *Attention and self-regulation: A control-theory approach to human behavior.* New York: Springer-Verlag.

Chaumeton, N.R., & Duda, J.L. (1988). Is it how you play the game or whether you win or lose? The effect of competitive level and situation on coaching behaviors. *Journal of Sport Behavior, 11,* 157-173.

Chidester, T.R., & Grigsby, W.C. (1984). A meta-analysis of the goal setting performance literature. In J.A. Pearce & R.B. Robinson, (Eds.), *Academy of management proceedings* (pp. 202-206). Ada, OH: Academy of Management.

Christensen-Szalanski, J.J.J. (1980). A further examination of the selection of problem-solving strategies: The effects of deadlines and analytic aptitudes. *Organizational Behavior and Human Performance, 25,* 107-122.

Csikszentmihalyi, M. (1977). *Beyond boredom and anxiety.* San Francisco: Jossey-Bass.

deCharms, R. (1976). *Enhancing motivation: Change in the classroom.* New York: Irvington.

Deci, E.L., & Ryan, R.M. (1985). *Intrinsic motivation and self-determination in human behavior.* New York: Plenum Press.

Diener, C.I., & Dweck, C.S. (1978). An analysis of learned helplessness: Continuous changes in performance, strategy, and achievement cognitions following failure. *Journal of Personality and Social Psychology, 36,* 451-462.

Dossett, D.L., Latham, G.P., & Mitchell, T.R. (1979). The effects of assigned versus participatively set goals, KR, and individual differences when goal difficulty is held constant. *Journal of Applied Psychology, 64,* 291-298.

Duda, J.L. (1985, October). *The relationship between motivational perspective and participation and persistence in sport.* Paper presented at the meeting of the Canadian Society for Psychomotor Learning and Sport Psychology, University of Quebec at Montreal.

Duda, J.L. (1986a). A cross-cultural analysis of achievement motivation in sport and the classroom. In L. VanderVelden & J. Humphrey (Eds.), *Current selected research in the psychology and sociology of sport* (pp. 115-134). New York: AMS Press.

Duda, J.L. (1986b). Perceptions of sport success and failure among white, black, and Hispanic adolescents. In J. Watkins, T. Reilly, & L. Burwitz (Eds.), *Sport science* (pp. 214-222). London: E. & F.N. Spon.

Duda, J.L. (1987, April). *Criteria underlying perceived success/failure among children with different pre-game goals.* Paper presented at the meeting of the American

Alliance for Health, Physical Education, Recreation and Dance, Las Vegas, NV.

Duda, J.L. (1988). The relationship between goal perspectives, persistence, and behavioral intensity among male and female recreational sport participants. *Leisure Sciences, 10*, 95-106.

Dweck, C.S. (1975). The role of expectations and attributions in the alleviation of learned helplessness. *Journal of Personality and Social Psychology, 31*, 674-685.

Dweck, C.S. (1980). Learned helplessness in sport. In C.H. Nadeau, W.R. Halliwell, K.M. Newell, & G.C. Roberts (Eds.), *Psychology of motor behavior and sport—1979* (pp. 1-12). Champaign, IL: Human Kinetics.

Elliott, E.S., & Dweck, C.S. (1988). Goals: An approach to motivation and achievement. *Journal of Personality and Social Psychology, 54*, 5-12.

Ewing, M.E. (1981). *Achievement orientations and sport behavior of males and females*. Unpublished doctoral dissertation, University of Illinois, Urbana.

Feltz, D.L., & Petlichkoff, L. (1983). Perceived competence among interscholastic sport participants and dropouts. *Canadian Journal of Applied Sport Science, 8*, 231-235.

Fox, K.R., & Corbin, C.B. (1989). The physical self-perception profile: Development and preliminary validation. *Journal of Sport and Exercise Psychology, 11*, 408-430.

Frankel, A., & Snyder, M.L. (1978). Poor performance following unsolvable problems: Learned helplessness or egotism? *Journal of Personality and Social Psychology, 36*, 1415-1423.

Frieze, I.H., & Weiner, B. (1971). Cue utilization and attributional judgments for success and failure. *Journal of Personality, 39*, 591-605.

Garfield, C.A., & Bennett, H.Z. (1984). *Peak performance: Mental training techniques of the world's greatest athletes*. Los Angeles: Tarcher.

Giannini, J.M., Weinberg, R.S., & Jackson, A.J. (1988). The effects of mastery, competitive, and cooperative goals on the performance of simple and complex basketball skills. *Journal of Sport and Exercise Psychology, 10*, 408-417.

Gill, D.L. (1986). Competitiveness among females and males in physical activity classes. *Sex Roles, 15*, 243-257.

Gill, D.L., & Deeter, T.E. (1988). Development of the sport orientation questionnaire. *Research Quarterly for Exercise and Sport, 59*, 191-202.

Gill, D.L., Dzewaltowski, D.A., & Deeter, T.E. (1988). The relationship of competitiveness and achievement orientation to participation in sport and nonsport activities. *Journal of Sport and Exercise Psychology, 10*, 139-150.

Gould, D. (1985). Goal setting for peak performance. In J.M. Wiliams (Ed.), *Applied sport psychology: Personal growth to peak performance* (pp. 133-148). Palo Alto, CA: Mayfield.

Gould, D., Feltz, D., Horn, T., & Weiss, M. (1982). Reasons for attrition in competitive youth swimming. *Journal of Sport Behavior, 5*, 155-165.

Hall, H.K., & Byrne, A.T.J. (1988). Goal setting in sport: Clarifying recent anomalies. *Journal of Sport and Exercise Psychology, 10*, 184-198.

Hall, H.K., Weinberg, R.S., & Jackson, A. (1987). Effects of goal specificity, goal difficulty, and information feedback on endurance performance. *Journal of Sport Psychology, 9*, 43-54.

Hardy, C.J., & Latane, B. (1988). Social loafing in cheerleaders: Effects of team membership and competition. *Journal of Sport and Exercise Psychology, 10*, 109-114.

Harkins, S.G., Latane, B., & Williams, K.D. (1980). Social loafing: Allocating effort or taking it easy? *Journal of Experimental Social Psychology, 16*, 457-465.

Harkins, S.G., & Petty, R.E. (1982). Effects of task difficulty and task uniqueness on social loafing. *Journal of Personality and Social Psychology, 43*, 1214-1229.

Harter, S. (1981). The development of competence motivation in the mastery of cognitive and physical skills: Is there still a place for joy? In G.C. Roberts & D.M. Landers (Eds.), *Psychology of motor behavior and sport–1980* (pp. 3-29). Champaign, IL: Human Kinetics.

Harter, S. (1985). *Manual for the self-perception profile for children*. Denver: University of Denver Press.

Heckhausen, H., & Strang, H. (1988). Efficiency under record performance demands: Exertion control—An individual difference variable? *Journal of Personality and Social Psychology, 55*, 489-498.

Hollingsworth, B. (1975). Effects of performance goals and anxiety on learning a gross motor task. *Research Quarterly, 46*, 162-168.

Ingham, A., Levinger, G., Graves, J., & Peckham, V. (1974). The Ringlemann effect: Studies of group size and group performance. *Journal of Experimental Social Psychology, 10*, 371-384.

Jackson, J.M., & Williams, K.D. (1985). Social loafing on difficult tasks: Working collectively can improve performance. *Journal of Personality and Social Psychology, 49*, 937-942.

James, W. (1890). *The principles of psychology* (Vol. 1). New York: Holt.

Johnston-O'Connor, E.J., & Kirschenbaum, D.S. (1984). Something succeeds like success: Positive self-monitoring for unskilled golfers. *Cognitive Therapy and Research, 10*, 123-136.

Kerr, N.L., & Brunn, S.E. (1981). Ringlemann revisited: Alternative explanations for the social loafing effect. *Personality and Social Psychology Bulletin, 7*, 224-231.

Kirschenbaum, D.S. (1984). Self-regulation and sport psychology: Nurturing an emerging symbiosis. *Journal of Sport Psychology, 6*, 159-183.

Kirschenbaum, D.S., Ordman, A.M., Tomarken, A.J., & Holtzbauer, R. (1982). Effects of differential self-monitoring and level of mastery on sports performance: Brain power bowling. *Cognitive Therapy and Research, 6*, 335-342.

Kirschenbaum, D.S., & Tomarken, A.J. (1982). On facing the generalization problem: The study of self-regulatory failure. In P.C. Kendall (Ed.), *Advances in cognitive–behavioral research and therapy* (Vol. 1, pp. 121-200). New York: Academic Press.

Kirschenbaum, D.S., Tomarken, A.J., & Ordman, A.M. (1982). Specificity of planning and choice in adult self-control. *Journal of Personality and Social Psychology, 41*, 576-585.

Kirschenbaum, D.S., Wittrock, D.A., Smith, R.J., & Monson, W. (1984). Criticism inoculation training: Concept in search of strategy. *Journal of Sport Psychology, 6*, 77-93.

Komaki, J., Barwick, K.D., & Scott, L.R. (1978). A behavioral approach to occupational safety: Pinpointing and reinforcing safe performance in a food manufacturing plant. *Journal of Applied Psychology, 64*, 434-445.

LaPorte, R.E., & Nath, R. (1976). Role of performance goals in prose learning. *Journal of Educational Psychology, 68*, 260-264.

Latane, B. (1986). Responsibility and effort in organizations. In P. Goodman (Ed.), *Groups and organizations* (pp. 277-303). San Francisco: Jossey-Bass.

Latane, B., Williams, K.D., & Harkins, S.G. (1979). Many hands make light the work: The causes and consequences of social loafing. *Journal of Personality and Social Psychology, 37*, 823-832.

Latham, G.P., & Baldes, J.J. (1975). The "practical significance" of Locke's theory of goal setting. *Journal of Applied Psychology, 60*, 122-124.

Latham, G.P., & Lee, T.W. (1986). Goal setting. In E.A. Locke (Ed.), *Generalizing from laboratory to field settings: Research findings from industrial–organizational psychology, organizational behavior, and human resource management* (pp. 101-117). Lexington, MA: Heath.

Latham, G.P., & Locke, E.A. (1975). Increasing productivity with decreasing time limits: A field replication of Parkinson's law. *Journal of Applied Psychology, 60*, 524-526.

Latham, G.P., & Locke, E.A. (1979). Goal-setting: A motivational technique that works. *Organizational Dynamics, 8*, 68-80.

Latham, G.P., Mitchell, T.R., & Dossett, D.L. (1978). Importance of participative goal setting and anticipated rewards on goal difficulty and job performance. *Journal of Applied Psychology, 63*, 163-171.

Lewthwaite, R. (1990). Threat perception in competitive trait anxiety: The endangerment of important goals. *Journal of Sport and Exercise Psychology, 12*, 280-300.

Locke, E.A. (1968). Toward a theory of task motivation and incentives. *Organizational Behavior and Human Performance, 3*, 157-189.

Locke, E.A., & Bryan, J.F. (1966). Cognitive aspects of psychomotor performance: The effects of performance goals on level of performance. *Journal of Applied Psychology, 50*, 286-291.

Locke, E.A., Cartledge, N., & Knerr, C.S. (1970). Studies of the relationship between satisfaction, goal setting, and performance. *Organizational Behavior and Human Performance, 5*, 135-158.

Locke, E.A., Frederick, E., Lee, C., & Bobko, P. (1984). Effect of self-efficacy, goals, and task strategies on task performance. *Journal of Applied Psychology, 69*, 241-251.

Locke, E.A., & Latham, G.P. (1985). The application of goal setting to sports. *Journal of Sport Psychology, 7*, 205-222.

Locke, E.A., Shaw, K.N., Saari, L.M., & Latham, G.P. (1981). Goal setting and task performance: 1969-1980. *Psychological Bulletin, 90*, 125-152.

Loehr, J.E. (1984, March). How to overcome stress and play at your peak all the time. *Tennis*, pp. 66-76.

Maehr, M.L. (1984). Meaning and motivation. In R. Ames & C. Ames (Eds.), *Research on motivation in education: Student motivation* (Vol. 1, 115-144). New York: Academic Press.

Maehr, M.L., & Braskamp, L. (1986). *The motivation factor: A theory of personal investment*. Lexington, MA: Heath.

Maehr, M.L., & Nicholls, J.G. (1980). Culture and achievement motivation: A second look. In N. Warren (Ed.), *Studies in cross-cultural psychology* (pp. 341-363). New York: Academic Press.

Mahoney, M.J., & Avener, M. (1977). Psychology of the elite athlete: An exploratory study. *Cognitive Therapy and Research, 1*, 135-142.

Manderlink, G., & Harackiewicz, J.M. (1984). Proximal versus distal goal setting and intrinsic motivation. *Journal of Personality and Social Psychology, 47*, 918-928.

Martens, R. (1987). Self-confidence and goal setting skills. In *Coaches guide to sport psychology* (pp. 151-169). Champaign, IL: Human Kinetics.

Martens, R., Burton, D., Vealey, R.S., Bump, L.A., & Smith, D.E. (1990). Competitive State Anxiety Inventory-2 (CSAI-2). In R. Martens, R.S. Vealey, & D. Burton, *Competitive anxiety in sport* (pp. 117-213). Champaign, IL: Human Kinetics.

Mento, A.J., Steel, R.P., & Karren, R.J. (1987). A meta-analytic study of the effects of goal setting on task performance: 1966-1984. *Organizational Behavior and Human Decision Processes, 39*, 52-83.

Miller, J.T., & McAuley, E. (1987). Effects of a goal-setting training program on basketball free-throw self-efficacy and performance. *Sport Psychologist, 1*, 103-113.

Morris, L.W., Davis, D., & Hutchings, C. (1981). Cognitive and emotional components of anxiety: Literature review and revised worry—emotionality scale. *Journal of Educational Psychology, 73*, 541-555.

Nemeroff, W.F., & Cosentino, J. (1979). Utilizing feedback and goal setting to increase performance appraisal interviewer skills of managers. *Academy of Management Journal, 22*, 566-576.

Nicholls, J.G. (1976). Effort is virtuous, but it's better to have ability: Evaluative responses to perceptions of effort and ability. *Journal of Research in Personality, 10*, 306-315.

Nicholls, J.G. (1984a). Conceptions of ability and achievement motivation. In R. Ames & C. Ames (Eds.), *Research on motivation in education: Student motivation* (Vol. 1, pp. 39-73). New York: Academic Press.

Nicholls, J.G. (1984b). Achievement motivation: Conceptions of ability, subjective experience, task choice, and performance. *Psychological Review, 91*, 328-346.

O'Block, F.R., & Evans, F.H. (1984). Goal setting as a motivational technique. In J.M. Silva & R.S. Weinberg (Eds.), *Psychological foundations of sport* (pp. 188-196). Champaign, IL: Human Kinetics.

Ravizza, K. (1977). Peak experiences in sport. *Journal of Humanistic Psychology, 17*, 35-40.

Roberts, G.C., Kleiber, D.A., & Duda, J.L. (1981). An analysis of motivation in children's sport: The role of perceived competence in participation. *Journal of Sport Psychology, 3*, 206-216.

Rosenberg, M. (1965). *Society and adolescent self-image*. Princeton, NJ: Princeton University Press.

Rosswork, S.G. (1977). Goal setting: The effects on an academic task with varying magnitudes of incentive. *Journal of Educational Psychology, 69*, 710-715.

Rothkopf, E.Z., & Billington, M.J. (1979). Goal-guided learning from text: Inferring a descriptive processing model from inspection times and eye movements. *Journal of Educational Psychology, 71*, 310-327.

Russell, W., & Branch, T. (1979). *Second wind: The memoirs of an opinionated man*. New York: Random House.

Sales, S.M. (1970). Some effects of role overload and role underload. *Organizational Behavior and Human Performance, 5*, 592-608.

Schrauger, J.S., & Rosenberg, S.F. (1970). Self-esteem and the effects of success and failure feedback on performance. *Journal of Personality, 38*, 404-417.

Schunk, D.H. (1983). Developing children's self-efficacy and skills: The roles of social comparative information and goal setting. *Contemporary Educational Psychology, 8*, 76-86.

Sears, P.S. (1940). Levels of aspiration in academically successful and unsuccessful children. *Journal of Abnormal and Social Psychology, 35*, 498-536.

Shavelson, R.J., Hubner, J.J., & Stanton, G.C. (1976). Self-concept: Validation of construct interpretations. *Review of Educational Research, 46*, 407-441.

Strang, H.R., Lawrence, E.C., & Fowler, P.C. (1978). Effects of assigned goal level and knowledge of results on arithmetic computation. *Journal of Applied Psychology, 63*, 446-450.

Terborg, J.R. (1976). The motivational components of goal setting. *Journal of Applied Psychology, 61*, 613-621.

Terborg, J.R., & Miller, H.E. (1978). Motivation, behavior, and performance: A closer examination of goal setting and monetary incentives. *Journal of Applied Psychology, 63*, 29-39.

Tharp, R.G., & Gallimore, R. (1976, January). What a coach can teach a teacher. *Psychology Today*, 75-78.

Tubbs, M.E. (1986). Goal setting: A meta-analytic examination of the empirical evidence. *Journal of Applied Psychology, 71*, 474-483.

Vallerand, R.J., Gauvin, L.I., & Halliwell, W.R. (1986). Effects of zero-sum competition on children's intrinsic motivation and perceived competence. *Journal of Social Psychology, 126*, 465-472.

Vealey, R.S. (1986). Conceptualization of sport-confidence and competitive orientation: Preliminary investigation and instrument development. *Journal of Sport Psychology, 8,* 221-246.

Weinberg, R.S., Bruya, L.D., & Jackson, A. (1985). The effects of goal proximity and goal specificity on endurance performance. *Journal of Sport Psychology, 7,* 296-305.

Weinberg, R.S., Bruya, L.D., Jackson, A., & Garland, H. (1986). Goal difficulty and endurance performance: A challenge to the goal attainability assumption. *Journal of Sport Behavior, 10,* 82-92.

Weinberg, R.S., Bruya, L.D., Longino, J., and Jackson, A. (1988). Effect of goal proximity and specificity on endurance performance of primary-grade children. *Journal of Sport and Exercise Psychology, 10,* 81-91.

Weiner, B. (1972). *Theories of motivation: From mechanism to cognition.* Chicago: Rand McNally.

Weiner, B. (1981). The role of affect in sports psychology. In G.C. Roberts & D.M. Landers (Eds.), *Psychology of motor behavior and sport—1980* (pp. 37-48). Champaign, IL: Human Kinetics.

Weiner, B. (1982). An attribution theory of motivation and emotion. In H. Krohne & L. Laux (Eds.), *Achievement, stress, and anxiety* (pp. 223-245). Washington, DC: Hemisphere.

Williams, K.D. (1981). *Social loafing and group cohesion.* Paper presented at the meeting of the Midwestern Psychological Association, Detroit.

Williams, K.D., Harkins, S.G., & Latane, B. (1981). Identifiability as a deterrent to social loafing: Two cheering experiments. *Journal of Personality and Social Psychology, 40,* 303-311.

Wine, J.D. (1980). Cognitive–attentional theory of test anxiety. In I.G. Sarason (Ed.), *Text anxiety: Theory, research, and applications* (pp. 349-385). Hillsdale, NJ: Erlbaum.

Wood, R.E., Mento, A.J., & Locke, E.A. (1987). Task complexity as a moderator of goal effects: A meta-analysis. *Journal of Applied Psychology, 72,* 416-425.

Yin, Z., Simons, J., & Callaghan, J. (1989, September). *The application of goal-setting in physical activity: A field study.* Paper presented at the meeting of the Association for the Advancement of Applied Sport Psychology, Seattle.

Yukl, G.A., & Latham, G.P. (1978). Interrelationships among employee participation, individual differences, goal difficulty, goal acceptance, goal instrumentality, and performance. *Personnel Psychology, 31,* 305-323.

Editor's Postscript

As I have read and reread the individual chapters in this book, I have constantly been reminded of two facts. First, sport psychology, as an academic area of study, has come a long way since its inception in the mid 1960s; that is, we have certainly accumulated much information concerning the behavior of individuals in sport and physical activity contexts. However, as the authors of the individual chapters in this volume have continually reiterated, we have only begun to identify and explore the multitude of interacting factors that affect sport and exercise behavior. Given the number of pages in each chapter allocated to a discussion of future research issues, it is obvious that many more questions remain to be answered.

Interestingly, when I first entered this field approximately 12 years ago, I sensed a rather euphoric optimism among our ranks that we, as

sport psychologists, were literally on the brink of answering all, or many, of the important questions concerning the behavior of sport and physical activity participants. After reading this text, the reader may be struck, as I was, by the recognition that our optimism, while still evident, has been tempered by the realization that human behavior remains a very complex phenomenon that cannot be easily understood. It appears to me that this state of affairs clearly illustrates the old adage, *The more you know about something, the more you realize how much you don't know.*

To leave this book on a positive note, however, it is truly my belief that while we, as sport psychologists, may not know all the answers, we are at least asking some very important questions! It is our collective hope that these questions will serve us, as researchers, well in the years to come.

Index

References to tables and figures appear in italics.